Social Work Treatment

SOCIAL WORK TREATMENT

INTERLOCKING THEORETICAL APPROACHES
Second Edition

Edited by

Francis J. Turner

With a Foreword By

EILEEN L. YOUNGHUSBAND

THE FREE PRESS
A Division of Macmillan Publishing Co., Inc.
NEW YORK

Collier Macmillan Publishers
LONDON

Copyright © 1979 by   The Free Press
                       A Division of Macmillan Publishing Co., Inc.

The Free Press
A Division of Macmillan Publishing Co., Inc.
866 Third Avenue, New York, N.Y. 10022

Collier Macmillan Canada, Ltd.

Library of Congress Catalog Card Number: 78-73027

Printed in the United States of America

printing number

3 4 5 6 7 8 9 10

Library of Congress Cataloging in Publication Data

Turner, Francis Joseph
   Social work treatment.

   Includes index.
   1. Social service--Addresses, essays,
lectures. I. Title.
HV37.T87 1979   361   78-73027
ISBN 0-02-932920-5

Copyright Acknowledgments

To Joanne

Contents

Foreword by Eileen L. Younghusband   **xiii**

Preface to the Second Edition   **xv**

Preface to the First Edition   **xvii**

Acknowledgments   **xxi**

About the Contributors   **xxiii**

1. Theory in Social Work Practice   **1**

     Francis J. Turner

2. Psychoanalytic Theory   **13**

     Eunice F. Allan

3. Ego Psychology   **33**

     Sidney L. Wasserman

4. Psychosocial Therapy   **69**

     Francis J. Turner

x Contents

5. Problem-Solving Theory   **93**

    David Hallowitz

6. Functional Theory for Social Work Practice   **123**

    Shankar A. Yelaja

7. Existential Social Work   **147**

    Donald F. Krill

8. The Client-Centered System Unfolding   **177**

    G. T. Barrett-Lennard

9. Cognitive Theory   **243**

    Harold D. Werner

10. Contributions of Gestalt Theory to Social Work Treatment   **273**

    Michael Blugerman

11. Transactional Analysis—A Social Treatment Model   **293**

    Denise Capps Coburn

12. Meditation and Social Work Treatment   **313**

    Thomas Keefe

13. General Systems Theory and Social Work   **333**

    Gordon Hearn

14. The Life Model of Social Work Practice   **361**

    Carel Germain and Alex Gitterman

15. Role Theory   **385**

    Herbert S. Strean

16. Communication Concepts and Principles   **409**

    Lotte Marcus

17. Behavior Modification: A Technology of Social Change   **433**

    Richard B. Stuart

18. Family Therapy   **449**

    Sanford N. Sherman

19. Task-Centered Treatment   **479**

    William J. Reid

20. Crisis Theory   **499**

    Naomi Golan

21. Interlocking Perspective for Practice   **535**

    Francis J. Turner

Index   **547**

Foreword

To many social work educators and practitioners the development of a usable, expanding and internally consistent theory of social work practice is both urgent and long delayed. To others it is an exercise in beating our breasts which fills a good deal of paper but is remote from the daily demands of practice. Is it then an exercise primarily engaged in by academics in their struggle to keep up with other academic Joneses? Or is it so crucial for the improvement of practice that we are rightly to be taken to task for elevating assumptions into theories or concentrating on practice without analyzing the common factors that could be discerned in that practice or testing the fruitful application of theory to it?

Probably the only useful way to resolve this debate is to ask what is the use of theory. The first point is that it must be a good theory, based not only on observation but also on hypothesis in which alternative possible explanations have been ruled out. For instance, an observer in the early nineteenth century noted that men who wore top hats did not die of starvation, and a society to provide free top hats was about to be launched, so it is said, before further observation ruled out the hypothesis. Similarly, in social work the enormous complexity of the scene with which social workers engage, the "big, buzzing confusion," to quote William James, may well have a good deal to do with our failure to develop theories of the right size, i.e., neither so comprehensive that they are of little use for every day purposes or so one-track that they leave most of the real world out of account. To produce usable theories of the right size over a sufficient range of commonly encountered persons in their major life experience is a formidable task. But once again "what's the point of it?" The first thing to be said is that theory is not an end in itself but a means to an end. That end is the objectives or goals of social work; however these may be expressed at any given time they are essentially concerned with enabling people to make a better go of it with themselves and others and to achieve or have provided for them more elbow room in their social circumstances. The hallmark of a good theory is, of course, its capacity to predict the outcome of any given action. It also provides a guide to what is the same and what different in a range of similar situations, and it should thus be a springboard for the development of further theory that sheds light on fresh interconnections. The point of a good theory is thus that it works in practice and in the very working generates more comprehensive, more powerful theory. The other overwhelming advantage of theory applied and tested in practice is that it is transmissible to other practitioners and is testable by them in a way that does not hold for wisdom acquired through practice or for assumptions.

The present study is significant, indeed a landmark, because it contributes to and springs from the new impetus to pioneer for social work the application of theory in practice without which it cannot advance as a profession—or, what is more important, in its capacity to deliver the goods—at this point in its development. The two-pronged attempt to elucidate theory and to study rigorously what actually happens in practice is now going forward, even if spasmodically, in several different countries. This is important, because we need to discover not only what theories reliably predict outcome within a given culture and circumstances but what in these is directly relayed to universals in human nature and is thus applicable, even by different modes of operation, in different cultures or in cultures within certain similar traditions. All the authors have illustrated from practice the theories they each discuss. This adds greatly to the values of the study from an international point of view. Other countries and continents where the practice of social work, and education for it, has spread rapidly in the last quarter century are greatly in need of studies like those which Dr. Turner and his collaborators have brought together here. It is to be hoped that this book will be widely read, not to be slavishly learned and regurgitated, but for use as a further stimulus to the well-planned study which must go ahead in other situations where social work is practiced. This is essential for the much needed cross-fertilization of well recorded and tested theories. In short, we must develop the attitude of mind that inspired this book, not only for the improvement of practice, but also for the vastly better education of social work students which is so urgently needed in the world as a whole.

Eileen L. Younghusband
Honorary President, International Association
of Schools of Social Work

Preface to the Second Edition

The decision to issue a second edition of *Social Work Treatment* was based on two factors. First was the growing awareness that the phenomenon of the rapid emergence of new thought systms marking the last twenty-five years seemed to be waning. Certainly in the past five years some new systems have begun to appear in the literature and to be talked about by practitioners. But, on the whole, these have not been as numerous as before. What is happening, rather, is that new developments are emerging from the established theories and thought systems. New interpretations of traditional thought systems are being made, enriching their utility for practice. At the same time, expanded applications of some of the newer systems, originally seen as having only narrow application, are also occurring. This search for the expansion of theories rather than the creation of new ones is of particular importance to the practice world. It reflects a healthy search for richer applications of available concepts, a process essential to the ongoing development, testing, reformulation and enrichment of practice.

It was the awareness that this type of enrichment was indeed taking place that led me to decide to give the original authors an opportunity to revise their chapters. All but two did indeed find it necessary to make revisions, and in several instances these revisions were extensive. Most added new items to their bibliographies, making resources even more useful than they were in the first edition.

The other reason for the decision to issue a second edition stemmed from the need to include some additional topics. These had been omitted from the first edition pending further development of their applicability in social work. The inclusion of five new chapters, each devoted to a new treatment approach, speaks to this concern.

Each of these new chapters is viewed as being of significance to current practice and as having become an integral part of the social work tradition. Certainly transactional analysis and gestalt have become widely known in all the helping professions and are increasingly becoming a part—in some cases the principal component—of many therapists' practice base. Task-centered practice is very much a product of social work, of particular relevance to practitioners seeking to make their practice more concrete, organized and predictable. Meditation as an approach to practice has long been viewed with some discomfort. There has been a lingering fear that it is not really a professionally based practice theory but, rather, a philosophical-religious world view. This concern has been largely dispelled by increasing awareness that it is possible to demonstrate measurable physical changes in persons in the meditative state. This empirically based understanding of meditation is only part of the emphasis now being given to the need for a closer understanding of the interconnection of biological and psychological man. The use of biofeedback mechanisms as a component of psychotherapy reflects this growing interest, and, undoubtedly in a further revision of this book, a chapter will be necessary on biopsychotherapy as a basis for social work practice.

The ecological or life-model approach to practice is the newest thought system in the book. It is based on the conviction that man cannot be considered apart from the environment in which he functions. In an interesting way, ecological concepts help to strengthen the utility of systems theory and the growing interest in biological man in therapy.

I have been most pleased by the reception accorded the first edition. Originally it was thought that it would be useful to the practitioner as a ready reference to the various thought systems available as resources to clients. This goal has been achieved, and for this I am grateful. But the first edition has also been useful to scholars at all levels: undergraduate, graduate and postgraduate. This trend reflects the continuing search for a stronger theory base for practice. I would caution, however, that a volume such as this one should not be used as the single authoritative source of information on a particular system. It is in an attempt to avoid this problem that particular stress has been put on the bibliographies, and that readers are urged to see them as essential to the book and its use. Clearly, each thought system requires a full-scale exposition in its own right. This book is intended, then, as a ready reference, not as a substitute for in-depth study.

It is evident that we are not yet at a point in practice where we can anticipate the emergence of a general practice theory. We are, however, certainly at a point where there is commitment to tap the rich resources of all systems and to continue the search for interlocking concepts. It is hoped that this second edition of *Social Work Treatment* will contribute to this needed trend.

F.J.T.
Waterloo, Ontario
June, 1978

Preface to the First Edition

The primary goal of this book is to expand and strengthen the theoretical base of social work clinicians. Implicit in this goal is the conviction that an expanded and strengthened theoretical base will contribute positively to the quality and effectiveness of therapy. The method by which this goal is achieved is to bring together in a readily accessible form the spectrum of conceptual viewpoints presently influencing current social work practice.

The rationale for assembling this range of conceptual viewpoints under one cover stems from a conviction that our profession has not been markedly effective in widely sharing with each other the diversity of ideas considered to have rich potential for practice. All of the approaches discussed in this volume have appeared somewhere in our professional literature. But this appearance has been in an uneven manner, so that the potential influence of each body of thought is greatly restricted. I do not suggest that each approach discussed in the book is of equal importance; I do suggest that each should be available to practitioners in a manner and style that will facilitate its examination and assessment for its usefulness.

In recent years the cry has been frequently raised that social work practice does not have an adequate theoretical base. Clearly, like all other professions practicing in the area of human adjustment, we do lack a sufficiently comprehensive and integrated body of theory necessary to understand and explain the myriad of situations we are called upon to assess. But no longer can we say we lack theories. At this point in our history our problem is a superfluity of conceptual frameworks rather than a dearth.

Indeed, it is this abundance of systems that makes current social work practice both exciting and frustrating. Exciting because unlike any other time in our history we do have a range of orientations on which to draw in our endless search for a structure by which we can order that almost infinite complexity of "person in situation." Frustrating because each new approach challenges us to reorder our thinking as we attempt to examine, assess, modify and, when appropriate, introduce such ideas into our conceptual armamentarium.

This diversity also challenges individual social workers to come to terms with a pluralistic conceptual base. Thus, must one become a free-floating eclectic? Or is it better to pick a framework that appears most appealing and ignore the others? Or, rather, does one attempt to synthesize all of them into some form of general all-encompassing theory?

We are probably not yet ready to answer these questions. Clearly, though, there is a suggested answer underlying the format of this book. It is my conviction that each of the conceptual systems addressed in this book has something of significance for practicing social workers. This conviction thus implies support for some form of synthesis which is neither eclecticism nor an all-encompassing grand theory. The task for each practitioner from my viewpoint is to develop a theoretical approach to practice with which one is comfortable and to build onto it or modify it as one becomes more knowledgeable about, experienced in and convinced of the importance and significance of other approaches. The task of further syntheses is not that of individual practitioners but the responsibility of our theoreticians.

But for practitioners to make full use of available thought systems the material must be readily available in a form that presents both differential approaches and perceived implications for practice. Thus, each author was asked to write against a common framework to facilitate comparison between chapters. Within this outline each author brought together available thinking about the body of thought he was addressing, his own views about it and in particular the perceived implications for individual, family, group and community practice.

The principal aim of this volume is to serve as an aid to practitioners. It is this segment of colleagues who most need a quick and ready access to a range of viewpoints to aid them in practice. It is hoped also that it will be of use to students, both those beginning their professional training and those at more senior levels where greater emphasis is put on critical examination and comparison of various stances. It is further hoped it will aid future scholarly studies that seek similarities and differences, gaps and trends, strengths and weaknesses in our theoretical base.

Since the primary target is to develop a useful resource for practitioners, there are some goals to which this volume does not aspire. Thus, in no way does it attempt to be an exhaustive analysis of the various thought systems, but a scholarly operational approach to them. Each author has included a selected bibliography to which the reader may turn who wishes to pursue more assiduously one or more of the topics. Each author has also included indicators of the direction in which further research might be pursued that could increase the understanding and utility of the conceptual viewpoint.

Other colleagues have identified the need for books such as the present one at this point in our professional history. Since the original idea of this book began to take shape, two related volumes have been published: *Theories of Social Casework* by Roberts and Nee and *Social Casework: Theories in Action* by Dr. Herbert Strean, one of the contributors to this volume. Further, the recently published *Encyclopedia of Social Work* also includes individual articles on some of the topics discussed in this book.

In selecting the topics for consideration no preference was given to thought systems that originated within our profession as opposed to those we have borrowed from without. Frequently the criticism has been made by colleagues, students and interested outsiders that we have relied too heavily on borrowed ideas from outside, rather than developing our own distinct body of knowledge. Although this viewpoint is usually presented as a criticism, it may soon be viewed as one of the strengths of our profession. This latter view is clearly my own conviction. With the current shift from closed thought systems to more open ones taking place in other disciplines, this quality of our knowledge base may well be one of our major hallmarks of respectability.

Whatever the outcome of opinion about borrowing, we clearly have borrowed, both frequently and consistently, both bodies of knowledge and interventive methods from other fields. But this borrowing has not been random, reckless or total. I think we can clearly demonstrate that when we borrow, as we will continue to do, we do so in a judicious manner, always trying to adapt the borrowed concepts and techniques to fit our available state of knowledge to achieve better the goals to which we are working.

This selective borrowing concept applies to the way we adapted psychoanalytic thinking to our practice without aspiring to become analysts, in spite of the popular straw man to the contrary. It is also true, more currently, in the way we are beginning to make use of the thinking techniques and skills of the behavioral school without claiming or aspiring to become behaviorists in any general way.

But, borrow as we do, we must never forget that we do more than this. It seems we frequently underestimate the amount and extent of original contribution we have made to the fund of human knowledge about human behavior in interaction with significant environments. Several of the topics considered in the following chapters substantiate this.

Fourteen bodies of thought are included in this book. At the point of beginning this project, these were judged to be those most influencing practice. Throughout recent literature other thought systems have been mentioned and discussed, some of which are experiential, gestalt, transactional, organizational, informational and games theory. Some of these were not included because they were not thought of as having had as yet significant impact on social work practice, others from a lack of adequate knowledge about them, and still others for semantic or conceptual reasons where a different title is used to describe a topic already included.

One of the difficulties experienced in developng the book's outline was the question of distinguishing between different schools of thought. As one examines the topics chosen, it can be seen that they range from headings that encompass the work of many people such as psychodynamic theory, or ego psychology, to those that represent the thinking of a single person, such as the client-centered system of Rogers. It is also expected that some will seriously question the separations that have been made for some of the chapters. For example, distinguishing psychosocial treatment from psychodynamic theory could be seen as artificial and indeed inappropriate. In the same way, separating ego psychology from psychodynamic thinking might be viewed as a presumptuous and distorted division.

In planning the book, choices for chapters to be included were based on usage in our professional literature rather than on conceptual differences: that is, the topics selected were the schools of thought that have been identified in professional circles as representing a particular approach to practice by identifiable segments of the profession, even though they may not in fact represent real differences. Thus, without doubt psychosocial theory is clearly a psychodynamic approach to practice, but so is problem-solving theory. But we know that there are practitioners who would identify themselves as ego psychologists and distinguish themselves from both a psychosocial orientation as well as a problem-solving one. It is because of these differences in usage that each contributor was asked to write against a common framework. This was done to help identify areas of difference, both overt and covert, as well as areas of commonality.

Certainly, in beginning this project one of the primary motivations was to attempt to establish how much of a common base there is to our practice and also to identify the differences: that is, are we a multitheoretical profession, or is there emerging a general theoretical orientation that permits a variety of specialized applications of this theory for specific situations, as for example crisis theory? Whether this book has helped in resolving this question must be left to the judgment of the reviewers and readers. Certainly it has helped the various authors who have participated and shared their thinking with each other.

In the beginning the title for the book was *The Theoretical Bases of Social Work Practice*. It was this title that was originally presented to the publisher and in the letters of invitation to the contributors. But it soon became clear that our profession has tended to be quite imprecise in the use of the word "theory." Clearly, many of the topics selected, although frequently designated as theories, do not fulfill all the requirements of the concept of theory. This point is discussed more fully in the first chapter.

If this book does help practitioners and students to expand their conceptual horizons and assists them in being more effective with their clients, the efforts of those involved will be justified. If it also encourages scholars in the continuing pursuit of stronger and better-knit theoretical bases for practice, our task will be fully rewarded.

F.J.T.

Acknowledgments

In sitting to write the acknowledgments for this book I am keenly aware of the strong collegial feelings I have for the group of coauthors who have contributed to it. Although there are several I have not met except through the process of correspondence in the last year, they have become an important component of my professional life. I am deeply appreciative of their assistance, their support, their cooperation, their promptness and their constructive help in various stages of the project.

I am also appreciative of the many students at Wilfrid Laurier University, Faculty of Social Work who have influenced this project. The idea for it emerged over a period of two years as I taught a comparative theory course in casework and found it a rich way to examine current practice requirements.

Finally, I am most grateful to my family for the understanding they have shown during the many hours related to the book's production. No doubt the willing assistance of Francis, Sarah and Anne Marie slowed the process somewhat, but certainly they made it a shared familial experience. Joanne has been, as always, an indispensable coworker throughout.

F.J.T.

About the Contributors

Eunice F. Allan

was formerly a Professor of Social Work and Director of treatment methods at Smith College School of Social Work. In addition, she has lectured at Simmons College School of Social Work. She has extensive experience in family agencies and psychiatric settings in the Boston area as well as in private practice. Dr. Allan's Master's degree is from Smith College and her doctorate in social welfare is from Columbia University. Her current interest is in adaptation of ego psychological theories to understanding the origins of social dysfunctioning and the development of treatment concepts. In education, she has been exploring learning theory and experimenting with its application to training supervisors as educators. Her practice is divided among direct treatment, conducting seminars on the uses of theory in practice and consultation on issues of professional education.

G. T. Barrett-Lennard

is presently a research Professor in the Faculty of Arts at the University of Waterloo, where his work has been primarily in the human relations and counseling studies sphere. He came to Waterloo in 1966 from a visiting professorship with the Rehabilitation Institute at Southern Illinois University, following several years' teaching in the University of New England in Australia. From western Australia, originally, Dr. Barrett-Lennard completed his Ph.D. thesis at the University of Chicago in 1958 under the sponsorship of Carl R. Rogers. His special interests include the study of client/patient-therapist *and* significant life relationships; intensive group processes on theory/research and practice levels; meanings of health and well-being from personal to organizational and community system levels; and human development, emphasizing the impress of culture and the lived world of persons through the life cycle.

Michael Blugerman

is a graduate and Fellow of the Gestalt Institute of Toronto. He has taught part-time in the Graduate School of Social Work at Wilfrid Laurier University and the Department of Social Work at York University. He provides consultation and supervision to the Counselling Service at Huntley Youth

Services and the group therapy program at Jewish Family and Child Services in Toronto. He has a private practice in marriage and family counselling and conducts training and professional development workshops. He received his B.A. from the University of Toronto and his M.S.W. from Waterloo Lutheran University.

Denise Capps Coburn

is on the Faculty of the School of Social Work at Michigan State University. She is a child welfare specialist, and her teaching and research interests involve children and families. Her specific current research interests are in the relationship between social stress, personality and body function. In addition, she carries a private caseload. Her graduate studies were completed at the School of Applied Social Science at Case-Western Reserve University. Her practice experience has been in child guidance, family and hospital settings.

She has extensive training, practice and teaching experience in transactional analysis. She is a charter member of the National Association of Social Workers, and is also a member of the Academy of Certified Social Workers.

Carel Germain

is a Professor at the University of Connecticut School of Social Work. Previously, she was Professor of Social Work at the Columbia University School of Social Work. Dr. Germain has also been on the faculty at the University of Maryland School of Social Work and School of Medicine, and was Acting Director of Psychiatric Social Work at the University's Psychiatric Institute. She received the B.A. in economics from the University of California at Berkeley and the M.S. and D.S.W. from the Columbia University School of Social Work.

Alex Gitterman

is a Professor of Social Work Practice at the Columbia University School of Social Work. He has written articles on social work practice purpose and method, and on supervision, and coauthored a book on social work practice. He received his doctorate from Teachers College, Columbia University, and his Master's from Hunter College School of Social Work.

Naomi Golan

is an Associate Professor at the School of Social Work, University of Haifa. Before coming to Israel, Dr. Golan was on the faculty of the School of Social Welfare, University of Wisconsin-Milwaukee. Prior to receiving her Ph.D. at the School of Social Service Administration of the University of Chicago, she practiced at the Adult Psychiatry Clinic, Milwaukee County Mental Health Center, and at the Jewish Family and Children's Service of Milwaukee. In Israel she taught at the Hebrew University and the University of Tel Aviv and she served as professional consultant to the ministries of Defense and Social Welfare. Currently, she is consultant to the Department of Social Services of the

National Insurance Institute and the Haifa Municipality, and she has given in-service training seminars throughout the country on crisis intervention and short-term treatment. She received her B.A. in psychology and her M.S. in social work at the University of Wisconsin.

David Hallowitz

is Associate Director and Chief Psychiatric Social Worker of the Child and Adolescent Psychiatric Clinic, Inc. A field instructor at the School of Social Work of the State University of New York at Buffalo, and previously at the Columbia University, University of Pennsylvania and University of Denver schools of social work, he has trained many social work students. He has also trained numerous staff caseworkers. He is Clinical Assistant Professor in the Department of Psychiatry at the State University of New York at Buffalo. In previous years, he conducted classes and seminars at the University of Buffalo School of Social Work, the State University College in Buffalo, the University of Manitoba and Smith College School of Social Work. In past years, he held casework and residential treatment positions at the Southard School of Menninger Foundation, the Denver Home for Asthmatic Children and Pleasantville Cottage School. He holds a Master's degree from Columbia School of Social Work, and is a Fellow of the American Orthopsychiatric Association. He has received awards for distinguished professional service from the University of Buffalo School of Social Work, the Erie County Mental Health Association and the Child and Adolescent Psychiatric Clinic, Inc.

Gordon Hearn

is Professor Emeritus at the School of Social Work, Portland State University. He was the founder and Dean of the school from 1962 to 1977. Prior to that time he was Professor, School of Social Welfare, and Assistant Dean of Students, University of California, Berkeley, from 1948 to 1962.

His academic interests include social group work, group dynamics and general systems theory. The interest in general systems theory and the general systems approach to theory building began during a sabbatical year in 1955–1956. The year was spent as Cassidy Research Visiting Professor at the School of Social Work, University of Toronto. A product of that year was *Theory Building in Social Work,* published by the University of Toronto Press.

Professor Hearn's practice experience was primarily in the Canadian YMCA, in the settlement field and in the National Training Laboratories, Institute of Applied Behavioral Science.

He holds a B.A. from the University of Manitoba, a M.Sc. from George Williams College and a Ph.D. from Massachusetts Institute of Technology.

Thomas Keefe

is an Associate Professor at the Department of Sociology, Anthropology and Social Work, University of Northern Iowa. Dr. Keefe received his B.A. in psychology at the University of Colorado and his M.S.W. at the University of Denver Graduate School of Social Work. He practiced in psychiatric and family settings and in a corrections and rehabilitation setting with the United States Air Force before returning to school to take a doctorate in social work at the University of Utah. Following his doctoral study, Dr. Keefe taught, practiced part time and served as the first Coordinator of the Social Work

Program at the University of Northern Iowa. His research and publications have included theoretical and empirical articles on empathy development, meditation, eastern philosophical perspectives and, more recently, theory development articles on the implications of economic-structural changes for direct practice.

Donald F. Krill

is presently an Associate Professor with the University of Denver Graduate School of Social Work. He is in private practice in Denver and a member of the American Academy of Psychotherapists. He has practiced in urban, suburban and rural mental health settings. His Master's degree is from the University of Denver School of Social Work.

Lotte Marcus

is Associate Professor at the University of McGill, School of Social Work. Her main teaching areas are Aging and Intergenerational Relations: Social Work in the Health Field. She has practiced mostly in hospitals, in family therapy, geriatrics and community mental health. Her doctorate is from Columbia University, her Master's degree from McGill University and her early social work training was at the London School of Economics.

William J. Reid

is the George Herbert Jones Professor at the School of Social Service Administration, the University of Chicago. After completing his doctorate in social welfare at Columbia University in 1962, Dr. Reid joined the faculty at the school, where he has taught social treatment and research, and has carried out studies in the areas of manpower, community mental health and task-centered practice. He has contributed over fifty publications to the professional literature. His most recent book is *The Task-Centered System,* published in 1978 by Columbia University Press.

Sanford N. Sherman

has just ended a tenure as Executive Director of the Jewish Family Service of New York, having helped that agency merge with the Jewish Board of Guardians of New York, creating the Jewish Board of Family and Children's Services, from which he is officially retired while still functioning as a part-time consultant on program integration. He is also doing other local consultant and teaching work. In a forty-year-plus career, he has worked in foster care, child guidance, residential treatment and, for the longest span, family service, as practitioner, supervisor and executive—but throughout has maintained an active practice. He served as clinical and adjunct Professor at graduate schools of social work at Adelphi, Columbia and Fordham universities. He coedited two volumes on family therapy and contributed a number of articles to books and journals on the subjects of family and group therapy, individual and marital counseling and professional training. His Master's is from Case-Western Reserve University.

Herbert S. Strean

is Distinguished Professor at the Graduate School of Social Work, Rutgers University. His doctorate is from Columbia University School of Social Work and his Master's degree in social work is from Boston University. He has practiced in a wide range of settings, including mental health, child guidance, public welfare, family and private practice. He is the author of ten texts in social work and over fifty professional articles. His most recent book is *Clinical Social Work: Theory and Practice.*

Richard B. Stuart

is currently a faculty member in the Graduate School of Social Work at the University of Utah. He is a former Professor in the School of Social Work and a Fellow at the Center for Human Growth and Development at the University of Michigan. His research interests have been in the areas of family and marital interaction and change, the management of obesity and behavior modification in the schools. Dr. Stuart's doctorate is from Columbia University.

Francis J. Turner

is presently Dean of the Faculty of Social Work at Wilfrid Laurier University. He has taught at the University of Ottawa and Memorial University of Newfoundland. He has practiced in mental health settings, family service agencies and children's aid societies—as well as private practice. His Master's degree is from the University of Ottawa, and his doctorate is from Columbia University.

Sidney L. Wasserman

is presently a private practitioner in England. Prior to this, he was a Lecturer at the University of Bradford, School of Applied Social Studies. Before coming to England, he was Associate Professor of Social Work at Smith College School for Social Work and taught earlier at Case-Western Reserve University. He practiced as a caseworker at Bellefaire Residential Treatment and Child Care Center and the Jewish Children's Bureau, Cleveland, Ohio. He received his doctorate and Master's degree from Case-Western Reserve University, School of Applied Social Sciences.

Harold D. Werner

received his Master's degree in social work from Columbia University in 1947 and worked for ten years in children's institutions and psychiatric clinics. He next served as Associate Director of the Mental Retardation Research Project at New York University. He was Chief Psychiatric Social Worker of the Morris County Guidance Center, Morristown, New Jersey, from 1959 to 1977. He has taught at Fairleigh Dickinson University. Current activities include private practice, editing a publication of Psychiatric Outpatient Centers of America and interest in the application of social work treatment in industrial settings.

Shankar A. Yelaja

is a Professor of Social Work at the Faculty of Social Work, Wilfrid Laurier University. He holds the D.S.W. from the University of Pennsylvania and has taught social welfare policy and services in schools of social work in the United States, Canada, Australia and India. His social work practice experience includes child protection work, medical social work, correctional services for adolescents, community organization and consultation to social agencies. He is the author of several publications, including two books, *Authority and Social Work* and *Canadian Social Policy,* and numerous articles in North American and international social work journals.

Social Work Treatment

1

Theory in Social Work Practice

by

FRANCIS J. TURNER

One of the major assumptions of this book is that the theories on which our profession is built should be essentially related to the nature and style of our practice. Most social workers would consider this statement to be self-evident and basic to any profession. Yet, though apparently obvious, would an examination of our practice reflect this assumed connection? Are our theories and techniques closely related in current practice? Does theory strongly influence practice, or indeed, one could ask, does it influence practice at all? The question here is not should it, but does it? The same question can also be raised in another way. That is, do our theories emerge from our practice experience as tested components of our practice, or do they serve as sympathetic "post hoc" explanations of our practice observations? If theory does emerge from practice, does this happen in a highly formalized way, or is there only a strong but unspecified connection, or indeed, is there any connection at all?

Or, is it possible that none of these alternatives reflects current reality? Might it be that theory and practice are two separate but necessary components of our practice, that what we do in our clinical practice is not based on our identified theoretical bases but on an experientially based framework not yet systematized? Or, further, is it even possible that at this point in our history the question is not relevant, that we do not have either singly or plurally an adequate theoretical base for practice?

This book presumes that there should be and must be a high level of connectedness between theory and practice, but it also assumes that this is still a goal to which our profession must aspire. It is further presumed that the absence of this connection does not mean that we function irresponsibly or ineffectively; our history dramatically discounts this. It may mean that as yet we haven't been able to, or been compelled to, or found it neccessary to develop a more rigorous conceptual framework on

1

which to build and order the wealth of knowledge we have.

It is not our intention to attempt to state definitely the connection between theory and practice on the current scene, but rather to examine tentatively the question from the viewpoint of our quest for theory. In beginning we will take as an assumption that there are some elements of available theory on which we can draw, and that there is some connection between what we know and what we do. At the same time we are aware that these are only assumptions and as such must be challenged and tested.

The approach to be followed will be to examine the material in a fourfold manner: What is theory? What have we said about it? What have we done about it? What can theory do for us?

1. What is theory?

Many of us who have been away from formal courses in research concepts and methods might not be able to give a precise textbook definition of theory and an accurate description of its component parts. Nevertheless, most of us would quickly remember the essential components of this concept. Thus, we would recall that the word "theory" is used to describe a logical explanation of the interrelatedness of a set of facts that have been empirically verified or are capable of being verified.

There are three terms usually identified as being essential to theory; concepts, facts and hypotheses.

Concepts are symbols developed by a discipline to describe the phenomena with which it is dealing. Concepts are thus abstractions and represent only descriptions of reality. Concepts are the labels (a term so unpopular in clinical practice) by which men communicate to each other. They are agreed-upon terms to describe the world in which we live. When referred to a body of theory and the practice of a discipline, concepts are presumed to have accuracy and

precision for a clear and effective communication between colleagues. Thus, responsible theoreticians and practitioners are strongly committed to sharpen constantly and specify the precision of the concepts used. The concept is not the phenomenon but a formulation about the phenomenon derived by logical abstraction from our experiences. As we all know, the frequent error of the practitioner and researcher is to treat the abstractions as concrete realities.

Examples of concepts in social work practice, although not necessarily ones with high precision, are such terms as relationship, personality strengths, mental mechanisms, homeostasis and self-identity.

Facts, on the hand, are concepts that can be empirically verified; that is, they are observations that we and others can make about the concepts with which we deal. Clearly, the whole question of what constitutes adequate empirical verification is an involved and challenging one, and the whole history of man's search for knowledge provides many examples of facts considered to have been proven being replaced by more updated proofs.

Theory emerges through the process in which facts are ordered in a meaningful way: that is, the relationship between facts is posited through observation, speculation, inspiration and experience, and as such relationships are observed and verified, theory is developed. Theory thus looks to the process of ordering facts and searching for relationships between facts.

New relationships between facts that are formally predicted in emerging theories are called hypotheses. When a hypothesis is developed and found through disciplined observation to be supported, then the theory has been further developed and tested.

One of the difficulties about theory building is that the terms and process can be defined and described in a clear and precise manner, and such descriptions can readily give the false impression that the process of theory building takes place in a clear, highly structured manner. The error in such an impression is that it fails to recognize that the process of developing new systematized knowledge is a complex and intricate human activity involving the whole spectrum of man's intellectual and emotional potential, as anyone knows who has tried to develop even a single testable hypothesis.

2. What have we said about theory?

In examining material for this chapter many references to the concept of theory were observed in the writings of our colleagues in social work and related disciplines. These references indicate a high degree of consistent understanding of the essence of theory as briefly summarized above. Thus, Gordon Hearn regards theory as "an internally consistent body of verified hypotheses" (7, p. 8). For Strean (31, p. 5) theory is described as "a more or less verified explanation of observed facts or phenomena." Goode sees theory as the relationship between facts, or the process of ordering facts in some meaningful way (5, p. 9). Baldwin refers to theory as the explanation of some class of events (1, p. 45). Merton (15, p. 89) states that theory is the logical interrelationship between propositions. Harold Lewis says, ". . . theory in social work is intended to provide explanations for the phenomena of practice" (12, p. 16). Lotte Marcus sees theory as ". . . a systematized and comprehensive set of assumptions" (14). Joel Fischer says that theory is ". . . a more or less formalized explanatory conceptualization of the relationship of variables" (3, p. 41). Theory for Carl Rogers is a ". . . fallible changing attempt to construct a network of gossamer threads which will contain the solid facts" (27, p. 9). Talcott Parsons describes theory in the following manner, ". . . a theoretical system in the present sense is a body of logically interdependent generalized concepts of empirical reference" (19, p. 212).

When the practitioner looks at theory, his goal is to develop and refine an intellectual structure by which he can understand and manage the complex array of facts encountered in our practice, so that the nature of intervention can be deduced and the effects of such intervention predicted. The clinician's principal interest is in the utility of theory: what can it tell me about this situation that will permit me to act effectively? It is, therefore, not knowledge for its own sake, but knowledge for use.

Although it is not difficult to demonstrate that in our professional literature we have manifested an understanding of the nature of theory, this attitude is by no means a universal one within our profession. The literature of social work practice, especially that of the last decade, has been replete with a dual emphasis: one, a loud decrying of the lack of a strong theoretical base, and, two, an equally voiced exhortation for the strengthening of this component of practice. Such exhortations underline the observation that we have not put into practice what we know about, the dimensions of, need for and utility of theory. It may be that this is a phenomenon common to segments of other related disciplines. Be that as it may, we clearly have not been consistent in our application of the theory concept.

Thus, for some of us, theory seems to be almost antithetical to fact. This attitude is summed up in statements like: "I am a practitioner, not a theoretician." The implication here seems to be that theory inhibits practice. For others, the term "theory" seems to be synonymous with value statements about the dignity of man, the desirability of participation in one's destiny, or the seeking of the public good as a desirable goal. For still others, theory seems to describe a form of speculation or a post factum explanation. Thus, a colleague might say, "I have a theory as to why this happened," or ask, "What's your theory about this situation?" In another vein, theory sometimes seems to be used in the sense of basic axioms or postulates from which a particular logical structure is developed.

When a group or discipline tends to be diffuse about the concept of theory, it is easy to understand why it would also be diffuse in the way it applies available theory. Thus, it is still said that the lack of available theory seems to be holding us back. But this does not appear to be accurate. This present work emerged from an awareness that many theories, or at least emerging themes, existed in current practice, and from a wish to bring them together in one book. Our weakness is not that we suffer from a shortage of theories, but that we have not made full use of what we do have. For example, I believe that the currently strong criticism of clinical social work's heavy reliance on psychoanalytic theory is a red herring. I suggest a more accurate criticism would be that this theory is not understood and thus is not correctly applied. Many social workers identified with this school really only use some of the general basis of this rich body and are even less well acquainted with the various subsystems and persons related to this theoretical approach. If so, much of the criticism of the alleged limitations of psychodynamic theory or of any other theories important to social work should in fact be criticisms of a lack of understanding. Thus, the criticisms should be leveled against practitioners who operate predominantly from an impressionistic ad hoc type of base rather than from one solidly built on available theory.

Clearly, the reasons for our oft-cited apparent disregard or at least diffuseness in our use of available theory are complex. Herb Strean discusses this in his recent book and speculates on some of the reasons for this apparent weakness in our practice. Among the ideas mentioned, he identifies our strong tradition of human service as being used as an explanation for failure to make full use of available theory.

Undoubtedly, our origins of service and traditions of individual human worth have influenced us and must partially account for our less than full enthusiasm for theory, especially if theory is thought to be antihuman and mechanistic. But I suggest that using our concern for individuals, groups and communities as a rationale for a disinterest in theory is in reality a denial of the problem. This stance also seems to have an indefensible presumptuousness about it, for it also seems to be saying that those who are interested in theory building, whether within our profession or without, are seen as being without human concern, and only those committed to ignore theory are truly concerned about people and their needs. Neither can we rule out the fact that it is only in the last fifteen years that we have had heavy demands put on us by society for what we are doing. Without this pressure, it was easier for us to trust our impressions that what we were doing was good rather than attempt to conceptualize and thus explain our activities.

But surely we have frequently and perhaps continuously talked about theory and its needs. Several of the major books in casework included theory in their titles, such as Hamilton's classic, *Theory and Practice of Social Casework* (6), Ruth Smalley's *Theory for Social Work Practice* (29) and, most recently, *Theories of Social Casework* by Roberts and Nee (26). A recent survey of ten years of ten social work journals turned up over fifty articles with the word "theory" in their titles. Although we have long been interested in theory, we also have an accompanying tradition of using the word in less than a precise way. Rather than applying the concept in a specific sense proper to a scholarly discipline, we have tended to use it in a much looser way. Thus, we frequently apply the word "theory" to describe such things as: basic tenets of practice; systematic formulation of ideas; approaches to theory; schools of thought or systems of thought; accumulated practice wisdom; post factum explanations of basic values; rather than the rigorous definition of theory usually used. Bernice K. Simon comments on this in a chapter of the excellent book, *Theories of Social Casework* (26). In the final chapter, she questions whether any of the approaches called theories in the book is, in fact, a theory.

3. What have we done about theory?

Originally, the plan was to review the significant clinical writings of social work that indicated a theoretical orientation and comment on each from the viewpoint of its proximity to our accepted definition of theory. This original objective was altered for two reasons: first, after a preliminary draft had been written, it was soon perceived that this was a highly complex task, one that could serve as material for a book itself; and, second, it was seen that such an approach would not produce the thread of ideas necessary for the rest of this book. What did emerge, though, was a tentative classification of our search for a theoretical base that appeared to mirror the development of our profession. This is presented here in hopes that other colleagues might wish to pick up on it and develop it further.

In our literature eleven different approaches to theory can be identified. Each of these eleven topics could be developed at length, but at this time will merely be identified with brief comments:

The first of these could probably best be referred to as pretheory. Included under this heading would be the first formal attempts by our colleagues to conceptualize definitions of practice, components of practice and classifications of treatment procedures and methods. Examples of these would be Mary Richmond's (24) work, *Social Diagnosis*, and Gordon Hamilton's (6) classic, *Theory and Practice of Social Casework*. In spite of the title, Dr. Hamilton uses the word "theory" only a few times in the book and even less frequently refers to the process of theory building through research. Rather than dicussing concepts and verified hypotheses, she talks about "basic assumptions which cannot be proved" (6, p. 3), axioms, values, attitudes and exhortations. She speaks comfortably and authoritatively from a rich practice experience, but not from a formal theoretical base. Thus, her book is more prescriptive than theory-based. These early writings were, of course, essential first steps at bringing together in a scholarly experience-based manner the practice wisdom of the profession.

The second type of appoach to theory that could be identified was that cluster of writings based on a framework accepted as a theory. I refer specifically to that rich range of writings so essential to the early development of clinical practice that were based on the various psychodynamic schools of thought. The authors of these writings accepted one or several schools of psychodynamic theory as proven theory and then speculated on their implications for social work practice. A long list of articles, monographs and books can be identified under this heading. Looking at the last fifteen years, two good examples of this type of writing would be H. Parad's two books, *Ego Psychology and Dynamic Casework* (17) and *Ego Oriented Casework* (18). Here the authors are not trying to develop a particular theoretical stance but using an accepted existing one to develop further its applications for clinical practice.

The third approach to theory building in clinical practice in social work can be observed in those authors who have used their practice experience base and presented a particular stance or conceptual approach that represents their own thinking. Admittedly, such authors draw heavily and explicitly, but not exclusively, on other bodies of thought: that is, they have taken one or several series of ideas and to these added their own and out of this present an unique approach to practice. In the casework field, Hollis's "psychosocial system" (8) and Perlman's "problem solving approach" (22) would be the two best known examples of this. In the group work field, the writings of Gisela Konopka (11) would also represent this approach. Both Hollis and Konopka present statements about the theoretical orientations on which their work is based, and Perlman gives a series of axioms or statements of principle as the substructure for her approach to practice. Although clearly these works are based on carefully thought out and well organized thought systems, no one of them would meet the precise parameters of theory. They represent a system of propositions from which hypotheses could be developed and a theory built.

The fourth identifiable characteristic of our efforts at theory building in clinical practice in social work has been to divide practice into discrete segments: that is, we have long operated from a conceptual framework that separated out various forms of treatment as individual methodologies with separate conceptual underpinnings. Thus, up to the recent past and obviously continuing into the present, our principal writings in clinical practice were developed from either a casework, group work or family therapy stance. Clearly, there are historical reasons for this trend related to the way in which the various methodologies emerged. Nevertheless, this tradition fostered an assumption that our sought-for theoretical base needed a pluralistic foundation related to the various treatment modalities, and until recently gave little attention to the commonalities of different models.

Although the preponderance of our clinical writings have been based on some form of psychodynamic and small group theory, in the recent decade we have seen emerging a trend in theory building that introduces new thought systems into practice. Hence, in the late 1950s and continuing through the 1960s we began to see a series of important writings stemming from a range of theoretical bases. Thus, we find Perlman writing a book from a role theory base (27), Parad editing two books from an ego psychology base (16) (17) and later one on crisis theory (18), Werner publishing a book on cognitive theory (35), Jehu (9) and Thomas (33) producing major writings from a learning theory approach and similarly Lutz (13) and

Hearn (7) from a systems theory base. Consequently, we begin to see an interest in broadening our conceptual base. Sometimes this was done in a scholarly, searching way and at other times in an exhortative way implying that finally the goal of our long search was reached.

As would be expected, once our clinical field began to move into a more diverse conceptual base, we began to wonder how these theories fitted or did not fit together and to begin to make comparisons between theories. This seeking for interconnectedness is the next characteristic of our theoretical thinking. As before, we have still tended to make such comparisons along methodological lines; thus, Stein (30) and her associates compare the various theories related to family theory, Roberts and Nee (26) look at diverse theories in social casework, with Strean (31) doing the same thing a year later. Florence Hollis' reedition of *Social Casework, a Psychosocial Therapy* (8) gave us an example of how her own thinking has begun to incorporate several of these newer approaches into her psychosocial framework. In the group field, we find Schwartz and Zalba (28) doing a study of the theoretical bases of this modality of practice.

Accompanying the above development, another less predominant yet highly significant group of writings aimed at improving our theory can be identified. These do not look at particular theories, but at the more basic concept of the nature of theory and theory building. These writings move away from our traditional approaches to theory building and urge us to look at the process in the abstract. Usually the abstractions are then related to current professional reality with exhortations to shift our approach. This strategy was considered most carefully by Lutz (13) and Hearn (7) both of whom, interestingly, then moved into the specific applications of theory concepts in a systems orientation. I think these two writings have made significant contributions to our growing understanding of the nature, purpose and dire need for theory in our practice; they have been the inspiration for a renewed and more explicit approach to theory formulation in social work.

A further strategy in theory building that can be identified in our literature approaches the traditional model of theory building, that is, the approach based on research activities. From this writer's viewpoint, this stance is one still greatly neglected by our field. In this mode, various concepts related to our field are operationally defined and tested through the formulation of hypotheses and the examination of resultant data. The Ripple studies (25), using the concepts of motivation, capacity and opportunity, are an excellent example of this, as is Reid and Shyne's (23) work on short-term treatment and Hollis' work on a testing of her paradigm of treatment methods devised from experience-based observations (8). Many more projects of this type are needed and can be expected in the next few years.

Another approach to theory building is represented in the present work. Like others, we are here bringing together a range of theories related to social work, but unlike other collections also asking the authors to apply their particular orientation to various treatment modalities used in clinical practice, including work with communities. It is hoped that this type of two-way analysis of theory and methods will serve to bring a different strategy of comparison and, hopefully, integration than we have had to the present. Equally clear is the need for more work that seeks both areas of similarity and difference between theories and methods of treatment.

Since the first edition to this book, another trend can be observed in the literature, a trend that has positive and important implications for practice. This is the increasing numbers of articles that are dealing with highly specific components of discrete theories. That is, rather than attempting to discuss total systems, authors are doing one of two things: (1) looking at a specific application of a thought system, such as the use of crisis theory in a schoolroom context, or (2)

discussing the application of a discrete concept from a thought system to practice—such as the specific application of the concept of homeostasis in work with married couples. Both of these trends indicate a healthy awareness that further progress in theory building will probably happen only on a slow step-by-step basis.

There can also be identified an additional viewpoint of theory that doesn't help develop theory, but might well be effective in slowing our progress along more traditional lines. Here I refer to the opinion that says theory is unimportant and indeed counterproductive to good practice. Effective treatment consists of a warm, understanding, respectful reaching out of one human being perceived in all respects to be the equal of the person to whom he is reaching. Quantifying, analyzing, testing and experimenting, the regular scholarly endeavors of an academic approach to theory, are disregarded and looked on with suspicion.

The above elevenfold division shows that we have used a wide range of approaches in our search for better integrated and tested thought systems from which we can develop and test theory. Although highly fashionable to engage in rhetorical contests of mutual recrimination for our lack of theory-building efforts, I think our field has demostrated that a significant and consistent tradition of persons committed to this task has always existed. Clearly, we are just beginning to succeed; perhaps more progress can be made if we direct our efforts more into the task of theory building and less into the commitment to criticize each other.

It is my assessment, possibly debatable, that at this point most, if indeed not all, of the conceptual bases of the various explanations of behavior, the descriptions of intervention and the axioms about indicators for treatment that have been presented as the theoretical base of our practice do not qualify for the title of a theory in the strict sense of the word. This has been said before, and repeated exhortations about this lack by still another author would not advance the cause. Neither should we despair, for considerable progress is being and has been made. We are certainly conscious of the need for better thought systems and better coordination and utilization of the immense store of practice wisdom acquired by our field. The purpose of this volume is both to bring more of this thinking to the field as well as to contribute to the search for a better integration.

4. What can theory do for us?

If we are still far from either a theoretical base or even a base of several theories, two questions must be examined: first, what can we hope for in aspiring to such a goal and, second, is theory really related at all to practice? The latter question could be put another way, "Is a strong theoretical base a necessary concomitant to effective therapy?" Are good therapists also good theoreticians and poor therapists poor theoreticians?

Let's first examine what theory should do for practice. For the clinician seeking to offer responsible, effective intervention, the most essential and important contribution of theory is its ability to predict outcomes, or, in other words, its ability to explain. The practitioner who consciously formulates a treatment plan based on an assessment of a situation is involved in either a theory-building or theory-testing activity. That is, a treatment plan aimed at achieving a specific treatment goal presumes a situation is understood to the extent that specific alterations of the situation can be made with predictable outcomes. Without the confidence in predicting outcomes based on a presumed understanding of situations and persons, practice remains for the most part in the area of guesswork and impressionistic responses. This is not to imply that the day is near at hand when we will be certain about the outcome of each of our cases, only that we can anticipate being able to be more sure about more of our cases than we are at present.

Theory also aids the practitioner to an-

ticipate future outcomes of some situations and to speculate on unanticipated relationships between variables: that is, theory should help us to recognize, understand and explain new situations. If we understand the phenomena with which we are dealing and their interrelationships sufficiently well, we should, therefore, have the conceptual tools to deal with some unexpected or unanticipated observations in the behavior we meet. To the extent that our theory is sound, we should experience fewer surprises in our practice.

Theory, of course, also helps us carry over from one situation to the next, in aiding us to recognize what is similar and what is different in our ongoing practice experience. This in no way detracts from the concept of individuality or self-determination; in fact, it can enhance these concepts by helping us see not only how the client or situation is like other clients and situations, but how he is different.

A sound and logically consistent theoretical structure permits us to explain our activity to others, to transfer our knowledge and skills in a testable, demonstrable way and to permit our activities to be scrutinized and evaluated by others: that is, if we have sound theories, then others can profit by our experience in applying the theory.

Theory further helps us to recognize when we have new situations that indicate gaps in our knowledge. Thus, when the application of a theoretical concept does not result in the expected outcome, we are made aware that we have misunderstood, or that what we have is not sufficient to deal with the situation at hand. Frequently practitioners, in meeting a difficult or new practice situation, overblame themselves, thinking that if they had been more aware they could have coped more effectively, when in fact there may be no available theoretical construct to explain the presenting phenomena. Hence, it is as important to know what we don't know, as to know what is known.

Theory also gives assurance to the worker. We all know the awesome responsibility of the practitioner. We have all experienced the haunting loneliness caused by the weight of the responsibility of our cases. Theory will never dispel it completely, but a firm theoretical orientation helps to give us a base on which to order what we do know. We must have a set of anchoring concepts from which to work to avoid the aimless, albeit benevolent wandering with the client that comes from lack of knowledge. Somewhat cynically, one might suggest that theory, whether it be sound theory or not, gives a sense of security to the therapist, thus increasing his certainty, thus increasing his effectiveness, even if what he does is not related to the theory he espouses. If this were true, it would give a new meaning to the saying attributed to Kurt Lewin, "Nothing works better than a good theory."

Theory, in addition, permits us to assess other theories: that is, if we are clear about which of our concepts are empirically verifiable and empirically connected, then we are in a much better position to compare what we know with other emerging iedas. In our field especially, there can frequently be several theoretical explanations for similar phenomena. Which is most useful and most effective, must constantly be tested. Other theoretical explanations from bases different from our own frequently help us better understand and indeed modify our own theoretical stance.

Intriguing as are these posited functions of theory for the clinician, there are some who would argue that our search for theory that would fully explain the "person in situation" is a search in vain. With some conviction, they say that the target of our concern is so complex, individualized and rapidly changing, that it cannot be either understood or manipulated in a predictable way. Whether this be so or not, and I choose to believe it is not, I think it is abundantly clear that man will continue forever his search for the key to the explanation of himself, his fellow earth travellers and the societies and systems in which we function or fail to function.

A more telling and troubling question to me

is whether at this stage in our practice development we need a theory except to serve as our anchor, as mentioned above. Although not a respectable question in a profession seeking increased recognition in the company of scholars, it is not to be discounted. Might it be that the complete therapist is not the theoretician but the artist whose theory is his intuition and skills his natural endowment?

I once suggested in another writing that one had to conclude that many social workers were in fact skilled diagnosticians, otherwise how to explain the myriad of highly successfully treated cases. I was strongly taken to task for this statement (20), as it was pointed out that it didn't follow that a successfully treated case meant that the worker knew what he was doing and why he was doing it, at all. This question has similarly been raised in discussions concerning curriculum models for teaching social workers. Should one teach theory and practice together, or separately? Or, put another way, can one teach techniques of interventions that have been found to be effective without presuming that such techniques can be directly related to a body of theory?

Perhaps the state of our practice is such that the artistic component is stronger than the knowledge base, and for the present we should leave the two separate. Although it is not something I believe or can be comfortable with, I think in our search for a better understanding of the therapeutic process, the how and why of intervention and the assessment of its outcome, we should at least consider the possibility that a person's practice is not related to the theoretical concepts that he holds. If so, we might learn more about practice and its base by studying what in fact practitioners do, not the reasons for which they say they manage cases in particular ways. Many of the discussions that take place among practitioners revolve around alleged theoretical differences, yet more than one research project has indicated that even when we fly different theoretical flags, we tend to act similarly when we are with clients who are alike in personality, need and life situation. Thus, practitioners who would claim to be diametrically opposed theoretically, are frequently found to do similar things in treatment while still claiming to be different. If it can be established that our practice does not reflect our stated theory base, perhaps one could develop a theory of intervention that is different from the theories of personality, learning and behavior with which we are familiar and which are the topics of subsequent chapters in this book. What I am suggesting is that at times we may be misled by the idea that our practice directly reflects the theory we hold. In fact, I think one could identify components of our various practice activities that contradict what we say we know about how people learn and behave and about how behavior is modified.

In summary, this chapter has identified that our field has long been cognizant of the nature of theory, although it has tended to be free in the use of the term "theory" and even more free in stating what our theories are and showing that we use them in our practice activities.

In subsequent chapters each of the various thought systems identified as being a part of our theoretical base will be presented, with comments on its present place in social work practice, its known implication for practice and the research challenges that it offers.

In the final chapter, we will discuss some interconnections between these various approaches and speculate on some of the implications for further developments in theory building in social work that might be expected in the next few years.

References

1. Baldwin, Alfred L. *Theories of Child Development*. New York: Wiley, 1968.
2. Eron, Leonard D. and Robert Callahan. *The Relation of Theory to Practice in Psychotherapy*. Chicago: Aldine, 1969.
3. Fischer, Joel. "A Framework for the Analysis and Comparison of Clinical Theories of Induced Changes," *Social Service Review*, December, 1971, pp. 440-454.
4. Ford, Donald H. and Hugh B. Urban. *Systems of Psychotherapy*. New York: Wiley, 1964.
5. Goode, William J. and Paul K. Hatt. *Methods in Social Research*. New York: McGraw-Hill, 1952.
6. Hamilton, Gordon. *Theory and Practice of Social Casework*, rev. ed. New York: Columbia University Press, 1951.
7. Hearn, Gordon. *Theory Building in Social Work*. Toronto: University of Toronto Press, 1958.
8. Hollis, Florence. *Casework, A Psychosocial Therapy*, 2nd ed., rev. New York: Random House, 1972.
9. Jehu, Derek. *Learning Theory and Social Work*. London: Routledge, 1967.
10. Kadushin, Alfred. "The Knowledge Base of Social Work," in Alfred Kahn (ed.) *Issues in American Social Work*. New York: Columbia University Press, 1959.
11. Konopka, Gisela. *Social Group Work: A Helping Process*. Englewood Cliffs, N.J.: Prentice-Hall, 1963.
12. Lewis, Harold. "Practice, Science and Professional Education: Developing a Curriculum, Responsive to New Knowledge and Values." Paper read at General Session of *Symposium on the Effectiveness of Social Work Intervention: Implications for Curriculum Change*. New York: Fordham University, 1971.
13. Lutz, Werner. *Concepts and Principles Underlying Casework Practice*. Washington, D.C.: National Association of Social Workers, 1956.
14. Marcus, Lotte. Personal communication to the Editor, January, 1972.
15. Merton, Robert K. *Social Theory and Social Structure*. Glencoe, Ill.: Free Press, 1957, Chapters I, II, III.
16. Parad, Howard J. (ed.). *Crisis Intervention: Selected Readings*. New York: Family Service Association of America, 1958.
17. ———. *Ego Psychology and Dynamic Casework*. New York: Family Service Association of America, 1965.
18. ——— and R. Miller. *Ego Oriented Casework: Problems and Persepectives*. New York: Family Service Association of America, 1963.
19. Parsons, Talcott. "The Present Position and Prospects of Systematic Theory in Sociology," *Essays in Sociological Theory*, rev. ed. Glencoe, Ill.: Free Press, 1954, pp. 212-213.
20. Perlman, Helen H. "Diagnosis Anyone." Book review of F. Turner (ed.) *Differential Diagnosis and Treatment, Psychiatry and Social Science Review*, 3, No. 8 (1969-1970), 12-17.
21. ———. *Persona: Social Role and Responsibility*. Chicago: University of Chicago Press, 1968

22. ———. *Social Casework: A Problem-Solving Process*. Chicago: University of Chicago Press, 1957.

23. Reid, William J. and Ann W. Shyne. *Brief and Extended Casework*. New York: Columbia University Press, 1969.

24. Richmond, Mary. *Social Diagnosis*. New York: Russell Sage Foundation, 1917.

25. Ripple, Lillian, Ernestina Alexander and Bernice Polemis. *Motivation Capacity and Opportunity: Social Service Monographs*. Chicago: University of Chicago Press, 1964.

26. Roberts, Robert W. and Robert H. Nee. *Theories of Social Casework*. Chicago: University of Chicago Press, 1970.

27. Rogers, Carl. "A Theory for Therapy Personality and Interpersonal Relationships as Developed in the Client-Centered Framework," in S. Koch (ed.) *Psychology: A Study of a Science*, Vol. 2, *General Systematic Formulations, Learning and Special Processes*. New York: McGraw-Hill, 1949.

28. Schwartz, William and Serapio R. Zalba (eds.) *The Practice of Group Work*. New York: Columbia University Press, 1971.

29. Smalley, Ruth E. *Theory for Social Work Practice*. New York: Columbia University Press, 1967.

30. Stein, Joan W. *The Family as a Unit of Study and Treatment*. Seattle: Regional Rehabilitation Research Institute, University of Washington, School of Social Work, 1969.

31. Strean, Herbert F. (ed.) *Social Casework: Theories in Action*. Metuchen, N.J.: Scarecrow Press, 1971.

32. Studt, Elliot. "Social Work Theory and Implications for the Practice of Methods," Mimeographed, C.S.W.E. Annual Programme Meeting, January 24, 1968.

33. Thomas, Edwin J. *Behavioral Science for Social Workers*. New York: Free Press, 1967.

34. Turner, Francis J. (ed.). *Differential Diagnosis and Treatment in Social Work*. New York: Free Press, 1968; second edition, 1976.

35. Werner, Harold D. *A Rational Approach to Social Casework*. New York: Association Press, 1965.

2

Psychoanalytic Theory

by

EUNICE F. ALLAN

Any practice profession must examine theories relevant to its purpose and master the task of adapting them to service use. Within the social work profession the subspeciality, clinical social work, must locate a range of concepts pertinent to a primary commitment to the restoration or enhancement of social functioning. Inasmuch as an individual or family in a stressful situation represents the confluence of inner and outer forces which have an impact on social functioning, the phenomena which must be explained are complex.

In consequence of this complexity, any intervention designed to enhance an individual's capacity to select and pursue options in the management of his life would appear to require two separate but related sets of concepts or theories. One set must make comprehensible the paths by which individuals sort out and respond to life experiences, influence and are in-

fluenced by what happens to them in life; in short, a general theory of personality development. Such a theory would need to provide a universally applicable framework for personality development, pose a model which would make it possible to explain individual differences in rates and modes of development and clarify how these factors influence both feeling and functioning. It must offer concepts for the seemingly invisible connections among an individual's biological equipment, the quality of nurturance experienced, real life opportunities and the resultant mode of dealing with object relations as well as with the functions accompanying these relations. The theory must be so constructed that its outer parameters hold firm even as details about its parts can be reordered or enhanced by new knowledge or insights. It must provide a basis for explaining past functioning and thus a basis for prediction of the future. In short, it must encompass all the data essential to explain the etiology of any given aspect of current functioning.

Theory of Causation

Increased focus on the relevance of cultural and environmental forces to personality development, influenced and supported by the observations of social work practitioners and sociological theorists, increases the range of data which a theory of personality must encompass and integrate. Such an increasingly complex theory of personality provides, in effect, "basic science" data from which any profession involving human relationships may legitimately draw. So long as there is no violation of the theory's internal consistency, a particular aspect may be extrapolated and adapted to the stated purposes of practice.

It is the writer's belief that the psychoanalytic theory of personality development provides the most rational, ordered explanations of functioning. Perennially incomplete, the logical links between its basic tenets have tolerated well and been enhanced by clarifications and variations contributed by creative theorists who have followed Freud (33, p. 103).

Most of Freud's theoretical formulations were developed retrospectively, in an attempt to account for the disturbances in feeling or functioning observable in therapeutic encounters with patients. The research method consisted of microscopic examination of associations retrieved from the patient's unconscious from which phenomena he drew his earliest formulations contained in the topographic, dynamic, economic, and genetic points of view. These concepts assigned a kind of geographic location to parts of the inner life (topographic), captured a sense of the presence of the drives (dynamic), the fluidity of shifting quantity (economics), and pointed to a calendar of psychic events (genetic).

Through these formulations Freud described development as characterized by parts of the personality warring with one another, with the ego as representative of reality and the whole summarized as "conflict." However, in relation to the ego, there were difficulties in tracing the path of reality influence which arose from the constraints inherent in the topographic point of view. If, as he observed, identifications were unconscious and the ego was made up of abandoned identifications, then it followed that the ego must develop gradually, invisibly, over time, and not in response to reality in the sense of the immediate external world. Rather than the inner life being a constantly seething cauldron of conflicting forces from within, by 1923 Freud had concluded that the ego seemed to develop more stable ways of dealing with the drives through unconscious processes which delayed or contained the drives and thus developed more lasting structures (13, pp. 29-30). In this context the assumptions underlying the topographic view became untenable and were replaced by the abstractions of id, superego, and ego viewed as stable structures in an anatomy of personality. With these constructs, it became possible for analytic theorists to study the paths by which these structures achieved their characteristics, the respective content of each part, and to examine the relationship of these parts to one another. Thus, the door was opened for the growth of a general theory of psychology. From this basic formulation later theorists—Anna Freud, Hartmann, Kris, Erikson et al.—continued the examination of the manner in which real life experiences (object relations) became interwoven with intrapsychic processes on the path to mastery of functions and achievement of autonomy in the perpetual (epigenetic) tasks which characterize man's entire life span.

Corollary to work in the area of a general theory of development, Kernberg (25), Kohut (28), and Masterson et al. (30) advanced understanding of the way in which disturbances in early object relations resulted in distortions in ego growth. Clarity as to the early origin of such distortion increased comprehension of a large group of individuals variously characterized as having narcissistic or borderline personality organization, helping to explain the difficulty encountered in therapy directed toward altering or repairing such organization. Perhaps the greatest value lay in the extent to which these formulations increased focus on ego organization as a central issue in adaptive or maladaptive functioning.

From practice wisdom and social science observations, social workers had become acutely aware of the lasting effect on functioning of attitudes derived from important relationships and experiences which reflected differences in social class, role, ethnicity. Ego psychological theories provided a way of comprehending the subtle process through which these varied reality experiences became integrated in the personality and thus improved the conceptual tools with which to examine ego functioning. Conceptually, these additional formulations reduced the gap between the inner psychic world and reality and enormously expanded the explanatory power of the theories of personality development. The change did not in any way suggest a reduction in the power of unconscious forces but provided intellectual tools "with which unconscious operations could be traced and a link sought between early ego organization and current social functioning. That refinement in formulation and adaptation to diagnosis and treatment proved of particular interest to clinical social work in its concern with social functioning."

Concepts of Treatment

The necessity to adapt these concepts to practice pointed up the requirement for a second, separate set of concepts in order to locate and explain causal connections between theories which explain the phenomena of functioning and the specific interventions designed to alter that functioning in the direction of a predetermined therapeutic goal.

It is widely accepted that a therapeutic rela-

tionship is central to the interventions which characterize the helping process. Like a marriage, it is created by two visible participants and a shifting population of invisible figures from the past. Its collaborative nature suggests that it cannot be imposed by either participant but that each one brings different life experiences, knowledge, and expectations. The client brings his "felt need" and characteristic way of responding to the dual demand inherent in his discomfort and his quest for help. The professional training of the practitioner should equip him with awareness of his own inner life and a body of knowledge which enables him consciously to direct and shape the therapeutic relationship in a manner to advance an agreed-upon treatment goal.

Intervention and the Therapeutic Relationship

Some helpful perspectives on the science and art of evoking a therapeutic relationship have enriched our literature. Richmond (35), who never accepted Freud's theories, assumed that the manner in which individuals responded to crucial life realities was connected with "character," a term which carried implications of moral rectitude or regrettable lapses. The treatment involved an effort to change the most noxious aspects of the social environment and by example and moral persuasion to use the relationship to encourage a change in the client's usual mode of response. However, during the late 1920s and the subsequent decade many caseworkers were learning psychoanalytic theory and using it to help explain disturbances in functioning and as a key to the mysteries of the therapeutic relationship.

In 1941 Garrett examined the unrealistic or transference element of the relationship, explored its sources and some of the techniques for keeping it within bounds appropriate to the goals of casework treatment (18). The paper indicated her awareness of our beginning understanding of ego psychology and she predicted that further developments in that area would yield new directions for the caseworker's use of the unconscious aspect of the relationship. In a passing reference, she suggested that "identification," which had been loosely used to cover every aspect of relationship, should be examined for more discriminating application.

In 1946 she resumed her study of the worker-client relationship, discussing transference phenomena more specifically in connection with dependence feelings stirred up by the client's request for help, while pointing up contraindictions for overdevelopment of transference feelings in encouraging the client's identification with the caseworker (17).

By 1948 Austin noted two major categories of casework "social therapy and psychotherapy, in both of which the worker-client relationship was considered the medium of help" (1). The intensity of relationship appropriate for each casework category was determined by the nature of the problem and the treatment goal. In her work, the essential factor was an orderly attempt to relate the caseworker's conscious direction of the therapeutic relationship to variables concerned with the severity of the client's internal pathology, as distinguished from environmental disturbances, and to examine the effects of these two variables upon the treatment goal.

For a number of years there appeared a hiatus in the literatue insofar as a consideration of the relationship was concerned, except as it was incidental to a discussion about role, or various forms of family or group treatment. The quest was resumed by Louise Bandler in 1963 (2) when she factored from the theories of ego development those elements which could be linearly arranged and subsumed under Hartmann's felicitous term "sublimatory process." She suggested this process as a model for casework treatment, on the basis of which the caseworker might provide a positive identification, thereby making neutralized energies available for sublimation, an avenue through which normal development takes place. She described, through case illustrations, the way in

which the caseworker could advance a positive identification by meeting the underlying need rather than exploring or posing demands in connection with the area of deprivation.

In 1964, Hollis (23) characterized the relationship as a mode of communication and a set of attitudes and responses in which realistic and unrealistic forces operate. In a discussion of the uses to which the relationship was put, she noted the frequency with which successful treatment was associated with the client's capacity to identify with a caseworker with whom he had a positive relationship.

Conceptual Problems

In Richmond's work the major weakness in the formulation as to causation was its failure to recognize that functioning could not be entirely understood through observable phenomena, for all reality experience had to be processed through an essentially invisible mental apparatus. The limited effectiveness of the intervention she prescribed reflected the basic flaws in the explanation of causation. Nonetheless, Richmond's writings did contain ordered though simplistic concepts of causation and separate but related concepts as to intervention.

Most of the later casework contributors assumed the relevance of psychoanalytic explanations to the intrapsychic causes of social malfunctioning. During the 1920s and 1930s, practitioners who relied upon the then extant analytic theories depicted personality development centered around conflict and its resolution. The theories were concerned with the drives, their fate throughout the early genetic stages, and examination of the defenses. Careful examination of a client's past did indeed make it possible to trace the course of a disturbance in development. In effect, the theories of causation provided the guidelines for gathering data from which diagnosis could be determined. However, a usual goal of casework treatment—improvement or restoration of social functioning—did not commonly follow the revival of old conflicts and resulted in disenchantment with treatment, which was essentially a misapplication of a psychoanalytic theory of personality in a miniature psychoanalytic model of treatment.

In the decades since the 1940s, practitioners turned to ego psychological theories with an emphasis on issues of normal development, maturation, and adaptation in the context of the "life" model. In applying these recent insights, practitioners have tended to relinquish direct exploration of early parental and sibling relationships close to instinctual feeling and to concentrate on current relationships supportive and ego building in intent. Associated with clinical diagnostic categories, social class, physical and intellectual capacities, education, and economic level, general guidelines have been developed as to what kinds of exploration to avoid as well as what to pursue. At professional meetings and in the literature, discussions have frequently been accompanied by case material which appeared to substantiate the appropriateness of these treatment choices.

Despite these substantial advances in understanding the differential ways in which a relationship might be used to advance growth, connection between theory to explain the influence of relationships in psychic development and the use of the relationship in the therapeutic intervention itself has been loosely drawn. Thus the links have been best examined on a case-by-case basis or by collectivities of cases grouped according to presenting complaint, diagnostic category, treatment goal, etc. Still elusive have been generalizable formulations usable across categories of diagnosis or goal, which would permit prediction of the probable effect of using the therapeutic relationship to give direct advice, explore or ignore sexual material, express interest in a man's job achievements or in his failure. A logical step in postulating concepts of intervention rests on examination of a specific aspect of psychoanalytic theory of development in a search for a rationale for equally specific treatment decisions, purposively made to in-

fluence a therapeutic relationship to advance growth in a specific area.

Aim of Chapter

A client's encounter with a caseworker is customarily precipitated by acute discomfort with a disturbed function or relationship and accompanied by additional anxiety related to the actuality of needing help. In this context the client draws upon the cumulative work of the ego and superego, the past identifications through which he has developed a repertoire of responses to human relationships and life situations. Consequently, the reponses apparent in interviews will reflect the extent to which the ego has mastered developmental tasks to date as well as revealing the functions and relationships threatened by the current stress. Through the feelings of self-worth or blame, expectation of approval or criticalness expressed, the responses will reveal also the characteristic of the superego. Inasmuch as early adaptational tasks are not erased by subsequent development and attitudes but coexist silently with them, these responses will reveal not only the present but the old feelings and attitudes which resurface in the therapeutic relationship (13, p. 69). It is from these old and new attitudes and needs that the practitioner must draw in engaging the client in an alignment for growth.

Such a "therapeutic alliance" is generally regarded as fundamental to effective treatment, although there is a difference of opinion as to whether it is best negotiated by formal contract or by implication. It is the writer's belief that whether accompanied by explicit contract or unspoken commitment there is an additional, less visible process, whereby the practitioner is able to influence consciously the relationship to mobilize a growth-enhancing aspect of the personality. Clinical experience and formal research findings suggest that the earliest interviews appear crucial in determining the fate of the alliance (29, pp. 106, 189).

The conceptual task, then, is to abstract

and adapt from the psycholanalytic theory of personality the process of normal development in connection with relationship formation. If it is so that the ego's adaptive capacity rests on the extent to which aims and objects are powered by energies freed from instinctual control, the corollary area of inquiry must be the path by which freedom from impulses, or neutralization, is achieved. This consideration led more specifically to focus on that part of the theory which traces the course of identifications and their role in neutralization of impulses, and to consideration of the impact of those identifications on the superego precursors and the crystallized superego itself.

In this context, an attempt will be made to trace a link between specific aspects of the theory explaining identification in influencing relationship capacity and equally specific therapeutic interventions. A convenient unit of study is the therapeutic relationship as it operates in the initial exploratory interviews, for it is in this crucial period that the therapeutic alliance is forged.

Interest in this problem is determined partly by practitioners' interest in the treatment issues themselves. Perhaps a more compelling basis of interest is the need to develop a simple model which would serve as a basis for repeatable efforts to link a particular aspect of a theory of development to an aspect of treatment. It may be that a "theory of treatment" can develop only through orderly accumulation of a series of related treatment concepts.

Theoretical considerations

Neutralization and Sublimation

In his paper "On Narcissism" (15, pp. 30-59), Freud used the term sublimation to describe the object libido's shift to a nonsexual aim, a process he considered a prerequisite to ego growth and achievable only through identification. In *The Ego and the Id* (13, pp. 64-65)

he expressed his belief that diffusion of libido accompanied every identification, making identification an essential ingredient of every sublimatory advance. Hartmann et al. (22, p. 226) extended the concept of sublimation to include aggressive drives and considered, therefore, that both libidinal and aggressive impulses could be neutralized through identification and thereby made available to the ego. In his "Notes on the Superego" (21, p. 47), Hartmann specified that sublimation, like all other defenses, depends upon a change in energic mode.

There is considerable difference of opinion as to whether or not sublimation constitutes a defense or a separate kind of resolution of primitive impulses. Freud (12, p. 163) defined defense as a "general designation for all the techniques which the ego makes use of in conflicts which may lead to a neurosis" and further comments that it exists in order to protect the ego from instinctual demands. In enumerating defenses Anna Freud (8, pp. 56-57) suggested sublimation, or "displacement of instinctual aims," as an additional defense, although she considered that it was more relevant to normal development than to neurosis. There seems to be no finally agreed-upon answer. However, since sublimatory activity uses neutralized energies which, by definition, are those already separated from their instinctual sources, sublimation does not seem to meet the requirements inherent in the definition of defense. It might be appropriate to consider sublimation not a defense, but a separate process inherent in normal development. Most recent theorists agree with Freud that the process, by whatever name, whereby impulses are neutralized and made available to the ego, is achieved through identification.

Process of Identification

At that point the agreement ends, for there are few aspects of psychoanalytic theory about which there are more disagreement and confusion than that which exists in connection with the meaning of identification and the process by which it is achieved. Freud (14, p. 159) originally used the term in "Mourning and Melancholia" to explain the manner in which a melancholic dealt with his feelings about a lost love object, by establishing an identification with the ego of the lost object and then directing the reproaches against that part of his own ego. In 1921 (11, pp. 105-108) he returned to an earlier idea that identification was a primitive form of object relation, the earliest in which a person attempts to mold his own ego in the image of the one he has chosen for a model. In the first instance, he was searching for an explanation for an illness but in the second, he appeared to relate identification to questions of development. In *The Ego and the Id* (13, pp. 36-40) he seemed to combine these two approaches by suggesting that mechanisms of melancholia, the substitution of an identification for an abandoned object cathexis, might be used in normal ego development. In this manner, he left within one definition an aspect of personality at once playing a part in pathology and in development. Implied in his different use of the term is the suggestion that identification is a process which can serve different purposes.

Fenichel (5, p. 100) agreed with Freud's definition in which identification is seen as an attempt to mold the ego in the image of another. He further emphasized its unconscious quality and noted that in therapy identifications are powerful and peculiarly resistant to "insight."

As the focus of psychoanalytic concern shifted somewhat from pathology to a greater interest in development, child analysts have paid special attention to clarifying the process and content of identification, as it appears of central importance in the development of the ego and the superego. Jacobson (24, pp. 46-48) distinguishes between introjective and projective elements in identification formation. She emphasized that introjection and projection refer to psychic processes through which self-images take on the characteristics of object images. In the early preoedipal stage of development when the boundaries between self and other are thin, the child's object relations are the result of the continuous operation of projective and introjective mechanisms and his self-image reflects those object relations.

Sandler (36, pp. 150-155) considers that the superego is formed through the introjection of the authority of the parent and that before, during, and after its formation identifications continue to operate so that the child's developing self-concept reflects the harshness or benignity of the parent model, diluted by subsequent experience with a greater variety of models.

It is apparent, then, that the way in which the term "identification" is used depends on how it is seen in relation to development. Perhaps it would clarify understanding of the term to trace it through the stages of psychic development, for much of its utility to treatment is determined by whether it provides greater precision in locating disturbance on a developmental continuum.

Identification and Development

Mahler (29) observed that from birth subtle interaction between mother and child determined the centrality of that relationship in each individual's "unique somatic and psychological make-up." Her studies of the mother-child interaction during the first three years of life enabled her to distinguish four subphases in the separation-individuation process and to suggest that the manner in which the subphases are negotiated has critical impact on the resilience of ego functions. In combination with well-established ideas about psychosexual development, recognition of the psychic tasks of these subphases provided a complementary set of ideas with which to follow early ego development through the achievement of object constancy, separation-individuation in the direction of autonomy.

In earliest development, balance in the child's frustration-gratification experience is determined by the earliest relationship with the mother which enables the child to share mother's affective responses, later to imitate her in a kind of global identification in which he plays at being mother. Even as early as this, how capable he will be of separating himself from mother and progressing in development will be influenced by the quality of parental feeling to which he has been exposed as well as by the particular biological equipment with which he is endowed. During the second stage of childhood, roughly from the second year until the resolution of the oedipal conflict, the child is able to develop true object relations. Through these object relations primarily with the parents, he is able to take in and make part of himself on an increasingly selective basis qualities and functions of the parents. This selectivity derives from the fact that the child's capacities for more realistic object and self-representations enable him to exercise greater refinement in his introjective and projective mechanisms. During latency, an increasing opportunity for a range of object relationships opens up a selection of models from which it is possible to draw for varied qualities and capacities in a discriminating way. For optimal developmental neutralized impulses need be drawn most heavily from positive libidinal impulses and most lightly from aggressive impulses. Such neutralization can take place only if the inevitable frustration to which the child must be subjected by a nurturing parent is motivated by positive nonerotic feelings.

At adolescence the increased pressures from libidinal drives threaten the autonomy the young person has been able to build. He must begin the final severance of childish ties to his parents and simultaneously establish himself as an autonomous adult, a task possible only as he can displace libidinal investments onto new objects and, building on past identifications, move to new identifications. As the adolescent or young adult enlarges the sphere of ego autonomy through a growing sense of his own identity, pursuit and mastery of intellectual and social aims, reliance on identification diminishes particularly on indiscriminate, introjective and projective mechanisms. However, here is no absolute ego stability and ego functions can be reinvolved in instinctual impulses if vulnerable object relations are threatened. What is vulnerable for one person will be determined by any of the many factors which influence the content and timing of identification. One factor in determining points of vulnerability may be found in the identificatory experiences which accompany the development of the superego, a psychic unit which exercises considerable influence over object relations and ego functioning (7, Ch. III; 24, Part I, Sections 3,4,5; Part II, Sections 6,7).

The superego

Its Development as a Structure

In the preoedipal years the child experiences a variety of self and parental images. In the progression from one developmental task to the next these images, through identification, begin to make fragmentary contributions to inner standards which the child makes his own. Because these developments take place through the medium of energies neutralized by superego identifications, there is an accretion of power as the embryonic superego takes on the capacity to modify the cathectic conditions and the discharge processes of the ego in general.

Current theorists (3, pp. 326-327, 336-338; 35; 24, pp. 70-86) emphasize that developments in ego maturation are what make possible substantial progress in mastery of the oedipal conflict. This maturation is exemplified by the ego's capacity to relinquish literal self and object images which are replaced by more selective recognition and comprehension of parents as separate personalities. There is a partial reduction of interest in and dependence on the real parents as the precursors yield an introject. Through this introject the relationship to the parental object is retained while the real parents cease to be essential to the standard-setting part of the personality. What has been introjected is parental authority and a separate unit of psychic organization is launched.

Implied here is a circularity in development which highlights the interdependence of ego and superego. Preoedipal ego development in itself rests on many factors: constitutional growth essential for locomotion, speech, fine muscular coordination, etc., and on neutralized energies. During the preoedipal period neutralization takes place partially through superego identification (at this point hardly distinguishable from ego identification) (35, 24, 3) and thus preoedipal superego precursors contribute energically to ego growth. In turn, ego growth creates one of the conditions necessary for the crystallization of the superego as a separate unit of psychic organization. The partial mastery of the oedipal conflict which heralds the final formation of the superego results in massive neutralization of instinctual drives, making available to the ego a vast reservoir of energies for further development.

Thus formed, the superego, in a position to modify the cathectic conditions and discharge of the ego, is a unit of personality exercising "enormous influence over our emotional thought processes and our actions" (24). Through its cathectic control, it is able to dictate signals not only in relation to specific impulses, but also to influence overall feelings of self-esteem. As Beres comments, "The superego can be defined in terms of attitude, not in terms of action" (3). It could be added that attitudes are conveyed by relationships and through those avenues influence action, although action itself we consider as being ultimately determined by the ego. It is, however, this connection with attitudes toward

self and the silent parental attitudes toward impulses which results in the superego's powerful influence in the therapeutic relationship.

Content of the Superego

Because the very stability of the superego as a structure appears to be strengthened or threatened in response to changes in its content, it is useful to examine how those changes come about. It has been noted that superego as well as ego development rests on the degree of neutralization of drives around each successive genetic stage. We have further noted that parental relationships, in which libidinal feelings transcend aggressive ones, make neutralization possible, and strongly color the affective tone of the identifications. Mindful of the hazards of oversimplifying, it is nonetheless useful to observe that at the oral stage identifications will be around the tasks of giving and receiving; at the anal stage, around those involving dependence and control; and at the oedipal period, around the myriad aspects of sexual identity.

The Superego and Developmental Stages

Practitioners interested in modifications which make possible improved functioning search for indicators as to the time and kind of intervention likely to advance modifications. At any stage, intervention would need to take into account the nature of the unfinished developmental business, for the residual mark of superego precursors will be present in the client's attitude toward his own impulses, his self-esteem, and parentlike figures of authority. Thus, although adult in chronological age and life experience, his perception of himself, of the therapist and his current felt need will reflect the identifications of the past as well as those of the present. Any relationship offered him must accommodate itself to these dual feelings about himself. Clues as to what attitude and behavior on the part of the therapist will encourage a growth-enhancing relationship can be derived from locating the partial stalemate or deflection in development and noting the characteristics of object relations accompanying that aspect of development.

Since most parents will be loving or hostile differently and in relation to different stages of development, a client will have experienced varied qualities of relationship and his identifications will reflect that variety. A mother deprived in her own growing may be unable to be loving around feeding, so that a child would have difficulties around giving and receiving which would interfere with all subsequent stages and cause him as an adult to assume other adults will be ungiving to him, just as he would be restricted in his own ability to give. Such deprivation tends to increase anxiety and distrust and delay genuine differentiation, leaving a child vulnerable to prolonged attachment. In adult life one would expect adequate though limited functioning to the extent that a symbiotic-like relationship was available or in defense against such a relationship, an isolated way of life relatively free of demands.

A mother may be able to give around feeding but unable to gratify the dependence of the two- or three-year-old, or is able to do so only by extracting complete compliance. Thus, a child might be comfortable in giving and receiving, more expectant that others would share with him in respect to more passive matters, but be uncomfortable about appropriately aggressive behavior with an expectation that aggression would bring retaliation through control or abandonment. Or, in Mahler's (29) terms, when a mother's hostile or ambivalent feelings make inescapable the child's failure to complete the tasks of rapprochement anxiety about closeness-distance, dependence-control persists, accompanied by defenses developed to contain the anxiety. Adult adjustment might be characterized by relationships and work situations which permit leeway for verbal expression, conflicted feelings, or living out of both sides of the ambivalence about closeness-distance, dependence-control. Threats to a tenuously held autonomy would likely be ill tolerated.

If a mother, able to meet the needs of the two earlier stages, feels unsure, unloved, and unappreciated in her femininity she will convey to the child her underlying anxiety about her sexual identity. The child then grows with a capacity to give and receive, to be appropriately dependent and assertive, but with respect to the tasks related to sexual identity will have uneasy feelings about himself. As an adult, one would expect discomfort with life tasks associated with sexual identity, i.e., invasion of the capacity to sustain mature love relationships and of parenting functions, particularly around issues related to sexuality. A relationship with such a client would need to take into account that the positive identifications which made possible neutralization and mastery of developmental tasks were connected with the two earlier stages, whereas those related to the oedipal period would be characterized by conflicted indentifications and the accompanying unneutralized, undefused libidinal and aggressive drives. Up to the point of successful resolution of the oedipal conflict all the developmental stages have in common that they are tentative, in a state of flux, and that their successful working out involves important relationships with parents or parental figures.

From the standpoint of treatment, these characteristics of developmental experience represent at once an opportunity and a hazard. The opportunity lies in the tentative, open-to-change quality of precursor identifications. The hazard is in the visibility of such early identifications, which tempts the practitioner to their direct exploration in a misuse of the psychoanalytic model.

Following the resolution of oedipal conflict and the accompanying establishment of the superego as a separate unit in the psychic system changes may continue to take place within that unit. The new authority will preside over the experiences of the ego and the id, just as the parents originally did, and subsequent identifications will continue to develop with the superego *in loco parentis.*

For the latency child whose world is widening, new identifications will be found in teachers, class, and playmates. These increasingly selective identifications with their attitudes and attributes gradually "dilute" the introject, further freeing the child to enlarge his ego capacities. As these growing capacities diminish dependence on the parents, he becomes increasingly capable of making true object relations.

At adolescence, the resurgence of instinctual feelings occurs at a time when the young person is needing to pull away from the very relationships which in the past have helped to neutralize and redirect his instinctual drives. In this reworking of the oedipal conflict there is a major difference from the task at age five or six, in that adolescence offers more immediate freedom of adult sexual choices, simultaneously requiring the relinquishment of childish aims and real assumption of adult responsibilities. The characteristics of the superego can be influenced by the attitude of the real parents toward their own sexual identity, plus those of other important adults and peers who provide different identificatory models. The superego is modified, reflects less the earlier identifications, and bears a closer affinity to reality. Positive feelings about his own sexual identity free his energies to pursue a wide range of object relations, learning and work opportunities through which he can experience adult life. The superego gradually recedes as a visible power, as expanding object relations and achievements develop from the enlarged reservoir of diffused drives. (6, pp. 255-276; 24, Part III).

Effect on Treatment

Assuming a client to have successfully mastered the three earlier stages of growth, he should be free to enlarge his sphere of functioning through the wide-ranging identifications described above. Real people, however, seem never to develop so tidily nor to come upon stress in precisely the order of the developmental stages. Even psychotic, borderline, and character-disordered clients who have suffered substantial disturbances in development may during latency and adolescence manage positive identifications, albeit of a tenuous nature. Conversely, apparently mature clients under stress reveal an unsuspected vulnerability related to partial failure of neutralization and mastery of adaptive tasks of an earlier stage of development. These complexities contribute to the difficulty in finding rules for assessing latent need and predicting prescriptions for the kind of relationship which will meet that need.

Nonetheless, it seems valid to attempt a formulation as to locating the major source of disruption in a client's growth. It would appear that a hostile or excessively indulgent relationship may occur at any point along the developmental continuum. The earlier it occurs, the more will the global identification which characterizes the precursors involve a wide range of relationships and functions in vulnerability to instinctual pressures. Similarly, the later the disturbance in relationship occurs, the more focused or limited will be the involvement of relationships and ego functions in vulnerability to instinctual pressures.

An essentially hostile or ambivalent parent offers an angry ambivalent identification which prevents neutralization, exposes a child to engulfment by aggressive feelings which not only interfere with mastery of ego tasks but lay down expectations of criticalness from later parental figures. An essentially loving parent not only provides the positive identification through which energies are neutralized and put at the disposal of the ego, but initiates in the child a sense of self which subsequently leads to expectations of approval from parental figures. In such manner, identificatory precursors accumulate and provide the bases for mastery of tasks and for subsequent relationships.

In conjunction with knowledge of a

therapeutic relationship, these factors warrant examination in order to determine whether from them will emerge concepts which would provide indicators for the management of a therapeutic relationship.

Dimensions of a Therapeutic Relationship

Any relationship has a structure comprised of the object component and a transferred (as distinguished from a transference neurosis) component. The object component, the end result of neutralization and identification, represents the ego's capacity to respond to another as he realistically is. The transferred component represents those affects and expectations which remain attached to earlier relationships and are inappropriately projected upon or transferred to another. These expectations may represent positive, libidinal or hostile, aggressive affects. In either case they represent the unpredictable parts of the relationship, tied as they are to the invisible past, rather than to the present.

A therapeutic relationship shares the elements common to all relationships but is characterized by a particular intensity because of the context in which it occurs. When the client initiates a request for help he is propelled by two separate but related anxieties. The problem which he cannot solve alone is one source of anxiety. The second has to do with how he views his own helplessness, how he expects that others, particularly the practitioner, will view it. Much of his feeling about helplessness in the face of the presenting problem will derive from the history of his progress from infantile attachment to autonomy. Old parental attitudes toward impulses which had become the core of the superego are revived, and thus color the client's feeling about himself and his anxieties about how the practitioner will perceive him. These attitudes will be expressed by the way in which the client discusses parental figures, in-laws, teachers, bosses, and perhaps the

therapist directly. In short, these attitudes will be "transferred" to the practitioner and will be a measure of the client's expectations as to approval, disapproval, of being helped or not helped. If a client indicates that he expects harsh or indulgent treatment with respect to a particular area of his life, it should suggest the stage in development at which he suffered deprivation, excessive indulgence, or intense ambivalence. Such location of miscarriage in positive identification and consequent failure in neutralization, stalemate in ego development, provides a specific clue to the affective losses or demands underlying the disturbance in affect and/or functioning which is the client's manifest problem.

In order to determine the utility of these concepts in advancing the positive identifications which promote growth, it is useful to reexamine the manner in which transference phenomena operate in a therapeutic relationship.

Practice experience demonstrates repeatedly that if in the early interviews the caseworker explores or expresses exclusive interest in the areas of deprivation, no matter how kindly his intentions, the client reexperiences the feeling associated with earlier relationships of not being given to, understood, or approved. The old expectations of being criticized, denied help, or controlled are reaffirmed, the angry negative aspect of identification is repeated, and the accompanying impulses are refocused on the therapist. In the absence of positive feelings, which are the mainstay of the object component, that aspect of the relationship diminishes and the therapeutic relationship takes on the discomfort of the earlier, troubled period.

In the analytic situation, the goal makes relevant a method in which the patient reenacts the initial parental relationship, working through the infantile feelings. One of the calculated risks is the temporary deterioration in the therapeutic relationships, in "outside" relationships, and in social functioning. In clinical social work where the goal is more immediate restoration or impovement in social funtioning, such mobilization of infantile feeling may be sufficient to terminate the relationship. The childlike residual expectations of being criticized, denied help, or controlled may be reaffirmed and the therapeutic, relationship itself embroiled in a revival of hostile, erotic infantile feelings. This proliferation of affect related to the past increases the likelihood of a repetition of the angry or ambivalent identification in which he feels himself the unloved, unworthy, or overindulged child. Thus, the relationship, rather than serving as a sensitive instrument for growth, becomes an arena in which the old struggles to extract gratifications are reenacted with the client's responses directed to provoke a repetition of the original experience.

Mindful of this powerful unconscious transference phenomenon, the therapist may use his knowledge of the areas of deprivation or excessive indulgence to guide him away from an exclusive focus on the conflictual content. If he drops back to an earlier period where need was partially met, or forward to a later time when identifications with derivative figures were achieved, the client is enabled to recall and share some of his experiences in mastery. This sharing appears to minimize the hostile or erotic residuals from earlier periods of deprivation and mobilizes the affect connected with more positive identifications. The client seems then to experience the practitioner not as the ungiving, neglectful, or controlling parent, but as someone who can be trusted to give, set limits without control, or approve appropriate sexual identification. In this context infantile anxieties over an angry, critical, and powerful parent begin to recede and are replaced by those positive feelings associated with more rewarding early relationships. These are the relationships through which the impulses were initially neutralized and placed at the disposal of ego growth, and they are the same ones which must be tapped to reneutralize impulses which have become reinvolved in the current conflict. Such reneutraliza-

tion appears essential to the resumption of interrupted or distorted growth.

In the earliest interviews the most prominent feelings are those related to the client's perceptions of himself, his relative helplessness. The affect will be related more closely to superego identifications which have greatest impact on feelings of self-esteem, particularly when the client must assess his performance in a relationship with a figure perceived as the "authority" or the "expert." Because feelings related to superego identification are somewhat closer to impulses they are more easily reinvolved in conflict. It is, perhaps above all, this factor which accounts for difficulties in implementing a therapeutic alliance. Decisions as to areas to explore and old identifications to tap are particularly important when the therapist seeks to solidify the relationship without denying or evading the conflict. It is crucial that the early interviews circumvent the harsh, disapproving identifications which result in ill feelings of self but, rather, engage those which are available for growth.

Discussion has focused on formulations only with respect to the earliest phases of relationship formation. However, it seems relevant to consider whether they have application to later periods in treatment. It is appropriate to question whether all of treatment consists in advancing positive identification or whether there is a point at which more direct exploration of conflictual material is indicated. It would appear that these two elements are not mutually exclusive. In real life maturity is not the absence of conflict but derives from the mastery of adaptive or conflictual tasks through the kinds of positive identifications previously discussed. Each experience in successful mastery provides momentum for addressing subsequent tasks. Similarly in treatment, success does indeed breed success. When the client has shared his mastery of tasks which have preceded or antedated the current problem it is productive to address directly the more conflictual issues, for in that context positive forces are most prominent in the relationship.

Summary

This chapter was undertaken in an attempt to articulate a critical formulation drawn from psychoanalytic theory of personality development and to examine its relatedness to a typical practice requirement in order to develop a model from which theoretically based treatment decisions might be made. Selected for exploration was the aspect of theory which delineates the path of identifications. The choice rested on recognition that identifications play a major role in development and constitute a potent factor in the therapeutic relationship, in itself the major treatment instrument.

Adaptation of Theory

The theory suggested that the client experienced a need for help in connection with discomfort in current relationships or disturbances in functioning connected with a developmental stage around which he had not enjoyed a positive, productive identification. Thus the current problem would revive the old discomforts and anxieties expressed derivatively as he talks of his job, his boss, his child's teacher, his spouse. In treatment the therapeutic relationship develops around the material discussed and reflects the growth-enhancing and growth-deflecting elements from the past. Depending on the major subject emphasis the relationship may revive the old feelings of anger and helplessness or, conversely, those of self-assurance of being valued and competent. Logic suggested, therefore, that the kind of feeling about himself which would sustain the therapeutic alliance would derive from a major emphasis on subject matter which remobilized in the client good feeling about himself and the corollary assumption that the practitioner would, therefore, find him a person of value who warranted help. While the specific subject matter would vary with each case, the generalizable principle would enable the practitioner through the language of derivative figures to recognize qualities which were characteristic of the persons in the past with whom the client had important relationships. Able to identify those which initially promoted growth and adaptation, the practitioner then has a conceptual tool through which to determine what a client would experience as supportive or ego building.

Other Treatment Modes

Exploration of the extent to which this formulation may or may not be adaptable to couples, family, or group treatment requires an exhaustive study beyond the scope of this chapter. Nevertheless, it seems useful to point to areas in which the ideas may have pertinence.

Assumptions which underlie all three modes are that the totality of the membership of the couple, kinship, and nonkinship groups constitutes the unit of treatment, that the well-being of the unit supersedes that of the individual members and that crucial communication and interaction is among the participants as well as with the therapist. In couples and family treatment there is an additional assumption that a goal of treatment is to strengthen and improve the relatively permanent unit and, failing that, to permit constructive separation of individuals from the unit. Only in group treatment is the unit seen as a transitional object used by all members as an instrument of growth, with the goal ultimate separation of each member from the group. In these contexts individuals bring idiosyncratic responses to the unit and extrapolate from the mutual work whatever understanding and change in behavior proves useful.

While the personality organization of individual members is not the major focus in the therapeutic sessions, it would appear a relevant element in determining the choice of treatment mode. For instance, in determining when a couple would find joint treatment the optimal mode, a useful assessment in relation to each individual should be the level of ego organization and the quality of object relations surrounding phases of growth and maladaptation. This kind of assessment conveys something of the kinds of identifications which have supported development and predicts the kind of therapeutic relationship which may stimulate and support further growth. For instance, it is unlikely that Mrs. B., still struggling with unresolved attachment to her own mother, would experience as supportive of growth a mode of treatment in which she would have to share with a husband the relationship with a therapist. Such a history might suggest the value of a period of individual therapy preliminary to treatment of the couple.

In family treatment, when membership in the unit is predetermined, understanding the level of ego organization in conjunction with the history of identificatory experiences may suggest a reasonable goal of treatment, help explain the varying degrees and kinds of participation of individual members, and suggest ways in which the therapist may deal with the differing transference expectations that each member will have of him. Thus, in a family in which three members are struggling with issues of separation and two have essentially completed those developmental tasks and are occupied with questions of sexual identity, the therapist and family must seek a commonly acceptable goal and the therapist a way to deal with the range of transference expectations.

In nonkinship groups, where the selection of members can be made by the therapist, the kind of assessment presented in this chapter may add an additional criterion to those which already influence assignment of members. It is characteristic of groups that the pull and tug mobilized by the different levels of ego organization of its members and the relentless pressure of transference expectations dictated by early object relations of each group member obtain, whatever the purpose or composition of the group. The ideas presented here may be useful in predicting an optimal fit between the purpose of the group and the selection of its members. After a group is formed, the ideas may help the therapist better understand the tension within the group. They may also alert the leader to the wisdom of finding the kinds of identificatory models available within the group membership as well as in the person of the therapist himself.

There are sets of ideas about roles, family and group systems pertinent to these units which influence the characteristics of these modes of treatment. However, the units are made up of individuals so that as there are improvements in clarity and explanatory power of ego psychological theories it seems useful to explore their applicability to these multiperson modes of treatment.

Conclusion

Any treatment method which aims to heal or promote progress in some part of a growth process must, perforce, tap the same materials of development. A therapeutic relationship need not reproduce the original developmental process but it must draw on some of the same resources.

It is apparent that the relationship can be used to provide positive identifications which resemble those which advance ego growth in normal development. Within a therapeutic relationship, the conditions which must be created to promote that kind of identification require the use of knowledge about the way in which parts of the psychic system operate to advance such growth. Practitioners have been aware of the importance of the ego, but have tended to refer to it as though it were an instrument in itself to be acted upon, in some manipulative way. It does certainly indicate the maturity already achieved and, throughout treatment, is an accurate measure of improvement. It might be useful to think of it as an ally and an accurate barometer of progress—an indicator of accumulated positive identifications.

Except to reflect on its negative restrictive qualities, practitioners have paid less attention to the superego. On closer examination of its role in development, it appears that in the context of nurturing relationships it participates constructively through its control over the neutralized energies which it makes available to the ego. Because, by definition, it is closer to infantile impulses, it is likewise more directly involved in the residual feelings available for transfer to or projection on the practitioner. Consequently, it is likely to reveal more about the irrational element of the relationship so prominent in the initial encounters. This information is a useful guide to the area of the client's life which will provide the milieu for the growth of a positive identification.

As this identification develops, the transferred element of the relationship diminishes, while the object component increases. This shift can take place only if the caseworker has a key to where the disruption occurred in the developmental chain of identification so that the therapeutic relationship can be used to provide the restorative identification at the appropriate place. As Jacobson cogently says: "The superego cannot be remodeled, reorganized and consolidated, and new personal and sexual relations, new ego structures and ego function cannot be built up and integrated unless these new formations are allowed to grow organically from those of the past" (24, p. 173).

A wide range of psychic mechanisms and reality factors influence the course of a therapeutic relationship. In this formulation there is no implication of an all-encompassing model but, rather, an attempt to develop a conceptual base for one element in treatment. Psychoanalytic theory of personality, albeit incomplete, is nonetheless a sophisticated, complex one in contrast to the fragmentary treatment concepts developed from it.

The lack of concepts to explain or direct effective treatment intervention is not the exclusive problem of clinical social work. In the analytic literature, Chassell (4) very recently reviewed a series of cases in an attempt to identify what aspects of therapy appeared to characterize patients successfully treated. He concluded that, without reference to symptomatology or diagnostic designation, his review revealed that "in running records of productive individual psychotherapy . . . the hallmark of the kind of procedure developed is to be found in the relationship required by the patient for his own resumption of growth . . . a growth which had been previously blocked or distorted." His conclusions are consistent with the experiences of clinical social workers but describe rather than explain.

In the field of sociology theorists have had comparable difficulties in systematizing unwieldy material. In assessing attempts to develop formulations from amorphous sociological data, Merton (31) attempted to reconcile his more ambitious colleagues to pursue modest "theories of the middle range" rather than "all-inclusive conceptual schemes."

Clinical social workers may have to be content with finding connections between a specific aspect of development and a planned intervention which predicts a desired goal. Rich theories of personality, increasingly orderly sociological observations, and a wealth of practice experience provide ample resources from which to develop a series of minimodels dealing with important issues in treatment. Each model in itself poses a challenging formulative task and undoubtedly the monumental undertaking of fitting the small parts together will have to be addressed. However, a more complete theory of intervention must wait upon clarification of ideas covering the myriad factors which comprise treatment as well as on research methods which can capture and accurately measure elusive variables. Meanwhile, there are immediate conceptual tasks awaiting only hard, cognitive labor.

References

1. Austin, Lucille. "Differential Trends in Social Case Work," *Principles and Techniques in Social Case Work, 1940-1950*. New York: Family Service Association of America, 1950.

2. Bandler, Louise. "Some Casework Aspects of Ego Growth Through Sublimation," *Ego Oriented Casework*. New York: Family Service Association of America, 1963.

3. Beres, David. "Vicissitudes of Superego Function," *The Psychoanalytic Study of the Child*, Vol. XIII. New York: International Universities Press, 1958.

4. Chassell, Joseph. "The Growth Producing Experience in Psychotherapy," *International Journal of Psychoanalytic Psychotherapy*, Vol. I, No. 2, 1972, pp. 99-100.

5. Fenichel, Otto. "Identification," *The Collected Papers of Otto Fenichel*. 1st Series. New York: Norton, 1953.

6. Freud, Anna. "Adolescence," *The Psychoanalytic Study of the Child*, Vol. XIII. New York: International Universities Press, 1958.

7. ———. *Normality and Pathology in Childhood*. New York: International Universities Press, 1965.

8. ———. *The Ego and the Mechanisms of Defense*. Trans. C. Baines. London: Hogarth, 1937.

9. Freud, Sigmund. "Observations on Transference," *The Complete Works of Sigmund Freud*, Vol. XII. London: Hogarth, 1959.

10. ———. "The Dynamics of Transference," *The Complete Works of Sigmund Freud*, Vol. XII. London: Hogarth, 1959.

11. ———. *Group Psychology and the Analysis of the Ego* (1921), standard ed., Vol. XVIII. London: Hogarth, 1959.

12. ———. *Inhibitions, Symptoms and Anxiety* (1926), standard ed., Vol. XX. London: Hogarth, 1959.

13. ———. *The Ego and the Id*. Trans. J. Riviere. London: Hogarth, 1957.

14. ———. "Mourning and Melancholia," *Collected Papers*, Vol. IV. London: Hogarth, 1950.

15. ———. "On Narcissism," *Collected Papers*, Vol. IV. London: Hogarth, 1950.

16. Garrett, Annette. "Modern Casework: The Contribution of Ego Psychology," in Howard J. Parad and Roger R. Miller (eds.) *Ego Psychology and Dynamic Casework*. New York: Family Service Association of America, 1958.

17. ———. "The Worker-Client Relationship," Howard J. Parad and Roger R. Miller (eds.) *Ego Psychology and Dynamic Casework*. New York: Family Service Association of America, 1958.

18. ———. "Transference in Casework," Cora Kasius (ed.) *Principles and Techniques in Social Casework, 1940-50*. New York: Family Service Association of America, 1950.

19. Hamilton, Gordon. "A Theory of Personality: Freud's Contribution to Social Work," Howard J. Parad and Roger R. Miller (eds.) *Ego Psychology and Dynamic Casework*. New York: Family Service Association of America, 1958.

20. Hartmann, Heinz. *Ego Psychology and the Problem of Adaptation*. Trans. D. Rapaport. New York: International Universities Press, 1958.

21. ———. "Notes on the Superego," *Psychoanalytic Study of the Child,* Vol. XVII. New York: International Universities Press, 1962.

22. ——— et al. "Notes on the Theory of Sublimation," *Essays on Ego Psychology*. New York: International Universities Press, 1964.

23. Hollis, Florence. *Casework: A Psychosocial Therapy,* New York: Random House, 1964.

24. Jacobson, Edith. *The Self and the Object World.* New York: International Universities Press, 1964.

25. Kernberg, Otto. *Borderline Conditions and Pathological Narcissism*. New York: Jason Aronson, 1975, pp. 3-68, 153-184.

26. ———. *Object Relations Theory and Clinical Psychoanalysis*. New York: Jason Aronson, 1976, pp. 19-138, 161-184.

27. Knight, Robert. "Introjection, Projection and Identification," *The Psychoanalytic Quarterly*, Vol. IX, July, 1940, p. 338.

28. Kohut, Heinz. *The Analysis of the Self*. New York: International Universities Press, 1971, pp. 37-73.

29. Mahler, Margaret A. "Thoughts About Development and Individuation," *The Psychoanalytic Study of the Child,* Vol. XVIII. New York: International Universities Press, 1963, pp. 307-324.

30. Masterson, James. *Psychotherapy of the Borderline Adult: A Developmental Approach*. New York: Brunner/Mazel, 1976, pp. 13-68.

31. Merton, Robert K. *Social Theory and Social Structure*. New York: Free Press, 1957.

32. Pine, Fred and Manuel Furer. "Studies of the Separation-Individuation Phase," *The Psychoanalytic Study of the Child,* Vol. XVIII. New York: International Universities Press, 1963.

33. Rapaport, David. "Psychological Issues," *The Structure of Psychoanalytic Theory*, Vol. II, No. 2, Monograph 6. New York: International Universities Press, 1960.

34. Reich, Annie. "The Early Identification as Archaic Elements in the Superego," *Journal of American Psychoanalytic Association*, Vol. II, 1954, pp. 218-238.

35. Richmond, Mary. *Social Diagnosis*. New York: Russell Sage Foundation, 1918.

36. Sandler, Joseph. "On the Concept of the Superego," *The Psychoanalytic Study of the Child,* Vol. XVII. New York: International Universities Press, 1960.

37. Sargent, Helen. "Intra-Psychic Changes: Methodological Problems in Psychotherapy Research," *Psychiatry,* Vol. XXIV, No. 2. Washington, D.C.: William Alanson White Psychiatric Foundation, 1961.

38. Stern, Max M. "The Ego Aspect of Transference," *International Journal of Psychoanalysis,* 1957, pp. 146-157.

Annotated listing of key references

FREUD, Anna. *The Ego and the Mechanisms of Defense.* London: Hogarth, 1937.

This small volume is an important basic work in understanding psychoanalytic theory and its relevance for social work practice. It served an essential role in bringing the ego on a par with the id and superego of earlier theoretical writings. Out of it developed the enriched understanding of the ego and its importance in healthy functioning.

FREUD, Sigmund. *Collected Papers.* London: Hogarth, 1950.

Ordinarily the Collected Papers of an author are not listed as key references; rather, selections are made from them. It is being done here to encourage persons wishing to pursue further reading in this theoretical orientation to use primary rather than secondary or tertiary sources.

GARRETT, Annette. "The Worker–Client Relationship," in H. Parad (ed.) *Ego Psychology and Dynamic Casework.* New York: Family Service Association of America, 1958.

This is an important and useful paper for social workers because of its focus on the transference components of the treatment relationship. The concept of transference is an essential contribution to current social work practice coming from psychoanalytic theory.

HAMILTON, Gordon. "A Theory of Personality: Freud's Contribution to Social Work," in H. Parad (ed.) *Ego Psychology and Dynamic Casework.* New York: Family Service Association of America, 1958.

One of the classical papers written by a famous social worker. It is important, as it traces the impact of Freudian thinking on social work practitioners in relation to the profession's prior history of treatment. It also touches on some of the issues that emerged from this impact, many of which are still a part of current professional dialogue.

HARTMANN, Heinz. *Ego Psychology and the Problem of Adaptation.* New York: International Universities Press, 1958.

The writings of Hartmann have made a significant contribution in helping move psychoanalytic theory to a general psychology. This author picked up on Freud's later writings about the ego and developed these concepts and their implications for healthy functioning and the role that the "conflict free sphere" of ego functioning plays in it. Hartmann doesn't discount the genetic viewpoint but, rather, shows how ego functions can become independent of these origins.

KERNBERG, Otto. *Borderline Conditions and Pathological Narcissism.* New York: Jason Aronson, 1975.

From the point of view of developmental theory Kernberg has advanced formulations as to the impact of early object relations on ego organization. In clinical research he has applied the for-

mulations to differential diagnosis, particularly as between narcissistic and borderline personality organization.

MAHLER, Margaret. "Thoughts About Development and Individuation,"
in *Psychoanalytic Study of the Child,* Vol. XVIII, pp. 307–324.
New York: International Universities Press 1963.
*Mahler's papers delineated phase-specific developmental tasks
of infancy and early childhood. Derived from twenty years of
observation, she postulated a causal link between these phases
and ego development. Her careful methods and penetrating
analysis of data inspired a whole generation of child analysts to
similarly careful study of early ego development. Her work has
vastly increased the knowledge from which social workers can
devise restorative treatment methods for developmentally impaired children and preventive planning to enchance normal
development.*

MASTERSON, James. *Psychotherapy of the Borderline Adult: A Developmental Approach.* New York: Brunner/Mazel, 1976.
*Derived from work on early object relations and his own exten-
sive clinical research, Masterson has concentrated on the
diagnosis and treatment of those suffering with borderline personality organization. His presentation is pertinent to social
workers who are responible for the treatment of large numbers
of individuals with that kind of maladaptive ego organization.*

3

Ego Psychology

by

SIDNEY L. WASSERMAN

Theory, historical origins, principal proponents

Some time ago, in clinical practice, I presented at a staff conference the case of a severely disturbed, acting-out, regressed adolescent. After the chaotic, unassimilated facts had been set before the treatment team and each member of the staff had presented his somewhat discouraging reports, the residential director of the treatment center pondered for some moments, heaved a sigh, and asked: "Well, what do we do until the ego comes?"

It is both intriguing and ironic that, similarly, the evolving of ego psychology theory followed a path of what appeared to be undifferentiated, unassimilated chaos. Though the concept of the ego had been present in Freud's writings as early as the 1890s, he did not expand on this aspect of his work until the early 1920s, as his concern and major preoccupation were with libido theory, the concept of the id,

instinctual drives, and their relation to psychoanalysis. Thus, the ego did not come into its own until considerable groundwork had been laid. The study of the personality came by way of the id with the emphasis on unconscious mental processes, instinctual drives, and psychic conflict (27). It is now recognized that the insights Freud and others gained from this early period of investigation were necessary precursors to the development of ego psychology. Freud's later formulations and modifications provided an important breakthrough for the post-Freudians to understand further and to build on ego progression and development.

In early theoretical development, there was a kind of insistence that the ego developed from the id. Yet, in one of Freud's last writings, he stated: "We have repeatedly had to insist on the fact that the ego owes its origin as well as the most important of its acquired characteristics to its relation to the real external world"(18). This led to further elaboration of superego development in that the ego gives up a part of the external world as an object and takes it unto itself, through identification, and observes the ego very much as the child's parents had done (19). This rediscovery of Freud's ego-external world statement appears to have brought about an expanded emphasis on object relations and its paramount importance to optimal ego development.

Freud perceived functions of the ego in relation to reality, its ability to organize, to control motility and perception (inner and outer), and to test reality, thinking and action (20). The later clinical findings, research and writings of Anna Freud (17), Heinz Hartmann (27), Erik Erikson (11), and P. Federn (13) have brought us to a clearer understanding of how the ego is shaped as it mediates between the intrusion of external reality and internal drives, and as it defends itself.

However, tracing this factor to its genetic base continues at a most elementary level. For example, Anna Freud points out how introjection is probably used innately in early weeks of life as a form of instinct gratification, and later evolved as a defense (17). She broadens understanding of ego defense mechanisms, demonstrating how a variety of such mechanisms (i.e., repression, projection, reaction formation) serve to ward off anxiety stemming from external threat, id impulse, and/or superego demands. The ego defensive system has been further extended and elaborated, along with a subsystem of defenses, by H. Laughlin (41). Hartmann (28) stressed the "autonomous factors" in ego development (e.g., aspects of the ego which are not traceable to the impact of either reality or the instinctual drives). The autonomous ego grows and matures as a result of experience, and may or may not remain in the conflictless sphere of the ego. Such executive functions include perception, motor equipment, intelligence, judgment, impulse control, self and body image, and thought processes. Though these "primary

autonomous" ego apparatuses are predisposed toward adaptation from birth and can be influenced by instinctual drives, secondarily they derive pleasure through experience, learning, and mastery. The reality ego (secondary autonomy) gradually evolves by maturing and freeing itself from the infringement of the instinctual drives, thus lending itself to adaptation. The autonomous ego is further utilized in the ego's defense against external reality and the demands of the superego.

In terms of adaptation to internal and external reality, the ego and its functions are directly related to the growth of the individual. As he develops the ability to cope, his ability to use skills increases as well. The maturing ego acquires a progressive sense of reality and a fuller ability to invest in (cathect) and sustain relationships, to tolerate frustration, to enhance impulse control, to increase communicative powers, to master cognitive and motor tasks, and to broaden integrative abilities (51). With such powers, the individual's sense of confidence, mastery, and autonomy in overcoming difficult situations increasingly strengthens his coping mechanisms. Thus, ego development becomes both a maturational and learning process.

The relation of ego development to structural psychology has been increasingly perceived as a continuum, progressing from its autonomous forestage, through narcissistic ego cathexis, to "desexualized and deaggressivized energy" of reality-ego functioning (29). The neutralization of instinctual energy is an indication of ego strength and the ego's capacity for neutralization becomes most relevant in understanding personality.

In Freud's later works (20), he elaborates on the self-perservative psychic tendencies comprising what is "useful" egoism, self-assertion, etc., inferring their relation to the ego system. These "ego interests" and tendencies (striving for what is considered useful) are rarely unconscious, as are the defenses, but are mostly preconscious and even conscious. They are highly interrelated to what the society and/or culture defines as "useful" (i.e., striving for status, wealth, education, etc.), and it is difficult to determine a form of structural hierarchy of ego functions which can be correlated to "healthy" functioning. In fact, Schmideberg (63), Glover (24), and Hartmann (30) speak of a "health neurosis." When the clinician or practitioner is prompted to use himself as a measuring scale of "normality" in observing another's behavior, the risk of prejudicial overstressing and exaggerating reactions is high. In the broad sense, a healthy person possesses the capacity to mourn, suffer, grieve, verbalize anger, and be depressed. What appears to be adaptive in the individual can be maladaptive. If the ego overdefends against loss, ill health, and trauma, the price to ego maturation can lead to maladaption. Equally, an overrestrictive, punishing superego can produce similar repercussions. Ego psychology and its grasp of the normal ego crises along the full spectrum of the life cycle underscore the importance of conflict and disturbances in adaptation (11). Satisfactory development of the ego is the key to inner sustainment, whereby the individual is capable of using his full resources to attain a sense of autonomy and competence (52).

The "ego interests" are but another aspect of ego qualities which can and do oppose each other in a conflictual manner. Though such contrasts within the ego exist, the aim is to oppose the drives and to seek gratification through reality assessment-identification-adaptation. Simultaneously, the ego must consider and mediate the demands of the superego. As a result, ego qualities and strengths are assessed on the basis of behavior in various situations, whether stress arises from id, superego, or external reality. In situations of stress, the degree to which the ego is pressed upon is central to the understanding of the individual personality and its characteristics. The functioning or malfunctioning of the defenses is determined by both the degree of press and strain, and the potential energy that can be drawn upon for integrative functioning. Concomitantly, an assessment of ego autonomous functions and the degree to which they can withstand intrusion is required.

Building on Freud's work, Erikson (11) postulated a sequence of phases of psychosocial development, paralleling that of libido development but extending to the full span of the life cycle. He outlined how, in each phase, a specific task must be solved, emphasizing that the solution, successful or unsuccessful, has been prepared in the previous phase. His concept of mutuality brought new dimensions and insights to the interactions between the individual and his social environment. He also extended his theory to how each society meets these phases of the life cycle by institutions, influencing the way in which the individual undertakes to solve and master the tasks of each phase.

David Rapaport (55), in his *Collected Papers*, divides the historical development of ego psychology into four phases. The first phase coincides with Freud's prepsychoanalytic theory, ending with 1897, the beginning of psychoanalysis. In this phase there evolved the concept of defense and, secondarily, its relation to external reality, which contributed so markedly to ego psychology. The second phase ended in 1923, with the development of psychoanalysis proper. The outstanding contributions to ego psychology in this phase were the conception of the secondary process, the reality principle, and the analytic process of repression. Insight into the secondary process provided a conception of reality relations, and the introduction of the reality principle provided the analysis of its means of functioning (reality testing). The third phase begins with Freud's publication of *The Ego and the Id* (1923) and extends to 1937. No longer was the ego perceived as totally subservient to the id, but as having genetic roots and energies of its own. Autonomously, the ego initiates defense, and a variety of defenses are concerned with reality relationships. Thus, external reality was brought into the center of the theory, and for the first time a conception of adaptation was implied. The fourth phase begins with the writings of Anna Freud (17), Hartmann (27), Erikson (11), Horney (34), and Sullivan (69), and extends to the present. A theory of object and interpersonal relationships has evolved, taking into account the ego's autonomous roots, development, and functions.

Path into social work, present status, and influence on current practice

In a sense, the "ego" was taken for granted as social work practice evolved. In the late nineteenth and early twentieth centuries, social work and social casework were perceived as one and the same. The focus and aim were for societal reform, the introduction of necessary social protections and services as proposed by Jane Addams (2), as well as reform of the individual. It was assumed that, through appeals to their rational thinking and compassionate minds, the legislators and the power structure, industrialists as well as the "downtrodden," would each be swayed by "the facts" and change would be initiated. When repeated resistance was encountered, social action was employed, with varying degrees of success. Parallel to Rapaport's first phase of ego psychology, the external reality was the area of social work attention—in the society, the community, and the individual. Economic, political, and social inequities were recognized, but there was little understanding of how systems reflect and act upon a broad gamut of human needs and, conversely, how human beings act upon institutions and structures.

The "friendly visitor" of that period was equally at a loss to understand why so many of the "poor" didn't follow what was assumed to be sound advice. By appealing to the individual's sense of logic and common sense, it was anticipated that reformation would take place. When this did not happen, the individual was

then perceived as either of low intelligence or poor moral character (8). Similarly, what was lacking was insight and knowledge as to how the system acted upon the individual and/or family, the client's and family's inner reality, and, concomitantly, how he and/or they acted upon the environment.

During and after World War I, Mary Richmond (58) was the first social caseworker to evolve and bring a beginning systematic approach in the form of a study-diagnosis-treatment framework to the needs of human beings and their situation. She believed that if we had "all the facts," solutions to problems would present themselves.

With the advent of psychoanalysis and its introduction to the American scene during the 1920s, social caseworkers could at last find an explanation and meaning for human behavior. The concepts of resistance, defense, repression, the unconscious, aggression, and sexuality were intellectually grasped and a psychoanalytic treatment model of "dynamic passivity" was applied on an almost universal basis. At a time of economic and political stagnation and reaction, the individual was frequently perceived as the sole creator of his "plight." By the worker's standing off, much like a reflective screen, and encouraging the release of undefended, unconscious sexual and aggressive fantasy, the individual (it was assumed) would be freed of self-defeating hangups. Resistance and defenses needed to be pierced to free him. Though much was learned about human personality and pathology, there was minimal understanding of ego processes, functions, and development. As a result, a kind of professional identity crisis was created for many practitioners who perceived themselves as junior psychiatrists performing a watered-down version of psychoanalysis. Like the early preoccupation of psychoanalysis with libido theory, id, and instinctual drives, so social casework became similarly overinvested—perhaps, in retrospect, as a necessary and painful growth process.

During the late 1930s and early 1940s ego

psychology came increasingly into its own. With growing understanding of ego autonomy, functions, and defenses, and of the conscious and unconscious aspects of ego and superego apparatuses, social casework moved into a necessary reassessment of its former knowledge and began to use this knowledge in a modified form, supplementing it with new understanding of ego integration and functioning. It was recognized that, though insights were essential to our understanding, ego functioning was influenced and affected by a continuum of external and internal stimuli. This necessitated further understanding of social, cultural, anthropological, economic, and political systems and forces.

In a paper written in 1941, Gordon Hamilton (26) articulated a set of concepts basic to social work practice by emphasizing that

> the social sciences allied with the physical sciences must increasingly throw light on social needs and social improvement.... Personality is both biological and cultural ... social study is important because cultural and economic factors are important and history is important because the history of the organism is the organism. Much of what is now inside a person was once outside.

She went on to say that workers who adhere to these concepts or assumptions

> would admit that when casework was assimilating new concepts into emotional life, when psychiatry itself had not yet assimilated its ego psychology, that there was a tendency in casework to minimize the immediate practical and emotional situation in favor of rather sterile research into early experiences.

Miss Hamilton underscored that, though the immediate situation must be dealt with, it is necessary to obtain "appropriate, selective, factual information, including relevant history," and that

only diagnostic ability can distinguish those maladjustments which arise chiefly from economic and cultural factors and those with more complicated psychosocial causality. Only diagnostic ability can ensure that services are given appropriately as well as responsibly.

Finally, she pointed out that both diagnostic and functional theorists concur "in giving a central place to the ego and the reality side of experience." Later, Lucille Austin pointed out how this new focus on the ego brought casework and psychoanalysis closer together in "their common aims" but noted that the ego is more accessible and useful to casework in its "efforts to influence adaptive capacities" (3).

Interestingly, in the 1940s, Annette Garrett (21) stressed the importance of continuing to understand more thoroughly the unconscious factors which are present but to combine this enhanced understanding "with a different method of handling." She points out that this shift in approach necessitated a greater understanding of ego psychology which meant

> learning ways of strengthening the client's ego instead of stimulating greater regression of infantile behavior-recognizing and responding to the client's unconscious demands without bringing them to consciousness on the client's part and, particularly in the area of transference, acquiring ways of keeping it under control and diluting it.

In the late 1940s, Miss Garrett (23) pointed out that the early literature of the 1860s revealed concern with distinguishing "the worthy from the unworthy" while the current immediate challenge (1940s) has been identifying of ego strengths and weaknesses and the achieving of "the best contemporary integration of psychoanalytic understanding and modern casework procedures." This emphasizing of the importance of "strengthening the ego" is still—thirty years later—inadequately understood in practice.

The misunderstanding of the concept of strengthening the ego has had some unfortunate historical twists and distortions. Just as casework was coming to a greater integration of ego psychology and a clearer grasp of its application in practice, it increasingly became the target of the social work profession's growing conscious frustration with the broad social-economic political problems of the 1950s and 1960s. Before enough practitioners could really test out their newly assimilated knowledge, along with expanding skills, ego psychology casework became suspect by various factions within the profession. It was perceived as too allied with psychoanalysis and the unconscious, too limited in its approach, too slow moving in bringing on change. Insufficient grounding in ego psychology and its application, however, frequently affected training and ultimately practice. As a result, the casework method—though referred to as "ego-supported casework"—had been too often misapplied and abused. Though the "unconscious" had become a dirty word, too many practitioners—instead of respecting ego defenses and working with and around such mechanisms—were making inappropriate interpretations of the defenses and resistances to remove "obstacles." Invariably, multiple unconscious power struggles developed between client and worker. On the other hand, to respond to basic reality needs, and overlooking the internal reality of the individual and family, too many practitioners were rushing into indiscriminate activity (as opposed to dynamic passivity) to the point of undermining the client's own potential resources for doing, achievement, and growth. Not listening to needs, demands, and requests on various levels only obstructed an understanding of what was occurring in the client's external and internal situation, as well as in the interaction between worker and client. As a result, minimal thought was being given to how each is being perceived, cognitively, and what is being recreated and reexperienced in the present for the client that necessitated corrective handling.

In spite of growing disquiet the 1950s and 1960s, Annette Garrett (22), Gordon Hamilton (26), Florence Hollis (33), Helen Perlman (53), Charlotte Towle (71), Beatrix Reiner and Irving Kaufman (57), Yonata Feldman (14), Lucille Austin (3), Norman Polansky (54), and Esther Clemence (7) contributed much to social casework's theoretical understanding and application of ego psychology. Building on earlier knowledge, casework had come to recognize the uniqueness of its method. Though knowledge needed to be continually gained from various disciplines, the application of this knowledge in terms of service to the individual client and his family was the evolving "specialness" of ego-oriented casework. In 1959, Isabel Stamm (64) pointed out that "special attention" must be paid to ego psychology as an "emerging theoretical base of casework." Though ego psychology expands intrapsychic aspects of personality, it expands equally upon concepts that include the individual's total functioning. She pointed out that casework practice requires the use of numerous frames of reference—social role, family interaction, ideals, and values, as well as instinctual drives and defense operations. Adding to this, Nancy Staver emphasizes that "we cannot work with part of a human being and decide to dismiss from our view the rest of him—the helping person has always to be planning his help in understanding of the whole person" (65).

This period is best summed up by Annette Garrett (22), who pulled together some of the implications and impact of ego psychology for practice.

A full appreciation of ego psychology reveals new meaning as we integrate the concept that the unconscious ego operations are manifested in a myriad of ordinary day-to-day characteristic ways of functioning. Putting the social back in social casework does not mean one whit less attention to and need for knowledge of unconscious and instinctual behaviour, but it does mean an enriched blending of both as the unconscious significance of the social aspects is increasingly appreciated, and practical manifestations of the unconscious are recognized in familiar, taken-for-granted activities.

By the mid-1960s up to the present day, ego-oriented casework—as well as social work practice as a whole—began to place much more conscious emphasis on adaptation to external reality, and on enhanced understanding and knowledge of object relations, role performance, and interpersonal-transactional relationships. Communication patterns of family members, their individual and collective ego perceptions of their assigned and ascribed roles took on new meaning and significance. Because the egos of both individuals and families continue to be receptive and open to new learning, this expanded understanding enriched the practitioner's diagnostic thinking. Equally important, new treatment methods and models began to be introduced (i.e., family-centered casework, crisis intervention, brief casework treatment) —albeit sometimes at the price of triggering a kind of bandwagon-panacea effect.

Finally, knowledge about ego processes and functions has made ego psychology closely allied to learning developmental theories. The human organism gains mastery through repeated efforts, and learning is an ego process (70). The teaching and findings of Piaget have enriched our understanding of the role of the intellect in ego development—how the ego perceives, assimilates, abstracts, conceptualizes, and accommodates. This complementarity— instead of diminishing ego psychology or other theories—has added to each. Developmental theory and its emphasis on task achievement and motor skills have given another dimension to the role of ego mastery and the attainment of control of one's environment. The ability to gain ego mastery spurs motivation toward greater maturity, as the ego strives toward attainment of enhanced self-reliance and self-approval.

Theoretical concepts, diagnosis, treatment

Florence Hollis (31) underlines the present psychosocial assessment process as "essentially a system theory" approach; that is, "the person-situation gestalt or configuration." This process necessitates understanding the human being "in the context of his interactions or transactions with the external world." To do this, particularly in the assessment of the individual, his personality and needs, the framework most operational and useful has been personality theory, "with emphasis upon the ego and its adaptive capacities"—understanding that aspect of the external world which acts upon the individual and gearing treatment, differentially, according to the understanding of the individual and of the assessed needs.

Katherine M. Wood (74) puts into proper perspective the significant contribution of ego psychology to casework practice in her statement:

> While the worker is responsible for diagnosing and understanding the areas and dynamics of conflict of the client, essentially what he, and the client, have to work with toward solution of the difficulty is the conflict-free portion of the client's ego. It is for this reason that casework lays such emphasis on inclusion of intrapsychic and situational strengths and resources, as well as limitations and pathology, in casework psychosocial diagnosis.

As to the treatment process, Wood (75) delineates eight concepts and techniques central to psychoanalytic psychotherapy and discusses their relevance and/or irrelevance in terms of ego-oriented casework practice. These included "free association," the therapist as a "blank screen," "the recovery of the repressed," interpretation of dreams, insight development, "working through," resistance, and transference-countertransference. Of these, the former three are not applicable to casework technique.

Interpretation, though occasionally used in modified form, has been overemphasized in the development of casework treatment. Direct interpretation is used only "when appropriate to the individualized needs of the client." For the majority of clients, interpretive techniques are not helpful; change, modification, and growth come about through and as a result of the casework relationship and its management (the "corrective experience"). Working through is an important concept for use in casework treatment. It is an awareness of the time factor involved in learning and integrating new patterns of behavior. There is a forward and backward movement to the treatment process which is necessary in the testing out and giving up of previous patterns. Also, plateaus in treatment are to be anticipated as preparation for future change and growth. Resistance is often closely aligned with repression but, within the casework context, can reflect the ego's means of protecting itself, as well as indicating that it is being overtaxed. Understanding the meaning of resistance (the client's perception of and need to ward off help) has been useful to casework understanding. Appreciating the client's need to resist, recognizing its positive, healthy aspects—even, as put forth by Strean, "joining the resistance"—has freed clients to engage in the problem-solving process.

The concept of transference-countertransference arouses considerable passions among professional groups but, nevertheless, it is central to the casework treatment process. It is a part of the human condition in that every human being brings into every new relationship and/or experience the sum total of his past. In a casework situation, the client frequently transfers to the worker "irrational elements" carried over from past meaningful relationships. Though encouragement of a "transference neurosis" and extensive regression is part of the analytic model, in casework the opposite approach is used. The reliving of past traumas and events, and regression, are not encouraged, although the meeting of some dependency needs is necessary in forming a relationship with the client. In casework one works with the transference as a means toward "corrective handling," thereby encouraging further growth. The application of sound ego-oriented casework necessitates the understanding of unconscious transference manifestations and how to work with these—to keep the relationship reality-focused. Handling the transference requires expanded self-awareness by the worker. To meet the client's need appropriately, to create an atmosphere conducive for working through and growth, the worker must be aware of his own responses associated with his past relationships and experiences (countertransference) which free or obstruct the client's ego development. Such self-knowledge becomes available for use to the client's benefit. It may require considerable disciplining of one's own needs and responses, but not at the price of one's warmth and ability to respond to the client's needs. To allow for optimal anxiety within the client to stimulate further ego growth can easily be misperceived as punitive and withholding. If the transference is recognized and worked with, along with the worker's awareness of his own countertransference reactions, then there is a sound application of ego psychology principles.

In addition to Wood's conceptual delineation, I would like to introduce further concepts and techniques which may tend to overlap, but which have been useful to casework understanding and practice as separate unto themselves. This interrelated list is probably quite exhaustive, but the following have been demonstrated to have particular significance: lessening of threat, ambivalence, repetitive themes, dependency-independence, identification-self-identity, separation-termination.

Though the *lessening of threat* is frequently associated with resistance, it is a dynamic unto itself. All new situations bring threat, consciously and/or unconsciously. Unless this is anticipated, recognized, and dealt with early in the treatment process, engagement of the client within a basic trust relationship is unachievable. Too often "resistance" has been diagnosed without giving proper weight to the threat of the new situation. Early underscoring of this on the worker's part—as, for example, "Perhaps you are wondering what I'm doing here"; "It must seem as though I'm here to remove your children from you"; "Getting to know a new person takes time"—begins to diminish and dent some of the rational and irrational fears. Further, it gives evidence to the client that the worker is sensitized to understanding what it must be like to be in the client's shoes. To tune in to "threat," the worker needs to anticipate and prepare for a broad range of reactions—even before encountering the client for the first time. Though initial threat can be allayed through appropriate handling, it is equally important to anticipate further threat at various points in the treatment process—particularly as the client gets ready for the next growth spurt and feels threatened by what he perceives to be the worker's expectations.

Ambivalence is a concept that workers may tend to take for granted, but they do not necessarily deal with it. In the early stages of treatment, the client's ambivalence is frequently parallel to his feelings of threat and of being intruded upon—even when the client has initiated a request for help. It is not uncommon for caseworkers to assess diagnostically the client's ambivalence and then divert from it. Some of this diversion is perhaps related to the worker's own anxiety at hearing the client verbalize: "No, I don't want your help." By avoiding ambivalence and not recognizing it as inherent and a necessary part of the beginning phase (as well as its ongoing recurrence throughout treatment), the client feels increasingly threatened. As threat is dealt with, it is also liberating for the client to hear the worker address the underlying ambivalence (i.e., "Perhaps you are having some thoughts as to whether you want this or not?"). Understandably, the client who is seeing a worker involuntarily would have strong negative feelings about such involvement, and it is often relaxing and relieving for him to hear the worker's understanding of this. Without dealing with ambivalence, a chain of "undoing" and/or conscious and unconscious sabotaging sets in on the part of the client. He needs, and has the right, to feel and to say no before he can shift energy into another more positive direction. Further, he needs to know that it is all right to have such doubts and that in spite of these misgivings, the worker wishes to help.

Repetitive themes tend to overlap and are often tied in with the working-through process. Both in the beginning, diagnostic phase, as well as during ongoing treatment, the client's need to repeat is most significant, and the themes are valuable. Yonata Feldman (14) discusses how the repetitions reflect symbolic messages of what went wrong. Something is unresolved for the client (repetition compulsion) which is associated with past events, and he is signaling the need for "emotional reeducation"—a corrective relationship. Repetitive themes of dirt-cleanliness, fights-weaknesses, sex-attacks, closeness- distance, God-devil are commonly heard in treatment. Though the worker's activity in terms of such content must be initiated on a differential basis, it can be helpful, especially in the early phase, for the client to hear the worker underscore this concern (i.e., "This has been something you have talked about before—it seems to concern you"). As Feldman points out, the repetitions may stop, or the client may start repeating in a different way. However, as threat is lessened and ambivalence is dealt with, gradually the client begins to fuse the ambivalence, and the splitting themes of the content lessen. As the client's ego is appropriately supported, he often begins to "record" within this safer trusting atmosphere, talking about "the other side" of himself—i.e., fear of closeness, wish to "mess" things up, or fear of vulnerability.

Dependency-independence is another "duo-bind" that the client is caught up in throughout the life cycle (though more apparent at certain phases than at other times). This unresolved struggle is invested and energized with considerable ambivalence by the client. On the one hand, the infantile, irrational part wants to be nutured and made up to for all the deprivations suffered, unconsciously expecting from a worker what he expected from his parents. He may endow the worker with power which he does not possess, and he may take flight if he invests too quickly, thereby becoming disenchanted if all his expectations are not realized; or he may take flight if overwhelmed by the intensity of his feelings (14). On the other hand, if he allows some of his needs to be met, will he give way to all infantile wishes, becoming totally dependent, helpless, and vulnerable? Many clients, feeling the press of this kind of bind, often present themselves in a pseudoindependent manner, insisting that they can manage on their own and do not need anyone. In such situations, the worker must sensitively assess the anxiety, carefully avoiding moving in too closely or usurping the apparent and potential strengths and resources from the client. When the client feels reassured, he may gradually let some of his needs be known. In other situations, some clients present themselves as totally helpless, incapable of self-assertion and active doing. Such persons frequently invite the worker to rescue them, to take over completely—almost as an all-powerful parent would do. In such instances, the worker must carefully choose to meet some appropriate needs, frustrate others, and encourage the client to fulfill some of his own needs. Regression and the development of a transference neurosis are discouraged.

Identification-self-identity are particular concepts which have been observed to be important aspects of the casework treatment process. Though Reiner and Kaufman (57) have projected these concepts in terms of treatment with the character-disordered client, the identification-self-identity process can be recognized and dealt with in all treatment situations. Gradually, as the client moves toward basic trust, as ego functioning (having been encour-

aged and supported) is expanded, and the client's ability to do and succeed is enhanced, the identification with the worker develops simultaneously. It is usually manifested in remarks of "wanting to be a social worker," or expressing a desire to please the worker on the basis of thinking how the worker would deal with a situation when under stress. On the observational level there is often a taking on of the worker's mannerisms, dress, and acts. Here such identification remarks or behavioral patterns must be differentially assessed, as there are instances of their being of a pseudoimitative, nonincorporative quality. The more unconscious the "taking in" of the worker, the more likely is the identification internalized, rather than being an imitative process. Remarks or observations of the identification process are not directly taken up. It is a necessary phase in treatment if the client is gradually to arrive at his own identity. Occasionally, neurotic, delinquent clients will let it be known that they are staying out of trouble—almost as a gift to the worker (72). It is often helpful at such times to accept the effort and self-control, but also to challenge the client's own identity: "Thank you very much, but what about yourself?" Repeated encouragement and support for the client's right to meet some of his own needs, for his importance as an individual, for his right to take pride in achievements often gradually leads toward a genuine, healthy caring for himself. This self-identity phase can be reflected when the client is demonstrating increased ability to form maturing relationships with others; acting upon his own behalf in a nonrebellious, self-assertive manner; coping in stressful situations with a growing ability to sort out and take action; and attaining his own value system, which enables an individual to adapt to, as well as to change, his own environment. Granted, few of us ever really achieve all of these in the fullest sense; still, in the ongoing treatment situation, the client will reflect some or all of the above factors in a relative sense. Overall, he will project a more totally integrated self.

Separation-termination is introduced and prepared for as increasing evidence is produced indicating a greater synthesizing of self-identity. No set time factor is associated with this. It will vary according to the assessed problem(s), the personality and needs of the client, the situation with its supports (or lack of supports), and the perceived goals toward which client and worker are working. The introduction of separation-termination will initiate and necessitate the reworking of earlier losses. Regression to the early phase of treatment often recurs and/or a defensive system of denial, avoidance, withdrawal, or displacement is triggered. Frequently, not enough time is allowed for working through and attaining a higher level of coping. All kinds of professional rationalizations and countertransference reactions can get set off within the worker, at the expense of the client's growth. In an extreme sense, this can take on a form of collusion—an implicit agreement that "we won't talk about it, certainly not in any way that will be upsetting." Moving at the client's pace, the worker observes the defensive reaction to the ending process, underscores repeatedly the "letdown" and disappointment it is for the client, allows for ventilation of loss, negatives, hurt, and anger. During the working-through process, encouragement of ongoing present areas of ego functioning is important, and they are carefully assessed and measured. To what degree is the client now somatizing, acting out, verbalizing his feelings? As he progresses through the painful letting-go process, has he been able to expand his observing ego capacities, and to what extent is his potential for investment in former and new objects manifesting itself? At the end of the process, it is helpful for client and worker to review progress throughout the treatment period, his areas still needing change, and acceptance of the unchangeable. Social casework draws much of its knowledge of the separation-termination phase from the functionalists, the works of Erich Lindemann (42), and, more recently, the theoretical enlightenments of Margaret Mahler (43). Progressively, it is recognized that the client tends to rework symbolically the earlier symbiotic relationship. Gertrude and Rubin Blanck (6), in their book *Ego Psychology*, address themselves specifically to Mahler's theory and its application. They emphasize and demonstrate how the various stages of the first thirty-six months of life are often replayed in treatment. They illustrate how clients, particularly borderlines, tend to have been severely traumatized during the rapprochement subphase when the child, once again, returns to the mother in a clinging fashion only to be rebuffed and/or signaled that it is unacceptable, even dangerous, to individuate. Instead of experiencing rapprochement as a prelude to letting go, such clients were forced to regress to earlier levels or remained fixed. Lackie (40) points out that in treatment the resolution of the rapprochement subphase results in enhanced self-esteem and a more benevolent superego. No client can be helped through such a process unless he implicitly senses that the worker's ego can tolerate his feelings of loss, hurt, separateness, anger, and grief.

Implications for types of clients and treatment approaches

Presently, there appears to be a rejection within the social work profession of the labeling of clients in terms of a clinical diagnosis such as "neurotic" or "character disorder." Unless the worker is clear in his assessment of the client's total situation (external and internal)—his ego strengths, intact areas, gaps, and weaknesses—his model for intervention will be affected by cloudiness, groping, and undifferentiated kinds of action (or inaction). Especially, it is the assessment of the client's ego functioning, his defensive structure and ability to cope with stress, anxiety, frustration-tolerance, reality testing, autonomous ego functions, and superego development, which determines the differential diagnosis and provides guidelines for differential intervention. If his external reality is the primary focus of intervention, then the worker's assessment should have good evidence and predictability that the client's potential ego functions will be reactively restored, enabling further ego progression once the external press is lifted and/or relieved.

And so it is the ego assessment which guides the worker's direction. The weaker the client's defenses, the more actively the worker will help support these defenses, getting behind and strengthening areas of ego functioning, encouraging repression of undefended, chaotic, irrational content, and refraining from probing, uncovering techniques. This broad, general approach has been most effective with borderline and ambulatory schizophrenic clients (Kaufman, 36; Colt, 9; Strean, 66; Stuart, 68; Weinberger, 73; Fauber, 12).

The client whose problems stem from a more characterological nature—impulse-ridden, acting out, lack of anxiety, or primitive superego development—will generally necessitate considerable activity on the worker's part in terms of the environment, the teaching of impulse control, the setting of limits, the pointing out of cause-effect relationships (as well as consequences), and partializing experiences which can be tolerated and assimilated (Reiner and Kaufman, 57; Strean, 66; Jackel, 35; Grossbard, 25; Scherz, 60). Such techniques are employed to make acting-out behavior ego-alien.

With the narcissistic personality and/or behavior-disordered client, there is presently a spirited and, I believe, fruitful dialogue going on within the field of psychoanalysis and ego psychology. Heinz Kohut (39) strongly believes that knowledge about the psychology of self must be applied in the treatment of such patients/clients. He stresses that the theory of self-psychology runs parallel and is complementary to the structural-drive-neurosis and object relations theories. He finds that such patients are increasingly prevalent in presenting themselves and that they are suffering from serious, deep-seated, early narcissistic injuries resulting in fragmented self-concepts. These injuries are dealt with by various defensive maneuvers which serve to cover the defect and/or by various forms of compensatory behaviors. According to Kohut, the treatment goals should be the restoration of self into a firm, cohesive identity, not aimed primarily toward the achievement of controls over infantile, sexual, and aggressive drives.

Otto Kernberg (38) and James Masterson (46), on the other hand, recognize the prevalence of narcissistic injury, but perceive this as part of early oral drive frustration and feel it should be addressed as such. This theoretical and clinical issue has yet to be resolved, but it is likely that we are heading for an integration of this "psychology of self" which is already enriching our clinical social work understanding and affecting our treatment approach to clients. In the past, we have found that confronting such clients with their defensive maneuvers has invariably brought on the full wrath of the clients' rage or, not infrequently, a flight from treatment. Still, many clients have been treated successfully by social workers intuitively treating the client's wounded self and not primarily focusing on the drive-object conflicts.

The client, functioning at a neurotic level, will manifest stronger ego development, and as a result treatment will be affected. An increasing encouragement of feelings to be verbalized, to clarify, connect, and at times interpret would be indicated. The development of self-awareness is often associated with the client's ability to examine previous "taboos" in relation to his thoughts, feelings, and behavior. What surfaces and is used during the treatment context is essentially suppressed, preconscious content. Depending on the strength of the client-worker relationship, as well as the client's ego readiness to be engaged, it is commonly observed that what might have been unconscious in the early phase of treatment emerges later into ego consciousness and is amenable for discussion-working through during later phases.

In all clients and their situations, the conflict-free areas are identified, assessed, and engaged within the context of a relationship with the worker, who lends his ego-superego (alter) until the client's own ego is strengthened and consolidated for his own utilization.

Implications for individuals, families, groups, communities

During the late 1950s and 1960s ego psychology theory had been expanded and extended in application beyond the individual and toward a broader spectrum, including families, groups, and community. For reasons such as administrative-organizational structure, social injustices, the client's demands, and cumbersome caseloads, crisis oriented, brief treatment has been examined, and is now readily used. No longer are clients and their situations being assessed consistently as long-term, ongoing treatment. At the risk of perceiving crisis-oriented, brief treatment as a panacea, it does offer an opportunity to apply ego psychology knowledge with individuals, families, groups, and communities. Social work's level of understanding and sophistication in terms of how this is done is not as refined and systematized with groups and communities as it is with individuals and families. Even with the latter, the profession is still in the early phase of differentiating the target groups that can most benefit from crisis-oriented, brief treatment (Rapoport, 56; Parad, 50). There appear to be two broad clusters: (1) those individuals and families who had relatively good ego functioning prior to the state of disequilibrium and who are reacting to considerable external stress, and (2) borderline individuals in whom encouraging changes in personality have come about as a result of active intervention which succeeded in forestalling further ego disruption. Ego-supportive treatment, in such instances, aims to restore and sustain ego functioning (56).

Though crisis intervention can be enhancing to human beings under stress, the approach can be misused and abused, especially with those individuals and families who suffer from serious and severe character-disordered problems. Crisis is frequently the theme of such individuals' lives; balance-steadiness is alien to them. Turmoil and upheaval have been incorporated into their ego structures in such a way that internal conflict is minimally perceived and acting out is ego-syntonic, while the individual's behavior creates conflict within the environment. The individual's awareness of conflict is limited to the external environment being obstructive or frustrating to immediate needs and gratifications. As Lydia Rapoport (56) warns: "The tendency has been to misconstrue the nature of crises and the power and limits of brief intervention and to misapply this theory in work with clients for whom life style crises are most frequently operative." It is well known that a large percent of caseloads are heavily weighted in the direction of work with such individuals and families who require more long-term approaches, as delineated by Reiner and Kaufman (57) and Mayer and Schamess (47).

Beyond the introduction of crisis intervention on a conceptual systematized basis, the changing dimensions of ego psychology have led to even broader changes in method, particularly in terms of the family. Dissatisfaction with the limitations of work with the individual, along with the all-too-frequent undoing by the family pathology, led to the family treatment model. The findings of cultural anthropologists and sociological small-group theory provided new insights into the dynamics of the nuclear and extended family. Scherz (62), Ackerman (1), Beatman (4), and Mitchell (49) all stressed the importance of directing attention toward the family interactional system and not just the sum of the individual diagnoses. The family is viewed as the patient and, as such, the "family ego" requires assessment. Primarily because of the works of Erikson (11), the family life cycle is perceived in terms of phases, each phase bringing its particular development crisis to be resolved within the family context. Concepts such as "scapegoating," alliances, communication, and family need-response patterns have taken on broader, in-depth meanings. Family strengths and vulnerabilities, the kinds of stresses (external and internal) impinging on the system, and patterns of conflict and resolution, along with the family's coping mechanisms, roles, and goals, are taken into consideration and worked with. Marital equilibrium (or lack of equilibrium), level of ego development, integration, and use of defenses are assessed and understood in relation to how the interactional behavior is reflected on each family member.

Group and community workers are making increasing use of ego concepts and applying their intervention techniques accordingly. As in individual and family functioning, areas of group and community breakdown are identified, as well as the external and internal stresses that they experience. Intervention is frequently introduced on the basis of active reaching out, mobilizing of resources (both internal and external), working with group and community conflict, assessing strengths and self-concepts, promoting autonomy, and time-limited problem solving (59). All or selected parts of these concepts and techniques are used as a means of promoting collective ego mastery on the part of groups and communities. Though these ego processes, within the community-societal context, have not necessarily always been identified as such, they are executive-autonomous functions which various forms of societal interventions and institutions relate to and work with (10). Group and community workers' knowledge of systems and organizational theories, including the sociological concepts of anomie and alienation, have more immediate application in the operational sense. In work with individuals and families (though such knowledge and concepts enrich our understanding in the diagnostic sense), their application is more limited. This remains an area for further research.

Gaps in knowledge and implications for research

As indicated above, ego-oriented social casework with individuals and families continues to struggle with application of knowledge derived primarily from the sociological and anthropological sciences. Considerable strides have been made in role systems and small group theory and their application to practice. It is axiomatic that the diagnostic process involved in studying the personality makeup of an individual, his symptoms and adaptive capacities, leads the practitioner to a broader understanding and grasp of the individual within his total environment—family, social group, community, society (10, 76). Though the worker is led to this multidimensional taking in of facts and knowledge, its direct, systematic use within the individual client remains blurred and undefined. The profession has yet to devise tools which match adequately the expanded knowledge gained of the client's problem(s). At the same time, the practitioner often suffers from a sense of inundation in trying to sort out usable knowledge. The market is presently flooded with what is labeled "new" knowledge, and thus the practitioner is at risk of being immobilized, or of blocking out excessive stimuli which cannot be assimilated, or of discarding all previous knowledge and skill and opting only for the new. In any of these broad approaches, the client generally gets short-changed.

It has been frequently stated that the problem of social work and social casework theory is not a dearth of knowledge, but the selection of the applicable and helpful from such a plethora of content. Up to the present, social casework research and its findings have not been particularly conclusive. Studies of effectiveness have left much to be desired in that certain questions have remained ambiguous and unanswered. Furthermore, in studies where ineffectiveness had been generalized from the results, there was also the question of whether an ego-oriented casework treatment method (or other treatment methods) had been applied appropriately according to assessed client needs. Too often, the design and problem formulations of such studies have been implicitly set up to confirm and validate the built-in bias of the investigating team. We have yet to come to a more objective exploration and to develop valid hypotheses.

Case examples

To illustrate best the application of ego psychology within a casework context, I have selected the following two cases. They are not the ultimate in either diagnosis or treatment, but they attempt to show the direct relationship between the understanding and use of skill, as well as the resultant effects of both. In each case, supplementary work was done with other members of the family, as well as with the family group as a whole.

Ego-oriented Casework with the Impulse-ridden, Character-disordered Client—The Case of Mrs. M.

In offering a "corrective emotional experience," the worker must invariably ask himself: "What does the client need now from the relationship?" Perhaps no group of practitioners have a broader range of knowledge and skills, in working with what have been termed "character-disordered" clients, than caseworkers. Such clients have experienced a lifelong pattern of receiving both psychologically and socially, and because of their own ego-superego deficiencies have been caught up in a repetitive pattern of self-defeating, acting-out episodes. A continuous cycle of reciprocal and negative reinforcement appears to set in between client and significant others. A kind of "I'll-get-you-before-you-get-me" behavioral pattern is triggered, whereby each (client and societal agents) draws on provocative-protective devices to ward off threat and intrusion from the other.

This pattern and the treatment process can best be illustrated by the case of Mrs. M., mother of Myron M. Initial intervention was implemented along the traditional approach of history-taking and fact-gathering related to early etiological factors.

Myron, age 12, black, was originally referred by the school because of his use of vile language, referring to the teacher as a "white bitch." He constantly chased other children, dragging them to the ground. Teacher and principal described mother as uncooperative, extremely hostile, "dangerous," insisting that the only recourse would be transferring Myron to an "adjustment" school. Mrs. M. disregarded all requests to come to school, and with the Attendance Officer, Mrs. M. displayed an attitude of indifference followed by vulgar, abusive language. At one point, the Principal warned Mrs. M. that Myron could not graduate, that he was "crazy" and needed help. Mother was unhappy about this and agreed to talk to a social worker.

Based on the above scanty facts, there appeared to be no understanding or questioning on the part of the school authorities during the period of deteriorating behavior: What precipitated or triggered the responses on the part of Myron? What does it mean to be an emerging adolescent black boy being taught by a white teacher? To what extent are we observing a psychologically upset child, and to what extent is the educational system triggering, exacerbating, and/or unable to meet the needs of this particular youngster? What would it mean for this black mother to come to a white-oriented school, at an expected appointed time, and then to be confronted with threats as well as a questioning of Myron's sanity? To what extent are we dealing with a teacher, principal, and educational system threatened by the unsubmissive, uncowed black (who attacks rather than retreats into apathy)? To what extent is his attack a disguised source of ego protection and potential resource and strength?

Mrs. M. came in for one interview after missing her first appointment. She was receiving AFDC assistance for her four children , Myron, Earl, age 5, and twin girls, one-year old. She recounted a succession of difficulties ("fights") with Dept. of Welfare investigators. She was critical of the school, and seemed unable to comprehend her son's difficulties there. In an effort to understand Mrs. M.'s apparent deprivation, the worker tried to draw out something about her early experiences. The worker gathered that Mrs. M. had grown up in South Carolina, reared by two women (not relatives) after her mother's death in Mrs. M.'s infancy. Her father saw her infrequently and finally disappeared altogether. She was not married to Myron's father and he did not support her or the child. It was necessary to "board him out" for the first several years of life. Mrs. M. came to New York City five years ago, since which time Myron had lived with her.

Mrs. M. failed several appointments following this interview. The investigator felt that Mrs. M.'s limited intelligence and emotional upset added to the problem. Due to staff shortages, no new activity was initiated until seven months later, at which time case was transferred to another worker.

One cannot help but ask what it must have meant to Mrs. M. to be "drawn out" about early life experiences at a time of multiple reality crises impinging upon her. Can one assess "limited intelligence" when the ego is being so heavily taxed and overburdened by a demoralizing and degrading social reality? To what extent was an overloaded investigator interacting, in a perfunctory manner, with a defeated, exhausted client, who answers such questions in a clouded, mechanical, rote fashion, devoid of meaning or affect? It is noted that no attempt was made to move in actively on the part of the investigator, by relating to Mrs. M. in the midst of her many crises—Myron and school, financial, Department of Welfare. Such activity on the part of the worker is vital in the beginning phase (57). Seven months later a new worker is assigned and the following is recorded:

Relationship Phase.

The family resides on top floor of a dilapidated tenement located on a site being cleared for Housing project. Many buildings are already vacant and streets are littered with debris and broken glass from abandoned buildings. The apartment is beyond repair. Mrs. M. did not greet me or invite me in, but instead stared angrily and stated: "I guess you're another one coming to tell me he's crazy." I said that I was another person coming to discuss Myron, but not to say that he is crazy. I asked if I might come in and if Mrs. M. had received the appointment letter. Mrs. M. gruffly admitted me and made much effort about finding some place "clean" for me to sit. I said I could sit and took the nearest chair. Mrs. M. did not sit, but busied herself with the dishes while she angrily poured forth a loud tirade. She got my letter but there was no use in talking. Myron isn't any more nervous than anyone else. That principal said he was crazy and wanted to have his head examined. He even wanted the boy sent away until he was 21. She would never sign for that. Myron acts sensibly at home. I said that of course he does, and he acts sensibly in school. I had not come because the school questioned his sanity nor had I come to make any suggestions about examination or placement. Mrs. M. asked, "Then what do you want?" I said I wanted to see if there were ways in which I could be of help to the family. The school did feel that Myron was sometimes troubled and nervous, but wasn't bad. Mrs. M. answered that she does the best she can. I was sure that she did and commented that it isn't easy to rear a family alone.

The new worker's observational capacities take in the social scene in her description of Mrs. M.'s environmental situation. From where can an individual and the family ego draw sustenance and/or replenishment when survival instincts are paramount? Understandably, Mrs. M. perceives the worker as another representative of white, formal authority who has come to criticize and attack. Interestingly, she reveals two pressing anxieties within the first few minutes of the interview: (1) Myron's "craziness" and (2) sending him away—separation. The worker sensitively moves in by consciously lessening threat on both these levels: (1) he's not crazy and (2) she did not come to make any suggestion about placement. She clarifies her reasons for coming, she recognizes Myron's worth ("He wasn't bad"), and she sympathizes with Mrs. M.'s plight in having to "rear a family alone." By going along with Mrs. M.'s defenses, not threatening them, and by stressing ego strengths (i.e., Myron's sensibleness, Mrs. M.'s strength in rearing a family alone), she elicits the first indication of lowering defenses—"I do the best I can."

> Mrs. M. then let go with a hostile outburst against Dept. of Welfare. They drive her crazy with visiting and prying, and accusation of working. She could cut Mr. S.'s (the worker's) throat. She heard there is a new worker and guesses this one will be worse than the last. She read in the paper that the city planned to wipe out the Dept. of Welfare, and she would be glad. Then they will just have to starve and die. I said that the Dept. of Welfare was not being disbanded. I thought Mrs. M. sounded very troubled and hopeless. What was the problem with the Dept. of Welfare? The worker is pressing for address of the twins' father. He already gives $10 per week, through court, but Dept. of Welfare wants to re-check his present situation and he refuses further contact. I asked what Mrs. M. had done about her present problem. She had told worker the man wouldn't give his address and that was that. In discussion, I proposed that there might be some other way of working this out, since now she was jeopardizing her eligibility. I thought that a periodic review might be necessary. I suggested that it may be possible to work things out so

> that he would not lose work time or be inconvenienced. Mrs. M. softened a bit and agreed that she had not asked about any other ways of straightening this out. When I offered to clear this with the Dept. of Welfare, Mrs. M. said sharply that she would be glad to have help, "but for God's sake don't do anything to make matters worse." I tied this up with my wish to help and with Mrs. M. perhaps not seeing at this point how anything could help.

In this part of the interview it is observed that Mrs. M.'s momentary lowering of defenses is quickly replaced by a hostile outburst—almost as though she had left herself open and vulnerable to hurt and further exploitation. Her ranting over the disbanding of the Department of Welfare carries a symbolic message of anticipating getting dropped and being abandoned once again. The worker gathers facts in relation to the immediate crisis—the Department of Welfare—while simultaneously clarifying and reassuring that disbanding is not planned. By relating to Mrs. M. in the midst of her crises, she starts where Mrs. M. is, upholds reality, and injects hope ("It may be possible to work things out"). This is followed by Mrs. M. softening and the worker then moving in by offering "to clear this with the Department of Welfare." Clients such as Mrs. M. have had prolonged and repetitive negative experiences with authority and an important, early-treatment technique is to intercede temporarily with authority in order to act as an advocate on their behalf.

> Mrs. M. began to cry, commenting on her long struggle in managing alone. She has no people, no money, everyone pushes her around. She guesses Myron would naturally be unhappy in a home such as his. He had no decent clothing and no T.V.; no opportunities for shows and trips like other boys. He did go to camp last year through Dept. of Welfare, but she guessed he wouldn't be sent again. I expressed interest in talking more about Myron as we went along. I purposely did not pursue discussion about the child at

this time as Mrs. M.'s own needs seemed so much in evidence. Mrs. M. did mention that Myron suffered an accident in school the day before by running into a post and injuring his nose. School refused to dismiss him early but sent a note for Mrs. M. to take him to the hospital where the doctor was impatient and rude. No x-ray was taken. The doctor pushed on the twisted bone and Myron could scarcely bear it. There is still swelling and dark bruising. She had not returned because the doctor refused her suggestion that Myron be "given a needle" before further examination. She had no further plans, but angrily did ask me to find out why the school did not dismiss Myron early. I agreed to do this and discussed the possibility of getting a further hospital check-up to prevent later trouble. Mrs. M. would consider this.

In the sequence, it is noteworthy that the worker's offer to advocate on the client's behalf and her underscoring Mrs. M.'s perception of hopelessness brings a breakthrough, an admission on Mrs. M.'s part of her difficulty in "managing alone." There follows a recognition that there is a problem in terms of Myron's material deprivations, and a beginning of clearer perception and thinking emerges. Though the worker expresses interest in talking about Myron "as we went along," she is clear in her recognition that Mrs. M. is the primary client, at this point in time. Mrs. M.'s description of the accident and hospital episodes must be weighed on various levels. Degrading, brutalizing experiences in emergency rooms of hospitals servicing disadvantaged areas do occur. At the same time, because of past experiences with personal and community authorities, to what extent are there ego distortions on the part of Myron and Mrs. M.? Once again, the worker agrees to intercede, thereby giving further evidence of interest and concern, but also suggesting follow-up with the hospital in terms of Myron's health. The suggestion is a form of encouraging the client's ego to begin to engage actively on her behalf.

Mrs. M. was somewhat more pleasant when I left. She said I was welcome to return at any time. She does not like to be nasty to people but is sick and tired of being "nagged and investigated." She accepted appointment for a home visit in two weeks.

By not invading defenses but going along with them, underscoring positives and strengths in terms of Myron's behavior and the mother's managing, upholding realities about the Department of Welfare, dealing with here-and-now issues, getting actively involved in the environment, using community resources, giving empathy along with suggestions, and injecting hope, the worker perceives a relieved, more approachable Mrs. M. by the end of the interview. The various sustaining techniques converge in order to create an atmosphere that provides for the planting of seeds of a trusting relationship. For Mrs. M., this is a change in attitude which begins to permit problem solving, development of basic trust, and a corrective working through of problems.

In succeeding home visits for the next two months, Mrs. M. repeatedly tested the worker in numerous ways. On one occasion there was a neighbor present with prolonged whispering going on in the worker's presence, or Mrs. M. would busy herself by the sink, noisily rattling dishes and drowning out any conversation. In these early relationship phase interviews, Mrs. M. turned discussion to material needs—clothing, a mattress, and then housing. She threatened to "fix" the Department of Welfare by withholding rent. Worker consistently balanced recognition of Mrs. M.'s distress with pointing out how her threats, if acted upon, would work against her. Instead, the worker offered to obtain household needs through the agency, to check into continuing eligibility, and to work with the Housing Authority as to the possibility of better living conditions. The worker introduced techniques of (1) balancing empathy with (2) the teaching of impulse control, the pointing out of cause and effect and the consequences of unplanned, unthought-through acts, as well as (3) remaining active in the environment. Mrs. M.'s need to test diminished, and her ability to trust increased. Worker always fulfilled her promises: reciprocally, Mrs. M., despite her anger at the hospital, took Myron back for a checkup, thereby beginning to test herself out in the community as a concerned and caring mother.

Identification Phase. In the third month of treatment there was a noticeable shift in content. The worker's setting of limits through the teaching of impulse control and the discouraging of acting-out, impulsive behavior (ego-alien), as a good parent would do, appeared to bring Mrs. M. to a more thoughtful state. As acting out began to cease, some depression and repeated reflective discussion of her relationship with Myron and her core separation problem gradually surfaced. It centered on Myron wanting to attend a recreation center and a summer camp. The worker carefully avoided these issues—instead, she offered to discuss possibilities "if this is something both mother and Myron wanted." Mrs. M.'s repetitive theme was that she would be receptive to any plan short of "sending him away." She was willing for him to register at the Community Center (but restricted his attendance to once a week) and kept raising the question of the Center's "distance from home." Worker made conscious effort to go slow on this emotive area, but underscored it as an area of concern for Mrs. M.

As a basic trust in the relationship with the worker consolidated, Mrs. M. was increasingly prepared for the worker's visits, and was more ready and strengthened to engage in participation, both in treatment and environmentally. She experienced a positive contact with the school and the Department of Welfare. She was impressed with the school's guidance counselor and she found the new welfare worker to be "very nice." She gave the address of the babies' father and his phone number at work. He had been in touch with the Department of Welfare and had sent in verification of his salary. The

Department then came through with various household supplies and Mrs. M. asked that the new mattress not be brought into the apartment until the family was rehoused. All of these were indicators of Mrs. M.'s growing ability to tolerate frustration, to delay, and to obtain gratification as she felt nurtured and supported in the relationship with the worker. By meeting some of Mrs. M.'s narcissistic and dependency needs on both a tangible and symbolic level, but not encouraging regression, the worker had freed energy for coping and problem solving.

> With these environmental successes, Mrs. M. kept returning to the theme of Myron's wish to go to camp and of her failure to register him. She persistently apologized for not doing so, even though the worker kept clarifying that they needed perhaps to talk more fully about this, as "something seems to be getting in the way." Mrs. M. would then inject that she "needs Myron at home" in case they move over the summer and when the worker would accept this, Mrs. M. would impulsively insist that she will register him at once. Gradually, the worker introduced the thought that perhaps Mrs. M. felt some pressure from her and that "We would not want to plan things this way." She talked of Myron being the oldest and that understandably, it might be hard for Mrs. M. to think of his being away for a few weeks. Mrs. M. appeared to avoid further discussion and suggested that the worker register him—"You just go ahead and do it for me." The worker indicated that this would not be a good thing, as she "did not wish to make a plan for Mrs. M." but wanted instead to help her and Myron carry out what they wanted. Mrs. M. then talked of how frightened she was last year when she had to go "across water" in order to pick up Myron, and she would "never do this again," as she is "scared to death" of water.

The worker did not go into the symbolic-primitive-phobic content, nor did she

attempt to uncover or interpret its annihila-
tion–separation meanings. Instead, she underscored Mrs. M.'s apprehension by recognizing it,
and held to the point that it is important to
understand if camp is what she really wants and
that perhaps she needs more time to think about
it before coming to a decision, one way or the
other. Here the worker reinforces secondary
ego autonomy processes for the impulse-ridden
client, underscoring the importance of thinking,
planning, and delaying in order to allow for the
expansion of ego abilities. In addition, the
worker carefully avoids controlling or usurping
the client's own efforts toward problem solving.
In the working-through process, the worker retains optimal anxiety within the client and allows
time for resolving the problem.

> The follow-up interview, once again,
> found Mrs. M. "cool, formal, busying
> herself with pots and dishes and then
> bursting forth with a long list of
> complaints about the house—the
> difficulties of housekeeping in a shack."
> She then slipped in the comment that
> with all the worry over the house, she
> had no time to see about camp for
> Myron—"He will just have to miss it this
> year." The worker underscored that Mrs.
> M. seemed pretty upset and that she (the
> worker) did not feel disappointed or
> upset because nothing had been done
> about camp. Mrs. M. let her know that
> she needs Myron to be with her until she
> feels "more settled"—that Myron is big
> enough to run out for help if someone
> bothers them. She began to cry,
> commenting that all her life she seems
> to be alone whenever she needs
> someone to help her. Now that Myron is
> getting bigger she had hoped he would
> be around so she would at least have
> someone of her own blood to turn to.
> Instead of that he always wants to be in
> the street, or to "go off somewhere," that
> he will be "under her rule" until he is 21.
> Worker empathized with how upsetting it
> is to feel so alone and that this would
> understandably make it hard to plan for
> Myron to be away from home. The worker

> then let Mrs. M. know that planning for
> camp was not nearly as important as
> trying to understand how we could help
> Mrs. M. feel less burdened and
> lonely—she has had such a hard time
> managing alone. Mrs. M. said it was not
> just doing for the children that was hard.
> All her life things had seemed to go
> wrong. Life is a "sorry thing" without a
> mother. The relatives who reared her
> gave her food and little more. Myron's
> father "tricked" her and then refused to
> marry her. She was lonely after they
> broke up and started to "hang out" with
> various women neighbors. Before she
> knew it she was playing cards and
> drinking during the day. Some mornings
> she wakes up and one look at her
> rundown apartment makes her feel blue,
> and then she drinks her wine or beer. She
> guessed she had been around the "low-
> down" people in her block so long that
> she got to be like them. She said
> tearfully, "I want to be decent just like
> other people, but everything I turn my
> hand to seems to go wrong." Worker said
> that Mrs. M. was a decent person, that
> making mistakes and having trouble did
> not make her less decent. The important
> thing was that Mrs. M. wanted to work
> things out in a better way. Things did not
> have to keep on going wrong.
> At the end of the interview, Mrs. M.
> thought she would tell Myron that she
> needed him this year, but she would
> promise that he could go to the Center
> several days a week during the summer.
> As the worker was leaving, Mrs. M.
> smiled very warmly, commenting, "You're
> such a nice size. I used to be small like
> that. Maybe one day I'll get rid of this
> stomach."

A crucial point has been reached in the
treatment process. Under stress, Mrs. M. again
needs to test and retest the relationship, and the
worker calmly points out the observed pattern
without interpreting its meaning. Also, the
worker carefully signals back that she is not
disappointed about camp, once again allowing

for Mrs. M. to come to terms with her own disappointment and loosening her projection as to the worker's expectations of her. What follows is conscious admission of her need for Myron's presence and protection and her ambivalent bind about his growing up. The worker stays with Mrs. M.'s feeling of being all alone, dismisses camp as the issue, and recommits herself to wanting to understand how to lessen Mrs. M.'s burdens, loneliness, and underlying depression. In coping, as a child, with such intolerable feelings of loss, low self-worth, rejection, and deprivation, a life cycle and behavioral pattern of acting out (drinking and gambling) was triggered to ward off depression. This time the content is not facts rendered by an apathetic client in response to a worker's questioning, as was seen in the first worker's interview. Only the sensitive handling of the transference—the corrective parenting which Mrs. M. was receiving within the present relationship with this worker—allowed for the emergence of what were previously unconscious, repressed feelings. The worker did not probe into early deprivation; rather, her support of a low self-image, and her careful introduction of "working things out in a better way" conveys to the client that though one can no longer do anything about the past, one can direct one's present and future. Ego progression is encouraged and enhanced.

Additionally, identification with the worker now openly emerges as well and the expression of "wanting to be like" is stated. It is often detrimental and professionally undoing to close the case once expressed identification has been attained. Too often, a kind of countertransference sets in (in such instances), where the worker's own ego gets narcissistically inflated around the need for successful endings, and the worker believes that the case is ready for closure. A kind of "my client is now ready to move on in that he or she is very nice, well behaved, decent, caring—just like me" sets in. In the other extreme, a worker's overinvested ego can militate against letting go when it is indicated. However, to close the case before the client has attained his own identity, values, and standards, can abort the whole process, undo and repeat for the client what he has invariably experienced in past, meaningful relationships— namely, that an investment means losing.

Self-Identity–Autonomy Phase.

During the next two months, the turning-point in treatment was followed by Mrs. M. using the worker to secure care for Myron's teeth at the Health Center's Dental Clinic. The worker also encouraged her to secure attention for her own eye condition. Myron stepped on a piece of glass during this period and Mrs. M. took him to the hospital, but worried that the Dept. of Welfare would question her for having paid the clinic fee. The worker pointed out that in such an emergency the Dept. would only expect a parent to get his child to the nearest hospital. Mrs. M. said she guesses she is in the habit of being hard on the Dept. of Welfare. She added that she had notified the school about Myron's absence. Sometimes she forgets to do such things, but the guidance counsellor was so nice to her and Myron is getting along better in school now, so she wants to do her part.

Though a kind of plateau appears to have been reached in treatment, actually much is going on subterraneanly. Mrs. M. seems to want to please the worker, but she is also beginning to talk about wanting to "do her part." It is noted that her observing ego is developing as she talks of having been "in the habit of being hard on Dept. of Welfare," as the worker supports her role as a mother and upholds the societal expectation as well. This plateau period was brought to an abrupt halt when a harsh reality crisis occurred.

The worker came for her regular interview, and Mrs. M. was highly upset about an incident with a neighbor woman. Upon seeing the worker Mrs. M. commented, it looked like the day for you to come would never get here." She had not phoned because she did not think anyone could do anything, but she just wanted to tell the worker about it. She said that the apartment plan had fallen through and on top of that disappointment she had a very frightening experience. Myron had a fight with a boy whose mother later struck Myron with a brick and stick. Mrs. M. ran out and Myron was bleeding from a scalp cut. Her first impulse was to go back and get a knife to cut the woman, "but something said to me, Katherine be decent—set a better example for your children." She tried to talk to the woman explaining that she had no right to hit Myron, that the boys had simply had a fair fight, in which neither boy was really hurt. The woman was very bold, cursed, threatened and challenged Mrs. M., who had to strain to keep from attacking her. Mrs. M. said she remembered the time when she would have cut the woman's head off, but she controlled herself. She, at the same time, didn't want Myron to feel that his mother wouldn't protect him; thus, she told the woman she was going to the police. She secured a summons and served it that evening. That night three men came to her home—one had a gun. They threatened to maim or kill her if she did not withdraw charges. Mrs. M. argued a little about her need to protect her child. The men left, but three to five of them came back for the next three nights. She felt so frightened, alone, and angry too. At first she wished she had brutally beaten the woman, but then she felt that this would have got her into trouble—it would be worse to go to jail and leave the children. She did go back to talk with the woman, suggesting the woman could have talked with her about her predicament and they could have settled things another way. She believed the woman felt ashamed of herself after their talk. Mrs. M. thought it really did

not pay sometimes to try to do things right. I thought it may seem that way at first glance; sometimes even when we do our best, there are circumstances that seem to get the better of us. I thought it was the way that we reacted to such experiences that was the important thing. I said that Mrs. M. certainly had done well, that she had set a good example for Myron in the way she handled things, and she had kept the well-being of her children in mind as she acted. Mrs. M. said proudly that she had been "more of a woman" than the other person. Mrs. M. plans to renew her search for an apartment so she can leave the neighborhood.

This horrific experience would have put the strongest of egos to the supreme test. However, numerous indices emerge which pinpoint and measure how far Mrs. M. had developed in terms of ego and superego growth. It is interesting to note that Mrs. M. "sat on herself" (ability to delay) and waited for the worker's visit to verbalize what had happened, indicating further growth of coping mechanisms. She verbalizes her aggressive thoughts and wishes toward the neighbor lady and puts it into a context which reveals a marked ability of her ego to neutralize and fuse aggression into verbalization. Her superego development is aligned with her ego ideal for herself ("Katherine be decent—set a better example for your children"), reflecting an enhanced self-image. Her "talking" to the neighbor, her recognition that beating up the woman would mean trouble for herself, her desire to protect her children, indicate (through identification) the incorporating and internalizing of many of the standards, values, prohibitions and controls of the worker and making them her own. Verbalizing has become her mode of functioning and she persists in using this in making contact with the neighbor. As a result, she perceives that in some vague way the neighbor experienced something different ("I think she felt ashamed of herself") after their talk. Though

Mrs. M. indicates it "sometimes doesn't pay to do things right," there is an implicit invitation for further ego and superego support for having done right, which the worker consciously reinforces. When this is forthcoming, Mrs. M. underscores her own identity as a "woman," perceiving herself as having "achieved" as well as continuing the process of "becoming." Ego energy is further freed for integrative functioning and renewed tasks, such as apartment hunting.

At the start of the interview, Mrs, M.'s remark about it "looking as though the worker would never get there" contained an element of criticism and anger at the worker. It is not to be overlooked that there continues an underlying feeling of being unprotected by the worker and having to cope on one's own. By the end of the interview, an increased awareness of her growing ability to cope and to function adequately as an autonomous adult becomes apparent. No longer is she helpless and vulnerable, subject to being annihilated and exploited. As harrowing as the above experience had been, she had not fallen apart.

> After the above crisis, Mrs. M.'s increased capacity to work out problems for herself continued. She followed through on eye care for herself, saying "It's time that I take better care of myself." As to the housing situation, she recently attended a meeting of site tenants—something she refused to do before. "Those people don't do anything but lie; they don't care what becomes of people." This time she decided to go and take a couple of women from the building. For the first time in her life she spoke at a meeting. She was nervous, felt ashamed of her lack of education and inability to put things "just right"; but, "I'm a human being, like everybody else, and have to have some place to live." She asked what would be done for those tenants who don't find places by the moving deadline. She told of her many efforts to find places and of the excessive rents. The man answered her

> very nicely, explaining the Housing Authority's plan of offering a place on another site. She was also advised to contact Dept. of Welfare about maximum rent as he thought the amount stated was not maximum.

Mrs. M.'s self-identity is consistently being consolidated, as the above experiences verify. As has been evident, her mode of functioning is no longer on an impulse-ridden, acting-out level. The diagnosis and treatment have shifted toward a more neurotic level of functioning. No longer is the worker employing holding action approaches in order to limit acting out; rather, there is fuller use of reflective techniques, concentrating on the person-situation, along with some discussion of dynamic and developmental factors (33). Mrs. M.'s ego ability to contain her anxiety and to channel it toward constructive "doing" is most apparent in her method of asserting herself and letting her needs be known. Because self-identity is being progressively synthesized, the worker can think in terms of timing the next phase—preparation for termination.

Termination Phase.

> Mrs. M. followed through on the advice of the Housing Authority and went to the Dept. of Welfare, only to learn that Mrs. F. is no longer there, but out on maternity leave. "I might have known I would lose her. Nothing ever lasts for me." Worker recognized that some past experiences may make Mrs. M. feel this way, but that this did not have to be so. Mrs. M. was handling things with Dept. of Welfare in such a way that the worker felt she could work smoothly with whatever worker came. Worker offered to clear about the rent, and about the new worker.

> As the worker was leaving, Mrs. M. commented about doing some summer cleaning, and used this to ask questions about the worker and her home life. Did she do housekeeping? Did she hate to

clean house? Did she have any children? The worker said maybe Mrs. M. was wondering how long she would have her, too? Mrs. M. responded that people come and go so much. Worker said she had no plans for changing, but thought the important thing was that Mrs. M. and she had been working together. She would be able to do this with any worker once they got together on what needed attention. Worker thought it was hard to trust people, but that Mrs. M. had shown much progress on this. The neighbor who had once come to Mrs. M.'s apartment before interrupted, and on seeing the worker withdrew—commenting she didn't know the investigator was there. Mrs. M. angrily called out, "I have told you a thousand times that she is not an investigator—she is a social worker."

As Mrs. M.'s ability to cope is enhanced, she nonetheless gets across her ever present vulnerability to separation, fearing that "getting better" means losing the worker. This worker cautiously clarifies and connects to past experiences but begins to separate what was from what is. In so doing, she upholds the difference from the past to the present and future. What is conveyed is that Mrs. M. is capable of further ego perception and change in attitude. She begins to introduce the concept of transfer and investment to other objects on the basis of Mrs. M.'s proven ability to relate—a kind of saying, "If you did this with me, you can do it with others as well." The worker tunes in to Mrs. M.'s underlying anxiety of separating from the worker, and questions her on this. Mrs. M.'s response indicates that the worker's hearing was accurate. Worker again underscores a vulnerability of Mrs. M., her difficulty to trust, but balances this with her progress in this area. In so doing, the stage is being set for the introduction of termination, timing it to the obtaining of better housing, preparing Mrs. M. for the move and its concurring upsets, and the settling into a new environment. The termination of therapy will trigger regressive responses, which will be ex-

amined in the discussion of the next case and will need to be dealt with. Mrs. M.'s perception of the difference between the past and the present ("investigator" versus "social worker") is further measurement of her progress. This tribute to the worker is the client's way of indicating that important basic needs have been met by someone who knew how to provide a "corrective emotional experience."

Ego-oriented Casework and Separation–Termination—The Case of J.

Evelyn F. Fox, Marian A. Nelson, and William M. Bolman (15) graphically point out that the method of dealing with termination-separation is directly correlated to the degree that gain will be sustained beyond treatment. When termination is introduced, the practitioner needs to be aware that, within the transference between client and worker, earlier experiences related to separation and loss will be reawakened. It has often been stated that the reawakening is not only experienced by the client, but also by the worker. This partially explains why termination has remained such a neglected aspect of treatment, and why positive results of therapy are often undone by avoiding it.

In the following case, separation from the worker and the transfer process will be examined. Three phases of grief—(1) denial, (2) expression of grief, hurt, and anger, and (3) working through—will be illustrated (14). Though J. had been told some months in advance that the worker would be leaving the agency, he did not begin to deal with it directly until the last eight weeks. Work with parents was also implemented, but will not be dealt with here.

J., age 18, was originally referred because of indecently exposing himself "with intent to insult females." There had been two previous similar charges. J. has two brothers: Peter, age 27 living abroad, and Lewis, age 21, chemist, and recently married. J.'s father, engineer, is an

Austrian Jew who emigrated one week before World War II began. He is described as "gentle and unassuming" by both J. and mother. Mother is Gentile, and describes her family as "the height of respectability," and feels severely affronted by J.'s behavior.

J. is intelligent, plans to go to university to study physics. He works part-time in a local clothing store. J. had been seeing the social worker on a regular weekly basis for the past ten months. After considerable testing and provoking the worker, he began to relate to her gradually on a trusting, meaningful level. The worker carefully focused on ego functioning areas: his part-time job, university plans, his interest in physics. The propping up of his strengths brought J. to the point of talking about his home situation—mother's need to control him, father's ineffectiveness, and his perception of university as a "complete break" from home. His need to expose himself in the community gradually began to be replaced with increased exposure of his feelings in treatment. At times of stress and quarrelling with his parents he would go out and drink in the local bar. Two months before the worker was leaving, the worker reminded him that their time together was drawing to a close.

It is important to note that in the ten months of working within the relationship and identification phases, the worker carefully aimed toward propping up J.'s sagging ego. Though his "offense" was not ignored, it was not uncovered or probed. J. frequently said his mother keeps "going on" about "it," and though he doesn't "forget it," he also "doesn't want to go on about it either." Through corrective parenting, by emphasizing his strengths, his defensiveness begins to loosen, his need to intellectualize lessens, and he slowly moves toward feeling areas. J. is aware that the relationship with the worker is time-limited, and it appears that this knowledge motivates him toward meaningful use of treatment time.

Denial Phase

When worker reminded J. that their time together was ending, J. simply grunted, then added that he was "not very pleased." Worker pointed out that he was now used to her, and it is understandable for J. to feel let down at the prospect of a change in workers. J. responded by saying he guessed he was really "quite angry." Worker indicated that she did not intend to disappear without introducing him to the new worker, but they would discuss this nearer to the time of her leaving. J. did not seem too pleased, and said that he "does not like everybody" and he might "not want the person he likes to go." Quite suddenly he moved on to talk about his bell-ringing, explaining the complexity of this hobby, saying he intends to keep it up when he goes on to university. He went into detail of how a local drama group was putting on a play and sent a messenger to the church to complain that the bells were so loud they could not hear themselves on the stage. J. proudly told how the leader of the bell-ringing group responded by telling the messenger they must shout. He then went into a discussion of noise, complaining that his mother always seemed to make a lot of noise when he didn't want her to. When he reads, she begins to vacuum the floor and he ends up shouting at her. Worker did not respond to this content and J. became more anxious and then told of a friend who recently suffered a serious accident while mountain climbing. It seemed that this young man is unlikely to walk again, and J. was considerably upset by the whole issue. The interview ended in a rather confused state, with the worker reminding him of their next appointment.

The worker reintroduces "ending," underscores ambivalence about change, and J.

responds by saying that he is "quite angry." From this point, the worker appears to be on uncertain ground, and the whole aspect of countertransference factors rears itself. She prematurely injects the new worker, which J. rejects. He goes into highly symbolic content to deny the issue, but the worker seems to be tuning out. By avoiding his hurt and anger, J.'s anxiety rises—even to conveying symbolically that he feels he will be left unable to walk, like his "friend." When separation is introduced, invariably the client will be conveying, directly and indirectly, attitudes and feelings, and unless the worker is aware of his own feelings, the content of the interview will become unstructured and diffused.

Behavioral–Emotional Reactions (Warding Off).

The next week we talked of my leaving, and J. exclaimed: "I'm not angry!" Worker pointed out that he sounded angry and could they discuss it and the change to a new person. He said he is afraid of a new person but he was most concerned about the worker going ... besides, there are some feelings he cannot talk about. Worker asked which feelings; he answered that anger and distress were quite easy to explain, but others were hard. "Others?" worker repeated, and he said: "Yes, like when you lose someone." Worker asked if this has happened before and he answered: "Yes, too often. . . . I have not lost anybody by death, but it is just the same when a girl friend leaves you flat." This has happened several times. He repeated that this had happened "too often," and the worker commented: "And now I am leaving you, too." J. said, "Yes, that's just the feeling and I don't want to think about it until you go." Worker pointed out that thinking and talking about it can help. J. admitted it, but added, "It will be very painful." Then, aggressively said: "Can't you understand? You said you

have lost people, too." Worker agreed and said that the feeling is different if someone leaves suddenly with no warning or preparation. J. then said he has never been able to talk to his parents about things that are near to his heart. His mother would explode, and his dad would pretend to but didn't really. He doesn't want to be part of the family like his parents would like him to be, but he wants to be an individual. He doesn't feel he is one person, but several—at school he is concerned with work; at home he is always frustrated and angry; in the office here he is able to sit and talk. He had a need to leave home and to find "J.—J. with long hair, if I want." He said the real J. is the intellectual together with the dating J., but people leave him too soon "just like you are doing." He added that he needs a "total break" from home, and is avoiding relationships with girls because of the pain of parting when he goes to university. Worker commented that it is also painful for him not to have these relationships, and that perhaps it would be better if he were able to bear separation. He agreed, but added that he must "run away from everything at home." Run away? "Yes, probably from my mother, and the hold she has over me." J. started to go into an academic discussion of growing up, and when the worker pointed this out he said: "I feel as if I am fencing with you." Worker agreed, and wondered what this was all about. He hesitantly answered that he wants to avoid answering her questions.

J.'s insistence that he is not angry is the overlapping and continuing phase of denial, a defensive attempt to ward off feelings of loss and pain. Worker uses her observation to provide an ego method of coping—discussion helping to neutralize aggression by the use of word symbols and by aiding in the assimilation process. Gradually, this leads J. to indicate that there are some feelings he cannot verbalize. Denial begins to break down as he talks about past losses, then reverts back to his "painful" feelings. The worker points out the difference between abandonment and separation by discussion and working through. This leads to his inability to communicate with his parents, and the growing recognition that he is caught up in a symbiotic tie which has prevented his developing toward individuation (43). He projects his failure in this development onto his parents and the worker. He feels he could be an individual, but because others prevent him from this, he has no choice but to make a "total break—run away—avoid relationships." The worker introduces alternative choices—pain can be faced and tolerated—indirectly conveying his underlying feeling of vulnerability and helplessness. His expression of grief and sadness gets intertwined with a need to "fence" with the worker to avoid pain, but he is not consciously aware of the pleasure aspects of such behavior. The grief process has begun, and gradual working through—letting go—is initiated as well.

> J. seemed rather confused this week. He spoke of his exams, and is now somewhat pessimistic about his chances of going to university. Worker attempted to discuss this, but he appeared to ward her off. Worker commented that they did not seem to be getting on very well and J. agreed, saying he thought he was going to fight with her again, and he didn't want to. "Fight?" He answered that he felt that was what he was doing last week. "You were trying to help me look at feelings." Worker commented that this had been painful for him, and he agreed, but then added that it had not been a waste of time. He would not enlarge on this, but said that he still wanted to forget about "Miss What's-her-name" taking over. Worker gave her name, and made no further comment. J. cut short the interview, saying he would come back next week, "if he remembers." He won't talk today.

In this process, regression appears to set in.

Environmental functioning is experienced by the client as ego depleting and exhausting. J.'s pessimism over university entry has a quality of threat to it—"If I fail, it will be your fault; look what you are doing to me." He prevents further discussion, and when the worker uses what she is observing ("We do not seem to be getting on very well"), he talks about his need to "fight." Once again the need to provoke and engage in an anal power struggle returns. In his perception, painful feelings call for defense and attack, and when the worker recognized his pain, he adds significantly that it has not been a waste of time. This is the client's way of indicating that the worker's approach is valid and helpful to him—in spite of the pain. He still needs to ward off the reality that a change in workers will be coming about, but does admit there is such a person, hinting at the beginning of acceptance. At the same time, basic trust has been dented. His tolerance for pain and anxiety is minimal.

Grief and Working Through.

> At the next interview, J. talked about an old girl friend of a year ago, whom he had never been able to forget. He blamed the worker for "opening the wound" when talking about parting. He had recently seen the girl, and since then has been very unhappy and depressed. He began to cry. J. slowly began to say he is pleased, that all this needed to come out and that he has bottled it up long enough. He was afraid of crying, and of his feelings. He doesn't know why he is like this. He went on to say how his girl friend had left him and for a day or two he was upset, and then forgot about it. However, recently all this has come back. He then commented that he thought I looked sad, and went on to tell me about his near-suicidal motorcycle ride to ease his feelings (a year ago) and then his success in forgetting all about it. It seems that he did make an attempt to contact the girl, but her mother intercepted the letter, telephoned him to ask not to write to her daughter again.

Since then, J. has not been able to talk to the girl, nor forget about her. Before leaving, the worker pointed out that if he continues to feel distressed, she would be able to see him later on in the week. J. commented that if someone had said that twelve months ago he would not have been where he is now. J. then expressed considerable fear of the new worker. Worker admitted that the adjustment may not be an easy one; it will take time, and they will need to discuss this.

The loss of the worker now brings J. to face up to a previous loss—that of his girl friend one year ago—when he began to expose himself in the community. He graphically describes how his use of repression worked partially. With the present separation and loss he "exposes" his emotions, and as he does so he comes to see he was unable to do this earlier. The worker's extension of support over this present difficult time brings forth J.'s recognition that this is what he needed desperately a year ago. The worker's offer makes the ending of this relationship more painful; but she confirms that she has not been destroyed by his exposure and that she is available to him. Once again, J. speaks of his fear of the unknown, and the present worker does not diminish the adjustment involved; instead, she admits that new relationships need to be worked on.

J. took up the offer of an extra appointment. He was depressed. He was supposed to take out a girl last night and didn't, because she was like the other girl. Worker stressed his being able to see this as positive and that, as a result, he had been able to make a decision for himself. J. said that he could not stand the feelings that he was experiencing any more, but what could he do? Worker pointed out that she is sure he now realizes it is not good to pretend that feelings do not exist. She could help him by discussing his options with him. They talk of his choices in relation to his old

girl friend: (1) he could ask her out again; (2) he could move forward and let her go altogether, which is not easy. J. said he didn't feel he could do either of these. At the end of the interview, he said he had made a decision. He said that he would not be able to do it until he had someone to lean on, and that the worker was such a person. Worker reminded him again of her leaving, and he started to cry. Worker again stressed that parting is painful, and that we could not make this disappear. J. seemed a little less distressed when he left.

In the resolution-termination process, the mourning and grief seem intolerable. J. is not just mourning the loss of the worker, but has transferred many of his feelings toward the "good" mother. He is mourning the loss of his parents, his youth, and his childhood, and resents that he didn't receive all that he wanted. To succeed, he reexperiences earlier losses. Through ventilation, he brings back memories of the "lost girl friend," and reveals his wishes for the worker to be the omnipotent, permanent parent, who can remove frustration and anxiety. Carefully, the worker dents the omnipotence and brings power and control back to J., supporting his autonomy and ability to make decisions for himself. J. denies he is capable of self-identity by insisting that he can make decisions only if she is there "to lean on." The worker upholds that the relationship is coming to an end, and J. cries again.

J. came for his appointment much less depressed. He said he had reached "rock bottom" the other day, but now was better, adding—"couldn't have done it without your help." Worker thanked him, but then pointed out that she doesn't have power over his feelings—that obviously he has more strength than he gives himself credit for. J. agreed somewhat uncertainly. They began to talk about the change in workers and J. was asked what he expected from Miss H. He said he didn't know, but that he got something quite different from what he expected when he was assigned to present worker, so he doesn't attempt to predict. He did indicate that he had expected a kind of retribution. Instead, he got what he expected least—help with his problems. It was arranged for J. to meet Miss H. the following weekend; they would be able to see each other for the last time after that. J. said that if he didn't like Miss H. he just would not talk or he would "fence" with her. Worker lightly indicated that this could be disturbing. He laughed and said, "Yes, I have done that with you a bit, haven't I?" Worker said she hoped that he would be able to talk to Miss H.

The crisis has dissolved, and a turning point has been reached. J. recognizes that he had hit "rock bottom," and the worker carefully places ego mastery and control into his own power when he attempts to attribute the improvement to her. He has now come to an early acceptance of change in workers as he is more ready to discuss this. Worker encourages recall of expectations of what present worker would be like, as a means of bridging from her to the new object. He speaks of his anticipation of punishment and condemnation, but he received the opposite. Facing up to meeting new worker arouses J.'s need to fence (anal power struggle), and when the worker indicated this could be "disturbing" J. removes himself through laughter. His observing ego affirms that this is how he tended to interact with worker when ambivalence was high. Worker reaffirms her hope that he will be able to verbalize feelings.

After having met Miss H. the previous day, J. came to his last appointment light-hearted, explaining that his exams were over, but he probably would be going to a junior college instead of university, as he did not feel he had done particularly well. Some time was spent in discussing exams, his plans for the future, and a job after university. He has thought of post-graduate work and research, because he doesn't think he wants to work; "University research is just cheap labour for the Government." It was apparent that J. was avoiding discussion of the new worker he met, and this was pointed out to him. He laughed, and then said seriously that he felt he was going to be able to work with her. He hesitated to say any more, and worker did not insist. After some silence he said that when he discovered that Miss H. was "human" he was all right. He was impressed that she, too, was willing to listen when he tried to explain something. He added that she had forced him once or twice to state an opinion, and he was amused when worker commented that sometimes an opinion is better not stated. J. wondered if there was anything left to do, saying that at last he faced up to something that had been bothering him for a long time, and life now seems trouble-free and easy. He agreed that "we" did not solve all his problems, and that "maybe" he and Miss H. would have something to work on—he isn't sleeping well, and he has an uneasy feeling when he thinks about himself. He had not mentioned this before, but now he felt he would be able to discuss it with Miss H.

J. faces up to separation and, instead of destroying and being destroyed, he is able to complete exams as well—albeit with a warning that he may not attain his original goal (university). Worker allows for discussion of his perceived future, which he depicts as potentially useless and corrupting. Worker avoids this area, asks about the new worker, a subject he has evaded. Though hesitant, J. speaks of his feeling that it will work out. He finds similar characteristics in the two workers (linking to the new object), and once again a disguised dependency asserts itself. He is aware that, though he continues to have problems, he has "faced up" to separation, which he couldn't do earlier. Having said this, he recommits himself to treatment and to Miss H. In fact, he will tell her things he never shared with this worker; the following letter (excerpts) was received by the worker:

> Dear Miss S.,
> . . . I thought you might be interested to hear how I am doing. It's been a year since we've seen each other. Since then, the probation order has been ended, but I've been seeing a worker regularly and voluntarily. I left home in October and entered university. I no longer desire to expose myself, nor do I have fits of depression. I now have a steady girl friend and I wish to give a little to other people. . . .
>
> Sincerely,
> J.

Conclusion

Given our present state of evolution, it is my bias that ego psychology theory, and its application to individuals and families, has come the closest toward an integrated system and body of knowledge which is readily applicable. It is far from all-inclusive nor a panacea, but, I feel, it is the best we have in dealing with human beings living within modern, complex Western societies, suffering from impersonal and dehumanizing experiences. The social work method of ego-oriented casework is one of the few means left that is concerned about the protection, care, and uniqueness of the individual. In a technological society, little is available that allows for the individualizing of human beings, and casework continues to say to the individual and his family: "You are special. You have a right to be listened to. You deserve attention."

In conclusion, I am reminded of a young student who, early in his training, was convinced that all types of social casework were "irrelevant." Though he continues to question its relevance and struggles with the incorporating of individualism within his broader scheme of thinking, he recently said: "You know, mankind began when man began to relate one to another, man to man. If and when mankind ceases to exist, it will be because man has stopped relating, man to man."

References

1. Ackerman, Nathan. *The Psychodynamics of Family Life.* New York: Basic Books, 1958.
2. Addams, Jane. "Charity and Social Justice," Presidential Address in Proceedings of the National Conference of Charities and Corrections, 1910.
3. Austin, Lucille N. "Trends in Differential Treatment in Social Casework," *Social Casework,* June, 1948.
4. Beatman, F. L. "Family Interaction: Its Significance for Diagnosis and Treatment," *Social Casework,* March, 1957.
5. Bergen, Mary E. "Emotional Stress in the Symbiotic Relationship," *Social Casework,* November, 1969.
6. Blanck, Gertrude and Rubin. *Ego Psychology: Theory and Practice.* New York and London: Columbia University Press, 1974.
7. Clemence, Esther. "The Dynamic Use of Ego Psychology in Casework Education," *Smith College Studies in Social Work,* June, 1965.
8. Cohen, Nathan E. *Social Work in the American Tradition.* New York: Dryden Press, 1958.
9. Colt, Ann. "Casework Treatment of a Borderline Client," *Social Casework,* October, 1967.
10. Edelson, M. *Ego Psychology, Group Dynamics and the Therapeutic Community.* New York: Grune and Stratton, 1964.
11. Erikson, Erik. "Identity and the Life Cycle," *Psychological Issues,* Monograph 1, Vol. 1. New York: International Universities Press, 1959.
12. Fauber, L. "Casework Treatment of Ambulatory Schizophrenics," *Social Casework,* January, 1958.
13. Federn, P. *Ego Psychology and the Psychoses.* New York: Basic Books, 1952.
14. Feldman, Yonata. "Integration of Psychoanalytic Concepts into Casework Practice," *Smith College Studies in Social Work,* February, 1960.
15. Fox, Evelyn F., Marian A. Nelson, and William M. Bolman. "The Termination Process: A Neglected Dimension in Social Work," *Social Work,* October, 1969.
16. Fraiberg, Selma. "Psychoanalysis and the Education of Case Workers," in Howard J. Parad and Roger R. Miller (eds.) *Ego-oriented Casework: Problems and Perspectives.* New York: Family Service Association of America, 1963. pp. 236–258.
17. Freud, Anna. *The Ego and the Mechanisms of Defense.* New York: International Universities Press, 1946.
18. Freud, Sigmund. *An Outline of Psychoanalysis,* standard ed., Vol. 23. London: Hogarth, 1964, p. 201.
19. ———. Ibid., p. 205.
20. ———. *New Introductory Lectures on Psychoanalysis,* standard ed. Vol. 22. London: Hogarth, 1964.
21. Garrett, Annette. "The Professional Base of Social Casework," *The Family, Journal of Social Casework,* July, 1946.
22. ———. "Modern Casework: The Contributions of Ego Psychology," Howard J. Parad (ed.) *Ego Psychology and Dynamic Casework.* New York: Family Service Association of America, 1958, pp. 38–52.
23. ———. "Historical Survey of the Evolution of Casework," Cora Kasius

(ed.) *Principles and Techniques in Social Casework, 1940-1950.* New York: Family Service Association of America, 1950, p. 395.

24. Glover, Edward. "The Concept of Dissociation," *International Journal of Psychoanalysis,* Vol. 24, 1943.

25. Grossbard, Hyman. "Ego Deficiency in Delinquents," *Social Casework,* April, 1962.

26. Hamilton, Gordon. "The Underlying Philosophy of Social Casework," *The Family, Journal of Social Casework,* July, 1941.

27. Hartmann, Heinz. *Essays on Ego Psychology.* New York: International Universities Press, 1964, p. 113.

28. ———. Ibid., p. 119.

29. ———. Ibid., p. 128.

30. ———. Ibid., p. 6.

31. Hollis, Florence. "The Psychosocial Approach to the Practice of Casework," R. W. Roberts and R. H. Nee (eds.) *Theories of Social Casework.* Chicago: University of Chicago Press, 1970, pp. 33-75.

32. ———. "Personality Diagnosis in Casework," Howard J. Parad (ed.) *Ego Psychology and Dynamic Casework.* New York: Family Service Association of America, 1958, pp. 83-96.

33. ———. *Casework: A Psychosocial Therapy.* New York: Random House, 1964.

34. Horney, Karen. *New Ways in Psychoanalysis.* New York: Norton, 1939.

35. Jackel, Merl M. "Clients with Character Disorders," *Social Casework,* June, 1963.

36. Kaufman, Irving. "Therapeutic Considerations of the Borderline Personality," Howard J. Parad (ed.) *Ego Psychology and Dynamic Casework.* New York: Family Service Association of America, 1958, pp. 99-110.

37. ———. "Maximizing the Strengths of Adults with Severe Ego Defects," *Social Casework,* November, 1962.

38. Kernberg, Otto. *Borderline Conditions and Pathological Narcissism.* New York: Jason Aronson, 1975.

39. Kohut, Heinz. *The Restoration of the Self.* New York: International Universities Press, 1977.

40. Lackie, Bruce. "Mahler Applied," *Clinical Social Work Journal,* Vol. 3, No. 1, 1975.

41. Laughlin, H. P. *Ego and Its Defenses.* New York: Appleton-Century-Crofts, 1970.

42. Lindemann, Erich. "Symptomatology and Management of Acute Grief," Howard J. Parad (ed.) *Crisis Intervention.* New York: Family Service Association of America, 1965.

43. Mahler, Margaret S. "Thoughts About Development and Individuation," *The Psychoanalytic Study of the Child,* Vol. 18. New York: International Universities Press, 1963, pp. 307-324.

44. ———. "On Sadness and Grief in Infancy and Chilhood: Loss and Restoration of the Symbiotic Love Object," *Psychoanalytic Study of the Child,* Vol. 16, 1961.

45. ——— and N. K. L. Perviere. "Mother and Child Interaction During Separation-Individuation," *Psychoanalytic Quarterly,* Vol. 34, 1965.

46. Masterson, J. F. *Psychotherapy of the Borderline Adult: A Developmental Approach.* New York: Brunner/Mazel, 1976.

47. Mayer, Herta and Gerald Schamess. "Long Term Treatment for the Disadvantaged," *Social Casework,* March, 1969.

48. McDevitt, John B. and Calvin F. Settlage. *Separation-Individuation: Essays in Honor of Margaret S. Mahler.* New York: International Universities Press, 1971.

49. Mitchell, C. "Family Interviewing in Family Diagnosis," *Social Casework,* July, 1959.

50. Parad, Howard J. "Brief Ego-Oriented Casework with Families in Crisis," Howard J. Parad and Roger Miller (eds.) *Ego-Oriented Casework.* New York: Family Service Association of America, 1963.

51. Parens, Henri and Leon J. Saul. *Dependence in Man: A Psychoanalytic Study.* New York: International Universities Press, 1971, p. 129.

52. ———. Ibid., p. 130.

53. Perlman, Helen. *Social Casework: A Problem-Solving Process.* Chicago: University of Chicago Press, 1957.

54. Polansky, Norman A. *Ego Psychology and Communication.* New York: Atherton Press, 1971.

55. Rapaport, David. *The Collected Papers,* Morton Gill (ed.), Chapter 58. New York: Basic Books, 1967, pp. 745-754.

56. Rapaport, Lydia. "Crisis Intervention as a Mode of Brief Treatment," R. W. Roberts and R. H. Nee (eds.) *Theories of Social Casework.* Chicago: University of Chicago Press, 1970, pp. 265-311.

57. Reiner, Beatrice S. and Irving Kaufman. *Character Disorders in Parents of Delinquents.* New York: Family Service Association of America, 1959.

58. Richmond, Mary E. *Social Diagnosis.* New York: Russell Sage Foundation, 1917.

59. Ross, Murray G. *Community Organization.* New York: Harper and Row, 1955.

60. Scherz, Frances. "Acting Out Character Disorders in a Marital Problem," *Social Work,* January, 1957.

61. ———. "Family Interaction: Its Significance for Diagnosis and Treatment," *Smith College Studies in Social Work,* Vol. 31, 1961.

62. ———. "What Is Family-Centered Casework?" *Social Casework,* Vol. 34, 1953.

63. Schmideberg, M. "After the Analysis . . . ," *Psychoanalytic Quarterly,* Vol. 7, 1938.

64. Stamm, Isabel. "Ego Psychology in the Emerging Theoretical Base of Casework," A. J. Kahn (ed.) *Issues in American Social Work.* New York: Columbia University Press, 1959, pp. 80-110.

65. Staver, Nancy. "The Concept of Ego in Casework," *British Journal of Psychiatric Social Work,* Vol. 8, No. 3, 1966.

66. Strean, Herbert F. "Casework with Ego-Fragmented Parents," *Social Casework,* April, 1968.

67. ———. "The Use of the Patient as Consultant," *Psychoanalytic Review,* Summer, 1959.

68. Stuart, R. "Supportive Casework with Borderline Patients," *Social Work,* January, 1964.

69. Sullivan, H. S. *The Interpersonal Theory of Psychiatry.* New York: Norton, 1953.

70. Towle, Charlotte. "The Contribution of Education for Social Casework to Practice," *Social Casework,* October, 1950.

71. ———. *The Learner in Education for the Professions.* Chicago: University of Chicago Press, 1954.

72. Wasserman, Sidney. "Casework Treatment of the Neurotic Delinquent Adolescent and the Compulsive Mother," *Social Casework,* November, 1963.

73. Weinberger, Jerome L. "Basic Concepts in Diagnosis and Treatment of Borderline States," Howard J. Parad (ed.) *Ego Psychology and Dynamic Casework.* New York: Family Service Association of America, 1958.

74. Wood, Katherine M. "The Contribution of Psychoanalysis and Ego Psychology to Social Casework," Herbert F. Strean (ed.) *Social Casework: Theories in Action.* Metuchen, N.J.: Scarecrow Press, 1971, p. 76.

75. ———. Ibid., pp. 88-105.

76. ———. Ibid., p. 107.

Annotated listing of key references

FELDMAN, Yonata. "Integration of Psychoanalytic Concepts into Casework Practice," *Smith College Studies in Social Work,* February, 1960.
This article demonstrates a conceptualized approach to clients who usually come to social agencies less motivated than patients who seek psychotherapy. Further, the article shows how the understanding and use of psychoanalytic concepts can engage the client's ego in establishing a therapeutic alliance which frees the client for problem solving.

GARRETT, Annette. "Modern Casework: The Contributions of Ego Psychology," Howard J. Parad (ed.) *Ego Psychology and Dynamic Casework.* New York: Family Service Association of America, 1958, pp. 38–52.
This is a classic paper in that it synthesizes and updates the ego-oriented casework approach. Also, it presents guidelines as to future direction and development. Miss Garrett's contribution in this paper is such that educators, students, and practitioners will continue to refer to it for years to come.

HOLLIS, Florence. "The Psychosocial Approach to the Practice of Casework," R. W. Roberts and R. H. Nee (eds.) *Theories of Social Casework.* Chicago: University of Chicago Press, 1970, pp. 33–75.
A clear, scholarly description of the psychosocial casework approach. An intelligent rationale as to the how and why of the approach, its strengths, its gaps, and its unsolved problems. At the same time, Miss Hollis allows for open-endedness, in both diagnostic thinking and treatment.

WOOD, Katherine M. "The Contribution of Psychoanalysis and Ego Psychology to Social Casework," Herbert F. Strean (ed.) *Social Casework: Theories in Action.* Metuchen, N.J.: Scarecrow Press, 1971, p. 76.
Probably the most definitive description to date of the contribution of psychoanalysis and ego psychology to social casework. A concise and logical description of the various concepts and their application to social casework. A marked contribution to the profession as a whole.

4

Psychosocial Therapy

by

FRANCIS J. TURNER

Introduction

The term "psychosocial" has deep, strong roots in the history of social work. Although originally a generic term, in recent years it has become very precise, attached to a particular approach to social work practice. It is a term that is fully the prerogative of our profession. If there is any concept that clearly sets out a function of social work treatment different from the focus of other professions it is this one. It is a concept that serves to prevent overemphasis on either the inner life of man or his relationships with society. When applied to a system of clinical practice, it refers to the body of theory that stresses the need for a dual and integrated focus on psychological and sociological man—that is, on intrapersonal man, interpersonal man and intersystemic man.

Psychosocial practice is a thought system that stresses the healthy development of man and has the interventive objective of establishing optimal conditions for human growth and development. It is also an essentially optimistic approach to the human condition. This optimism stems from an increasing understanding of and wonderment at the potential of the human being to recover from serious deprivation and, in the face of overwhelmingly rejecting situations, continue to progress and develop. In this chapter we will present an overview of this theory rather than a detailed examination of each of its component parts, relying on the bibliography to assist the reader who wishes to pursue this material more deeply.

Historical origins

Civilized man, whatever his origins, has always known that to survive and prosper a balance of physical, emotional, human and spiritual nurture is needed. Yet this knowledge has been only vaguely understood and rarely used in a planned, universal way. Social work, with its formal origins in the traditions of the Charity Organization Society movement, is one of many channels through which society has attempted to formalize and use this awareness. In looking at psychosocial practice as it exists today, we can see this tradition reflected, going back to the beginning of the profession. Its present profile can be traced through the work of such social workers as Mary Richmond, Gordon Hamilton, Annette Garrett, Lucille Austin, Florence Hollis and many others. The term itself seems to have been used first by Frank Hankins, a faculty member at Smith College, in 1930 (22). It was then picked up in Gordon Hamilton's early writings (20) and used in the writings of Florence Hollis (25). The term "psychosocial" can also be found in the writings of a wide range of other social scientists and practitioners as an important bridging concept. To date, however, it is only the social work literature that has developed it into a thought system.

The theory also reflects the tradition in social work of being richly influenced from outside. As will be discussed below, the list of those who have influenced this approach is long and sparkling.

Undoubtedly, the impact of psychoanalytic theory has been strong and lasting. For some this strong influence is seen as a weakness in the current scene, while for others it gives the approach legitimacy. Other important sources have been the later ego psychology thinking of psychoanalysts such as Erik Erikson (11), Heinz Hartmann (23) and others, as well as the theories of sociologists Talcott Parsons and Robert Merton and anthropologist Clyde Kluckholn, to name only a few, and the later influence of learning theory, family theory, systems theory and crisis theory, so prevalent in today's practice. Thus, one of the distinguishing characteristics of the psychosocial approach is its openness to development and change. This in turn makes it considerably broader than its

origins would indicate and vastly richer and more flexible than its critics would acknowledge.

Theoretical base

Overview

The psychosocial system of therapeutic help builds from an understanding of biopsycho development, interpersonal influence, the influence of significant others, and the influence of significant environments and systems as essential characteristics in the development and maintenance of healthy and fulfilling human living. From this it follows that the knowledge bases of practice are drawn from the biological, psychological and social components of human growth and development and their interaction. To these components are joined an understanding of the interrelatedness of the spectrum of systems in which man functions, their strengths and weaknesses, their potentials and limitations. On this knowledge base are developed skills in engaging responsibly and effectively in therapeutic and helping relationships with individuals, families, groups and significant environments to bring about planned change in human functioning. As mentioned earlier, the psychosocial approach holds an optimistic view of human potential. But this optimism is not a blindly naive one; our experience has all too clearly helped us to understand the complex and manifold ways in which human development may be curtailed, warped, damaged and distorted.

The general objective of psychosocial practice is the fostering of healthy growth patterns. It is understood that the structure and content of healthy psychosocial growth are complex; growth is developed, or hindered, through a combination of biological, material, physical, personal and interpersonal factors in interaction with a wide range of significant environments. Because of this, psychosocial practice is strongly committed to an ongoing search for a fuller understanding of man in his psychosocial situation to help him better achieve his potential in a satisfying, fulfilling way.

Value Orientations

One of the interesting phenomena of contemporary practice is the widespread interest in values and value orientations and their influence and importance in the therapeutic process. No longer are therapy and the therapist held to be value-free, nor is discussion of values with the client to be avoided. Thus any approach to practice must be aware of the values, implicit and explicit, of each thought system.

Psychosocial therapy is based on the general social work commitment to the importance and worth of each individual human person. Flowing from this is the related commitment to the goal of human betterment, both materially and emotionally, and to the development of human potential. Because each person is considered to be important and of inestimable value there is a strong belief in individual responsibility and the related concept of the importance of the individual's participation in his destiny. Since man is a social animal who fully reaches his potential through relationships and identity with family, friends, small groups and communities, the concepts related to individual worth, responsibility and participation are also transferable to family, group and community.

Such value orientations are the content and product of millennia of theological, philosophical and sociological thought. People can come to accept them through many pathways; regardless of their origin, they serve as the essential value orientation of psychosocial therapy.

Following on these is another set of commitments that rest somewhere between value orientations and the pragmatic outcome of experience. Included in this category are the familiar ideas of acceptance, permissiveness, uncondemning attitudes, congruence, confiden-

tiality, respect and controlled emotional response (9, 49). Originally, these qualities of practice emerged from our basic respect and commitment to individuals. Additional support for them came from experience. Thus we know from practice that work with an individual or a group more readily and effectively achieves its goal if a commitment to these qualities is demonstrated; that is, they are both philosophically and pragmatically sound.

Basic Assumptions About Human Behavior

Psychosocial therapy is also established on a series of assumptions about human behavior. It begins with the assumption that basic human nature is good. Human nature is also free, but not in an absolute way, for people are greatly affected by their histories. But even though free within limitations, human behavior can be understood and predicted. Even though we are all individuals, there is much about us that is common, knowable and predictable. Man is seen, therefore, as being somewhere between the "invincible master of his fate" and the "powerless pawn of destiny."

It is also assumed that human behavior can not only be understood (this, of course, in a relative and developing way) but also influenced and changed in a predictable way. In addition, available knowledge of human behavior can be transmitted through cognitive methods: that is, other people can be taught to understand and influence behavior. From this it follows that it is possible to hold individuals accountable for the misuse or nonuse of knowledge when there is community-sanctioned responsibility to use it.

In addition, psychosocial therapy is strongly committed to a scientifically built and tested body of knowledge. It does not claim that all of its present concepts are of this nature, but it is committed to the pursuit of such a foundation. Related to this idea is a conviction that a structured approach to theory building is fully compatible with a humanitarian concern for the people we serve.

It is assumed that human behavior is and can be influenced in a variety of ways. Physical, human and situational agents have differential impact on individuals, groups and communities. These influences are intersystemic, so that changes in one aspect of a person's functioning or reality has reverberating influences on other segments of his psychosocial condition. In our present state of knowledge the extent or limitations of this intersystemic influence is not fully known.

A further assumption of this theory is that a person's past is important. Thus, in seeking to understand a person's current behavior the important though nondetermining, influence of his earlier history must be acknowledged. Just as a person's ability to function adequately and successfully in a current situation results from skills, knowledge, attitudes, reflexes, perceptions and experiences from the past, so can unsuccessful and stress-producing problem behavior be similarly influenced. But the interest in a person's past is to help him understand and cope effectively with the present and thus with the future. Understanding past influences can bring about restored balance to current behavior. When either by chance or direction new and successful patterns of coping are acquired, future behavior will be influenced. A person who is helped to cope more effectively with a current situation, therefore, can thereby also be helped to deal with future situations only remotely resembling the original situation with which he was helped.

This historical component of human functioning and its importance in psychotherapeutic endeavors has been the source of considerable professional dispute. The controversy has ranged from an almost total dependence on understanding the past to its almost total disregard. The former position is best exemplified in the exasperated statement of a colleague in a case conference: "How can you expect me to understand this man if I don't know how he was toilet-trained?" The latter position is exemplified by colleagues who want to know nothing of the client's past, from others or the client, and in fact will make it clear to the client that nothing of the past is relevant to the situation under consideration.

Surely, the most elementary observation of non-therapy-based human interaction clearly indicates the importance of talking out, talking about and reflecting on the past as an aid to current functioning, whether this be the sharing of a guilty secret with a close friend or detailed examination of a prior experience with a knowledgeable associate to try to understand and learn from it.

An additional essential assumption of this theory relates to nonconscious phenomena. That is, an individual is not fully aware of all the historical and present intrapersonal influences on his or her current functioning. Awareness of some experiences, attitudes, emotions and memories is only partial, except in special circumstances or through the agency of specialized techniques. Yet unconscious components of a person's experience influence, although they do not determine, behavior.

This question of the impact of the unconscious and preconscious on current behavior and its relative importance for psychotherapy is variously accepted in the spectrum of current clinical social work. This topic has been fully and masterfully dealt with by Hollis (25) and by Allan in her chapter in this book. Undoubtedly, one of the trends in psychosocial therapy has been a reassessment of the significance of the unconscious in practice. In this reassessment there has been no deemphasis on the importance of understanding the potential influence of unconscious and preconscious material on behavior. There has, however, been growing appreciation of the fact that considerable growth and healthy functioning can and do take place without direct use being made of this material. Undoubtedly, many clients are helped by social workers who have little sympathy with the concept of unconscious mental mechanisms. But we also know that clients can fail and treatment can be rendered ineffectual because the unconscious, preconscious and historical components of the clients' reality are not considered, understood or permitted to enter the purview of treatment in situations in which these influences have been a significant part of the problem.

Psychosocial practice early found psychoanalytic theory its major source for understanding the individual and his relationship with society. This theory was modified and greatly strengthened by the developments of ego psychology and considerably enriched by the improved understanding of genetic endowment and by current sociology and psychology. All this has been integrated with the valuable insights and understandings derived from casework's own accumulated experience, practice wisdom and formal research.

But man is not only a rational, psychodynamic and interacting person, he is also a physical entity. Hence some understanding of biological man is stressed in this practice theory. All of us are aware how great can be the influence on our functioning of even as simple a thing as the common cold. Thus in practice we must always have some understanding, limited as it might be, of our client's physical state, both chronic and transitory. In recent years we have become aware of a much closer connection between man's emotional state and his somatic functioning. This further emphasizes the need to be closely attuned to our client's physical well-being.

In applying these understandings of man in interaction with his situation, psychosocial therapy has developed the following structure of intervention. These interventive resources are most easily dichotomized into those elements of treatment that consist of direct contact with the client and those elements consisting of activities by the social worker with other components of the client's life. The latter may be significant individuals and groups, environments or material realities which are variously manipulated to bring about sought-for change.

Direct methods

Relationship

The essential component of direct work with the client has always been identified as the professional relationship that is fostered between the client and the social worker. To such an extent has this been considered the pivotal point of treatment that, for some, the effectiveness of treatment has tended to be measured by the intensity of the relationship.

This emphasis on the importance of the relationship between client and social worker is based on awareness and appreciation of the extent to which human growth and development are related to the nature of interpersonal experiences. That is, once basic biological and nutrient needs are met, it is the influence of human relationships that results in both successful and unsuccessful development and functioning. Hence, considerable stress has always been put on the focused management of relationships between clients and social workers. To this end, consistent efforts have been made to learn from healthy human experience the qualities of helping, curing, growth-producing human relationships, as well as what qualities and experiences can be detrimental, hurtful and destructive. Even though each relationship between two or more persons is in some way unique there are general characteristics that apply to all relationships which can be observed and transmitted. It is known, for example, that concern, understanding, competence and congruence are essential qualities that a person must experience for a relationship to be helpful (6, 49).

I think we frequently forget the power of our concerned, knowledgeable, trustworthy reaching out to clients, which becomes almost automatic to experienced social workers. Over and over again we meet persons in our practice who have rarely had an opportunity in their lives to sit down and talk freely about themselves to someone who in a sincerely concerned way can hear, understand and respond from a background of learning and experience that encompasses the combined history of many experiences. Too often we forget how helpful even a single such experience can be in a person's life. Most of us on reflection can recall occasions when an hour with a person significant to us has dramatically affected us and our subsequent life choices.

Several years ago, I was involved in a project with a family agency that had developed a long waiting list of people, each of whom had been seen once at intake. Our task was to pick up on these people and offer a brief service to them. Many of these persons on recontact indicated there was no need for further service, describing changes in attitude, perception or behavior that had taken place from their one contact with the intake worker. These were described with quotations, examples and a sincerity that were certainly different from the responses of the client who does not wish to involve himself in treatment.

The potential positive effects of relationships are such that many persons can be helped by individuals not trained or consciously skilled in formal psychotherapeutic processes. This phenomenon unfortunately gives weight to those who argue against intensive and lengthy training for practice.

But important as is the formal helping relationship, it is not in itself sufficient for practice. It is the skillful and understanding way in which this phenomenon is used and the length, intensity, frequency, content and forms of interaction that are added to it that result in responsible, effective treatment.

Transference

One specific relationship component of interest in the psychosocial tradition is that of transference and countertransference (17, 24). This concept in current thinking is today not being given the focused attention it received in the 1940s and early 1950s. Nevertheless, it is still an important concept which, if ignored, can create difficulties and problems in the course of treatment. Certainly, there has been development in this concept, and some components of relationship previously interpreted as transference reactions can be better explained in terms of values or cultural and other life experiences. It is not held that all transference reactions that take place need be identified for the client or examined in treatment; what is important is that when this phenomenon is present its occurrence and strength be recognized, controlled if necessary, utilized when appropriate and worked out if required.

Since each person, including the therapist, brings to new relationships the experiences of his own relationship history, it is essential in psychosocial practice for the therapist to be aware of himself and his own reactions as well as to try to understand those of clients. We know that we do not all relate identically to all people; we know that there are kinds of people and situations that make us uncomfortable, anxious, guarded or defensive. It is hoped that training and experience teach us to understand and appropriately adjust. It is because of this awareness to the influence of one's relationship history on all new relationships that psychosocial thinking stresses the need for a high degree of self-awareness on the part of the therapist. Hence it gives a particular emphasis to the need for supervision, consultation and indeed at times one's own therapy to meet the need for objectivity in relationships.

Direct Treatment Procedures

In the past decades considerable attention has been given to identifying and classifying the range of procedures and techniques that describe the interactions that take place between social workers and clients. The work of Hollis and her associates has greatly assisted progress in understanding the specifics of these interactions (29). This development, and the content-analysis techniques that are a part of it, provide rich potential both for more precise understanding of this system and for comparison of various approaches to practice.

In the Hollis schema emphasis is put on the twofold necessity of having the client look both inward and outward and reflect on the interconnection of these two components of his reality. In doing this, six major forms of interaction are identified as taking place between clients and their social workers. Since these have been fully described in recent literature it will suffice to list them without description or comment.

The six major headings of worker–client interaction are:

1. Sustaining Procedures
2. Procedures of Direct Influence
3. Procedures of Ventilation, Description and Exploration
4. Procedures That Encompass Reflective Consideration of the Current Person–Situation
5. Procedures That Encompass Reflective Consideration of Patterns of Personality and Behavior and Their Dynamics
6. Procedures That Encompass Reflective Consideration of the Past and Its Effect on Current Functioning

Each of these categories has specified subdivisions which permit precise quantification of the client and worker verbal content in interviews.

An important component of this system and its subdivisions is the way in which it draws attention to the twofold use of reflection on intra- and extracomponents of a situation. Examination of practice has shown the importance of helping a client focus on selected areas of his situation to understand his own contribution to his problem and the related problem-solving and decision-making work. No one of the various items is considered to be of any more importance or value than another. Each has its place in practice. The challenge and responsibility for each practitioner in relation to his cases, and for the field in relation to its body of knowledge, are

to search for the optimum combination and blend of these procedures suitable for the treatment objectives established for individual cases or groups of cases.

Using this schema, recent research has demonstrated that patterns can be identified that indicate commonalities in practice (10, 27, 39). A brief overview of these findings indicates that the majority of interview content revolves around a combination of ventilative material and refective consideration of the current situation, with important but limited use of the other procedures. Further, it has been found that sustaining, ventilation and description are important in early interviews. Use of pastfocused material and efforts to elicit such material are not nearly so extensive as some practitioners have thought. It has also been clearly demonstrated that in spite of our traditional discomfort about the use of direct influence with clients we do use such procedures. When this is done effectively it is in a highly selected manner and in company with considerable sustaining material. Other research has demonstrated that clear and patterned differences can be observed in examining the interview content of situations where clients and workers are from different value orientations or from different ethnic groups (55).

Not as much precision is available in psychosocial therapy about other components of direct work. We know, of course, that factors such as the timing, length and frequency of interviews, the setting of interviews and the physical surroundings in which interviews take place all differentially affect interviews and their outcome. The locale of interviews is also an important variable in treatment—the use of office interviews, both formal and informal, home visits, and informal settings such as restaurants, cars, street corners and park benches. Frequently, the decisions about use of these variations are made on the basis of pragmatics, agency policy, or at times on the basis of preference or desire to be nontraditional rather than on the exigencies of the case. Thus, we find colleagues who will interview only in a formal across-the-desk situation while others will never interview in such a setting, insisting on a highly informal situation. Clearly, both have their place but this should be decided on the basis of case-related objectives rather than value preference.

There is considerable practice experience available to us that could give us a much clearer understanding of the use of these variables. Such material would be helpful to the entire field. We have not given sufficient attention to these aspects of our practice even though there are extensive data available in other fields on such things as the effects of office setting, physical comfort, time and attention span, sound, influence of locale and design. A cursory overview of current practice procedures indicates how studiously we have chosen to ignore such factors. In a similar way, considerable additional attention has to be given to understanding more fully the differential use of joint and family interviewing, the selection of content themes, the focus of treatment and the specification of goals. Some of the recent work on length of treatment and on short-term intervention is an important beginning in this area (46).

Technical Aids

Another set of resources that is beginning to find its way into direct psychosocial treatment is the use of technical equipment as aids to treatment (3). Considerable progress has been made in understanding how equipment such as tape recorders and closed-circuit television can be used in observing, teaching, research and the recording of practice. Less attention has been given to the ways in which these resources can be used as adjuncts to treatment itself. Some work has been done on letting clients in marital situations listen to themselves on audiotape. Some therapists have had families watch themselves on videotape and use the reactions of the various family members to this self-observation as the content of subsequent interviews. As mentioned earlier, there are awareness, understanding and familiarity with the importance of reflective consideration of various aspects of the present-person-in-interaction-with-situation. Having the opportunity to observe self and significant others in interaction through the medium of these resources provides a rich opportunity for this type of reflective thinking.

In addition to these recording procedures, there are other types of equipment beginning to be seen as adjuncts to therapy. Although just in the beginning stages, it is clear that increasing use is going to be made of computers, not only as a way of storing and retrieving large amounts of data about clients and groups of clients, but also as direct aids to practice. For example, it is already possible to build programs that permit clients to give a great deal of their history through interaction with a computer. This might be particularly useful for very withdrawn or hostile clients. Use is also being made of various forms of stress measures, relaxation aids and apparatus to assist in biofeedback procedures.

Although traditionally social workers have not made use of technical equipment in treatment, there is no reason why we shouldn't. A psychosocial orientation, with its commitment to openness, stresses that anything that will help a client should be used. Clearly clients can be helped in this manner, and it follows that we should be more attentive to this type of resource.

Indirect Work

Although an essential and significant aspect of psychosocial therapy is practiced in the setting of direct contact with clients, an equally essential and significant component includes work with significant others, systems and material aspects of a client's life. As mentioned, this direct involvement in the client's outer reality in conjunction with work with the personality is the distinguishing mark of this school, and indeed gives it its name.

Although always an essential segment of

psychosocial practice, work in the client's environment has tended to be given secondary importance in practice. Two factors seem to have contributed to this. The first is sociological in that at present our society gives high status to the model of psychotherapy that uses the format of the intense clinical office-based type of interpersonal contact. With this valuation has been a related idea that this form of interpersonal helping requires skills and training at a level beyond environmental work.

The second factor stems partially from the first and is more a semantic one. In our tradition we have tended to collapse the complex, multifaceted external environment of the client into single terms such as "milieu," "situation," "environment" or "external reality." This has resulted in a tendency to oversimplify these components of realtiy.

A result of this two-faceted underestimation of the importance and status of environmental work has been a corresponding underuse of these components of treatment, a tendency to take understanding of their dimensions for granted and to fail to give them the same detailed study that is given to direct client contacts. There has been some increased interest in this aspect of treatment stemming from the recent renewal of concern for clients' rights, advocacy and the damaging effects of some components of established systems on people. Even here, though, only partial components of the client's environment have been stressed, rather than the total spectrum. Thus, for some colleagues all work in the environment must be carried out in a stance of advocacy or confrontation. Important as these strategies are, they do not have an inherent preferential place. They are valuable only when they are appropriate for the situation and goals of treatment. Just as inappropriate use of sustaining techniques can be detrimental to a client, so can an inappropriate use of any of the skills in environmental intervention.

The knowledge of human behavior, social systems and their interaction required to intervene efficiently and effectively in the client's external reality is just as demanding as that re-quired in direct work with him. Not only is this aspect of treatment just as demanding, it can also be just as effective. For example, highly developed skills are required to understand and work with an employer already overburdened with his own problems to help him also understand and work with a troubled adolescent trying to find his way in a first employment situation. Such an intervention can have healing and growth potential for the young man as significant and long-lasting as many weeks of one-to-one treatment. (As a side effect, such intervention may have positive results for the employer as well.)

A particulary useful and indeed powerful component of indirect help consists in work with significant others in a client's life such as friends, family and close associates. Sometimes this is done on a case-by-case basis, although there is increasing awareness of the benefit of utilizing the potential of volunteers and indigenous workers on a regular basis.

An excellent formulation of the functions and roles in this external component of treatment is presented by Hollis (26). She discusses this material from a threefold approach: the types of communications used, the range of resources that are called upon, and, most importantly, the range of roles that can be employed. It is this last component that has been given the least critical attention in practice. We have frequently and variously identified the range of resources used in practice, but we have tended to underestimate the range of roles we have used by a failure to identify them specifically. The roles identified by Hollis are those of provider, locator, creator, interpreter, mediator and aggressive intervener (26, p. 155). To this list can be added the role of broker, which describes that cluster of activities in which the social worker serves as coordinator and manager of various services and resources in which the client is involved, a most essential role in today's multiservice practice.

The challenge for the therapist related to the indirect methods of practice is to identify the various components of environmental treatment, understand their interconnectedness and collate knowledge of the differential use of these roles for specific clients and clusters of clients.

There is also the additional challenge of further developing an understanding of the balance between direct and environmental procedures best suited for individual cases. Finally, there is the challenge of insuring that these facets of practice are given proper weighting as effective therapeutic resources. The persistence of a pattern of thinking that downgrades environmental work with the concomitant tendency to relegate responsibility for it to nonprofessionals is a source of continuing stress and disservice.

Psychosocial History and Diagnosis

The foregoing pages have presented a highly condensed summary of the range of resources and roles available to the psychosocial practitioner. The task for today's practitioner is to appreciate the component parts of this range, to understand their potential and limitations and the exigencies of the situation, and from this to structure, with the client, a pattern of interaction that will best achieve the case goals.

To make most efficient use of this spectrum of psychological, sociological and material resources, psychosocial therapy emphasizes the necessity for understanding each situation that is treated as completely as is appropriate—that is, a full assessment and diagnosis. It is this aspect of treatment that causes some to designate this school "the diagnostic school." Also it is this component of practice, or rather a misunderstanding of it, that has been the focus of considerable criticism. For some the term "diagnosis" as applied to social work practice is a pejorative. This negative approach has been strengthened by the current reaction against classifying human behavior and the misuses to which classifications can be put. In a related way, but not as extensively, the emphasis that psychosocial treatment has put on the psychosocial study, or history, is also under criticism.

Focus on these two components of practice

is based on the premise that the decision as to which of the many available components and procedures are to be used in a particular situation must be based on adequate knowledge and understanding of the person and situation. This in no way implies that the client is excluded from such decisions, or that treatment is chosen categorically. It does mean that for the social worker to make most effective use of his knowledge and skills to achieve the goals mutually arrived at he must come to some clear decisions as to who the client is, what he needs and wants, what are the strengths and limitations of the person and situation that can help or hinder, what resources are available and what knowledge can be brought to this situation from other similar or dissimilar experiences. The purpose of the psychosocial study and diagnosis is to bring together the available components of the situation in an orderly, economic manner that permits an adequate assessment to be made and responsible decisions to be arrived at.

But, like all components of practice, diagnosis must be related to the nature of the case and setting. Thus its nature, content and detail will vary according to the time available, the type of problem, the nature of the request, the services available, the setting and the skill of the worker.

Diagnosis, as both a process and a fact, is not by definition a voluminous enterprise. In both psychosocial study and diagnosis the law of parsimony applies. Only that amount of information is required which is necessary to reach the conclusions demanded by the situation. Thus a person inquiring of an agency about available resources for institutional care of an aged relative need not be expected to give a complete history of all components of his history nor need the social worker involved prepare a lengthy detailed diagnosis. This doesn't imply that the worker ignores other questions the client may wish to ask, other potential areas of difficulty related to the request, other aspects of the client's life that may be affected by the request, other needs the client may have, other services the client might be able to use. These areas will be thought of against the worker's experience in similar situations, his assessment of the client's wishes and the perceived adequacy of the client's functioning out of which decisions are made as to planned procedures.

Thus a twenty-minute interview skillfully conducted usually represents a bewilderingly complex array of assessments, judgments, categorizations and decisions by the social worker, many of which are almost intuitive. That is, the worker is constantly engaged in a diagnostic process.

Social workers are often accused of making things too complex, of looking for pathology when it isn't there, or involving clients in complex processes when simple ones would suffice. Such criticisms are not to be automatically disregarded, but neither should they be unquestioningly accepted. Life is complex; problems do have multiple and differential impacts; individuals do vary in their ability to cope with situations; people do disguise requests in a variety of ways. I shall never forget a client I saw at intake a few years ago who, in a quiet, controlled way, was inquiring about getting help for his wife whom he described as depressed, worried and acting strangely. Following this interview, in which the situation was clarified, alternatives considered, help offered and a plan made to see the wife, the man went home and a short time later committed suicide. His last unrecognized appeal for help had been disguised in a request for help for his wife.

Frequently the criticisms of the diagnostic component of psychosocial therapy are in reality legitimate criticisms of the misuse of diagnosis, that is, of the fact of diagnosis, not the process. One still meets colleagues for whom diagnosis seems to be identified with assigning a single-term label; the responsibility of arriving at a clear and precise assessment of clients-in-situations is misunderstood to mean narrow categorization. Clearly, this is not possible; if attempted it is irresponsible practice. But this type of criticism of diagnosis has by now been overstated and too

often repeated. It seems to me to be more and more a rationale for avoiding the highly complex and awesome responsibility of reaching decisions about other human beings, the inescapable responsibility of anyone in a helping profession.

Settings

Psychosocial treatment is not restricted as to the settings in which it is best used. Assuredly there are settings which offer more opportunity to use the entire spectrum of attitudes, knowledge and skills than others, but any setting committed to the improved psychosocial functioning of individuals permits the application of this method. Some settings with a strong, controlling authoritarian or social-control commitment create difficulties in the nature of client involvement, the setting of goals and objectives and the range and kind of resources available to the social worker. Similarly, in some settings the worker may seriously question policies and practice or feel constrained by the limitations in resources that restrict the scope of intervention. But commitment to an open approach, as in this orientation, implies commitment to an ongoing search for ways of making more effective use of the settings in which psychosocial therapy is practiced, as well as a search for making the settings more useful for treatment.

Methods of Psychosocial Practice

In discussing this form of practice, its strong historial interest in the casework tradition and its earlier emphasis on one-to-one treatment must be considered in view of the developing readiness of social workers to use a wider range of treatment modalities and to move comfortably from individual to joint, family, group and community-based practice. The theories and methods of psychosocial therapy are not restricted to one-to-one practice, but are fully applicable to practice that utilizes joint interviewing as well as family and group methods. The knowledge required to understand clients in interaction with others and their situations includes by definition the spheres of familial and group dynamics and their interactions. The goals of much of group and all family practice are fully consonant with the goals of psychosocial treatment. This is not to imply that psychosocial theory encompasses all forms of group and family treatment, but that this theory and practice base are sufficient and adequate preparation for a practitioner wishing to utilize a group and family modality of practice. If one's training and experience have been directed to a single form of practice, then additional supervised experience is required to develop other methodologies. But if an individual's training has been based on psychosocial theory and has included experience in a range of treatment modalities, the person is then well equipped for the multimethod demands of current practice. The profile of direct and indirect interventive methods, the understanding of relationship and its multiple manifestations, the emphasis on use of self in treatment are all applicable and essential to a multimethod approach.

It is not being suggested that individual, joint, family and group practice are identical. A minimum of experience quickly will show how different are the demands put on a practitioner in a family interview as compared to an interview with a single member of that family. There are differences between methods, just as there are vast differences between cases treated on a one-to-one basis. Each modality creates specific demands and patterns related to the use of time, content and focus of interviews or sessions, relationship patterns and difficulties, transference manifestations, use of resources, contract, setting objectives and goals and termination, but all of these are within the present perspectives of psychosocial treatment.

Research done on the use of the Hollis typology with joint interviews showed it to be conceptually applicable, although, understandably, technically more difficult (10). It was found that the same kinds of interactions and the same opportunities for understanding of self and others take place in family-group interviews, and these could be classified within the sixfold system and its subcategories. Similarly, some experimentation has been done applying the typology to group interviews, and it has been found useful in analyzing the process and content of these interviews. Clearly, in multiple client interviews complex communications, relationship and transference alignments occur and differential use is made of the procedures. But it is important to see that these are not totally different treatment methods requiring differential theoretical bases. As mentioned earlier, a person who has limited his experience and practice to a single mode of treatment might well be weak in some elements of theory as well as skill, but these are individual limitations, not limitations in the system itself.

These ideas are not fully accepted by everyone; in many ways they go against our strongly established traditional terminology of casework and group work. In this age of terminological confusion one hesitates to suggest new terminology, especially if it deemphasizes already well-established terms. Certainly we should never lose the rich and separate traditions from which casework and the clinical elements of group work emerged. What is suggested is that the term "psychosocial" does contain all the elements of the demands of today's clinical practice in social work and overcomes the difficulties arising from a separate tradition of casework and group work and the more recent one of family therapy. There are, of course, many theoretical differences among group workers and among family therapists, but those who find the psychodynamic theory of value are close to psychosocial thinking.

In advocating a common procedural base for all methods of clinical social work practice, I am not suggesting that all practitioners need to be equally skilled in all methods. Just as some social workers are more interested, comfortable and competent in working with specified kinds of clients and situations, so some of us will use different patterns of treatment. But we do a disservice to our clients if we restrict ourselves exclusively to a single modality, be this individual, family or group. We can greatly extend our skills and make ourselves more helpful to clients by introducing a range of treatment alternatives into our practice. In those instances where practitioners prefer to concentrate on one mode of practice, they need to associate themselves with colleagues who can supplement with other modes if needed.

Community

These ideas do not apply as easily to work with communities as with groups and families. There still is a clear division between practice with individuals, families and groups seeking to achieve improved psychosocial functioning for themselves and their families and practice aimed at helping sections of the community or the entire community to organize and develop resources needed to achieve community goals and aspirations.

Since these areas are all a part of social work, we should not be surprised that the distinction between these two streams of practice is not a precise one. Although in the heat of battle between clinical social workers and resource-development social workers there seems to be little in common, the clinical psychosocial tradition has always associated itself with community organization and development, social action and social change. This has been especially true in the family agency field. There are few experienced practitioners who have not committed much of their professional and personal time and resources to this broad area of concern.

In the psychosocial tradition there is a clear commitment to concern for and at times direct work with communities. Certainly in our diagnostic activities it is essential that we seek to understand the reality and impact of the various systems and subsystems both as they exist and as they are perceived by the client. To make

these assessments requires knowledge of community structure, power, systems, history, tradition and values. Beyond assessment and diagnosis, in moving into environmental work the same knowledge helps us to evaluate the potential and limitations of the components of the client's significant others. Only with this knowledge can we plan realistic goals with the client.

It is easy to underestimate how crucial such knowledge can be for clients. Tremendous relief and security can be provided clients by our knowledge of a community, its exigencies and foibles, its strengths and resources.

But more than just knowledge about communities is involved; frequently it is necessary to intervene actively in these communities. To be effective in such endeavors necessitates knowledge of systems, their functioning, ways in which they can be altered and an accurate diagnosis of and assessment of each specific situation.

One of the roles earlier identified in environmental work with clients was that of creator of resources. In our practice we frequently involve ourselves or our agencies in efforts aimed at meeting identified gaps in resources needed by our clients; when successful in these efforts we have also contributed to the needs of the entire community. A particular facet of this resource-development role that is being given particular attention in current practice is work with groups of clients who themselves have identified a community need and set out to meet it. An example was experienced in a family agency where the social workers became aware from their caseloads of serious gaps in community services for single-parent families. Out of this awareness developed a project conducted by the single parents themselves aimed at both improving services and changing community attitudes.

Thus the psychosocial practitioner has a responsibility for understanding community functioning, for being aware of community organization and development skills and for achieving some competence in skills related to the needs of the clients for which he is responsible.

Relationships to Other Theories

Because of the aforementioned interest in other theoretical orientations, psychosocial treatment has been open to and positively influenced by virtually all the systems considered in this book; this point is clearly indicated in the second edition of Hollis' classic book on *Casework* (25). In the ten-year interval between the two editions the influence of systems theory, role theory, communications concepts, family theory, learning theory and crisis theory can be observed as well as developments internal to the system, resulting from increased experience, research and reconceptualization. These influences do not represent radical changes in the system; they do indicate an enriched understanding, a realigning of concepts, clearer systematization of ideas, more precise categorization of methodology and a clearer awareness of interrelatedness of concepts. These developments are the sought-for signs of any healthy developing system. It is presumed that as efforts at reconceptualizing continue more precise integration from other schools of thought will take place.

It is not being implied that this is the only theory open to outside influence. As the other chapters in this volume indicate, this type of mutual influence is taking place in virtually all areas and approaches to sound practice. The phenomenon of interinfluence is an exciting one for social work, although at the same time frustrating when trying to sort out and identify conceptual differences between schools of thought.

A good example of this influence can be seen in learning theory. Within the past ten years or so this body of theory and its related applications in behavior modification have had a marked impact in some areas of social work practice. Accompanying this influence have

been strong claims that this approach to practice is antithetical to traditional therapy. It is interesting to note how shortlived have been these criticisms and how quickly there has developed a growing comfort, acceptance and understanding of these concepts and techniques. Clearly much additional work is required to appreciate fully what knowledge, formal training and added experience are needed by practitioners wishing to make full use of this material. The work of Jehu et al. should add to this growing acceptance and understanding (30).

Some of the immediate influences of the behavioral school on practice have been increased awareness of how even the most client-centered therapy uses both positive and negative reinforcement techniques and how some of our behavior with clients, both in interviews and in provision of services, has contradicted the goals of treatment, and, most importantly, the necessity for clear and highly specified treatment goals. It is expected that in the future other sound theoretical developments will similarly influence psychosocial therapy just as this theory has a reciprocal influence on them.

Present Status

It is difficult to identify any component of current social work practice that is not and has not been influenced by psychosocial thinking. Both the intensity of this influence and the extent to which individuals acknowledge it vary, but to a continuing degree the generic concepts of psychosocial thinking form the base for much of current clinical social work practice, especially in the field of casework. This strong influence of psychosocial thinking is not a recent phenomenon but a long-standing one. What is different is the nature of its influence. Within the profession it describes a practice position not always acceptable to all. In past years when the psychological components of human behavior were being stressed and interest in the psyche, psychodynamics and psychotherapy were to the fore, this term helped us keep a balanced focus. Now that the pendulum has swung back and the social components of behavior and its influences are in the limelight it serves the opposite role of keeping man's inner functions in perspective.

For some retaining an interest in, concern for and declared competency in the understanding and management of psychological man is said to be an immature holding on to a relationship with psychiatry and a medical model of psychopathology. This approach would have our profession identify only with the social concept. Within this purview the principal concern of social work is man's social condition, including the people, systems and resources that variously influence it. These areas are and always have been an essential part of the warp and woof of social work. What is dangerous about the stress on the term "social" in an exclusive way is the concomitant conclusion that man's psychological life and functioning are not directly included in the scope of professional activity and intervention. Few, of course, would deny an interest and concern in these areas, only that we have a direct responsibility.

Another aspect of the current status of this theory is a tendency to see it in a narrow deterministic sense that interprets all current functioning in terms of early developmental influences. Undoubtedly, there was a time when considerably more emphasis was put on the influence of past experiences on present behavior, but the extent to which this took place in practice has been grossly exaggerated. Practitioners of this persuasion have long known that overemphasis on the influence of early years creates too narrow an expectation for people and a sense of finality about a person's potential.

Essential as is an understanding of the early years of development, we know that this is not the only period of growth. The maturation process continues all through life. Some of the effects of this increased understanding of human potential can be seen in recent work with groups of retarded persons, with highly deprived families and with aged individuals.

Related to this is a continuing tendency to see this approach to practice as based on a single theoretical orientation to the exclusion of other theories. As discussed earlier, this viewpoint overlooks the richness of psychosocial thinking. In fact, one of the current weaknesses of this approach is that at this point in our history we are being strongly influenced by such a wide range of thought systems that it is difficult to give precise boundaries to the term "psychosocial." Rather than call this a current weakness, perhaps it is better expressed as a possible area of criticism. For being open to many sources of influence is this school's greatest strength and potential. A commitment to openness, of course, creates a gigantic challenge of assimilation, integration, synthesizing and reformulation.

A related type of criticism is the suggestion that present psychosocial thinking is really only a collection of borrowed concepts and techniques and in fact has contributed little of its own. Such an attitude underestimates the tremendously rich contribution that this approach to social work practice has made in the skillful management of individual, family and group relationships, the enlargement of our understanding of the human potential and increased perception of the dimensions of interaction of person and person, and person and situation and the intersystemic interaction of significant environments. In addition, there have developed enlarged knowledge and skill in making maximum effective use of society's resources, both material and personal. A further contribution that must be noted is the importance that has been placed on understanding and focusing on the here and now in the client's life. Finally, and perhaps most importantly, credit must be given to the great progress that has been and is being made in the classification and categorization of patterns of psychosocial problems and methods of intervention and their interconnectedness. It is out of these developments that new theoretical formulations can be made and tested.

Because of its long tradition, a tradition that

is longer than that of most of the other approaches discussed in this volume, there is a tendency in current discussions to refer to psychosocial theory as "traditional casework thinking." Since there is currently a fad of disparaging things traditional (for some this means anything more than five years old) frequently psychosocial therapy is used as a point of departure for new ideas based on other theoretical bases. Too often in such comparisons differences are overstated, particular concepts are stressed that magnify differences, similarities are ignored or underemphasized and, even more serious, it is not acknowledged that many of the newer developments are actually further elaborations of a psychosocial base.

One point that must be emphasized in this discussion of current influences stems from the traditional association of this approach with casework and the casework tradition. This, in turn, has also tended to be identified principally with one-to-one intervention. Casework has long had a broader scope than one-to-one intervention and, as the recent writings of Hollis indicate, currently has an even broader base than in recent decades (25). Nevertheless, for many, the concepts of casework and one-to-one intervention are synonymous. One of the unfortunate consequences of this mistaken view is that colleagues with an individual orientation to practice who wish to expand their treatment armamentarium to include modalities of joint, group, family and community work sometimes think that they must turn to other theoretical approaches and other schools of practice for their orientation to these additional interventive modalities, failing to appreciate the fact that these modalities are now available in the psychosocial approach itself.

It is, of course, appropriate to turn to other thought systems available in both theory and practice, as the various chapters of this book indicate. What does create problems for the practitioner is the persistent misconception that other treatment styles are totally separate from

casework as it is commonly known; that is, once again the emphasis is on differences rather than similarities. This tendency to encapsulate treatment modalities is further reinforced by our tradition of personifying practice methods. Thus we still refer to caseworkers, group workers and family therapists rather than to social workers who utilize these methodologies in practice.

Fortunately, this tendency has not taken place to the same extent when theory is being considered. We tend to be much more comfortable in incorporating bodies of theory even though we may continue to use a particular practice form. Thus, even the most committed one-to-one therapist will agree that knowledge of group theory and family dynamics, communication concepts and social systems, to name but a few, is essential to work effectively with a client even though the process being used is one-to-one.

Although traditionally associated with the casework field psychosocial theory, as discussed above, has equal relevance for practice that uses family, group and some community methods. As has been said, this system is an open one, committed to an ongoing search for more sensitive ways of understanding people in interaction with situations and, equally important, to a search for more effective ways of achieving the goals of intervention. An open-thought system has to be prepared to alter and modify ideas, beliefs and techniques, cherished though they may be, when others are found to be more relevant, productive or economical and effective. From this it follows that this approach to practice needs to be committed to an ongoing and active research thrust, including responsible experimentation with and evaluation of approaches and techniques both new and traditional.

In examining the present status of psychosocial therapy the risk of becoming conceptually overextended must be kept in mind. To be equipped to practice in this framework in its fullest context requires knowledge and skill in a wide range of areas. It is this necessary dependency on a multiple skill and knowledge base that creates the great contemporary challenge for social work practitioners and educators.

This approach to practice must seek to find a balance between several choices or directions: one, to focus on a broad overview of knowledge of many fields, theories, techniques and viewpoints; two, to follow a narrow monolithic commitment to method and theory; or three, an even more dangerous alternative, to develop a cynical anti-intellectual stance that professes there is no certitude, no available useful tested knowledge upon which one can draw. If this third option is elected, the only recourse in practice is to a present-oriented, impressionistic reliance on the outcome of a spontaneous, concerned human encounter. There is, in addition, a fourth option, which consists of oversimplifying practice. Since psychosocial therapy is strongly committed to making use of all aspects of a client's life, many of which are the mundane factors of daily living, there is a risk of seeing such activities as being uncomplicated and requiring little more than good will and human concern. Because these facets of treatment are indeed commonplace, they create a particular challenge to the therapist seeking to use them in a planned effective way.

Overall Assessment

A responsibility of any approach is to examine its own weaknesses and strengths. Thus, although psychosocial therapy is committed to an open approach to knowledge, this does not imply that the system has no boundaries. It would be presumptuous to claim for psychosocial therapy all knowledge and all skill in human behavior.

One of the risks in a volume that seeks to present a spectrum of approaches to social work practice is the risk of overstating or overselling one's own viewpoint. This is a particular risk for the psychosocial approach since it is established on a broad and developing base. It can easily aspire to become all things to all people or to present an approach that implies that all that is worth knowing is contained within this framework.

To date, this approach has tended to understress the physical functioning of man except in settings directly related to health. However, as indicated earlier, this is changing and with growing understanding of intersystemic functioning will change still further. Similarly, in direct work with clients, the psychosocial therapist does not seek to examine extensively the unconscious components of personality structure. Thus, it follows that this theory of practice does not use the full range of psychoanalytic techniques. Neither does it use hypnosis as a part of its range of treatment procedures.

Nor has this approach to practice made direct use of the resources of psychometrics, except in a highly limited way. Although we have always worked closely with psychologists and their psychometric skills, we have not considered it necessary to equip ourselves with these competences.

In a similar way, psychosocial treatment is limited by the scope of its interventive targets. Vast and rich as has been the experience of this school of practice, it in no way claims to be competent in dealing with all existing psychosocial difficulties. Clearly this type of treatment cannot cure many of the serious physical, emotional, mental and social handicaps of people. Frequently, it is able to help persons function more comfortably and satisfyingly within such limitations without undoing them. In a more specific area psychosocial therapy does not claim to treat more serious forms of mental illness, although, again, it does contribute to the alleviation and modification of some of the precipitating and aggravating circumstances, frequently with dramatic results.

This system of therapy, to date, has not been dramatically effective in dealing with family systems that are marked with multifaceted long-term serious problem functioning although some progress has been made with this challenging group.

For a long time psychosocial practice seemed to have avoided intensive concern with the wide range of sexual problems, concerns and difficulties experienced by many of our clients. This is not to say that this important area of the human condition was avoided; rather, we tended to see sexual problems as symptomatic rather than as areas for direct intervention. Happily, this is changing rapidly and to an increasing extent therapists can be found highly skilled in assisting persons with a wide range of sexual difficulties (19).

On the positive side, psychosocial therapy has shown itself to be highly effective with a wide range of emotional, personal, interpersonal, situational and intersituational problems. Although there has been a tradition to see this approach as highly problem- and pathology-focused, in current practice a growing emphasis can be observed on strengths, potential and healthy functioning.

Another of the strengths of this theory lies in its tradition of borrowing, incorporating, rethinking and reformulating knowledge from without and adding to these its own insights, experiences and tested concepts. But this is also its vulnerability, in that it is continually being tempted by new perceptions and formulations, even before we have fully integrated and understood what we know about psychosocial functioning from our own knowledge and experience. I think among our colleagues who would identify themselves with this school would be found a wide range of theoretical and conceptual viewpoints. These viewpoints are frequently not contradictory or mutually exclusive but, rather, represent emphases on different components of this theory. But this does not imply in any way that these are negligent or biased practitioners. These are colleagues who are strongly committed to ethical, responsible practice and achieve enviable results in practice. It does imply, though, that all of us can enrich our practices to the extent that we can fully appreciate the implications and resources of this practice system.

From without, our greatest challenge is to demonstrate in a scientifically acceptable way the differential results of our activities. By now enough has been made of the apparently disappointing results of some well-known evaluative projects of recent years. It is essential that we continue to focus on well-designed, thoroughly conducted outcome studies. We must continue to improve the whole structure of available research methodologies and experiment with ways of adapting them to our practice. We have been remiss in describing what we do in precise and accurate terms. We have not as yet made sufficient use of available audiovisual technology to record our contacts with clients. These processes give us rich opportunities to develop and test paradigms of interventive activities.

We have been particularly remiss in declaring the goals we establish with our clients in a format that permits examination and comparisons with outcome and patterns of intervention. As has been pointed out by others, when we do not do this, others do it for us and often in an inappropriate way. Thus, an overall goal for practitioners in this school should be to put heavy stress on documenting practice more specifically. This in two ways: presenting clearer formulations of our diagnostic thinking and its development through the life of the case, and specifying goals for treatment. We must also begin to make more antefactum statements about our choice of treatment emphases and resources related to our diagnosis and goals.

The prior points have been made before, as has the appeal for continuing and expanded research of high quality. In the past two decades we have trained a large number of skilled researchers. We still seem to be expending considerable energy on exhortations about our shortcomings rather than on hard clinical research. We cannot be dissuaded because of the unfavorable results of some projects. As committed researchers we have to be ready to accept findings, whether favorable or unfavorable. Only by continually and directly studying our therapeutic activities will we better understand when and why we are effective and when and why we are not.

One of the pressing difficulties in current research is the lack of a system of describing and classifying cases into groupings that permit more accurate comparison of input and outcome and thus specify the differential effectiveness of various clusters and emphases of intervention (54). This has become more of a challenge to us as we broaden the spectrum of significant environments included in assessments. In turn, this necessitates different kinds of classifications and interclassifications of persons, problems, resources, symptoms, behavior patterns and treatment goals. Thus, our overall research challenge is to bring to the fore the strengths of the system by improving and testing our conceptual framework.

Summary

Psychosocial therapy is and has been a significant component of the history of social work. At its present stage of development, it both reflects the tradition of the profession and responds to the demands of current practice in terms of available conceptual and practice resources. It is committed to modify and improve its effectiveness and scope, the soundness of its theoretical base and the communicability of its knowledge and skills. It is an orientation to practice that can be proud of its achievements to date yet should be fully aware of its limitations and the conceptual and research tasks still to be accomplished.

References

1. Ackerman, N. W., F. L. Beatman and S. N. Sherman (eds.) *Expanding Theory and Practice in Family Therapy*. New York: Family Service Association of America, 1967, pp. 109-124.
2. ———. *The Psychodynamics of Family Life: Diagnosis and Treatment of Family Relationships*. New York: Basic Books, 1958.
3. Alger, Ian and Peter Hogan. "Enduring Effects of Videotape Playback Experience on Family and Marital Relationships," *American Journal of Orthopsychiatry*, 39, No. 1 (January, 1969), 88-94.
4. Appel, Gerald. "Some Aspects of Transference and Counter-Transference in Marital Counseling," *Social Casework*, 47 (May, 1966), 307-312.
5. Bahn, Anita K. "A Multi-Disciplinary Psychosocial Classification Scheme." *American Journal of Orthopsychiatry*, 41 (October, 1971), 830-845.
6. Barrett-Lennard, G. T. "Significant Aspects of a Helping Relationship," *Canada's Mental Health*, Supplement 47. Ottawa: Department of National Health and Welfare, July-August, 1965.
7. Bartlett, Harriett M. *The Common Base of Social Work Practice*. New York: National Association of Social Workers, 1970.
8. Berkowitz, Sidney. "Some Specific Techniques of Psychosocial Diagnosis and Treatment in Family Casework," *Social Casework*, 36 (November, 1955), 399-406.
9. Biestek, Felix B. *The Casework Relationship*. Chicago: Loyola University, 1957.
10. Ehrenkranz, Shirley M. "A Study of the Techniques and Procedures Used in Joint Interviewing in the Treatment of Marital Problems," Doctoral Dissertation, Columbia University, School of Social Work, New York, 1967.

11. Erikson, Erik H. *Childhood and Society.* New York: Norton, 1950.
12. Fantl, Berta. "Integrating Psychological, Social and Cultural Factors in Assertive Casework," *Social Work,* 3 (October, 1958), 30-37.
13. Freud, Anna. *The Ego and the Mechanisms of Defense.* New York: International Universities Press, 1946.
14. Freud, Sigmund. "The Unconscious" (1915), in *Collected Papers,* Vol. 4. London: Hogarth, 1949, pp. 98-136.
15. Friend, Maurice R. and Pollak, Otto. "Psychosocial Aspects in the Preparation for Treatment of an Allergic Child," *American Journal of Orthopsychiatry,* 24 (January, 1954), 63-72.
16. Garrett, Annette. "Modern Casework: The Contributions of Ego Psychology," in Howard J. Parad (ed.) *Ego Psychology and Dynamic Casework.* New York: Family Service Association of America, 1958, pp. 38-52.
17. ———. "The Worker-Client Relationship," in Howard J. Parad (ed.) *Ego Psychology and Dynamic Casework.* New York: Family Service Association of America, 1958, pp. 53-72.
18. Glasser, William. *Reality Therapy.* New York: Harper and Row, 1965.
19. Gochros, Harvey S. "Sexual Problems in Social Work Practice," *Social Work,* 16 (January, 1971), 3-5.
20. Hamilton, Gordon. *Theory and Practice of Social Casework,* 2nd ed. New York: Columbia University Press, 1951.
21. Handel, Gerald (ed.). *The Psychosocial Interior of the Family: A Sourcebook for the Study of Whole Families.* London: Allen and Unwin; 1968.
22. Hankins, Frank. "The Contributions of Sociology to the Practice of Social Work," in *Proceedings of the National Conference of Social Work,* 1930. Chicago: University of Chicago Press, 1931, pp. 528-535.
23. Hartmann, Heinz. *Ego Psychology and the Problem of Adaptation.* New York: International Universities Press, 1958.
24. Hellebrand, Shirley. "Client Value Orientations: Implications for Diagnosis and Treatment," in F. J. Turner (ed.) *Differential Diagnosis and Treatment in Social Work.* New York: Free Press, 1968, pp. 615-624.
25. Hollis, Florence. *Casework: A Psychosocial Therapy,* 2nd ed., rev. New York: Random House, 1972.
26. ———. "Personality Diagnosis in Casework," in Howard J. Parad (ed.) *Ego Psychology and Dynamic Casework.* New York: Family Service Association of America, 1958, pp. 83-96.
27. ———. "A Profile of Early Interviews in Marital Counseling," *Social Casework,* 49 (January, 1968), 35-41.
28. ———. "The Psychosocial Approach to the Practice of Casework," in R. Roberts and R. Nee (eds.) *Theories of Social Casework.* Chicago: University of Chicago Press, 1970, pp. 33-75.
29. ———. *A Typology of Casework Treatment.* New York: Family Service Association of America, 1968.
30. Jehu, D., P. Hardiker, M. Yelloy and M. Shaw. *Behaviour Modification in Social Work.* London: Wiley, 1972.
31. Josselyn, Irene M. *Psychosocial Development of Children.* New York: Family Service Association of America, 1948.
32. Katz, Alfred H. "Some Psychosocial Problems in Hemophilia," *Social Casework,* 40 (January, 1959), 321-326.

33. Kendall, Katherine A. (ed.) *Social Work Values in an Age of Discontent.* New York: Council on Social Work Education, 1970.

34. Kluckhohn, F. and J. P. Spiegel. "Integration and Conflict in Family Behaviour." *Group for the Advancement of Psychiatry Report,* No. 27. New York: G.A.P., 1957.

35. Littner, Ner. "The Impact of the Client's Unconscious on the Caseworker's Reactions," in Howard J. Parad (ed.) *Ego Psychology and Dynamic Casework.* New York: Family Service Association of America, 1958, pp. 73-87.

36. Lutz, Werner A. *Concepts and Principles Underlying Social Casework Practice.* Washington, D.C.: National Association of Social Workers, 1956.

37. Merton, Robert K. *Social Therapy and Social Structure.* Glencoe, Ill.: Free Press, 1957.

38. Meyer, Carol H. *Social Work Practice: A Response to the Urban Crisis.* New York: Free Press, 1970.

39. Mullen, Edward J. "The Relation Between Diagnosis and Treatment in Casework," *Social Casework,* 50 (April, 1969), 218-226.

40. Parad, Howard J. (ed.) *Crisis Intervention: Selected Readings.* New York: Family Service Association of America, 1965.

41. ———. *Ego Psychology and Dynamic Casework.* New York: Family Service Association of America, 1958.

42. Polansky, Norman A. *Ego Psychology and Communication.* New York: Atherton Press, 1971.

43. ——— and J. Kounin, "Clients' Reactions to Initial Interviews: A Field Study," *Human Relations,* 9 (1956), 237-264.

44. Pollak, Otto, Hazel M. Young and Helen Leach. "Differential Diagnosis and Treatment of Character Disturbances," *Social Casework,* 41 (December, 1960), 512-517.

45. Pollitt, Ernesto, Aviva Eichler and Cee-Khoon Chan. "Psychosocial Development and Behavior of Mothers of Failure-To-Thrive Children," *American Journal of Orthopsychiatry,* 45 (July, 1975), 525-537.

46. Reid, William J. and Ann W. Shyne. *Brief and Extended Casework.* New York: Columbia University Press, 1969.

47. Richmond, Mary E. *What Is Social Casework?* New York: Russell Sage Foundation, 1922.

48. Roberts, Robert W. and Robert H. Nee (eds.) *Theories of Social Casework.* Chicago: University of Chicago Press, 1970.

49. Rogers, Carl R. "Characteristics of a Helping Relationship," *Canada's Mental Health,* Supplement 27. Ottawa: Department of National Health and Welfare, March, 1962.

50. Russel, A. "Late Psychosocial Consequences in Concentration Camp Survivor Families," *American Journal of Orthopsychiatry,* 44 (July, 1974), 611-619.

51. Salomon, Elizabeth L. "Humanistic Values and Social Casework," *Social Casework,* 48 (January, 1967), 26-39.

52. Sherman, Sanford N. "Joint Interviews in Casework Practice," *Social Work,* 4 (April, 1959), 20-28.

53. Turner, Francis J. *Differential Diagnosis and Treatment in Social Work.* New York: Free Press, 1968; second edition, 1976.

54. ———. "The Search for Diagnostic Classifications." Unpublished Paper. The Learned Societies, University of York, 1969.

55. ———. "Ethnic Difference and Client Performance," *Social Service Review,* 44 (March, 1970), 1-10.

56. ———. *Psychosocial Therapy.* New York: Free Press, 1978.

Magraw-Hill

1-800-338-3987

College Text
Div.

4th

Woods, —

ISPN

· 49.84 —

$57.53 ·
_____

7³/₄
_____

ordered 2/28/94

Jodi — contact
person

Annotated listing of key references

HAMILTON, Gordon. *Theory and Practice of Social Casework,* 2nd ed.
New York: Columbia University Press, 1951.

This book, now a classic in the casework field, brings together both a theoretical base for psychosocial practice as well as a specification of the major components of such practice. It was written during the period when psychodynamic theory was the principal theoretical base underlying clinical social work practice.

HOLLIS, Florence. *Casework: A Psychosocial Therapy,* 2nd ed., rev.
New York: Random House, 1972.

This is currently the most up-to-date text on psychosocial therapy in which is presented the theoretical base of practice, a precise outline of treatment procedures and the supporting developments in research. Of particular interest is the development of a multifaceted theoretical basis of practice; this represents a shift from Gordon Hamilton's work that had been based on a single theory.

PARAD, Howard J. (ed.). *Ego Psychology and Dynamic Casework.* New York: Family Service Association of America, 1958.

Although written from an ego psychology viewpoint, most of the articles in this collection highlight components of psychosocial therapy. Here can be observed the broadening of the theoretical base of practice from a more restricted base on which renewed stress on the importance of social science material is underscored. The other themes in this book reflected in current psychosocial practice are the stress on research and the consideration of differential treatment ap[ ] categories of clients.

RICHMOND, Mary E. *What Is Social Casewor[ ]* Sage Foundation, 1922.

An important historical source book for [ ] In this short, well-written book can be fou[ ] current practice within this tradition. M[ ] still relevant today, and most of the tre[ ] are anticipated, although expressed in [ ]

TURNER, Francis J. *Differential Diagnosis a[ ] Work,* 2nd ed., New York: Free Press, 1976.

This book contains a collection of over seventy articles, each of which deals with a specific client type or problem, principally within a psychosocial framework. The unifying concept in the book is that effective treatment necessitates diagnostic understanding of the client and a specific selection of a profile of procedures and resources to achieve the identified goals of treatment within the client's strengths and limitations.

5
Problem-Solving Theory

by

DAVID HALLOWITZ

Problem solving exists in all aspects of casework: the rendering of concrete services; counseling and guidance with respect to immediate reality problems requiring planning decisions; interventions of an advocacy nature; drawing teachers, probation officers and other professionals into a broadened treatment program; treatment of marital and parent–child relationship conflicts through individual, conjoint and family interviewing processes; and treatment of individuals with internalized emotional disturbances. Yet, except for Perlman (8), problem solving as a clinical entity has not been comprehensively examined. Betz (1) showed that there was a positive correlation between problem solving and improvement in schizophrenic patients. Hallowitz (3) discussed the problem-solving component in family therapy. Haley (2) did this more extensively. Spitzer and Welsh (11) focused upon diagnosis, treatment and action-oriented interventions, mostly in relation to clients beset with social problems. The relative dearth of writings on the subject is understandable because problem solving is embedded in, and interwoven with, the dynamics and processes of casework diagnosis and treatment. Hollis (7), Hamilton (6) and others make only brief mention of problem solving. Perlman presented problem solving extensively. Spivak et al. (12) present cognitive skills in social adjustment as guidelines to research and intervention.

Perlman's concepts

It is first necessary to specify Perlman's concepts in their essence, which I will briefly do by quoting selectively from her book. The reader is asked to bear in mind that I am merely touching upon Perlman's major points and am thereby not doing justice to her book. Perlman stated:

In casework practice, our effort is to maintain the relationship on the basis of reality . . . transference manifestations need to be received, identified and dealt with as they occur, but the effort is to so manage the relationship and the problem solving component as to give minimum excitation to transference. (p. 78)

The casework process sustains, supplements and fortifies the functions of the client's ego. (p. 86)

. . . much in the problem solving work is on an unconscious or only partly conscious basis; that is, it happens spontaneously in the empathic interaction between caseworker and client. But all of it . . . centers about some problem consciously brought by the client and affirmed by the caseworker —a problem to be solved by joint effort. Problem solving must include then, conscious, focused, goal-directed activity between client and caseworker. (p. 87)

The work of problem solving in the caseworker's mind must . . . be a systematically organized process. He will hardly play it out in its logical outline because he will measure it to the client's capacities and needs. But he must be clear as to what must happen in order to move from dilemma to solution or from stalemate to decision; the facts that constitute the problem must be known, thought and feeling must be brought to play upon them and choices and means for dealing with them must be considered and decided upon. (p. 88)

The work of problem solving as it is experienced by the client . . . may be recognized chiefly as a stimulation to mobilize himself to think about himself and his situation in some protected and orderly ways. (p. 88)

The first part of the casework process, as in all problem solving, is to assert and clarify the facts and the problem. The second aspect of casework problem solving grows out of and is interwoven with the ongoing eliciting of facts: it is thinking through the facts. (pp. 89–90)

In each case, the caseworker has his own problem solving task: . . . this mental work of examining the parts of the problem for the import of their particular nature and origin, for the interrelationships among them, for the relationship between them and the means for their solution—this is the diagnostic process. Diagnosis . . . must result in a design for action. (p. 164)

. . . the dynamic diagnosis may be a simple or a complex formulation. Psychological factors may be dominant in one instance, social in another. (p. 171)

Additional concepts

I will now present additional concepts of my own to develop further the theoretical foundation for the use of problem solving in casework practice. (The term "client" is used throughout this chapter to represent an individual or two or more persons involved in a joint or family process.)

1. Problem solving is generally conceived in a narrow sense: that of the worker helping the client rationally to think through a discrete problem. However, this is only one segment of a spectrum of problem-solving situations. Perlman's concept that problem solving takes place on an unconscious or partly conscious level will be brought to the forefront for fuller consideration. This will be done also with her concept that problem-solving work goes on in the mind of the worker, which is of the utmost importance because this determines the differential diagnostic assessment, the worker's awareness and dealing with his own transference and countertransference feelings and his trying and the course and dynamics of counseling and treatment. The worker's problem-solving thought processes may never be verbalized during the helping process but may be implicitly and experientially understood by the client. In other words, there are two kinds of problem-solving work: that which is overt, tangible and conducive to rational solution; and that which is intangible and subject to the coming-to-grips with, and resolution of, inner conflicts and resistances toward achieving maturational growth and change. The two are often interwoven.

2. A problem-solving orientation on the part of the worker requires a component of self-assertion with the client in the context of a positive therapeutic relationship. Let us refer to this as an "assertive counseling component" (4). The worker's activity thereby has the following elements:

a. Crisis intervention: The worker intervenes in chaotic and critical situations in order to halt or at least reduce unbridled destructiveness and thereby fosters a climate that is conducive to further treatment. The worker's active, assertive intervention represents the intensification of therapeutic effort that is required to help a family or an individual in a desperate situation.

b. Correction of disparities between perception and reality: The worker helps the client accurately to perceive external realities.

c. Dealing with discrepancies between behavior and goals: The worker confronts the client with the ways in which short-sighted, impulsive, momentarily gratifying behaviors block the attainment of his desired goals. He helps the client see the undesirable consequences of his actions and become aware of the dynamics that determine his maladaptive functioning.

d. Taking a position: The worker expresses his observations and understanding in a forthright manner. When necessary, he takes a stand on vital issues for the purpose of providing the client with something tangible to react to in working out his own

direction and solutions. The client's specific requests for advice and guidance are often not turned back to him but directly answered. They are accepted at face value as indicative of gaps in the client's experience and knowledge.

e. Active direction-finding: The worker recommends, suggests or implies by his questions the objectives toward which the client may strive and the concrete measures by which the client may achieve his objectives. He thus leaves the decision-making responsibility to the client. This active direction-finding is done by means of discussion in which the client's own ideas are fully elicited and supported.

f. Direction–implementation: When decisions have been made about the modes of behavior and the specific steps that are needed to achieve the desired objectives, the worker suggests that they can be concretely implemented during the period between interviews. In a sense, he gives the client "homework." As the client moves toward constructive change, the worker provides substantial support, encouragement and recognition. His aim is to help the client make the new experience growth-producing. The client will experience delight in the expansion of his ego and be better able to cope with later crises. The educational concept, the use of repetition toward mastery, is basic to the maturational process. The client finds out by experiencing one little success at a time that the new behavior is really worthwhile, and progress in treatment is advanced.

It must be borne in mind and reemphasized that the assertive counseling component is embedded within the framework of generic treatment methods and processes. Its selective and appropriately timed use requires the same high level of skill, creativity, sensitivity and judgment. In other words, in order to be constructive, the assertive counseling component must be accompanied by accurate perception within the framework of basically sound treatment. It is not a treatment modality and may easily be destructive if used in isolation from the mainstream of skilled casework treatment.

3. When interpersonal relationship problems (in multiple interviewing) constitute the content of treatment, and efforts are being made to solve them, this becomes the medium through which positive and negative feelings, misunderstandings and conflicts in these relationships are expressed. Problem-solving work in the realm of relationship conflicts can contribute to the development of better understanding and feeling between the people concerned, and this in turn generates even more productive problem-solving effort. As in individual treatment, change for the better with respect to relationship conflicts can take place without explicit discussion of reality problems. Nevertheless, it should be recognized that this change is an outgrowth of the client's relationship with the therapist and the particular treatment process, and that agreements and decisions are being made implicitly with the worker and between the client participants. More often than not, the problem-solving process explicitly becomes a vital part of joint and family interviews.

In this area of interpersonal relationship problems and in most other areas of casework endeavor—including individual treatment—problem-solving content may become predominant at any point in the treatment process. This depends upon whether deeper and more complex emotional and psychopathological factors and forces exist that may first have to be worked through or, if possible, encapsulated to permit constructive and practical work on immediate reality issues. Early problem-solving efforts may be undermined and thwarted by these factors and forces, which often operate on a preconscious or unconscious level. The worker can use problem solving as a lead-in to the deeper conflicts by pointing out that something in the client is obstructing the particular problem-solving efforts and wondering what this might

be. On the other hand, it is also possible that the client could have some success with the surface and immediate issues despite the existence of deeper pathological forces. This would have therapeutic value because the client can gain confidence, and his energies become freed, thereby enabling him to go into the more central and underlying conflicts.

Although there is considerable variability and interrelationship between deeper conflicts and immediate reality problems, the problem-solving work generally emerges into prominence fairly early in the treatment process when there is a greater degree of health and strength in the client. It emerges later in the process when these factors are minimal.

4. There is a considerable amount and variability in the problem-solving work that is done in child therapy. It is not possible to present all of this, and the contexts of the various treatment approaches and processes with children. Just one approach will be presented—that of a sharply focused concentration on the child's symptomatic reactions to the vicious cycle breakdown in the relationships with the parents. Responsibility is placed on the child for doing something constructive toward correcting and changing the behavior which inevitably stirs up in the parents feelings of rejection. The use of a specific behaviors chart enables the child to visualize and keep in the front of his mind the concrete troublesome behaviors. The incentive held out to the child is that of winning the love and good feeling of the parents and, implicitly, the approval of the worker, whom he has come to like, trust and respect.

There are a multiplicity of cases and situations in which the worker is doing problem-solving work in the privacy of his mind and overtly within each interview and in the total treatment process. It is impossible to cover the waterfront. Nevertheless, I will try to approximate this by dividing the various problem-solving situations into the following eight categories: (1) intrafamilial relationship problems; (2) problems between a parent and a child; (3) marital problems; (4) school and home behavior problems; (5) problems in juvenile delinquency; (6) problems of individual clients with internalized emotional disturbances; (7) environmental problems: intervention on behalf of the client; (8) problems with respect to future planning and direction. A particular case can often fit into more than one of these categories. However, a particular category was chosen for illustrative purposes only.

In each category, I will present one or more vignettes of problem-solving situations in the context of the treatment dynamics and process. The focus will be upon the worker's thought processes and methods. The first vignette is presented in verbatim excerpts to show, in as live a form as possible, the problem-solving work prevalent in all the vignettes. After each vignette, I will identify the worker's problem-solving efforts, from which additional concepts will be drawn. The summary section of the chapter will consist of a delineation of all the problem-solving concepts covered.

1. Intrafamilial Relationship Problems

Vignette: Stealing and General Relationship Breakdown. Stealing and general disobedience on the part of the six children, ranging in age from six to nineteen years, were symptomatic of long-standing mental illness in the mother; relationship breakdown between the parents and the children; and between the children. Indeed, the family was in a state of near chaos at the time help was sought for Tom and Carl, seventeen and fifteen years of age. These two youngsters were involved in delinquent gang activity and placed on probation by the Family Court. Julie, thirteen, was developing a pattern of ungovernable behavior verging on delinquency, similar to that of her older brothers. The two youngest children, six and nine years old, were disobedient and troublesome but minimally under control of the

parents. The nineteen-year-old daughter was mostly away at college, but in intense conflict with her adolescent siblings whenever she was home on vacation.

Family treatment was undertaken with Tom, Carl, Julie and the parents. The deeper dynamics were discussed with intense emotion by these family members: the effects upon the children and family of the mother's past mental illness and extensive hospitalizations; the father's ineffectualness in exerting discipline and control over the children, not only during those years but in the present as well; Tom's having felt rejected by his parents throughout his life, especially when they sent him to military school five years ago; the mother feeling that the children did not really care for her; and the lack of teamwork and unity between the parents in relation to the children. Helping the family members bring out these and many other feelings that had been stored up within them not only in relation to each other, but as individuals unto themselves, constituted the core of the family treatment process.

Yet, it was essential for the worker to involve the family members in problem-solving work of a specific nature in order to rebuild their relationship and bring order out of chaos. The rampant stealing within the household was one of several major discrete problems with which the family came to grips. The problem-solving work with respect to this particular problem will be briefly presented through verbatim excerpts as follows:

Father: (to worker) Is this problem of stealing in our home worth working on?

Worker: It certainly is. It's the whole matter of being able to trust each other.

Mother: This is it; there really is a lack of trust in the family.

Julie: (to Carl) If something of yours is taken, do you know who's taken it? (Carl: No.) All right, and do you ever find out? (Carl: No.)

Mother: I can't leave money around the house. You've got to carry your purse around with you no matter where you go. Or your cigarettes, anything valuable, you've got to lock up somewhere. And even the locks are picked. We really have a talented group in that you can't hide anything. This is a terrible way to live.

Father: I never know whether Carl and Julie are telling me the truth.

Worker: (to all) What are some of your ideas as to why this problem exists in your family?

Tom: Whenever I saw something I wanted, I took it.

Worker: Do you think that's what it is?

Tom: I used to think that I could get away with it.

Worker: What is it with you, Julie?

Julie: I don't know. I just want it and I don't think about it until after it's done. I put my conscience aside.

Worker: How about you, Carl?

Carl: The same as her. I wanted it and I didn't think about it until after it was done. I just wanted it and I'd forget about what would happen if I got caught. Feelings about it started to bother me afterward, but then it started to be a habit.

Worker: Sometimes we find that kids will steal not so much because they want something, but because it's a good way of punishing somebody or getting even. You can get rid of your angry feelings that way.

Tom: That's not it; we have better ways, like messing up someone's room.

(Spontaneous narrations of various stealing incidents followed, with a concentration on Carl's smooth operations.)

Worker: Let me get back to Carl for a moment. I just want to check something out. The way it sounds to me, you're describing Carl almost like a con man. Is that what you are? I mean, do you put the charm on to get something?

Carl: Yeah.

Worker: How come you agree so readily?

Carl: Because it's true.

Mother: Well, I think you fooled us all once too often. I mean, we've all been taken in, I, probably, more than anybody else.

Julie: You keep trusting him and I don't do that any more.

Worker: My next question, Carl, is: Do you really want to continue being this way—the con artist?

Carl: I don't want to grow up to be a con artist. But right now I really don't use my connery as much as I used to. If I try to work with my parents better and my brothers and my sisters better, no one will believe me. So how can anyone try and do something right when you have the reputation of being a con artist? You can't.

Worker: That's a real problem. Carl wants to change and win your confidence. How can he go about it? How can he overcome the reputation he's built up?

Julie: I think if he would be good for a long period of time, he would gain our trust back.

Father: We were asked if we can do anything about the stealing. If we decide that it has to stop, then maybe we should all start putting things on the table and trust that it's going to be there. And start trusting each other all the way.

Carl: I'll never be trusted, so I may as well just keep going on.

Julie: We don't know when this trust will begin, and you guys just won't know unless we all try together.

Problem-Solving Work in Vignette Above: The worker entered into the problem-solving phase, as exemplified by the discussion about stealing, after the family members had reached each other at a deeper feeling level—i.e., in terms of what had gone wrong and what they have been missing in their relationships with each other and in their family life. Even the discussion about the stealing problem had some deeper roots, namely, the distrust that has long existed in the intrafamilial relationships. By helping the family members work on the stealing problem, the worker opened up further avenues of communication. They talked with each other about their respective contributions to the problem and the need for everyone now to exert the effort to put an end to the pattern of stealing from each other. The worker made an attempt to help the family members think about the origins of the problem; the possible psychological reasons for its existence. What became clear to him was that the stealing was characterological in nature in the sense that the children stole things for narcissistic reasons and were deficient in their capacity to recognize and respect the feelings of the other family members. Solving the stealing problem in the family would not only have the beneficial effect of eliminating one source of internal family chaos, but also of inducing further growth toward maturation on the part of the family members, especially the children. The worker and the family members made Carl aware of the fact that he was like a "con artist." This kind of confrontation had the potential of helping him begin to do something about this aspect of his personality, about which he had some concern. The family was able to work together successfully on the stealing problem and several other major problems which they tackled. This furthered the relationship-building process between them and gave them more of a feeling of self-worth individually and collectively. The verbatim excerpts above do not make clear the fact that the worker stimulated and encouraged the father to assume more and more of his rightful role. The worker had to be aware of the growing relationship between himself and the family members and the particular psychodynamic meaning that he had to them. Perhaps, in a transference sense, the worker was a respected relative or good, close family friend.

2.   Problems Between a Parent and a Child

Vignette: Negativism in a Four-year-old Girl Toward Mother. Kim became extremely negativistic toward her mother when the latter was pregnant with the second child two years ago. Kim was constantly disobedient and resisted the mother's efforts to reach her through play and overt affection.

I engaged Kim in play activity and found her to be a bright, well-coordinated, secure, friendly, affectionate and likable little girl. I then met jointly with Kim and the mother, having Kim sit on my lap. I talked in very simple terms to Kim about her being angry at the mother because of the birth of the two-year-old sibling; really needing the mother's love; pushing the mother away and not listening to her. Kim was making it impossible for her mother to show her love. Yet, her mother loves her very much and wants to play with her, hug her, kiss her and tuck her into bed. I then suggested to Kim that at home she let her mother play with her and show her affection and love. Talking to the mother, also in terms that Kim could understand, I explained that she has felt frustrated, angered and rejected by Kim, which has made it hard for her to provide the love Kim needs. Yet, I added, she must have given a good deal to Kim for her to be such a friendly, likable and secure little girl.

Spontaneously, Kim went to her mother, sat in her lap, hugged her and kissed her several times. The mother responded with genuine affection to Kim. She said that this is the first time in two years that Kim has done this. I then planned with the mother on having individual interviews with her so that she could work on some of the feelings within herself that she had already mentioned and which fed into her frustration and resentment toward Kim—e.g., her having become pregnant with Kim before marriage. I suggested that the mother try once again to reach out affectionately to Kim, playing with her whenever appropriate. I stressed that she do this consistently, not allowing herself to become discouraged and not giving up if Kim should reject her overtures.

Because Kim had the symptoms of stumbling and falling for no apparent reason, I had advised the mother at the very beginning to have a complete medical examination. This resulted in glasses being prescribed; in Kim's vision becoming improved; and in the disappearance of the stumbling and falling. I also had our psychiatrist evaluate Kim neurologically. His findings were negative.

Problem-Solving Work in Vignette Above:

The worker's problem-solving work had the following elements: working out in his own mind the dynamics of the mother–child relationship conflict; his helping the mother and Kim to gain this understanding as well; his developing the treatment plan of working primarily with the mother; and his suggesting the direction the mother and Kim can take in order to overcome the vicious cycle breakdown (3) in their relationship. The stumbling was handled medically.

Vignette: An Eighteen-year-old Adolescent's Need for Adult-level Communication with His Father.

Chris was in treatment with me because of depression and a suicidal attempt. He was unable to become clearly aware of the underlying reasons, which remained nebulous. However, he expressed himself meaningfully about related concerns: the fear of losing his girlfriend which precipitated the suicide attempt; his deep feelings of insecurity and inadequacy; and his fear of being drafted. Chris made significant progress in treatment, achieving a better feeling about himself and a higher level of morale and functioning.

He now brought up his feeling of discontent about the relationship with his father. His father still treats him as a child, confining conversation to such practical matters as chores and Chris's monetary needs. Chris has tried to talk with him about personal concerns, but the father did not seem to be interested. Chris said that he could do without a closer relationship with his father, because he is on the threshold of adulthood and independence. Yet, he felt that he would be missing something important in his life. Chris accepted my suggestion of a joint interview.

In this interview, Chris expressed his feelings directly and frankly to his father and a good discussion ensued. A subsequent joint session revealed that father and son were now talking much more meaningfully with each other. Thereafter, Chris reported that the breakthrough in their relationship was being sustained.

Problem-Solving Work in Vignette Above:

The worker accepted the validity of the problem Chris presented and offered an approach to it. He viewed the potential of an improved father–son relationship as a significant supportive element with respect to Chris's original problem of depression and suicidal tendencies. The problem-solving effort was that of having father and son face and deal with the distance that had existed in their relationship with each other.

3. Marital Problems

Vignette: Sexual Problem in a Young Married Couple. Mr. and Mrs. J. had been married for one year and felt their relationship to be deteriorating. The ostensible cause was Mr. J.'s dissatisfaction with the sexual part of the relationship. His wife did not "turn me on" sexually as did the "beautiful dolls" with whom he had had intercourse prior to marriage. He realized that his wife was not as attractive as these other females, but she had all the other qualities that he sought in a wife: intelligence, understanding, and real love. He found his wife to be goodlooking from the waist up, but the shape of her legs repelled him. He could not refrain from constantly making critical comments to his wife, even though he knew that this was a physiological characteristic which could not be changed. Mr. J. believed that complete sexual compatibility and gratification in the marriage was primary. Mrs. J. had the opposite point of view, that the sexual part of the relationship would achieve fruition as a function of the development of the total marital relationship. Her husband's constant criticism of her physical appearance was eroding her self-confidence and making her angry at him; she was tense and ungiving towards her husband sexually, as a result.

Initially, in joint interviews, I helped Mr. and Mrs. J. frankly to express their feelings. I also explored their earlier life background in order to gain more understanding of them individually and help them to some beginning understanding of themselves as well. In my own mind, I struggled to determine where the key to the marital conflict lay: was it in the interrelationship between the two, or was it within one or the other or both individuals? I came to the conclusion that the major problem existed within Mr.

J.; that his extreme emphasis on the sexual part of the relationship was tied in with a basic and long-standing feeling of inadequacy. His conquests of beautiful women prior to marriage and his expectations from his wife sexually seemed to be a reaction formation against his feelings of low self-esteem. I discussed my view about the locus of the problem with Mr. and Mrs. J. and suggested a course of individual treatment for Mr. J. This was accepted.

The work with Mr. J. thereafter centered upon talking about his earlier life experiences, especially in relation to his parents, that made him feel inadequate and insecure. He expressed the angry and bitter feelings stored up within him about the constant criticism to which he was subjected by his father. He gained insight into the meaning of his earlier sexual conquests and the high expectations sexually he held towards his wife, as an outgrowth of his basic feeling of inadequacy. He was then able to shift his order of priorities in the marriage, coming to realize that the sexual part would become increasingly gratifying as the basic relationship grew and developed. In a more specific problem-solving discussion, Mr. J. decided that he would refrain from criticizing his wife's legs, emphasize to himself and to her the attractive aspects of her physical appearance, and above all contribute to the building of the companionship part of the relationship.

Problem-Solving Work in Vignette Above: The worker tried to solve the problem of where the locus of the marital conflict existed, doing so in his own mind and then sharing his thinking with the marital pair. The solution to the marital problem seemed to require a course of individual treatment of the husband. His part in the sexual problem was symptomatic of deeper emotional problems consisting of feelings of low self-esteem. This was dealt with not in a concrete problem-solving way but in the broader sweep of the treatment process. A practical and concrete problem-solving approach to the sexual problem was then formulated by the client with the worker's help and support.

Vignette: Past Incest Discovered.

Mr. C. was extremely upset about the imminent breakup of his marriage. He also feared that he might have a mental breakdown. His wife had just learned from the twenty-one-year-old married daughter that Mr. C. engaged her in sexual intercourse and fellatio for three years, starting when she was fourteen years of age. Mrs. C. left the home to stay with her mother and immediately initiated steps to obtain a divorce.

In the first interview, Mr. C. cried throughout and was obviously a distraught and broken man. He pleaded with me to do what I could to save the marriage, and he also wanted to determine if he was mentally ill.

My first problem-solving task was to check my own feelings towards Mr. C. Initially, I felt repelled by him because of what he had done, but this quickly passed. I found that he was a very disturbed person emotionally and mentally, in need of help.

I enabled him to express all of his feelings, not only about the incest, but about the marital relationship and himself as a person. I did the same in subsequent interviews with the wife.

The thought of ending the relationship was very painful to Mr. C. despite the fact that for the past six years he had been thinking of divorce. For many years, the relationship between his wife and him was cold and distant. Their sexual relationship was mostly barren. He felt that his wife withheld sex from him because of her anger. He had tried to be a good father and a successful provider. On the other hand, he knew he was very strict with his children, often inflicting brutal physical punishment.

Mr. C. had a very difficult childhood. His father and mother had been separated and he lived with his father while the latter was living with another woman. He observed open sexual relations of all kinds between them.

My diagnostic assessment of Mr. C. was that he was mainly a character- or personality-

disordered individual. Indicative of this, in part, was that, at the time of the incest, he felt that there was nothing wrong with it and was not upset. He must also have had many hostile and sadistic impulses. There was also the likely dynamic factor of his acting out against his wife for denying him sex. On the positive side, he had many strengths, as evidenced by his success at work and by his taking good care of the family from an economic and material point of view.

Psychiatric evaluation, supported and enhanced by diagnostic assessment, was as follows:

> Diagnostically, Mr. C. is an extremely insecure individual with an easily threatened masculine ego. There is also a question of an underlying psychotic process and the danger of a mental breakdown. He seems pretty well compensated and has the definite idea that he would never do anything sexually with the younger daughter now at home.

The initial therapy sessions and the psychiatric interview enabled Mr. C. to regain his equilibrium psychologically and emotionally. The fear of mental breakdown dissipated. He turned his full attention to trying to effect a reconciliation with his wife.

Now I had the problem-solving task of determining how I could be of help in this regard. I gave Mr. C. the responsibility of exploring with his wife whether or not she was interested in meeting with me.

During the three sessions I held with her she moved to the point of being willing seriously to consider reconciliation, provided that her husband continued living apart from the family in order to give both of them a chance to reestablish their relationship. At first, Mr. C. accepted this plan. Subsequently, he reestablished himself forcefully in the home.

In further sessions, separately with Mr. and Mrs. C., I found to my surprise that not only did Mrs. C. accept the new situation forced upon her but that she had actually developed positive feelings towards her husband. They resumed sleeping together and for the first time in many years had satisfying sexual relations with each other.

One would naturally ask why Mrs. C. accepted her husband back into the fold. There are several psychodynamic and practical factors. Psychodynamically, there probably was and continued to be a sado-masochistic relationship between the two. Through work with me, Mrs. C. advanced to being less submissive to her husband, demanding more from him in terms of consideration of her feelings and giving her respect. Mr. C. was able to change sufficiently in this regard. Finally, there was the practical consideration of Mrs. C. being unable to support the family without the help of her husband: that is, a divorce might have resulted in his acting out against her by not providing financial support for herself and the children.

The Problem-Solving Elements Were as Follows:

1. Examining my own feelings towards Mr. C. The incestual acts were initially reprehensible to me; but realizing that I was dealing with a very disturbed person in need of professional counsel helped me to accept him.
2. Intervening therapeutically on a crisis basis in view of the rapid deterioration that was taking place in Mr. C. mentally.
3. Providing strong support and acceptance of him despite the incestuous acts he committed, of which he was profoundly ashamed.
4. Enabling him to express the many important feelings and events in his life that led to his seeking professional help.
5. Arranging for psychiatric evaluation and consultation at an early point in the process.
6. Working out in my own mind the diagnostic formulation that Mr. C. represented a personality or character disorder. This was partially borne out by the psychiatrist who evaluated Mr. C., but he also discerned an underlying, but arrested, psychotic process.
7. Working out the strategy of involving Mrs. C. in an exploration of reconciliation despite her original decision to proceed with divorce, and providing therapy to her as well.

Vignette: Nine-year-old Withdrawn and Fearful Boy. Bob was not accepted by the other children in the classroom; they constantly called him names. He cried in class a good deal, hid under desks, including the teacher's, and would not do his schoolwork. He was withdrawn from family relationships as well and had no friends in the neighborhood. He was described by teachers and parents alike as being constricted, fearful and withdrawn. His behavior was disruptive in the classroom and his uncooperativeness and negativism at home evoked feelings of resentment on the part of the parents, especially the father. Diagnostically, I viewed Bob as a neurotic child.

The parents were constricted in their personalities and the relationship between them lacked closeness and warmth. These latter qualities also characterized their relationship with Bob. Bob's difficulties had begun six years earlier with the birth of a younger brother; they were aggravated two years ago with the birth of a younger sister. One of the major dynamic factors in his emotional disturbance was that he no longer was the center of parental attention. The vicious cycle breakdown in the parent–child relationships had become intensified over the six-year period. Bob's specific behavior difficulties fed into the vicious cycle.

Because the parents needed help with their own relationship conflicts and the constrictions in their own personalities, which inhibited their ability to give of themselves in a relationship with Bob, they were seen in a separate therapeutic process. I worked with Bob in individual therapy. Brief conferences with the parents' therapist served to coordinate our efforts.

At first afraid of me, Bob soon got over this

and began to enjoy coming. We played games and chatted lightly. He was not able to express himself verbally to any considerable extent. His behavior difficulties in school had become so severe that the faculty did not know how they could continue to keep him in a regular class. I had tried talking with Bob about the specific behaviors over which he must gain control, but to no avail. This spurred me to work out a specific behaviors chart with Bob, to be used each week. We prepared a chart for the home as well. These were weekly charts with a column for each day of the week and a rating scale. Bob formulated each of the items.

A = Excellent
B = Good
C = Fair
D = Not good

School Chart
Running out in the hall.
Rolling around on the floor.
Hiding behind the teacher's desk.
Stop making it hard for the teacher to
    teach.
Doing my work.
Try to ignore them when they call me names.

After we constructed the school chart, Bob and I wrote a letter to Bob's teacher. I had a telephone conference with her the next day. She was most understanding and we collaborated with each other thereafter, via the telephone and in direct conference at the school.

There was an immediate dramatic change for the better in Bob's behavior at school, and at home too. He proudly showed me his school and home charts, which had many As and Bs, and a few Cs and Ds. Each week he took pride in showing me the charts, which soon became replete with As. On the school chart of the seventh week, the teacher pasted on a small bunny rabbit, smiling broadly as he held a carrot. In large letters, she wrote: "BOB, IT'S GREAT TO SEE SUCH A HAPPY SMILE ON YOUR FACE. YOU MAKE THE PEOPLE AROUND YOU VERY HAPPY."

The main therapeutic process was to give Bob an experience in a relationship with me wherein he could feel genuinely liked and accepted. In the games we would play, there was a modeling effect in that I would be naturally exuberant, enthusiastic, disappointed when I lost and so forth. In time, I found that Bob was expressing himself similarly in our play interactions. He never became able to talk in any depth about troubled feelings. However, he derived much emotional support and gratification from the praise he received from me, his parents and his teacher, as he improved upon his behavior, as seen in the weekly charts.

Home Chart
Listen to my mother.
Being good.
Try not to listen to brother and sister when they
    call me names.
Keep my room clean.
Help my mother clean the house.

The Problem-Solving Elements Were as Follows:

1. Determining diagnostically that Bob was a neurotic child, and that his parents were comparably disturbed as individuals, and as a marital and parental pair. The treatment plan, therefore, was for Bob to be in individual therapy, and for the parents to have a therapist of their own.

2. Discerning the need for crisis intervention in view of the school's inability to cope with Bob's disruptive behavior. The worker focused on his difficulties in school through the use of the specific behaviors chart. This was extended to the home as well.

3. Developing the basic therapy process with Bob, which consisted mostly of the

therapeutic relationship itself. The worker did not rely on verbal discussion of Bob's feelings and problems, having previously learned through problem-solving experience that this is not necessary with nonverbal children.

4. Working collaboratively with the teacher.
5. Building teamwork with the parents' therapist.

Vignette: Nine-year-old Boy on Brink of Removal from Foster Home. George had been living in his present foster home for five years. In the past two years, his behavior had become increasingly difficult. He would be negativistic and uncooperative with the foster parents. When angry, he would break household articles, punch his younger foster brother and stay away from home. In school, he had many fights with other children, most of which were unprovoked. The teacher and principal were hard put to know how to handle George and were quite concerned about the physical safety of the other children. The foster parents were quite upset about the school behavior, because they would receive frequent calls from the principal.

Much of George's behavior was directly attributable to the failure on the part of his father and stepmother to visit him. The father's previous mental illness and the divorce from George's mother had made foster home placement necessary.

The case was referred by the child welfare worker at the point when the foster parents wanted George removed from their home. Rather than accept the case as a complete referral, I conferred with this worker about our working collaboratively with George, the foster parents and the natural parents.

She and I held an interview with the foster parents. I explained at the outset that we did not wish to persuade them to keep George but felt the need to get the full benefit of their experience with him so that we could have a better understanding of the boy and his situation. If

their minds were not completely made up and they wanted to consider trying further with George, we would certainly wish to explore this with them. In that connection, we could also consider the possibility of my meeting regularly with George so that I would be of direct help to him. The foster parents brought out all of their frustrations about George and their fear that in due time he could become physically assaultive to the other members of the family. They had the specter of George becoming a full-blown delinquent when he becomes an adolescent. The child welfare worker and I were understanding and accepting of their predicament and their inclination to surrender George. They were still in conflict about whether or not to give up with George but, a few days later, decided that they would try further with my direct intervention.

When I met with George, it was apparent that he was not a verbal child, capable of expressing his feelings. I drew him out as much as I could but, for the most part, I put into words what I thought his feelings really were. I knew previously that George was aware of the fact that his foster parents had decided to have him leave their home and told him that I knew all about this. With much empathy, I talked about George's upset feelings about his father and stepmother not visiting him, and more basically about his not being able to live with them. George displayed through the tears that welled up in his eyes that I was in tune with his feelings.

I then asked George if he wished to stay with the foster parents and opened up for consideration the possibility that he might not really care for them and might prefer living in another setting. Perhaps this might even be better for George, I added, if there was not much left in their relationship. George said that this was not so, that he did care for the foster parents and they cared for him, and that he really wanted to stay. I proceeded to explain that it was now mostly up to George. He was able to specify the ways in which he had been behaving at home and in school which caused the foster parents to think in terms of giving him up. I asked George if there was something he could do about this, and he felt that he could. I explained that I wanted to help him. We would meet together each week and talk over what was happening in the foster home and in school; I would be in close touch with his worker, the foster parents and the school, so that I could let him know what they were observing and experiencing too; and we could also play together. I took a liking to George and he to me in that first hour. The positive relationship grew as we continued to meet.

George made very noticeable efforts to get along better in the foster home and in school. There were some critical points along the way when he tended to slip back, but the overall trend was one of significant change for the better. The foster parents decided to keep George with them. This added to the boy's feeling of security within the foster family.

Early in the treatment process, the child welfare worker and I met with the father and stepmother, helping them understand the importance of maintaining consistent contact with George. We also had a conference with the school principal and teacher so that all of us worked together as a team.

Problem-Solving Work in Vignette Above: One aspect of problem solving was the worker's carrying the case jointly with the child welfare worker. The problem-solving approach to the foster parents consisted of extending acceptance and understanding to them and giving them the feeling that whatever decision they made—either to keep George or to give him up—would meet with our approval. Indeed, the two workers gave them much commendation and recognition for their five-year investment in George which truly represented a major contribution to his growing up, even though at the moment his behavior difficulties seemed to overshadow everything. In regard to the treatment process with George, the worker felt that he had to discuss forthrightly and di-

rectly with him the fact that he was responsible for his own behavior, which was causing the foster parents to move in the direction of having him placed elsewhere. Workers generally shy away from this kind of direct approach with young children, who cannot always be shielded from responsibility for problems they themselves create and which to a large extent they can solve. Finally, the father, the stepmother and the school were drawn into the total problem-solving and treatment effort.

5. Problems in Juvenile Delinquency

Vignette: Characterological Delinquency—Larceny in a Fifteen-year-old Boy. Jim was apprehended in family court and placed on probation because he was caught by the police with fairly expensive machine tools. He had stolen them from a store into which he had broken and entered. To the knowledge of the authorities and the parents, this was Jim's first transgression.

The initial interview was with the parents and Jim. They brought out additional problems that Jim had had: his being suspended from school for frequent fighting; his poor cooperation at home; and his remaining away from the family beyond reasonable hours. Exploring the family relationships not only in the present but in the past, I learned that these had not achieved much depth and that for circumstantial reasons there was much emotional deprivation in Jim's life. Jim seemed to be on his guard in the family interview. I, therefore, met alone with him as part of the same hour.

Jim at once opened up with me. He confided that the theft of the machine tools was only one of a long series of thefts over the past several years. He and a friend would sell their stolen goods and made a substantial amount of money as a result. When I explored with Jim the various dynamic possibilities that might underlie the stealing, Jim could see no connections. He felt that it had nothing to do with his parents or his family in general. "I wanted the money," was the explanation he gave again and again. Jim would also engage in petty stealing—e.g., cigarettes—and once again his explanation was similar: "I wanted it."

Jim had asked me not to reveal the secrets about which he told me, and I gave my assurance that I would not do so. I asked Jim if he wanted to do anything about the problem of stealing. He replied that he really does; that he does not want to end up in jail. He proceeded to say that it is going to be hard for him to "break the habit" but he wants to try. He was interested in my being of help to him in this regard. He liked talking with me. I supported Jim in his desire to try to give up the stealing, agreeing that it could lead eventually to his being sent to jail. As we met each week, Jim told me with some pride about the many opportunities he had to steal and how he resisted these temptations. When he succumbed to temptation, he told me about this as well.

At one point in the treatment process, Jim expressed his anger about his inability to talk with his father: "My father always cuts me off; always knows the answers, and does not let me tell him what's on my mind." The father was also quick to doubt and disbelieve Jim even when Jim would be telling the truth. When I suggested that Jim, his father and I discuss this problem, Jim at first refused but when I offered to meet alone with the father, acting as Jim's spokesman, he thought it better to express his feelings directly to his father. The joint interview that followed achieved the desired result. The father could see that Jim was right, and both decided that they would work on this problem together at home.

Problem-Solving Work in Vignette Above: In the worker's problem-solving approach to Jim's delinquency, he first had to assess diagnostically its essential nature. Was it a form of acting-out behavior against the parents? Was it a symptom of some deep psychopathology? Was it characterological in nature—i.e., poor impulse control, inability to postpone

gratifications, narcissism, weak superego development, poor reality testing, etc.? When the worker came to the conclusion that Jim's problem was predominantly characterological, it followed from this that constructive use could be made of the authoritative control that the family court had begun to exert upon the boy. The worker felt it was justifiable to make use of Jim's fear of eventually going to jail as a lever to encourage him to give up his self-destructive delinquent behavior. Because of the earlier emotional deprivation, Jim's psychosocial development had been arrested or slowed down. Providing the relationship experience with the worker and helping father and son to come closer together in their relationship were seen to be ways of making up some lost ground in Jim's emotional and psychological maturation.

Vignette: Neurotic Delinquency— Sixteen-year-old Boy Involved in Gang Fights. David had been taking a central part in brutal and violent gang fights and was brought into court for resisting arrest. His sister and brother-in-law engaged and paid for extensive legal help, which resulted in the case being dismissed. The sister and brother-in-law had recently obtained custody of David from the natural mother and stepfather, from whose home he had run away several times. The stepfather was misusing funds which belonged to David resulting from the war death of his father, at which time David was three years old. The sister and brother-in-law prevailed upon him to come to the clinic. They were concerned not only about his gang activity but about his being depressed and suicidal. They sensed that David was full of angry feelings, mostly stemming from mistreatment by his mother and stepfather, and that he was suppressing these feelings. David would scarcely communicate with his sister and brother-in-law. They became alarmed when David put a loaded gun in his mouth, toying with the idea of killing himself. David resisted coming to the clinic because he had thoughts that maybe he was going crazy and this would be discovered.

In the initial family session with David, his sister and brother-in-law, much of his emotional problems as described above were brought to the fore and elaborated upon by all. I made the diagnostic determination that David's delinquent activity with gangs was symptomatic of an intrapsychic disturbance—suppressed anger, depression and suicidal tendencies. The family session had the effect of David and his relatives talking with each other about important feelings and problems for the first time. Nevertheless, I explored with them whether they wished to continue these family sessions or have me and David meet together in an individualized process. The decision was left to David, and he preferred meeting just with me.

In subsequent interviews, he told me much about the frustration and anger he experienced with his mother and stepfather and how this led him to run away. He realized, with my help, that the running away represented both an attempt to get back at his parents, but also to shock them into caring more for him. He went into the gang fights and what this meant to him—getting a sense of enjoyment and fulfillment out of beating up other youngsters. He came to realize, in our discussion, that he would really like to beat up his mother and stepfather. When problems came to the fore about David's relationship with his sister and brother-in-law, he agreed with my suggestion that we resume having sessions with them as well. The course of treatment consisted of individual sessions with David as well as family sessions to include his relatives.

Problem-Solving Work in Vignette Above: David's problems had some characterological elements, but for the most part they were intrapsychic in nature in terms of an underlying depression and suicidal inclinations. The problem-solving approach was that of treating the underlying pathology and not the symptoms of delinquency. This was done through a combination of individual and family therapy.

6.   Problems of Clients with Internalized Emotional Disturbances

Vignette: Depression and Nonfunctioning in a Young Man. Bob, age twenty-three, became deeply upset and depressed when he discovered that his wife was having an affair with another man. Blaming himself and finding rationalizations for his wife's behavior, he denied having any anger toward her. He slept and ate poorly, gave up his job and depended upon his parents for financial support. He ruminated in an obsessive way about the earlier apparent happiness with his wife and the love that he had felt and stills feels for her.

Treatment over several months consisted of helping Bob bring out the repressed intense anger against his wife and grapple with the conflict of whether or not to work toward a reconciliation. Part of his conflict was also in relation to their one-year-old child, for whom he cared deeply. Gradually, the depression lifted but the passivity and dependence persisted. When I would broach the subject of his considering finding work or completing his college education, this would be met with intellectual concurrence but no action.

Consequently, I confronted Bob strongly. I gave full recognition to the great distress in which he had found himself and with which he was still struggling in relation to his wife's unfaithfulness to him and the blow that this represented to his self-esteem, with resultant feelings of inadequacy. In the course of treatment, I continued, Bob had done a good deal of work in regard to his feelings about himself as an individual, his feelings of inadequacy, particularly in regard to sex, his long-standing resentments and rebellious feelings against his parents and his slowly coming to the realization that he had built up an idealized image of his wife and was now seeing her as a person for whom he could no longer have feelings of love and respect. I then told Bob forthrightly that if he was to make further progress he would now have to break out of the rut of being passive and dependent in relation to his parents, that he would have to start functioning once again. To remain passively inactive, I pointed out, would ultimately result in a deterioration of his emotional and mental stability and health. It was time, I stressed, for him to start living again—to work, study, if this is what he wants, to meet people, develop friendships with men and women, and so on. The confrontation was a turning point.

Problem-Solving Work in Vignette Above: The worker's treatment efforts up to the point of the confrontation were valid and helpful. Bob had made substantial progress in sorting out and working through basic feelings in relation to his marriage, his child, himself as an individual and his parents. The problem facing the worker was: Would Bob move out of his dependent and passive state in due time as a result of this progress? As the worker observed that Bob was on a plateau, he came to the conclusion that further progress—in terms of Bob's getting back into the mainstream of life—would not automatically ensue. Hence, the confrontation.

7. Environmental Problems: Intervention in Behalf of the Client

The following vignettes illustrate the application of certain problem-solving principles. In making the decision to intervene on behalf of the client with respect to environmental problems, the caseworker must determine in his own mind whether or not the client has the ego strength independently to take the required steps to alter the environmental situation; whether or not the outside persons in authoritative positions would pay attention to the client; and whether or not the worker's intervention would be consonant with, and enhance, the treatment process. Because these principles are self-evident in the vignettes, there will not be separate discussion of them.

Vignette: Helping a Mother Gain Acceptance into a Training Program. Mrs. T. was in casework treatment because of the emotional disturbance in her eight-year-old son. The child was born out of wedlock, and the father had deserted them. The mother had withdrawn from social relations with others, particularly men. She had need for male companionship and eventual marriage but was afraid of getting hurt once more. She had been channeling her energies into the relationship with her son, overprotecting him to a great extent. Moreover, she would displace upon him her personal frustrations. A central theme in the treatment process was that of helping the mother to become aware of the overprotection and displacement problems and to fulfill her personal needs for male and female companionship.

Mrs. T. had an opportunity to enter a training program offered by the welfare department so that she could become self-supporting. I viewed this as a potential enhancement of the treatment process. With my encouragement, Mrs. T. took the necessary steps toward making an application for this training program but the authorities procrastinated and then were about to reject her. I encouraged Mrs. T. to talk with the authorities. She did so, but their attitude remained negative. I then asked Mrs. T. if she would like me to intercede for her. With her eager consent, I talked with the man in charge. I explained the importance of Mrs. T. being given the opportunity to undergo this training, in relation to the purposes for which she and her son were coming to the clinic. Further, I conveyed my impression that Mrs. T., an intelligent individual, would most likely succeed in the training. Mrs. T. was then accepted.

Vignette: Mother's Application for Housing Project Admittance, Rejected. I was seeing Mrs. S. and her nine-year-old son in a combination of family and individual treatment. Divorced from her husband, Mrs. S. was raising four children and was also engaged in a welfare department training program. A major theme in the treatment process was her gaining insight into the ways in which she was contributing to her son's emotional disturbance. She was able to alter her feelings and relationship with him, thereby contributing to the boy's progress.

From time to time Mrs. S. would become overwhelmed by her life situation and would discuss the specific problems with me in this regard. One of these was an urgent need to move out of the inner city because of gangland violence, including a murder in the immediate vicinity. She had accordingly filed an application with the governmental housing authority. An opening in a particular housing project occurred; she immediately went to the manager to work out the arrangements, but was told that she had to move immediately. When she explained that she would need a few weeks' time, because she had to find a babysitter for her young children and because otherwise her training program would be disrupted, she was flatly told that she would lose her opportunity for admission to the housing project.

When Mrs. S. told me what happened, I asked if she would like me to call the manager. She consented at once. I talked with the manager but, despite all my efforts, he steadfastly held to the rules about immediate occupancy. I then telephoned the person in higher authority and explained the situation to him. This resulted in his prevailing upon the manager to give the client the additional time she needed to move into the project.

Vignette: Legal Action Against a Mother for Impulsive Acting-out Behavior. I was involved in a long-term treatment process with Mrs. C. An intelligent and capable person, she nevertheless felt herself to be worthless. She was involved in a common-law relationship with a man who had sado-masochistic characteristics. Despite the fact that they would have violent physical fights from time to time, they remained together.

One of the threads of a complicated treatment process, in which the transference dynamics were a major component, was my working with Mrs. C. on her drinking problem and the violently aggressive, destructive outbursts that she would have when intoxicated. There was a marked reduction in the drinking and in the impulsive outbursts.

However, one night she was in a restaurant with her common-law husband; they had been drinking; they had a quarrel; and Mrs. C. went on a rampage, breaking dishes, smashing chairs and tearing pictures off the wall. The restaurant keeper filed an official complaint and Mrs. C. was summoned to court. She urgently called me, asking if I could do anything to prevent her from being arraigned before the judge. I decided that Mrs. C. could not handle this herself and that my intervention was necessary because a heavy fine or imprisonment would have a devastating effect on her. With Mrs. C.'s permission, I went to the restaurant and talked with the owner who had filed the complaint. He had known Mrs. C. in the past and was glad to learn that she was receiving professional help. A reasonable and understanding person, who at one time in his life needed and benefited from psychiatric care, he accepted my suggestion that he withdraw his charges and allow Mrs. C. further opportunity to work on her problems.

8.   Problems with Respect to Future Planning and Direction

Vignette: Dilemma in a Sixteen-year-old Boy About Dropping Out of School. I had been working with Ed ever since he was eight years old. Because of a chaotic family situation, he had suffered a good deal of emotional deprivation. His problems were primarily characterological. One recurrent major problem was his being the leader of a delinquent gang and his having gained the reputation of being unbeatable in fist fights. His preeminence in this regard was constantly challenged in much the same way as this occurs in western movies. My relationship with Ed had much significance to him in a transference sense; perhaps I was a father figure. The treatment process was continuous for the first two years. Thereafter, Ed would turn to me from time to time whenever he found himself in a critical predicament or needed some help with a problem.

He came to me with the problem of whether or not he should drop out of school, which now would be legally permissible. I drew Ed out on his own feelings and ideas, but he was unable to resolve his conflict. I then proceeded to give Ed my point of view: "I'll tell you what I think, Ed. You should quit school. You're still at the fourth grade level and you don't have a prayer of catching up. Besides, you hate school and you've been suspended and expelled once or twice every year. You are strong, you like to work, and I think it would be far better to leave and get a job. After a while, you may want to go to night school to get your elementary school diploma and some vocational training. Also, there is a way of getting apprenticeship training. I can tell you about it if you are interested."

Problem-Solving Work in Vignette Above: The worker's approach to this specific problem was first to turn it back to the boy, stimulating him to think it through himself. When the worker saw that the boy could not resolve the issue, he presented his own views. It was a frank and forthright appraisal of the problem, but the decision was left with the boy.

Vignette: A Man in Conflict About Remarriage. Mr. J. came to see me because he was in conflict about marrying a woman with whom he had fallen in love and she with him. His three boys, aged ten to fifteen years, were living with their mother from whom he was divorced.

I had Mr. J. tell me fully about the relationship with the woman in question. Although they loved each other, he was not sure the marriage would work out successfully, because she was a dominating person. Mr. J. was also very much in conflict about his three boys, with whom he maintained a rather close relationship. To remarry would mean his moving to another part of the country, far away from his sons. He asserted that his first loyalty was to them.

My approach in the two sessions I had with Mr. J. was that of having him struggle with his conflicts. He seemed to resolve them for himself but asked me point-blank what I thought. I put into words what I felt he himself had come to: that his first loyalty was to his sons, and he did not want to weaken that relationship; and that he had some negative feelings about the new woman in his life and some real doubts that the marriage would work out successfully. It therefore seemed to me, I said, that Mr. J. had virtually come to the conclusion himself that remarriage to this woman at this time was not what he really wanted.

Problem-Solving Work in Vignette Above: The worker in this situation essentially rendered a consultation service to the client. He withheld until the very end rendering his own opinion and, in so doing, merely put into other words the conclusions to which the client himself had come. Yet, it also had the quality of independent thinking and recommendation on the worker's part.

Summary of problem-solving concepts

1.   Definition of Problem Solving

Tangible and discrete problems that the client brings to the worker can be taken at face value; the worker may discern additional related problems and bring them to the fore. Problem-solving work is mostly on a rational level, but the worker also helps the client with feelings that impair his ability to deal with the problems at hand—e.g., anxiety, conflict, resistance. He encourages the client to do the problem-solving work to the fullest possible extent. When the limits of this are reached, he contributes his own thinking and suggestions. The worker tries to leave the client with the feeling that he has carried the responsibility, and has done the major part of the work in achieving the ultimate decision or resolution.

Problem-solving work on discrete and tangible problems can take place without words, i.e., without discussion. These problems have been verbally defined, when it was understood that sooner or later they will require solution. However, the worker's helping the client with underlying emotional disturbances and feelings and therapeutically meeting his emotional needs enables him independently to go on to solve the problems.

An enormous amount of problem-solving activity goes on in the privacy of the worker's mind during both the course of the interview itself and before, after and between interviews. A few of the many major questions that cross the worker's mind in the course of an interview may be: Is the verbalized problem the real one? Did the client really feel like meeting with me, or did he come because of external pressure? The client seems unhappy and depressed—should I comment upon this and encourage him to talk about his upset feelings, which may not be germane to his primary reasons for coming to see me? The client seems angry and resistive—should I comment on this now or continue to draw him out on the problems about which he came? I am feeling anger or annoyance at the client, should I express this, tying it in with his problem? I am feeling repelled by the client because of his reprehensible behavior or qualities—e.g., incest, prostitution—how can I resolve such feelings?

Then there are the countless other miniature questions: Should I put what I have to say in the form of a question or a comment? Should I allow the heated interchanges between the family members to go on, or should I intervene? Should I allow for silence in the interview or try to stimulate further expression on the part of the client? Should I open the interview by keeping quiet and waiting for the client to take the initiative, or should I make the opening statement? If so, should it be something specific or general? All of these major and minor questions that enter the worker's mind require rapid thinking and decision making on his part—problem solving. In this internal problem-solving work, the worker shifts, sorts, differentiates, analyzes, evaluates and synthesizes a multitude of stimuli, communications and pieces of information that emanate from the client, gearing all of this into that which he already knows and understands about him. And yet, at the same time, the worker has to be sensitive to the client's feelings, to be in tune with him emotionally and to be warm, giving and empathetic. The considerable amount of thinking that the worker must do while with a client should not and must not impair the naturalness and spontaneity of his self-expression and his giving of himself emotionally. This is a tall order.

2. The Contexts in Which Problem Solving Takes Place

The worker tries to discern the full range of problems besetting the client and to gain a diagnostic and dynamic understanding about their origins and current manifestations. The presenting problems may have their roots in deeper ones. The worker then tries to define with the client the particular problems for which he wants the worker's help. The two then reach an understanding about what they will work on together. Of course, this understanding often cannot be explicit. Moreover, as the casework relationship develops, the client may decide to enter problem areas which he had previously ruled out of consideration.

Based upon his diagnostic understanding of the client, the worker formulates in his own mind the essential nature of the treatment dynamics and process. It is in this context that problem-solving work takes place. Problem solving, therefore, is not an independent entity but a function of basic casework treatment. Similarly, it is an outgrowth of the client expressing and dealing therapeutically with deep-level feelings about himself and those close to him, such as parents, spouse and children, about whom he is troubled. Conversely, a beginning focus upon specific problems may be a necessary step for getting into vital deep-level feelings.

The problem-solving work is done at the level of conscious awareness and with an orientation to the client's reality situation. The developing relationship between the worker and the client can contain unconscious transference elements. More often than not, it is sufficient only for the worker to be aware of the transference and nonverbally to make use of it. On occasion, it may be necessary to talk about it.

3. The Assertive Counseling Component

The worker's capacity to use himself to the fullest extent possible in problem-solving work with the client requires a philosophic and attitudinal disposition to assert himself interactively with the client when this can be therapeutically helpful.

The client who is capable of insightful self-exploration and who is able to translate this into positive action, does not need assertive interventions by the worker. Yet, even such self-reliant clients may genuinely want the worker's point of view on a given issue or some specific suggestions. By complying with the request, the worker would not be detracting from the client's strong tendencies to be self-reliant and independent. That is, the worker would be providing his own perceptions and thinking to which the client would react in the process of working out his own solution to the particular problem at hand.

A great many clients do not have much capacity for self-exploration and insight; are confused and overwhelmed by their inner emotional disturbance and/or extremely stressful environmental situations; and do not have sufficient ego strength to solve particular problems and issues without a substantial amount of help from the worker. He helps the client face and think through the problems and issues that require resolution. He may do this by raising questions, by suggesting approaches, by posing alternatives, by judiciously using confrontation and occasionally by offering some definite advice.

Whatever the form of the worker's self-assertion may be, its essential quality engenders genuine respect and caring for the client, making it very clear that the ultimate responsibility in decision making is the client's.

4. Problem Solving in Relationship Conflicts

In conflicts between a parent and a child, between several members of the family and between marital pairs, the worker first determines diagnostically whether the locus of the problem lies within a particular individual or if it is truly a mutual problem between the persons concerned. This diagnostic differentiation determines the treatment approach of choice—a problem which the worker must solve for himself, usually with the participation of the client.

When the treatment modality is that of meeting with two or more persons in order to help them with their relationship conflicts, the worker develops several aspects of the treatment process which are generally intertwined. He helps the participants to bring out into the open their feelings toward each other; helps them now to reach each other with respect to these feelings at the levels of mutual compassion and understanding; helps them gain a dynamic perspective about how the conflicts came into being and how they have subsequently become intensified; and, finally, helps them find new and more constructive ways of relating to each other. The worker develops the treatment process, over time. The participants work through deep feelings of pain, anger, mistrust and unhappiness and increasingly devote their energies to specific problems that must be resolved if they are to come closer together in their relationship. Conversely, the worker may help the participants come to the realization that the breakdowns in the relationships are ir-reparable—as may be the case in chronic marital situations—and reach the point where they can separate from each other.

The primary problem-solving task is to help the participants find for themselves the direction they wish to take: either to build the relationship or to terminate it temporarily or permanently. In relationship conflicts between parents and children, the course they almost invariably take is that of building the relationship. In marital conflict situations, the direction decided upon after they have been helped by the worker honestly to face their deeper feelings toward each other may be either to rebuild or to separate. Once the course and direction are set, the client is helped to work upon reality problems along the way.

5. Problem Solving in Individual Treatment

With respect to the treatment of emotional disturbances in individuals, a large part of the worker's problem-solving work takes place in his own mind. He tries to determine diagnostically the nature, origins, depth and dynamics of the disturbance. From this, he conceptualizes the kind of treatment approach and process to be developed if he is to be of therapeutic help. It is not totally a unilateral problem-solving effort because, to a considerable extent, the worker engages the client's participation, especially in the area of understanding and insight. The worker may formulate verbally the treatment plan in order to arrive at a mutual agreement about whether or not to undertake it. Beyond this agreement, the worker may encounter problems of resistance: conflict between himself and the client, discouragement and wish to end treatment prematurely on the part of the client, etc. Such problems have to be recognized, brought to the fore and discussed with the client.

The client may be distressed and perplexed about not making progress in treatment with respect to such incapacitating aspects of his disturbance as depression, anxiety, feelings of inadequacy and the like. Continuing to turn his questions about this back to him has validity up to a point. It may then be necessary for the worker to make some direct interpretation; or to resort to confrontation; or just to wait, providing a good deal of empathy and support. These are problem-solving decisions which the worker must make when encountering apparent im-passes in the treatment process.

As the client gains in self-understanding and works through deep and complex feelings about himself, his original presenting problems and symptoms may disappear and his function-ing may generally improve. On the other hand, this may not occur. It may be necessary for the worker to help the client in a direct fashion to make the transition from understanding to ac-tion. This may consist of the worker taking the initiative of pointing out the need for the client to surmount this vital hurdle, raising for his con-sideration specific problems with which he must deal or, on occasion, resorting to direct confron-tation when the gentler approaches prove not to have sufficient impact.

6. Problem Solving with Respect to Symptomatic Behavior

A sharply focused, problem-solving ap-proach to specific behaviors is often valid and ef-fective in the treatment of relationship conflicts. Within the family, for example, the behaviors on the part of parents and children may have to undergo a change for the better if the vicious cy-cle breakdown in their relationship is ever to be broken. The vicious cycle may persist despite the fact that the dynamics have been fully ex-plored and understood and that there has been considerable expression and discussion of the negative and angry feelings involved. The worker would then move to a concentration upon the continuing behavioral manifestations of the disturbed relationships.

The worker and family members together spell out what each must concretely do to change the behavior. The worker shows what the beneficial effects of this would be in terms of better feelings coming about in the relationship. He would explain the child's need for love and affection from his parents, for example, which would be forthcoming if the child would cease to behave in the ways that are so distressing and annoying to the parents. Conversely, he would help the parents determine the specific ways in which their behaviors toward the child would concomitantly have to change. The worker also makes conscious use of his positive relationship with the particular family members. In his own mind, he reasons that because they like him and trust him they may respond positively to his suggestions in order to please him.

The foregoing principles constitute the theoretical rationale for the use of the specific behaviors chart. A systematic method of monitoring unacceptable behavior can be a useful device, not only to check upon whether or not change is taking place, but to provide a medium in which the family members can review and discuss the recorded ratings and the happenings during the day upon which they are based. Material rewards are not used. The basic motivation would be for the child to want to please the parents and the therapist to break the vicious cycle relationship breakdown and for parents and child to win each other's love. This specific behaviors chart can be most effective with young children in individual and family treatment processes, and also when conducted by the teacher and the child in the classroom with the worker's involvement.

A sharp problem-solving focus upon antisocial behaviors beyond the family is also essential in crisis situations brought on by the individual being apprehended by law-enforcement authorities. It can also be valuable in noncrisis situations when it is already clear that the an-

tisocial behavior is destructive in the sense that the client eventually will be apprehended by the law-enforcement agencies, to say nothing of the harm done to the people against whom the delinquent acts were committed.

A problem-solving focus upon specific behaviors in marital and intrafamilial conflicts and conflicts between the client and society, is especially indicated for character-disordered individuals whose ego, superego and general maturational development has been impaired.

7. Broadening the Treatment Team

The worker can enhance the problem-solving and general treatment process by drawing other professional persons beyond the agency into the treatment program.

For example, if a child's problems are manifested in the school as well as in the home, the teacher and other members of the faculty can play a vital therapeutic role in collaboration with the worker. To make full use of this potential therapeutic resource, the worker must overcome resistances and blind spots that he might have in order to take the initiative and perhaps provide the leadership for creating and developing a broader team effort. In addition to conferences with the school faculty members, unimpeded and systematic telephone communication between the worker and the teacher is essential. The worker would first discuss with the client his desire to work with the school and gain his approval. The specifics of the collaborative relationship would also have to be spelled out to the client. The worker would bring into the interview with the client the significant information he has gained from the school. In crisis situations, the worker might talk directly with the child in the school setting or with the teacher, via the telephone, in the child's presence.

The same principles and procedures would be applicable to involving the probation officer, the physician, the clergyman and other significant professional persons in the life of the client, in a broadened treatment program.

8.   Environmental Problems in Need of Solution

In the course of treatment, the client may encounter environmental problems which may be peripheral to the purposes for which he originally came to the agency for help; or, conversely, constitute a major causal component. When a particular environmental problem comes to the fore, the worker determines in his own mind, as well as in discussion with the client, whether or not it is within his power to do anything about it. If so, he has to come to grips with such questions as: Can the client handle the problem himself with support and encouragement by the worker? If not, would it be therapeutically helpful to intervene on the client's behalf? If the worker decides that his intervention is essential, he would do so with the full participation and consent of the client, allowing the latter to take as much responsibility as possible for this kind of decision. The interventions may consist of the worker taking action by telephone, letter or meetings with persons in positions of power and authority.

Pitfalls and Counterindications

The foregoing problem-solving concepts contain, by implication, several pitfalls and counterindications which should be made more explicit. The major ones are as follows:

1.   Problem solving, as previously stated, is not a treatment modality but rather an integrated component of treatment processes, whatever the particular modality may be. When problem solving is done out of this context, harm to the client and treatment setbacks can occur. For example, at one point in the treatment process, the worker referred a young woman for vocational counseling. Her poor self-image was a significant area in the treatment process. The worker tried to interpret this to the vocational counselor, but it was misapplied. The counselor advised her to take a course in beauty culture to gain a better feeling about herself and to prepare herself for job-seeking activity later on. This had a devastating effect upon the client. It confirmed for her the conception she had of herself as being an ugly and unattractive person. This was out of context with the treatment process. The worker had been making progress in helping the client come to realize that there was a great disparity between her self-concept and the reality of her being a lovely and attractive young lady. At a deeper level, the worker had been helping her work through feelings of being a bad and worthless person, which stemmed from early and more recent life experiences. This example is not to be construed as critical of vocational counseling; it can happen in casework treatment as well.

2.   The worker should not intrude upon the problem-solving work that the client is doing on his own as a function of coming to grips with deeper psychological and emotional conflicts. For example, the worker made an interpretation to a depressed, middle-aged woman who had become unable to continue her work and support herself economically. This was to the effect that she was angry about, and rebelling against, having had to carry a great deal of responsibility as a child in her family and having to do the same for herself for many years after her divorce from her husband. She had decided subconsciously, the worker added, that at long last she was going to have her relatives take care of her. This hit home. The client accepted the interpretation and proceeded to plan toward becoming independent once again, doing the problem-solving work in this regard with minimal help from the worker. Once she became angry at the worker for proposing a solution to a specific problem, asserting that she wanted to do it herself!

3.   There is a fine line between judiciously stimulating and guiding problem-solving work on the part of the client and the worker's doing this for him. Stepping over this fine line can at the very least be unhelpful and, at the worst, harmful. An example of this fine line can be seen in the worker's trying to help a young man with his conflict about committing himself fully to his girlfriend through engagement and eventual marriage. The worker had to become aware first of his own subjective feeling that it would be good for the client to so commit himself; that the client's girlfriend could meet effectively his relationship and sexual needs. The worker had to struggle against his own strong impulse to advise and persuade the client to make a decision that would be "good" for him. The worker was able, however, to control this impulse and relate instead to the client's conflict. His focus was that of helping the client separate out his real underlying feelings from a pattern of intricate intellectualizations which had been a problem for this young man in other aspects of his life and in the treatment process itself. Essentially, therefore, the worker helped the client define the conflict and the issues within it; helped him become more clearly aware of his feelings in contrast to intellectual processes; and left the responsibility for resolving or not resolving the conflict with the client. To have imposed his will upon the client, which the latter might have accepted, would have been potentially damaging and dangerous because he would have entered into a full relationship with his friend without fully dealing with the conflict that might eventually destroy that relationship.

Summary

Problem-solving theory reported in the literature was reviewed and then new concepts were added. Putting it all together, it would seem that discrete problems presented by the client in the course of treatment require diagnostic assessment by the worker: Can they be taken at face value? Do they represent defen-sive, diversionary maneuvers to shield more personal and sensitive problems from the worker? Are they symptomatic of deeper and more extensive emotionally incapacitating problems and conflicts? These and innumerable other questions of a diagnostic, treatment, strategic and tactical nature require continual problem-solving work on the part of the worker in the privacy of his own mind or in interactive discussion with the client. The definition of problem solving is consequently a broad one which includes not only direct work with the client in this regard, but unilateral, internal problem-solving activity by the worker. Problem-solving work is woven through the continuum of diagnosis and treatment, whether this be in individual, multiple or family interviewing. That is, problem-solving work should take place in the context of the individual's or family's underlying problems, conflicts and upset feelings—i.e., as an integral part of the treatment dynamics and process. The flow can be from deeper levels of disturbance to the problem-solving level or vice versa. To use himself to the fullest possible extent in the problem-solving dimension, the worker's philosophic and attitudinal orientation should contain an ability to assert himself with a client—i.e., an assertive counseling component in treatment enhances problem-solving work. These and other concepts in problem-solving theory were elucidated. Some pitfalls and counterindications were also presented and discussed. Case vignettes were used to illustrate the application of problem-solving concepts in various treatment areas: intrafamilial relationship problems; problems between a parent and a child; marital problems; school and home behavior problems; problems in juvenile delinquency; problems of individual clients with internalized emotional disturbances; environmental problems which may require intervention on behalf of the client; and problems with respect to future planning and direction.

References

1. Betz, E. J. "The Problem Solving Approach and Therapeutic Effectiveness," *American Journal of Psychotherapy*, 1966, 20 (1), 45-56.
2. Haley, J. *Problem Solving Therapy: New Strategies for Effective Family Therapy*. San Francisco: Jossey-Bass, 1976.
3. Hallowitz, D. "The Problem Solving Component in Family Therapy," *Social Casework*, 1970, 51 (February), 67-75.
4. ———, R. Bierman, G. P. Harrison and B. Stulberg. "The Assertive Counseling Component of Therapy," *Social Casework*, 1967, 48 (November), 543-548.
5. ———, and B. Stulberg. "The Vicious Cycle in Parent-Child Relationship Breakdown," *Social Casework*, 1959, 40 (May), 268-275.
6. Hamilton, G. *Theory and Practice of Social Casework*. New York: Columbia University Press, 1940.
7. Hollis, F. *Casework: A Psycho-Social Therapy*. New York: Random House, 1969.
8. Perlman, H. H. *Social Casework: A Problem Solving Process*. Chicago: University of Chicago Press, 1957.
9. ———. "Social Casework: The Problem-Solving Approach," in *Encyclopedia of Social Work*, Vol. II. New York: National Association of Social Workers, 1971, pp. 1206-1216.
10. ———. *Perspectives in Casework*. Philadelphia: Temple University Press, 1971.
11. Spitzer, K., and B. Welsh. "A Problem Focused Model of Practice," *Social Casework*, 1969, 50 (June), 323-329.
12. Spivack, G., J. Platt and M. Shure. *The Problem Solving Approach to Adjustment, A Guide to Research and Intervention*. San Francisco: Jossey-Bass, 1976.

Annotated listing of key references

BETZ, Barbara J. "The Problem Solving Approach and Therapeutic Effectiveness," *American Journal of Psychotherapy,* 1966, 20 (1), 45–56.
Psychotherapy is essentially a problem-solving process. Good results are equated with the successful resolution of crucial, underlying problems accurately recognized from the start. The problems considered in this paper are those that pertain to diagnostic and dynamic clinical issues. Working hypotheses are derived therefrom. The therapist's personality is seen as a therapeutic variable. The author discusses these concepts in relation to therapy with psychotic patients, especially schizophrenics.

HALEY, J. *Problem Solving Therapy: New Strategies for Effective Family Therapy.* San Francisco: Jossey-Bass, 1976.
Haley's problem-solving approach to therapy focuses on "solving a client's presenting problems within the framework of the family. The emphasis is not on a method but on approaching each problem with special techniques for the specific situation. The therapist's task is to formulate a presenting symptom clearly and to design an intervention in the client's social situation to change that presenting symptom. Although the book focuses on problems, the approach here differs from other symptom oriented therapies in that it emphasizes the social context of human problems."

The therapeutic focus is on the social situation rather than on the person. Problems are viewed as a "type of behavior that is part of a sequence of acts between several people." The therapist must view himself as part of the "social unit that contains the problem. The therapist must be considered as part of the social dilemma of the client . . . . A presenting problem includes the professional world in which the problem appears, as well as the larger society."

The therapist's task is to "define the social unit that he can change to solve the presenting problem of a client." The therapist must recognize that any situation contains the potential for a better arrangement for the client. The therapist must be able to formulate problems and plan for intervention in human relationships to solve these problems.

Haley presents "simplistic formulations of social situations that can help a therapist recognize typical interchanges and determine what to do."

HALLOWITZ, D. "The Problem-Solving Component in Family Therapy," *Social Casework,* 1970, 51 (February), 67–75.
Family therapy usually has a practical and realistic problem-solving component that is embedded in and grows out of deeper-level discussion of breakdowns and conflicts in intrafamilial relationships. The therapist provides guidance and leadership in helping the family members work out different

ways of handling issues that have previously driven them apart. This is integrally connected with the family therapy process. The problems brought into the therapy situation and the family's efforts to cope with them constitute the medium through which the positive and negative feelings, misunderstandings and conflicts in the relationships are expressed. The problem-solving component contributes to the development of better understanding and feeling in the family relationships, and this development in turn generates even more productive problem-solving work.

HALLOWITZ, D., R. Bierman, G. P. Harrison and B. Stulberg. "The Assertive Counseling Component of Therapy," *Social Casework*, 1967, 48 (November), 543–548.

The component of assertive counseling is developed and applied in the context of a positive therapeutic relationship. The following are essential: (1) Crisis Intervention—the therapist tries to bring a halt to the unbridled mutual destructiveness in families. (2) Confrontation—the therapist points out the disparities between the client's perception and objective reality. (3) Acceptance of responsibility—he expresses his observations and understanding in a direct manner and takes a stand when necessary on vital issues, leaving the decision making to the client. (4) Active direction-finding—the therapist helps the client formulate objectives for himself. (5) Direction-implementation— he suggests that decisions and specific steps be implemented during the period between interviews. The assertive counseling component is embedded within generic treatment methods and processes and requires a high level of skill, creativity, sensitivity and judgment.

HALLOWITZ, D., and Burton Stulberg. "The Vicious Cycle in Parent-Child Relationship Breakdown," *Social Casework*, 1959, 40 (May), 268–275.

Regardless of the specific diagnosis of a child's emotional disturbance, an element almost invariably present is the child's feeling of being rejected. This paper does not deal with the devastating effects of total and frank parental rejection, but with the effects of other forms of rejection: partial rejection accompanied by a substantial component of parental love; and the impairment of parental expression of love as a result of various circumstances, which is misinterpreted by the child as rejection. The child's feeling of rejection generates a vicious cycle in the parent–child relationship. The child becomes anxious and insecure about whether or not his parents really love him. He then tests them, retaliates, rebels, or withdraws. The parents, in turn, feel unappreciated and rejected, and their negative, hostile and rejecting feelings are further stirred up, aggravated, and intensified. The treatment of the child and parents, aimed at breaking the vicious cycle, is described.

PERLMAN, Helen Harris. *Social Casework: A Problem Solving Process.* Chicago: University of Chicago Press, 1957.

Perlman examines intensively and extensively the problem-solving process in casework practice. She states: "Much in the problem solving work is on an unconscious or only partly conscious basis;... it centers about some problem consciously brought by the client.... Problem solving must include then, conscious, focused, goal-directed activity between client and caseworker" (p. 87). "In each case, the caseworker has his own problem solving task:... this mental work of examining the parts of the problem for the import of their particular nature and origin, for the interrelationships among them, for the relationship between them and the means of their solution—this is the diagnostic process. Diagnosis ... must result in a design for action" (p. 164).

SPITZER, K., and B. Welsh. "A Problem Focused Model of Practice," *Social Casework*, 1969, 50 (June), 323–329.

A conceptualization is presented of a problem-focused approach to social work practice designed to deal with the rapidly changing demands and needs of today's fast moving society. Large numbers of social workers, recognizing the need for more comprehensive service provision, have adopted an increasingly expanded practice role. However, conceptualizations of such comprehensive forms of practice have been singularly lacking in social work literature. The proposed approach provides a framework for problem solving consisting of an identification and definition of the social problem(s) with which the worker or work group is dealing as the basis for determining objectives, the appropriate level(s) at which intervention(s) should occur, the range of interventive methods to be used, the tasks to be performed and the corrective feedback mechanisms to be developed.

SPIVACK, G., J. Platt and M. Shure. *The Problem Solving Approach to Adjustment: A Guide to Research and Intervention.* San Francisco: Jossey-Bass, 1976.

This book proposes a beginning statement about the nature of healthy human functioning and a set of working postulates relevant to social adjustment and the ways in which certain cognitive skills function in social adjustment:

1. A key and common element in any theory of adjustment is the quality of social relationships (capacity to relate to and deal with other people).

2. A significant and heretofore largely neglected determinant of the quality of social relationships is a group of mediating cognitive processes that define abilities to solve interpersonal problems.

3. These processes, while perhaps delimited in their broad outline by general intellectual ability, are not the same as abstract, impersonal intellectual ability.

4. These essential mediating processes are learned from experience in our culture (family childrearing).

5. Given the above, any educational therapeutic interventions that enhance or "free up" these processes will enhance the quality of social adjustment.

It identifies and measures, over a broad age span, interpersonal cognitive problem-solving skills, to appreciate their meaning within the broader question of what defines healthy human functioning, and explores how intervention programs may enhance that operation.

6

Functional Theory For Social Work Practice

by

SHANKAR A. YELAJA

Introduction

Functional theory for social work, its origin and development, are attributed to the School of Social Work at the University of Pennsylvania. The two pioneers of this theory, Jessie Taft and Virginia Robinson, both taught at the Pennsylvania School of Social Work. Influenced by the philosophy and teachings of Herbert Mead and John Dewey, and later by Otto Rank, they laid the foundations of what became known in social work literature as a "functional school of thought." The pioneering work of Taft and Robinson was sustained by Kenneth Pray and later on by Ruth Smalley whose book, *Theory for Social Work Practice,* is a milestone in the history of functional social work. The old but imposing gothic building at 2410 Pine Street in Philadelphia (the home of the Pennsylvania school from 1943 to 1966, which still stands) is the place where it all began.

The period from 1930 to 1955 in social work history is enlivened by a controversy and debate over "legitimate" theory for practice. The two schools of thought—diagnostic, as it came to be called, and functional—differed with each other in several important respects, including the underlying assumptions about human growth and development, the nature of the worker-client relationship, the purpose of social work, and consequently the theoretical base for practice. It was a conflict that stimulated lively and meaningful debate. It compelled all social workers, especially caseworkers, to examine their practice. The new generation of social workers perhaps do not care to know much about that conflict, and might prefer to see that it is left to the archives of social welfare history. Social workers in the 1960s and 1970s have developed an appreciation of the similarities and differences in many theories that have had an impact on social work practice.

Contemporary social work practice is influenced by a wide range of theories; even within the single domain of personality theories the influence of psychoanalytic, behavioral and humanistic theories is strongly felt—not to mention, of course, a large segment of social theories. Social work practitioners and educators are confronted with the formidable task of developing a systematic theory for practice which is testable and usable. The theory-building efforts are at a crossroads: whether to test existing theories against practice situations or whether to test the practice against the rigor of the theories. Divergent approaches to theory building are suggested. Thus social workers of the future, in looking back upon that debate, might very well wonder and ask, What was the fuss all about?

In this chapter I shall neither analyze nor defend the past controversy. Rather, my intention is to restate and recapitulate functional theory as it has evolved, then consider its relevance for the many challenges confronted by the social work profession in the 1980s and in the future. In the context of this chapter I have used the word "theory" not in the strictly scientific sense of a closely drawn hypothesis which can be tested and proved or disproved, but more loosely, in the dictionary sense of a "plan for action" or scheme for practice based on a set of identified principles which are interrelated and which derive from a common basis in relevant knowledge.

Historical origins of functional theory

In order to understand the functional theory for social work, it is important to be aware of its historical origins, the fomentation of thought around the time of its inception, and the landmarks contributing to its development and refinement.

Influenced and paralleled by a revolution in the "pure" sciences against the mechanistic Cartesian stance of traditional science, the functional approach developed out of a growing negative reaction to the mainstream of social work, a movement which was totally caught up in the sweep of psychoanalytic thought gaining momentum in the 1920s and early 1930s and which came, as the opposition grew and the rift widened, to be known as the diagnostic school of social work.

Heavily influenced by Freudian concepts of personality development and psychoanalytic treatment, the diagnostic school, to which the great mass of social workers, including some of the future founders of the functional school, claimed allegiance, had adopted wholesale both concepts and methods and were attempting, regardless of setting, to perform a function barely distinguishable from Freudian psychotherapy.

Social work had progressed from its philanthropic Lady Bountiful beginnings through its first systematized, sociologically oriented phase under Mary Richmond in 1910-1920 to a psychologically oriented stage which was to dominate the field wholly for the next decade or so, and which continues to influence it to varying degrees at the present time. Not least among those carried to new and exciting heights of hope and enthusiasm for the helping potential in the Freudian approach were two individuals who more than any others can be credited with founding the functional school of social work, Jessie Taft and Virginia Robinson. In a paper discussing the influence of psychiatry on the field of mental health, Jessie Taft recalls the thrill of her first encounter with the "modern psychiatric viewpoint," the seemingly boundless prospect it introduced of bringing mental disease "into the realm of the knowable" (37, p. 60), and the promise heralded by the birth of the psychiatric social worker. In time, however, and under the decisive influence of Otto Rank, a disciple of Freud who had parted ways with the master, Robinson* also turned aside from the main path of social work thinking, adopting and

---

*Virginia Robinson, in *A Changing Psychology in Social Casework*, was one of the first social work writers to identify the portent of the new psychological insights for what could be truly a social work method.

developing a psychological position which was in many vital aspects diametrically opposed to what was later identified by contrast as the functional school of social work.

Psychoanalytic (diagnostic) social work in its earlier form, unmodified by the influences of the more optimistic neo-Freudians such as Anna Freud and Heinz Hartmann, is based on the principle of scientific determinism, the assumption that man is the product of his past and that only through understanding and acceptance of the influences that have molded him can he be led to psychological salvation. This emphasis on the past and on the efficacy of probing the unconscious mind to bring to light and so overcome blocks to normal, healthy functioning and fulfillment casts both therapist (social worker) and patient (client) into particular roles. The client is assumed to be psychologically ill, in need of treatment in preparation for which he will be diagnosed and tentatively categorized, and of which he will be the passive recipient. The immediate presenting problem is regarded as merely a symptom of a deeper, all-pervading psychological condition, the proper domain of the caseworker-therapist, who assesses and treats over an indefinite stretch of time, assuming sole responsibility for the goal and direction of treatment, operating paradoxically not in dynamic interaction with the client but, rather, from a stance of dynamic passivity, reflecting, encouraging the client to dredge up from the dim reaches of the unconscious mind origins of fears and anxieties, receiving, interpreting, and deflecting revived hostilities, but always as a neutral, basically uninvolved figure. The effect of past influences is regarded as irreversible, so that what is sought in treatment is not change but adjustment. The Freudian view of human change potential in its earlier days was essentially pessimistic. It was only in the 1950s that the Freudian analytic group, through its emphasis on ego psychology, reflected a more optimistic view of man which conceived him to be the creator of himself as well as the created.

It is this view, first developed for psychotherapy by Rank and later corroborated and developed elsewhere by a considerable body of writers and scientists in a variety of disciplines, which contributed to the thinking of the "functional school" from its beginning.

This describes, then, in brief outline, precisely what functional casework as it evolved was not. Before presenting, in equally broad delineation, what it, by contrast, did constitute, it would be well to examine some of the influences that directly and indirectly bore upon the thinking of Jessie Taft and Virginia Robinson and their close associates in the Pennsylvania School of Social Work, within which the functional theory of social work practice originated and with which it has remained identified.

As dramatically as the impact of Freud's discovery of the unconscious revolutionized the field of psychiatry and, by adoption, the field of social work, the winds of change were sweeping, in quite another direction, over the entire arena of scientific thought in the early decades of this century. There was, as Peter Drucker records, "a philosophical shift from the Cartesian universe of mechanical cause to the new universe of pattern, purpose and process" (9, Preface, p. xi). The static, deterministic view of the physical world was giving way to a new concept of bodies in motion, the stance of predictive certitude to one of probability. In the face of the old, predictable, and rigidly irreversible cause-and-effect order, leaders in the sciences were experiencing a Copernican turnabout and recognizing with increasing clarity that the only thing truly predictable in the universe is unpredictability itself, that change is the essence of all matter and all living organisms. The concept of "being" as a process, but a process with a universally recognizable purpose, was being elaborated by scientists in every field. If change was the one constant, it was also recognized that its polar counterpart, purposive pattern, was an equally universal phenomenon. It was seen that every living cell, every organism, and, by wider application, every person demonstrated a "recurrent patterning of a sequence of changes over time and in a particular direction" (15, p. 15) as opposed to random, chance changes with no interrelationships. Scientists like embryologist George W. Corner (6) and biologist Edmund Sinnot (41) were emphasizing a concept of human growth that expresses purpose and constitutes a process. Dr. Corner's description of embryonic life in his classic work, *Ourselves Unborn* (6), laid a base for understanding (1) the nature of human growth in its purposiveness and orderly progression; (2) respective roles of the environment and endowment in their interaction on the course of growth; and (3) the origin and nature of difference between man and other species, and between man and man. Sinnot's writings on human biology opened relatively new vistas for understanding the process of human growth and development. Sinnot considered living things as seekers and creators, striving for goals as the essence of all life. He referred to the organizing, goal-seeking quality of life and each human being as "an organized and organizing center, a vortex pulling in the matter and energy and knitting them into precise patterns never known before " (41, p. iii). Sinnot also recognized the influence of environment on the life of the organism. Thinkers in such diverse fields as physics (F. C. S. Northrup) and business administration (Peter Drucker) were calling for the abandonment of the concept of fixed causality and promoting the concepts of relativity, energy, particularity, emergence, and potential, relating them to the nature of process, the essence of being. These ideas were also being developed by Banesh Hoffman (14), Julian Huxley, Hans Selye, John W. Gardner, and Floyd W. Matson, whom Hofstein (15) credited with the best analysis he had encountered of the development of modern concepts of process.

Recognition by these men and a growing number of others of their persuasion, that the goal-directed whole of any organism transcends the sum of its parts, that each being is unique despite common patterns, that the observer affects the observed despite rigorous striving for scientific objectivity and impersonality, and that will and freedom do exist and play a significant

role in the unfolding of a human being, had vital implications for thinkers in the field of human services. Psychologists such as Prescott Lecky, with his theory of the unity and consistency of the self, were similarly discovering the error of mechanistic psychological explanations, based on the assumption that man is simply "a machine moved by forces," and were calling for a new view of man, to be thought of as "a unit in himself, a system which operates as a whole. His behavior must then be interpreted in terms of action rather than reaction, that is, in terms of purpose" (27, p. 88). Gordon Allport contrasts the outdated Lockean philosophy, which saw man as a purely passive reactive "tabula rasa,"with the Leibnitzian view, which recognized the person as the activist, the source of acts, not merely the reactor. Human activity, he contended, was not simply the result of pushes by internal and external forces, but was purposive.

> To understand what a person is, it is necessary always to refer to what he may be in the future, for every state of the person is pointed in the direction of future possibilities. (2, p. 12)

The development of the human personality is a "process of becoming," a continuous striving toward the realization of all its capacities, toward individuation which means the formation of certain structures—moral conscience, self-conception, hierarchy of interests—unique to each person. Other psychologists and personality theorists—Abraham Maslow, Karen Horney, Andras Angyal, Clark Moustakas (27)—were expanding upon the same theme, the human capacity for positive growth and change, the uniqueness and variation of human nature, the individual self, not static and preshaped by early forces, but by being and becoming. It was a new view of man as "order-maker, working consistently through the anticipation, control and direction of change" (9, p. 23). Helen Merrell Lynd (21), exponent of a psychology of potential abundance in reaction to the psychology of scarcity or theory of compensation which had been dominating the scientific scene; Marie Jahoda, with her view of human maturation through a proscribed sequence of capacities to be, each developing through the use of different life opportunities; and Erik Erikson, with his conception of the unfolding process of the life cycle in distinct phases, each offering its peculiar crises, tasks, and opportunities—all these theorists were known to Jessie Taft and Virginia Robinson and the early functionalists and all contributed to the birth and evolution of this new theory of social work practice.

It was the catalytic influence of Otto Rank, who served on the faculty of the Pennsylvania School of Social Work, however, and his dynamic influence in the lives of Taft, Robinson, and the community of social workers in Philadelphia, that shaped the basic ideas of the functional school (with the exception of the use of the social agency function, a pivotal concept, which was the contribution of Jessie Taft alone; it will be discussed at greater length in this chapter). As Rank reassessed and rejected many of the Freudian tenets and built in their place his own philosophy and therapeutic method, so did the functionalists turn decisively and diametrically away from Freudian dominated social work theory and practice.

Rank was not, of course, the only dissenter from Freudian theory. The names of Alfred Adler and Carl Gustav Jung must be mentioned for their powerful dissenting ideas. Adler had a profound social consciousness; he was particularly moved by the grievous social problems and deplorable living conditions of the underprivileged working class in Europe.

Moved by his own personal experiences and a growing awareness of social environments and their effects on human beings, Adler developed a new therapeutic approach with a basis in redirecting the life style of patients. Jung probed the mysteries of fantasy and the unconscious. He had a fundamental disagreement with Freud regarding the libido theory. Jung's most vital contribution to psychoanalytic theory was the distinction he made between neurosis and psychosis and his search for a "soul" as an ego developer in the development of human psychology.

Each of the three men—Adler, Jung and Rank—felt constrained by his Freudian ties and strove for the release of his own creative potential. In the process, they inevitably separated themselves from Freud's teaching and leadership. Each found his own niche. Adler found his "style of life," Jung his "soul," and Rank his "creative self-expression." With the contributions of these men to psychoanalytic theory a new era in the understanding of human psychology had already begun.

Virginia Robinson (who, in close collaboration with her lifelong friend and colleague, Jessie Taft, and like her influenced by the teaching of Dewey, Mead, and later Otto Rank, was among the first social work writers to recognize the significance of the Rankian direction in psychological thought) notes in her milestone work, *A Changing Psychology in Social Casework,* that the "concept of fixed causality in mental and social phenomena has yielded to a conception of a functional correlation between the factors studied" (38, p. 121). No longer could the nucleus of thinkers associated with the Pennsylvania School accept the scientific determinism base of diagnostic social work. The view of man as the hapless product of interacting external and internal forces had given way to a positive, hopeful view of man, the fashioner of his own fate, capable of creatively using these inner and outer experiences to shape his own ends. A psychology of illness was rejected and in its place a psychology of positive human potential and capacity for change gave impulse and direction to a new method in social work. Turning its back decisively on the diagnostic preoccupation with the past, functionalism placed new and creative emphasis on the present experience and its power to release growth potential. The concept of treatment was replaced by the concept of service, of a helping process in which the use of the relationship, the dynamic interaction of the social worker as helper and the client as determinant of the process, was paramount. The center of change was no longer seen to be in the worker-therapist, but in the client. It was a positive acceptance and adoption of

> Rank's concept of the analytic situation as a dynamic situation in which the patient works out his own "will," his conscious desires and his unconscious and unaccepted striving against the attitude of the analyst. (38, p. 122)

The attitude of the analyst, or rather the caseworker, as the concept was adapted to social work, was in contrast to the diagnostically conceived role which assigned to the worker complete responsibility for both setting and carrying out treatment goals. An attitude of complete acceptance of the client as he presented himself and his problem, a recognition of his difference, his uniqueness, of the meaning to him of accepting help, and of his ability to use the present situation, the helping relationship, to release an innate capacity to organize experiences and so to resolve his immediate problem were the most essential principles of functional social work. In contrast to the diagnostic approach with its global problem parameters, concentration was directed toward only a phase, or "fragment," of the client's total problem, the presenting problem which he defined within the limits of the service offered, the assumption being that change in any one hurting area of his life could work a salutary effect on his total psychological equilibrium. As Kenneth Pray points out:

> In helping to relieve pressure of conflict at this point [i.e., the point of the immediate problem], the worker may be releasing energies and opening insights that reach far beyond this moment or this episode. (28, p. 185)

In the second assumption, that one of the main sources of human problems was the destructive use of relationships, the client took a fundamental step toward basic positive change through the experience afforded by the casework relationship of a new and constructive way of using the self in therapy.

The importance of time as a dynamic element in the helping process marks another departure from the diagnostic approach. More will be said about this later, but briefly, the premise was offered that time symbolizes the whole problem of living in that it represents simultaneously both the need to accept limitation and the difficulty in doing so.

> It is upon this universal reality of the meaning of time to the individual human being that functional casework bases its use of time in the helping process, with its emphasis upon the present moment and the present relationship, and its dynamic use of the ending of that relationship. (17, p. 26)

Before turning to the core concept of "function" in the functionalist approach to social work practice, it is vital to consider the rejection of diagnosis as it was understood and employed by the diagnostic school in an integral relationship to all the foregoing. In Freudian practice a thorough, although not necessarily definitive, diagnosis based on an extensive collection of facts—particularly of the client's past—was the prime prerequisite of the treatment plan developed by the worker on the basis of his diagnosis and in accordance with the goals he had set for the client. The functional social worker does not regard diagnosis as a disparate step in the treatment process, but as inextricably woven throughout the process with the client's participation actively enlisted and an open sharing along the way. Diagnosis is

> a developing process, worked out by the client himself, as he uses the agency service made available by the worker and as he tests his own capacities and needs

in accepting or contesting the conditions and responsibilities he faces in using that service and so in dealing with his own problems. (28, p. 185)

The worker bears responsibilty not for the diagnosis nor for the outcome of the service relationship, but for his own self-disciplined fostering of "the process that goes into it—the process by which the recipient of help is enabled to face freely and steadily the alternatives open to him" (28, p. 14). This in no way minimizes the importance of a thorough understanding on the part of the worker of the factors affecting human development and behavior in general and in application to each individual client, nor does it imply a rejection or devaluation of the hard-won psychological insights to date. Without this knowledge base a worker could not hope to be in command of his part in the helping process. The difference lies essentially in rejection of helping from a stance of superior wisdom, assuming the source of understanding and therefore, of solutions, to reside solely in the worker. Certainly diagnostic observations can and should be made and shared, but this is neither the basis nor the substance of the helping process.

Generic principles for social work practice

One of the significant contributions to conceptualizations of social work practice appears in the writings of Ruth Smalley. In *Theory for Social Work Practice*, Smalley lists five generic principles for social work practice and emphasizes that these principles can be applied to the various forms of specialized practice (casework, groupwork, and community organization) rather than to combinations and mergers in practice.

The principles may be paraphased as follows:

1. Diagnosis should be related to the use of services, should be developed as services are given, should be changed as the phenomenon changes, and should be shared with the client.
2. Time phases in the social work process (beginnings, middles, and endings)* should be fully exploited for the use of the client.
3. The use of agency function gives focus, content, and direction to social work processes, assures accountability to society, and engages the client in the process characterized by partialization, concreteness, and differentiation.
4. Conscious use of structure, related to function and process, introduces "form" into the relationship of client and worker.
5. All social work processes involve a relationship in which *choices* or *decisions* are made by the person being helped, and the relationship must be of such a character as to further the making of purposive choices and decisions.

The Function in Functional Social Work Practice

If one had to single out the distinguishing characteristic, the fundamental dynamic, of the functionalist approach, it would be the place and use of agency function in the helping process.

It was Jessie Taft who first recognized the philosophical and psychological implications of the creative, positive acceptance of social agency parameters and who introduced agency function as the unifying, direction-giving concept in social work practice. Although Otto Rank exercised the greatest direct influence on all the

---

* Smalley defines the social work process in this way:

Process is the use of a special method by the worker in a relationship with "others" which leads to a characteristic process marked by engagement in movement towards a mutually affirmed purpose as that purpose finds expression in a specific program or service. (44, p. 16)

other significant concepts of functional social work, the early functionalists, and Jessie Taft herself, were careful to exclude Rank from involvement or influence in the development of this pivotal principle. Rank was unable to appreciate the concept, never having worked in an institutional setting.

While social work may be regarded, by and large, as an "institutionalized profession," there are two widely divergent ways of regarding the institution, the social agency through which the services of the profession are delivered. Those claiming allegiance to the diagnostic school tend to identify only in a secondary way with the purpose of the agency, the primary focus being on individual therapy, the treatment of the totality of client need regardless, as already noted, of practice setting. For the functionalists, who do not accept agency service limitations as a necessary evil, the function defined by the social agency provides reality boundaries within which the client can test and discover his ability to work out his problem and make a satisfying adjustment or readjustment to the wider realities.

The social agency is seen as "the place where the interests of society and the interests of the individual are joined" (22). Both the need to be served and the form of service deemed most effective to meet that need have been identified by society, which delegates responsibility for service delivery to the agency. The worker, as representative of both agency and society, operates with a clear understanding of his role and the delineation of the service he embodies.

> The worker sets up the conditions as found in his agency function and procedure; the client . . . tries to accept, to reject, to attempt to control, or to modify that function until he finally comes to terms with it enough to define or discover what he wants, if anything, from this situation. (47, p. 8)

Far from being stultifying, restrictive, or repressive, the secure, stable parameters of agency function offer the creative basis, the functionalists should argue, for truly effective social work practice which makes active use of limits on the philosophical and psychological premise that conscious, positive acceptance is the keystone of therapy. It is clear that the purpose and form of service, once defined, cannot remain static, but require continuous review, and that complete identification with agency function on the part of the worker both assumes this timeliness and appropriateness of goals and places upon him partial responsibility for ongoing assessment. Kenneth Pray points out that, although social workers cannot carry responsibility for knowing everything that goes into the formulation and implementation of sound social programs, they are in a very special position to bear witness to their effects.

> And we have a corresponding obligation not only to make these specific contributions from our experience, when occasion presents itself, but also to use our influence to its last limit, to see that the legislative and administrative processes involved in the formulation and execution of policy shall allow full consideration and use of these basic human interests and relationships. (28, p. 16)

The concept of agency function, as agency service or role responsibility within the organization (it means both), is the substitute for the transference phenomenon within the worker-client relationship. It was conceived as the professional control factor. The stress on agency function kept the relationship professional and objective and helped to maintain the clear difference between worker and client.

The economic depression of the 1930s had a profound impact on social services. Social agencies were called upon to reassess their services—including their purposes, goals, and delivery—to meet the rapidly growing demand for service as a result of social and economic crises created by the depression. To what extent the introduction of the social agency as a base for functional practice within the functional school of thought is influenced by the economic events of the 1930s is still far from clear. But it is interesting that Taft in her paper, "Function as the Basis of Development in Social Work Processes," at the American Association of Social Workers National Conference in June, 1939, made a statement which gives us a clue to the basis for her thinking. She stated:

> Although some agencies under extraordinary leadership had begun to differentiate individual helping from the responsible and skillful exercise of a specific function, it was not until public relief and assistance forced social workers into clarification through actual numbers and pressures of work to be done for taxpayers as well as clients, that we came, at least in Philadelphia, to a realization of the relation of function to social work practice that seemed little short of revelation. (37)

The functional view of man and societal relationships

George Herbert Mead, whose writings, as noted, deeply influenced the foundations of thought of the Pennsylvania School through and beyond Jessie Taft, noted that "a self can arise only where there is a social process within which the self has had its initiation. It arises in that process" (24, p. 384). The important distinction which the functionalists make, however, in their view of that process is in emphasizing the active as opposed to the merely reactive role of the individual in the development of his own unique self.

We have considered emerging concepts of man, the purposeful, change-oriented, potential master of his own fate, as these were understood by the early functionalists increasingly dissatisfied with the restrictive, fundamentally pessimistic Freudian view of man, the product of biological and environmental forces. Although the influence of these forces is by no

means minimized in Rankian thought, it is his revolutionary concept of will and self-determination which provides the point of departure and gives direction to the new therapeutic approach upon which functional social work is built. The rationale for this approach, as it identifies and seeks to mobilize the self-helping capacity of the human will, is expressed by Smalley as follows:

> In short, the psychological base for functional social casework practice is a view that the push toward life, health and fulfillment is primary in human nature, and that a person is capable throughout his life of modifying both himself and his environment according to his own changing purposes and within the limitations and opportunities of his changing capacities and changing environment. (45, p. 198)

The basic assumption is that there is not only an ability to change but an innate striving toward psychological growth in each person, and a creative push toward a fuller, more integrated self. As the individual reaches toward growth and change, he fears and resists it because of the simultaneous pull in the opposite direction toward the security and safety of the known and the stable.

> Only at points of growth crisis, where the pressure for further development becomes strong enough to overcome the fear of change and disruption, is the ordinary individual brought to the necessity of enlarging his hard-won integration. (48, p. 5)

The point at which a troubled client summons his courage and resolve to seek help with an immediate problem is just such a point of growth crisis and, as such, provides the basic ingredient for the kind of mobilization toward self-help that functional casework offers. As each person is unique, so has each developed his own peculiar pattern for meeting critical experiences; first through his own particular weathering of what Rank refers to as the "birth trauma," the first separation, or beginning, and then through his meeting every subsequent growth change, separation, beginning, and ending. It is through relationships that these beginnings and endings, these growth-producing (or growth-limiting) inevitable separation experiences, are encountered: "The Ego needs the Thou in order to become the Self" (30, p. 290). If past relationships, particularly the earliest and most vital relationship with the mother, have been positive and constructive, the will has learned to accept the inevitability of separation and to adopt reality limitations as its own. If these formative experiences have been negative and destructive, the will has developed a pattern of refusing to accept separation and of repeated and futile attempts to complete the self through the other person in the relationship. Regardless of how negative a client's growth experiences may have been, however, the casework relationship, premised on an implicit trust in the growth potential, provides a unique opportunity for the release of the potential. It provides this opportunity through a consistent attitude of respect for and faith in the worth and strength of the client and a consequent setting up of an atmosphere in which he can feel safe and free to be truly himself.

The concepts of conflict, counterwill, and resistance are to the functionalist not only inevitable but necessary for movement and growth. Conflict is inherent in the development of the human organism, conflict between the individual and others and with society. The counterwill, the negative aspect of the will, orginates in opposition to the will of others and against reality in general and carries with it a heavy guilt connotation. Resistance, the unavoidable phenomenon in the beginning casework relationship, is not only a natural and essential attempt on the part of the individual to maintain his personality, but is, as noted earlier, the sign of a strength of will indispensable to new growth. The caseworker-therapist

represents not only the human counterwill, a needed reality, but the human counterwill which for perhaps the first time in a client's experience offers almost no counterprojection, setting up rather "a situation so safe, so reassuring that none of his defenses is needed and, therefore, fall away, leaving his underlying fears, loves and jealousies free to express themselves" (37, p.113). As Angyal points out, the very foundations of a patient's neurosis begin to crumble when he learns to trust the worker's attitude of complete acceptance and he can, therefore, no longer "uphold the fiction of being unloved and unworthy, undeserving of love" (27, p. 57). In being safe to express hitherto suppressed negative feelings, the client performs the valuable function of bringing "unconsidered isolated impulse" into relation with "conscious will and intelligence" (37, p. 139). Similarly, in the vital symbolic act of separation which takes place in a planned constructive way in the ending of the casework relationship, the client dares to trust his own will without feeling the need to justify it morally to the caseworker or to feel guilty about it as in previous encounters with other individuals. He dares, in other words, to be himself and to endure consciously the pain of separation through resolute, confident, guilt-free willing.

> The true self reveals itself . . . always only in the other self, that which we want to be, because we are not, in contrast to that which we have become and do not want to be. (27, p. 70)

This discovery and reaffirmation of the true self, or at least a sufficient glimpse of it to remobilize the client's own resources to cope with that limited piece of his life which he brings to the casework situation, is the goal and substance of the helping relationship. There is in the entire functionalist approach an implicit faith in the innate striving of each person to be truly human, to be healthily social, and to act in a manner consistent with his own values and with a confidence that a consciously controlled relationship of unqualified empathy and acceptance can and does provide a healthy basis for each client's social growth. As the term "functionalist" holds always before us, the therapeutic aspect of the service inheres "incidentally, within the limits of a concrete function" (37, p. 157).

Major concepts of functional social work practice

Although most, if not all, of the major concepts and principles of functional theory have been incorporated into the foregoing, they will be pulled together and presented here for concise examination and specific relation to social work practice.

The significance of process in the functional approach refers to the life process itself, with its inherent qualities of emergence and unpredictability, the microcosmic portion of it nurtured in the casework relationship and the helping relationship per se. The concept "process" and the elements of human growth potential and condition as espoused by the functionalists have already been discussed, albeit cursorily, and attention will be focused here only on the use of time in all three phases of the helping process.

1.   The Importance of Time

The universal reality of time, as identified by Rank and adopted by the functionalists, has been alluded to earlier in this chapter. Taft saw time as "only a name for the inmost nature of man, his own medium, which can sustain as well as confound him. It is his own element if only he will yield to it instead of fighting it" (37, p. 316). It is recognized in the functional approach that the client brings a dual attitude to the beginning phase of the process—a strength of will to grow or change in some degree through help, and a fighting resistance to the pain of growth and to accepting the needed help. The helping role of the social worker is, as noted, that of a counterwill presented in such a

way that it will strengthen, not break, the will of the client. The strengthening is effected through an acceptance of resistance, along with a firm faith in the client's ability to work through this resistance to a positive affirmation of the will to grow. It is helped further by a planned use of this particular time phase to overcome in the client the fear of the unknown, and to acquaint him with the limits of the service offered and help him to decide, through partializing his problem, whether and how he can use the service, accepting the boundaries of time tentatively and judiciously set. Once this vital initial phase has been completed and the "climax of acceptance" passed, the direction of the helping process begins to veer toward preparation for the ending, the separation which, as we have seen, can complete the final and self-perpetuating therapeutic effect of the entire process by allowing the client to experience, perhaps for the first time, a guilt-free leaving of a significant other and of a growth phase willed by himself and propelled by his own rediscovered strength to cope. The middle phase might be considered to comprise no more than the turning point from beginning toward ending. The separation phase reintroduces in full force the struggle between wanting and not wanting and again, in order that this struggle may be carried out within the safety zone of a preestablished time limit, the skill of the worker is challenged to work out, not only for but with the client, an appropriate present ending point. The therapeutic value of endings, as Taft identified it,

> consists primarily in this fear-reducing heightening of the value of the present and the releasing discovery that an ending willed or accepted by the individual himself is birth no less than death, creation no less than annihilation. (37, p. 170)

Perhaps the most succinct summary of the meaning of consciously guiding the client's use of service phases is this quotation from Rank:

Experience has taught...that as the therapist can only heal in his way, the patient also can only become well in his own way; that is, whenever and however he wills, which moreover is already clear through his decision to take treatment and often enough also through his ending of it (31, p. 99)

2.   Freedom of Choice

As has been repeatedly discovered in this review of basic functionalist concepts, the cornerstone of the social work process is the unshakable belief

in the existence of a natural impulse toward better organization of the self, which, however blocked or confused, provides the basis for a new orientation to living, once a situation is encountered which can disrupt the habitual pattern and release, for the formation of a new integration, the underlying growth tendencies. (37, p. 329)

The growth-releasing situation is the helping relationship which either engages the voluntary commitment of the client or is rejected by him, but it cannot be imposed on him from without if it is to be effective. The significance of choice and self-determination on the part of the client is central. Anita Faatz (10), who has written extensively about the nature of choice in social casework, points out that only when an individual chooses to grow or change can growth occur and that self-chosen growth is possible only when an individual's inner strength remains intact. The decision to approach a social agency with a problem is already a choice to change, but the inevitable persistence, which further solidifies the internal strength to maintain, has first to be worked through in the process and the desire to change strengthened to the point of the second vital moment of choice, which is the climax of the beginning phase, the choice to ac-

cept and use the service personified by the worker in the casework relationship. In order that the ending, the crucial positive separation from the helping person, really free the client to use his rediscovered, newly mobilized inner resources, it is imperative that his choosing be enlisted in the decision to end the process.

What man resists, above all, is external interference with any phase of his living before he himself is ready to abandon it. It is not the leaving, but the lack of control over leaving, that he fears. If he can possess to some degree the ending phase of even the deepest relationship, so that he feels as part of himself the movement toward the new, then he cannot only bear the growth process, however painful, but can accept it with positive affirmation. (37, p. 106)

3.   The Place of Agency, Structure, and Authority in Functional Theory

The central place of the agency in functional theory has already been discussed. In choosing to accept the limitations of the agency's service, the client identifies with the social purpose the agency represents and so discovers, rediscovers, or confirms his ability to deal responsibly with reality in the pursuit of his own particular ends. Similarly, in his conscious decision to work within the parameters of an agency's function, the worker accepts a circumscribed area of service, not in resignation, chafing at the boundaries or secretly resolving to stretch them in the wider interests of the client, but recognizing and using them as the most valued, basic tool in his armamentarium.

Arising from and determined by the function of the agency are the structure and form of service delivery, the conscious and knowing use of which is the principal dynamic in the helping process. The time structure, as we have seen, is neither mere expedient nor simple necessity, but a deliberate plan with a particular philosophical and psychological rationale. The form adopted for beginnings and endings—the way they are set up, the application, intake, registration and assessment forms, the content—is consciously designed in functional practice for maximum effectiveness of the social work processes. The form and structure of the place are regarded as a similar tool, affording, if truly suitable to the discharging of the particular agency's function, a center of stability which further facilitates the processes. Agency policy too, itself a structure, provides a center from which all other form and structure arise. It is recognized, however, that structure faces the constant danger of rigidifying and so requires unceasing creativity and imagination in use and ongoing assessment. As the client in functional social work is helped to accept limitations and to exploit them creatively for his own purposes, so are the positive acceptance and use by the worker of form and structure seen to be the royal road to the achievement of social work goals.

The relationship between choice and limitation is easy enough to see in the situation where a client freely seeks out an agency service and as freely takes or rejects that service. Not so obvious, however, is the scope for free and voluntary engagement in an authoritative setting, where the service must be seen, to the uninitiated, at any rate, to be imposed by social rules enforcing conformity with no place for choice. Kenneth Pray, a large part of whose experience was with just such settings in the field of corrections, has written a great deal about this apparent dilemma, arguing cogently that freedom and authority are not only by any means mutually exclusive, but can, in the functionalist view, be seen to be completely compatible. Pray identifies two conditions in the authoritative setting both essential and conducive to the potential success of the social work process. The first is the fact that the authority reflects not an individual will but the social will, and the second is the element of the freedom to

choose, the freedom to accept the authoritative bounds and so to find fulfillment within them or to continue to balk against them and so to reject the service the captive client has not freely sought out.

> The function of social casework in facilitating social adjustment is not . . . to free the individual from all limitation; it is not to assist him to achieve, without hindrance, any or all of the ends to which he might aspire, but rather it is to help him to face, to understand, to accept, and to deal constructively and responsibly with certain realities of his own situation—his own capacities and also the facts of his social setting. (28, pp. 165–166)

The kind of authority embodied in social agencies is a rational authority which, as Fromm has defined it,

> not only permits but requires constant scrutiny and criticism of those subjected to it. It is always temporary, its acceptance depending upon its performance. The source of irrational authority, on the other hand, is always power over people. (59, p. 13)

The earlier quotation in this chapter from Pray, emphasizing the obligation of social workers to maintain constant vigilance over legislative and administrative processes, feeding in from direct experience to ensure that goals and procedures truly reflect social needs, is stressed throughout the literature.

Application to group work and community organization

Clearly, although a generic application of the central concepts of functional theory has been implied throughout this review, the focus has repeatedly gravitated toward social casework where the principles can be most readily demonstrated. A brief examination, therefore, should be made of the other two primary methods: group work* and community organization† as functional social work practice.

Ruth Smalley (44), in her definitive work of pulling together the many threads of functional theory as it has evolved over the past four decades, has woven into her synthesis five generic principles of functionalism, already cited earlier in this chapter. Smalley is careful to point out that group work and community organization must be understood as phenomena in their own right. The great parrallel potential for functional application is seen to be the general recognition of the power within groups for defining a purpose and moving toward it. In other words, the group as an organism, whether it be a foster parent group in a child placement agency or a welfare rights group under the aegis of a governmental body, is essentially the same as a person, as an organism or a microscopic cell. All are in process, striving toward fulfillment of a self-appointed purpose. The helping agent, the worker, is there to facilitate that process through a helping relationship, but clearly within the limits defined by the function of the agency he represents.

Kenneth Pray reminds us that the objective of social work is not to make over environments or people but to introduce people to a process of dealing with problems of social relationships or social adjustment which would lead to "solutions satisfying to themselves and acceptable to the society of which they are a part" (28, p. 277). In

---

* Helen Phillips made a major contribution to the application of functional theory to social work practice with groups. For further details see Helen U. Phillips, *Essentials of Social Group Work Skill* (New York: Association Press, 1957).

† The writings of Harold Lewis on community organization, although in a beginning stage of conceptualization, are significant in exploring the application of functional theory to community practice. For further clarification of this see Harold Lewis, "Toward a Working Definition of Community Organization Practice" (Philadelphia, 1961), unpublished.

casework or even in group work, by and large, it is easy enough to see how agency purpose as it is embodied in the service might be clearly presented to the client unit and either accepted or rejected. The goal could be either social adjustment or social agitation. The responsibility of workers remains within the parameters of agency function and purpose. If the social worker considered that the present agency function was not suited to the group goal, he would have to work toward bringing desired changes in agency functions as part of his group process and work with clients. In community organization it is equally easy to see a dilemma arising for the worker as the client group evolves its purpose, which may well be to make radical inroads on agency goals and structure, even to the point of seeking to overthrow them. It may be less easy to assume that such groups will always readily recognize the congruence of society's interest as the agency purports to represent it and their own. This may, of course, also happen with individuals and with small groups set up within the agency's purpose, but the self-perpetuating power evoked and fostered in a community group might conceivably end by biting the hand that fed it. Certainly the functional approach can be seen as applicable to these two methods and Smalley, as other functionalists before her, presents some quite telling arguments that it is indeed.

Current and future perspectives

Functional theory for social work practice made its impact at a time when the profession was still under the influence of psychoanalytic thinking and vestiges of personality theories. Because of the historical period in which the functional theory emerged its potential contribution to the refinement and reexamination of practice theory has not been sufficiently exploited, at least in my view. Let us therefore explore the contribution of functional theory to current and future social work practice.

1. Integrated Conception of Social Work Practice

The social work profession historically and even to some extent today is caught up in the dilemma and duality of its practice. The dilemma, discussed in numerous professional writings as cause and function (Lee, 18) or social action versus service delivery (Rein, 32) has led to a dichotomy in the conception of social work practice. Professional practice is defined, on the one hand, as delivery of service by a competent social worker for the individuals, families, groups, or communities. On the other hand, social change, including institutional change and/or reform, are considered outside the purview of the professional's immediate job and responsibility. These activities are either relegated to one's own off the regular hours of professional work or to an organization (political, church, action group, etc.) with a socially sanctioned purpose and a mandate. Social workers are concerned over this dichotomous division of their professional obligations. Some social workers have sharply questioned it. There is no denying the fact that the internal fight within the profession has been divisive and harmful to both the social workers and their client systems.

The increasing awareness within the profession of the consequences of dichotomy has led to a renewed search for and development of an integrated conception of social work practice. Integrated social work practice has been understood as an integrated totality involving provision and delivery of service and strategies of social change within clearly defined areas and directly related to social work competence and responsibility. Thus, the participations in social change will flow from practice and be supported by clear-cut knowledge from professional involvement at the proper level in the social

system. It will not be directed toward those broader areas of change with which social workers must be concerned as informed citizens, but which cannot be their sole and special prerogative as professionals.

In functional theory, particularly its conceptualization by Smalley, method and social purpose are interrelated and inseparable. Consequently, there is never a split in thinking or action, and both client interests and broad social welfare interests are served. Thus, there is no schism between social change and service delivery objectives of the profession. They are complementary, not contradictory to each other. The following definition of social work proposed by Smalley puts forth a cogent argument for an integrated conception of social work practice.

> The underlying purpose of all social work effort is to release human power in individuals for personal fulfillment and social good, and to release social power for the creation of the kinds of society, social institutions, and social policy which make self-realization most possible for all men [and women]. (44, p. 1)

The full potentials of an integrated social work practice are beginning to be recognized. Some schools of social work are redesigning their curricula to capture the essence of this practice. Social work practitioners are reexamining their roles and fuctions. Caseworkers are no longer satisified that they cannot effect a policy change without it's being counterproductive to their casework effort. By the same token, social welfare policy makers and administrators are wanting to know more about how the policies and programs affect society at the grass roots level. They are interested and concerned over the gap between policies and their desired effects. Who else would know better about this situation than a caseworker and a client?

Social work practice in the 1980s will be far different from the current and past realities. Increasingly, the traditional roles of a social worker are being questioned. Social workers are moving into hitherto unexplored roles and responsibilities. New service delivery patterns and organizations are continuously emerging and will continue to emerge as unmet social welfare needs are recognized and acted upon. In this fast-paced and dynamic world of social work practice what is needed are a reexamination and refinement of practice theory to serve as an anchoring frame of reference. The concept of an integrated social work practice seems to offer a potentially useful approach for further development.

2. Institutional Context for Practice

Functional theory is perhaps the only theory in social work that introduced the concept of a social agency as an important element influencing practice. To date, social workers have paid very scanty attention to the institutional context of their practice. Social casework theory for a long time has suffered, and to some extent continues to suffer, from an absence of concepts from modern organizational and administrative theory.

The absence of organizational concepts in social casework theory, according to Wasserman, impoverishes our understanding of what are the possibilities and limitations of our work as practiced in a variety of environments, which in themselves represent a spectrum of facilitative and constraining conditions. The working environment for social work practice is not value-free. Consider, for example, the following questions raised by Wasserman in his review of the contributions of functional theory.

What are the effects of legislation, policies and regulations and rules upon a social caseworker's potential helping efforts vis-à-vis the client? Do they facilitate or impede his efforts? Is it possible that in some organizational contexts the policies which derive from legislation or therapeutic ideology or a dysfunctional hierarchical system prohibit a solid therapeutic effort on the part of the social worker? In brief what are the indispensable conditions under which social casework can be praticed? (55, p. 188)

For a long time social work practice theory has assumed that the institutional context of practice is no more than a series of neutral stimuli and inputs. But can we afford to hang on to this assumption, particularly when there are new pressures, financial and political, to name only a few, on the social agencies within which we practice?

The institutional context for social work practice will assume enormous significance if the present trends of financial restraints in social services continue. And there is every reason to believe that the "new realities" in financing social services will be more or less permanent as governments at all levels cut back on their funding. This trend is reinforced by diminishing contributions to social welfare by private and philanthropic organizations. Social workers must learn to deal with the effects of this reality on their services. They must examine their practice against the harsh realities to differentiate between essential and nonessential services. They must be committed to an evaluation of their services. They must question the assumptions of the present service delivery, agency objectives and functions. Under these conditions the institutional context of their work is raised to the level of a "critical decision"—critical in regard to the future directions and possibly the survival of social work as a profession. If social workers fail to make some of the decisions alluded to them in the aforementioned concerns, these will be made for them by others outside the profession.

3.   Unity in Diversity or Diversity in Unity: Which Way to the Future?

The search for a unifying concept and model for social work practice has a long history in the social work profession. For example, in 1929 the Milford Conference addressed itself to the task of defining and stating social work practice. There has been a resurgence of interest and impetus to examine practice, as evidenced from a number of studies, including those by Pincus and Minahan, Goldstein, Bartlett and Siporin, to mention only a few. The push for a systematic appraisal of practice appears to have been influenced by several factors. These include: a growing awareness of the fragmentation of social work practice by methods, fields of practice, objectives, etc.; an awareness of the limitations of a practitioner trained only in one method of helping; the creation of multiservice agencies and new advents in the delivery of services (e.g., social workers operating in teams with other professionals); and finally a recognition that "practice wisdom" does not always work, given the enormous complexity of the scene with which social workers engage.

The development of a usable, expanding, and internally consistent theory for social work practice is not an academic exercise but, rather, an urgent necessity for social work if it is to survive as a profession. One hardly needs to emphasize that social work practice must be based on *good, testable* and *usable* theory which acts as a "springboard for the development of further theory that sheds light on fresh interconnections. The point of a good theory is that it works in practice and in the very working generates more comprehensive, more powerful theory" (60).

But can social work ever build a unitary (single) theory that has all the aforementioned attributes? Or should it even try and build one? In what way should the future directions for theory building take us? If we accept the fact that the social work scene is both complex and diverse, then it is clear that a single theory for pratice is a fairytale dream never to be realized. Social workers have defied attempts to force them into a mold. They appear never to be satisfied with a singular theory. The profession has borrowed and continues to borrow from other professions and their knowledge bases.

If there is unity in diversity, there is also diversity in unity. The duality of social work referred to earlier is only one example of such a diversity. The level of training and education of social workers, the contexts of their practice, ranging from employment in a public agency to private practice as an autonomous practitioner, the diverse nature of professional commitments, are but a few illustrations of this diversity. Social work practice theory has just begun to recognize and take note of this in the formulation of theories. Compared to conceptualization and theory-building efforts in social casework, other practice areas such as community organization, social planning, and administration have not received adequate attention. Because of this, the practitioners have parted ways and looked to other disciplines for leadership. This trend has contributed to further diversity within the profession.

So, then, which way should the practice theory take us? Should we build one global theory which enables social workers to deal with the enormous complexity of the social work scene? Or should we follow separate routes in terms of theories for a variety of our roles and practice modalities? Furthermore, what directions should we follow in theory formulation and development? On the one hand, social workers might wish to concentrate their energies on selecting and testing theoretical orientations that are appropriate to social work objectives. In this way they can approach the theory building as an integration of practice with theory. On the other hand, social workers might expend their efforts at surveying, examining, and studying different theoretical approaches that have had an impact on practice, and integrate them into a new social work theory or theories. This approach calls for a multiple theory base and a continuous examination of practice to determine which theory has relevance and application for a variety of practice situations. Obviously, there are advantages and disadvantages in following either of these choices. As a profession, we have yet to agree on the choice and direction for further theory building. There are no pat answers. But it is certain that the road to theory development in social work, to paraphrase Aptekar's remarks, is paved with many different truths, must traverse many streams of conflict in point of view, and must wend its way over great mountains of strong opposition. The enormous task of theory building requires consideration of all choices (3, p. 342).

Conclusion

It is my belief that a clash in therapeutic doctrines is not a disaster but an opportunity. There are both commonalities and differences in theoretical approaches. Until we are able to come up with a testable and usable theory for

social work practice, we must try and relate theories to different client situations, problems, and needs. Through this process of searching, examination, and reexamination, perhaps one day we will come up with a good theory, or theories, for practice.

Although functional social work theory originated as an opposing force to the prevailing diagnostic school of thought in social work, its contribution to the conceptualization of practice must be seen in a broader perspective. The theory helped to widen the psychological and social bases for understanding man, the social environment, and the concept of social agency. Throughout the history and development of functional theory the emphasis has remained on the refinement of the "helping process" of social work. The task of building a scientific theory base for social work practice is enormous. It calls for recognition of the contributions different theories can make to unraveling the phenomena called "social work."

Functional theory has much to offer to the understanding of the complex realities of social work and it would be a sad day for the profession if we failed to recognize the importance of this contribution.

References

1. Allan, Frederick, M.D. "Dilemma of Growth," *Archives of Neurology and Psychiatry*, Vol. 37 (1937). Reprinted in Frederick Allan, *Positive Aspects of Child Psychiatry*. New York: Norton, 1963.
2. Allport, Gordon W. *Becoming*. New Haven: Yale University Press, 1955.
3. Aptekar, Herbert. "Theory for Social Work Practice: Book Review," *Social Service Review*, Vol. XLI, No. 3 (September 1967).
4. ———. *The Dynamics of Casework and Counselling*. Boston: Houghton Mifflin, 1955.
5. Briar, Scott and Henry Miller. *Problems and Issues in Social Casework*. New York: Columbia University Press, 1971.
6. Corner, George W. *Ourselves Unborn*. New Haven: Yale University Press, 1944.
7. Coyle, Grace L. *Group Work with American Youth*. New York: Harper, 1948.
8. ———. *Social Science in the Professional Education of Social Workers*. New York: Council on Social Work Education, 1958.

9. Drucker, Peter. *Landmarks of Tomorrow*. New York: Harper and Row, 1952.

10. Faatz, Anita J. *The Nature of Choice in Social Casework*. Chapel Hill: University of North Carolina Press, 1953.

11. Faith, Goldie Basch. "The Elements of Functional Practice in Casework." Mimeographed, Library of University of Pennsylvania School of Social Work, 1961.

12. Gardner, John W. *Self-Renewal: The Individual and the Innovative Society*, 1st ed. New York: Harper and Row, 1964.

13. Gardner, John W. and Rosa Wessel. *Professional Education Based in Practice*. Philadelphia: School of Social Work, University of Pennsylvania Press, 1953.

14. Hoffman, Banesh. *The Strange Story of the Quantum*, 2nd ed. New York: Dover, 1959.

15. Hofstein, Saul. "The Nature of Process: The Implications for Social Work," *Journal of Social Work Process*, Vol. XIV (1964).

16. *Journal of Social Work Process*, Vols. I–XV. Philadelphia: University of Pennsylvania Press, 1937–1966.

17. Kasius, Cora (ed.). *A Comparison of Diagnostic and Functional Casework Concepts*. New York: Family Service Association of America, 1950.

18. Lee, Porter. *Social Work as Cause and Function and Other Papers*. New York: Columbia University Press, 1937.

19. Lewis, Harold. Outline Statement in Response to "Statement in Progress to Draft Statement Towards a Working Definition of Community Organization Practice." Mimeographed, Philadelphia, April, 1961.

20. ——. "The Functional Approach to Social Work Practice—A Restatement of Assumptions and Principles," *Journal of Social Work Process*, Vol. XV (1965).

21. Lynd, Helen Merrell. *On Shame and the Search for Identity*. New York: Harcourt Brace and World, 1961.

22. Marcus, Grace. "The Necessity for Understanding Agency Functions." Unpublished manuscript, School of Social Work Library, University of Pennsylvania, Philadelphia, 1937.

23. ——. "The Need and Value of Supervision for the Experienced Caseworker," in Dorothy Hankins (ed.), *Journal of Social Work Process*, Vol. X (1959).

24. Mead, George Herbert. *Mind, Self and Society*. Chicago: University of Chicago Press, 1962.

25. ——. *Movements of Thought in the Nineteenth Century*. Chicago: University of Chicago Press, 1936.

26. ——. *On Social Psychology*. Chicago: University of Chicago Press, 1964.

27. Moustakas, Clark (ed.). *The Self: Exploration in Personal Growth*. New York: Harper and Row, 1956.

28. Pray, Kenneth L. M. *Social Work in a Revolutionary Age and Other Papers*. Philadelphia: University of Pennsylvania Press, 1949.

29. Rank, Otto. *The Trauma of Birth*. London: Paul, Trench, Truber and Harcourt, Brace and World, 1929.

30. ——. *Beyond Psychology*. (Published privately, 1941.) New York: Dover, 1958.

31. ——. *Will Therapy and Truth and Reality*. New York: Knopf, 1947.

32. Rein, Martin, "Social Work in Search of a Radical Profession," *Social Work,* Vol. XV, No. 2 (1970), pp. 13-28.

33. Roberts, Robert W. and Robert H. Nee. *Theories of Social Casework.* Chicago: University of Chicago Press, 1970.

34. Robinson, Virginia P. *The Dynamics of Supervision under Functional Controls.* Philadelphia: University of Pennsylvania Press, 1950.

35. ——. "The Meaning of Skill," in Virginia P. Robinson (ed.), "Teaching for Skill in Social Casework," *Journal of Social Work Process,* Vol. IV (1942).

36. ——. *Supervision in Social Casework.* Chapel Hill: University of North Carolina Press, 1936.

37. ——. (ed.). *Jessie Taft, Therapist and Social Work Educator.* Philadelphia: University of Pennsylvania Press, 1962.

38. ——. *A Changing Psychology in Social Casework.* Chapel Hill: University of North Carolina Press, 1930.

39. ——. "The Administrative Function in Social Work," in *Four Papers on Professional Function.* New York: American Association of Social Workers, 1937.

40. Selye, Hans. *The Stress of Life.* New York: Viking, 1961.

41. Sinnot, Edmund W. *Cell and Psyche.* Chapel Hill: University of North Carolina Press, 1950.

42. Smalley, Ruth E. "Distinctive Knowledge and Skills in Child Welfare: A Symposium," *Child Welfare,* April and May, 1955.

43. ——. "Freedom and Necessity in Social Work Education," *Proceedings Annual Program Meeting, 1963.* New York: Council on Social Work Education, 1963,

44. ——. *Theory for Social Work Practice.* New York: Columbia University Press, 1967.

45. ——. "Social Casework: The Functional Approach," *Encyclopedia of Social Work,* 16th issue. New York: National Association of Social Workers, 1971.

46. ——. "The Significance of Believing for School Counsellors," in Grace Lee (ed.), *Helping the Troubled School Child.* New York: National Association of Social Workers, 1959.

47. Taft, Jessie. "The Relation of Function to Process in Social Casework," *Journal of Social Work Process,* Vol. I, No. 1 (1937).

48. ——. "A Conception of the Growth Process Underlying Social Casework Practice," *Social Casework,* October, 1950.

49. ——. "Function as the Basis of Development in Social Work Processes." Presented at Meeting of American Association of Psychiatric Social Workers, NASW, June, 1939.

50. ——. "Living and Feeling," *Child Study,* January, 1933.

51. ——. *Otto Rank, A Biographical Study Based on Notebooks, Letters, Collected Writings, Therapeutic Achievements and Personal Associations.* New York: Julian Press, 1958.

52. ——. "Some Specific Differences in Current Theory and Practice," in *Role of the Baby in the Placement Process.* Philadelphia: Pennsylvania School of Social Work, 1946.

53. ——. "The Relation of Psychiatry to Social Work." Address given at New York City Conference of Charities and Corrections, May 12, 1926.

54.   ———. *The Dynamics of Therapy in a Controlled Relationship*. New York: Macmillan, 1933; Dover, 1962, 2nd ed.

55.   Wasserman, Harry. "Social Work Treatment: An Essay Reivew," *Smith College Studies in Social Work,* Vol. XLV, No. 2 (February, 1975), pp. 183–195.

56.   Wessel, Rosa. "Training for Skill in Casework Through Professional Education in a school of Social Work," *Compass,* Vol. XXV, No. 5 (September, 1944).

57.   ———. "Implications of the Choice to Work for Mothers in the ADC Program," in *Training for Service in Public Assistance*. Washington: U.S. Bureau of Public Assistance, 1961.

58.   ———. "Family Service in the Public Welfare Agency—Focus or Shift," *Public Welfare,* Vol. XXII, No. 1 (January, 1963).

59.   Yelaja, Shankar A. *Authority and Social Work: Concept and Use*. Toronto: University of Toronto Press, 1971.

60.   Younghusband, Eileen. "Foreword" to *Social Work Treatment,* 1st ed. New York: Free Press, 1974.

Annotated listing of key references

LEWIS, Harold. "The Functional Approach to Social Work Practice: A restatement of Assumptions and Principles," *Journal of Social Work Process,* Vol. XV (1965).
A consise statement on basic assumptions and principles of functional theory considered in an objective and scholarly manner.

PRAY, Kenneth L. M. *Social Work in a Revolutionary Age and Other Papers.* Philadelphia: University of Pennsylvania Press, 1949.
A collection of papers, speeches, noted articles, etc., by Pray, one of the major exponents of functional theory. His contribution to functional theory is notable for its extension to other areas of social work practice including administration, community organization, and social policy and planning. Pray's writings have illuminated a serious consideration of social policy. Along with this, he devoted major attention to the role of authority in dealing with captive client populations.

ROBERTS, Robert W. and NEE, Robert H. *Theories of Social Casework.* Chicago: University of Chicago Press, 1971.
In this collection of various theories for social casework appears a chapter on functional theory by Ruth Smalley. This chapter is more or less a condensed version of her book, Theory for Social Work Practice. *However, this chapter must be considered an additional source of information on functional theory because of a section on unresolved issues in social work theory and practice.*

ROBINSON, Virginia. *A Changing Psychology in Social Casework.* Chapel Hill: University of North Carolina Press, 1930.
A fairly definitive work on the early beginnings of the functional approach to social work practice. Psychological bases of social work practice are explored and stated within functional theory. Historically, this book must be seen as a turning point in breaking new ground in social work theory and practice.

ROBINSON, Virginia (ed.). *Jessie Taft, Therapist and Social Work Educator.* Philadelphia: University of Pennsylvania Press, 1962.
A collection of papers by Jessie Taft, one of the major architects of functional theory. The book is a most comprehensive source of material on major concepts and ideas of functional theory. This can be used as a major reference book on functionalism.

SMALLEY, Ruth E. *Theory for Social Work Practice.* New York: Columbia University Press, 1967.
This book is a definitive source of an overview of functional theory, its historical background, development, and application to practice. In this scholarly book, Ruth Smalley sets forth the theoretical foundations of functional theory and explores its application to social work practice.

SMALLEY, Ruth E. "Social Casework: The Functional Approach,"

Encyclopedia of Social Work, 16th issue. New York: National
Association of Social Workers, 1971.
*A slightly revised but condensed version of the functional approach to social casework. An excellent and detailed account of
the historical origins and development of functional theory.*

7

Existential Social Work

by

DONALD F. KRILL

The impact of existential philosophy upon the social work profession is at the moment most unclear. Only one short book has been published on the subject. Less than a dozen articles have appeared in United States journals and about half as many in Canadian journals of social work. The topic of existentialism has yet to make entry into a national conference of social workers.

On the other hand, those social workers familiar with the existential viewpoint emphasize that this perspective speaks to the profession's most pressing needs: for more effective treatment of the poor and minorities; for more present-focused, experiential, task-oriented short-term work with families and individuals; for a more flexible and eclectic use of varied treatment techniques; for a lessening of categorization of people and of paternalistic efforts by therapists to adjust the values of clients to those of their therapist or those of the established society. The existential perspective is

even seen as providing an important humanizing effect to social workers' present experimentation with social change.

The failure of the existentialist to attract major attention among social work professionals may be twofold. In the first place, writings of this type by philosophers, psychologists, theologians and social workers tend to present a terminology that seems foreign to the average practitioner (Being, Nothingness, the Absurd, Dread, I-Thou, Bad Faith, etc.). Social workers have tended to be doers rather than theoreticians and even the theorists tend to be pragmatic rather than philosophical. Secondly, existential social work writers have proposed a more philosophical perspective rather than specific working techniques. This is primarily because there does not really seem to be an existential psychotherapy per se. To be more accurate, one might say there is an existential philosophical viewpoint of how one sees oneself, one's client system and what can happen between them. Various theoretical approaches may then be used to provide techniques compatible with this philosophical perspective.

The existential stance

Modern existentialism was born in the ruins, chaos and atmosphere of disillusionment in Europe during and following World War II. Earlier existential writers, such as Kierkegaard and Dostoevsky, reacted against what they believed to be false hopes for the salvation of men and the world through a philosophy and politics of rationalism in their times. In the United States, with its boundless faith in achieving the good life through continued growth in economic productivity and scientific advancement, the interest in existentialism has been slower in coming.

Today we seem to have arrived somewhere, sufficiently uncertain and chaotic that our sensitivities to existential themes are stimulated. Not only are the Kennedy brothers dead, and Martin Luther King, Jr., but the life of God himself has been called into question by some who are supposedly up on his existence or nonexistence. The blacks, browns, reds, poor, students, far left and far right are angry and at times in lawless revolt, and now even our women take up the march and bullhorn.

Existentialism has been termed a "philosophy of despair," partially because of the fact that it seems to emerge from disillusionment. But we may view this emergence as the origin and rooting of existentialism and a turning away from a primary allegiance to those idols and values that have fallen. Where it goes beyond this point depends upon which particular writer, theologian, philosopher or film director one chooses to follow.

In most of the philosophical literature on existentialism four themes seem to recur: the stress upon individual freedom and the related fundamental value of the uniqueness of the person; the recognition of suffering as a necessary part of the ongoing process of life—for human growth and the realization of meaning; the emphasis upon one's involvement in the immediate moment at hand as the most genuine way of discovering one's identity and what life is about (not in any finalized sense but, rather, in an ongoing, open way); and the sense of commitment that seeks to maintain a life of both discipline and spontaneity, of contemplation and action, of egolessness and an emerging care for others.

The existentialists disagree with those who hold man to be either essentially an impulse-driven animal or a social animal of learned conditioning. Both of these ideas deny man what is, for the existentialists, his source of dignity: the absolute value of his individual uniqueness. Man discovers his uniqueness through the way he relates to his own subjective experience of life. Sartre points out that this subjectivity is man's freedom; it is something that is there; it cannot be escaped from or avoided; one can only deny one's own responsibility for choices made within this freedom. From the existential view, psychoanalytic theory is sometimes misused by encouraging man's denial of responsibility on the basis of impulsive forces; similarly, sociological and learning theory may be misused by excusing man on the basis of totally determining social forces.

Characters from fiction, drama, mythology and philosophical tradition have portrayed the existential posture. Stoicism, courage and individualism are common attributes. The existentialist hero is often characterized as living on the edge of the traditions, values, and enticements of his society, prizing the preservation of his own uniqueness and authenticity above all else. He commonly suspects the motives of others, bordering on the cynical, and therefore avoids complete identity with any group espousing a "good cause." He is tough-minded in holding to his own code, evaluating it and preserving its integrity. He refuses to be "put down" by dehumanizing social forces through conformity or by selling himself out to their rewards. He is against system efforts to suppress the individuality of others in his society. His values are concrete and inseparable from situations: certain arising social or political issues, loyalty to friends, unfolding creative potentials, honesty and sincerity in relationships. He lives forever with a clear awareness of life's limits, the absurd, the tragic, yet maintains a committed faith in his groundings of freedom—the springboard for unique assertion. His interaction with life defines who he is rather than the acceptance of some definition of himself imposed by an outside authority, such as family, church or economic system. The rhythm of responsive life-swinging-in-situation is his sole guide.

Existentialism is rejected by many as a narcissistic withdrawal from life when disappointments arise. At first glance, this might appear true as we hear the existentialist proclaim his own consciousness, subjectivity, uniqueness as the sole absolute: "truth is subjectivity," said Kierkegaard. The existentialist does reject the world, in one sense, in his new commitment to his own deepest self. What he rejects, however, is not life—its conditions, limits, joys and possibilities—but the mistaken hopes and expectations he had held about life, which, under closer examination, failed to fit with the reality of his life.

What is real does shatter cherished yearnings in us all—about love, about divine protection, about our own abilities and goodness. Yet in surveying the landscape of rubble from broken aspirations and beliefs, we find that we still have a choice of how to relate to these realities. We can allow ourselves to be driven to despair, or to choose new illusional hopes, or we can accept the reality and go from there.

The Hemingway hero is a portrayal of this. We might expect him to say, "We lose in the end, of course, but what we have is the knowledge that we were going great." One's manhood, the sense of realistic pride, comes from the engagement with, and assertion of, one's own uniqueness. Each must discern what is right for him in terms of talent and skill, what

is of value and what is enjoyable. This becomes his own private personal perspective for which he alone is responsible. It changes throughout life, but it remains always his own, and hence truly unique.

The black conception of "Soul" has been defined as "the force which radiates from a sense of selfhood, a sense of knowing where you have been and what it means. Soul is a way of life—but it is always the hard way. Its essence is ingrained in those who suffer and endure to laugh about it later."* Soul is the beauty of self-expression, of self-in-rhythm. One swings from inside and in response to what is outside as well. Soul is mind operating free of calculation. It is humor and spontaneity and endurance. This concept of soul is consistent with the existential aim of authenticity.

Subjectivity

What is this subjectivity, this freedom, which holds the devotion and loyalty of a man? To Sartre, freedom is "no-thingness." For Kierkegaard, it is the human encounter with the Transcendent—man's "moment before God." Buber sees this as the "I" meeting the "Thou" of life. Kazantzakis speaks of the cry from deep within the human personality. To respond to it is man's sole possibility of freedom.

Yet this subjectivity, while termed by some as an encounter with the transcendent, cannot be considered as God itself. Each of us is all too soon aware of the finite nature of subjectivity. It is not all-knowing, and subjectivity is different in each person and constantly in the process of change within the same person. Subjectivity exists as a unique responsive relation to the world. Its primary activity is the conveyance of meaning through thought and feeling, intuition and sensation, and the assertion of this unique perspective through creative acts.

It is this relationship between one's own

---

* "Lady Soul: Singing It Like It Is" (article on Aretha Franklin), *Time Magazine,* June 28, 1968, p. 26.

subjectivity and the outside world which is the basis for responsible freedom instead of narcissistic caprice. One's inner subjectivity encounters outer reality again and again in the form of limits set up by life which challenge certain beliefs and meanings one has concluded about about oneself. One experiences failures, misjudgments, hurt of others, neglect of self, conflict and guilt. There is inevitable death, uncertainty and suffering. These limiting situations, this suffering, becomes a revealing, guiding force of one's life. In a similar way one realizes one's potentials. A person senses in the world some expectation of response from himself. He feels called upon to choose, to act, to give and imprint himself upon the world. This awareness of both limits and potentials is the foundation upon which one can judge one's own unique perspective and readjust it when necessary. The ongoing encounter between subjectivity and the outside world may be looked upon as a continuing dialogue, dance, responsive process of inner and outer reality, continually affecting and being affected by the uniqueness of all forms involved.

Each must assume the burden of responsibility for his own freely chosen perspective and the associated consequences of his actions. To be a man is to assert one's uniqueness, knowing that one does not have an absolute knowledge of truth and that one may hurt others or oneself; one's efforts will often end in mistakes or failure. One must assert this uniqueness again and again—choosing courage or cowardice and knowing that suffering is often inevitable as one's perspective conflicts with the limits of life.

We fail, finally, in our resurging hopes, the existentialist might say, but then we are a brotherhood in this—not only with others, but with all of nature. For there is a striving everywhere, a fight, and, in the end, only the remnants of our struggles—and a little later there are no longer even the remnants. Our loyalty is to the thrust behind this struggle in all things. What is this thrust? A mystery! A meaningful silence! Can we be sure it is meaningful?

Who is to know? The questions of salvation or an afterlife must be held in abeyance. They can no longer be certainties.

The mystical flavor of life is shared by both existential believers and nonbelievers alike. It affirms life as meaningful, not because it has been clearly revealed as such through science or Scripture, but rather because one has sensed a deeper or clearer experience of reality in certain moments. These moments are not dismissed lightly, but are preserved as precious and illuminating even though the full meaning of their revelation may be unclear. Such experiences as love, beauty, creative work, rhythm, awe and psychic phenomena suggest seeing "through a glass darkly."

The bond with others

If subjectivity and its unique development and expression is valued in oneself, it must be valued in others as well. Since there is no absolute subjective perspective, each person's unique view and contribution contains an intrinsic value. The existentialist feels a bond with others and is responsive to their needs and to friendship, for he respects their subjectivity as being as valid as his own. He also knows that the assertion of courage is difficult and often impossible without occasional affirmation from others. Human love is the effort to understand, share and participate in the uniqueness of others. It is validating in others that which one also values within oneself. Love is sometimes an act of helping, at other times a passive compassion. At times it reaches a total merging which takes one beyond the fundamental awareness of isolation. Afterwards, one settles again into the separation that is one's lot.

But the existentialists realize, too, the dangers in human relationships. Just as one guards against self-deceptions that tempt one towards a narcissistic idolization of oneself, so one remains on guard in relation to the institutions of society. The assertion of individual uniqueness is often a threat to others and to a smoothly functioning social group. This is because such assertion will frequently defy those rules, patterns, habits and values which are sources of defined security for others, or a group. Thus society and subgroups within a society will again and again attempt to suppress arising individual uniqueness out of a sense of threat or an inability to comprehend. Conformity is urged. It happens with family, friends, neighborhoods, church, professional and political groups. The existentialist often finds himself estranged from others because of his own creativity and authenticity. Even when there is a relationship of mutual respect, with moments of unity through love, there will also come the moments of threat and misunderstanding because of the impossibility of one person's subjectivity fully comprehending that of another.

Yet conflict and threat in relationships do not move the existentialist into a schizoid withdrawal. He may display a touch of cynicism as he hears others identify themselves wholly with some group effort or as they proclaim the hope of man to be in his sensitive and loving interchange with his fellow man. But he knows that his own growth depends upon both affirmation from others and their occasional disagreement with him. The same interchanges are true for their growth. He believes in the beauty and warmth of love even though it is momentary. He knows that people must stand together in respecting and validating the uniqueness of one another and resisting the forces of those who believe themselves blessed with an absolute truth that justifies their using other people as things instead of as valued, unique personalities.

The philosophical position described has stressed both faith and commitment to a perspective of life deemed valid as a result of one's direct and sensitive involvement in the life process. It is in opposition to establishing a life perspective by accepting some theoretical explanation of life as defined by some outside authority—whether parental, religious, scientific or political. The subjective involvement of the whole person is essential to the life perspective

one finally concludes is his reality. This perspective is also in opposition to those who use fragmented life experiences as the ground for a total life perspective (as is sometimes found in the superficial assessments of the meaning of a weekend sensitivity group experience, or the realization of the "rightness" of a cause by a budding social activist). Human life is highly complex and one must seek an openness to its totality of experiences if his search is to be legitimate. This effort should not neglect an opening up of oneself to the meaning of experience as described by others as well.

What becomes apparent is a movement in personal awareness—from egotistical strivings to self-understanding; then to I-Thou relationships with one's immediate surroundings; and finally in the incorporation of some overall principle where man and universe are joined. Both discipline and spontaneity are essential elements on this road of increasing awareness. Disillusionment, freedom, suffering, joy and dialogue are all important happenings along the way. The end of this process does not really arrive until death. It is a continuing way that requires again and again the reaffirmation of that personal perspective called "truth."

Professional contributions

These ideas can be found in philosophical and religious writings as well as in motion pictures, plays, novels and poetry labeled "existential." One of the earliest examples of existential literature is the Book of Ecclesiastes in the Old Testament. From the Orient, Zen Buddhism is often compared with Western existential thinking.

Existential philsophy as we know it today had its initial comprehensive presentation by Soren Kierkegaard (1813-1855), whose writings were a passionate reaction to the all-embracing system of Hegelian philosophy. Later developments included the thought of Friedrich Nietzsche and Henri Bergson. Modern-day existential philosophers include Martin Heidegger, Jean-Paul Sartre, Albert Camus, Simone de Beauvoir, Miguel de Unamuno, Ortega y Gasset, Nicholas Berdyaev, Martin Buber, Gabriel Marcel and Paul Tillich. This array of names suggests the widespread interest in existentialism among several European countries.

Much of existential psychology had its ideological rooting among the phenomenologists, most notably Edmund Husserl. Two European analysts, Ludwig Binswanger and Medard Boss, were constructing an existential psychology during Freud's lifetime.

Viktor Frankl, a Viennese psychiatrist, developed his "logotherapy" following his imprisonment in a German concentration camp during World War II. Logotherapy is based upon existential philosophy, and Frankl remains one of the most lucid writers in conveying existential thinking to members of the helping professions.

Rollo May's monumental work *Existence* (46), published in 1958, was the first major impact of existential psychology upon American psychiatry and psychology. May presented the translations of existential psychologists and psychiatrists from Europe, where such thinking had become popular and in many places had replaced psychoanalytic thought. There was a readiness in America for existential thinking and it quickly became part of the third force or humanistic psychology movement. This group included people such as Karen Horney, Carl Jung, Clark Moustakas, Carl Rogers, Abraham Malow, Gordon Allport, Andras Angyal and Prescott Lecky.

Two journals devoted specifically to existential psychology and psychotherapy began quarterly publication in the United States in the early 1960s.

Today existential thought is also being related to gestalt therapy (Frederick Perls), the encounter movement (Carl Rogers and Arthur Burton), rational-emotive psychotherapy (Albert Ellis) and R. D. Laing's recent provocative writings labeled "antipsychiatry."

Perhaps the earliest social work writings with a decided existential flavor were by Jessie Taft, of the functional school. The functional school had its roots in the psychology of Otto Rank.

More recently, social workers, some of whose training had been in psychoanalytic-oriented schools, began to relate to existential thinking. Gerald Rubin's article of 1962 appeared in *Social Work*. Andrew Curry was publishing articles in the existential psychiatry journals. In the late 1960s, several articles appeared in various social work journals written by John Stretch, Robert Sinsheimer, David Weiss, Marjory Frohberg and myself. These papers were specifically related to the application of existential philosophy in social work thought and practice.

There were also several social work papers published during this period which did not specifically emphasize existentialism but which related to similar concerns of the existential social work group. These writers included Elizabeth Salomon, Mary Gyarfas and Roberta Wells Imre. The first book at this writing on the subject of existentialism in social work was published in 1969 by Exposition Press. It was Kirk Bradford's *Existentialism and Casework*. Its subtitle expresses its intent, *The Relationship Between Social Casework and the Philosophy and Psychotherapy of Existentialism*. It should be considered an introductory and integrative work rather than a comprehensive or prophetic book. In 1970 Alan Klein related existential thinking to social group work in his book *Social Work Through Group Process*. A second book was published in 1975 by Dawson College Press of Montreal authored by David Weiss and titled *Existential Human Relations*. This was a more comprehensive work applying existential thought to various aspects of social work practice.

While there appears a rising, if somewhat limited, interest in existential philosophy in social work literature, it would seem that the interest is far more widespread among social work students and younger professionals. Many of the newer therapeutic approaches being performed by social workers are closely akin to the existential view of the therapeutic process. As we shall see shortly, gestalt therapy, the reality therapies, encounter groups, communications theory, transactional analysis and psychodrama all reflect existential perspectives.

Therapeutic Concepts

The philosophical perspective discussed earlier suggests five organizing concepts of existential thought: disillusionment, freedom of choice, meaning in suffering, the necessity of dialogue and a stance of responsible commitment. These same concepts can provide a way of viewing the therapeutic process (39).

1. Disillusionment. In existential thinking one can move from a life of "bad faith" to one of authenticity. To do this one must risk the pain of disillusionment. Similarly, in psychotherapy, change can be viewed as a result of giving up those very defensive beliefs, judgments, symptoms or manipulations that interfere with the natural growth process. This growth process would be seen as the emergence of unique personhood through responsive acts in relation to one's surroundings. Realistic needs and potentials begin to be the source of choice and action instead of neurotic, self-deceptive security needs.

An important therapeutic task, then, is to help a client experience disillusionment with those various security efforts that block his own growth. Disillusionment will seldom result from a rational exploration of one's past with the hope of realizing causal factors of present defensive behavior. It is rare that one gives up security patterns because they are viewed as irrational, immature, or no longer applicable. Disillusionment occurs through the pain of loneliness and impotence. On the far side of such despair arise the possibilities of new values and beliefs. It is the therapist's concern that these be more

human values than those abandoned. The therapist acts as a midwife for the release of the natural growth energies within personality so that what is wholly and individually unique may emerge. Any tampering with this natural direction, once begun, is likely to do more harm than good.

2. Freedom of Choice. Sartre characterizes consciousness as "nothingness," for it is an awareness of oneself that transcends or goes beyond any fixed identity one might have concluded about oneself. Personality is always emerging. To view it as static or secured is an act of self-deception (bad faith). This conception of consciousness as freedom is a break with conceptions of personality as being totally ruled by an "unconscious" or by early learned behavior.

Despite one's past, despite any diagnostic label pinned upon a person, he always has the capacity to change himself. He can choose new values, or a new life style. This does not always necessitate years or months of "working something through"; it may occur within days or weeks.

Choice is for action and differs from intellectual meandering or good intentions. Chosen actions occur in the present. Therapy is therefore present-focused and task- or action-oriented. People learn from experience, not from reason alone.

The critical ingredient for change is the client's wish to do so. Therapy must therefore be designed to clarify quickly the nature of change sought by the client and the therapist must be able to work within this framework, rather than seek to convince or seduce the client into redefining his problems and aiming for some type of change goal that pleases the therapist but is only vaguely understood by the client.

A therapist's belief in the client's capacity for change is a message of positive affirmation conveyed throughout treatment. There is no question but that a therapist's focus upon unraveling the intricacies of past relationships conveys a deterministic message that is a commentary upon the weakness and helplessness of a client.

3. Meaning in Suffering.

Just as existentialists see suffering as an inherent part of a life of authenticity based upon responsibility and freedom, so, too, the existential therapist does not seek to discredit or eliminate anxiety and guilt in his clients. He, instead, affirms such suffering as both necessary and directional for a person. He will help reveal what real anxiety and guilt may lie disguised behind neurotic (unrealistic) anxiety and guilt. But he would not seek to minimize or eradicate realistic anxiety and guilt. Such efforts would themselves be dehumanizing, unless used to prevent decompensation.

4. Necessity of Dialogue.

Man does not grow from within himself alone. His emergence happens in responsive relation to his surroundings. He creates his own meaning in response to situations, and these meanings become the basis for choices and actions. However, his own meanings are no more absolute than those of any other person. His own growth has to do with the continued reassessment of personal meanings, and he depends upon feedback from his environment (particularly human responses) for this reassessment activity. In order to gain honest feedback, one must allow others to be honest and free in their own expression. In therapy, therefore, it is critical to help a person open himself to relationships with others wherein he gives up his manipulative or "game" efforts in order to invite free responses from others. In doing this he not only allows himself experiences of intimacy, but he also realizes that his own emerging sense of self requires such honest transactions with others.

5. Commitment.

A client's recognition of and commitment to his own inner emerging unique lifestyle is a hope of the existential therapist. The client realizes this commitment through his experience of the therapists's own affirmation of the client's world view. This unique world view is affirmed from the beginning in the therapist's acceptance of how the client perceives his symptoms, problems, conflicts—how he perceives change and what he wants changed. His uniqueness is also affirmed during the course of treatment by the way a therapist relates to "where a client is" in each interview. The theme of a session comes as an emerging force from the client, rather than as a rationally predicted starting point made in advance by the therapist. Both the goal-setting process and the activity of centering upon and working with an interview theme are therefore client-centered rather than therapist-centered. This in no way crimps the therapist's operation as a skilled professional with "expertise," but he acts out of this expertise rather than displaying it in a manner that will inhibit the process of therapy.

The client's awareness of and respect for his own unique lifestyle might be described as a turn away from self-pity and impotence. Rather than complaining about his lot in life, he discovers that he is intricately involved in the life process itself. He learns to listen to what life says to him and finds meaning in the response that is unique to himself. This is what is meant by the existential concept of dialogue and commitment.

Related Therapeutic Approaches

As suggested earlier, there are obvious differences among those therapists claiming the existential label. This becomes more understandable if we consider the above therapeutic principles and note how they may be activated in a number of differing ways. A consideration of the ranging techniques that may fit with the principles outlined will also clarify how other treatment theories tend to be compatible with the existential view. Existentialism claims no technique system of its own and needs none. Its affirmation of the uniqueness of each client results in a perspective of each treatment situation being also unique. Whatever techniques can be used, from whatever treatment theory, become the tools toward accomplishment of the unique goal chosen. In this sense existentialism is thoroughly eclectic. Techniques are always placed secondary to the uniqueness of the client and the puzzle he presents to the therapist.

Several therapeutic systems are compatible with existential thinking. Some are not, and these will be considered later. The reality-oriented therapists (Glasser, Ellis, Mowrer, Frankl and Morita) all stress choice and specific behavior change. They are present-focused and commonly propose specific tasks for clients wherein the client is expected to put into immediate practice a decision for change. They tend to use reason to aid the decision for change, but then stress action. The action is usually expected to occur outside of the therapy interview (often as homework assignments) but its results are brought back for further discussion. The reality therapist focuses upon the disillusionment process by clearly identifying "faulty or irrational beliefs" that are responsible for problematic behavior. He affirms the client's freedom to choose and encourages a value shift through action.

Gestalt therapy, psychodrama, client-centered therapy and encounter group techniques all stress a heightening of a client's awareness through action in the here and now. They seek the immediacy of experience as a thrust for change rather than a rational process of analyzing causal connections. They differ from the reality therapies in that the stress is upon choice and action which is more immediate; it is to occur in the here and now of the therapy meeting itself. Whether the client seeks to make use of this experience in his outside daily life is usually left up to him. There is less effort to deal rationally with the disillusionment process of beliefs and manipulations. These are dealt with experientially as group members are encouraged to give direct and open feedback to the attitudes and behavior expressed by others. The activity of dialogue is stressed.

Transactional analysis is a third therapeutic system that is in many ways compatible with

existential principles. The way of viewing pathology is as a life script consisting of games and other manipulative maneuvers to control meaningful others. This is an excellent description of how existentialists perceive the development of dysfunctional behavior. The disillusionment process occurs in transactional analysis both experientially, as others give direct and honest feedback, and rationally, as one is taught game terminology that aids in "pegging" what is dysfunctional maneuvering. But in contrast to psychoanalytic ego psychology, this process of insight occurs very quickly, with little time given to past cause-effect linkages, and clients are believed to be immediately capable of choosing a nonmanipulative lifestyle to free themselves from the game behavior. Nothing must be re-lived and "worked through" repetitiously in order to bring a person to the point of change. He is viewed as capable of change now, and therapy very soon becomes present-focused and task-oriented.

Communications theory presents a therapeutic approach highly compatible with the existential framework. A linkage between communications theory and existential theory has been described by Ruesch and Bateson (59). Virginia Satir's use of communications theory in family interviewing combines the use of reason and task activities, discussed above with the reality therapist, with the heightening of client awareness in the interview situation, used by gestalt and encounter therapists. Satir is present-focused and task-oriented and stresses the need to work with the family, for the family is the person's most immediate and intense relationship system of daily living. Work with the entire family together can ideally combine here-and-now heightened awareness in the interview situation with ongoing homework task expectations.

Jay Haley, another communications theorist, accomplishes the same two-pronged goal of Satir, but with less stress on reasoning out dysfunctioning patterns. His "strategies" are aimed at action both within and outside the family-interview situation that will move clients toward change and experiential awareness with a minimum of intellectualizing about this process. In Haley's approach, the therapist remains more in the background. While he very much becomes an influential part of the family system, he works very directly with the symptom brought in by the client and in line with the client's manner of wanting to work and change. The therapist may be direct or indirect in his behavior; this decision is based on the best strategy possible to help the client experience change rather than the therapist's need to be an expert, such as model, interpreter, teacher, etc.

Haley's "strategies" are often criticized as "manipulative," which they clearly are. Haley's response is to declare all forms of therapy manipulative, and it is preferable to be manipulative in terms of the client's stated needs and symptoms than the therapist's needs of how he wants clients to perceive their problems and make use of therapy of adjust to society. With this, the existentialist would agree.

There is strong similarity between Haley's strategies and behavior modification therapy in that both begin with the presenting symptom itself. The major difference appears to be that Haley views the symptom as always a manipulative effort to control a meaningful other person; therefore, his focus is on the family relationship system. He is expectant of an alteration in the family system of roles and interaction once the symptom is changed. The shift may necessitate further therapeutic strategies to help the family move toward growth, as a result of the shifting balance; otherwise there is the danger of the family returning to the same symptom or adoption of a new one in order to restore the neurotic equilibrium. This perspective is largely ignored by the behavior modification people who tend to see the symptom as a problem of previous faulty learning that can be altered by effective learning of a different behavioral response. While the behavior modification therapists allow that when a symp-

tom is altered, the person's experience of the nature of his problem may shift and a new symptom may be presented for treatment, this is much more of a happenstance activity than with Haley. This point of difference also accounts for the greatest danger of behavior modification (in the eyes of the existentialist). This is that a person's problem may be defined by someone else (schoolteacher, parent), and the modification of that person's behavior may result in an adjustment to the expectations and wishes of some person in a authoritative role, who has no interest in facing up to his own problems in the dysfunctional relationship system. Treatment then becomes a means of tyrannical repression rather than being humanistically growth-directed.

From the foregoing comparisions of therapeutic approaches, as they relate to existential thought, several areas of existential theory become more clear-cut. We shall look at these in more detail, considering the therapeutic relationship, nature of personality, concept of change, use of historical data and diagnosis and treatment methods.

The therapeutic relationship

The therapist's use of himself and the type of relationship he seeks to foster with a client will be considered from two vantage points. First, the attitude of the therapist toward the client and his problems; and second, the behavior of the therapist as he interacts with the client—his use of himself as a unique person in his own right.

There is a critical difference between a therapist who sees the client as a complex of defenses or learned behaviors that are dysfunctional and a therapist who views the client as a unique, irreplaceable world view that is in the process of growth, emergence and expansion. The latter is an existential position. It views the problems and symptoms of a client as his own efforts to deal with the growth forces within himself and the risks these pose to him in relation to his self-image, relationship with significant others in his life and his role in society.

The writings of R. D. Laing are aimed at clarifying the critical differences between the two types of therapists (43). He points out that the therapist who sees the client as a mass of complexes, defenses and dysfunctional learnings sees himself as the authority. His task is to diagnose the nature of these "dynamics" and convey these insights to the client either through verbal commentary or through specific behavioral tasks he gives the client. But in doing so, he also acts as another societal force which seeks to adjust the client to someone's definition of the functional personality. Such a therapist tends to support the view that the client's symptoms and problems identify him as ill (even "dysfunctional" implies that he is out of step with his surroundings). The therapist often becomes another dehumanizing force in the client's life in the sense of urging the "patient" to adjust to his family, his instincts, his needs, society's needs, etc.

In contrast to this position, the existential therapist has no prescriptions of how the client should live. He sees his task as that of a midwife, an agent who has knowledge and skills to aid in the unblocking process that will allow the client to resume his own unique growth and emergence—whether this puts him in further conflict with his family, friends and society or not. While the therapist may point out the potential risks and consequences of an emerging lifestyle, he will not negate its potential value.

The existential therapist's attitude affirms the inherent value of the client as a unique person with a very special world view or lifestyle that is his alone to charter. The client is also aware that the therapist sees in him the power of free choice. Instead of being helplessly at the mercy of forces beyond his consciousness, he can see the significant choices in his present life situation and has the power to decide which way he will proceed in the shaping of his life.

In one sense the existential therapist does stand for a particular lifestyle—but it is one based upon his belief in the nature of humanness rather than a cultural viewpoint of how a person should pursue his role in his family or his society. The values conveyed by the existential therapist are these: human beings have the capacity for free choice; they are of fundamental worth in their own unique perspective of life and their assertion of this perspective; they require an open interaction with their surroundings in order to grow—emergence is a responsive and interactive process; suffering is an inevitable part of the growth process for emergence involves risks and unknowns, and self-deception is a potent force.

These values are in opposition to several values supported by society at large; that man is a helpless creature both at the mercy of an unknown unconscious and of utter insignificance in the complex mechanisms called society; that man can and should find happiness through avoidance of suffering and pain and by means of the distractions and pleasures offered him at every turn; that a man is what he is so he should fulfill his role in his family or social system as best he can and be satified with his already finished identity; and that since there are groups of men considered ultimately wise in politics, universities, at the executive level of business and the military, in churches, and in medical buildings, Mr. Citizen should essentially consider a conforming obedience to what these soothsayers say is best for him.

The behavior of the existential therapist reflects his philosophical–psychological attitudes toward the client. If he is not the authority with the answers, what is he? The therapist does see himself as an expert, but his expertise has to do with his skills and talents of empathy; understanding; appreciation of/and compassion for individual human beings and their struggles; experience in the process of self-deception, having struggled with the growth-defensive process within himself; and affirmation of the value of the unique soul, having himself been disillusioned with all the society-made authorities who offer solutions, happiness, etc; and an open honesty that offers the client the possiblity of genuine dialogue, if the client seeks to engage in such.

He may exhibit a type of detachment. But this detachment is not the cool aloofness of the objective mechanist who is dissecting and re-forming the patient. The detachment of the existential therapist is an expression of his profound belief in the freedom of the client. The client has a right to his own lifestyle. If he chooses not to follow a direction of personal growth, but chooses to maintain his defensive posture for security or other reasons, so be it. The therapist's sense of worth is not in the client's hands but within himself. His detachment is from results, even though his actual activity in the helping process will be quite open and involved.

The relationship between therapist and client is seen by many existential writers as the essential ingredient of change. The concepts of individual growth and genuine encounter with others are interdependent in the thought of Martin Buber. David Weiss emphasizes this same connectedness in his discussion of healing and revealing (77). This I-Thou relation need not be seen as mystical. Carl Rogers's description of this activity suggests that the therapist provides an atmosphere for growth by means of a non-threatening, affirming, understanding responsiveness (55). But this does not mean the therapist remains passive. On the contrary, Rogers emphasizes the importance of the therapist being himself in the expression of important arising feelings. To offer a dialoque is at least to present one side of it in an open, honest fashion. The therapist reveals himself in another manner at times. He shares some of his own struggles, disillusionment and experiences wherein he, too, sought growth in the face of pain. In both these examples of the therapist's openness, we see that the therapist sees his own unique world view as an important experience to share with his client—not in a "go and do likewise" spirit, but rather showing himself as a fellow traveler on the rocky road of human existence.

Human personality

Freudian theory proposed the ego as a balancing, organizing, controlling, harmonizing agent among the demands of the superego, the pressures of the "outside world" and the cravings of the id. Behavior theory suggests a passive psyche that is primarily molded by outside forces. What one learns from others is what one is. Both roles render the individual practically helpless to resist the many forces that work upon him.

Two key concepts differentiate the existential view from those above. The first is the idea of an integrating, creative force for growth at the core of the personality. The second is the belief that every individual has the capacity to shift his style of life radically at any moment.

In terms of the human dynamo, the existentialists would not disagree with Freud's formulation of the id as a composite of Eros and Thanatos, or life and death instincts. To this is added, however, the notion of a force that moves man toward meaning and toward relations with his surroundings on the basis of meanings concluded. There is an integrative, unifying, creative force within man that synthesizes his experiences, potentials and opportunities and provides him clues for his own direction of growth. No matter how emotionally disturbed a patient may seem, there is this integrative core within him that prompts him in the direction of experiencing and expressing his own uniqueness (realistic needs and potentials). He may shut himself off from such integrative promptings; he may refuse to listen or mislabel such messages as dangerous. But they are with him always.

The existential idea of a core of integration and creation suggests a conflict-free portion of personality that survives and transcends any dysfunctioning that may possess a person.

Such a force toward integration and meaning need not be considered separate from id. It is an expression of id activity. Teilhard de Chardin posits such a force as existing in all forms of existence: animals, plants and even inanimate matter. Chardin sees in man the fruition of this drive toward complexity, and it is experienced as man's need for meaning and for love. Martin Buber, too, suggests a force in man that permits him to enter the realm of relation with nature, ideas, other men and God. This is a force that transcends what otherwise appears to be his limited, finite, individual self. This thinking helps distinguish the existential view of the creative force in man from what the ego psychologists have attempted to add to basic Freudian theory to explain creative functioning through certain basic powers of the ego.

The second major distinction has to do with the power of free choice possessed by every person. Even the most disturbed individual is not solely at the mercy of chaotic, irrational, destructive forces—an id gone wild. Nor is he at the total mercy of environmental forces that seek to identify, coerce, dehumanize, conform or destroy him. The individual personality is always in the process of change and emergence. Sartre defined human consciousness as a "no-thingness." Since it is always in the process of becoming, it is never fixed and completed. This no-thingness is an openness to the new, the unknown; it is forever moving beyond whatever identity one has concluded about oneself. Sartre sees this as an essential human construct. One may deny one's freedom and find ways of avoiding responsibility for this very process of change and emergence, but the process itself goes on. Pathology is not the arrestment of growth but the self-chosen distortion of growth (3).

Human consciousness is itself freedom—for it is a force that moves forever beyond whatever one has become as a fulfilled identity. As such, it is the power within man to change, to alter his lifestyle, his direction and his sense of identity. It is an ever-present potential for a conversion experience. "To find one's self, one must lose one's self."

If one has the capacity for free choice and also some awareness of integrative promptings toward growth from the very core of his psyche, then why should one choose dysfunctioning, defensive symptomatology or madness?

Freud's concept of the superego and his view of defense mechanisms and pathological symptomatology are seen by the existentialist in a more holistic manner. The existential idea of bad faith is man's activity of denying his nature of freedom and emergence for the sake of a sense of security and identity. He deceives himself by a set of beliefs that define specifically who he is and what he can expect from others. This belief system contains both positive and negative judgments about oneself and suggests how one must relate to other people. It is the center of man's defensive control efforts, of his symptomatology, of his manipulations of relationships and of his fostering myths about who he is. *He chooses* to believe certain notions about himself when he is quite young and undergoing the socialization process with his parents, teachers, peers, etc. The beliefs he holds to are used to maintain a sense of secured identity. He is tempted somehow to reassure himself of the solidity of his identity whenever he feels threatened. This he can do through manipulations of others, physical or psychological symptomatology and reassuring beliefs about himself. The belief pattern may change over the years, so that ideas implanted by parents may become more personalized beliefs, but it is the rigidity and response to threat that characterize his security image, rather than the nature of the beliefs themselves.

This defensive belief system, or security image configuration, has its values too. It helps the young, developing ego with limited experience and judgment conclude a manner of survival in a family constellation. The beliefs concluded about self and others provide habit patterns that furnish a sense of security so that one can use one's energy for other achievements as well. Even the adult ego is occasionally on the verge of exhaustion and needs to resort to the security image patterns of reassuring contentment. One will at times choose security image behavior, even when one knows it to be irrational and defensive, simply as a means of enduring and managing under considerable stress.

Security image patterns take the form of outer identifications, as well as inner passions. Outer identification includes all ways by which a person uses others to conclude who he is as a fixed identity—using his parents, spouse, children, friends, employer, profession, politics, church, race, social norms, etc. Inner passions have to do with feeling responses to life's situations that also fulfill a sense of identity, so that certain feelings become fanned into possessing passions. For the self identified as "Top Dog," irritation can become rage. For the self identified as "Don Juan," sensual excitement can become lust. For some people, competition becomes greed. For others, pride becomes a quest for power. In the outer identifications, one identifies with beliefs and roles; in the inner passions, one identifies with specific feelings. In either case, the sense of self is experienced as fixed, solidified, defined, rather than flowing, free and emerging. *

The process of change

If you want to know who you are, don't conceptualize upon it. Look at your actions, your behavior, your choices. Existentialism is a philosophy rooted in personal experience. "Truth is subjectivity," Kierkegaard's slogan, and "existence precedes essence," Sartre's assertion,

---

* This description of security image operation is similar to other conceptions of defensive functioning: Perls's "maya" and "hole" and associated "top dog and underdog" behaviors; Berne's life script with its games played out of certain "parent and child" ego states; Horney's "self idealization" and "self glorification."

are both ways of rooting identity in personal experience—one's active and unique response in a situation. Being-in-the-world is a concept of Heidegger's that asserts the same notion.

There are two components commonly accepted as necessary for the change process, one rational and the other experiential. Almost every form of psychotherapy includes both these components, despite their occasional assertions to the contrary.

The experiential component has to do with the client experiencing himself in a new and different way. He may discover that he is being dealt with differently by a significant other person in his life. He may also find new kinds of feelings or symptoms arising within himself. The rational component has to do with self-understanding through the process of reflecting and conceptualizing about oneself—the cause-effect relationships in his background, evaluating how he handled recent situations, considering the meaning to him of a new way he has experienced himself, etc.

The existentialists see values in both components of change—one reinforces the other when both occur. The existentialists, however, are particularly wary of the common self-deception of intellectualizing about oneself—of dwelling on self-evaluation and introspection in a manner that negates any action or choice in the here and now. The existentialists, therefore, stress the experiential component of change as of primary importance. The rational component is secondary and is most useful in either preparing oneself to act now in a new way, or else in evaluating the meaning of an experience wherein one did act differently. Several forms of experiential activities can occur in therapy:

1. The attitude of the therapist toward the client can present a new type of affirmation by a significant other person that the client has never experienced.

2. The therapist's skill with empathy may provide the client an experience of being understood more intensely than by others in his life.

3. The openness of the therapist about himself as a revealing, engaging person provides an invitation for the client to the dialogical experience. It can also offer an experience of an authority figure as human and of equal status. Such openness by a therapist may constructively take the form of provocative, negative feedback to the client about his appearance, attitudes, feelings and behavior. Here the client experiences a candid honesty that may be otherwise denied him in his everyday world of interactions.

4. Techniques designed for here-and-now heightening of awareness, such as in gestalt, psychodrama and encounter groups or the dealing with "transference" interactions between therapist and client, are obviously aimed primarily at the experiential component of change. Similarly, efforts to vitalize new interactions between group or family members quickly stir new areas of individual awareness.

5. Action tasks for the client to perform outside of therapy sessions provide new behavioral experiences.

Compatible with the existential therapist's emphasis upon experiential change is his lack of interest in historical data. Some history may be of value in the early interviews to help the therapist see the client in a more human, better rounded perspective, so that the therapist is less inclined to make superficial judgments about the client in response to the stereotype the client usually presents to other people. But the therapist often does not even need this aid. It is far more important to understand the dynamics of the client's present struggle, and what his symptoms or complaints reveal about his efforts to grow and meet his own needs (the present beliefs and activities of his defensive belief system).

If the client himself brings up historical material, the existential therapist will often seek to make it immediately relevant. He may do this by relating the past experience to present choices, or else (using gestalt techniques) by asking the client to bring the early parent figure into the present interview session by role playing the past interaction which the client is describing.

The existential therapist is in agreement with Glasser's position that an intent focus upon early historical material plays into the client's feelings of helplessness and his efforts to rationalize his own impotence.

Dynamics, diagnosis and world view

Clinical diagnosis has its value as a shorthand way of communicating to peers about clients, in terms of areas of conflict and types of defenses. Other than this, it is of questionable value in the eyes of the existential therapist and commonly results in more harm than good. The danger of diagnosis is the categorization of a client, so as to provide the therapist some "objective" way of defining prognosis, goals, the role he must play as he interacts with the client and his decision about termination. Such "objective" efforts based upon generalizations about clients with a similar history-symptomatology-mental status constellation miss what is unique about a particular client. A further danger described by R. D. Laing is that diagnosis is often used as a way of agreeing with the family that this client is "sick" and in need of readjustment to the demands and expectations of the family.

This depreciation of the value of clinical diagnosis, however, does not suggest a disregard for understanding the nature of a client's present struggles, conflicts, strivings and fears. Dynamic understanding remains of key importance. Here the existentialist differs with the behavioral modifier who relates himself only to a specific symptom without regard for its meaning and the client's present lifestyle.

It is critical to understand the unique "world view" of the client. This consists of patterns of relating to meaningful others and expectations of them. It also includes beliefs about oneself, both positive and negative judgments and assumptions about oneself and how these affect the way one meets one's own needs and handles one's frustrations of need satisfaction. It is important to see how the client is interfering with his own growth, and this includes both the beliefs he holds about the sort of person he is and the notions he has about how he must deal with the significant people in his life. It may even include how he evaluates forces of society that play upon him and attempt to conform his behavior into some stereotype that is useful to society's needs (employers, church, racial attitudes, etc.).

This type of dynamic formulation stresses the here-and-now lifestyle—the client's present being-in-the-world. How he gets this way is of questionable significance. The values of dynamic formulations are twofold. First, they provide the therapist with an understanding of his unique client and how his present symptoms are ways of handling a particular stress or conflict area. Second, dynamics give the therapist somewhat of a guideline to assess his own work with the client, particularly when he discovers that his therapeutic efforts are bringing no results.

The dynamic formulation of the existential therapist will emphasize family dynamics (interactions, scapegoating, alliances, etc.). For these usually make up the most significant area of the client's lifestyle functioning. Intervention efforts will frequently involve other family members for the same reason.

Even when the problem is not set forth as family or marital in nature, the therapist will tend to see the presenting symptom as a means of dealing with significant others in his life. An interpersonal appraisal of symptoms is attuned to the absence, loss, breakdown or dysfunctioning of important human relationships in the person's life. Therapeutic work will commonly be addressed to the creation, the restoration, or the improvement of such relationships. This interpersonal focus upon symptomatology need not neglect the individual's subjective experience of attitudes, values and feelings. The two are ob-

viously interdependent. However, the existential therapist sees catharsis and self-understanding as a vehicle for altering the person's world of human relationships, which is the fundamental goal.

Dynamic formulation, just as we will see with goal setting and treatment technique selection, are focused upon how the client is experiencing his present stress. He is not "talked into" viewing his problem as having "deeper" meanings. It is his problem, not the therapist's problem. He is not there to please the therapist by pursuing those insights deemed crucial by the therapist. He is there because he wants change and his motivation for change is experienced in the stressful symptom or condition itself. This highlights another viewpoint of the existential therapist mentioned earlier. A client is capable of changing his life by choice and action, no matter what diagnostic category we may label him. The sole factor and prognosis for change is the client's desire to change. This does not disregard the client's usual ambivalence about change. Ambivalence may be used to point out that the client has not really concluded what he wants to change, and it is this decision that is necessary if therapy is to proceed toward an agreed-upon goal.

To validate the client's view of his problem may appear inconsistent with the therapist's concern with improving the client's significant other relationships. This need not be a problem. Therapists must have a way of understanding symptom dynamics, whether interpersonal, intrapsychic or a combination of the two. Without emphasizing either insight or interpersonal needs, a therapist can work on problem alleviation, within the client's own frame of reference, in such a way as to produce enhanced relationships. A client who views his problem solely as alcoholism, for example, may be asked to participate in Alcoholics Anonymous as an adjunct part of his therapy. It is not uncommon for a careful exploration of any symptom to reveal the interpersonal component of it—its manipulative intent. When this becomes apparent, the client will oftentimes request that some significant other be involved. At such a choice point, the existential therapist would usually encourage rather than discourage such involvement.

Treatment methods

It is difficult to talk of treatment methods without first considering the types of clients and problems for which the methods are used. In one sense, the existential perspective is loyal to no particular treatment system. It is eclectic and uses whatever techniques will best meet the needs of a particular client. In another sense, the existential therapist may be considered best equipped to work with clients whose problem involves a loss of direction, a value confusion, a shaken identity in a swirling world of anomie. For these clients, certain techniques have been developed to focus precisely on such difficulties. However, it should be clearly understood that the existentialist works out of his unique philosophical persective with all clients, and he should not be viewed only as a specialist with clients experiencing personal alienation.

There are three principles of treatment that clarify the therapeutic approach of the existentialist. These are:

1. A client-centered orientation
2. An experiential change emphasis
3. A concern with values and philosophical or religious perspectives

1. The client-centered focus has already become apparent in our introductory comments on the existentialist's antiauthoritarian stance. Client-centeredness was also the major issue in the discussion on diagnosis and dynamic formulation. Two other areas exemplify client-centeredness: these are goal formulations and work with an emerging theme in any given interview.

Goal formulation involves the therapist and client working out a mutual agreement in the early interviews as to the purpose of future treatment. What must be guarded against here is the type of therapeutic dogmatism that seeks to convince the client as to the "true implications" of his symptoms or problem, so that he will work in the manner the therapist wishes. The most important initial step in treatment, following the age-old social work principle, is to "start where the client is." This adage refers to focusing on how the client is experiencing his problem, what it is that he wants changed, and other ideas as to the type of help he is seeking.

Elsewhere, I enumerated a framework of possible goals from which social workers may proceed with treatment (41). These are:

a. Provocative contact
b. Sustaining relationship
c. Specific behavior (symptom) change
d. Environmental change
e. Relationship change
f. Directional change
g. Combinations of the above

The type of goal left off this list is the extensive insightful analysis that a client who enters psychoanalysis may be seeking. Whether or not he ends up with any more significant change through insightful analysis than in some of the above-mentioned goals is highly questionable at this point in time, considering research efforts into the effects of treatment.

The above-stated goals can be briefly differentiated by considering the client's view of change in each category.

Provocative Contact. The client seeks neither change nor help of any kind. The caseworker assertively seeks to provoke a client into wanting change. This occurs often in protective services, in residential treatment centers for children and in the "back wards" of psychiatric hospitals and institutions for the retarded. It is also common with the "hard-to-reach" families who present various problems to the community via the schools and police departments. Just how far a caseworker should go in his provocative efforts is itself an ethical decision related to the right of a client to his own unique lifestyle. Nevertheless, provocative efforts are often justified insofar as they provide an outreach effort and offer an opportunity that the client might otherwise never consider.

Sustaining Relationship. Here the client seeks help, in that he is lonely and wants an affirmative, interested contact in his life. But he has no hope for changing his lifestyle in any way and will resist any such efforts. His need is for an affirming relationship without expectations of changed behavior.

Specific Behavior (Symptom) Change. The client is distressed with a particular troublesome behavior. He has no interest, however, in widening his problem area by seeing how this particular symptom is related to his past or present lifestyle and system of relationships. His motivation is restricted to symptom alleviation.

Environmental Change. The client sees his difficulty in relation to the environment beyond his family. The problem may have to do with employment, education, social contacts, community forces that he experiences as dehumanizing. He does not see himself as part of the problem. He seeks help in dealing with social institutions and systems.

Relationship Change. Here the client experiences difficulties in relationships with significant others in his life—his spouse, children, parents, relatives, friends. He realizes his own involvement and wants to alter a relationship pattern.

Directional Change. The client's sense of identity, of values, of personal direction is confused. He has difficulty in making choices and feels impotent in relation to his immediate future. The conflict is experienced as within himself.

The mode of therapy used (individual, couple, group, family) or the types of techniques (reality, behavioral modification, encounter, psychoanalytic ego, gestalt, etc.) will vary, of course, in accordance with the interest of the client, the skills of the therapist and the nature of the treatment setting itself. However, certain techniques are obviously more appropriate for certain goals. Behavior modification would be particularly useful with the goals of provocative contact and specific behavior (symptom) change. Social work literature provides many useful approaches to accomplishing the goal of environmental change. The goal of relationship change can be dealt with using communications theory (Satir, Haley, Jackson), other family and marital therapy models, transactional analysis, and encounter-group approaches. Directional change can be effected by techniques described by Carl Rogers, Frank Farrelly, the Gestaltists, reality therapy, and psychoanalytic psychotherapy. The critical point here is that the therapeutic approach must fill the unique goal and needs of a client rather than fitting clients into some pet system of psychotherapy, and dismissing the misfits as "unmotivated."

What is important to understand in this goal framework is that it provides a starting point for treatment in a manner that recognizes the unique experience of the client as valid. The goal may change during treatment as the client begins to experience his problems in some other light. The goal must also be tested out in early interviews so as to ascertain whether the goal agreed upon is merely a verbalized goal of the client, or whether it is indeed the way in which the client experiences the need for help and hope for change. With this framework, the therapist engages the client in a manner by which they can both "talk the same language" and have similar expectations for what is to follow.

There would appear to be a contradiction

between some of the above-mentioned goals and what has previously been described as the existential focus upon disillusionment, freedom of choice, finding meaning and suffering, discovering the growth value of dialogue and coming to a sense of personal commitment in relation to one's future. Such a focus seems most applicable to the goal category of directional change. The existential therapist, however, is not bound to pursue such a focus, if it does not seem appropriate. The existentialist concern with client-centered treatment and an emphasis upon experiential change enables him to assert his philsophical perspective to a degree in all goal categories described.

The other client-centered activity deals with the interview theme of any given session. The client is not a problem to be solved, a puzzle to be completed. He is a person who is undergoing constant change from week to week, day to day. Change occurs in his life for both the good and the bad apart from what happens during his therapy sessions. For the therapist to preplan an interview, picking up where the last one ended or getting into what the therapist considers to be an area of increasing importance, is often presumptuous.

The interview begins and the therapist listens to both verbal and nonverbal expressions of the client. He is alert to possible inconsistencies among what the client says, his feeling state and behavior. The therapist's most important listening tool is his capacity for empathy. In the initial stages of the interivew, the therapist must free himself of preconceptions about the client and preoccupations with himself in order to open himself to the whole person before him.

From various client communications, the therapist discerns a common thread of concern and feeling state that seems predominant in the client's presentation of himself. This is the emerging theme—where the client is today; how he is experiencing himself in relation to his problem and to the therapist. Sometimes the interview theme will be clear quite early; other

times it will be well disquised and only understood, in Reik's words, by the therapist "listening with his third ear." Here the skill of empathy is a necessity, and the therapist who hears only content and seeks to reason out helpful suggestions from this communication level will often be lost. Empathy includes a listening to the feeling state of the client and responsive feeling states in oneself. Sometimes one's own feeling response will be the only clue to what is happening within the client.

As the feeling state becomes more clear to the therapist, he may use his diagnostic understanding of the client to clarify further for himself the possible meanings related to the feelings. This is the therapist's rational response to the experience occurring and can only be considered a diagnostic activity in the broadest sense, since he may not actually reflect upon his dynamic conceptualization of the client. For instance, he may wonder if this feeling state is somehow a reaction to the last interview; or if it is a repetitive reaction pattern related to a recent event that was quite important but alluded to only casually in the client's discussion today. As the therapist comes to a better understanding of what the feeling is and what it might mean (which may often involve further questioning and refocusing of the interview) he is in a better position to make vital contact with the client. Vital contact involves making the client aware that his primary, felt concern is known and understood by the therapist. It may be that the moment this contact is made the therapist can only express awareness of the client's feelings but that he does not himself understand the source of meaning of the feelings.

How the theme is made known as well as how it is dealt with are related to the goal of therapy (thinking in terms of the goal framework described earlier) and what particular therapeutic approach a therapist favors for work on such a goal. The therapist and client work together from the point of theme clarity. Techniques aimed at experiential insight, self-understanding or both, may be used depending upon the goal, therapeutic approach and needs and capacities of the client at that particular moment. On the other hand, the client may steadfastly deny the theme as clarified by the therapist, and if the therapist believes this to be client resistance, the work of the interview will proceed in terms of working on the resistance itself.

It is this process of making vital theme contact that results in interview satisfaction for both therapist and client. They realize themselves to be "on the same wave length" and therefore working together. Even the resisting client feels himself to be understood by the therapist who has genuinely detected resistance.

Theme contact will vary from interview to interview. Sometimes it will occur quite early in the session while at other times not until the end. Sometimes it will fail to occur at all and it will be important then for the therapist to express his own frustration and ignorance at the end of the session. In some instances theme contact will occur, therapeutic work will proceed, a resolution will result and a new theme will arise within the same session.

This entire process of theme contact and subsequent therapeutic work can operate at times in a totally intuitive fashion. When this occurs, there is little need for the therapist's rational reflection upon how he needs to proceed. The therapist experiences empathetic awareness followed by his own need for vitalization of the interview. Vital theme contact, then, occurs with the therapist experiencing a certainty of action, using techniques that are fully appropriate. The response of the client either validates his intuitive activity or else faces him with his own erroneous assumptions. Here we have therapy as art.

2. The experiential emphasis has already been discussed. The activities encouraging experiential change included: attitude of therapist, empathy, therapist's openness or transparency, heightening of here-and-now awareness, tasks for choice and action. In the earlier discussion of

how various theories of therapy reflected various existential points of emphasis, it was apparent that techniques could be tapped from many theoretical sources.

It is clear by now that the existentialist is radically concerned with the here-and-now encounter between a person and his world. For it is in this moment of responsiveness, of being-in-the-world, that one experiences his freedom of choice and meaning making. Who he is stems from what he does—the choice he activates—and does not stem from the intellectual conceptualization he holds about himself, nor from any dogmas or groups to which he holds allegiance in exchange for some bestowed identity.

Theoretical material regarding the therapist's attitude toward the client, his empathic activity and his openness or transparency are presented by Carl Rogers, Robert Katz and many leaders in the encounter movement, such as Arthur Burton.

Techniques on heightening here-and-now awareness are best illustrated by gestalt therapists, encounter-group leaders, and transactional analysis. Psychoanalytic psychotherapy also deals with this activity in relation to identifying transference manifestations.

The emphasis upon choice and action is seen in a number of varied theories of treatment: behavior modification, communications theorists (Haley, Satir, etc.), reality therapy, rational-emotive psychotherapy, directive therapy (Thorne), transactional analysis and many of the writings of existential therapists (Frankl, May, Sutherland).

3. The concern with pinpointing, challenging, clarifying values and philosophy or religious perspectives is also dealt with by various writers. There are strong similarities between the rational-emotive psychotherapy of Albert Ellis and the morita therapy of Japan. Both pinpoint "irrational" or "unrealistic" beliefs the client holds to and specifically propose other more realistic and human beliefs in substitution for the dysfunctional beliefs. Hobart Mowrer's

integrity therapy follows a similar course, where the emphasis is upon helping the client see that there is a contradiction between the values he holds in common with his "significant others" and his behavior or actual lifestyle. Viktor Frankl has developed two techniques, dereflection and paradoxical intention, that are designed to help a client reexamine and alter his philosophical perspective so as to affirm a new way of viewing himself in relation to his symptoms, choices and life direction.

These "reality-oriented" approaches include four common ingredients:

1. Pinpointing specific values (attitudes, beliefs, judgments about self and others) manifested by the client's lifestyle.
2. Clarifying how these very values are interfering with his own growth and intimacy needs or efforts.
3. Helping him substitute more realistic, human values and beliefs for the dysfunctional ones so his realistic growth and intimacy needs can achieve more direct satisfaction.
4. Encouraging decisions, choices and actions (often as homework assignments) in order to activate the new values concluded to be more valid.

This therapeutic emphasis upon values and philosophical perspective is designed for certain types of clients—those whose working goal is directional change. There is a growing recognition of the effects of anomie in modern culture with resulting personal alienation from the roots of human needs and human strivings. C. G. Jung reported this phenomenon forty years ago and existential novelists, philosophers, and psychologists have been emphasizing the extent of alienation ever since World War II.

The American culture has finally felt the same impact of alienation that shook Europe during and after World War II. In America, this awareness was helped along by the revolt of the youth, minority groups and poor people. At this point, it is unclear whether alienation is a problem of a particular client population or whether it is really at the root of all emotional distress. The writings of R. D. Laing and others suggest the latter view.

Considering the three therapeutic principles discussed (the client-centered orientation, focus upon experiential change and concern for values and philosophical perspectives), it becomes clear that the existential caseworker seeks to work with all types of clients and human problems and that he could function with any kind of social agency or therapeutic setting, provided he was given the administrative approval to work as he wished. It is also clear that the existential position is in opposition to those therapeutic practices that seek to adjust clients to family and social norms or to those prognostic norms stemming from the rigid use of diagnostic categories. The authoritative misuse of behavior modification and psychoanalytic theory is a major concern of the existential social worker.

Considering the eclectic use of treatment approaches suggested by the existential perspective, it is also apparent that social workers can make more creative and varied use of the existential perspective than can either psychiatrists, psychologists, ministers or nurses. This is because of the wide-ranging problem activities that engage the efforts of social workers, necessitating a manner of work that includes multiple skills. While there is still a lack of research verification, it appears that work with a middle-class clientele will commonly involve techniques aimed at heightening here-and-now awareness, as well as dealing with values and philosophical perspectives. Clients from the lower classes, who are considered unresponsive to traditional treatment approaches, would appear most responsive to task-oriented techniques emphasizing choice and action.

The modes of therapy (individual, couple, family and group) are all effective ways of conducting an existential-oriented treatment. Application to individual counseling has been elaborated upon, particularly by Carl Rogers,

Frank Farrelly, Rollo May, Viktor Frankl and Frederick Perls. Work with groups with an existential perspective has been described by Helen Durkin, Carl Rogers and Arthur Burton. The social work writer, Alan Klein, relates the group work approach to existential thinking. Family therapists whose approaches are highly compatible with the existential perspective include Jay Haley, Virginia Satir, John Bell and Carl Whitaker.

Case example

The following could be considered an example of the existential social work approach. The case described is short-term casework with an individual from the goal framework of specific behavior change. It should be clear from the previous discussion about differing goals and the eclectic use of treatment techniques, that other case examples would take much different forms from the one described. The three existential principles of client-centered focus, experiential change and value focus are illustrated in this case.

An attractive Spanish-American woman, aged thirty-four, came to me complaining of a severely inhibiting depression. In the course of the evaluation, it appeared that she had little interest or sensitivity for seeing any connection of her symptoms to her past or present living situation. She was somewhat troubled over a divorce of a year ago. There was also a problem with her mother (living across the street) who tried to dominate her and provoke her guilt and who often took care of her two teenage daughters. Some rebellion in the older daughter was apparent. She also believed herself "hexed" by her mother-in-law. These were areas of complaints, yet she saw no prospects for changing them. Her concerns for change were very concrete; she could not do her housework or cook the meals or discipline the children, for she would usually go to bed soon after she returned from work. In bed, she would either sleep or fantasize

about how bad off she was, and the running of the house was left to the children, particularly the rebellious older one. She feared losing her job as a nurse's aide with the local hospital and had already missed several days of work because of feeling too tired. She had given up going out with her boyfriend and felt extremely alone and worthless.

Within ten interviews, seen on an alternate week basis, the depression had lifted. She managed her housework well; disciplined the children—the older one was much less rebellious; she could stand up to her mother on a realistic basis; she was dating again; and she was taking a training course to become a practical nurse. The goal was specific behavioral change, although its successful accomplishment resulted in a broadening of this woman's constructive activity in several areas of her life. My techniques dealt primarily with the symptoms of depression and helplessness. In the second interview, I emphasized what I sensed to be her inhibited potential: I said that she could make herself get out of bed (or refuse to enter it) by performing the tasks of her housework and by going to her hospital work every day, no matter how tired she felt. I recognized that feelings of depression were strong within her, but pointed out that they represented a part of herself that seemed to be trying to convince her that she was no good. In the third interview, I dealt actively with a defensive belief, challenging its validity and questioning her need to be dominated by it. She thought the depression resulted from being "hexed." I told her that I did not believe in the magic of hexing and if there was anything to it, it had to do with her own reaction to the notion that she had been "hexed." I linked this belief with the part of her that was trying to convince her that she was helplessly useless and inadequate. As sessions went on, she did bring up material about her mother, husband, children, job and relatives, but this was more from the standpoint of content for discussion in what she felt to be a positive, affirming relationship. The actual therapeutic effort, in terms of pinpointing her problem and a way of dealing with it, was primarily in relation to the depressive symptom described. The techniques used were my ways of responding to her area of concern and view of change. We could communicate through the goal of specific behavior change. She was able to see the depression as being a self-defeating part of her. This freed her from the belief that the depressive symptom was a condemnation and failure of her *whole* personality, which had been implied in her notion of "being hexed." While this was a limited shift in the belief system of this woman, it could still be a significant one. Furthermore, her resumption of responsibility in the family had its rewarding feedback responses from the children, as well as from her own mother who was closely involved with her family

Note the three principles involved: a client-centered focus in terms of goal selection and interview management; emphasis upon experiential change through use of task assignment as well as through the attitude of the therapist regarding the client's potential strengths; and finally, an effort to deal with the woman's value system, specifically suggesting that she did have some capacity for free choice and need not identify herself completely with her symptom (feelings of fated helplessness).

This case raises an interesting cultural issue in relation to the client's view of the change process and how she views change as possibly occurring. An alternative approach might have been a referral of this woman to a curandero to handle the "hexed" issue. Had she been unresponsive to my rational efforts to deal with her belief about "being hexed," I would have considered such a referral. Since she had sought out my help, I chose to deal with this belief issue in this more personal, challenging way.

Existentialism and the community

Existentialism is sometimes criticized as an individualistic philosophy lacking a social ethic. This is a misnomer. Philosophers such as Camus, Berdyaev, Tillich and Buber have written extensively on the application of existential thinking to social issues. Members of the helping professions have also related existential philosophy to social concerns. Edward Tiryakian, a sociologist, compares existential thought with that of Durkheim. Lionel Rubinoff's *The Pornography of Power* is a critique of modern philosophical, psychological and sociological thought on the subject of the individual and his relationship to society. Rubinoff's basic premises are existential. R. D. Laing also uses an existential framework in his critique of society and of the helping professions as dehumanizing extensions of society's values.

Beginning with the existential belief that truth is not found in any objective fashion, within a doctrine or within a group of people, we find some implications for a view of society and social change.

In the first place, the existentialist stands against tyranny in any form—not only by politically conservative, status quo-oriented leaders, but also by the rational social engineers who would seek to establish the utopian society necessitating many controls and committed to adjustment of individuals to a "properly functioning" society. The existentialists are a prime opponent of B. F. Skinner in his appeal for a society that meets men's needs by limiting freedom and nonconformity.

The existentialists know that power corrupts and that much of the evil perpetrated by all men is unpredictable at the moment of its inception. If, on the other hand, there is an effort to decondition evil-producing behavior, this effort itself, if successful, would result in the most profound evil of all—the dehumanization of people by depriving individuals of freedom—the only valid source of their sense of personal meaning and dignity.

On the other hand, an appeal for a completely free and open society, such as proposed by Reich's *Greening of America,* is again a naive position founded upon a disregard for the self-defeating, the aggressive and the evil-producing behavior of men. Spontaneous "doing one's own thing" is too simple a commitment. Man can be defeated by his own instincts and self-deceptions as easily as by his efforts to organize and construct the happy state.

Power itself results in an increased effort toward solidification and self-perpetuation. Society must be a dynamic, growing system, just as the individual is a being of responsive emergence. The healthy society is one attuned to the creative ideas and efforts of individuals and groups within its structure that propose change and new ideas. A participatory democracy is an expression of the existential affirmation of the unique perspective of each individual. In a participatory democracy, groups are seen to possess their own truths, which will differ from the attitudes and values of others who have not had the same life experiences. The minority groups are correct in claiming the right to speak for themselves. On the other hand, this does not mean that any single minority group possesses the final truth and wisdom for all men either, as many guilt-ridden whites seem to believe.

The direction for a society's emergence stems from the sufferings and potentials of its people, and not from an elite group of rebels or social organizers. Eric Hoffer was right in saying that the most creative and innovative shifts in a society stem from its outcasts, nonconformists and those who experience the failures of its present functioning. The existential model for social change would be one wherein the very people who suffer from dehumanizing social forces would be the indicators of what sorts of changes are needed. The community organization social worker would have a facilitating, clarifying, enabling role here, perhaps, and once a direction is clear he may use his knowledge of power structure and change tactics in order to mobilize the social change effort.

The "anti-existential" community organizer would be one who decides for himself what change other people really need and then uses his knowledge and skills to "educate," seduce and pressure a disadvantaged group into deciding what their problems are and the change indicated. The worker's basic notions of change, here, come either from his own needs, or his rational, analytical conclusions of what this group or community lacks in comparison with some ideal he holds about how people should live. The impetus for change is worker-oriented rather than community-oriented.

The opposite extreme, also anti-existential, is sometimes seen in community mental health clinics. Although such clinics are committed, by their very purpose (and federal funding), to a community outreach stance, there is little genuine effort at dialogue with those needy members of the community who do not enter the portals of the clinic itself requesting some specific help. In contrast, the genuinely committed community mental health clinic is actively seeking contact with those groups in its community who are known through police, welfare and schools to have problems but who are not availing themselves of any helping services. Primary prevention at times of family or neighborhood crisis becomes a major way of help, and this most often takes the form of consultation with police, welfare workers, teachers, nurses, ministers and doctors.

As discussed earlier, the existentialists see many of the forces of society as being in opposition to the individual's effort at an authentic lifestyle—establishing his unique direction out of an awareness of his own freedom, responsibility and what he learns through personal suffering. Modern society encourages anomie and personal alienation by its forces of seduction and oppression. Insofar as the economic–political system uses people as objects in order to preserve its own efficient functioning, it may be said to be dehumanizing. Various social institutions combine their efforts to achieve this goal. Certain roles in the system are rewarded with status, financial remuneration and prestige while others are ignored. Happiness is defined in such a way as to keep the public at large an active consumer of economic goods. An attunement to personal suffering is discouraged through the various tranquilization forms of drugs, alcohol, treadmill activities and a work ethic that implies a solution to all one's problems with the purchase of the next automobile, house or packaged vacation plan. Such writers as Erich Fromm and Henry Winthrop have elaborated upon the multiple forms of social dehumanization that are too numerous and complex to mention here (24, 81).

The helping professional is faced with a critical choice in relation to social dehumanization. He can become a part of this system that is a purveyor of anomie by the very way he performs his helping role. Or, on the other hand, he can be a member of a vanguard actively in touch with many of society's victims, who can help bring individuals and groups to an active awareness of themselves as free and responsible beings despite the negative forces bestowed upon them by society. Beyond such awareness, he will help them toward personal direction and action that affirms human dignity in the face of tyrannical and dehumanizing social forces.

The institutions of society can and do provide constructive, affirming forces for individuals and groups, of course, through education, employment, protection, health and welfare care as well as valued traditions, a sense of history and a national spirit that affirms a set of values that is generally accepted and may be quite compatible with the freedom, responsibility and valuing of uniqueness and personal dignity that characterize existentialism. The existential helping professional realizes, however, that the constructive forces of society cannot in themselves bring an individual to authenticity. The matter of personal choice and acceptance of responsibility for one's own world view and lifestyle remain essential. The existentialist is, therefore, cynical in response to social utopians who seek to construct a society of need-met, happy people.

Research and knowledge gaps

Recurring themes in existential thought have to do with freedom, uniqueness and emergence. B. F. Skinner claims that man's bondage to such concepts about himself has actually impeded the development of society (63). Existentialists argue that Skinner's controlled society of institutional conditioning is itself a dehumanizing idea. In such a dispute between faiths further research is in order. Whether research can actually reveal the existence and value of human freedom and emergence is another question. It is clear, however, that research with rats and dogs cannot provide answers to questions about the human dynamo.

Theoretical speculation and argument about the nature of intrapsychic processes may be an exercise in futility for researchers. On the other hand, behavior, interactions between people and responses within the therapeutic interview are observable data for study. Research into the results of treatment must be more carefully explored. Studies to date seem to indicate no treatment method as superior to any other. This may imply the value of a more eclectic use of treatment methods, based upon the needs of clients rather than treatment preferences of therapists. In further studies perhaps the skilled eclectic therapist should have the results of his work compared with that of a single-therapy-method therapist.

On the other hand, it may be that the results of treatment are completely independent of the therapeutic (even eclectic) approach used. This could suggest that a successful therapist is one who has arrived at a level of wisdom which expresses itself in response to a client's needs regardless of the treatment method used. This may suggest, as Jay Haley does, that therapeutic success has to do with the effective use of strategies that alter the interpersonal processes in a client's lifestyle. A wise therapist may intuitively sense the most effective strategies and apply from whatever therapeutic method is most familiar. But then there is a new question, What constitutes a wise therapist and how does he develop?

How are social work education programs preparing students for present practice? Do they foster those ingredients that may eventually result in a wise practitioner, given a few years additional experience? Here the existentialist has serious concerns. An educational tradition has existed for many years in social work that has emphasized the analytic, diagnostic, rational-authoritarian approach. Teachers have often viewed students in this categorical manner and have in turn urged students to view their clients in a similar manner. This has been the phony guise of "scientism" that has sought to identify social workers as "scientific" when in fact the "objective nature" of most of their knowledge would be scoffed at by physical scientists. Many students, in their insecurity, seek comfort in categorizing clients according to the knowledge system taught them. Other students, rebelling against what feels like a rigid authoritarianism, will completely abandon dynamic understanding of any type and naively seek to provide "band-aid" answers to problems posed by clients. It would appear that students need to be somehow "humanized" rather than "object-ified." Self-awareness has been a goal of social work education, but it would seem that new educational approaches need to be devised to achieve this goal more effectively. Only by an appreciation of one's own personal complexity can one begin seriously to understand the complexities of others.

In conclusion, the existential stance provides a philosophical perspective that can be related to the many avenues of social work practice. One does not need a profound acquaintance with existential philosophy in order to benefit from this perspective. One might, instead, view the existentialists as emphasizing a sense of direction and a style of working that are primarily concerned with a greater humanization of the social work profession. From their emphasis upon the value of the uniqueness of the individual there comes an affirmation of a client-centered focus and an awareness of the dangers of anomie in a mechanistic society. From their view of growth through choice and action there comes a primary effort aimed at experiential change with clients. From their model of man as a meaning-making being there comes a recognition of the importance of values, philosophy and religion as ingredients of the casework process. From their emphasis upon dialogue there comes the concern for therapist transparency and authenticity as well as the valuing of a participatory democracy. And from their appreciation of the powers of self-deception at work with human beings, there comes an emphasis upon personal commitment in the face of suffering and uncertainty, as well as a suspicion about any authority that establishes itself as knowing how other people should live their lives.

References

1. Allport, Gordon. *Letters from Jenny.* New York: Harcourt, Brace and World, 1965.
2. Angyal, Andras. *Neurosis and Treatment.* New York: Wiley, 1965.
3. Barnes, Hazel. *The Literature of Possibility: A Study of Humanistic Existentialism.* Lincoln: University of Nebraska Press, 1959.
4. Barret, William. *Irrational Man.* Garden City, N.Y.: Doubleday, 1958.
5. Berdyaev, Nikolai. *Slavery and Freedom.* New York: Scribner, 1944.
6. Binswanger, Ludwig. *Begin in the World.* New York: Basic Books, 1963.
7. Borowitz, Eugene. *A Layman's Guide to Religious Existentialism.* New York: Delta, 1966.

8. Boss, Medard. *Psychoanalysis and Daseinsanalysis*. New York: Basic Books, 1963.

9. Bradford, Kirk A. *Existentialism and Casework*. Jericho, N.Y.: Exposition Press, 1969.

10. Buber, Martin. *Between Man and Man*. Boston: Beacon Press, 1955.

11. ———. *The Knowledge of Man*. New York: Harper and Row, 1965.

12. Burton, Arthur (ed.) *Encounter*. San Francisco: Jossey-Bass, 1969.

13. Camus, Albert. *The Rebel*. New York: Knopf, 1969.

14. Curry, Andrew. "Toward a Phenomenological Study of the Family," *Existential Psychiatry*, Vol. 6, No. 27, Spring, 1967, pp. 35-44.

15. Durkin, Helen. *The Group in Depth*. New York: International University Press, 1964.

16. Ellis, Albert. *Reason and Emotion in Psychotherapy*. New York: Stuart, 1962.

17. Farber, Leslie. *The Ways of the Will*. New York: Harper Colophon Books, 1966.

18. Farrelly, Frank. *Provocative Therapy*. Madison, Wis.: Family, Social and Psychotherapy Service, 1974.

19. Ford, Donald and Hugh Urban. *Systems of Psychotherapy*. New York: Wiley, 1964, Chapter 12.

20. Frankl, Viktor E. *The Doctor and the Soul. From Psychotherapy to Logotherapy*. New York: Knopf, 1965.

21. ———. *Man's Search for Meaning: An Introduction to Logotherapy*. Boston: Beacon Press, 1962.

22. ———. *Psychotherapy and Existentialism. Selected Papers on Logotherapy*. New York: Simon and Schuster, 1967.

23. Frohberg, Margery. "Existentialism: An Introduction to the Contemporary Conscience," *Perceptions* (School of Social Work, San Diego State College), Vol. 1, No. 1, Spring, 1967, pp. 24-32.

24. Fromm, Erich. *The Sane Society*. New York: Rinehart, 1955.

25. Glasser, William. *Reality Therapy*. New York: Harper and Row, 1965.

26. Gyarfas, Mary. "Social Science, Technology and Social Work: A Caseworker's view," *The Social Service Review*, Vol. 43, No. 3, September, 1969, pp. 259-273.

27. Haley, Jay. *Problem Solving Therapy*. San Francisco: Jossey-Bass, 1976.

28. ———. *Strategies of Psychotherapy*. New York: Grune and Stratton, 1963.

29. Heinecken, Martin J. *The Moment Before God. (A Study on the Thought of Kierkegaard.)* Philadelphia: Mulenberg Press, 1956.

30. Hoffer, Eric. *The True Believer*. New York: Harper, 1951.

31. Imre, Roberta Wells. "A Theological View of Social Casework," *Social Casework*, Vol. 52, No. 9, November, 1971, pp. 578-585.

32. James, Muriel and Dorothy Jongeward. *Born to Win: Transactional Analysis with Gestalt Experiments*. Reading, Mass.: Addison-Wesley, 1971.

33. Jourard, Sydney. *The Transparent Self*. Princeton, N.J.: Van Nostrand, 1964.

34. Jung, C. G. *Modern Man in Search of a Soul*. New York: Harcourt, Brace, 1933.

35. Katz, Robert L. *Empathy*. New York: Free Press, 1963.

36. Kazantzakis, Nikos. *The Saviors of God*. New York: Simon and Schuster, 1960.

37. Klein, Alan F. *Social Work Through Group Process.* Albany, N.Y.: School of Social Welfare, State University of New York, 1970.

38. Krill, Donald F. "Existentialism: A Philosophy for Our Current Revolutions," *The Social Service Review,* Vol. XL, No. 3, September, 1966, pp. 289-301.

39. ———. "Existential Psychotherapy and the Problem of Anomie," *Social Work,* Vol. 14, No. 2, April, 1969, pp. 33-49.

40. ———. "Psychoanalysis, Mowrer and the Existentialists," *Pastoral Psychology,* Vol. 16, October, 1965, pp. 27-36.

41. ———. "A Framework for Determining Client Modifiability," *Social Casework,* Vol. 49, No. 10, December, 1968, pp. 602-611.

42. Kuckelmans, Joseph J. *Phenomenology. The Philosophy of Edmund Husserl and Its Interpretation.* Garden City, N.Y.: Doubleday, 1967.

43. Laing, R. D. *The Politics of Experience.* Baltimore: Penguin, 1967.

44. ———. *The Divided Self.* Baltimore: Penguin, 1964.

45. Maslow, Abraham H. *Toward a Psychology of Being.* Princeton, N.J.: Van Nostrand, 1962.

46. May, Rollo, E. Angel and H. F. Ellenberger (eds.). *Existence: A New Dimension in Psychiatry and Psychology.* New York: Basic Books, 1958.

47. May, Rollo (ed.). *Existential Psychology.* New York: Random House, 1961.

48. ———. *Psychology and the Human Dilemma.* Princeton, N.J.: Van Nostrand, 1967.

49. Moustakas, Clark (ed.). *The Self: Explorations in Personal Growth.* New York: Harper and Row, 1956.

50. Mowrer, O. Hobart. *The Crisis in Psychiatry and Religion.* Princeton, N.J.: Van Nostrand, 1961.

51. Nuttin, Joseph. *Psychoanalysis and Personality.* New York: Mentor-Omega, 1962.

52. Perls, Frederick S. *Gestalt Therapy Verbatim.* Lafayette, Calif.: Real People Press, 1969.

53. Reich, Charles. *The Greening of America.* New York: Random House, 1970.

54. Reinhardt, Kurt F. *The Existentialist Revolt.* New York: Unger, 1952.

55. Rogers, Carl. *On Becoming a Person.* Boston: Houghton Mifflin, 1961.

56. ———. "The Group Comes of Age," *Psychology Today,* Vol. 3, No. 7, December, 1969, p. 29.

57. Rubin, Gerald K. "Helping a Clinic Patient Modify Self-Destructive Thinking," *Social Work,* Vol. 7, No. 1, January, 1962, pp. 76-80.

58. Rubinoff, Lionel. *The Pornography of Power.* New York: Ballantine, 1969.

59. Ruesch, Jurgen and Gregory Bateson. *Communication: The Social Matrix of Psychiatry.* New York: Norton, 1968.

60. Salomon, Elizabeth. "Humanistic Values and Social Casework," *Social Casework,* Vol. 48, January, 1967, pp. 26-32.

61. Satir, Virginia. *Conjoint Family Therapy.* Palo Alto, Calif.: Science and Behavior Books, 1964.

62. Sinsheimer, Robert. "The Existential Casework Relationship," *Social Casework,* Vol. 50, No. 2, February, 1969, pp. 67-73.

63. Skinner, B. F. *Beyond Freedom and Dignity.* New York: Knopf, 1971.

64. Stretch, John. "Existentialism: A Proposed Philosophical Orientation for Social Work," *Social Work*, Vol. 12, No. 4, October, 1967, pp. 97-102.

65. Sutherland, Richard. "Choosing as Therapeutic Aim, Method, and Philosophy," *Journal of Existential Psychiatry*, Vol. 2, No. 8, Spring, 1962, pp. 371-392.

66. Taft, J. "A Conception of the Growth Underlying Social Casework Practice," *Social Casework*, Vol. 21, 1950, pp. 311-316.

67. Teilhard de Chardin, Pierre. *The Phenomenon of Man*. New York: Harper and Row, 1959.

68. Tillich, Paul. *The Courage to Be*. New Haven: Yale, 1952.

69. ———. *Love, Power and Justice*. New York: Oxford, 1960.

70. Tiryakian, Edward A. *Sociologism and Existentialism*. Englewood Cliffs, N.J.: Prentice-Hall, 1962.

71. Watzlawick, Paul, John Weakland, and Richard Fisch, *Change: Principles of Problem Formation and Problem Resolution*, New York: Norton, 1974.

72. Weiss, David. "The Ontological Dimension—Social Casework," *The Social Worker*, C.A.S.W., June, 1962.

73. ———. "The Existential Approach to Social Work," *Viewpoints*, Montreal, Spring, 1967.

74. ———. "Social Work as Authentication," *The Social Worker*, C.A.S.W., February, 1968.

75. ———. "Self Determination in Social Work—An Existential Dialogue," *The Social Worker*, C.A.S.W., November, 1969.

76. ———. "Social Work as Encountering," *Journal of Jewish Communal Service*, Spring, 1970.

77. ———. "Social Work as Healing and Revealing," *Intervention*, No. 50, Summer, 1970.

78. ———. "The Existential Approach to Fields of Practice," *Intervention*, No. 55, Fall, 1971.

79. ———. "The Living Language of Encountering: Homage to Martin Buber 1878-1965," *Intervention*, No. 57, Spring, 1972.

80. Wheelis, Allen. *The Quest for Identity*. New York: Norton, 1958.

81. Winthrop, Henry. "Culture, Mass Society, and the American Metropolis; High Culture and Middlebrow Culture: An Existential View," *Journal of Existentialism*, Vol. 8, No. 27, Spring, 1967, p. 371.

Annotated listing of key references

BARNES, Hazel. *The Literature of Possibility: A Study of Humanistic Existentialism.* Lincoln: University of Nebraska Press, 1959.
A thorough introduction to the basic concepts of existentialism through both the literature and philosophy of Sartre, Camus and de Beauvoir.

BRADFORD, Kirk A. *Existentialism and Casework.* Jericho, N.Y.: Exposition Press, 1969.
A short review of existential thought in terms of its philosophical development and its entry into the field of psychology. A comparison and integration of existential psychology and social casework concepts.

BUBER, Martin. *The Knowledge of Man.* New York: Harper and Row, 1965.
Articles relating Buber's philosophy of dialogue to the psychotherapeutic relationship.

CURRY, Andrew. "Toward a Phenomenological Study of the Family," *Existential Psychiatry,* Vol. 6, No. 27, Spring, 1967, pp. 35–44.
The effects of existential despair upon family life, described as a "web of unrelatedness."

FRANKL, Viktor E. *The Doctor and the Soul. From Psychotherapy to Logotherapy.* New York: Knopf, 1965.
A very readable development of existential psychology in comparison with other psychologies and its application in therapeutic practice.

RUBIN, Gerald K. "Helping a Clinic Patient Modify Self-Destructive Thinking," *Social Work,* Vol. 7, No. 1, January, 1962, pp. 76–80.
Application of Frankl's logotherapy in casework practice. Emphasis is upon the discovery of meaning in suffering.

SINSHEIMER, Robert. "The Existential Casework Relationship," *Social Casework,* Vol. 50, No. 2, February, 1969, pp. 67–73.
Concepts from existential psychology are related to the casework relationship in terms of the I–Thou dialogue and encounter.

STRETCH, John. "Existentialism: A Proposed Philosophical Orientation for Social Work," *Social Work,* Vol. 12, No. 4, October, 1967, pp. 97–102.
Existentialism provides a view of life that accepts the perennial crises of people as opposed to utopian hopes of a secured society.

SUTHERLAND, Richard. "Choosing as Therapeutic Aim, Method and Philosophy," *Existential Psychiatry,* Vol. 2, No. 8, Spring, 1968, pp. 371–392.
The applicability of the concept of freedom of choice in specific techniques of psychotherapy.

WEISS, David. "Social Work as Healing and Revealing," *Intervention,* No. 50, Summer, 1970.
Development of Buber's philosophy of dialogue according to the concepts of Being, Becoming, Belonging and Sympathy, Empathy and Compathy.

8

The Client-Centered System Unfolding

by

G. T. BARRETT-LENNARD

In 1939, as World War II began, a book entitled *The Clinical Treatment of the Problem Child* was published by an unusually talented but, as then, largely unknown working clinician in Rochester, New York. Based on over a decade of field experience working with children, parents and families in difficulty—spanning a period that included the Great Depression and Roosevelt's New Deal—the book was an original and substantial resource to other workers in this field. While he was formally trained in psychology, it was evident that the author's professional activity and principal influences (at that time) were equally associated with the field of social work. His book was a major factor in Carl R. Rogers' appointment the next year to a full professorship at Ohio State University.

A further book was soon in progress and appeared in 1942 (111) already drawing on research studies completed and in progress at Ohio State, and presenting a distinctive orienta-

tion to theory and practice in therapeutic counseling. As the war continued and it was clear that large numbers of veterans would require personal, psychological assistance in coming home and readjusting to civilian life, Rogers became involved in national programs of selection and training of special counseling personnel to serve as accessible and effective helpers with returning servicemen (181).

By 1945, when Rogers moved to the University of Chicago as professor of psychology and human development and head of the newly established Counselling Center there, it was clear that he was strongly in the process of founding a new school of theory and practice in personal counselling and psychotherapy. This became known as client-centered therapy in keeping with the (then) distinctive and strong emphasis (a) on the counselee leading the way consistently so far as the content of therapy interviews was concerned, and (b) on the complementary aspect of the counselor focusing consistently on the client's frame of reference rather than introducing an outside viewpoint.

The present work will further sketch the emergence of this approach, describe the subsequent flowering of client-centered therapy as a major "school," and outline developments beyond the school phase. Main concepts of human nature and personality, principles of therapeutic change in particular, and connected thought regarding a fixity-fluidity continuum of personal functioning *and* process and change in experiencing, will be examined. At the level of practice, attention shall be focused separately on the helping interview, therapy with children and in families, work in intensive groups, and applications in teaching and education. The writer will conclude with a careful distillation of substantive developments, and significant shifts in concern and vision, during the post-school period of the client/person-centered movement.

Origins and early development of client-centered therapy

1.   Background Influences and Sources

As a distinct school of thought, systematic inquiry, and practice, client-centered therapy was founded and fathered by an immensely energetic, determined, and creatively resourceful innovator-parent. By the middle 1940s the lusty offspring was also surrounded by the growing adoptive family of Carl Rogers' associates and students, who increasingly influenced and contributed to its further development. The parentage and central influence, however, remained unmistakable.

The elements uniquely combined and developed in the early phase of client-centered therapy did not of course arise *de novo*. Their most direct source lies in the spectrum of influences, ideas, and learnings during Rogers' "Rochester years." These spanned a twelve-

year period, overlapping the completion of his Ph.D. at Columbia University and culminating in his move to Ohio State.

In Rochester, Rogers worked in a professionally staffed, community child, and family service unit eventually organized, under his leadership, as the Rochester Guidance Center. In a personal biographical statement, he reports:

> For at least the first eight of these years, I was completely immersed in carrying on practical psychological service, diagnosing and planning for the delinquent and underprivileged children who were sent to us by the courts and agencies, and in many instances carrying on "treatment interviews." It was a period of relative professional isolation, where my only concern was in trying to be more effective with our clients.
> . . . There was only one criterion in regard to any method of dealing with these children and their parents, and that was "Does it work? Is it effective?" (156)

The preceding comment, and others in the same source and vein, clearly reflect the strongly practical, pragmatic outlook that carried over into the development of client-centered therapy itself.

There was little in common during this period between Rogers' work and interests and those, for example, of faculty-teaching psychologists at the University of Rochester or, for that matter, the professional establishment in psychology as represented at that time in the American Psychological Association. Between this fact and, for Rogers, the more relevant and innovative work coming, especially, from the Pennsylvania School of Social Work and Philadelphia Child Guidance Clinic, his identification with psychology attenuated, and he became active in social work circles. In his own words:

> The psychiatric social workers
> . . . seemed to be talking my language,
> so I became active in the social work

profession, moving up to local and even national offices. Only when the American Association for Applied Psychology was formed [1937-1938] did I become really active as a psychologist. (137, p. 12)

In his 1939 book Rogers describes and discusses methods of intensive, personal therapy—conceived as *one* important avenue in assisting children and families—first within a section titled "The Means of Changing Parental Attitudes" (110, pp. 184-220) and, later, in a chapter on "Deeper Therapies" with children (110, p. 332 ff.). He writes as a careful reporter, seeking to present the central ideas and operational features of the main existing approaches to therapy. The "deep therapy" approaches he distinguishes are identified as interpretive therapy (in general) and psychoanalysis (in particular) *and* "relationship therapy."

Rogers' personal leaning toward relationship therapy is indicated here not so much by the direct content of his statements as by the care, discrimination, and "warmth" of his discussion and illustration, and by his appreciative references to the work, particularly, of Otto Rank (on a practical, treatment process level), Jessie Taft, and Frederick Allen. In retrospect, Rogers' discussion of relationship therapy (in places he uses the term "passive therapy") directly foreshadows most of the therapeutic principles he set forth and elaborated over the next three or four years. His discussion of this therapy with parents includes these points (in Rogers' words):

a. It applies only to those parents who have a desire to be helped.
b. The relationship between the worker and the parent is the essential feature. . . . The worker endeavors to provide an atmosphere in which the parent can come freely to experience and realize his own attitudes. The worker creates this atmosphere by her acceptance. . . .
c. The effect of this relationship upon the parent may be characterized by

the terms "clarification of feelings" and "acceptance of self." . . .
d. . . . another characteristic of this viewpoint is its reliance on the parent himself to determine independently the manner of dealing with the child.

The aim of such a passive approach is to bring about a higher degree of integration and self-realisation in the parent. . . . It will be difficult, under any circumstances, to determine the effectiveness of this method.
. . . Indeed it seems likely that its major value may be, not in the percentage of cases assisted, but in the fresh viewpoint of noninterference and reliance upon the individual's own tendency toward growth which it has emphasized. (110, pp. 197-200)*

In discussing relationship therapy with children, Rogers makes the additional point that

it deals entirely with present situations and makes no attempt to interpret or explain past reactions. Furthermore it is primarily those feelings which center on the worker which are the core of the process. . . . Because the child has learned to live successfully in one segment of his experience, the treatment relationship, it is expected that he can adapt himself more successfully in other segments of his life. (110, p. 343)

Rogers emphasizes that the last point is a hypothesis whose validity, or limits of application, are not yet known. He also emphasizes that relationship therapy depends on a certain viewpoint and philosophy in regard to others "and cannot therefore be picked up or laid down as a mechanical tool of treatment." (110)

---

* Later in the same work, Rogers suggests that relationship therapy may turn out to be a "more practical method" than psychoanalysis, given the latter's more ambitious and demanding character but similar aim.

2. Early Development

Rogers took up his appointment at Ohio State in January, 1940. In December of that year he gave an invited talk at the University of Minnesota entitled "Newer Concepts in Psychotherapy"—later revised to form Chapter 2 of his 1942 book, *Counseling and Psychotherapy* (111). His 1940 presentation is described by Rogers as the point in time at which it might be said that client-centered therapy was born:

> I was totally unprepared for the furor the talk aroused. I was praised, I was attacked, I was looked on with puzzlement. By the end of my stay in Minneapolis it struck me that perhaps I was saying something new that came from *me*. . . . I began to believe that I might personally, out of my own experience, have some original contribution to make to the field of psychotherapy. (147)

In his revision of this talk (111, Ch. 2) Rogers includes essentially the same points in characterizing the "Newer Psychotherapy" as in his earlier account of relationship therapy. The therapeutic relationship as a direct medium and vehicle for growth and change is emphasized; and within this relationship effective movement and change are seen as generated by the individual's own drive toward growth and health. Greater stress is placed on the emotional-feeling aspects and focus, as against intellectual-knowing aspects of the client's experience, and the immediate situation rather than analysis of the past is stressed. The author takes the further step of presenting a differentiated outline of the way these qualities translate into characteristic steps in the treatment process. Unlike his earlier statements, Rogers expresses sharp advocacy of the new approach as against "older methods." This quality, and the substance of Rogers' more detailed discussion of the therapy relationship, is well conveyed in a chapter summary from his book:

> The counseling relationship is one in which warmth of acceptance and absence of any coercion or personal pressure on the part of the counselor permits the maximum expression of feelings, attitudes, and problems by the counselee. The relationship is a well-structured one, with limits of time, of dependence and of aggressive action which apply particularly to the client, and limits of responsibility and of affection which the counsellor imposes on himself. In this unique experience of complete emotional freedom within a well-defined framework the client is free to recognize and understand his impulses and patterns, positive and negative, as in no other relationship. (111, pp. 113–114)

Rogers' founding statement of the new therapy does not, in this writer's view, stand out at the levels of theoretical or philosophical originality. As a how-to-do-it manual, in the best sense, for counseling practitioners and students, as a documentary source for research workers and others interested in studying the actual phenomenon and process of therapy, and also as a lucid, articulate, demystifying, educative, and humanly encouraging statement in its field for intelligent lay readers, the book was without peer or serious rival. One of the innovative and strikingly effective features lay in Rogers' extensive use of illustrative documentation from actual transcripts of recorded therapy interviews—including the famous verbatim record of a complete eight-interview therapy case! He was also able to draw on the first of the formal therapy research studies stimulated by his work—of which a notable example is E. H. Porter's doctoral dissertation, focusing on systematic analysis and comparison of the interview behavior of counselors independently classified as clearly directive or as nondirective in orientation (99).

Several additional students completed

graduate thesis studies with Rogers during his Ohio State period, each study typically a discovery in method, technique, or theoretical formulation in the still uncharted field of empirical therapy research. Victor Raimy's work on the self-concept in counseling and personality organization (101, 102) helped to initiate the development of self-theory as a central axis in Rogers' later theoretical system. William Snyder's research on "the nature of nondirective psychotherapy" (190) was another foundation stone. Papers on a variety of topics and in various journals flowed from Rogers' own pen: for example, on the use of sound recordings of interviews as a learning medium (112), a new paper in his earlier field of interest–therapy in guidance clinics (113), a report supported by direct empirical data on insight in the counseling process (114), papers on adjustment problems and counseling with returning servicemen (115, 117), and a presentation (for sociologists and others) of the potential of nondirective interviewing as an effective technique for gathering unbiased information in social research (116). With Rogers' move to the University of Chicago, in 1945, nondirective client-centered therapy was effectively recognized as a new "school" and Rogers as an outstanding leader in his field.

The "school" phase: growth and change

Client-centered therapy evolved and flourished as a relatively unified system of thought, research inquiry, and professional practice for a period of approximately twenty years (circa 1945–1965). Carl Rogers remained the undisputed leader and principal advocate and integrating influence in the school he had founded. Most visible new developments originated with the group centered at the University of Chicago, and after Rogers moved to the University of Wisconsin in 1957, from that setting as well. There was in this period a quality of strongly experienced identification with a philosophy and value system, a distinct but unconfining and evolving theoretical viewpoint and (most of all in the Chicago group) a mode of helping practice of a sharply defined and highly consistent nature. Adherents of the client-centered school who had worked or trained with Rogers or with his previous close associates and students, generally experienced a strong personal and professional sense of belongingness with other "members" during this phase. Rogers' immensely communicative and articulate writing, published in many contexts, and the generally searching, original, and often eloquent presentations of other "Rogerians," attracted the interest and often the adherence of a growing circle of readers beyond the field of professional counseling or the loose boundaries of actual "membership" of the school.

The client-centered school, by the nature of its philosophy and practice, has provided very fertile ground for innovation and diversity. The idea of fixed doctrine or ideology, or of disciples following the footsteps of the master, has been abhorrent to Rogers (85).* The labels "nondirective," "client-centered," "group-centered" and, most recently, "person-centered", are associated with principles and modes of practice designed to release inner forces or tendencies toward growth, to enhance personal freedom, and to facilitate creative, self-transcending development. Given such values and aims, coupled with the naturally increasing geographical separation and continued development of original members of the client-centered group (and of their close associates and students in turn), it was inevitable that client-centered therapy would not remain a cohesive *school*. Instead, the client-centered system is now a broad and diversified movement increasingly connected with other currents in therapy and help-

---

* For example, when the *Journal of Client-Centered Therapy* was instituted, Rogers opposed its formation and dissociated himself from the enterprise, which lasted only a short period.

ing relationships, in many contexts. The contexts include counseling (psychology), social work, the field of educational guidance and education itself, pastoral psychology and counseling, psychiatry, aspects of nursing and medical practice, small-group work and segments of the human potential movement, organizational life and development, and the gradual infiltration of humanistic viewpoints in the behavioral sciences.

A number of important subphases and milestone developments, in which Rogers' work stands out but is strongly complemented by other exponents and contributors to client-centered therapy, may be distinguished during the school phase.

1. Refinement and Perfection of Nondirective–Reflective Psychotherapy

In a searching examination of the emergence and nature of nondirective therapy, published in 1948, Raskin (104) outlined Rogers' special achievements (in part) in the following terms:

> He introduced into therapy the systematic use of the recognition of feeling response. . . .
>
> In so doing . . . he gave to the Rankian "client-as-central-figure" philosophy a definite technique, which Rank, Raft and Allen had pronounced impossible.
>
> At the same time, he gave a new, more exact and deeper meaning to the concept of "acceptance" of the client. . . .
>
> Thus the function of the therapist, with Rogers, becomes specifically . . . to recognise and accept the attitudes of the client at the moment.

In what was probably his own sharpest

statement of the last-mentioned point, Rogers wrote: "The therapist . . . must concentrate on one purpose only; that of providing deep understanding and acceptance of the attitudes consciously held at this moment by the client as he explores step by step into the dangerous areas he has been denying to consciousness" (118).

The emphasis on refining and "purifying" the meaning and method of nondirective-reflective therapy remained the central issue and focus in client-centered therapy practice into the early 1950s. More concretely, the focus was on accompanying the client with continuous, accepting awareness and expressed recognition of his feelings and personal meanings—*by means of reflective restatement and clarification of these feelings and meanings.* Research studies, such as those of Snyder (190)* and Seeman (184), reflect this focus of interest *and* provide direct evidence that the frequency of nondirective responses by Rogerian therapists rose through the 1940s, while lead-taking, directive, and "semidirective" statements diminished correspondingly (184).

Client-Centered Therapy, Rogers' third major book (121, Part 1), vividly and effectively portrays the rationale and *process* of reflective therapy, in which the counselor's responses are targeted consistently on the internal frame of reference and experiencing of the client. In addition, however, his account reveals an incipient but very important shift in emphasis. While the *way* the therapist proceeded at the level of his (verbal, responsive) behavior and technique was still central, Rogers also emphasized strongly that this behavior needed to be supported and accompanied by a genuinely client-centered attitude; more specifically, by a perspective on man, a value-system, sensitivity, and style of expression that corresponded with the overt behavior. How the therapist experienced himself

---

* Snyder's 1947 *Casebook of Non-Directive Therapy* (191) is also a pertinent source, containing annotated interview transcripts from the work of five therapists.

and *felt* toward his client and the relationship of these to his behavior, were discussed directly as "growing-edge" issues among client-centered therapists. In a 1952 article, Raskin goes further in the same direction:

> Very recently, many therapists with a client-centered orientation have been groping for a formulation of counselor attitudes which will go beyond the possesion of a genuine client-centered attitude. There is an attempt here to see the counselor as a whole person, in the therapeutic relationship. (105)

Other ideas and formulations cited by Raskin indicate even more sharply that some client-centered writers had begun to focus strongly on the *therapist's* experience and personal functioning in the helping relationship. In retrospect, it is clear that a new way of viewing the importance of the therapist's frame of reference and expressiveness in therapy was emerging. Nondirective–reflective psychotherapy had reached its peak and significant modifications were in the wind (96, 120).

2. The First Phase of Research: Systematic Description of the Therapy Interview Content and Movement

The essential issue providing the main starting point of substantial research effort by client-centered investigators was: What is therapy itself, as a phenomenon—viewed in terms of the content and patterning of events in a sequence of therapy meetings? Is it *a* phenomenon in the sense that there *are* consistent patterns that form meaningful regularities in the behavior of the interview participants and sequential unfolding of the process? The most representative set of studies in this first, descriptive–inductive phase of interview-process analysis was published in 1949, as an entire issue of the *Journal of Consulting Psychology* (177). This composite report of the "Parallel Studies Project" opens with a uniquely informal and lively "Non-Objective Introduction" by Carl Rogers. Raskin introduces the six relatively crude but ground-breaking studies—and adds a concluding, integrative analysis. The component study by Seeman focuses on the analysis of counselor technique (now 85 percent "nondirective" in form), of client *content* categories (such as problem descriptions and insight statements), and of client *feeling* categories (for example, positive and negative attitude expressions toward the self, counselor, and other persons and situations). Sheerer examined client expressions of self-acceptance and respect, and of acceptance of others, and found that these expressions increased during the course of therapy, and that they were intercorrelated. Stock conducted a related study focusing on feelings toward the self and others. Haigh and Hoffman studied defensiveness and maturity of behavior, respectively, from client statements over the course of therapy. *One* study (by Carr) examined pre-post outcome data, foreshadowing the next main focus and phase of client-centered research.

3. Development of Self-Theory

As the above-mentioned investigation of the content and patterning of events in therapy interviews proceeded, a related current of development was flowing and gathering force. To explain and adequately connect the events of therapy, a view of human personality was needed. The events themselves were highly suggestive in regard to fundamental aspects of personality. The temptation was great, and major theory-building began. The first mature fruit of this work, presented as a general theory of personality, forms the last chapter of *Client-Centered Therapy* (121). The theory is arranged as a series of nineteen interlocking propositions, first postulating basic properties of the human organism (e.g., that the organism has one basic tendency—to actualize, maintain, and enhance itself) and then dealing in particular with the origins, properties, and functions of the self (proposition 8, for example, indicates that the self is a portion of the individual's total perceptual field which becomes discriminated as "me," "I," "myself," and in development is differentiated to an increasing degree from the environment or "not-self").

The development of self-theory had begun with Raimy's dissertation (101) and was first focused on by Rogers in an address he gave in 1947—as retiring President of the American Psychological Association—under the title "Some Observations on the Organisation of Personality" (119). By 1948, Raskin was able to say that "The client's concept of self is now believed to be the most central factor in his adjustment and perhaps the best measure of his progress in therapy"(104). Two articles, by Elizabeth Sheerer (186) and by Dorothy Stock (196), in the 1949 "parallel studies" project focused directly on self-attitudes and feelings, and Hogan's dissertation (87) and Haigh's report on defensive behavior in therapy (177) effectively drew on the developing self-theory. Rogers' nineteen-proposition statement was a further order of development and established his school of therapy as a new source of an articulated, psychological perspective on human personality and nature.

Further research focusing on the self-concept, in the 1950s and 1960s, notably by John Butler and collaborators (32,34), has further illuminated the nature and functional significance of the self-concept, self-ideal, and related constructs and variables. Most of the principles of self-theory are embodied also in later, broader-based theoretical statements, particularly, that of Rogers in the mammoth series *Psychology: A Study of a Science* (133).

4. The Focus on Therapy Outcome: Does It Work?

By the early 1950s therapy research data were being collected (in the Chicago Counseling Center) in multipurpose blocks for grant-supported programs of investigation, as well as for use in more independent studies. The first major, multistudy project to be formally designed as a whole was devoted primarily to the investigation of therapy outcome. By now it was clear that client-centered therapy was a relatively consistent or lawful phenomenon in terms of the interview behavior of the participants. In effect, systematic knowledge was accumulating in regard to the "interior" characteristics of therapy. Its actual "exterior" characteristics or consequences were relatively uncharted. It was possible and timely to seek to remedy this limitation.

In an extensive program reported as a whole in 1954 (175), a team of investigators developed a control-group project to compare changes in personal functioning with and without an intervening therapy experience. Some clients served as their own controls, being tested at the beginning and end of a two-month interval before therapy began, as well as at the end of therapy and six to twelve months later. A partially matched control sample of "normal" volunteers not in therapy was tested at the same intervals as the in-therapy sample. The overall trend of findings was positive. The investigators concluded "that various changes in self-perception of the client, in his personality organisation and in his daily behavior occur as a concomitant of a period of client-centered therapy. It appears . . . that the psychotherapy is the effective agent of change, since changes of comparable magnitude do not occur in a control group or in our clients during a control period" (175, p. 433).

5. Development of New Concepts: Unconditional Positive Regard and (Therapist) Congruence

In 1954, Standal (195) completed a *theoretical* Ph.D. thesis in psychology (itself a rarity) focusing on a postulated, fundamental "need for positive regard" in human beings; and carefully developing a system of explanatory ideas and constructs centrally including that of "unconditional positive regard." Simply stated, the concept refers to a felt attitude of respect and caring for another person, with no "strings" attached; or a "prizing" of the other as a whole person. Earlier, related concepts included acceptance and warmth. Unconditional positive regard of the counselor toward his client was advanced as a quite basic and primary ingredient of the therapeutic relationship, and this concept rapidly became a part of the thinking and language of other client-centered workers.

About the time that Standal was completing his thesis, another major new concept in therapy had begun to germinate. Used initially in reference to consistency between a person's view of himself and of his ideal or wanted self, "congruence" began to take on another meaning as a core factor in therapeutic interaction (and human relationships more broadly). During the mid-1950s the quest to portray and refine the idea and importance of the therapist being himself—that is, as a real genuine person in his therapeutic mode or role—culminated in the revised meaning and application of the concept of congruence (126). Referring to consistency within the person in the sense that (a) his primary, immediate experience, (b) conscious perception and (c) outward behavior all matched or were of one piece, the congruency of the *therapist* (in the therapy interaction) was postulated as a fundamental therapeutic ingredient.

From a practical standpoint, the emphasis was on the therapist avoiding incongruence. Lack of congruence would be associated, for example, with unclear or mixed messages from the therapist, less accurate perception of the client's feelings, and diminished trust, self-disclosure, and self-exploration on the client's part. From its first clear articulation, personal congruence was seen as being of central importance in interpersonal communication, influence, and facilitation generally, not only in therapy as such (129).

6. The Conditions and "Equation" of Therapy

As early as 1946, Rogers presented a major paper clearly embodying the idea of an "equation of therapy," without using that term. In this paper, he set forth a set of six "conditions" of therapist attitude and behavior which, he argued, led predictably to a pattern of described qualities of therapy process and outcome. In Rogers' words "If these (listed) conditions are met, then it may be said with assurance that in the great majority of cases the following results [also listed] will take place" (118). This early statement foreshowed to a remarkable degree one of the most outstanding milestones in Rogers' own writing, the client-centered school and, quite possibly, the history of psychotherapy.

Ten years after his 1946 article, Rogers formulated his now-classical statement of the "necessary and sufficient conditions of therapeutic personality change" (127). The intervening decade of theoretical development and research had set the stage for an explanatory focus on what it is, basically, that generates and sustains a healing or constructive change process in therapy (e.g., 30, 175, 195). In his breakthrough statement Rogers proposed that if a few specified, primary conditions exist in the client-therapist relationship an orderly, definable process will be set in motion, leading to a predictable pattern of outcomes. The author made it clear that his hypotheses referred to psychotherapy generally, not just client-centered therapy. Controversy, even furor, as well as intense interest, occurred widely in relevant professional circles, and a whole new phase of research opened up, aimed at testing, refining, and extending the new conception. Implications for practice in a wide range of helping situations were numerous and important. Much more will be said bearing on these developments, in the course of this total account.

7.   Level of Process in the Helping Context

In 1956, The American Psychological Association honored Rogers—and, indirectly, the client-centered school—by means of a Distinguished Scientific Contribution Award (in a series of awards that *began* that year).* His "repayment" involved an address to the A.P.A the following year, entitled "A Process Conception of Psychotherapy" (130). This and the more fully worked out statements that soon followed it (134, 136, 206) comprise another milestone development. Essentially the process conception is a broad-gauge ("multistrand") systematic description of an entire spectrum of individual difference in personality functioning, within an interpersonal context in which the individual is psychologically "received." It originated in the study of client functioning and development within the course of therapy, as manifest in the client-therapist interviews.

Rogers' definition of the process continuum, and his careful account of the spectrum of distinguishable levels or stages of functioning, grew in large part from a process of intensive, reflective "immersion" in interview recordings from different clients and stages in therapy. The essential overall direction of change that he discriminated was *from* a fixed, closed, self-perpetuating mode of functioning *to* a state of fluid, open, but integrated changingness; briefly, from a condition of stasis to one of process.

---

* The award was bestowed on Rogers "for developing an original method to objectify the description and analysis of the psychotherapeutic process, for formulating a testable theory of psychotherapy and its effects . . . , and for extensive systematic research to exhibit the value of the method and explore and test the implications of the theory. His imagination, persistence, and flexible adaptation of scientific method . . . *have moved this area of psychological interest within the boundaries of scientific psychology.* [Italics added]" *American Psychologist, 12,* (1957), 128.

The process conception and directly related work, particularly by Gendlin (49, 66), provided the major foundation for the study of in-therapy process change during Rogers' Wisconsin years. The whole approach and substance of this work are quite different from the early interview-analysis research by Snyder (190), Seeman (184), Sheerer (186) and others. The change reflects the rapid evolution of knowledge and investigative methods rather than any basic modifications in scientific interest, general philosophy of human nature, or mode of helping practice.

8.   Client-Centered Therapy with Schizophrenics

Soon after Rogers moved to Wisconsin, he was joined by a former student-associate from Chicago, Dr. E. T. Gendlin, among the most outstanding younger exponents and original contributors in the client-centered school and tradition. Gendlin and Rogers undertook the development of a massive study of psychotherapy (broadly, client-centered) with hospitalized schizophrenic patients. Most client-centered workers had little prior experience with deeply disturbed individuals and the opportunity for intensive, carefully researched application of his therapy with psychotic clients was a major motive in Rogers's move to Wisconsin. His academic-teaching affiliation with the Department of Psychiatry and association with the Wisconsin Psychiatric Institute also gave him the opportunity for direct involvement and impact in medical education and in psychiatric and related medical practice with seriously troubled persons.

Within two or three years, important articles by client-centered workers from this new context of practice, theory, and research were being published. Perhaps the most outstanding of these, in terms of its sensitivity and influence on the reader, is by Dr. John M. Shlien, another leading exponent of the client-centered viewpoint and a member (at the time) of the Chicago group. Shlien's article concludes with a richly documented case study of psychotherapy with a deeply disturbed hospitalized client (187). Articles by Rogers (138) and by Gendlin (50), at about the same time, also included direct and sensitive portrayals of the human condition of the schizophrenic person.

The "Schizophrenia" project ran throughout the period of Rogers' Wisconsin years and beyond, finally receiving full publication in a major, multiauthored volume from the University of Wisconsin Press, in 1967 (154). Long before that time, Gendlin had returned to the University of Chicago. The research team suffered internal vicissitudes but regained the working integration necessary to accomplish completion of another landmark contribution, signaled by the volume mentioned—after the client-centered "school" began to diversify into a many-sided movement.

9. The Widening Circle of Nontherapy Applications

By the early 1950s, theoretical and value principles and methods of the client-centered system were being extended and applied in a variety of contexts beyond the confines of counseling and therapy. In view of the educational setting in which the system was evolving and the involvement of its principal exponents in formal teaching and supervision, it is not surprising that education was an early and continuing context for extension of client-centered principles. As usual, Rogers' own first statements in this area (121, 122) aroused considerable controversy—particularly his presentation in a conference on "Classroom Approaches to Influencing Human Behavior" at Harvard University in 1952. (122, 137) Besides trenchant criticism of prevailing educational practice, Rogers has offered proposals and documented innovations, in contexts from elementary education to graduate school. His principal writings concerning education, from the early 1950s to the mid-1960s, are drawn together in a volume entitled *Freedom to Learn* (161).

Another relatively early and continuing focus of application is the area of leadership and administration. Major contributions in this field were made initially by Thomas Gordon (73, 74). The influence of Gordon's and Rogers' work, and that of others from the client-centered school, is to be found in literature and practice within the fields of educational administration and management studies and in selected work concerned with organizational functioning and community studies and development.

The area of family life and relationships has understandably been another focus of interest and contribution by client-centered workers—for example, via application of principles of interpersonal communication and facilitation both in "normal" families and those in difficulty. In a 1953 paper Rogers discussed the nature and effects of actual openness and honesty and their lack in family relationships; the relationship of openness to the ability of family members to listen and to know each other's feelings; and ways in which increasing acceptance and helpful caring among family members may develop (124). Writings by Van der Veen and collaborators (95, 107, 204) and Gordon (75, 76) are among the helpful and important contributions of client-centered workers in the area of family process, change, levels of functioning, "parenting," and related aspects.

Work concerned with the understanding and resolution of tension or conflict between groups and larger social systems has received significant, increasing attention in the client-centered school. Rogers launched his direct contributions in this area with a conference paper given in 1951, later "twinned" with a presentation by the distinguished industrial psychologist, F. J. Roethlisberger, for publication under the joint title "Barriers and Gateways to Communication" (178). Twelve years later, Rogers returned to a similar focus and theme in another major conference paper, subsequently published in the first issue of the *Journal of Applied Behavioral Science* (148). Intergroup and intersystem tension and conflict "resolution" is emerging as a strong thrust in the diversified post-school phase of the client-centered movement, with increasingly versatile use of face-to-face groups being a major context (163, 172, 174, 183).

In the broad area of the social uses of psychological knowledge (or behavioral science knowledge), Rogers and other client-centered writers have spoken eloquently and urgently of the dilemmas, dangers, and enormously consequential choices involved. Rogers' presentations include the notable sequence of debates with B. F. Skinner, broadly concerned with the control of human behavior (180, 189), and several other papers presented from the late 1950s on (132, 139, 148, 162, 168). The present writer has contributed to discrimination of issues in this area (10).

Human nature, personality, and change: the theoretical perspective*

1. General Orientation to Human Nature and Knowing

Client-centered theorists have portrayed a strongly "holistic" and humanistic view of man clearly belonging, for example, in the "third force" cluster of viewpoints distinguished by Maslow (92). This membership implies important contrasts, for example, both with the behavioristic and the Freudian analytic perspectives—in respect to such basic issues as the ways human activity is conceived to be generated or "powered," the processes by which significant *change* in attitude or conduct occurs, and the nature and role of conscious experience in human functioning (10, 144).

Client-centered thinking *stresses* that human beings act on and respond to reality as they individually experience and perceive it to be; that man is continually relating to his phenomenal field or environment, of which part of the core is his own self-perceived identity. An individual's perceptions are influenced by a variety of factors, including his expectancies, needs, the behavior of others, and nonpersonal events. However, whatever goes into the "mix" from which the person's view of reality emerges, it is this view by which he acts. This emphasis has led to the system being described as phenomenological in character (188). Another generic designation is that the viewpoint is broadly an existential one. It emphasizes, for example, the importance of first-hand experiential knowledge as against simply knowing about something or possessing an "intellectual" awareness of the end-products of the learning and discovery of others. Man's potential for personal freedom and his responsibility to define and transcend himself, his separateness *and* deep connection with others, and his capacity for knowing commitment are stressed (29, 54, 146, 189). In the course of a symposium presentation in the early 1960s, Rogers spoke directly of the phenomenological–existential movement in psychology and related fields. His summing up of the thrust of this movement leaves no doubt as to his own stand:

> Here is the voice of subjective man speaking up loudly for himself. Man has long felt himself to be but a puppet in life—moulded by economic forces, by unconscious forces, by environmental forces . . . [and] enslaved by persons, by institutions and by theories of psychological science. But he is firmly setting forth a new declaration of independence. He is discarding the alibis of *un*freedom. He is *choosing* himself,

---

* Subsections 1 through 4 in this section *and* in the next (on "Principles in Practice") are largely unchanged from the first edition—written when the author was less sensitive to sexist connotations of English language conventions. As a feasible adjustment, in this revision the use of masculine and feminine pronouns to refer to persons in general, is alternated from one subsection to the next among the eight referred to. (The subsection entitled "The Person in Process," and most of the final main section "The Post-School Period," were newly written for this second edition.)

endeavoring, in a most difficult and often tragic world to *become* himself—not a puppet, not a slave, not a machine, but his own unique individual self. (144).

While stressing—with argument and passion—the importance of personal psychological freedom, self-determination, and individuality, client-centered writers have by no means eschewed the principle of determinism applied to human experience and conduct. In fact, the application of this principle to the experiential realm has been strengthened by the determined and highly resourceful efforts of Rogers and others to bring psychotherapy into empirical, scientific daylight. In his 1955 article "Persons or science: a philosophical question" (125) Rogers first publicly shared the two-sided commitment and tension he felt between (a) his profound involvement in and respect for human subjective experience—including the experience of choice and freedom, and of subjective encounter and knowing of another, and (b) his search for objective, verified, scientific knowledge—including his belief in determinism and the basic methodology of science. Both the (a) and (b) sides are forcefully presented, and the author proceeds via a searching inner debate to a partial integration. This is developed somewhat further in subsequent papers, although a measure of paradox explicitly remains. In Rogers' own, later words:

> [The] experience of freedom . . . exists not as a contradiction to the picture of the psychological universe as a sequence of cause and effect, but as a complement to such a universe. . . . The free man moves out voluntarily, freely, responsibly to play his significant part in a world whose determined events move through him and through his spontaneous choice and will. (146)

The quotation is poetically rich in meaning and invites further working out. In discussing the experience of freedom and the countervailing assumption of lawful causation in human awareness and conduct, the particular view of human nature explicated by Rogers and associated writers *has within it* implications which can contribute to a resolution. To take one example, when man is seen as *inherently* active, directional, curious, and self-generating it follows that his built-in freedom is of a different order than if he is viewed as essentially molded, patterned, and "determined" by his environmental history. As the present writer formulated this issue, in a debate on the control of human behavior:

> If, in accordance with the behaviorist learning theory orientation, we view man as an essentially reactive agent, as being conditioned by external forces . . . then a concept of inner freedom or true choice does become meaningless. But if we take the contrary view that man is *inherently* active, that he is motivated essentially to develop his potentialites and exercise his capacities, then concepts of inner freedom and choice can be deeply meaningful. If this second description is accurate and providing the tendencies are not blocked or distorted* one would expect man to *feel* free and responsible. He would *be* free in the sense that the essential initiative for what he does and strives to become arises from an inherent tendency to maintain, express and actualize his experiencing being. (10)

In the preceding quotations and discussion, several fundamental characteristics of man and

---

* Man's freedom is also a function of the quality or level of his functioning. A major effect of successful therapy, from the client-centered standpoint, is that of achieving a new level of inner freedom (e.g., 10, 141, 143). Rogers and others have emphasized that the defensively organized, "structure-bound," "low-process" person is relatively unfree, compared with the fully functioning, highly self-actualizing, or "high-process" person. Expanded awareness, discrimination, and experiential knowledge increase an individual's autonomy, mastery, and freedom. The flexibility, scope, and balance of influences change, but a complex, causal system remains.

of the human condition, underlying the more specific features of client-centered theory, are implied:

First and foremost, a person is an experiencing (feeling, inquiring, thinking, willing, self-aware) being with a highly differentiated multilevel consciousness linked closely to his history of communication and relationships with other persons. Human consciousness is the apex of a vastly complex intrapersonal system, and the primary "seat" of man's individual being and identity. While much of this system is, normally, largely self-regulating, consciousness is its highest integrating and controlling center or subsystem.† To be alive *means* to be conscious—potentially, if not at the moment. Having desired *experiences* and achieving certain qualities of consciousness are ultimate values in man.

Second, reality is variously perceived, discriminated, and construed by different groups and individuals. Each acts according to his present view of the nature and relevant features of this reality. Man is better understood from his own "pictures" than from some impartial or external mapping of the terrain he faces.

Third, man is inherently active rather than merely *reactive*. His mind is not a tabula rasa, passively acquiring its content and contours by sensory stimulation and associative mental processes. Nor is he simply controlled by complex patterns of reward and punishment. Rather, as mentioned, he is active, curious, purposive, and directional in his inherent nature, prone to organizing and reflecting on his primary experience, to expanding his capacities and actively changing his world according to his own needs or goals (10). He devotes great energy, directly, to his own development.

A fourth point, related to the last, is that a person *grows into being*. His life depends for its existence and fruition on growth and developmental processes which themselves evolve.

† An antireductionist stance, while not discussed directly by most client-centered theorists, is strongly implied (188).

Human beings do not act *primarily* to restore internal equilibrium or homeostatic balance. While they may be said to have survival-type needs, a primary focus on such motivation is held to be invalid. An underlying or explicit growth principle is central in formulations and discussions relating to human motivation, learning, and change, by client-centered writers.

Finally, for a living thing to grow certain basic supporting conditions and nutrients are necessary. Given these nourishing conditions, the organism will develop according to its own nature as a species and individual. Even a plant takes "initiative" in spreading its roots and leaves to expose itself to the life- and growth-giving elements it requires. Higher animals have vastly greater versatility in acting to sustain and, often, to partially create conditions necessary to their growth and well-being. Man has unique potential for knowledge (and also for confusion or self-deception) in regard to his own nature, and for actively pursuing positive self-realization. The primary conditions for full human growth include certain basic qualities of interpersonal experience associated with genuine, "unearned," regardful, and perceptive caring of another.

2.   The Human Organism

Client-centered writers have formally postulated a number of more specific, basic properties of the human organism as a total entity and system. Some of these follow directly from the principles already advanced, while others are a distinct, further, conceptual step.

a. Rogers has held to a unified concept of human motivation since his serious theorizing began. As initially formulated, the human organism "has one basic tendency and striving—to actualize, maintain and enhance the experiencing organism" (121). In Rogers' later formulations, the term "actualizing tendency" explicitly subsumes and includes the "maintenance" aspect of satisfying needs for food, water, oxygen, and the like (which are nutrients for growth as well as for preservation). More generally and importantly, the actualizing tendency "involves development toward the differentiation of organs and functions, expansion in terms of growth, expansion of effectiveness through the use of tools, expansion and enhancement through reproduction. It is development toward autonomy and away from heteronomy, or control by external forces" (133).*

b. The organism functions as an organized whole, responding to its own (moving) perceptual field. This field is its reality, and includes the immediate, fresh incoming data of experience as well as the "map" of reality charted and built up over time by the organism (121, 133).

c. Through its *behavior*, the human organism interacts with perceived "outer" and "inner" reality in the service of the actualizing tendency. This tendency may be thought of as a (directional) energy system, organized to promote life-preserving, -developing and -enhancing processes.

d. As a major aspect of its functioning, the human organism (in infancy or as a well-functioning adult) engages in an "organismic valuing process." Experiences tending to maintain or enhance the organism are valued positively and the converse, negatively (133, 142, 145). Under certain conditions—to be mentioned under discussion of the *self*—the organism may develop strong inhibitory tendencies ("defensive processes") that block the flow of certain kinds of experiential data, impair and restrict the organismic valuing process, and reduce the organism's functional integration.

---

* Rogers has argued vigorously *against* the systematic use of systems of specific motives, drives, needs, or similar "whys" of human behavior—on the grounds that they are simply not useful in advancing knowledge (142). He prefers, for example, to identify "conditions" that contribute or give rise to certain important effects. In reference to one such condition, to speak of general "need" for empathy or a drive to be personally understood, while not necessarily wrong, would not be useful in an explanatory or knowledge-generating sense.

e. "In line with the tendency toward differentiation, which is part of the actualizing tendency, a portion of [the young organism's] experience becomes differentiated and symbolised in an awareness of being, awareness of functioning. Such awareness may be described as self-experience" (133, p. 223).

f. The organism's awareness of its own being and functioning "becomes elaborated, through interaction with the environment, particularly the environment composed of significant others, into a concept of self"—forming part of the organism's experiential field (133, p. 223).

g. The organism engages in complex, moving, felt processes, embodying and leading to symbolic meanings, to which the term *experiencing* is given. In an important mode of experiencing, extensively studied and articulated by Gendlin (49, 53), the conscious organism engages in "direct reference" to inner felt meanings and concretely or bodily sensed qualities (which form the primary data or substrata of experience). In effect, the conscious self "listens" to and "talks" with the images, sensings, and "shapes" of bodily experience. If and as the "conversation" goes on, unfolding interactive movement and change on both levels take place. There is a step toward preservation or increase in the differentiated wholeness of the organism.

3. The Self

Client-centered theory postulates that as the individual's awareness of self (which evolves into an elaborated and organized self-picture or concept) emerges, a need for the *positive regard* of others develops or becomes apparent in his experience and behavior (133, 195). This need is potent and pervasive in the young individual's social behavior and it can override the organismic valuing process or full expression of the actualizing tendency.

As the individual continues to develop, a need for *self-regard* (self-esteem, self-worth, etc.) evolves. Personal behaviors originally associated with regardful and rejecting responses from others now have similar force in satisfying or frustrating the individual's need for *self*-regard. In effect, the person "experiences positive regard or loss of positive regard independently of transactions with any social other. He becomes in a sense his own significant social other" (133).

As implied, the link between the positive and self-regarding needs is such that self-experiences (behaviors, attitudes, and perceived expressions of the self) which significant *others* define as "good" or "bad" lead to positive and negative self-regard. When a self-experience is avoided or sought solely because of its effect on self-regard the person is said to have acquired a *"condition of worth"* (133).

An effect of conditions of worth is that the individual is no longer freely "open to experience." His perception is selective in that experience consistent with his conditions of worth is accurately represented in his awareness while experiential data contrary to these conditions are denied or distorted in awareness. More specifically, behaviors and inner states of the person may not be recognized as *self-experiences* and in this sense not owned by the individual and not organized into his self-structure. This implies *incongruence* between self and experience, involving a state of "vulnerability" and a measure of potential or actual maladjustment.

The vulnerable person is divided in that while part (or much) of his activity is consistent with his self-concept and is accurately perceived *and* actualizing to the self, some of his behavior will tend to maintain and even actualize those aspects of his experiential being not admissible to the self-structure. When there is a pattern of behaviors or inner responses contrary to the person's conditions of worth, these responses must be denied or set apart from his acknowledged "real" self, in order to maintain or satisfy his need for self-regard. In this process, there is potential or "subceived" threat and the reaction may be described as psychological defense. Its

effect is to keep the individual's perception and evaluation of his own activity and characteristics consistent with his self-structure and its implied conditions of worth (133). The theoretical problem that remains is that of how this cycle is broken and forward change takes place.

4. Dimensions of Therapy and Personal Facilitation

In order for the process of defense to be reversed, that is (in Rogers' terms), "for a customarily threatening experience to be accurately symbolised in awareness and assimilated into the self-structure," there must be a decrease in relevant conditions of worth and a corresponding increase in the range of (self-) activity consistent with positive self-regard (133, p. 230). This can happen through the communicated unconditional positive regard of an empathically understanding significant other. The individual must actually and substantially experience these qualitative aspects in the significant other's response for her own conditions of worth and self-regard to change. Assuming this happens, the customarily threatening experiences are now openly perceived or discriminated, and integrated into the individual's owned and acknowledged self. Further, she is now relatively less vulnerable, more congruent, her positive regard for herself and others is increased and her functioning is more fully or more often reflective of an organismic valuing process.

In the client-centered view of therapy, and healing/helping relationships more generally, this process and cycle repeated many times, around the "same" and different conditions of worth (or conflict) areas, is the nucleus of therapy. The primary ingredients or "conditions" of the process, particularly those over which the therapist–facilitator has at least partial control, consist of about four dimensions of personal–interactive functioning and response in the formulations of client-centered workers (5,

7, 9, 31, 52, 127, 133, 135, 138, 140, 151, 152, 154, 187, 205).

In Rogers' previously mentioned, classical statement of the conditions of therapeutic personality change (127), six components altogether are distinguished. The first of these, that "two persons [here called client and therapist] are in psychological contact," is implied in the later ones and is not singled out in subsequent research and writing. The second condition refers to the state of the client and simply specifies that she "is in a state of incongruence, being vulnerable or anxious." Vulnerability implies conditions of worth, such that the individual is prone to being threatened. When actual threat occurs—by the individual, in effect, breaking the rules of her own conditions of worth with actions she cannot avoid discriminating and *owning* to some degree—the active, inner tension state of anxiety exists. In one or other of its forms, and in some (varying) measure, this second condition would seem bound to apply to anyone voluntarily in therapy—and, indeed, to most people. Further, client-centered therapists do not deliberately work at inducing anxiety or directly controlling the client's anxiety level. For these and perhaps other reasons—including the difficulties of operational definition and measurement—this condition has not been a major focus in subsequent research.

The third condition centers on the state of the therapist, specifying that (in contrast to the client) she be "congruent or integrated in the therapy relationship." Rogers makes it clear that he does not mean that the therapist needs to be a paragon of self-actualizing virtue exhibiting this quality of integration and wholeness in every area of her life or even *continuously* in therapy.

The fourth and fifth conditions refer directly to qualities of the therapist's response to the client. In keeping with the formulations already outlined, the therapist needs to experience unconditional positive regard (or "prizing") for the client and an empathic understanding of the client's internal frame of reference.

Finally, the requirement that the client, to some degree, actually register the therapist's unconditional positive regard and perceive the therapist's empathic understanding, was distinguished as a sixth necessary condition.

As soon as Rogers' conditions of therapy formulation were made known to his associates, this writer and another investigator each began to plan projects designed to test the main features of the theory. The theory itself evolved further, in some aspects, in the course of this research. The other worker, Halkides, whose unpublished study (83) is reported in outline by other writers (e.g., 7, 131, 151), effectively focused on the third, fourth, and fifth conditions as presented by Rogers (and another that she added). Using scales that she devised, observer-judges rated unconditional positive regard, empathy, and therapist congruence from segments of recorded therapy interviews. A similar method, building on the same theoretical foundation, was used soon afterwards—and in extensive later work—by Truax (154, 201, 202).

The present writer employed a different approach—involving development of a questionnaire instrument known as the *Relationship Inventory*, answered directly by client and therapist (7, 17, 19, 20, 82). His theoretical position

took as its starting point, the logical presumption that it is what the client himself experiences that affects him directly. It follows from this that the relationship as experienced by the client . . . [rather than the therapist or an external judge] will be most crucially related to outcome of therapy. Moreover, although it is not supposed that a client's conscious perceptions would represent with complete accuracy the way he experiences his therapist . . . his own report, given under suitable conditions, would be the most direct and reliable evidence we could get of *his actual experience* (7, p. 2).

The client's perceptions were conceived as resulting, in turn, from the interaction of her own characteristics with the therapist's "actual" response. In the hypothetical case of two clients with identical characteristics, the differential response of the therapists would be wholly responsible for the different perceptions of clients and, hence, for differences in therapy outcome (7). Thus the therapist's response remained as a principal contributory factor in generating the client's experience relevant to the therapeutic conditions' variables.

The conditions' variables themselves, perceived broadly as basic dimensions of a helping relationship, were freshly formulated in the course of the writer's research. These formulations were a further refinement, and underlie extensive work by other investigators (e.g., 20, 154, 161, 82, 205). The further delineation of the four main variables is briefly as follows:

a. Empathic understanding was defined (in part) as

> an active process of desiring to know the full present and changing awareness of another person, of reaching out to receive his communication and meaning and of translating his words and signs into experienced meaning that matches at least those aspects of his awareness that are most important to him at the moment. It is an experiencing of the consciousness "behind" another's outward communication, but with continuous awareness that this consciousness is originating and proceeding in the other (5, 7, 17, 82).

Recently, the writer has suggested that a sequence of five distinct, necessary steps are involved in a complete empathic process or "cycle" (17). However, the extent to which the *client feels* that the therapist is deeply with him in sensitive, accurate personal understanding remains as the core aspect of empathy in the sense of being most directly related to client change.

b. The (theoretically focal) interactive quality of unconditional positive regard was logically and operationally difficult to handle as a single variable. The writer separated the concept into two component aspects or dimensions: Level of Regard *and* Unconditionality (of Regard). A's level of regard for B is conceived as the net balance—at a given stage in their relationship—of all the various qualities and strengths of A's personal (positive, negative, or "indifferent") feelings and attitudes toward and in reference to B. Positive feelings include respect, caring, appreciation, affection, and others. Negative feelings include dislike, disapproval, expressed indifference, impatience, contempt, etc. More precisely, level of regard was defined as the "composite 'loading' of all the distinguishable feeling reactions of one person toward another, positive and negative, on a single, abstract dimension" of which the "lower" extreme "represents maximum predominance and intensity of negative-type feeling, not merely a lack of positive feeling" (7, 82).

c. Unconditionality is the degree to which A's basic attitudinal-feeling response to B is *not* contingently altered by expression of different "sides" (or new features) of B's identity or qualities as a person. Conversely, conditionality of response implies that A's regard for B does vary according to the light that B shows herself in, or to differing (perceived) qualities that she spontaneously expresses (19). B's *self-awareness* and acceptance are prone to be selective in any event, in accordance with her own conditions of worth. To the extent that A responds conditionally in *keeping with B's own "self-conditionality"* she would tend simply to reinforce the status quo in B's functioning. If, on the other hand, A responds in a strongly conditional fashion along *new* lines, she may lay the seeds for new conditions of worth in B.

d. The reader may recall that *congruence* refers theoretically to wholeness, integration, inner consistency—that is, consistency between primary experience, symbolized awareness, and outward behavior or communication. The concept is theoretically centered on consistency between the first two of these mentioned levels, this being considered the main determinant or condition for congruence between awareness and communication. Congruence is defined basically as an intrapersonal state (or condition) or quality of person functioning. In his classical paper Rogers did not speak of congruence needing to be communicated—as he specified in reference to empathy and unconditional positive regard (127). The writer treated congruence in the same way as empathy, regard, and unconditionality, that is, as a further relational dimension, with the central issue being the *client's perception* of the therapist's genuineness, transparency, honesty with herself and the client, and other congruence-related qualities.

An enormous range and quantity of research, *starting* with mentioned work by the writer (5, 7) and by Halkides (83), has been spawned by concepts of the conditions of therapy or interpersonal facilitation, stemming from Rogers' 1957 classic (127) and related writings (133, 140). In the more voluminous part of this work, short excerpts of interaction between client and therapist (or parent and child, etc.) have been rated by external judges for level of empathy and other conditions, communicated by the responding person (202, 203). In the language of this approach, the focus is on (therapist) interpersonal skills, manifest in the degree to which the conditions are "offered" (to the client), as "objectively" judged from communication samples (203). The other main approach, drawing directly on the participant's own experience and perceptions of the response of the therapist (or parent, etc.), generally recorded and quantified using versions of the writer's *Relationship Inventory*, is the more direct expression of the theory as outlined (7, 127, 139, 151; 82, p. 505). In terms of results, there is a high degree of consistency in numerous studies in the finding that empathy, congruence, and level and/or unconditionality of regard—*particularly when measured from client perceptions of therapist response*—are

significantly related to indices of client change over the course of therapy (82). An important related focus of research, developed in the monumental Wisconsin investigation of psychotherapy with schizophrenic clients (154), is a relatively fine-grained examination of levels of therapist empathy and other conditions in relation to developmental change in client functioning within the therapy relationship. This work was based on further new developments in client-centered therapy, forming the writer's next focus.

5. The Person in Process: Experiencing and Related Concepts

As mentioned earlier, the development of Rogers' "process conception" of the direction and discernible stages of change in therapy, a new *kind* of concept of variation in personal functioning—especially taken in conjunction with powerful new description and thought regarding the nature of experiencing articulated by Gendlin—represented another evolutionary advance in the client-centered system. Rogers' conception took form following development of the "conditions of therapy" theory (just outlined), and basically extended the equation of therapy on the "outcome" side: if X (the change-generating therapy conditions), then Y (before-to-after change effects *or* in-therapy process movement) (6, 136, cf. 133)

The process conception is a systematic framework and model, anchored in close description and examples, within which to identify a client's level of functioning, using as data features of his or her behavior in the client/therapist interaction. In order to regard the behaviors as client characteristics, it is necessary to assume (with justification) that relevant ambient conditions—particularly, basic qualities of therapist attitude and response—are relatively constant. Rogers proposed that this constancy needed to reside in the client being psychologically *received*, in the sense of the other's response being highly empathic, congruent, and unconditionally regardful (134; 137, Ch. 7). In practice, and for reliable comparison from one occasion to another or one client to another, the more important factor would be the consistency, rather than level, of the conditions.

The central discrimination underlying and contained in the process conception was that significant change in therapy was not a movement from one kind of fixed but faulty structure to another kind of stable but adequate structure, not a change from one kind of invariant organization to another. Rather, the essential direction was *from* a (more or less) fixed, closed, self-perpetuating structure *to* a quality of open, flowing, integrative emergence; from fixity and recycling motion to a formative changingness; briefly, from a condition of stasis to one of process (6; 134; 136; 137, Ch. 7). The process conception partly draws from and reflects the influence of Gendlin's early work on experiencing (48, 68, 134)—this in turn drawing from Rogers' thought and encouragement (63, p. 223; 134, p. 106). While the continuum was at first described (130), and initially subject to measurement (206), as a single multifaceted dimension, a number of separable component "strands" were soon identified (134). Of these, the most distinctive were concerned (a) with the way the individual related to feelings and personal meanings, (b) the manner (later, the level) of experiencing—particularly, in terms of immediacy and of interplay between symbolizing awareness and preconceptual experiencing, (c) qualities of awareness and application of personal constructs—including level of self-recognition of construing and attributing processes, and fixity versus flexibility of constructs, (d) the relationship to problems—including "problem" recognition and ownership versus regular external location of difficulties, (e) qualities of perception and communication of self (related to all four elements mentioned), and (f) manner of relating, especially in terms of ability to be present and expressively in contact in terms of immediately felt experience and meaning (134; 136; 137, Ch. 7).

Rogers arbitrarily chose to distinguish seven levels or stages for the continuum as a whole or for any component strand, regarding each strand as much more separate and distinct at the lower end of the continuum than in the integratively functioning "process" person at the other extreme. The following passages provide a succinct account of the two ends and further illuminate the dimension as a whole.

> At one end of this tentative scale or continuum we find the individual living his life in terms of rigid personal constructs. . . . He has little or no recognition of the ebb and flow of feeling life within him. . . . His communication, even in a receptive and acceptant climate, tends to be almost entirely about externals, and almost never about self. The form tends to be: "The situation is . . .," "They are . . .," "They say . . .," [or, possibly] "My characteristics are . . .," but he would almost never say "I feel . . .," "I believe . . .," . . . He does not recognise himself as having problems. He does not perceive himself as a responsible agent in his world. He exhibits no desire to change and, on the contrary, shows many signs of wishing to keep himself and his environment as unchanged and stereotyped as possible. (134, pp. 96–97)
> At the other end of this continuum we find the individual living in his feelings, knowingly, and with a basic trust in and acceptance of his feelings as a guide for living. His experiencing is immediate, rich and changing. . . . The ways in which he construes his experience are continually changing in the light of further experiencing. He communicates himself freely as a feeling, changing person. He lives responsibly . . . [in an open] fluid relationship to others and to his environment. He is aware of himself, but not as an object. Rather it is reflexive

awareness, a subjective living in himself in motion. (134, p. 97)

Not surprisingly, one finds in Rogers' other writings, shortly before and in the period following his differentiated articulation of the stasis-process continuum, very clear reflections of the same basic vein of thought. An early example is his paper "A Therapist's view of the Good Life" (128) which, while overlapping and echoing principal features of his earlier written work on the fully functioning person (141), uses language much more attuned to a "process" way of thinking. Another 1957 article subtitled "A Therapist's View of Personal Goals" (in 137) discusses change away from and toward qualities of functioning in terms that bridge earlier expression of his thought and the forming nexus of the process conception.

In taking up a related theme five years later, in an important paper on optimum valuing processes (145), Rogers' discussion under such headings as "Restoring Contact with Experience" and "Valuing in the Mature Person" closely draws and builds on features of the earlier creative work on process and experiencing. "The Emerging Person: Spearhead of the Quiet Revolution," as he or she is graphically portrayed in the last chapter of Rogers' latest book (174), lives very clearly in accord with (although not simply reflecting) the upper levels of the continuum discriminated twenty years earlier.

Following its first formulations, further refinement and empirical "translations" of the process conception evolved as the primary vehicle for the study of client process in therapy, in the monumental Wisconsin program of research on therapy with schizophrenic patients (67, 88, 154). Up to four separate scales, representing differing component strands, were used in tracing and analyzing client process levels and movement in therapy. Central among these was the "Scale for Rating of Experiencing" (67; 88; 154, Appendix C). This scale continues in use, due in part to its connection with another major

development in the client-centered system: Gendlin's theory of personality change (53).

The originality and richly differentiated nature and complexity of this theory prevent adequate distillation in a short space. Key qualities, concepts, and pointers include the following.

In the context of concern to understand and explain change, Gendlin rejects existing views of personality that emphasize contents, states, or entity characteristics, viewing current theories of repression (by whatever name) as incompatible with regarding the individual as a process and comprehending change in process qualities. There is no unconscious in terms of a depository of repressed events. It would be seriously inaccurate, in this view, to speak of experience being driven underground out of awareness, where it remains or resides, ready in some circumstances to burst forth again, full blown. On the other hand, it would be quite consistent to speak of a process, involving experience, being stopped or incomplete—or "structure-bound" (53, 68).

Gendlin posits an *implicit, preconceptual* level of inner life process. While occurring at an unsymbolized, undifferentiated level of awareness, this process is by no means ephemeral, but is the directly felt datum or referent substrate of experience. It includes unarticulated bodily felt processes, "gut reactions" for which no words have (yet) formed, images without clear shape, *sensed* emotion, and energies, and meanings not yet born in symbols. Ordinarily, to know of and begin to engage with this inner process or direct referent simply requires attending to it. A special (or full) way of attending leads to the process that Gendlin refers to as focusing, which comprises the core of his theory of change (53).*

In the initial "direct reference" phase of focusing a person attends to a definitely felt but

---

* The nucleus of this change process, in normal development, was mentioned at the end of a subsection of this chapter, entitled "The Human Organism."

vague or elusive, unformulated referent. This is a form of active, inner listening and communication, with a quality of excitement as the person increasingly recognizes, "puts a finger on," and articulates the form of this felt inner referent. When or as this happens, the unfolding process merges into the next phase of "referent movement," referring to a perceptible "give," yielding or releasing shift in what is concretely felt. An exclamation, or sudden light and mobility in the person's expression, may signal this shift; then, often, followed by many words, pointing to core elements, facets, and details of what the person is now symbolizing in experience. Like the slight turning of a chandelier, a small underlying shift may reveal a myriad of new facets of "light" or personal meaning. As focusing is sustained and the unfolding process continues, a third phase of "wide application" typically occurs, as the rich variety of implications and applications to differing situations comes to mind. What at first seemed unitary now has many sides or faces. As either a further phase, or as an outcome of focusing, an additional step of "content mutation" is described, in which the person sees differently and reidentifies the essential content or connection that initially excited him or her (53, 63). The focusing process can freshly begin with some new unclear felt referent, over and over again, with continuing integrative change in the person's lived world; and focusing itself becomes a recognized, basic resource modality in experiencing and development (57, 58, 63).*

Gendlin sees the essential ingredient processes encompassed in focusing, proceeding in a recurring (spiral-like) cycle, as the nucleus of a therapeutic or enabling change process; and the transformation of experiencing that results from this process, as the central outcome of therapy. The nature of this transformation is essentially in keeping with the stasis-to-process continuum, as

---

* Gendlin (and collaborators) describe the four-phase sequence somewhat differently in the two major papers referenced, embracing this conception (53, 63). The writer has worked to integrate the essential, strongly overlapping features, in this account.

already outlined. While some people can engage in focusing much more readily than others (63), the qualities of interpersonal response that strongly enable or facilitate this process are in keeping with versatile living expression of the "conditions of therapy" principles already outlined, especially finely tuned (empathic) listening, and also a further implied condition that this writer would call "availability" (9)—centrally expressed in responsively *active* willingness to lead or guide the other person into the focusing mode (57, 58, 63).

The reader is reminded that the account just given is an all-too-brief *illustration* of key features of Gendlin's total thought and rich array of concepts, in the sphere examined. This section as a whole has focused on theoretical perspectives and developments essentially within the school phase of the client-centered system. Additional, recent, and emerging frontiers of systematic thought are referred to and implied in the final section of this chapter. In the meantime, attention is turned to principles and developments, through the 1960s, within the main areas of practice.

Principles in practice

1. The Helping Interview

Client-centered therapy, far from being a passive or largely reactive process on the therapist's part, involves a very active, concentrated focusing of purpose, attention, skill, and energy. Consistent with the principle of congruence, this involves a *devotion* by the therapist or helper to activity that is not a *task* to be performed or a self-denying means to exterior ends but which is, certainly, a form of highly concentrated, dedicated, and skillful "work." This work has several major aspects, framed and described here with the previously mentioned principles in mind. Insofar as there has been development over time in principles of practice, the present aim is to provide a largely contemporary view, drawing on sources from the 1960s.* (The letters T and C in the following passages refer to Therapist—or counselor or facilitator—and Client, or counselee, respectively.)

a. The initiative for the topical *content* of the communication lies largely with the client. On the other hand, the nature of the relationship between T and C and, particularly, the salient *qualities of interaction* in the interview, are to a large extent in T's hands. There are no rules, however, against T expressing feelings and meanings of his own, or directly inviting C to focus on a particular issue; nor is C without influence on the nature or qualities of the helping relationship, especially as he perceives them. The mentioned balance of differential initiative has to do with the differing respective objectives and "set" of the participants. C, for example, knows best where he is hurting, conflicted, or wanting to move beyond his present functioning and consciousness. T has functional knowledge of ways of being and responding that can be helpful to C, who is struggling with or "stuck" in his difficulty. Broadly, these ways of being and responding involve a *living* of the therapy conditions in the helping relationship.

T may expand his range of initiative with withdrawn or deeply troubled persons—as, for example, Gendlin (50, 51, 52, 54) and Rogers (138, 154) describe in their work with schizophrenic clients. This may also be true with children and younger adolescents. Such initiatives, however, are an active *offering* of relationship, direct indications of the living, attentive presence and personhood of the therapist, direct suggestions of what C and T might do together that would provide a further vehicle for the helping engagement. T's broadened initiative and expressiveness, in such contexts, retains a nonimpositional quality and as C

engages and gains momentum, T moves with him.

b. The participants' attention, expression, and responding in the interview is *experientially* focused. Gendlin uses the term "experiential response" to refer in a generic way to what T does (56). This implies a focus on personally felt meaning—not on disembodied feelings (without their referent underlying, context or meaning) *or* observations and description "washed" of emotion, but on emerging discriminations imbued with the full coloration of present unfolding feeling. As expressed by Gendlin, "A therapeutic response always aims at the client's own directly felt sense of what he is talking about" *and* "aims to carry the client's experiencing further" (56).

The experiential mode has the quality of immediacy (63, 136). The client partner in the helping interview is optimally communicating felt meanings that are "surfacing" in words and nonverbal expressions *as he goes along*. Effectively, T is doing this also. Communication is emergent, not rehearsed, and the process is in many ways just the opposite of planned reporting or recitation. Much of the familiar terrain and pathways of C's construed world of experience and meaning are allowed to recede as he gains security and mobility in the new "environment" of the therapy-helping relationship and engages in a process of experiential inquiry and growth with a companion who greatly encourages and aids his search but does not try to conduct it.

c. T engages in active, concentrated, perceptive, empathic listening. He tries "to hear the sounds and sense the shape of the other person's inner world" (161). He asks himself, "Can I resonate to what he is saying, can I let it echo back and forth in me so deeply that I sense the meanings he is afraid of yet would like to communicate as well as those meanings he knows?" (161, p. 223). For C, the effects of such depth of understanding can be very powerful—"It may be as though something that had stopped inside him had begun to move and live again, that some part of his loneliness is a world of imperfect communication and knowing had

---

* Effectively, representing the culmination of the school phase; and still in keeping with the work of most client–person-centered therapists.

dissolved, or that some vital connection he had been unable to bring into focus had become suddenly and vividly clear to him" (13). The processes of deeply attentive, sustained, sensitive listening and resonation *and* of apt, expressive, empathic experiential responding may be said to comprise the manifest "work" of the therapist–interviewer (152).

What T hears, while it is drawn from, activated by, and pointed toward C's experience is, of course, also something that is going on in him and influenced in some measure by his own characteristics. The interviewer, at best, always indicates or implies in some way that it is his own consciousness or *perception* of the other's experience that he is reflecting, pointing toward, building on, or responding to in some experiential way. He does not suggest that he has complete, exact knowledge of any aspect of the other's experience or inner patterning; or that he knows with total assurance what it feels like to be the other person at a given moment. He responds to the other in terms of his "best understanding of his meaning at the moment, with the *attitude* that this understanding is continuously open to correction and change. This not only increases the possibility of accurate [empathic] comprehension . . . but helps to free the other to change his way of perceiving or formulating his experience, to consider other possibilities, and to discover new, deeper, and more integrated and personally valid meaning in his experience" (9).

T informs C, in any of a variety of ways that may fit the particular styles and language of both participants, that his communicated understandings are an expression of himself as well as of C. He implies that it is important for him to know whether his understanding is accurate, partially right, or quite "off target" in reference to C's immediate felt experience and meaning.* T also shows that he knows that C is moving in his experiencing and that he wants to go by C's sense of his "experiential track" (56).

d. Through his deeply empathic listening and experiential responding, T may go significantly beyond C's directly expressed messages. While staying with the client's experienced world, it is not the case

> that the client-centered therapist responds only to the obvious in the phenomenal world of the client. If that were so, it is doubtful that any movement would occur in therapy. . . . Instead the . . . therapist seems to dip from the pool of implicit meanings just at the edge of the client's awareness. (152)

In this passage, Rogers alludes to the similarity between this aspect and quality in the client-centered therapy interview and the aspect of skilled analytic interpretation as characterized by Fenichel, who stresses that "effective interpretations can be given only at one specific point, namely, where the patient's immediate interest is momentarily centered" and some new awareness "is striving to break through" (46). Gendlin also speaks in similar terms:

> The client-centered response at its best formulates something which is not yet fully formulated or conceptualized. . . . It formulates the meaning which the client has not yet symbolized explicitly but which he does now feel and which is implied in what he says. Sometimes it formulates the felt whole which the client has been trying to get at by various different verbalisations. (49)

---

* The cues are often implicit—even nonverbal—as for example, in a subtle quality of invitation in T's tone of voice for C to set him right, if necessary, or a response framed as an assertion but delivered with an implicit question mark. Examples of more explicit cues are qualifying or questioning phrases such as: ". . . it's kind of . . . isn't it?," "As though . . . ," "It seems to me you are saying . . . " "That this is a scary thing, is that what you mean?" (137, Ch. 6). Further examples from interviews with a deeply troubled and withdrawn client are: "And I guess your silence is saying . . ." "It's hard for me to know . . . but it looks . . ." "Just feel you are no good at all, huh?" "I guess . . . if I get it right . . ." (154, pp. 401–416). Often, C's next statement begins with "Yes," "That's right," or some other "reply" that confirms or corrects T's stated understanding of C's message.

e. In the nature of the helping interview situation, C is in a position of perceived or acknowledged need as a person. His "neediness," in effect, provides the occasion for his association with T (in the helping context). Conversely, if C's neediness is taken as a given, T's motives, identity, and resources as a helper are a major determinant of their association. These circumstances, and the associated limits and scope of the commitment and responsibilities each one undertakes in their relationship, contribute to the further focal aspects of the helping interview.

One such major aspect is the evocation of real feelings of warmth, interest, and caring on T's part toward C as a person. In the client-centered interview, personal detachment or distance militates *against* the helping process. Feelings of compassion, warmth, respect, or admiration, interest or liking and other positive feelings toward C as a person usually arise in T and are allowed to show (150). T is generally accepting and nonjudgmental toward C and, at best, there is a steady "prizing" quality to his feelings and attitude. At times, however, a helper will experience negative feelings toward the other and, if these feelings become strong, they are almost certain to be communicated in some way. In these circumstances, client-centered workers have increasingly favored "owning up to" rather than "covering up" such feelings, either directly with C or with another enabling-consulting partner—or perhaps with a helpful consultant *and* then with C (152). This relates directly to the emphasized aspect of personal congruence on T's part, with C. Broadly, T is "all there" in the helping interview. He is not presenting a contrived, cultivated, but non-integrated role or part of himself. He is totally *with* his deeply attentive listening and understanding, and his regardful, experientially focused, empathic responding.

The described pattern of qualities is distinguished as constituting a special "helping" interview and relationship partly because it is atypical (particularly, on a sustained basis) of everyday life. It is the view of client-centered workers that the elements involved are fundamental nutrients in human development and actualization and *should* be substantially present in each person's interpersonal life. This issue becomes *a* main focus in the last section of this chapter.

2. Client-Centered Therapy with Children and in Families

In 1947, the first major work on child therapy from the client-centered school was published (3). Virginia Axline's *Play Therapy* was soon a classic in its field and has remained an important resource. Play is taken by the author, as by other child therapists before her [including Taft and Allen (1, 199), who had influenced her work] as a young child's most natural medium of self-expression and, hence, a primary vehicle for personal communication. Through use of suitable materials—puppets, a doll family, finger paints and clay, sand box and basins, mugs, nursing bottles and running water, toy animals, cars, soldiers and weapons, a toy telephone, cutting out materials, and other items—in a robust, unconstricting play environment and in company with a therapist-person and possibly other children, the young child expresses and plays out his or her feelings, experiments and explores in safety, and discovers, learns, and grows inwardly and in relationships. Such, in briefest terms, is Axline's portrayal.

Eight working principles of nondirective play therapy—falling in two clusters, in this writer's perception—were discriminated by Axline and richly illustrated from records of play therapy sessions and the author's eloquent commentary. Four of the specific working principles advanced are concerned directly with interpersonal qualities and communication. Foremost is the aspect of establishing "a warm, friendly relationship" with the child, as soon as possible. This does not mean that the therapist-helper is pressing to form a close, affectional tie with her child client, but that there is ready opportunity for the child to know that the therapist likes to see her, is accepting in attitude, has an understanding and sympathy for child-people, certainly is not harsh or hostile and actually *wants* to be in company with the child in the play sessions.

Further principles are that "the therapist accepts the child exactly as he is" and establishes a relational atmosphere such "that the child feels free to express his feelings completely." Axline makes it clear that there should be no grounds for the child to feel threatened by anything the therapist actually does, or for a trial of strength to develop between them. In no way should the child be "crowded"; and praise for particular behaviors is seen as the other side of the same coin as disapproval or rejection. The qualities of positive regard and unconditionality are closely foreshadowed. In the counterpart of empathy, Axline saw the therapist's basic task (in line with adult therapy) as being to recognize and reflect the child's feelings "in such a manner that he gains insight into his behavior."

The further group of principles in Axline's portrayal are concerned essentially with issues of control and responsibility; with the therapist *avoiding* direction *or* the temptation to "push things along," maintaining a genuine attitude of respect for the child's ability to make responsible choices and find *her* solution to her problems and, consistent with this, communicating and maintaining some minimal, necessary limits in the therapy situation. In regard to the last-mentioned aspect, the therapist establishes (only) "those limitations necessary to anchor the therapy to the world of reality and to make the child aware of her responsibility in the relationship" (3, p. 76). The principal limits are those concerned with the bounded duration of play sessions, the proscription against physically attacking the therapist, and avoidance of willful destruction of the play materials or environment. When necessary, the therapist makes it clear that she will not accept the *behavior* of breaking such a limit. If she has to stop such

behavior, she continues to show her awareness and respect for the child's *feelings*.

Axline's portrayal gives only brief attention to the parents of children in play therapy. While the author feels that parents or parent-substitutes usually have considerable responsibility for the child's difficulties, she firmly asserts that "it is not necessary for the adult to be helped in order to insure successful play therapy results" (3, p. 68). She observes that as the child changes she sees a different world, and her new vision produces changes in the ways significant others respond to her. This observation (among others) is extended in the next general statement on client-centered play therapy, by Elaine Dorfman.

Dorfman's principal contribution (40) forms an extensive chapter in Rogers' 1951 book (121). In connection with the last-mentioned point, she proposed that a child's "stimulus value" to other persons can change significantly as she engages in therapy. "Once he is differently perceived, he is differently reacted to, and this different treatment may lead him to change further. Thus, the child may initiate a cycle of change . . . (We have found] that many children have benefited from play therapy without concurrent parent therapy" (40).

In her discussion of the child therapist's role, Dorfman cites a case Axline had reported. Three eight-year-old boys were in a play therapy group together. One of them, Herby, suddenly asked the therapist about her work. Ronny asked him what he meant, and Owen joined in. Herby continued:

"I mean I wouldn't know how to do what she does. She doesn't seem to do anything. Only all of a sudden I'm free— inside me, I'm free." (He flings his arms around.) "I'm Herb and Frankenstein and Tojo and a devil." (He laughs and pounds his chest.) "I'm a great giant and a hero. I'm wonderful and I'm terrible. I'm two, four, six, eight, ten people . . . " [The therapist begins to speak, and there is a brief interchange between Herby and Ronny] The therapist continued to speak to Herby—"You are all kinds of people in here. You're wonderful and you're terrible and you're dopy and you're smart"— Herby interrupted exultantly—"I'm good and I'm bad and still I'm Herby. I tell you I'm wonderful. I can be anything I want to be!" (3, 40)

Not all children were as articulate or exuberant as Herby in this passage. Dorfman refers also to those who were still or silent for long periods, where little overt interaction took place or where the child's activity was not visibly self-disclosing or exploratory. To a surprising degree, in these instances as well, the therapy hours were important and eventful episodes from the child's point of view, with effects visible to others.*

In 1953, Clark Moustakas published his first book, *Children in Play Therapy* (93), drawing particularly on the client-centered school as well as on the work of Taft and Allen and others. While his specific, creatively evolving perspective does not lend itself to labeling, the basic philosophy, style and working practice portrayed in Moustakas' eloquent and influential writing are strongly in the client-centered tradition. His second book focusing directly on play therapy (94)—written for a wider audience than the first—substantially complements Axline's and Dorfman's work. As these authors have done, Moustakas richly illustrates his work from therapy process and related records, particularly in the context of therapy with disturbed, "normal," "creative," and physically handicapped children, counseling with parents, and direct work with teachers and children in schools.

In Moustakas' discussion of major issues in child therapy, the matter of limits again receives

---

* Dorfman also outlines the first formal research studies on client-centered child therapy, including R. E. Bill's careful early investigation of nondirective play therapy with retarded readers (27).

careful attention. His view is that limits should be allowed to *emerge,* in varying patterns, according to the particular child, therapist, and situation:

> When I set a limit in psychotherapy it is an aspect of my being, an expression of who I am at a particular moment in time. It is my limit, a boundary for me. When the child accepts the limit a bond is formed between us. The limit is then a structure or boundary of our relationship. It is a reality held in a relationship. . . . The child confirms me and together we accept a structure through which our relationship can develop. (94, p. 15)

Within the Chicago group itself, following the heyday of Axline's work (and then her departure) and of Dorfman's cited contribution, child therapy became a somewhat less active and visible focus of development. Interested staff and students continued to work with children, and some significant studies and contributions to practice, including the report by Seeman, Barry, and Ellinwood (185), still appeared. By the mid-1950s, Charlotte Ellinwood was coordinator and principal contributor to the work that was continuing.

Although Axline (and others) had concluded that direct parental involvement was not essential for effective therapy with children, Ellinwood observed that, in practice, child clients were often withdrawn prematurely from therapy if there was no ongoing concurrent contact with a parent. It appeared that parents were often being "left out" unless they actively sought help for themselves, and also that "unsolicited therapy" for parents generally did not work out (41). Ellinwood examined the position and attitudes of both parents and therapists in such situations, in the light of current theory (41, 127, 133, 134).

Clearly, many of the parents who brought their children for therapy saw the difficulties as external to their own functioning and agency. Other parents felt the opposite, even to the point of seeking direct help solely for themselves. Parents of the former kind seemed to be functioning near the "stasis" or low extreme on Rogers' "process" spectrum. This quality of functioning and associated attitudes toward what "help" meant, coupled with what therapists expected of a "therapy client," loaded the situation against establishing the conditions of a helping relationship. Ellinwood's careful analysis ended with a number of suggestions for working with parents more literally from "where they are" in their attitudes and needs and for related research investigation (41).

By the mid-1960s, Axline's second book, *Dibs: In Search of Self* (4), had made its eventful appearance. It is a lovingly executed, indepth presentation of part of the life of an individual child, in therapy with the author several years earlier. The author speaks as far as possible through the words and actions of Dibs, of other important people in his life, and of her own interaction and feelings with him. It is a gently powerful story, full-bodied and evocative. The emergent patterning of events and meaning is consistent with the principles earlier advanced by Axline, but freer in regard to the forms and depth of response by the therapist. (It is perhaps *more* consistent with Rogers' view of the helping relationship, a decade after Axline's original work.)

At the point *Dibs* appeared, a new approach in client-centered child therapy came into view via Bernard Guerney's first published work on "filial therapy" (80). As early as 1957, Rogers' daughter, Natalie, had published an account of home play therapy sessions undertaken with her own daughter (47). In his 1959 book, Moustakas mentions this case and others involving parents in therapy play sessions with their own children (94).

Guerney and his associates (80, 81) developed procedures based on client-centered principles in which parents of young children are trained and assisted in the conduct of therapeutic play sessions with their own child. The children involved in the development of filial therapy were real clients, referred or brought for help as a result of distressing difficulties. The distinctive rationale of filial therapy (added to the conditions and goals of a helping relationship) begins with the assumption that parent–child relationships have been influential in causing or maintaining the child's difficulties. From this starting point, Guerney et al. propose that (a) difficulties acquired within the context of the child's association with her parents could most effectively be unlearned or resolved under similar conditions, (b) the parents' involvement and motivation are likely to be strongly mobilized by the process of developing resources to be of direct help themselves (where before they had been "failing" or ineffective), (c) as a parent experiments with a different pattern of response to her child, even for short times, and experiences new consequences, this brings changes in the whole relationship, and (d) if and as the parent successfully consolidates the new ways of relating and being with her child, favorable long-term prospects are maximized.

The actual filial therapy method as reported by Guerney and others (80, 81, 197) involves a phased experiential learning sequence including, in each phase, regular parent group meetings with a therapist. The sequence begins with discussion meetings designed for the parents to develop their awareness of the principles involved in client-centered play therapy—based on the therapy conditions—followed by demonstration play sessions and continuing discussion between therapist and parents. Each parent then brings her own child for sessions observed by, and discussed with, the rest of the group. After perhaps twenty meetings parents begin play sessions at home, while continuing with their own therapist-led parent group for a period of several months or longer. At least one of Guerney's reports includes a fairly detailed, illustrative case outline (81).

Therapy in *family groups* has not been extensively practiced and studied by client-centered workers. Van der Veen and collaborators have been active in research on family processes, adjustment, and change, including a focus on the study of family self-concepts (95, 204). The same author has reported family therapy practice, notably in an article with Raskin. Raskin and Van der Veen describe and advocate the flexible introduction of family therapy meetings, when consistent with the attitudes of family members already in contact with the therapist. The family group that is directly involved in therapy may then be further modified, according to the reactions of the participating members (107, p. 349). The authors illustrate with a case in which the two parents first meet jointly with the therapist, followed by meetings in which one or both of their two children participate as well, therapy sessions with one child alone and then with the parents again. Both client and therapist initiatives were involved in this varying pattern. The reported therapist interventions are very much in the empathic, nonconfrontational, client-centered, but self-expressively "immediate" and congruent mode.

Marital counseling is a related area in which client-centered therapy and principles have had very wide impact. Rogers and other leading exponents—as Raskin and Van der Veen's portrayal suggests—developed a flexible approach in working with individuals and couples troubled, estranged, or in conflict in their marriages. At first, Rogers advised against meeting with couples together, in view of the difficulty of maintaining a truly unjudging, nondirective attitude in working closely with potential combatants holding very divergent perceptions (117). His theory and practice soon grew beyond this constraint, and he became actively concerned with *direct* facilitation of communication, new awareness, and actual change in relationships—in various situations of interpersonal tension and conflict (148). Client-centered therapy, however, on the whole has had a more individual than relational or interactional focus.

Over time, the trend has been from the former toward also including the latter. The title of the following section is in keeping with the main emphasis. *

3. Helping Individuals in Groups

For the first decade in client-centered therapy, interest was focused principally on dyadic helping contexts. During the early to mid-1950s, considerable interest was developing in small-group contexts, as well. This interest included group therapy as such and also an emerging interest in working groups or teams, and in ways that such groups could be facilitating both to the individual members and from the standpoint of problem-solving and productivity. These developments first came into prominent view through contributed chapters in *Client-Centered Therapy,* by Nicholas Hobbs (86) and Thomas Gordon (73).

Hobbs's article, entitled "Group-Centered Psychotherapy," was concerned with individual-centered therapy in a small-group context. The main principles were in common with individual therapy, with the group providing distinct and unique therapeutic potentialities:

> It is one thing to be understood and accepted by a therapist, it is a considerably more potent experience to be understood and accepted by several people who are honestly sharing in a joint search for a more satisfying way of life. . . . [This] is the something added that makes group therapy a qualitatively different experience from individual therapy. (86, p. 287)

At the level of therapist technique and attitudes, group and individual therapy were closely similar. Groups, Hobbs observed, were more evocative for many people. Sharing of experience by one member helped to trigger

---

* Applying especially, through the school phase. Further strong, emergent thrusts are described later in this report.

another member's self-expression and exploration. There was opportunity and stimulus to express and try out emergent new perceptions and behaviors. The group fostered changes in self-awareness and self-concept via an environment of significant others, resembling "that which initially created the need to distort the perception of self, and of the self in relation to others" (86, p. 291). The realism and therapeutic potential of the group situation was seen as enhanced by the fact that a participant could be a giver of help at the same time as receiving help.

Hobbs discussed the analysis of the therapy group process in terms of themes, drawing the analogy of a rather loosely constructed musical composition, and referring to Gorlow's systematic research use of the theme concept (79). Diaries kept by members after each meeting were seen as one valuable source of descriptive understanding of the process and effects. Besides an early report by Peres (98) the main research cited by Hobbs was a cluster of studies by Gorlow, Hoch, and Telschow, later published together under the title "The Nature of Non-Directive Group Psychotherapy" (79). These authors used the transcribed protocols from three different therapy groups as their principal (and massive!) data source, and applied carefully worked out content analysis procedures. Hoch's study of process found the groups very similar in overall pattern, consistent with considerable variation between individuals —in terms of the categories and trends examined.

Gorlow's component study, concerned with "The Behavior of Members as Therapists," was in some ways ahead of its time. Relevant group-member responses were coded (in much the same way as those of the therapist-leaders) in categories including "clarification of feeling," "restatement of content," "simple acceptance, " etc. It was found in effect that members became better therapists during the course of the group experience.[*] Telschow focused on the (highly nondirective) therapist-leaders.

Later in the 1950s, Ends and Page reported their investigations of several forms of group therapy used with hospitalized alcoholics (42). The authors expected a learning-theory-based method to be most effective, but found instead that client-centered group therapy resulted in significantly greater remission of alcoholism—both in terms of immediate post-therapy results and effects a year and a half later. A neoanalytic form of group therapy came a close second in effectiveness, with the sample and criterion involved.

In 1961, Truax reported his original study of group therapy with hospitalized patients (201). The therapists involved varied in orientation and style, but the investigation drew largely on client-centered theory in the concepts and hypotheses involved. The central aim was to test relationships between (a) *postulated therapeutic conditions* rated from the therapist's response and also from the responses of group members, and (b) *associated levels of self-exploration* (or "therapeutic behavior") of clients, measured from Rogers' process scale and other indices. From among the scales he devised and used, Truax found that the rated conditions of "accurate empathy" and "self-congruence or genuineness" together with the factor of "concreteness or specificity" of discussion were most consistently related to the indices of self-exploration, in the group therapy context.

Since the early 1960s, with the mushrooming development of growth-oriented groups associated, especially, with the human relations training and human potential movements, the line between client-centered group therapy and client-centered forms of sensitivity-encounter group experience has become a very fine one. [†]

---

[*] Hobbs leaves open the possibility that this may have been a result of learning from the leader, "absorbing his attitudes and sensing the reasonableness and helpfulness of what he does," or an effect of personal therapeutic change, or both. (86)
[†] An intriguing study by Betty Berzon and collaborators in the early 1960's, concerned with "The Therapeutic Event in Group Psychotherapy" (25), indirectly reflects this convergence, judging from the described group situation and results.

The latter has evolved jointly from the former and from earlier applications of client-centered principles in administrative leadership training workshops and other nontherapy group contexts, as initially described and advanced by Thomas Gordon.

At the time of Gordon's first reported work, the group-process-oriented experimental training programs of the National Training Laboratory had recently been initiated at Bethel, Maine. The Tavistock Institute for Human Relations in London, England, was becoming a source of important new ideas and exploration in such areas as leadership and organizational functioning. Gordon acknowledged these and related developments as contributory influences in his thinking and work. (73). His 1951 report included a series of general propositions regarding the behavior and "adjustive capacity" of groups. He posited, for example, that forces within nearly any group produce, over time, some degree of instability or disequilibrium. Adjustive behavior is that which tends to reduce such disequilibrium, and this behavior best involves the participation and effective contribution of all group members. A group has the adjustive capacities or potentials to increase its internal harmony and productivity and, given certain conditions, it will move toward effective or fuller use of these capacities. Some of the crucial conditions have to do with qualities of leadership. (Other conditions of possible importance were not examined.)

Gordon discusses leadership extensively, taking the position that the group-centered leader does not accept responsibility *for* the group but proceeds with confidence that most of the functions and responsibilities associated with central leadership can be taken over and shared by members of the group. The author is careful to point out that this state of affairs cannot be accomplished by fiat (and any such attempt is likely to be seen as subtle or inverted imposition) but is itself a developmental process in which the leader may have a crucial facilitating function. Such a leader's primary values, as portrayed by Gordon, are "the ultimate development of the group's independence and self-responsibility, and the release of the group's potential capacities" (73, p. 337). Gordon also suggests that "the group-centered leader sees the group or organization as existing for the individuals who compose it" (73, p. 338). In the writer's view, the requirement of this attitude, literally interpreted, would greatly limit the range of application of Gordon's concept. Many groups, for example, have vitally important service responsibilities to others, which places the group and leader in a different position than that of groups who do exist literally for the individuals directly involved.

Gordon discriminates a number of functions of the group-centered leader, including those of conveying empathy, warmth, and acceptance (consistent with his real limits and situation), of being closely attentive to and understanding of meanings and intents of other members, and of carrying out a "linking function" in regard to the communications and contributions of other members. The last aspect involves a persistent effort to perceive the connection or linkage between each new comment or initiative and those already in view, and to convey this relationship to the group. To the extent that the leader is effective in all of these ways, the functions are gradually taken over and developed by the group members.

As the group-centered process unfolds, in Gordon's portrayal, salient aspects include: (a) members relate to each other with acceptance and understanding not formerly present, (b) far less attention and energy are used up in reactive response to authority, (c) members experience responsibility for evaluation of their individual and collective work as lying within themselves, and (d) participation becomes less ego-centered and more altruistic or group-centered.

In his subsequent book, *Group-Centered Leadership* (74), Gordon presents a self-contained statement of the philosophy behind the group-centered approach and of its broader social implications in a society subscribing to democratic ideals. A very fully documented case study of an intensive training workshop conference, conducted in accordance with the principles advanced, is the book's centerpiece. This workshop itself focused on leadership and, while the workshop leaders "practiced what they preached," their role and situation were relatively more like that of a "trainer" (in the human relations training sense) than that of a leader-administrator in an ongoing organization. A contributed chapter by another author does give a fascinating glimpse of such leadership in a functioning industrial organization.

In the early 1960s—a full decade after the workshop experiment Gordon had reported—client-centered workers began to engage, in experimental and distinctive ways, in the emerging sensitivity/encounter group movement. By this time, individuals from the client-centered school or broadly sharing this orientation were spread out in a variety of locations in the United States and represented in other countries. Their involvement in intensive groups, outside a formal counseling or therapy context, often came about independently—evidently as a natural further expression of shared interests and similar viewpoints—in conjunction with broader movements in social consciousness and practice. The writer's work is a case in point and a convenient example to cite.

From a background of earlier experience with the Chicago group—which functioned along group-centered lines—and experience in student-centered teaching as well as in therapy, the writer set out in 1962 to organize a residential "Workshop in Therapeutic Counseling" for people with existing background in the mental health-related disciplines in Australia. The setting for the workshop was a provincial university in a small center, on which participants (if any!) would have to converge from various distant points and where they would be in residence together. The workshop—the first such in Australia, with its focus on experiential learning from the data generated in agendaless small-group sessions conducted along client-centered lines—finally and successfully took place, at Ar-

midale, starting a series in that setting and sparking related developments elsewhere. A major stated goal of the early workshops was "to assist those taking part to further develop their capacities to engage in psychologically helpful relationships with other persons." It was further promised that participants "would not be confronted with a pre-arranged syllabus or programme of topics, and every effort would be made to ensure that the specific content of the workshop experience grows out of the thinking and concerns of the persons choosing to engage in it." Prospective members were advised that, to make good on this promise, "there will be provision for regular intensive discussion meetings in small groups" (11). The "intensive discussion meetings," as they developed in practice and as the available terminology evolved, turned out to be of the "basic encounter" variety, in terms of process, member goals, and outcomes. (11, 159). Data for evaluation and more basic research were gathered from the members of several workshops and are the origin of several later reports (12, 16, 21).

During the period of the writers' involvement in the Armidale workshops, Rogers moved from Wisconsin to the Western Behavioral Sciences Institute, an independent organization concerned with research and demonstration projects in the human relations field, co-founded by a former (Chicago) student and associate of Rogers, Richard Farson. From this point (1964) the area of intensive group experience and process became a primary focus in Rogers' subsequent work. Besides his activities at "home," he conducted intensive group workshops abroad, including one organized by the writer in Australia and others in France and Japan (in the 1960s).

Rogers's first major article in this new field (159), written in the mid-1960s, presented a developmental outline of the basic encounter group process, also published in his later book, *Carl Rogers on Encounter Groups,* and in other contexts. Some fifteen overlapping elements, which the writer suggests organizing in three broad groupings or phases, are discriminated in this report. The first phase might be termed *engagement*. It is always present in some form, tends to be difficult and demanding for those unfamiliar with the intensive group experience and, quite often, for experienced participants as well. Rogers describes and illustrates typical aspects of initial "milling around," expressions of fear and other resistance to personal expression and exploration, and a cautious venturing into past feelings and present outward-pointing negative feelings.

In the second phase, of *trust and process development*, there is significant "expression and exploration of personally meaningful material," here-and-now interpersonal feelings in the group are shared and the quality of immediacy develops, and group members become resources to one another (in Rogers' terms, a healing capacity develops in the group). Such development does not occur magically, smoothly, or without persistence, risk-taking, and committed effort and "work" by participants. The process involves going "beyond the organised, practiced styles and contents of communication and relationship to the level of deeply sensitive, protected or unexplored areas of self-perception and response to others" (11). Developing trust is a crucial ingredient and, as the necessary safety and trust are felt (but typically with back-and-forth swings), group members progressively share more of their individual process, more of the "immediate, unedited, self- and other-related emotions, assumptions, thoughts and concerns" that each experiences (11).

In the third phase of *encounter and change*, the experiential group and learning process becomes full-fledged. There are likely to be shifts in actual self-acceptance and self-regard of some members. Feedback processes, and also confrontation and demands to drop residual fronts or facades, typically occur. Helping or supportive relationships outside group sessions frequently develop between members. Episodes of deep sharing and encounter occur, and there is experience and expression of positive and close feelings between group members. Actual changes in behavior become noticeable in the group.

Rogers' portrayal was written in advance of directly pertinent research data or systematic descriptive-theoretical accounts by other client-centered workers, and of his own extensive further experience. The formulation stands as a valuable first approximation to one main vantage point from which to view the total phenomenon of the group experience and process. This writer has distinguished at least four significant vantage points or levels of analysis *additional* to the developmental-sequential perspective (16)—which itself has been a focus of further important contributions, especially by Beck (24) and Braaten.*

Proceeding from a client-centered base, further work concerned with process delineation and outcome effects, with investigation of variation and alternatives in regard to leadership, group composition and temporal arrangements, and with special applications in educational systems and a variety of other contexts, has all occurred on a growing scale. Two of the best collections, which include relevant work by associates and past students of Rogers, are Solomon and Berzon's *New Perspectives on Encounter Groups* (193), and *New Directions in Client-Centered Therapy* edited by Hart and Tomlinson (85). Further discussion of recent and contemporary work in the intensive group sphere appears in the final, main section of this chapter.

4. Client-centered Principles in Teaching and Education

From the start and throughout the "school phase" of the client-centered approach, its founder and principal exponents almost all were, or had been, engaged in university teaching and in research that was closely linked with their counseling or therapy practice. The

---

* L. J. Braaten, "Developmental Phases of Encounter Groups and Related Intensive Groups," *Interpersonal Development*, 5, 1974–1975, 112–129.

largest group among their clientele were students; and a large proportion of their student-clients, and nonclient students, became teachers or counselors in educational settings. As well, significant involvement and concern with school-age children, as parents or in other personal or professional ways, would have been typical. Under this confluence of circumstances, it was a very natural step for serious interest to develop in teaching and education as a further sphere for application of client-centered (or student-centered) principles. This fact, and the reader's likely concern with education in the helping professions and with the effects on children of different qualities of classroom and educational experience, have beckoned the writer strongly in preparing a concise outline of this area of contribution and the working principles involved.

In his "launching" statement on teaching and learning (121, Ch. 9) Rogers referred to important related work by several contemporaries, including Cantor (36), and acknowledged that "in one sense our experience is a rediscovery of effective principles which have been stated by Dewey, Kilpatrick, and many others, and a rediscovery of effective practices which have certainly been discovered over and over again by competent teachers" (121, p. 386). Having taken these (honest) bows, the author proceeded with preliminary conceptual mapping and practical illustration to suggest that a revolution in formal education and teaching was necessary and possible.

While it may not have been Rogers' prior intention to shock his readers and listeners (for example, in the 1952 Harvard conference—122) it is clear that he was not displeased with the controversy and ferment his presentations evoked (137, pp. 273-274). More rewarding still was the growing flow of practical application and research on "student-centered teaching" (28, 91, 200). The stimulus of Rogers' own contributions increased with his 1959 article "Significant Learning in Therapy and Education" (135), his well-known paper from the Wisconsin era "Learning to Be Free" (143),

his probing and provocative outburst on leaving Wisconsin (declined for publication by the Editor of the *American Psychologist*) entitled "Graduate Education in Psychology: A Passionate Statement" (85, Ch. 26; 161, Ch. 8), a cluster of papers embracing education and teaching in *schools* (153, 155, 157, 158), and then his book *Freedom to Learn* (161). This book contains several of the articles mentioned, others concerned with the application of student-centered teaching from the sixth grade to the graduate level, and several papers concerned with the broader value system and human developmental goals implicit in the author's approach to education.

The teaching–learning enterprise in education embraces, on the one hand, the values, purposes, and goals to which this enterprise aspires or, in practice, which it expresses. Complementing the aspects of goals is that of the conditions, methods, resources, and processes available and actually applied toward achievement of these goals (8). In outline, the interrelated *objectives and goals* emphasized in student-centered teaching and learning include:
a. The development of functional or working knowledge, a "knowledge of" rather than simply "knowing about," an organically connected, interwoven enlargement of the knower's consciousness in which the new elements are organized in active, dynamic interconnection among themselves and in relation to the person's prior experience and meanings. The new knowledge, in effect, is an extension or growth in awareness and capacity such that the learner's subsequent perceptions and behavior in related problem situations are necessarily different.
b. Inquiry and learning that are purposeful, subjectively meaningful, and actually relevant to the learner's own quest, goals, values, or present objective. In terms of its purposeful and meaningful nature, the effects of the learning are directly satisfying, self-enhancing, and, at best, an expression of the individual's actualizing tendency and process.
c. Learning experiences that have the effect of

awakening, nourishing, or enhancing the individual's curiosity, desire to know, to discover, or to gain new capacity in doing. Outcomes that involve the individual remaining at least as "turned on" to her learning as before. Effects in which any prior dependence on external goading or indirect (extrinsic) incentives is diminished rather than strengthened.

d. Learning that is individualized, releasing, enlivening, and of a quality that involves or leads to emergent, original, or creative products.

e. A learning how to learn, or "meta-learning." Learning that increases one's capacity to identify and to solve problems, that is concerned with fruitful processes of inquiry, that increases resourcefulness in gaining knowledge and desire to use these resources.

f. The development (or preservation) of experienced self-responsibility for one's learning and for assessing effective progress and products of this learning. Necessary external appraisal becomes feedback to the learner, who experiences herself as the final source of evaluational judgments regarding her accomplishments, capacities, and action decisions.

The *conditions and methods* conducive to achieving the goals just outlined, as emphasized in varying configuration by Rogers and other client-centered workers in education and teaching (161), fall into two subclusters. The cluster most systematically and consistently portrayed are qualities in the teacher-student relationship corresponding to the relational conditions of therapy. In their extended form, these qualities are conceived as core conditions in any interpersonal context intended to foster positive developmental or actualizing processes. In a teaching context, these conditions—stated in brief outline and relative terms—are:

a. The degree of congruency or realness of the teacher. The extent to which she presents and shares herself openly, without pretense or facade. The extent to which the teacher "comes across" as a real, alive, whole person, absorbed in what she is expressing, responding to, and calling forth from herself and others.

b. The extent of the teacher's multilevel experienced and communicated understanding of the learner, as the latter directly or indirectly expresses herself in the learning situation and relationship. The extent to which the teacher is able to sense both feelings and attitudes *and* see the subject-matter issue or problem-solving process from the student's point of view. The extent to which the teacher is as ready to tune in to the student's system of meanings as to express her own.

c. The degree to which the teacher-facilitator actually experiences and shows positive feelings for the student as a person. The extent of her respect, interest, warmth, appreciation, and caring in relation to the other.

d. The extent to which the teacher is basically accepting and nonjudgmental toward the student as a person. The degree to which the student is accepted and appreciated as a *separate* person, on her own track (or seeking this track) in *her* development.

e. The extent to which the teacher is able to perceive the student's own drive for growth and development as a trustworthy, primary motivation for learning. Some students will be outwardly passive and dependent, at first. In such circumstances, this condition involves the extent to which the teaching person is able to sense the need and potential in the other to be alive again in her curiosity and growthful, active search for relevant meaning and knowledge.

f. The teacher's "availability," that is, the extent to which she is ready to share information and knowledge which she has and to communicate meanings which do originate in her, in response to the other's desire for this (9). The extent to which she *responsively* contributes from that which she knows, as this is helpful to the other in achieving what she wishes to know.

In addition to these (and perhaps other) attitudinal-relational qualities, further relevant conditions and processes from the student-centered perspective include:

g. Contact with problems, issues, and processes that are real and important to the learner, relevant to her purposes, that engage and involve her, and that leave her more knowing in ways that make a self-valued difference in her thinking, perception, and action.

h. Provision of resources; of "all kinds and relevant raw material for use by the students, together with clearly indicated channels by which the student can avail himself of these resources" (143). Relevant resources may be of many kinds, from those to be found in a library, those needed to stimulate or reproduce processes the learner is studying, resources available in places where the knowledge she is seeking is applied and practiced, human resources from within and outside the learning group.

i. Additional arrangements which help to maximize self-initiated, goal-oriented, integrated learning by reducing threat and increasing self-targeted, self-monitoring, and self-appraising processes. Two such possible methods are the use of learning "contracts" and of self-evaluation procedures. One or the other of these and related procedures in any of a variety of forms—usually involving a clear sharing of responsibility and/or pooling of judgments by teacher and student—are typically associated with student-centered teaching.

j. The use, where possible, of small "facilitator-learning" groups (161) or their equivalent as an alternative or complement to other kinds of "class" or "course" meetings. Such groups may be varied in their specific characteristics, goals, and level of interaction, consistent with a basic facilitation model.*

If this outline statement on principles applied in education has stimulated the reader and, especially, if it has evoked and left the

question "But how does the full approach actually work in practice?", the best *group* of descriptions—largely in the original words of three different authors and teachers—that the writer can point to, are presented in the first part of Roger's *Freedom to Learn* (161). Some of the relevant research literature, including studies using forms of the writer's *Relationship Inventory* in classroom contexts, is also cited and referenced in this work.

The post-school period: development and vision

The time of transition of the client-centered system from a school of thought and practice primarily associated with personal counseling and therapy, and with an evolving but cohesive orientation, to a broad-gauge "post-school" movement is dated by the writer as the *mid-1960s.** By that time, exponents of the viewpoint had been working relatively independently in various locations for a significant time period (seven, ten, even fifteen or more years). Rogers was not involved directly in individual therapy *or* in conducting empirical research, as primary activities. (Very clearly, with the ending of the Wisconsin project, client-centered *research* was no longer focally represented by or "in orbit" around one luminary center of intense creative work.) For Rogers and many others, the focus of helping activity had shifted from dyadic therapy to intensive groups and further contexts. Working for personal development, integrated learning, and system change in education had become a visi-

---

* Wilkinson, for example, has investigated the effects of "optimal" and "nonoptimal" combinations of student preference and group placement in facilitation-learning groups operating at low, medium, and high "intensity levels" (209). Results tended to support the hypothesis that personal-educational gains were maximized at quite different intensity levels in groups with the same leader-facilitators, depending on the prior attitudes and preferences of the learning-group members.

* This dating applies in North America. Particularly in non-English-speaking countries where client-centered therapy has been influential—such as Japan and Germany—a similar transition probably did not occur until the early or mid-1970s. In areas where the client-centered/person-centered approach has only become widely known or influential in the 1970s—for example, Brazil (173, 210)—in terms of local experience the school phase is either quite different or not a meaningful identification.

ble, central interest for some main exponents of the approach. Broad-scale social issues and problems were becoming a consuming concern in subcircles within the client-centered movement. Needed overhaul of the philosophy and practice of behavioral science had emerged as a live, major issue. Counseling and therapy practice was less unique and more varied than in the school phase, especially in the visible aspects of form and technique. Other new thinking and developments of a diverse nature were coming into view or just over the horizon, in the concerns and contributions of client-centered workers (58, 76, 84, 166, 168, 171) and of others drawing from this system (37). A new era in regard to the emphasis and scope of theoretical and scholarly developments strongly rooted in the client-centered approach was brewing, and would become strikingly evident, for example, in the publication of *Innovations in Client-Centered Therapy* (208).

The writer has selected for brief review several of the focal beachheads and burgeoning thrusts in the post-school period. As areas of active concern and development these foci are not exclusive to the client-centered movement, but they are distinctive in their combination, qualitative character, and particular contributions.

1. Recent Theory and Application in Group Encounter: Beyond Self-Actualization

Recent work by Rogers and others involves the application of intensive group experience for purposes that encompass but extend beyond the goal of enhancing the *personal* development and well-being of participants. One such important purpose, to which client-centered workers who are simultaneously interested in groups and in teaching and supervison of trainee helpers have been responding for some time, involves the use of experiential groups in professional education. The context in which such a group is formed—for example, that of classmates in a "course" in small-group processes or social problems, members of a seminar in organizational or community development, or students in a counseling practicum—may naturally lead to distinctive structural arrangements and process emphases. Given that such variations are in accord with the personal qualities as well as the educational-professional objectives of participants, they help to enhance or sharpen relevant outcomes—for example, in the area of facilitative group leadership attitudes and skills.

Rather wide attention has been given to the use of intensive groups in organizational contexts—to assist organizations in remedial or developmental ways.* The relevant experience of client-centered workers has been largely in human service organizations and educational systems, and is not (yet) extensively documented in terms of system-level effects. Rogers has pointed out that serious introduction of encounter groups in organizations is likely to disturb, shake up, and alter the functioning of the system, *not* simply to have a tension-reducing, stabilizing influence. His own relevant work has centered on the application of group encounter processes in educational systems— and will be further discussed.

Encounter-type groups composed of members of differing social communities or subcultures, separated by prejudice, communication failures, and/or active conflict, form an area of new exploration of potentially great importance that has received mounting and sometimes dramatic attention (163, 172, 179). Rogers' most recent summary of work on this level—a chapter in his latest book (174)—includes information on the follow-up activity "back home" of a group he had led, composed of Catholic and Protestant members from Northern Ireland. Although not focusing on groups in active conflict, the Cross-Cultural Communications project coordinated by Charles

---

* A classic source is E. H. Schein and W. G. Bennis, *Personal and Organisational Change Through Group Methods* (New York: Wiley, 1965).

Devonshire, and involving other client-centered resource persons, has sponsored workshops in a number of countries since the early 1970s. These have focused on encounter experience in intensive small groups of multinational, -cultural, and -language membership (39; 89; 174, Ch. 7).

Solomon and Berzon and their associates (26, 192) and Richard Farson (43), among others, have developed and implemented differing kinds of leaderless (or leader-absent) small-group programs, from which the available evaluation data has been *almost* as promising as that in groups with a leader-facilitator present. Gendlin has been active in working with and sponsoring open experiential groups in special community settings, during much of the post-school period (64, 70). Called "Changes," the most unique aspects of this program relate to community rather than to groups as such, and it will be further mentioned.

In 1972, Bebout and Gordon published an initial "chapter" report on a massive research program aimed at the "comprehensive evaluation of outcome, process and leadership in more than 150 non-professionally led encounter groups" (22). Data had been already gathered from 100 completed groups involving over one thousand persons, and preliminary analyses focused on outcome and group typology. Most leaders were recruited internally from the membership, and received further in-service training. Of six group types, the most productive was described as "group-centered; highest on measures associated with a working, expressive encounter and with an attitude of acceptance." Leadership in this type was facilitating but not confrontive and not strongly centralized. Reported outcome effects include a range of salient positive changes in personal and interpersonal well-being, but no clear overall gain in regard to "productivity, work and school problems"—which were not objectives but might have been spinoff effects (22). A complementary, later article by Bebout strongly presents and illustrates (from group session protocols) his

own concept of encounter, from an existential Rogerian standpoint. In particular (for example), he discriminates "experiential communality" as a crucial, powerful form of coexperiencing, approximating a deep reciprocal empathy and "feeling-together-with-each-other," between persons. This basic experience and process are illustrated from encounter groups and other life contexts (23).

Beck (24) has recently presented—and is continuing to develop and test in her research—the most careful, systematic, differentiated conception of the sequential phases in the process structure of therapy and encounter groups so far advanced by a client-centered (or perhaps any) investigator. She distinguishes nine phases, each identified in regard to the group level issues or focus, the characteristic form of the process, and the distinctive leadership roles and development. Her crafted account ends with an outline of defining features of successful development of group process structure, which bear an interesting qualitative resemblance to the stasis-process conception of Rogers.

An unusually comprehensive, systematic view, concerned with built-in structural conditions, within-group processes, *and* direct and indirect effects of intensive groups has been advanced by this writer (16). In this work, "the centerpiece is concerned with ways of looking at the within-group *process*, and ranges over several complementary perspectives and levels of analysis"—*one* of these being the sequential view exemplified in Rogers' (159) and Beck's (24) work. The linked, original examination of issues and approach in the study of outcome was developed *in part* as the foundation for a long-term follow-up investigation (in progress) of meanings and consequences, within the individual's larger life journey, of participating in intensive residential human relations learning workshops (198). The structural features identified as contributing determinants of group process and outcome include several aspects of group composition, of formal leadership, and of "time structure, setting and associated activity." As the writer hints in concluding, this compact work could (and may) also be developed as a book (16).

Much remains to be done in terms of further illuminating encounter-type group processes and their effects, in an expanding range of contexts. Clearly, investigation and new developments in theory and application in this area are a *major* continuing thrust in the post-school era of the client-centered movement. One principal context of application of experiential groups has been in formal educational settings, involving, during the post-school period, increasing concern with system-level change.

2. The Focus in Education

Educational systems provide an enormous potential for contribution to human well-being; they are at the same time (mostly) in need of major overhaul, in the larger context of shifting social consciousness and priorities. In a paper first published in 1967, Rogers presented "A Plan for Self-Directed Change in an Educational System" (155). An essential feature of this plan was that some (at least) of the top administrative officers and active board members of any prospectively involved system would be willing and interested to take part in an intensive experiential learning group. With this condition met, the first step in implementation would be a residential workshop for the administrators and board members, focusing on small-group interaction and supplemented by topical meetings of a stimulating, strongly participatory nature. Certain important changes in attitude and administrative process would be expected to accrue from this experience—including increased openness, and ability to work toward possible change in organizational structures within the system.

Proposed as the next step was a multigroup workshop composed of teachers willing (with no coercion) to participate—from which the ex-pected effects would include increased concern and ability to listen and relate responsively to students, and more openness to innovation and change. Following this would be an intensive group experience for each participating class or course unit, from which crucial effects would also be expected. Groups would also be made available to interested parents.

The next main phase would involve vertical groups, in which persons from all levels in the educational system would meet together, and where (for example) developing changes in attitudes, new channels of communication, and new interpersonal awareness could be carried forward and strengthened. Rogers also discussed provisions for continuing, self-perpetuating facilitation and change within the system, and the need for a substantial program of research to track and evaluate the multifaceted process and effects.

Most aspects of this plan were first implemented in an intensive project in a parochial school system in Los Angeles. Rogers' preliminary report (161), while affirming the general feasibility and impact of the scheme, includes a number of learnings by the project team. One such learning was a rather clear gradation of difficulty in initiating the process of encounter groups, according to the participants' level in the organizational hierarchy. It seemed that "the more prestige and status and intellectual expertise the person has to defend, the more difficult it is for him to come to real encounter with other persons" (161, p. 339). Another learning resulted in an overall change in emphasis: "We have come to recognize that we are not simply studying the impact of encounter groups on an educational system. . . . [Rather] *we are studying the impact of a dedicated group of individuals who are interested in facilitating communication between persons . . . upon an educational system"* (161, p. 340). From this standpoint the encounter group was merely one important vehicle, and not consistently the most relevant and effective context for facilitation.

In his serious, lively book, *Groups, Gimmicks and Instant Gurus* (38), William Coulson, another leading member of the "Immaculate Heart Project," provides a long, highly communicative account of the project and its meanings. While the massive encounter group program conducted during the first six months was individually releasing and helpful to many (perhaps most) who took part, by itself it was an institutional disaster—in Coulson's view. The existing structure of the system did not evolve but fractured; and the encounter group medium (at least, as implemented) was repudiated by the majority, including some initially eager advocates. Coulson's evaluation is not wholly negative. There were very substantial indirect gains which some members of the resource team played a crucial part in continuing to facilitate, through persevering, caring consultation in various forms long after the group program subsided. There was considerable attrition, the system went through a fascinating metamorphosis, and eventually it was welcomed back again into the schools of the Los Angeles diocese, as the Immaculate Heart *community*.

While acknowledging that much of the learning occurred through trial and error and mistakes, Rogers later reported a considerably more optimistic evaluation of both the means and the ends, and cited the observations of outside assessors in support of some of his conclusions (170). The writer sees only a small range of direct incompatibility with Coulson's view, but the two perspectives complement each other in crucial ways. "Project Transition," an even more ambitious system-change program largely designed around the use of small groups in an educational context, followed the project just described. The (very different) setting was the city school system as a whole in Louisville, Kentucky. Rogers served as a consultant, the primary initiative being taken by the newly appointed superintendent—with school board backing and federal funding (163, pp. 144-148). The need for change was critical, the symptoms including exceptionally high student

dropout rates, delinquency levels, and teacher turnover, and very low and falling educational achievement (167). The nature, means, and speed of truly remedial change were unknowns. It was a high-risk situation for innovative intervention, and one where the rewards of success would be very great. Although enthusiastic, Rogers predicted that "as change is brought about, an increasing degree of turbulence and criticism [will occur] in the whole educational system" (163). Exciting and releasing developments took place, but this prophecy was borne out in ways that helped to abort the project. While the writer has seen no follow-up reports, informal indications are that at least one large school within the system, with crucial assistance from involved parents (and an "all deliberate speed" approach), has been able to maintain and/or build on a strong legacy of "Transition" features.*

Among other ongoing innovations is the Teaching Effectiveness Training program developed by Thomas Gordon and Noel Burch, initially as an outgrowth of Gordon's influential parent effectiveness program—mentioned further. The primary source is a manual for teachers, in book form (77), which presents, in concept and application, a model for learning- and growth-facilitating teacher-student relationships. Most extensively translated and illustrated in diverse schoolteaching and problem contexts is Gordon's key concept of *active listening*— linked to a variety of communication issues and specific processes. Gordon's style, concern with attitudes, and discussion of rationale make the jointly prepared work more than a cookbook or technology—although there is *some* risk that teachers could selectively learn techniques of active listening in the service of control, quite contrary to the author's aims.

---

* In a lead article (169) to a special journal issue, centering on the work in education of Rogers and associated contributors, he refers again to the Louisville project and his estimation of its value. An article in the same issue of *Education*, C. F. Foster and J. Back, documents in detail the evolution and metamorphosis of the particular school referred to.

Rogers' current work, and that of Coulson and others, relevant to education and the small-group sphere, involves a context of concern for the development and meanings of community. It is a very recent development in client-centered circles for community as such to be emerging as a primary, direct focus of interest.

3. The Search for Community: Action Experiment and Theory

The Center for Studies of the Person, of which Rogers and Coulson were key founding members, sponsors a rich variety of self-contained projects of which only two can be mentioned here. For over ten years the La Jolla Program has been conducting regular workshops in San Diego, with emphasis on intensive group experience in multigroup "communities," with gradually increasing interest in the community-of-the-whole, and experience and learnings explicitly related to community (90, 163). Rogers first describes this program, including the conscious beginning of experiential community meetings—and the fertilization of his own interest in community-person-centered workshop experience—in his 1970 book on encounter groups (163, Ch. 9). He writes, "I vividly recall one such meeting at which I was privileged to be present. The whole community of over ninety persons became [in effect] a live and deep encounter group." This was made possible, he felt, by the members' experience in the small, intensive (literal) encounter groups.

Four years later Rogers, John Wood, and others launched a new series of workshops under the general heading "The Person-Centered Approach," in which experiential learning in community formation, processes, and meanings became the central focus. Small-group contexts remained important but the unique, most magnetic feature was that of intensely involving community encounter experiences in meetings of up to two hundred persons or more (800 in a Brazilian workshop, early in 1977) (173). Early reports of these community-focused workshops include presentations by Rogers, Wood (210), and the present writer (18). Rogers' vividly descriptive statement is a chapter in his latest book (174, Ch. 8), the first of his works to include an explicitly "political" theme.* He outlines the *way* in which the initial nucleus of three people proceeded together to select the final staff of ten, how these ten jointly prepared the workshop announcement, the application of the sliding fee system that left each member with final responsibility for his or her precommitted fee, and the participatory reception of members—drawing everyone from the start toward shared responsibility in their collective happening. Of the 136-member, 16-day residential workshop itself, Rogers writes as an acutely attentive and deeply involved participant-observer, broadly charting the course of events and turning points, especially in the big meetings, and bearing witness as a seasoned explorer in an unfamiliar ocean to the difficult, hazardous, exhilarating voyage of discovery of a new *human* habitat—not a place, but a way.

What of this way? How was it qualitatively distinct, and was there a larger continuity and direction of change from earlier client/person-centered voyages? In his paper "Shadows of Surrender," John K. Wood ("director" of the Workshop) searches to discriminate the fundamental continuum and emergent new quality. He starts with the discovery, in one-to-one therapy, of the power of nonjudgmental, empathic listening and the helper's "surrender [of] the security of being regarded as the all-knowing expert following a clear-cut plan," surrender of the fear of destructive potentialities in place of depending on integrative growth forces in the person, surrender of primary reliance on rational thought in order to give equal place to feeling and intuition, and surrender of an external view to open contact from center to center of helper and client. In group encounter more was surrendered and more added to the situation

---

* Titled in *draft* form, "Empowering the Person: The Quiet Revolution."

and experience of the formal helper/facilitator. However, there remained direct awareness and connection between the participants, and a certain linearity and logical order to the process and its development. In the very large group, these things no longer apply, and new features appear. Complete facilitative responses by one "helper" are largely surrendered and a series of persons may combine in a "single" releasing expression. Even so, the energy and awarenesses of the many are articulated by relatively few, especially in a single meeting; and the form and motion of the process oblige the helper "to surrender dependence on manageable conversations and begin to trust in intuitive faculties to digest the meaning of more holistic expressions" (210).

Wood's total construction complements that of Rogers as well as work by the present writer—who was also a member of the workshop of which Rogers speaks. This work includes a (draft) paper "Toward a Person-Centered Theory of Community" (18). After offering a general working definition of community, the paper touches on strikingly relevant work and thinking outside the client-centered literature* and proceeds to the first of two main foci: the writer's own experience of, and pilot research on, the person-centered approach workshop. *One* of the given, defining features of community is "a certain uniqueness and associated homogeneity—in ways that are important to members"—insured, in the present case, by the workshop announcement and Rogers' involvement. Announced goals included, for example:

> The aim will be to build a workshop
> around an approach . . . which
> recognises that the potential to learn and
> the power to act lie within the
> person . . . [and to] provide a place
> where people who believe in the worth

and dignity of the individual and in each person's capacity for self-direction can come together to create a community. . . .

It is hoped that the experience will not only lead to inner personal growth but to an increased understanding of one's responsibility in the world, and how one can act on that sense of responsibility. (182)

In practice, early in the course of the big group's difficult, suspenseful birth and becoming as a community, this writer found that "the likenesses were far less apparent in the sharply felt present than the uneven chasms of difference and apartness"; and he wondered "whether these chasms were of our *like-minded* making" (18). Reference is made to his troubled concern about the lack of any organized investigative or evaluative component to the workshop; and to the way in which this was partly resolved through inner shifting and the discovery of others with related positive interest, and also through effects of the forming community becoming "self"-knowing and inwardly receptive. Via interest-group activity, an "End-of-Workshop Process Questionnaire" was devised—rough-formed but emergent from the workshop crucible itself—which the writer now felt the sanction and support to ask everyone to answer. One question was concerned with judged early-to-late change in, and the perceived relative importance of, 15 "selected indications of community." The results for several elements led to the conclusion (for example) that truly having "one's *presence* felt, recognised and acknowledged" was of special importance for the development of experienced community.

From answers to a further question, it was clear that members saw their experience in encounter groups as even more important than the community meetings—which ranked second—for their overall sense of membership in the community. One-to-one meetings were seen as

---

* For example, in Redfield's *The Little Community* (108), and Spiro's *Kibbutz: Venture in Utopia* (194).

by far the next most important context for sense of community—with topical interest groups, social events, and "alone times" also relevant but all lagging well behind. On the average, members estimated that their noncasual individual meetings and contacts had involved them with about one person in four from the total membership.

The writer's second main focus is to offer a number of tentative and preliminary formal propositions toward a theory of community as such. Examples follow:

2a) A community forms and evolves as a collective of persons, interconnected in a network of associations among individuals and sub-groups that have reciprocally valued elements for members. The more—in quality and extent—that potential linkages evolve such that community members are 'significant others' in each other's lives, the stronger and more fully-formed the community tends to be. . . .

3. Formed communities tend to sustain if not also to enhance themselves; to (each) have a distinctive identity, character or ethos with which members identify; . . . to satisfy human needs for affiliated belonging and presence with others; and to have corporeal reality and existence in the lived worlds of their members.

4. A well-functioning community would be an open system in interface with other systems (especially living systems), organically responsive to new external data and to fresh information and initiatives from within, continually 'in process' or motion, enlarging in scope, subtlety and wisdom of communal or collective consciousness, and characterised by an organismic egalitarianism. . . .

6. A community is an emergent whole with a life of its own and normally seeks to maintain itself. In effect, it is an emergent life form, and should not lightly be conceived, aborted, subverted or destroyed. (18)

It is argued that "a functioning community, properly identified as such, while it lacks a genetic code, has properties by which we identify life forms of a high order." From this view, it follows that the discrimination of "communicide" (by analogy with homicide, invented to refer to destruction of the life of a community), and of its commission through history and in the present, is a critically needed addition to human consciousness.

While writing this section, the author encountered a valuable, distinct, and separate contribution to the systematic, action-relevant understanding of community systems and change by William (unrelated to Carl) Rogers (183). Presented first—somewhat in the style of Carl Rogers's original "self-theory" of personality (121)—are a series of propositions, offered (with elaboration) as a client-centered concept of community as such, and of community decay and "pathology." Illustrative primary statements are:

1. Individuals seek a community of belonging, understanding and mutual support that will enhance the actualization of life.

2. Every community develops its own distinctive symbolization or myth of itself. . . .

5. Some elements of the community are "owned" as important to the identity of that community,

while other elements are denied
or distorted in the common
awareness. . . .

10. Particularly under conditions of
abrasive and heterogeneous
groups in a community, . . ., a
sequence of deterioration
develops [described by the
author]. (183)

Rogers' direct concern is with regional or
neighborhood (settlement) communities, particularly in an urban context. From this context,
he presents a client-centered perspective—and
schematic model—on the facilitation of social
change toward community health. To start with,
implicit in any approach to change is an
"ideology" regarding the nature of community
and of positive system change; of which the
assumption of a "community growth principle"
analogous to the concept of self-actualization is
a relevant example. Normative concepts, embodied in decision and governance principles,
form another component of this ideology, as do
process assumptions such as "the importance of
listening deeply to the needs and concerns of individuals and groups within the constituent communities." These assumptions have a vital bearing (for example) on the crucial step of problem
identification— in respect to which the change
agent/helper's task includes "facilitating community self-perception," "facilitation of communication among divergent groups," and
assisting in "identification of community goals."
A range of further, identified aspects is involved
in the total scheme of sequential steps and
critical decisions, to the end stage of assisted,
community-designed change toward an increasingly responsive and fulfilling social system
(183).

Sharply differing in context and direct aim
from the work referred to is the self-helping,
community-based experimental development
called "CHANGES," initiated by Gendlin,
Glaser, Henderson, and others in 1970 (61, 69,
70). Identified as a therapeutic community, the
emphasis in CHANGES has been strongly on
interpersonal processes and individual development, in special group settings and cocounseling
contexts, with concern to maintain maximum
organizational fluidity and responsiveness but
otherwise to devote little direct attention to
structures or system issues (69, 70). As expressed by Glaser and Gendlin, "For us, community is a bunch of people with whom you can
carry your living forward in a growing way, and
take the steps that are next in your life." Further,
"There isn't a line for us between psychological
and situational troubles, either way it's about trying to live." And, "Community is where you can
be in touch with all parts of yourself. . . . This
means needing a place that allows experimentation, that allows the old ways to go slowly, that
tolerates crumminess . . . [and that reflects]
great tolerance for differences. . . . On all our
differences—whether about money, therapy,
responsibility, leadership, etc.—if we talk
openly, listen carefully, give the other side
respect and feel that we don't have to go one
way or the other, a good process seems to
evolve" (70).

The last-mentioned phrase is a key one;
"process" referring to what goes on among, between, and within persons—in order of increasing importance. CHANGES is intended,
foremost, to be a place where fruitful processes
can happen for a wide range of people—ideally,
anyone who comes. Many of the process-value
aspects emphasized bear a striking resemblance
to features discriminated in the Person-Centered
Approach workshops (18, 70, 174). As of this
writing, direct attention to roles, structures, and
system thinking on organizational and community levels is incipiently emerging as an addition to the earlier perspectives and concerns
(61, 69). The context of this emergence is the
transition of CHANGES itself into a more defined and wider working organization, increasingly aware of its distinctive identity; and with an
aspect of direct concern to help illuminate and
enhance the human community condition in
diverse life settings.

4. Current Work on Personal Process and Change

While there has been recent, radical expansion in the range of phenomena and issues that are of serious and direct interest to client-centered workers, personal/professional and scientific concern with the experiencing individual, and with personal recovery and growth processes in particular, is still the central and strongest base. This is strikingly expressed in the psychotherapy-related contributions in the edited volume *Innovations in Client-Centered Therapy* (208). The greater part of this work consists of emergent translations, interpretations and/or extensions of basic features of client-centered thought and practice; producing creative syntheses with other systems from information-processing theory to Gestalt theory and practice. Reference has already been made to three of the five chapters outside the sphere of individual therapy (23, 24, 183). Ten chapters are focally concerned with psychotherapy.

Rice begins her individual contribution with the cogent remark that "client-centered therapists sound very much alike to outsiders but very different to themselves." This writer would go further. At the level of theory, as represented in this book, some of the authors would now sound very different to outsiders as well. Taken as a whole, this work is perhaps the clearest indication to date that the "school phase" *is* over, and that client-centered scholar–practitioners, at least, are doing their innovative work in a variety of languages lending themselves to distinctly differing modes of thought.

The book opens with prescient "Remarks on the Future of Client-Centered Therapy" by Rogers (171), written in substance ten years earlier. The article distinguishes several features seen by Rogers as saliently characteristic of client-centered therapy in the past, and in the emerging future as well. First, he observes that "a willingness to change, an openness to experience and to research data has been one of the most distinctive features of client-centered

therapy . . . [setting] it apart, almost more than anything else I know, from other orientations to therapy." Second, is the emphasis on seeing "the unique, subjective, inner person as the honored and valued core of human life"—viewed by Rogers as directly at odds with the major trend in American psychology—a trend that he sees as "mechanistic, atomistic [and] deterministic" in literal, confining ways—ways that fail to do justice to the potential of scientific method as a *tool* in the service of achieving humanly important, subjectively chosen goals. Further distinguishing aspects include "the stress on the enormous potential of the individual," and the increasing recognition that a profound hunger and need for deep human relationships are ubiquitous in our time. Rogers believes that recognition "of the need of every individual for free, spontaneous, mutual, deep communicative relationships is one of the major reasons why . . . client-centered therapy has an enormous potential in the field of prevention" he links this to the emphasis on "wellness," on the development of more fully functioning persons, and on qualitative enhancement of interpersonal relationships.

The chapters that immediately follow strongly express *most* of the features that Rogers emphasized—except that they do not all clearly avoid the prevailing "mechanistic, atomistic" stance from which Rogerian theory has rebelled. Anderson (2) and Wexler (207) work to apply the main features of information-processing theory (developed in relation to studying cognitive processes and higher-order learning) to systematic understanding of experiencing, and to self-actualization and growthful change in therapy. In this view, all stimuli impinging from outside or inside the organism on the sensory–perceptual systems constitute (potential or actual) information input; and the passage of this information up to or through various levels of selection and reception, initial coding, central organization, and "storage" constitutes information processing. The description, elaboration, and extension of these aspects are the main realm of the theory. Both Anderson and Wexler stress that this approach implies a view of the human organism as inherently active—more strongly and clearly so, in Wexler's opinion, than does classical Rogerian theory. His view is strongly put: "The Rogerian man is basically seen as recipient of experience and not as an active agent who is the creator of his own experience"—a paradoxical view for a position emphasizing the proactive nature of man (207, p. 55).

Anderson speaks of personal growth as including "the individual's expanded view of the inexhaustible informational riches contained in stimulation and of options and possibilities open in making use of this stimulation" (2, p. 32). He draws for illustration on Rogers' process continuum, proposing that as one goes "up" the process scale different rules and schemas for processing information are used and that a great deal more attentive capacity is devoted to internal events. He asserts that "the tools of personal growth turn out to be the uses of attention and [of] a store of extracted rules and schemas." The therapist's role is interpreted to include "the retraining or reeducation of attentive capacity" and assisting the client to become aware of his own information-processing rules and so to develop the capacity to transcend them. The author suggests in concluding that all perception, imagery, and memory are constructions, or "caricatures" (of the reality out there?). "The only question is: Do we produce or help others produce good or bad caricatures?" Certainly, client-centered therapists *do* differ!

Wexler provides the most extensive, consistent, thoroughgoing, and (given his premises) creative application of information processing to the phenomena and concepts of client-centered therapy—with radical revision of constructs such as self-actualization, whose prior definitions are seen as not susceptible to translation in Wexler's theoretical framework. In reference to the origins of feelings, it is asserted that affective states are *generated* in the process of organizing information (in some circumstances). A client in

therapy is always "engaged in a process of organizing information and structuring some portion of his life space." Further, "an optimal style of client experiencing . . . *consists of the activity of elaborating and organizing information so as to create change and reorganization in his field*" (207, p. 66). Such change involves complementary processes of differentiation and integration and, at best, experiencing "is the *activity* of differentiating and integrating meaning so as to *create* a richness of experience" (207, pp. 77-78). Wexler focuses in detail on reinterpreting the way that empathy—more specifically, empathic responding—works: "An empathic response is basically [superior] organization of information generated by the therapist and held out to the client" (207, p. 97). In effect, the therapist is a "surrogate" information processor, and his responses serve attentional, organizing, *and* evocative functions. Wexler acknowledges that his theoretical language is not evocative [!], but holds that it refers systematically to processes and qualities "that make people human."

Zimring's work—originally closely linked to that of Gendlin—in effect is a bridge between the kind of position Wexler exemplifies and client-centered humanistic theory, as so far put forward by Rogers and most other exponents. Included is an original discrimination of centrally distinctive aspects and implications of the *practice* of client-centered therapy. For example, most therapy approaches "attempt to move the client from a state of blindness to one of truth," with varying particular conceptions of both elements in this duality. In practice, the client-centered therapist is not trying to judge what the client's blindness is, or to redirect the client toward a particular truth. What the therapist *is* doing is consistent with earlier description in this chapter and with what follows. Zimring, too, advances a cognitive view of therapy, using some information-processing language, but with a sense of useful metaphor rather than wholly literal application; and he argues for consistency between concept and practice, which he believes would lead to therapy theory focusing on "the moment-to-moment interaction of client and therapist as its sole concern" (211, p. 136). He proposes that what is retained by successful clients is increased *ability* to organize experiential data—implying capacity for fuller, richer experiencing. While not self-knowledge in most of its meanings, this development implies a very important form of process knowing.

Rice also draws strongly on information-processing thought but is more directly concerned here with therapy practice and, like Zimring, her work expresses a more positive blending with Rogerian thought and concepts. Her purpose is not (like Wexler's) to reconstruct client-centered therapy theory but to systematically elucidate and describe a view of therapy practice centering on "the method of *evocative reflection*." She sees the central problem in therapy as finding a way in which clients can reprocess important life experiences to reduce distortion and generate new schemes (or organizing cognitive and affective structures) that are effectively relevant to a wide variety of situations. Broadly in keeping with a now-familiar vein, the therapist seeks (by evocative reflection) "to bring to life vividly [more *vividly* than the client has] what it is like to be the client in that situation" (referred to by the client) (109, p. 300). The therapist's reflections "tend to induce in the client a kind of *inner tracking,* and intense concentration on what it's like." Aided in the *process,* the client leads the way in content, in an unfolding reconstruction and fresh organization of his or her experience. The aspects of "Particularity," "Subjectivity," and "Use of Sensory, Connotative Language" in the therapist's response and what it evokes are emphasized and illustrated. Such qualities in action "bear a striking resemblance to . . . poetry that is moving and impactful" (109, p. 310).

In a sense the new thought and language outlined in this all-too-brief account have come full circle from a seemingly dissonant, relatively mechanistic beginning to a clear, strong "lineal connection" with an expanding expression of the distinctive core and flavor of the "parent" thought and practice system. Even in Anderson's and Wexler's work, with the consistent use of Rogers', and substantially also of Gendlin's, work as the initial base line and point of departure (and of return, in some descriptions of practice), it is as though the parentage on one side is very clearly "Rogerian" while the offspring of the marriage are working to establish a clearly separate identity—potentially a very distinct new branch of the family. The other parent of this particular marriage is the mainstream discipline of psychology in its scientific ethos, and a broad newer development in cognitive psychology in terms of its particular content. It is not clear to the present writer whether the further potential of this marriage lies in another breakthrough development of client-centered theory and practice emphases or in the direction of "humanizing" the information-processing viewpoint and theory—or both.*

In their introduction to the section of their book concerned directly with therapy practice (and opening with a chapter by Gendlin), Wexler and Rice distinguish three common features that they believe "promise to characterize client-centered therapy as it continues to change and develop." The first of these features, also cogently expressed by Gendlin, is that the "client-centered reflective response that attempts to stay *constantly in touch with what the client is experiencing* is the basic fabric of client-centered therapy." Second, the client and therapist are seen as engaged "in a joint process of exploration and reorganization." With some difference in roles, the relationship is one of an equalitarian partnership—effectively and crucially "the quality of two colleagues engaging in a variety of tasks that are acceptable and

---

* In a sense, Gendlin's work is also a unique offspring of the same parentage on one side but another quite different (perhaps distantly related) ancestral line on the other. As half-brother, his work in some ways is closer to the developments just outlined and in some other ways to the parent views—which he also influenced.

understandable to both." The third common aspect reflects the tradition of demystification of psychotherapy—particularly of the process of therapy. In the past, and in the new developments reported, it is essentially the processes of therapy and change about which hypotheses are formed and generalizations made. Further, the emphasis in therapy training and supervisory contexts on client, therapist, and interactive *processes* in the therapy hour is very pronounced and distinctive (208, pp. 208-209).

It is not feasible to outline further individual contributions in this 1974 volume, except for brief reference to newest features in the chapter by Gendlin. The author discusses client-centered and experiential psychotherapy—the latter conceived as a wider approach virtually inclusive of the former, which both helped to give birth to experiential therapy and was greatly influenced by it. Gendlin works first to "reformulate" client-centered therapy in experiential terms—in which form he believes that it ought to be part of every therapist's way of working. He strongly suggests (a) that "hardly anyone [anymore] practices only client-centered therapy, purely" and (b) "that the essence of client-centered therapy has not yet been learned by the field" (of therapy practice) (60, p. 213). What is this essence? It is held that true client-centered responding is a baseline for all therapy to work from and return to. This core feature is listening acutely, accurately, in the most finely tuned ways to the specific quality, context, and essential whole meaning or substance that is immediately "living" in the other and that the other is *trying* to make heard (or give a voice to) in therapy, *and* it is responding in a wholly, unreservedly listening way, a response that "reflects" (ideally) a total accuracy of hearing. Provided that this is happening, other kinds of responsive work which are also real expressions of the therapist's awareness and knowing can be added or interspersed.

Experiential therapy, in Gendlin's concept, flows from a "philosophy" about life or human nature as a process, and of experiencing as a core aspect of life that fruitfully involves *interaction* between whatever is being concretely, inwardly felt or sensed, and active symbolizing, conceiving, and articulating processes. From this base, experiential therapy centrally involves inclusion of the whole process of focusing, earlier outlined. How this works, where it leads, and what makes it applicable to diverse therapy contexts are further elaborated, illustrated, and brought up to date in the ensuing discussion (60).

In a work in press, entitled "The Inner Act," written for a wider audience, Gendlin lucidly portrays through everyday illustration the nature, texture, and sequential form of experiential intra- and interaction subsumed under the rubric of focusing. His aim is to help readers learn how to use their latent abilities to self-engage in a healing and growthful mode of experiencing. A large part of the work is explicitly a teaching/learning manual intended to bring the inner core of "psychotherapy" into the culture (62). In this respect, it is a bridge to the next step or section in this discussion.*

The outline just presented brings into sharp relief an already implied distinctive feature of client-centered therapy, namely, that it is an approach which thrives on diversity of thought and style rather than being fractured by it, a movement which is more like the person "high" on the process continuum than the structure-bound "stasis" person. As a system approaching midlife in human terms, the vigorous "child" of the early forties has become a mature adult, with the

---

* Among further recent contributions in the therapy sphere to which the writer regrets not being able to give attention, as well, are Butler's original formulation "The Iconic Mode in Psychotherapy" (33); a research study by Raskin systematically comparing dimensions and emphases in therapy interviews conducted by a leading exponent of client-centered therapy and each of five other principal orientations (106); and a paper by this writer centrally presenting and illustrating a theoretical model of relational empathy as an interactive sequence, involving a cycle of several quite distinct steps or phases (17).

same "genes," memory, and family likeness but a greatly developed, expanding consciousness and repertoire.

5. Social Crises and Interpersonal Cultural Change

It is probable that the client-centered movement both embraces and speaks to a growing number of persons in psychology, social work, education, and numerous other fields who are profoundly concerned with the tearing social issues and crises of the time, and who are desiring or working to contribute toward desperately needed social transformations. While sustaining focal concern with the *person,* in terms of inner life processes and interpersonal relations and change, exponents of the client-centered movement are pointing increasingly strongly to the larger social movements and systems into which individuals are so often locked in ways that profoundly influence the quality of their lives. An expression of this wider concern is the serious interest in community, already discussed.

In 1968 the American Board of Professional Psychology conferred on Rogers an award for outstanding contributions to professional psychology. His short acceptance speech drew a standing ovation from most of his audience; others remained dismayed and silent in their seats. He presented "some comments, positive and negative" on the involvement of psychologists in social problems, calling his fellow professionals to task for conservatism and inaction and mentioning some of the areas of burning need and possible working and investigative approach (162). He elaborated, with hard-hitting passion, in a later paper (167) from the same era. The key issues on which he focused were race relations and racism ("Running like a fever through our culture are the attitudes we hold, mostly at the unconscious level, toward blacks, Chicanos, Indians and other minorities—including women, who while not a statistical minority are treated as one"); the continuing worldwide population explosion and its

devastating potential effects; the desperate and dehumanizing condition, but continuing magnetism, of the big cities; (U.S.) international relationships (then) involving the "obscene war" in Vietnam and other more covert interventions abroad; and the evident trend toward authoritarianism, and even the specter of a police state, at home—which Rogers warned that violent protest would further fuel.

How to respond to such massive and dangerous problems? While suggesting possible remedial steps in some areas (including the sphere of international relations), the author is more concerned in these particular papers to help sound an effective alarm. He refers to a talk "The person of tomorrow" (164), and to his perception that a new kind of individual is emerging in the culture, in small numbers but with potent, unique strengths and resources, who will constitute the effective change agent of the future. Prominent among described qualities of these emerging persons is an abhorrence of pretense, sham, phoniness, hypocrisy, double-talk, and concealment. The message "Tell it like it is"—expressed loudly or bluntly in relevant public forums, or softly as an aspect of being authentic in relationships—is more than a slogan but an integral dimension of their living. Education, in most of its institutionalized forms, is seen by the new man and woman as frequently irrelevant and futile, usually deadening curiosity rather than fertilizing it, and as being preoccupied with instruction (and evaluation) but disinterested or incompetent in the facilitation of learning. Such persons maintain the initiative in the learning and discovery that matters to them, inside and outside the system(s). They are also intolerant of most highly structured forms, of set doctrines, and of orthodoxies and "sacred cows" of all kinds. Nevertheless, they are deeply concerned with values—especially with *living* in moral and ethical ways—and with mysteries of life, frontiers of human consciousness, and the search for the meaning of existence. Personal and collective human consciousness is seen as ever evolving, incompatible with promises of allegiance to any preestablished creed. While certain that they know no final truth, such persons are devoted to living the unfolding truth that they experience.

Persons of this new cultural genus Rogers speaks of are open individuals, keenly aware and perceptive of their own feelings and the lived thoughts and feelings of others, able to communicate with themselves much more freely than persons in previous generations and, perhaps, in human history; and their vision is clear as they search to discern the features and patterns of the world around them. They are seen to have the needed capacity to establish deep contact with others and to form close, intimate, communicative relationships quickly; and to separate humanely and with a minimum of mourning. They are evolving new life-giving forms of community, and are themselves vitally alive, spontaneous "process" persons. They are not always changing. but sometimes resting, digesting, and preparing for the (often unknown) next step into a future that belongs (in the words of René Dubos) to the "unique, unprecedented and unrepeatable person" (174, p. 263). The new women and men, found now in nearly all sectors of society, particularly threaten those who are most afraid of change and who are sinewed by control (and submission), repetition (and circular motion), and fixed (unquestioning) belief.

Rogers' concept of the person of tomorrow—a composite person not necessarily found in "pure" form, and not a new elite so much as the visible front of a tide rising in the culture—took form in the late 1960s; and its literal expression was prominent in his thought for about five years—during the later phase of the multilevel agony of the war in Vietnam, and of the "Watergate" presidency in the United States. It is not implausible that the kind of persons—or person qualities—that Rogers describes were a vital force, among others, in bringing the mighty machine of war, and the ultimate power of the presidential administration, to their respective ends. Under the heading

"The Emerging Person: Spearhead of the Quiet Revolution," in his most recent book, Rogers updates and refines his initial vision, gives many new current examples, and points to the supporting evidence of fascinating convergencies with other contemporary observers of the human condition (René Dubos, G. B. Leonard ["The Transformation"], Jonas Salk ["Man Unfolding"], Richards and Richards ["Homonovus: The New Man"], and many others).

The "emerging person" is now explicitly viewed by Rogers in his and her *political* dimension, as a force for change in the manner and directions in which society is "run," including the aspect of consistency between actuality and ideals—as manifest in the workings of government, business, education, legal and law enforcement systems, medicine and the human services, and many other spheres. The new person is found working outside *and* inside established systems; learning to be effective in diverse contexts, and to move freely in time perspective; and developing and fostering consciousness that is at once planetary and very local. In the span of his book, Rogers' discussion of the emerging person is a culmination that concentrates meanings and themes developed throughout. A central thematic feature is a power analysis, or power relations, perspective, applied to the understanding of interpersonal relationships and interactive human process generally, and to self-attitudes centering on assumptions of agency or of powerlessness. This perspective is applied to differing therapy styles and contexts; to family and marriage-partner relationships; to diverse approaches in education, administration, and management; to intercultural tensions and conflict resolution; to work with underprivileged or oppressed groups, and others *apparently* powerless. The actualizing tendency is restated as the foundation principle and inner source (effectively) of self- and other-empowering development or regeneration. In total thrust, the work is more evocatively descriptive than systematic, emphasizes a new way of *seeing* rather than modified principles of doing, and embraces new arenas with continuity in basic approach. An applied innovation outside the range that Rogers mentions (which *could* additionally be viewed through his new lens is embodied in the "companionship therapy" program developed and researched by Gerald Goodman (71, 72).

A major feature of Goodman's main (very thoroughly) reported project was to locate and identify "therapeutic talent" among young men of varied backgrounds, willing to invest in preparatory experience and in being counselor-companions to younger, needy boys in the community. The initial assessment-selection procedure involved interaction, in the roles of "discloser" and "understander," around real problems, in structured small-group contexts; followed by ratings of each candidate by all others in the group on such items as "I feel that he understands what others really mean." About 70 percent of the applicants "passed" on this procedure and were further identified, for example, as "quiet" or "outgoing," for matching purposes with child companions. Following a sensitivity/encounter group or alternative pre-training experience, the counselors began contacts with their child partners, meeting two or three times a week in the children's homes and in the context of expeditions and activities of various kinds. Extensive data were gathered for research evaluation. A clear overall finding was that the counselor-companions themselves had a valued and growthful experience. Results for the child partners were more equivocal, with follow-up reports from parents providing the clearest indication of beneficial outcome (72, pp. 169-172). Goodman's main report is a mine of information in regard to original, specific procedures and their careful evaluation (72).

Another community program ultimately concerned with the interpersonal life and well-being of children, is the system of Parent Effectiveness Training developed by Thomas Gordon (75, 76). This program is mounted in a university extension course context, and combines conceptual and experiential learning of a series of basic normative principles in interpersonal behavior and relationships. Included are the aspects of acceptance and of active listening, with illustrations of the many ways in which parents negate or fail to convey these qualities as well as alternative ways in which they may be communicated. Gordon's book, entitled *Parent Effectiveness Training* (76), is a very widely used, practical manual, designed as a potential aid to parents and others who are concerned to enhance their resources in relationship to children. A follow-up volume (78) reports an extensive descriptive-evaluation study of the program in action, and documents its working qualities and value.

In 1970—the year that the CHANGES program began—Gendlin offered a number of "forecasts" relating to the extension of the therapeutic principles into the culture at large. Through new social and educational programs, he predicted that learnings from therapy will be applied to society as a whole. Children in school, for example, are envisioned as learning the basic skills and resources now associated with therapy, as part of their "curriculum." The CHANGES program is, broadly, a prototype implementation of Gendlin's further suggestions, embodying kinds of helping-supportive relationships and group-community process and belonging that he foresaw becoming universally available. The essential direction of this and of a number of other predictions and developments, including proposals by this writer (15), may be described as the cultural assimilation of basic ingredient processes of professional psychotherapy—particularly, the more (explicitly) humanistic and equalitarian experiential therapies. An example from the writer's crystal ball is that "more and more people in the community—professional and nonprofessional—will be effective experiential helpers. Individuals will tend to form experiential therapeutic partnerships (besides forms of partnering we now know); and small groups will be the other dominant therapeutic medium" (15).

In his book *Birthrights* (45), Richard Farson—a student, to the mid-fifties, and subsequent colleague of Rogers—presents a vivid, searching, original picture of the structure of the world in which children develop and have their being in North American society. The author emphasizes arbitrarily discriminating, inherently oppressive, and largely "self-defeating" (especially where "self" refers to the selfhood of children) characteristics of child "care" involved in a wide band of social institutions (family, educational, legal, political, etc.) and life activity contexts. Farson's work includes a philosophy of the "rights" of the younger *persons* which, if implemented, would require a fundamental redesign of the social order. His perspective is startingly unorthodox, surprisingly plausible via cogent information and evocative comparisons, and undoubtedly of a kind to bring out basic and strong polarities among any broad cross-section of readers. The author suggests no easy solutions, acknowledges that most people are in "marginal" or special-need groups in some important way, and disavows confidence in social reform undertaken only in the interests of a single group—even children, as a whole-within the total social organism (or human family).

Farson's book has an overtly political dimension. He is the author also of "Carl Rogers: Quiet Revolutionary"—a portrait-article in which the artist paints his subject in wholly compelling likeness but with features not quite seen before, not made obvious by the needed eye and angle of view (44). Indeed, this statement by Farson, and his influence in other ways, was important in helping Rogers to see that his view of man implicitly contains a strong, evolving political manifesto—as in any strongly advanced conception of human nature and potential, involving directional or normative principles—vivified by contrasts with the more dominant ethos "in place" in the culture.

While basically optimistic, in ways that include his choice, or leaning, among possible alternative scenarios for the future, Rogers—as well as Farson and others—has also emphasized broad-ranging destructive realities and poten-

tialities, and specific future dangers for humankind. He would acknowledge that we have a long, uncertain way to go for the more positive trends and potentialities projected in his now ten-year-old article, "Interpersonal Relationships: U.S.A. 2000," to come to fruition (160). However, in keeping with some of his predictions, evidently profound changes are continuing to occur in man-woman relationships—in directions that include expanding areas of equality, significant evolution in communicational, affectional, and sexual dimensions, and rapidly increasing exploration and open variation in forms of partnering (later illustrated in his well-known book *Becoming Partners: Marriage and Its Alternatives*—166). The forecast that schools, as we know them, "will be greatly de-emphasized in favour of a much broader, thoughtfully devised *environment for learning*" cannot come to pass, on a large scale, as Farson makes clear, without many other, interrelated social transformations. Nor can teachers rely on being able to function as "facilitators of learning," although often sensitized to this concept and to some of its dimensions-in-action in their training and through such programs as Gordon's "T.E.T." (77). Consistent with Gendlin's vision, Rogers saw personal-interpersonal learning as a growing direct focus in schools. While (usually) cautious movement in this direction is detectable, it is clear now that such a focus cannot effectively be "tacked on," and could not flourish without systematic changes in which, for example, schools became resource "centers for learning and development."

The transition *from (a)* a literal client/person-centered viewpoint (i) focusing on individual development and interpersonal relations growth and change, and (ii) implicitly viewing broader social-cultural processes and evolution as *dependent outcomes* of the spread of self-actualization and fulfilling interpersonal relationships, *to (b)* a full-fledged conception of personal/interpersonal dimensions in complex *inter*dependent relationship with characteristics of organizations, communities, and the social organism in a larger sense (all with their own dynamisms and active life-form qualities) has *begun.* Provided this transition is effectively carried forward, an extremely powerful, integrated system of thought, theory, and practice will result. A synergistic blending of most present theory and a humanistic systems perspective is a nascent pathway to the further development envisaged. In this emerging conception and practice, "clients" may literally be persons, couples, families and other small groups, organizations, communities, and larger interwoven systems. On all levels, actualizing change or process level fit together; and the well-being of systems has meaning only (but, then, strongly) in synchrony with the well-being of persons.

6. The Client-Centered Facilitator–Change Agent: Helper, Explorer, and Quiet Revolutionary

Exponents and practitioners of the client-centered viewpoint have, in effect, generally fallen well to the "left of center" of the overall spectrum in their professional groups—whether in psychology, psychiatry, social work, education, or other contexts. This remains true, although *some* of the grounds for such positioning have changed during the life of this movement and system. Psychology is still predominantly behaviorist in orientation and logical–positivist in scientific outlook and method. In the client-centered viewpoint, experiential events and interactive processes in the lived worlds of persons are effectively the *primary phenomena* of interest and concern. Even where the focus is on human systems, concern with "consciousness " (climate, ethos, interperceptions, and communication within the system, and the flow of awareness and exchange with other systems) and with process (with the *working* of the system and with its structures as they effect this working), and with change in these respects, is predominant. Such emphases run counter to the bases on which

behavioral psychology emerged from the original "science of mind," and to its tendency to deal with molecular units either as causes or effects. Moreover, client-centered writers have not supported the concept of a value-free science, any more than they denied the existence of normative principles in the goals and processes of their work as facilitators (10, 139, 145, 149).

In psychiatry, client-centered practitioners stand quite to one side of the center of gravity of the profession, in order to respond on a basis of equal responsibility and transparent humanity with "patients" or others with whom they work and serve. In giving of him- or herself in equalitarian facilitating partnership with clients, and in not slipping into a paternalist stance or acceptance of doctrine, the client-centered-leaning social caseworker, too, has been in a minority position in the field. And so on, for those in other formal groupings.

The client-centered facilitator who is seriously and *actively* concerned to be a direct resource at the level of organizational functioning and system change is in a different place than most of his or her counselor–therapist–caseworker colleagues, particularly those heavily involved in the practice of intensive therapy. Much (perhaps all) of the facilitator–change agent's work, even with individuals and small groups, is not in a formal therapy context at all. And when working to further understand human systems and apply this understanding and associated helping skills in enabling ways, his or her repertoire and role encompasses but extends beyond direct interpersonal facilitation. It may include, for example: helping to identify and open vital new channels of communication among subgroups within the system, or effective ways through which participants can discover key aspects of the way their (human) system is actually working; facilitating new levels of consciousness of ways in which members are affected *by* system and subsystem qualities, and of differential effects *upon* the particular system of members and groupings of varied characteristics; and aiding clear identification of outside influences on the working and the health or growth of the system, and of its own contribution to the quality of the "space" it inhabits.

In the context of this account as a whole, it is clear that the client-centered worker's values, sensitivity, and resourcefulness center at (or centrally include) the level of personal-interpersonal experience and process; and there seems every indication that this will continue to be so. There is also clear indication that more and more persons of this orientation are concerned or working to become change agents in a wider sense. As change agents, their endeavors and influence (would) strongly incline toward system changes that enhance the working process

qualities of these systems such that they become more internally open and receptive to the resources and needs of their members, distinctly more visible in terms of system features to participants, more integrated or organismic in quality of functioning, and more humanly and personally beneficial for their contributing constituent members and groups. Such is this writer's vision, in an area of major challenge to individuals qualified and concerned to contribute to self- and social knowledge and well-being; and now learning to do so on a multilevel basis of which a principal goal is growthful symbiosis between individual person functioning and human/social systems functioning.

References*

1. Allen, F. H. *Psychotherapy with Children.* New York: Norton, 1942.
2. Anderson, W. "Personal Growth and Client-Centered Therapy: An Information-Processing View," in *Innovations in Client-Centered Therapy*—listed ref. 208, pp. 21-48.
3. Axline, Virginia M. *Play Therapy.* Boston: Houghton Mifflin, 1947.
4. ———. *Dibs: In Search of Self.* Boston: Houghton Mifflin, 1964.
5. Barrett-Lennard, G. T. "Dimensions of Perceived Therapist Response Related to Therapeutic Change." Unpublished Ph.D. dissertation, University of Chicago, March, 1959.
6. ———. "Recent Developments in Client-Centered Theory, Research and Practice." Armidale, Australia: University of New England Library, 1961. (Mimeographed, circulated article.)
7. ———. "Dimensions of Therapist Response as Causal Factors in Therapeutic Change." *Psychological Monographs,* 76, No. 43, 1962. (Whole No. 562.)
8. ———. "Student-Centered Teaching." Paper presented to the New England Group of the British Psychological Society, at the University of New England, Armidale, Australia, March, 1963. (Mimeographed.)
9. ———. "Significant Aspects of a Helping Relationship," *Mental Hygiene,* 47, April, 1963. (Also in *Canada's Mental Health,* 13, July-August, 1965: Supplement No. 47.)
10. ———. "Professional Psychology and the Control of Human Behavior,"

---

* Twelve principal sources from within this list, selected by the writer, are printed in bold-face type. This selection includes edited volumes and actually *contains* more than forty of the listed references. Significant information about numerous contributions additional to those cited here may *also* be found in these sources.

Australian Journal of Psychology, 17 (No. 1, 1965), 24–34. (Also in *New Directions in Client-Centered Therapy*—listed ref. 85, pp. 422–452.)

11. ———."Experiential Learning in Small Groups: The Basic Encounter Process," *Canadian Association of University Student Personnel Services. Proceedings of the Ottawa Conference,* November, 1971, pp. 2–12.

12. ———."Group Process Analysis from Post-Session and Follow-up Data." University of Waterloo: *Group Process Study Papers,* 1972, No. 4. (Mimeographed.)

13. ———. "The Intensive Group Experience: Process Description and Guidelines," *Canada's Mental Health, 21,* January–February, 1973: Supplement No. 73.

14. ———."Outcomes of Residential Encounter Group Workshops: A Descriptive Analysis of Follow-up Structured Questionnaire Data," *Interpersonal Development, 5,* 1974–1975, 86–93.

15. ———. "Future Directions of Experiential Psychotherapy." Presented at the Annual Conference of the American Psychological Association, August–September, 1975. University of Waterloo. (Mimeographed.)

16. ———. "Process, Effects and Structure in Intensive Groups: A Theoretical-Descriptive Analysis," in C. L. Cooper (ed.) *Theories of Group Processes.* London: Wiley, 1975, pp. 59–86. (Corrected, soft-cover reprinting, 1976.)

17. ———."Empathy in Human Relationships: Significance, Nature and Measurement," *Australian Psychologist, 11,* July, 1976, 173–184.

18. ———. "Toward a Person-Centered Theory of Community." An address to the Annual Conference of the American Psychological Association, August, 1977. (Mimeographed.)

19. ———. "The Relationship Inventory: Later Development and Adaptations." *JSAS Catalog of Selected Documents in Psychology, 8,* 1968.

20. ———, J. A. Bond, and D. A. Taylor. Resource Bibliography of Reported Studies Using the Relationship Inventory: Part A (Reference List) and Part B (Abstracts). University of Waterloo, 1972. (Mimeographed.)

21. ———, T. P. Kwasnik, and G. R. Wilkinson. "Some Effects of Participation in Encounter Group Workshops: An Analysis of Written Follow-Up Reports," *Interpersonal Development, 4,* 1973–1974, 35–41.

22. Bebout, James and Gordon Barry. "The Value of Encounter," in *New Perspectives on Encounter Groups*—listed ref. 193, pp. 83–118.

23. Bebout, J. "It Takes One to Know One: Existential-Rogerian Concepts in Encounter Groups," in *Innovations in Client-Centered Therapy*—listed ref. 208, pp. 367–420.

24. Beck, A. M. "Phases in the Development of Structure in Therapy and Encounter Groups," in *Innovations in Client-Centered Therapy*—listed ref. 208, pp. 421–463.

25. Berzon, B., C. Pious, and R. E. Farson. "The Therapeutic Event in Group Psychotherapy: A Study of Subjective Reports by Group Members," *Journal of Individual Psychology, 19,* 1963, 204–212.

26. ———, L. N. Solomon, and R. Riesel. "Audio-Tape Programs for Self-Directed Groups," in *New Perspectives on Encounter Groups*—listed ref. 193, pp. 211–223.

27. Bills, R. E. "Nondirective Play Therapy with Retarded Readers," *Journal of Consulting Psychology, 14,* 1950, 140-149.

28. ———. "An Investigation of Student-Centered Teaching," *Journal of Educational Research, 46,* 1952, 313-319.

29. Braaten, L. J. "The Main Themes of 'Existentialism' from the Viewpoint of a Psychotherapist," *Mental Hygiene, 45,* January, 1961, 10-17.

30. Butler, J. M. "The Goals of Counseling." Paper presented to the American Personnel and Guidance Association, St. Louis, Missouri, 1953. In *Counseling Center Discussion Papers, 2,* No. 20, 1956. (University of Chicago)

31. ———. "Client-centered Counselling and Psychotherapy," in D. Brower and L. E. Abt (eds.) *Progress in Clinical Psychology, Vol. 3: Changing Conceptions in Psychotherapy.* New York: Grune and Stratton, 1958.

32. ———. "Self-Ideal Congruence in Psychotherapy," *Psychotherapy: Theory, Research and Practice, 5,* Winter, 1968, 13-17.

33. ———. "The Iconic Mode in Psychotherapy," in *Innovations in Client-Centered Therapy*—listed ref. 208, pp. 171-210.

34. ——— and G. V. Haigh. "Changes in the Relation Between Self-Concepts and Ideal Concepts Consequent upon Client-Centered Counseling," in *Psychotherapy and Personality Change*—listed ref. 175.

35. ——— and L. N. Rice. "Audience, Self-Actualization and Drive Theory," in J. M. Wepman and R. W. Heine (eds.) *Concepts of Personality.* Chicago: Aldine, 1963.

36. Cantor, N. *The Dynamics of Learning.* Buffalo: Foster and Stewart, 1946.

37. Carkhuff, R. R. "Toward a New Technology for Human and Community Resource Development," *The Counseling Psychologist, 3,* No. 3, 1972, 12-30.

38. Coulson, W. R. *Groups, Gimmicks and Instant Gurus.* New York: Harper and Row, 1972.

39. Devonshire, C. M. and André Auw. "A Cross-Cultural Communication Workshop." Unpublished report, February, 1973. California: College of San Mateo and Center for Studies of the Person. (Mimeographed.)

40. Dorfman, Elaine. "Play Therapy," in *Client-Centered Therapy*—listed ref. 121, Ch. 6.

41. Ellinwood, Charlotte. "Some Observations from Work with Parents in a Child Therapy Program." *Counseling Center Discussion Papers, 5,* No. 18. (University of Chicago Library, 1959.)

42. Ends, E. J. and C. W. Page. "A Study of Three Types of Group Psychotherapy with Hospitalized Male Inebriates," *Quarterly Journal of Studies in Alcohol, 18,* 1957, 263-277.

43. Farson, Richard. "Self-Directed Groups and Community Mental Health," in *New Perspectives on Encounter Groups*—listed ref. 193.

44. ———. "Carl Rogers: Quiet Revolutionary," *Education, 95,* Winter, 1974, 197-203.

45. ———. *Birthrights.* New York: Macmillan, 1974.

46. Fenichel, O. *The Psychoanalytic Theory of the Neurosis.* New York: Norton, 1945.

47. Fuchs, N. P. "Play Therapy at Home," *Merrill—Palmer Quarterly, 3,* 1957.

48. Gendlin, E. T. "The Function of Experiencing in Symbolisation." Unpublished Ph.D. dissertation, University of Chicago, 1958.

49. ———. "Experiencing: A Variable in the Process of Therapeutic Change," *American Journal of Psychotherapy, 15,* 1961, 233-245.

50. ———."Initiating Psychotherapy with 'Unmotivated' Patients," *Psychiatric Quarterly, 34,* No. 1, 1961.

51. ———. "Subverbal Communication and Therapist Expressivity: Trends in Client-Centered Therapy with Schizophrenics," *Wisconsin Psychiatric Institute Discussion Papers, 1,* No. 10-g, 1962. Also in *Journal of Existential Psychiatry, 4,* 1963, 105ff.)

52. ———. "Client-Centered Developments and Work with Schizophrenics," *Journal of Counseling Psychology, 9,* No. 3, 1962, 205-211.

53. ———. "A Theory of Personality Change," in P. Worchel and D. Byrne (eds.) *Personality Change.* New York: Wiley, 1964. (Also in *New Directions in Client-Centered Therapy*—listed ref. 85, pp. 129-173.)

54. ———. "Existentialism and Experiential Psychotherapy," in C. Moustakas (ed.) *Existential Child Therapy.* New York: Basic Books, 1966, pp. 206-247. (Also in *New Directions in Client-Centered Therapy*—listed ref. 85.)

55. ———."Values and the Process of Experiencing," in A. R. Mahrer (ed.) *The Goals of Psychotherapy.* New York: Appleton-Century-Crofts, 1967, pp. 180-205.

56. ———. "The Experiential Response," in E. F. Hammer (ed.) *The Use of Interpretation in Treatment: Technique and Art.* New York: Grune and Stratton, 1968.

57. ———. "Focusing," *Psychotherapy: Theory, Research and Practice, 6,* Winter, 1969, 4-15.

58. ———."A Short Summary and Some Long Predictions," in *New Directions in Client-Centered Therapy*—listed ref. 85, pp. 544-562.

59. ———. "Therapeutic Procedures with Schizophrenic Patients," in M. Hammer (ed.) *The Theory and Practice of Psychotherapy with Specific Disorders.* Springfield, Ill.: Thomas, 1972.

60. ———. "Client-Centered and Experiential Psychotherapy," in *Innovations in Client-Centered Therapy*—listed ref. 208, pp. 211-246.

61. ———. "Beyond Roles." University of Chicago, April, 1977. (Mimeographed manuscript.)

62. ———. *Focusing.* New York: Everest House, 1978.

63. ——— et al. "Focusing Ability in Psychotherapy, Personality and Creativity," in John M. Shlien et al. (eds.) *Research in Psychotherapy,* Vol. 3. Washington, D.C.: American Psychological Association, 1968.

64. ——— and J. Beebe. "Experiential Groups: Instructions for Groups," in G. M. Grazda (ed.) *Innovations to Group Psychotherapy.* Springfield, Ill.: Thomas, 1968.

65. ——— and J. M. Shlien. "Immediacy in Time Attitudes Before and After Time-Limited Psychotherapy," *Journal of Clinical Psychology, 17,* 1961, 69-72.

66. ——— and T. M. Tomlinson. "Experiencing Scale." Wisconsin Psychiatric Institute, University of Wisconsin, 1962. Revised version in *The Therapeutic Relationship and Its Impact*—listed ref. 154, pp. 589-592.

67. ——— and T. M. Tomlinson. "The Process Conception and Its Measure-

ment." In C. R. Rogers (ed.) *The Therapeutic Relationship and Its Impact*—listed ref. 154, pp. 109-131.

68. —— and F. Zimring. "The Qualities or Dimensions of Experiencing and Their Change." *Counseling Center Discussion Papers, 1*, No. 3. (University of Chicago Library, 1955.) (Mimeographed.)

69. Glaser, K. "A Story About Changes: Looking Back from the Future." *Changes Discussion Paper, 1*, No. 7, 1977.

70. —— and E. T. Gendlin. "Main Themes in Changes: A Therapeutic Community." 5655 S. University, Chicago: Changes, ca. 1976-1977. (Printed manuscript, abridged and revised from January, 1973, publication in *Rough Times*.)

71. Goodman, Gerald. "Companionship as Therapy: The Use of Non-Professional Talent," in *New Directions in Client-Centered Therapy*—listed ref. 85, pp. 348-371.

72. ——. *Companionship Therapy: Studies in Structured Intimacy.* San Francisco: Jossey-Bass, 1972.

73. Gordon, Thomas. "Group-Centered Leadership and Administration," in *Client-Centered Therapy*—listed ref. 121, Ch. 8.

74. ——. *Group-Centered Leadership.* Boston: Houghton Mifflin, 1955.

75. ——. "A Theory of Healthy Relationships and a Program of Parent Effectiveness Training," in *New Directions in Client-Centered Therapy*—listed ref. 85, pp. 407-425.

76. ——. *Parent Effectiveness Training.* New York: Wyden, 1970.

77. —— and N. Burch. *T.E.T., Teacher Effectiveness Training.* New York: Wyden, 1974.

78. —— and J. G. Sands. *P.E.T. in Action.* New York: Wyden, 1976.

79. Gorlow, L., E. L. Hoch, and E. F. Teleshow. *The Nature of Non-directive Group Psychotherapy.* New York: Bureau of Publications, Teachers College, Columbia University, 1952.

80. Guerney, B. G. "Filial Therapy: Description and Rationale," *Journal of Consulting Psychology, 28*, 1964, 304-310.

81. ——. L. F. Guerney, and M. P. Andronico. "Filial Therapy," in *New Directions in Client-Centered Therapy*—listed ref. 85, pp. 372-386. (Reprinted from *Yale Scientific Magazine, 40*, 1966, 6-14.)

82. Gurman, A. S. "The Patient's Perception of the Therapeutic Relationship," in A. S. Gurman and A. M. Razin (eds.) *Effective Psychotherapy: A Handbook of Research.* Oxford: Pergamon, 1977, pp. 503-543.

83. Halkides, G. "An Experimental Study of Four Conditions Necessary for Therapeutic Change." Unpublished Ph. D. dissertation, University of Chicago, 1958.

84. Hart, J. T. "Beyond Psychotherapy—The Applied Psychology of the Future," in *New Directions in Client-Centered Therapy*—listed ref. 85, pp. 563-595.

85. ——. **and T. M. Tomlinson (eds.) New Directions in Client-Centered Therapy. Boston: Houghton Mifflin, 1970.**

86. Hobbs, N. "Group-Centered Psychotherapy," in *Client-Centered Therapy*—listed ref. 121, pp. 278-319.

87. Hogan, R. "The Development of a Measure of Client Defensiveness in a Counseling Relationship." Ph.D. thesis, Univeristy of Chicago, 1948. (Condensed publication in W. Wolff and J. A. Precker [eds.], *Success in Psychotherapy.* New York: Grune and Stratton, 1952, pp. 112-142.)

88. Kiesler, D. J., P. L. Mathieu, and M. H. Klien. "Process Movement in Therapy and Sampling Interviews," in C. R. Rogers (ed.) *The Therapeutic Relationship and its Impact* — listed ref. 154, pp. 221-250.

89. Kristal-Andersson, B. "Intercultural Communication Encounter Groups." *Invandrar Rapport, 3,* No. 7, 1975. (Stockholm Immigrant Institute.)

90. *La Jolla Program,* The Printed Announcement of the "1977 Summer Institute." La Jolla, Calif. Center for Studies of the Person, 1977.

91. McKeachie, W. G. "Student-Centered versus Instructor-Centered Instruction," *Journal of Educational Psychology, 45,* 1954, 143-150.

92. Maslow, A. H. *Toward a Psychology of Being.* Princeton, N. J.: Van Nostrand, 1962.

93. Moustakas, C. E. *Children in Play Therapy.* New York: McGraw-Hill, 1953.

94. ——. *Psychotherapy with Children: The Living Relationship.* New York: Harper and Row, 1959. (Republished by Ballantine, New York, 1970.)

95. Novak, A. L. and F. Van der Veen. "Family Concepts and Emotional Disturbance in the Families of Disturbed Adolescents with Normal Siblings," *Family Process, 9,* June, 1970, 157-171.

96. Pentony, P. "The Therapist's Function in Client-Centered Therapy," *Australian Journal of Psychology, 11,* No. 1, 1959, 106-112.

97. ——. "Persons as Teams: An Analogy," *Comparative Group Studies, 2,* August, 1970, 211-268.

98. Peres, H. "An Investigation of Nondirective Group Therapy," *Journal of Consulting Psychology, 11,* 1947, 159-172.

99. Porter, E. H. "The Development and Evaluation of a Measure of Counseling Interview Procedures." Ph.D. thesis, Ohio State University, 1941. (Published in two parts in *Educational and Psychological Measurement, 3,* 1943, 105-126, 215-238.)

100. ——. *An Introduction to Therapeutic Counseling.* Boston: Houghton Mifflin, 1950.

101. Raimy, V. C. "The Self-Concept as a Factor in Counseling and Personality Organisation." Unpublished Ph.D. dissertation, Ohio State University, 1943.

102. ——. "Self Reference in Counseling Interviews," *Journal of Consulting Psychology, 12,* 1948, 153-163.

103. Rank, O. *Will Therapy.* New York: Knopf, 1936.

104. Raskin, N. J. "The Development of Non-Directive Psychotherapy," *Journal of Consulting Psychology, 12,* 1948, 92-110.

105. ——. "Client-Centered Counseling and Psychotherapy," in Daniel Brower and L. E. Abt (eds.) *Progress in Clinical Psychology,* Vol. 1. New York: Grune and Stratton, 1952.

106. ——. "Studies of Psychotherapeutic Orientation: Ideology and Practice." *A.A.P. Research Monograph,* No. 1. Orlando, Fla.: American Academy of Psychotherapists, 1974.

107. —— and F. Van der Veen. "Client-Centered Family Therapy: Some Clinical and Research Perspectives," *Institute for Juvenile Research (Chicago) Research Report, 4,* No. 14, (1967). Also in *New Directions in Client-Centered Therapy* — listed ref. 85, pp. 387-406.

108. Redfield, R. *The Little Community.* Chicago: University of Chicago Press, 1960. Phoenix edition (including "Peasant Society and Culture").

109. Rice, L. N. "The Evocative Function of the Therapist," in *Innovations in Client-Centered Therapy*—listed ref. 208, pp. 289-311.

110. Rogers, C. R. *The Clinical Treatment of the Problem Child.* Boston: Houghton Mifflin, 1939.

111. ———. **Counseling and Psychotherapy. Boston: Houghton Mifflin, 1942.**

112. ———. "The Use of Electrically Recorded Interviews in Improving Psychotherapeutic Techniques," *American Journal of Orthopsychiatry, 12*, 1942, 429-434.

113. ———. "Therapy in Guidance Clinics," *Journal of Abnormal and Social Psychology, 38*, 1943, 284-289.

114. ———. "The Development of Insight in a Counseling Relationship," *Journal of Counsulting Psychology, 8*, November-December, 1944, 331-341.

115. ———. "Psychological Adjustments of Discharged Service Personnel," *Psychological Bulletin, 41*, December, 1944, 689-696.

116. ———. "The Non-Directive Method as a Technique for Social Research," *American Journal of Sociology, 50*, January, 1945, 279-283.

117. ———. "Counseling with the Returned Serviceman and his Wife," *Marriage and Family Living, 7*, Autumn, 1945, 82-84.

118. ———. "Significant Aspects of Client-Centered Therapy," *American Psychologist, 1*, October, 1946, 415-422.

119. ———. "Some Observations on the Organization of Personality," *American Psychologist, 2*, September, 1947, 358-368.

120. ———. "The Attitude and Orientation of the Counselor in Client-Centered Therapy," *Journal of Consulting Psychology, 13*, April, 1949, 82-94.

121. ———. **Client-Centered Therapy. Boston: Houghton Mifflin, 1951.**

122. ———. "Personal Thoughts on Teaching and Learning." Prepared for the conference on "Classroom Approaches to Influencing Human Behavior" held at Harvard University, April, 1952. (Later published, for example, in *On Becoming a Person*—listed ref. 137.)

123. ———. "Some Directions and End Points in Therapy," in O. H. Mowrer (ed.) *Psychotherapy: Theory and Research.* New York: Ronald, 1953, pp. 44-68.

124. ———. "The Implications of Client-Centered Therapy for Family Life." Paper presented to the International Society for General Semantics, Chicago chapter, April, 1953. (In *On Becoming a Person*—listed ref. 137.)

125. ———. "Persons or Science: A Philosophical Question," *American Psychologist, 10*, 1955, 267-278.

126. ———. "Client-Centered Therapy: A Current View," in Frieda Fromm-Reichmann and J. L. Moreno (eds.) *Progress in Psychotherapy*, Vol. 1. New York: Grune and Stratton, 1956.

127. ———. **"The Necessary and Sufficient Conditions of Therapeutic Personality Change," *Journal of Consulting Psychology, 21*, 1957, 95-103.**

128. ———. "A Therapist's View of the Good Life," *The Humanist, 17*, 1957, 291-300.

129. ———. "A Tentative Formulation of a General Law of Interpersonal Relationships." University of Chicago, 1957. (Mimeographed.) (Also in *On Becoming a Person*—listed ref. 137.)

130. ———. "A Process Conception of Psychotherapy," *American Psychologist, 13*, 1958, 142-149. (Revised version in *On Becoming a Person*—listed ref. 137.)

131. ———. "The Characteristics of a Helping Relationship," *Personnel and Guidance Journal, 37*, 1958, 6-16.

132. ———. "The Growing Power of the Behavioral Sciences," *Counseling Center Discussion Papers, 4*, No. 4, 1958. Also in *On Becoming a Person*—listed ref. 137, pp. 364-383.)

133. ———. **"A Theory of Therapy, Personality and Interpersonal Relationships, as Developed in the Client-Centered Framework," in Sigmund Koch (ed.) *Psychology: A Study of a Science,* Vol. 3: *Formulations of the Person and the Social Context.* New York: McGraw-Hill, 1959.**

134. ———. "A Tentative Scale for the Measurement of Process in Psychotherapy," in E. A. Rubinstein and M. B. Parloff (eds.) *Research in Psychotherapy*. Washington, D.C.: American Psychological Association, 1959, pp. 96-107.

135. ———. "Significant Learning: In Therapy and in Education," *Educational Leadership, 16*, 1959, 232-242. (Also in *On Becoming a Person*—listed ref. 137, pp. 279-296.)

136. ———. "The Process Equation of Psychotherapy," *American Journal of Psychotherapy, 15*, 1961, 27-45.

137. ———. ***On Becoming a Person.* Boston: Houghton Mifflin, 1961.**

138. ———. "A Theory of Psychotherapy with Schizophrenics and a Proposal for Its Empirical Investigation," in J. G. Dawson, H. K. Stone, and N. P. Dellis (eds.) *Psychotherapy with Schizophrenics*. Baton Rouge: Louisiana State University Press, 1961, pp. 3-19.

139. ———. "The Place of the Person in the New World of the Behavioral Sciences," *Personnel and Guidance Journal, 40*, 1961, 442-451.

140. ———. "The Interpersonal Relationship: The Core of Guidance," *Harvard Educational Review, 32*, Fall, 1962.

141. ———. "The Concept of the Fully-Functioning Person," *Psychotherapy: Theory, Research and Practice, 1*, August, 1963, 17-26.

142. ———. "The Actualizing Tendency in Relation to 'Motives' and to Consciousness," in M. R. Jones (ed.) *Nebraska Symposium on Motivation*, Vol. 11. Lincoln: University of Nebraska Press, 1963, pp. 1-24.

143. ———. "Learning to Be Free," in S. Farber and R. H. L. Wilson (eds.) *Conflict and Creativity: Control of the Mind*. New York: McGraw-Hill, 1963.

144. ———. "Toward a Science of the Person," in T. W. Wann (ed.) *Behaviorism and Phenomenology*. Chicago: University of Chicago Press, 1964.

145. ———. "Toward a Modern Approach to Values: The Valuing Process in The Mature Person," *Journal of Abnormal and Social Psychology, 68*, No. 2, 1964, 160-167.

146. ———. "Freedom and Commitment," *The Humanist, 24*, No. 2, 1964, 37-40.

147. ———. "Introductory Remarks." Symposium on the Future of Client-Centered Therapy. American Psychological Association Annual Conference, Los Angeles, 1964. (Mimeographed. See Also *Innovations in Client-Centered Therapy*—listed ref. 208, pp. 7-9.)

148. ———. "Dealing with Psychological Tensions," *Journal of Applied Behavioral Science, 1,* 1965, 6-24.

149. ———. "Some Thoughts Regarding the Current Philosophy of the Behavioral Sciences," *Journal of Humanistic Psychology, 5,* 1965, 182-194.

150. ———. "Client-Centered Therapy (filmed interview with "Gloria"), in E. Shostrom (ed.) *Three Approaches to Psychotherapy.* Santa Ana, Calif.: Psychological Films, 1965.

151. ———. "The Therapeutic Relationship: Recent Theory and Research," *Australian Journal of Psychology, 17,* August, 1965, 95-108.

152. ———. "Client-Centered Therapy," in S. Arieti (ed.) *American Handbook of Psychiatry.* New York: Basic Books, 1966.

153. ———. "To Facilitate Learning," in M. Provus (ed.) *Innovations for Time to Teach.* Washington, D.C.: National Education Association, 1966.

154. ———. **(ed.) *The Therapeutic Relationship and Its Impact: A Study of Psychotherapy with Schizophrenics.* Madison: University of Wisconsin Press, 1967.**

155. ———. "A Plan for Self-Directed Change in an Educational System," *Educational Leadership, 24,* May, 1967, 717-731.

156. ———."Autobiography," in E. G. Boring and G. Lindzey (eds.) *A History of Psychology in Autobiography,* Vol. 5. New York: Appleton-Century-Crofts, 1967.

157. ———."The Facilitation of Significant Learning," in L. Siegel (ed.) *Contemporary Theories of Instruction.* San Francisco: Chandler, 1967.

158. ———. "The Interpersonal Relationship in the Facilitation of Learning," in R. Leeper (ed.) *Humanizing Education.* Washington, D.C.: National Education Association, 1967. Also in *New Directions in Client-Centered Therapy*—listed ref. 85, pp. 468-483.

159. ———."The Process of the Basic Encounter Group," in J. F. T. Bugental (ed.) *The Challenges of Humanistic Psychology.* New York: McGraw-Hill, 1967, pp. 261-278.

160. ———. "Interpersonal Relationships: U.S.A. 2000," *Journal of Applied Behavioral Science, 4,* No. 3, 1968, 265-280.

161. ———. ***Freedom to Learn.* Columbus, Ohio: Merrill, 1969.**

162. ———. "The Increasing Involvement of the Psychologist in Social Problems: Some Comments, Positive and Negative," *Journal of Applied Behavioral Science, 5,* 1969, 3-7.

163. ———. *Carl Rogers on Encounter Groups.* New York: Harper and Row, 1970.

164. ———. "The Person of Tomorrow." San Rafael, Calif.: Big Sur Recordings, 1971. (Phonotape.)

165. ——— (facilitator and narrator). *Carl Rogers Conducts an Encounter Group.* (Film includes demonstration of phases of the group process.) Washington, D.C.: American Personnel and Giudance Association, 1972.

166. ———. *Becoming Partners: Marriage and Its Alternatives.* New York: Delacorte Press, 1972.

167. ———. "Some Social Issues Which Concern Me," *Journal of Humanistic Psychology, 12,* Fall, 1972, 45-60.

168. ———. "Some New Challenges," *American Psychologist, 28,* May, 1973, 379-387.

169. ———. "Can Learning Encompass Both Ideas and Feelings," *Education*, *95*, Winter, 1974, 103-114.

170. ———. "After Three Years: My View and That of Outside Evaluators." Part III, "The Project at Immaculate Heart: An Experience in Self-Directed Change." *Education, 95*, Winter, 1974, 172-189.

171. ———. "Remarks on the Future of Client-Centered Therapy," in *Innovations in Client-Centered Therapy*—listed ref. 208, pp. 7-13.

172. ——— (facilitator). *The Steel Shutter*. (From a filmed encounter group composed of Catholic and Protestant members from Northern Ireland.) La Jolla, Calif.: Center for Studies of the Person, 1973.

173. ———. "Some New Learnings About Learning." An address to the Association for Humanistic Psychology, San Francisco, 1977.

174. ———. **Carl Rogers on Personal Power. New York: Delacorte Press, 1977.**

175. ——— **and R. F. Dymond (eds.) Psychotherapy and Personality Change. Chicago: University of Chicago Press, 1954.**

176. ———, W. McGraw, and R. S. Farson, *Journey into Self*. LaJolla, Calif.: Western Behavioral Sciences Institute. (16 mm. documentary sound film of weekend encounter group.)

177. ———, **N. J. Raskin, et al. "A Co-ordinated Research in Psychotherapy," Journal of Consulting Psychology, 13, No. 3, June, 1949, 149-219. (Reports of a set of studies by client-centered investigators, comprising the "Parallel Studies" project, occupy this whole issue of the Journal.)**

178. ——— and F. J. Roethlisberger. "Barriers and Gateways to Communication," *Harvard Business Review, 30*, July-August, 1952, 46-52.

179. ——— and A. Rose (facilitators). *Because That's My Way*. (From a filmed encounter group with drug-involved, black and white members.) Lincoln: Great Plains Instructional Television Library, University of Nebraska, 1971.

180. ——— and B. F. Skinner. "Some Issues Concerning the Control of Human Behavior," *Science, 124*, November, 1956, 1057-1066.

181. ——— and J. L. Wallen, *Counseling with Returned Servicemen*. New York: McGraw-Hill, 1946.

182. ———, J. K. Wood, N. Rogers, et al. "A Person-Centered Approach: The Process of Individual Growth and Its Social Implications." La Jolla, Calif.: Center for Studies of the Person, 1975. (Mimeographed workshop announcement.)

183. Rogers, W. R. "Client-Centered and Symbolic Perspectives on Social Change: A Schematic Model," in *Innovations in Client-Centered Therapy*—listed ref. 208, pp. 465-496.

184. Seeman, Julius. "A Study of the Process of Nondirective Therapy," *Journal of Consulting Psychology, 13*, June, 1949, 157-168.

185. ———, E. Barry, and C. Ellinwood. "The Process and Outcomes of Play Therapy." *Counseling Center Discussion Papers, 3*, No. 14. (University of Chicago Library, 1957.)

186. Sheerer, E. T. "An Analysis of the Relationship Between Acceptance of and Respect for Self and Acceptance of and Respect for Others in Ten Counseling Cases," *Journal of Consulting Psychology, 13*, June, 1949, 169-175.

187. Shlien, J. M. "A Client-Centered Approach to Schizophrenia: First Ap-

proximation," in A. Burton (ed.) *Psychotherapy of the Psychoses*, New York: Basic Books, 1961, pp. 285-317.

188. ——. "Phenomenology and Personality," in J. M. Wepman and R. W. Heine (eds.) *Concepts of Personality*. Chicago: Aldine, 1963, pp. 291-330.

189. Skinner, B. F. and C. R. Rogers. "Skinner-Rogers Dialogue" (Education and the Control of Human Behavior). Tape Library, American Academy of Psychotherapists, Vol. 10 (1962). (Sound recording.)

190. Snyder, W. U. "An Investigation of the Nature of Non-Directive Psychotherapy," *Journal of Genetic Psychology, 13*, 1945, 193-223.

191. ——. *Casework of Non-Directive Counseling*. Boston: Houghton Mifflin, 1947.

192. Solomon, L. N. and B. Berzon. "The Self-Directed Group: A New Direction in Personal Growth Learning," in *New Directions in Client-Centered Therapy*—listed ref. 85.

193. —— (eds.) *New Perspectives on Encounter Groups*. San Francisco: Jossey-Bass, 1972.

194. Spiro, M. E. *Kibbutz: Venture in Utopia*. New York: Schocken Books, 1970. Augmented edition.

195. Standal, S. "The Need for Positive Regard: A Contribution to Client-Centered Theory." Unpublished Ph.D. dissertation, University of Chicago, 1954.

196. Stock, Dorothy. "An Investigation into the Interrelations Between the Self Concept and Feelings Directed Toward Other Persons and Groups," *Journal of Consulting Psychology, 13*, June, 1949, 176-180.

197. Stover, L. and B. G. Guerney. "The Efficacy of Training Procedures for Mothers in Filial Therapy," *Psychotherapy: Theory, Research and Practice, 4*, 1967, pp. 110-115. (Also in B. G. Guerney (ed.) *Psychotherapeutic Agents: New Roles for Non-Professionals, Parents and Teachers*. New York: Holt, Rinehart and Winston, 1969, pp. 534-544.)

198. Szeto, E. "Formative Life Episodes: An Exploratory Study." Unpublished Master's research essay, University of Waterloo, 1977.

199. Taft, Jessie. *The Dynamics of Therapy*. New York: Macmillan, 1933.

200. Tenenbaum, S. "Carl R. Rogers and Non-Directive Teaching" and "A Personal Teaching Experience," in *On Becoming a Person*—listed ref. 137, pp. 299-313.

201. Truax, C. B. "The Process of Group Psychotherapy: Relationships Between Hypothesised Therapeutic Conditions and Intrapersonal Exploration," *Psychological Monographs, 75*, No. 7, 1961.

202. —— and R. R. Carkhuff. *Toward Effective Counseling and Psychotherapy: Training and Practice*. Chicago: Aldine, 1967.

203. —— and K. M. Mitchell. "Research on Certain Therapist Interpersonal Skills in Relation to Process and Outcome," in A. E. Bergin and S. L. Garfield (eds.) *Handbook of Psychotherapy and Behavior Change: An Empirical Analysis*. New York: Wiley, 1971, pp. 299-344.

204. Van der Veen, F. et al. "Relationships Between the Parents' Concept of the Family and Family Adjustment," *American Journal of Orthopsychiatry, 34*, January, 1964, 45-55.

205. ——. "Client Perception of Therapist Conditions as a Factor in Psychotherapy," in *New Directions in Client-Centered Therapy*—listed ref. 85.

206. Walker, A., R. Rablen, and C. R. Rogers. "Development of a Scale to Measure Process Changes in Psychotherapy," *Journal of Clinical Psychology, 16,* 1960, 79/85.

207. Wexler, D. A. "A Cognitive Theory of Experiencing, Self-Actualization and Therapeutic Process," in *Innovations in Client-Centered Therapy*—listed ref. 208, pp. 49-116.

208. —— **and L. N. Rice (eds.)** *Innovations in Client-Centered Therapy.* **New York: Wiley, 1974.**

209. Wilkinson, G. R. "The Application of Differentiated Small-Group Processes to Developmental Learning in an Educational Setting." Unpublished Ph.D. dissertation, University of Waterloo, 1972.

210. Wood, J. K. "Shadows of Surrender: First Notes on Person-Centered Approaches." La Jolla, Calif.: Center for Studies of the Person, 1977. (Mimeographed article.)

211. Zimring, F. M. "Theory and Practice of Client-Centered Therapy: A Cognitive View," in *Innovations in Client-Centered Therapy*—listed ref. 208, pp. 117-137.

9

Cognitive Theory

by

HAROLD D. WERNER

Summary of theory

A cognitive approach holds that the principal determinant of emotions, motives and behavior is an individual's thinking, which is a conscious process. The problems that clients bring to social workers are considered to be problems of consciousness. The essence of cognitive theory is that it requires the practitioner to discard the concept of an "unconscious" as the primary force in the psychic life.

It should be emphasized that cognitive theory is not a body of ideas created by one or two individuals. Rather, it is a general category which can be clearly defined and into which the concept systems of several theorists will fit. Each practitioner, on the basis of his personality and style of work, can put together his own treatment technique from components within the category. He may make more use of some components than of others, stressing or omitting par-

ticular aspects. All the concepts that are appropriately included in the category of cognitive theory are consistent with each other: the category does not have internal contradictions. As a result, this kind of choosing from within the category has nothing in common with the eclecticism of those social workers who try to combine contradictory elements from psychoanalysis, behavior modification and other non-Freudian systems.

Included in cognitive theory are approaches that go by the names of "rational," "reality" or "phenomenological."

The main features of cognitive theory are:
1. Behavior is determined by thinking. We observe situations, other people and ourselves in action, arrive at conclusions or judgments about what we have observed, and act accordingly. In the words of Alfred Adler, "A person's behavior springs from his opinion." Inaccurate perceptions lead to inappropriate behavior.
2. An important kind of thinking that human

beings do concerns their immediate and long-term goals. The goals we set up for ourselves in turn influence our life style, our basic patterns of behavior. We develop the life style we believe will bring us to our goals.

3. An individual's life is not controlled by unconscious forces. However, a person can be unaware of the origins of current attitudes, of the impression he is making, or of the effect of his behavior on others.

4. There are instinctual drives, but aggression is not one of them. Aggression is seen instead as a reaction to feelings of threat or frustration or as the life style of a person who has chosen anti-social goals which cannot be attained without it.

5. Man is not doomed to be dominated by his instinctual drives. When important goals provide sufficient incentive, he defuses or modifies those drives which are inconsistent with his chosen objectives.

6. Most behavior is not a manifestation or sublimation of the sex urge. The sex drive is just one of several, and should not be automatically assumed to underlie a particular problem.

7. Emotions also trace back to thinking. The conclusions we draw about something we have perceived decide whether our emotional response will be fear, anger, guilt, love or joy. By definition, an unconscious emotion cannot exist. Unconscious guilt, for example, is not possible, because the development of guilt is a conscious process requiring a judgment.

8. Motives likewise cannot be unconscious. A motive is a goal or objective which we choose on the basis of a personal conception of what is necessary for our welfare, happiness or success. Motives (called goals in No. 2) can come into being only through a cognitive (i.e., conscious thinking) process.

9. Treatment focuses on the thoughts, emotions, expressed motives and behavior of the client. No unconscious content is postulated.

10. Cognitive theory is socially oriented. The principal determinant of emotions, motives and behavior is thinking, which in turn is primarily influenced by an individual's society, immediate environment, human relationships and experiences in general.

11. Every person is inherently creative, has resources of strength and courage, with a basic tendency to strive for competence and a sense of completion. Maslow referred to this tendency as a need for self-actualization, a need "to become everything that one is capable of becoming."

12. Change consists of expanding or modifying individual consciousness until perception more nearly approximates reality. This is done by talking to the client and/or guiding him into direct experiences that will alter his distorted thinking.

Historical origins

It might be said that cognitive theory began around 1911, when Alfred Adler and Sigmund Freud went their separate ways after a close association in Vienna for many years. Fundamental differences arose between them, and Adler proceeded to develop his own conceptual framework, which he named "individual psychology." Adlerian theory was in disagreement with Freud's division of the psyche into sections and Freud's concept of the continual war going on between the id and the superego. Adler saw the human personality as a unified whole never in conflict with itself. (This came to be known later as the "holistic" approach.) Conflicts in people were not within themselves but with the world around them and resulted from antisocial or distorted thinking.

Adler seems to have been the original proponent of the cognitive approach, by virtue of his contention that each person's behavior was shaped by his notions of what constituted success and by the goals he set up to achieve it. We have here, in elementary form, the main tenet of cognitive theory: thinking shapes behavior. In the 1920s and 1930s, Adler's ideas were widely accepted in many parts of Europe, and also had some following in the United States. For about twenty years after his death in 1937, there was a decline of interest, but this has been increasing steadily again since the publication in 1956 of a collection of his writings (4).

Principal proponents

The decade of the 1950s saw the appearance of other writings which made contributions in varying degrees to the substance of cognitive theory. A synonym for the cognitive approach is "rational psychotherapy," and perhaps the first use of this term in a book was made by Joseph Wortis in 1953:

> The closest descriptive term for the kind of psychotherapy I would think best is rational psychotherapy, based primarily on an appeal to consciousness and reason, with a true appreciation of the great role of experience, and with an acceptance—at least by adults—of a large degree of individual responsibility for one's behavior. (50, p. 181)

Joseph Furst, in a work published in 1954, viewed neurosis as a distortion or limitation of consciousness.

> The essence of cure lies in a profound change—a widening—of the patient's consciousness, resulting in a far more accurate understanding of the social process and causing his behavior to take a more constructive form, one that corresponds to the facts of external necessity. (14, p. 242)

The year 1955 witnessed the first issue of *Psychotherapy,* the journal of the Robbins Institute in New York City. The Institute was made up of psychiatrists who had received orthodox psychoanalytic training but were moving away from Freud. An article in this publication stated:

> Cure is change; cure is the development of rational consciousness. The Institute

does not subscribe to the thesis that consciousness is a knowledge of the "unconscious." . . . Change is recognized as unalterably related to awareness—an expansion in knowledge and experience. Such awareness must represent a correct consciousness on the part of the patient of his real nature as a person, as distinguished from what he conceives it to be: of the real nature of his environment, both natural and social, as distinguished from the previously false one: of his real connection with the outside world as differentiated from an illusory one. (10, pp. 91-92)

It was in 1956 that the American Psychological Association heard a paper on rational psychotherapy for the first time at one of its annual meetings. It was in this presentation that Albert Ellis described emotion as a "strongly evaluative kind of thinking," a result of the sentences we say to ourselves. Formulating it another way, he viewed thought as taking the form of "self-talk," "internalized sentences" or "self-verbalization." Irrational or unrealistic thought produced distorted and disturbed emotions and behavior. In such cases, Ellis believed that

> clients must be shown that their internalized sentences are illogical and unrealistic at certain critical points and that they now have the ability to control their emotions by telling themselves more rational and less self-defeating sentences . . . . Through exerting consistent interpretive and philosophic pressure on the client to change his thinking or his self-verbalizations and to change his experiences or his actions, the rational therapist gives a specific impetus to the client's movement toward mental health. (11, pp. 39, 48)

In the 1960s and up to the present time (1979), the earlier literature has been augmented by additional works which elaborated on cognitive theory, expanded it and specified additional treatment techniques. Albert Ellis enlarged upon his priminary ideas in two books: *A Guide to Rational Living* (co-author: Robert A. Harper, 1961) and *Reason and Emotion in Psychotherapy* (1962). William Glasser published *Reality Therapy: A New Approach to Psychiatry* (1965) and postulated two basic human needs: to give and receive love, to behave in such a manner as to feel worthwhile to oneself and to others. Glasser believed that clients seeking professional help are people who through their actions have failed to satisfy these needs. He did not regard them as sick but as weak and requiring assistance in order to change. The reality therapist's task was to force the client to judge his behavior for what it was, and then to educate him to take responsibility for fulfilling the aforementioned needs.

The author of this chapter was responsible for *A Rational Approach to Social Casework* (1965) and *New Understandings of Human Behavior* (1970). The first was an attempt to outline a cognitive theory with treatment procedures for social workers; the second volume was a collection of non-Freudian readings for practitioners and students in all the treatment professions, with major emphasis on cognitive theory. The writer appears to be the only social worker thus far who has written about cognitive theory as a distinct entity and identified it as such. Psychiatrists and psychologists have either formulated entire conceptual systems which fall into this category, or have discussed particular aspects of them. Nevertheless, a recent book, *Social Casework: Theories in Action* (1971), edited by Herbert F. Strean, a prominent social work theoretician, gives no attention to cognitive theory, nor to a single one of the cognitive theorists who are mentioned in this chapter.

The eminent psychologist Abraham Maslow died in 1970, shortly before the appearance of a book summing up his major ideas. This was Frank G. Goble's *The Third Force* (1970). A brilliant thinker, Maslow's original ideas ranged far and wide, did not usually have a treatment orientation and were not well systematized. Goble was able to simplify and structure Maslow's concepts, drawing them together from all of Maslow's complex writings. As a result, it has become clearer that Maslow belongs in the cognitive camp: he believed that man's thinking is important and that he is not controlled by his instinctual drives or his habits as are other animals; furthermore, whatever innate tendencies man has were mostly constructive rather than destructive.

We came full circle with the publication of *Techniques for Behavior Change* (1971). Edited by Arthur G. Nikelly, who also wrote some of the chapters, it is a collection of writings about Adlerian theory and its practical applications to treatment. It simplifies Adler's principal concepts and brings them up to date. Because of its clarity and brevity, it can serve as one of the basic textbooks for social workers who want a practical introduction to cognitive theory. The book's basic premise is that maladjustment stems from an incorrect evaluation of oneself and others, from excessive striving and mistaken goals, from discouragement and an inadequate interest in cooperation with others.

Maxie Maultsby's *Help Yourself to Happiness* (1975) reinforced previous writings by himself and others on the importance of mental imagery in cognitive treatment. Maultsby pointed out that people do not see and react to actual external events, but to the image of them that our brain makes in the neocortex. The brain does not automatically distinguish between images it makes of real external events and images it makes from our imagination or memory of old happenings. One can react to his memory or imagined image of an event with as much intensity of emotion as he reacts to the actual event itself (28, p. 88). For example, an individual can become very upset by a radio report of a tragic accident. Maultsby has his clients use what he calls "rational emotive imagery" to practice correct thinking, feeling and acting. In his view, it is the brain's mental image, from whatever source, that controls emotional and physical reactions.

Therefore, he will instruct people to imagine systematically and repeatedly acting effectively and feeling calm in anxiety-provoking situations.

In *Multimodal Behavior Therapy* (1976), Arnold Lazarus described imagery as various "mental pictures" that exert an influence upon our lives. He recommended utilizing imagery as an aid in assessing a client's problems. He himself asks clients to picture three things in their mind: their childhood home, a tour from room to room in this childhood home and a special safe place. He probes for details, information about other people involved, and associated feelings (26, pp. 37–38). In general, Lazarus ascribed great importance to imagery:

> It must be stressed that image formation is a crucial component of thinking. In other words, cognitive processes involve various levels of construct formation, abstract reasoning, intentions, plans, decisions, expectancies, values, belief systems, internalized rules, and mental imagery—innumerable events, scenes, people, and places drawn from past experience. Any cognitive schema that ignores imagery is bound to be incomplete. (26, p. 90)

Nineteen seventy-six also witnessed the publication of Aaron Beck's *Cognitive Therapy and the Emotional Disorders*. This is the definitive work on cognitive theory to date (1978), written by a leading psychiatrist who was originally trained as a psychoanalyst. Beck pulled together the ideas and formulations of many who preceded him. He set down in succinct but scientific fashion a body of principles and the cognitive therapeutic techniques appropriate for each of the major emotional disorders. In all cases he held that thought shapes emotion and behavior, and that the task of therapy was to reshape the erroneous beliefs which produced inappropriate emotions and behavior. He contended that the concept of "free-floating anxiety" was a fallacy, since anxiety was the consequence of a specific thought.

> The principle that there is a conscious thought between an external event and a particular emotional response is not generally accepted by the major schools of psychotherapy. . . . It is not difficult, however, to train subjects or patients to focus on their introspections in various situations. The person can then observe that a thought links the external stimulus with the emotional response. (6, p. 27)

Path into social work; principal social work proponents

Although cognitive theory, as a complete system, has to date not been written about by social workers other than this author, it has slowly been extending its path into social work in other ways. Many social workers use aspects of a cognitive approach in their daily practice, and some have written about these cognitive techniques in social work journals. However, in both cases, neither the practitioners nor the writers seem aware of the larger identity of these components, have seldom designated them as cognitive nor realized they are actually part of a theoretical system. It is the intent of this chapter to delineate that system.

Meanwhile, it may be of interest to review some recent journal articles which deal with cognitive techniques as fragments without awareness of their larger identity.

Gottlieb and Stanley (1967) stated the following:

> Treatment in casework should be based on goals that are consciously established and mutually agreed upon by the client and the worker. . . . This process occurs within the framework of the caseworker-client relationship on a conscious level. . . . Emphasis on the importance of mutually agreed-upon goals leads to a more disciplined approach to treatment, provides focus, and allows for the testing of hypotheses

as well as any timely reformulation. (18, p. 471)

These authors went on to warn against situations in which the worker's set of goals and the client's set of goals are not even remotely connected.

> If the worker sets up objectives for treatment without sharing them with the client, he runs the risk of losing the client or of losing the focus of treatment because the client does not know why he is in treatment or has unrealistic expectations. (18, p. 472)

Gottlieb and Stanley declared that the responsibility of the worker in treatment was to "feed back" pertinent diagnostic data, to help the client achieve new perceptions of himself and his situation, and to enable him to reformulate or expand goals (18, p. 473). Finally, they suggested the following working definition of social casework:

> Social casework treatment consists of mutually agreed-upon, goal-directed activities, engaged in by caseworker and client, the purpose of which is to bring about constructive changes in client dysfunctioning or distress and personality growth. (18, p. 476)

Gottlieb and Stanley in this paper recognized the importance of working with consciousness, helping the client to achieve new perceptions of himself and his situation, and dealing with the client's strengths rather than with his pathology. They seem to be well aware of the part goals play in shaping relationships, and they anticipate that personality growth will result from a process that occurs on a conscious level. These techniques and beliefs all flow directly out of cognitive theory.

According to Hallowitz, Bierman, Harrison and Stulberg (1967), there can be an assertive counseling component in therapy. One of its elements is confronting the client with disparities between his perception and reality and offering alternatives to inaccurate perception. Another element involves showing the client discrepancies between his stated goals and actual behavior, caused by shortsighted, impulsive, pleasure-seeking acts which block the attainment of desired long-term goals. In assertive counseling, the therapist may suggest concrete measures by which the client might achieve his objectives. Thus, he gives the client "homework" to do between interviews, guiding him into growth-producing experiences. Always the client's own ideas are elicited and utilized.

> When necessary, the therapist straightforwardly expresses his understanding of the problem as he begins to see it, and he proposes the direction and the steps that he thinks are necessary to change the client's maladaptive functioning. (20, p. 547)

At the same time, these authors emphasized that

> the assertive counseling component is embedded within the framework of generic treatment methods and processes. . . . It is not a treatment modality and may easily be destructive if used in isolation from the main stream of skilled psychotherapy. (20, p. 544)

Cognitive theorists would disagree with this last statement. "Assertive counseling" as described above *is* a treatment modality, a cognitive approach, and can stand independently rather than be regarded only as a fragment. It succinctly sums up much of Ellis's rational-emotive psychotherapy, which is a self-sufficient cognitive conceptual system, and even borrows from him the concept of therapeutic "homework."

Sunley (1968) was the first to use the term "cognitive casework." However, in so doing, he did not refer to an overall treatment approach but, rather, to a limited helping process dealing specifically with clients who exhibited cognitive deficiency.

> Cognitive deficiency, a term little known in casework, broadly refers to the lacks many people suffer in the normal development of their thinking processes. For the most part, although not exclusively, such deficits occur among the poor regardless of nationality or race. Perhaps of most significance for caseworkers, the results of cognitive deficits (or cultural deprivation) are rather constant despite the individual's emotional condition. Help with emotional problems, then, whether the client is 4 or 40, does not appear sufficient to overcome such handicaps. It has been pointed out that such deficits seriously impair the young child's development of rational thought and self-control. . . . Recent research has pinpointed certain areas of deficiency fairly well, such as auditory and visual discrimination, memory, language use, classification, and symbolic thinking. (43, p. 71)

Sunley believes that caseworkers should take responsibility for developing new ways of reaching out to clients, and one of these new dimensions he designates as cognitive casework. Cognitive casework should deal with those early-level cognitive deficits which deprive individuals of the basic tools of skills necessary for thinking. It should deal with the *processes* of thinking and the use of language, rather than with the *content* of thinking (opinions, conclusions, etc.). The goal of cognitive casework should be the improvement of the client's thinking processes. Specifically, those with cognitive deficiency lack the ability to find the right words for naming and classifying things. They have much difficulty in transferring what they have learned in one situation to another that is similar. It is hard for them to put problems into

words and to see alternative solutions. Sunley takes the position that it is valid for casework to concern itself with teaching clients how to use language, how to think systematically, how to observe, remember and generalize. Thus, he affirms some of the main tenets of cognitive theory: language is the unique possession of man which sets him apart from all other animals; mastery of language makes possible rational thought; expansion of consciousness, which includes how an individual goes about his thinking, is required when limitations in the thinking process produce problems in living.

Epstein (1970) discussed brief group therapy for parents in a child guidance clinic, describing a philosophical orientation which fits into the cognitive category, but not identifying it as such. He referred to the great amount of time and energy that was being spent elsewhere, with questionable returns, in attempts to resolve infantile conflicts.

> This investment of energy has often been predicated on the belief that the problems of children and parents evolve from their respective unresolved infantile conflicts. This questionable assumption, unsupported by any known hard-core research, has been accompanied by the mystical correlate that meaningful resolution of behavior is dependent on insight into the conflictual antecedents. The implication is that neither parent nor child is capable of accepting responsibility for his behavior and changing this behavior without insight and the working through of the unconscious conflicts. (13, p. 34)

Epstein went on to explain that treatment in his clinic was geared to helping people live more comfortably. The therapist did not focus on transference, countertransference, and the working out of problems through resolution of a countertransference relationship. The agency's follow-up program found no evidence that symptom removal necessarily led to symptom substitution, a formulation that is central to the more traditional analytical conceptualizations.

> Parents and children are not perceived as victims of unrelenting needs that are compelling them toward maladaptive behavior. A crucial premise of therapy is that perhaps one of the most difficult life tasks is that of parenthood, for which society provides no meaningful formalized educational experience. Parents often function with respect to their children out of a lack of knowledge of what to do in situations that are open to several alternate responses. (13, p. 35)

White (1970) described casework with reluctant welfare clients and how to circumvent hindrances to effective casework. He favored the experiential approach to therapy, in which *why* questions are never asked. The orientation is to the client in the interview here and now: what he is doing, how he is acting and feeling, what he dislikes about his current situation, how he is trying to solve his problem and what prevents him from solving it.

> The primary function of the caseworker is to present the client with the opportunity to consider his behavior and to decide whether this behavior is in his best interest. . . .
> Experiential therapy attacks defenses because this school of thought is predicated on broadening self-awareness, whereas defenses are employed most frequently by those persons well-conditioned to the art of fleeing from reality and consciousness. . . . People achieve better emotional health through heightened consciousness derived from functional thought and communication. This heightened consciousness is dependent on understanding the *what* and *how* of one's behavior as it occurs in the context of the here and now. (49, p. 617)

White's approach contains the essence of cognitive theory. Cognitive theory deemphasizes probing for the *origin* of current feeling and behavior. Instead, it emphasizes understanding the *quality* of that feeling and behavior: are they constructive or destructive, appropriate or inappropriate, effective or ineffective? Cognitive theory and White are in agreement in relating better emotional health to the expanded consciousness which results from accurate perception.

Siporin (1972) urged social workers to adopt a situational perspective in their efforts to help the client. Discussing the definition of a situation by an individual, he wrote:

> It is a mental, symbolic construction of a situation and of its meaning. It consists of the perceptions, explanations, attributions, expectations, attitudes, and feelings about a situational gestalt and its elements: the setting, the people, the interaction, the events, and one's self. The definition is the unique personal meaning, the felt experience and consciousness of a situation. . . .
> It is the situational definition or consciousness that influences or calls the actor to action, that guides the selection of stimuli to which one responds, and that cues expectations and obligations for specific role performance and identity negotiation. (41, p. 96)

Siporin went on to state that behavior change requires, among other things, "change in a person's situational attitudinal definitions" (41, p. 99). Personality change likewise "concerns a new consciousness and definition of one's life situation" (41, p. 99). He concluded by urging social workers to adopt "an explicit and conscious situational perspective" which will enable them to "achieve a richer and more valid understanding of clients in the context of the social realities of their lives and problems" (41, p. 109). Siporin pointed out that this would represent a return to a psychosocial outlook in social work that was lost for a while when psychoanalytic theory became dominant. He noted that the return to situational approaches in social work has in part been stimulated by "phenomenological, existentialist trends in philosophy and psychology" (41, p. 93). (The reader is reminded that "phenominological" is a synonym for "cognitive.") Siporin's situational perspective fits completely into the cognitive framework, with its focus on the close relationship between a person's behavior and personality and his perceptions of reality.

Present status and influence on current social work practice

Cognitive theory is a general category within which are included Adler's individual psychology, Ellis' rational-emotive psychotherapy, Glasser's reality therapy, this writer's rational casework and the ideas of others who regard emotions and behavior as the products of thinking. Philosophically, it is closely related to Mary Richmond's psychosocial orientation, which insisted that the caseworker had to understand both the individual he sought to help and the situation in which that client lived.

In the 1920s, Mary Richmond's ideas were washed away by the tide of psychoanalysis, whose focus was entirely on the client's inner dynamics. This concentration on the individual psyche was fostered in part by the prevailing political climate in the United States at that time, characterized by illusions that this was the best society possible and by resentment against any efforts to criticize or change that society. In such an atmosphere, personal problems and breakdowns were regarded as the consequence of individual weakness or pathology; the possibility of societal defects as a causal factor was not given much consideration. Borenzweig has supported this interpretation:

> Concern with sexual behavior and the unconscious led to the neglect of balancing psychological theories, particularly those concerned with the more rational cognitive processes of mind. Finally, the repudiation of social reform caused by the political climate of the 1920s reinforced a preoccupation with the individual psyche. (7, p. 16)

Following twenty years of psychoanalytic domination, there was a shift in emphasis again in the 1940s, after the Depression and World War II made it clear that preoccupation with the unconscious was ineffective in helping people to deal with massive pressures and anxieties generated by the world around them. The shift was to "ego psychology." The new emphasis on the "nonconflicted ego functioning" of the client was testimony to the fact that social work intuitively had moved back to working with the consciousness of people. The conceptualization of consciousness as "nonconflicted ego functioning" was an attempt to preserve Freudian terminology and framework. Nevertheless, this represented recognition of Adler's view that personality is a holistic phenomenon, that the psyche functions as a unit. Thus, the cognitive orientation made itself felt in the 1940s, although the new adherents of ego psychology never called it by that name.

From that time until now, cognitive theory has continued to influence social work practice, sometimes in the same anonymous way, but more recently with increasing frequency of identification. While many workers still use cognitive techniques on the sole basis that they make "common sense," others are now able to identify a treatment method as coming from Adler or Ellis or Glasser.

Whether identified or not, methods flowing out of cognitive theory are widely used by social workers today. This is true when a worker does any one of the following things:

1. Relates to the client on the basis of his behavior and his stated thoughts, emotions and goals, without postulating unconscious forces.

2. Makes a diagnosis in terms of the distortions or limitations in the client's thinking.
3. Looks for the client's strengths rather than his pathology and puts those strengths to use.
4. Guides the client into trying selected experiences which may alter his inaccurate perceptions.
5. Recognizes that each client's behavior is shaped by his personal goals rather than by universal biological drives.
6. Works to achieve the changes the client wants by expanding his consciousness of self, others and the world around him.
7. Requires the client to take responsibility for his behavior, not allowing the past or the "unconscious" to excuse present conduct.

Connection with other theories

Existential and functional theory have elements which are compatible with the cognitive orientation. In fact, existential theory would seem to fall completely within the cognitive category. It has not been so classified in this chapter only because it is the subject of a separate chapter in this volume.

According to Van Kaam, the existential viewpoint holds that the essential difference between one individual and another is the degree of readiness which each has developed to be open to whatever he encounters in his environment. The whole life of a person is built upon the decision he makes either to face or to avoid the truth about himself, e.g., his weaknesses and limitations. Only when an individual opens himself to all of significant reality and to the many modes of his existence can he understand his authentic self and fulfill his potentials and responsibilities (45).

Hora, in explaining existential psychotherapy, states that complete understanding of one's mode of being tends to bring about a changed attitude toward life. Change occurs when a person can see the totality of his situation. Hora contends that "change is the result of expanding consciousness" (22, p. 37).

The existential therapist and the cognitive therapist thus share an identical conviction: change in the client results from being helped to perceive himself, his world, and his relationship to that world more fully and more accurately.

Functional (Rankian) theory insists, as does cognitive theory, on the primary importance of consciousness. Smalley tells us that the push toward growth and fulfillment is primary in human beings; the innate purpose in each of us is to grow (42). This conception is shared by Adler, Maslow and others in the cognitive category. Otto Rank himself was especially interested in the will, which he considered to be a significant component of consciousness. Functionalists believe their task is to help the client use his will positively toward his own self-chosen ends. The cognitive practitioner has in mind a similar concept when he helps the client to understand his situation, assert himself, and confront whatever needs to be faced. Rank maintained that individuals are understood through their present experience, where their whole reaction pattern, past and present, is apparent. The cognitive practitioner uses the same kind of "here-and-now" approach. Finally, Rank placed considerable emphasis on the process of choosing between alternatives, a conscious act which each person carries out repeatedly throughout his lifetime.

For Rank, will and consciousness were primary. We remember what we *will* to remember. We will unconsciousness to escape facing the present (35). Cognitive theory, with its view that the *content* of man's behavior is usually based on what he thinks, recognizes that the *intensity* of his acts depends on the strength of his will. Adler, for example, gave much importance to the cultivation of courage in the client.

General therapeutic concepts

With the coming of Freud, thinking and reasoning were relegated to a minor role in the mental life of human beings. As Brenner stated, Freud believed that "the majority of mental functioning goes on without consciousness and that consciousness is an unusual rather than a usual quality or attribute of mental functioning" (8, p. 15). Interestingly, John B. Watson's behaviorism took the same stance and regarded behavior not as a product of conscious thinking, but mainly as the conditioned consequences of external events.

Psychoanalysis and behaviorism had their first major impact on this side of the Atlantic at about the same time in the 1920s, and they became the dominant psychological trends. This meant that social work, in its formative years, had a choice between two theories, both of which emphasized the animal nature of man. Freud saw man's behavior as controlled by inner biological drives; Watson saw it as conditioned by external events. Both regarded thinking as a minimal factor in determining behavior, and therefore in effect ignored the unique characteristic of man which sets him apart from, and above, other animals: language. Behaviorism also minimized the importance of emotions in human behavior, which may have been one of the reasons why social work was not attracted to it at that time and chose psychoanalysis for its theoretical framework.

The cognitive approach is based entirely on the fact that man does have language. It is language that makes it possible for man to reason, calculate, think abstractly, solve problems, make predictions, generalize and communicate his conclusions to others. In sum, it is language that makes thinking possible, and it is thinking which brings into being behavior, emotions and motives. Change in a person's behavior, emotions or motives is accomplished by effecting change in his thinking.

To use Maslow's phrase, cognitive theory is therefore a "third force," a psychological approach that does not see behavior as shaped either by unconscious biologically determined inner drives or by externally conditioned habits. The cognitive approach asserts that man's thinking intervenes continuously to deactivate or modify instinctual drives and learned responses. Ansbacher confirmed this in a recent paper on Adler:

> Today the entire movement of humanistic and existential psychology and psychotherapy is founded on this "third force," namely, the self-determination of the individual, as opposed to the other two determining forces: Freud's psychogenetic determinism and the environmental determinism of behaviorism. While Adler was far from denying the importance of biological determinants or environment, he insisted that the individual is not passively shaped by them but "uses" them in accordance with his style of life. (2, p. 779)

The reader may question this cognitive premise that instinctual drives and entrenched habits do not shape behavior, because it appears to be self-evident that they do. In this chapter, the word "shape" is used in the sense of "having the critical influence upon" behavior. Obviously, an inner urge or a strongly conditioned response starts us moving in a particular direction, but, except for those with psychoses, phobias or severe addictions, the movement or action is not completed unless our conscious thought processes support it. It is for this reason that cognitive theory maintains that thinking is the principal determinant of behavior.

In a very interesting recent development, Arnold Lazarus, a principal figure in contemporary behavior therapy, moved away from the school of orthodox S-R-oriented behavior therapists. He now (1979) views classical behaviorism as too limited in its approach to solving human problems, with its belief in automatic and autonomous conditioning and its eschewal of most cognitive processes. He summed up his position as follows:

> But our current view is that in humans, conditioning does not occur automatically and is in fact cognitively mediated. The non-mediational model cannot account for vicarious learning, semantic generalization, and other "exclusively human" functions such as imaginal response patterns and symbolic processes. . . . To account for behavior solely in terms of external rewards and punishments overlooks the fact that human beings can be rewarded and punished by their *own thinking*. (25, p. 552)

Lazarus also asserted (1977) that, while orthodox behaviorists remained opposed to the idea that behavior can be influenced by cognitions, the field of behavior therapy was currently becoming increasingly "cognitive." He regarded the stimulus–response "learning theory" basis of behavior therapy as passé, claiming that a distinctly cognitive orientation now prevailed, which did not deny consciousness and recognized that conditioning was produced through the operation of higher mental processes. Meanwhile, Lazarus himself had moved ahead to develop a more comprehensive framework for assessment and treatment, which he named "multimodal" and which included cognition and several other modalities in addition to behavior per se (26). When focusing on the modality of cognition with clients, Lazarus recommended emphasis on exploring the categorical imperatives ("shoulds" and "musts") that people impose on themselves, perfectionism and refusal to accept fallibility, and tendencies to attribute to external events.

While the psychotic, phobic and severely addicted constitute exceptions to the "rule" that thinking is the principal determinant of behavior,

they do not invalidate the concept. Maslow made an important contribution to the process of theory building in dealing with this same point: you cannot understand very disturbed people until you first understand more healthy functioning. Goble stated that

> Maslow was highly critical of Freud's concentration on the study of neurotic and psychotic individuals, and of the assumption that all higher forms of behavior were acquired and not natural to the human species. It is Maslow's belief that one cannot understand mental illness until one understands mental health. Not only Freud, but Hamilton, Hobbes, and Schopenhauer, reached their conclusions about human nature by observing the worst rather than the best of man. (17, p. 14)

Maslow himself wrote: "It becomes more and more clear that the study of crippled, stunted, immature, and unhealthy specimens can yield only a cripple psychology and a cripple philosophy" (27, p. 180). Maslow believed that a healthy individual's motivation was stronger than most instinctual drives. He felt that the power of these drives had been overestimated, and reclassified them from "instincts" to "instinctoid impulses" (27, pp. 77–95).

Krill supported the same view when he concluded:

> For the existentialists, man's biological drives are important and must be understood, but they do not fully explain man's nature. As a matter of fact, emphasis on the primacy of instinctual drives is a way of viewing human beings at their minimum level of functioning rather than their maximum level. At this maximum level man has freedom, the power to transcend his egotistical strivings, courage to venture, and a capacity to endure (24, p. 49).

The aforementioned three special situations, in which the axiom "thinking shapes behavior" does not apply, will be more fully examined further on in the section entitled "Counterindications for Use of Theory."

The cognitive practitioner sees each client as a person who perceives himself, other people, his world and his relationship to that world in his own special way. Experience consists of sensory inputs which the client interprets and evaluates. The combination of sensing and judging is what we call "perception." If perception is accurate, emotions and behavior will be appropriate. If perception is not accurate, emotions and behavior will be inappropriate. This is illustrated by the child who sees a friendly dog, perceives it accurately, reacts with a happy feeling and goes over to play with it. Perception, emotions and behavior are appropriate, but they would not be if the child perceived the same dog as dangerous, felt frightened and began to cry.

It is perception, a conscious thinking process, which generates emotions and behavior. Thinking is also necessary for the development of motives, which in cognitive terms are defined as objectives or goals chosen by the client out of his conception of necessity. Emotions, behavior and motives are therefore all viewed as conscious phenomena. In the cognitive framework, it is not possible for a person to have unconscious fear, because the emotion of fear is the product of the conscious processes of becoming aware of something and evaluating it.

A complete definition of emotion also takes into account the individual's physical reactions to a given object or situation. In cognitive theory, then, a full definition of emotion would be the following: Emotion is the feeling a person experiences after estimating what an event means to him and reacting with a set of involuntary physiological responses. Such responses include flushing, sweating, trembling, stiffening, relaxation, increasing of heart rate, and many more. The more pronounced the physiological responses are, the stronger the emotion is considered to be.

Arnold supported this concept when she wrote:

> We have seen that emotion is an experience in which the person appraises the object as affecting himself. Such an appraisal of the object results in a felt attraction or aversion, and eventually (if no other motive interferes) in approach or avoidance. Perception is completed by an intuitive appraisal that arouses emotion. . . . Summing up our discussion, we can now define emotion as the felt tendency toward anything intuitively appraised as good (beneficial), or away from anything intuitively appraised as bad (harmful). This attraction or aversion is accompanied by a pattern of physiological changes organized toward approach or withdrawal. The patterns differ for different emotions. (5, Vol. I, p. 182)

Confirming the cognitive view of emotion as a conscious phenomenon, Arnold also stated:

> We can like or dislike only something we know. We must see or hear or touch something, remember having done so or imagine it, before we can decide that it is good or bad for us. (5, Vol. II, p. 33)

As we have said, inaccurate perceptions or appraisals generate inappropriate emotions. Ellis stated this another way when he maintained that man's

> emotional or psychological disturbances are largely a result of his thinking illogically or irrationally; and that he can rid himself of most of his emotional or mental unhappiness, ineffectuality, and disturbance if he learns to maximize his rational and minimize his irrational thinking. (12, p. 36)

Ellis went on to specify a number of irrational ideas which can lead to emotional disturbances. These irrational ideas are taught and transmitted either by the culture as a whole, the family, and/or significant others:

1. It is a dire necessity for an adult to be loved and approved by most of the significant people in his environment.
2. One is not worthwhile unless he is virtually perfect in all repects.
3. Certain people are bad and should be blamed and punished for their badness.
4. It is terrible when things are not the way one would like them to be.
5. Human unhappiness is externally caused and people have little ability to control their sorrows.
6. One should keep dwelling on the possibility of dangerous things happening and be deeply concerned (e.g., being in a car accident).
7. It is better to avoid difficult situations or responsibilities than to face them.
8. One should depend on someone else, for we each need someone stronger on whom to rely.
9. One's past history is an all-important determiner of present behavior, and a significant past event will indefinitely continue to influence us.
10. We should become quite upset over other people's problems or disturbances.
11. There is a correct and perfect solution to human problems and it is catastrophic if this perfect solution is not found. (12, pp. 60–88)

Within the cognitive framework, aggression is not regarded as inherent in man. Cooperative behavior is not regarded as something that can only be achieved by man's repression of his true nature, because cognitive theory does not view his true nature as aggressive. On the contrary, cooperative behavior is seen as an inborn potential which, if cultivated by family and society, brings man to his highest level of functioning. Bertha Reynolds, the great social work teacher, wrote after her retirement:

I have come to challenge too much reliance on Freudian psychology with its assumption that neurosis is preconditioned by civilized society. A different view of history is that man is a part of nature and healthy adjustment to it is "natural" for man. (36, p. 16)

In examining Adler's ideas about aggression, Ansbacher stated:

Adler was fully aware of the frequently observed aggressive and hostile behavior of men toward one another. However, he did not see this behavior as one of the signs of an instinct of destruction that must find an outlet. Rather, he saw aggression as a way in which the individual mistakenly pursues the goals of personal superiority and power. Far from assuming an innate aggression and hostility, Adler assumed that a positive capacity for social living is an innate component of human nature. Once this capacity has been properly developed, beginning in early childhood, it becomes social interest that assures a constructive life. (3, pp. 269–270)

In recent years, Lorenz, Ardrey, Morris and others have been affirming their support of the "naked ape" concept: man is just another savage animal who kills to get what he wants. This is the modern version of Freud's contention that man is born "a wolf unto other men," driven by the same biology as jungle animals. On the other hand, it has been pointed out for a long time by many other investigators, of whom Alland is one of the latest, that the evidence is against the theory of inherent aggression. For example, if all individuals are born aggressive, then all societies should be aggressive, but they are not. There are many nonviolent societies. Alland contends that man is born with the biological *capacity* for aggression. However, he claims that the major determinant of behavior is culture, which has the decisive effect on whether or not aggressive behavior actually occurs, and on the form in which aggression is expressed. "The evidence tells us that man is not driven by instincts but rather that he is born with a set of capacities, potentials which are developed or thwarted and given direction by early learning and the cultural process" (1, p. 165).

The cognitive approach to aggression, therefore, is to consider it not an inborn quality but a reaction or a chosen life style. It is a reaction to feelings of threat or frustration: one responds forcefully if he thinks he is in actual danger, may attack first to secure an advantage over potential aggression from another, asserts himself if he believes he is being deprived of what is due him, or explodes when pressures become too great. Aggression becomes a life style for those whose greed for possessions or power is so great and so in conflict with the environment that their goals cannot be attained without aggression.

From the cognitive point of view, neurosis is a way of living based on unrealistic fear, guilt or anger. The individual is aware of these emotions, which are not necessarily associated with sexuality, but can relate to any of several important aspects of life. The neurotic person is saturated with anxiety, a state of apprehensiveness accompanied by somatic tensions, which is actually, as Krauss expressed it, "the dread of a future event" (23, pp. 88-93). Some of the future events that people commonly dread are rejection by others, loss of self-control, physical harm, failure, deprivation of power and exposure of their weaknesses. Rollo May saw anxiety as "the apprehension cued off by a threat to some value which the individual holds essential to his existence as a personality" (25, p. 191). Sarbin further enriched the concept of anxiety by depicting it as cognitive strain. He defined "cognitive strain" as large increases in cognitive activity produced by a person's inability to fit a new situation or object into his perceptual framework, find his place in society, or evaluate his performance of life tasks (38, pp. 635-638).

Finally, the concept of a substantive "unconscious" plays a minor role in cognitive theory. It is not seen as the controlling force of our mental lives. One can be unconscious (i.e., unaware) of certain facts, of the impression he is making on others, of the origins of his current ideas, of his own potentialities, or of a thought he has forgotten or deliberately put out of his mind. However, in the cognitive view, material out of awareness does not exert any influence over our behavior. Consciousness is not a knowledge of the "unconscious" but of the realities of our world and ourselves.

This new way of regarding the unconscious has considerable support. May wrote:

> The "unconscious," then, is not to be thought of as a reservoir of impulses, thoughts, wishes which are culturally unacceptable; I define it rather as those potentialities for knowing and experiencing which the individual cannot or will not actualize. (29, p. 688)

Rado described the unconscious as a "non-reporting (in contrast to the conscious mind which is reporting) organization of causative links between processes of which we are aware" (34, p. 182). Adler concluded: "The unconscious is nothing other than that which we have been unable to formulate in clear concepts" (4, p. 232).

The cognitive attitude toward the concept of an unconscious has important immediate theoretical consequences. As the author has written elsewhere, "This viewpoint does not recognize the existence of an 'unconscious' serving as a repository of ideas, emotions, drives, and conflicts of whose existence we are unaware but which determine our behavior without our knowing it" (47, p. 21). Consequently, the cognitive practitioner cannot regard anxiety as a danger signal warning that repressed material is breaking out of the unconscious. Dreams are not what Freud called "the royal road to the unconscious," but instead are seen as reflections of situations or problems we fail to master in our waking existence. Ullman suggests that the distorted content of dreams is due to the fact that parts of the brain which select, organize and systematize stimuli are inactive when we sleep (44, pp. 30–60).

In addition to dreams, Freudians view behavior under hypnosis and multiple personalities as further evidence of the existence of a substantive unconscious. Ernest Hilgard, however, claims that his studies of people under hypnosis suggest that what takes place is a division of consciousness into parallel parts instead of higher and lower levels. He finds that, under hypnosis, consciousness is split vertically, so that the hypnotized part can be instructed to become deaf or feel no pain, while a parallel process in another part of consciousness, "the hidden observer," registers spoken words or physical discomfort. Hilgard refers to Pierre Janet's theory of dissociation in characterizing dual personalities as a similar division of consciousness, a dissociation of some part of the personality from the primary personality, but on a single level. The secondary or hidden personality manifests itself in conscious behavior exactly as the normal one usually does, and knows all about the primary personality, although the primary person has no awareness of the second one. The barrier between the two parts is interpreted as an inability to recall, an amnesia by the conscious part for the split-off part that on occasion may become conscious. It does not seem necessary to postulate the existence of the unconscious on a different, deeper level. In cases where the hidden personality is healthier, therapy attempts to bring about an integration based on the secondary personality, not the primary one.

Hilgard believes that the mind as a whole has unity, though one's acquaintance with it is always partial. He concludes from his studies that in hypnosis the experimenter can deliberately inhibit certain cognitive systems. These systems, although they are not now represented in consciousness, continue to register and process incoming information.

When such a system is released from inhibition, consciousness uses this information as though it had been conscious all along. This is the clinical picture we find in cases of multiple personality; it is the laboratory picture when the hidden observer is brought to light. (21, p. 49)

Ansbacher has provided the following succinct summary of cognitive therapeutic concepts:

It follows directly from man's creative power that he is not blindly driven by instincts, but is guided by his goals or anticipations. Psychotherapy is not as concerned with discovering causes as with changing the individual's goals and interpretations, and thereby his actions.... Successful therapy is based on a cognitive reorganization; the criterion is a change in behavior. (2, p. 779)

Theoretical concepts: the therapeutic relationship

An experience reported by Mayer and Timms illustrates one of the key issues regarding any therapeutic relationship. They described a British family agency where social workers were trying to provide clients with some psychological insight into their difficulties. The clients were working-class people complaining about another member of the family. They were not interested in the causes of their problems but in obtaining specific advice or in getting their worker to take steps to reform the offender. However, the workers took a nonactivist approach and probed into the past. The clients found this strange and puzzling, and interpreted it as a lack of interest or understanding. Many dropped out. Mayer and Timms made the following comment:

It is our impression that the social workers were unaware that the clients entered the treatment situation with a different mode of problem-solving and that the clients' behavior during treatment was in part traceable to this fact . . . there is a pervasive, although possibly decreasing, tendency in the field of social work to rely on psychodynamic concepts in explaining behavior. As a consequence, cognitive elements (beliefs, thoughts, opinions) receive little attention and are apt to be viewed as epiphenomena, as derivatives of something deeper, and therefore unlikely to produce any decisive effects of their own on behavior. (31, pp. 37–38)

Since cognitive theory holds that cognitive elements are in fact the decisive influences on behavior, its practitioners as a matter of principle would have easily avoided the client disappointment and treatment termination mentioned above. The cognitive practitioner deals with the client's view of the situation, not his own. He establishes a therapeutic relationship based on working as a partner with the client to achieve the client's goals and to provide the type of help the client wishes. If the cognitive worker believes that the client's goals or the type of help requested will not serve the client's own interests, this becomes a matter of open discussion between them until the matter is resolved.

Cognitive theory regards the goal of treatment to be the expansion and changing of consciousness so that the client's perceptions more closely approximate reality. Accurate perceptions of reality, plus the ability to act on the basis of this accurate understanding, are the prime components of mental health. Therapeutic relationships should be of such a nature as to facilitate the expansion of consciousness and the performance of rational behavior.

Since the cognitive approach is reality-oriented, it calls for a therapeutic relationship in which the client perceives the social worker realistically. The worker should discourage any tendency on the part of the client to perceive the worker either as a parent/lover symbol who is omniscient and virtually perfect or a symbol of others in his life who have been too controlling or rejecting. Such fantasies should be challenged immediately. It is more fundamental to deal with the client's misperceptions about himself and his real world than with transference reactions to the worker which have been deliberately allowed to develop.

The worker should become a friend the client can trust, with all the implications this has for mutual respect, complete openness and informality. As a part of the therapeutic relationship, the client needs to have complete confidence in the worker, who in turn must exemplify any positive concept or quality he discusses. This applies particularly to courage, to which social workers have not paid sufficient attention in the past. If the therapeutic relationship is to enable the client to see things more accurately and to undertake difficult action which may be necessary, it must include the cultivation of courage within the client. Confronting reality and attempting acts which previously were feared can be extremely painful, and require courage.

The therapeutic relationship should be based on consciousness. The ideas the client expresses, the emotions he describes, the motives he states, and the behavior he exhibits are true delineators of what he is. It is not neccessary to speculate about unconscious conflicts, forces or problems. It has become fashionable in recent years to declare that psychoanalytic concepts apply to working-class clients as much as they do to the so-called upper classes, that poor people have an unconscious just like the more affluent have. The cognitive practitioner would claim that the reverse is true: all clients have a consciousness and can be understood only in terms of their consciousness.

The final important element in the therapeutic relationship is the professionalism of the worker. While conducting himself with warmth, spontaneity and friendliness, the worker must always maintain the maximum objectivity. What he does should always flow out of a sound knowledge of the theory of his choice, and out of his experience with other clients. When theory or past experiences do not apply or are lacking, he needs the courage to utilize his intuition, so that in the end his treatment of the client becomes a blending of science and art. The professionalism of the worker also must include a full understanding of the client's world. Since cognitive theory emphasizes the client's perceptions of reality, the worker will be unable to judge the accuracy or significance of these perceptions unless he knows the culture from which the client comes. In principle, a worker should disqualify himself in favor of another more appropriate colleague if he does not have an essential grasp of the life situation of his client.

Theoretical concepts: the nature of personality*

If we synthesize cognitive concepts about the nature of man into a systematic presentation, we emerge with the proposition that a person's behavior is mainly determined not by unconscious forces but by his thinking and willing. He evaluates himself, others and the world around him; sets up goals to achieve; and behaves in ways he thinks will attain his objectives and otherwise give him maximum satisfaction. The strength of an individual's will, and the direction in which it is applied, affect the amount of effort he expends and the progress he makes toward his goals. He has the ability to control and deactivate instinctual drives which interfere with his purposes. He normally feels and acts according to the thoughts he presently holds concerning significant factors in his environment.

People have to make choices all their lives:

_____

* The text of this section originally appeared in the writer's *New Understandings of Human Behavior* (New York: Association Press, 1970). It is reproduced with the kind permission of the publishers. A few minor changes have been made.

between dependence on others and independence; between clinging and separating; between conformity and originality; between accepting and challenging limits; between goals on the destructive and on the useful side of life; between avoiding and facing all the implications of their existence.

Emotional distress can develop in various ways. A man's goals may be destructive or antisocial, in which case the life style he evolves to reach these goals will bring pressure, rejection, or retaliation from his society. If an individual is afraid to reveal his authentic self for fear of being found imperfect by others, he erects defensive structures behind which to hide what he really is, becoming anxious and draining his emotional energy in the process. Emotional strain may be experienced in making any of the crucial choices listed in the preceding paragraph. In other cases, individuals become upset as a result of blaming themselves too severely for mistakes they commit just by virtue of being human. Some of us suffer acutely when significant people do not approve of us, or when we encounter disagreement in the world at large. Some of us become disturbed when we are unable to give love, receive love, or behave so as to feel worthwhile to others and to ourselves. There are all kinds of fears and guilt feelings, realistic and otherwise, which prevent people from enjoying a measure of inner peace. Finally, strongly conditioned responses which a person cannot stop even though he knows they are inappropriate can cause great distress.

The cognitive conception of man's nature views him as not born either good or evil but trainable in either direction. He is not seen as inherently aggressive; cooperation with a society in which he believes does not repress his true nature but develops it. Man is creative, possesses an innate purpose to grow, and has a basic tendency to strive for competence and a sense of completion. His sex drive is not primary but just one of several drives. Attachments or hostilities to parents, neurosis and anxiety do not inevitably trace back to sexuality and are more often reactions to all types of life situations. Each person is unique, differing in some ways from all other persons, and comprehensible only in his own terms. Diagnoses and labels can at most contribute only a partial understanding of an individual.

Theoretical concepts: the nature of personality change

Man's principal activities are the pursuit of chosen goals, dealing with new situations according to the way he perceives them, and solving problems. Choosing goals, evaluating events and solving problems are conscious cognitive processes intimately associated with personality. Change in goals, in perceptions of reality, or in degree of success in problem solving—i.e., cognitive reorganization—result in personality change.

A client whose goal in life is success in a highly competitive business exhibits a belligerent personality which would undergo a change if this goal were replaced by one completely different. Another client, convinced other people are all potential enemies ready to take advantage of him, presents a suspicious type of personality which can change if his perceptions of people change. A third client, whose personality is withdrawn because he fails frequently in his living or job situation, can experience personality change if he begins to have more success in solving his problems.

When a client changes his goals or perceptions, his behavior changes, and he engages in experiences that he avoided before due to ignorance, lack of interest or fear. The client who overcomes a basic distrust of others is able to try reaching out to people. A client, whose success after previous failure engenders new confidence and self-esteem, has a changed perception of himself, is likely to revise his goals and can be encouraged to try unfamiliar experiences. Change in behavior is not a superficial result in treatment. New behavior leads to new experiences which can reinforce the client's recent insights, make his future thinking more realistic and thus alter basic personality attributes.

Implications of theory for psychosocial history and diagnosis

Diagnosis asks the question: What is the problem? Cognitive theory implies that the answer should be given in terms of the client's goals, his perceptions of reality and his life style. This means that the cognitively oriented worker tries to determine whether the client's goals are constructive or destructive, what distortions or limitations there are in his evaluations and judgments, and what the nature of his life style is. In order to accomplish this, the worker will be interested in the kind of psychosocial history which provides material in these areas.

In that part of the history-taking which focuses on the client's goals, the worker can utilize the projective technique of Early Recollections (ER), which is economical in terms of time and cost. Nikelly and Verger believe that ERs can help the therapist understand the client's purposes, repetitive patterns of behaving, and the unity of his life. The client is simply asked to think back as far as he can and state the earliest memory from his childhood (33, p. 55). In assessing the client's goals, it is important to find out who are the principal opponents in his life and whether the goals represent an attempt to compensate for a lack or an inferiority feeling.

If the worker observes that the content of the client's evaluations of himself, others and his world are distorted or limited, part of the psychosocial history should contain information about the family atmosphere, which can be a prime cause of maladjustment. Dewey has worked out the following classifications of family atmosphere: rejective, authoritarian, martyrdom, inconsistent, suppressive, hopeless, indulgent, pitying, high standards, materialistic, competitive, disparaging and inharmonious (9, pp. 41-45).

Another cause of distorted perceptions of reality is what Adler called "private logic," a faulty *process* of thinking which leads to inaccurate conclusions. This is related to the "cognitive deficiency" described by Sunley earlier in this chapter. In taking the history, the worker should be alert to any evidences of a faulty private logic.

Other factors in distorted perceptions for which the worker should probe in taking a history include severely traumatic experiences, the client's ordinal position in the family (first, middle, last, only child), physical unattractiveness or handicap at any time, and what being a male or female of a certain color, nationality and religion has meant to the client within his particular family and surrounding environment.

Life style, the third basis for diagnosis, is the way the client goes about his quest for personal significance, his pattern of living, his "style of acting, thinking and perceiving" (Adler). Nikelly, in discussing psychotherapy from the Adlerian point of view, stated: "Instead of deciphering unconscious wishes and motives, as the psychoanalyst would do, the therapist looks for the basic pattern by which the client moves through life (32, p. 31). The psychosocial history should include sufficient clues from the past so that the worker, by combining these data about past behavior with his own observations of the client's current behavior, can reach an assessment of the client's life style. Some varieties of life style are : pampered, withdrawn, self-sacrificing, controlling, inadequate, joyful, obsequious and altruistic.

To sum up with an illustration, a cognitive practitioner takes a psychosocial history on a new client to arrive at a working diagnosis, which of course is always subject to revision. The client comes for help because he feels tense, overwhelmed and anxious. The history which the worker takes is designed to elicit goals, distortions of perception and life style. These are the three bases of diagnosis. He may ask the client for early recollections. He will probe for indications as to the client's chief op-

ponents in life. He will look for evidence that goals which are based on the client's conception of success may have developed out of a strong need to compensate for a specific lack or a specific kind of inferiority feeling. The worker will obtain data about the family atmosphere, any handicaps the client has suffered, his ordinal position, traumatic events and any problems created by gender, race or other ethnic characteristics. Finally, the worker will evaluate the soundness of the client's private logic.

In this case, the worker obtains a picture of a man who, because of a sickly childhood, fell behind in school and never matched the educational achievements of his four siblings, among whom he was the middle child. His parents, who overvalued both college education and material possessions, did not conceal their disappointment, and the client developed feelings of failure and inferiority. His earliest recollection was being left behind for misbehaving while all his siblings were taken on a special family trip. Because of the family atmosphere, he came to equate success with monetary wealth, and he set up for himself the compensatory goal of making lots of money in business any way he could. His private logic permitted bending or breaking the law, taking advantage of associates, cheating customers and using people for his own purposes. Anyone who stood in his way was his opponent. He used the fact that he was a member of the majority ethnic and religious group in his community to beat out business competitors by appeals to bigotry. His manipulating life style finally became clear to a significant number of people, who began to challenge him, block him and retaliate with all kinds of pressures. He sought professional help when he could no longer cope with his increasing anxiety, which was triggered off by the threat to one of his essential values—business success.

The diagnostic impression of this client is anxiety reaction in a person with antisocial goals whose manipulating life style has finally evoked from society retaliation, which he cannot handle. Impelled by an urgent need to overcome his feelings of inferiority through the attainment of a family-approved type of success, a limited and distorted perception of himself and his situation has led to equating self-worth and success with the accumulation of wealth in any way possible. Cognitive treatment will include helping the client to adopt a more constructive life style by having him reevaluate his goals. The reevaluation of goals, however, can only take place when, through the treatment process, the client alters his perceptions of his world to approximate reality more closely.

Treatment methods and techniques

The treatment methods and techniques that flow out of cognitive theory can be described simply and clearly. This writer, in a previous work, began such a description as follows:

> I ask my client to pinpoint his problems and goals. Then I work with him to accomplish the changes he chooses. I show him when his behavior defeats his own stated purposes. I try to help him reach the point where he can see things as they really are and act on the basis of his correct understanding. The focus is on the present and on what the client himself can do to overcome his difficulties. (48, p. 267)

In the process of treating a client, the cognitively oriented worker bases his activity on these premises:

1. Change in perception alters emotions, motives (goals) and behavior.
2. Change in goal is especially influential in altering behavior.
3. New activities and new kinds of behavior alter perception.

As can be seen, there are reciprocal relationships among perception, emotions, goals and behavior. It follows logically that treatment techniques include contradicting the client whose perceptions of self, others and society are not accurate. Evidence supporting more realistic appraisals is introduced whenever necessary. When the client's problems are the consequences of antisocial or self-destructive goals (e.g., the case presented in the previous section), the worker points out the connection between the client's distress and his choice of goals. The worker then has the therapeutic task of helping the client to reorient himself with a different set of goals. Finally, since the client himself has chosen the objectives he wishes to achieve in treatment, the worker does not hesitate to recommend new experiences or behavior which may bring him closer to those objectives.

This last point was given strong support by Shepard (who was trained in traditional psychoanalysis) and Lee:

> Nonbehavioral therapists are apt to forget or overlook the importance of activity and to lapse into the role of pseudo-philosopher or emotional historian, devoting unnecessary time to the study of feelings and their place in the life of man. Regardless of what patients bring to their therapeutic sessions, the antiaction therapist, feeling safe in the rut of his classical training, invariably directs the discussion to one of emotional reaction. (40, pp. 58–59)

Designating a similar type of practitioner as a Tell Me Why therapist, Shepard and Lee went on to say:

> Yet the TELL ME WHY therapist is not interested in the facts. He is concerned with proving that he is one step ahead of the patient. He can hide his ignorance of life-solutions by relying on a long analysis of Why, rather than launching into WHAT and WHAT-TO-DO-ABOUT-IT. (40, p. 62)

Glasser, one of the new cognitive theorists, who calls his treatment technique "reality therapy," also emphasized behavior, believing that it is much more important than feelings. He stated that the emphasis in treatment should not be on the client's attitudes and feelings but on what he is doing at present and what he is planning for the future. He contended that feelings will change when behavior changes; they do not change merely by discussing them. Glasser's treatment technique focuses on compelling the client to judge his own behavior realistically and to determine if it is meeting his basic human needs: giving and receiving love, achieving self-respect and respect from others. The therapist then has the task of educating the client to adopt better behavior, that is, to take responsibility for fulfilling those basic needs which he has not yet met. A client knows that a therapist cares about him when he demands responsibility and a high standard of behavior from him (16).

Consciousness-altering activity is also part of the "rational-emotive psychotherapy" practiced by Ellis, who gives his clients "homework" to do between interviews. This might involve participating in a social activity about which the client has been apprehensive, confronting a spouse with a grievance or taking a job for which one feels inadequate. Successful self-assertion is also very effective in diminishing anxiety.

The cognitive practitioner does not postulate unconscious emotions, conflicts or ideas. Remembering that the unique characteristics of man are language and the ability to think and reason, he makes use of these in the way he conducts his treatment. The client is asked to put into words what he has been saying to himself about significant events and problems. He is encouraged to describe his emotions, his goals in life and his current behavior. What the client says combined with what the worker observes is considered to be a valid basis upon which to develop a treatment plan. As treatment progresses, the client will be making basic decisions about his future. It is one of the responsibilities of the worker to be sure that the client has all the facts and concepts necessary to make judgments that correspond to reality.

Most people have untapped strength and courage. Under conditions of stress, they need to discover these resources within themselves and use them. It is most important in treatment that the therapist put the client in touch with this aspect of himself. This can be done only if the therapist concerns himself primarily with the client's strengths rather than his pathology. Such a treatment orientation is called for by the emphasis which cognitive theory places on the potential for growth inherent in every person. The cognitive worker uses what the client reveals about himself to foster a sense of worth, pointing to past accomplishments or successes to give him courage for the future. However, as we know, the client often denies that he has any competence.

Scarbrough discussed this issue in an article concerning his treatment of depressed and phobic patients. He reported very effective results in overcoming impasse situations when he shifted tactics from a neoanalytic approach to one in which he allied himself with unrecognized strengths the patient already possessed. An analytically oriented clinical psychologist, Scarbrough commented that "the historical development of psychoanalysis and psychology had understressed the competent side of the personality." (39, p. 298) He described his treatment technique as follows:

Whenever the patient pauses to take a breath, I interrupt him, seeking to uncover and dig out any elements of competence in his history, everything surrounding whatever successes he has had. In some patients previous competent functioning has not been very great; in others it is striking, and the patient works hard to deny the extent of it. Whether the history of competence is striking or minimal, I begin to dig it out. (39, p. 297)

Scarbrough suggested some reasons why an individual might refuse to admit previous success or to seek future success: success may be equated with perfectionism or having to achieve a paralyzing level of ability; with aloneness due to abandonment by the parent who wants him to be helpless; with disapproval by significant others; or with conformity to a parental ideal. The cognitive worker helps the client either to correct any such perceptions that are inaccurate or to take action on those situations which the client has evaluated realistically.

For further information about cognitive treatment techniques, the reader is referred to the annotated bibliography.

Types of clients, problems and settings most appropriate for this theory

Cognitive theory is a psychosocial theory, viewing each person on his own terms and stimultaneously as a reflection of his environment. It is oriented to each individual's particular reality. It would therefore seem to have an across-the-board validity that makes it equally appropriate for most types of clients, illiterate or educated, naive or sophisticated, poor or affluent, presenting a problem of long standing or reacting to an immediate situation. However, there will be difficulty with the nonverbal client, both child and adult, who cannot talk about his reality perceptions, emotions, goals or the way he behaves.

The cognitive worker is not required to fit the client into a preconceived universal blueprint. The uniqueness of each individual is stressed, instead of the concept that there are universal characteristics common to all. Cognitive theory holds that we are all different rather than that we are all the same: each client presents a different combination of goals, perceptions and life style.

Since each individual is unique, the dynamics of each case are different. The nature of the problem and what needs to be done will vary infinitely from person to person. One of the aims of cognitive treatment is for the client to achieve insight into the realities of his world, other people and himself. A further aim is to enable the client to decide what he should do about his problem and then to do it. These aims are in sharp contrast with other schools of thought, in which the aim of treatment is for the client to achieve insight into his unconscious and/or accept one of two or three universal explanations for his problems. Such theories do not work well with many types of clients, because they simply cannot meet these criteria for successful treatment.

As indicated previously, phobias, addictions and psychoses are types of problems best treated by other approaches. (See section on "Counterindications for Use of Theory.") Otherwise, cognitive theory is applicable to all other types.

In regard to the settings which are most suitable for applying cognitive theory, we would say that the reality orientation of the theory makes it appropriate to use in any kind of social or mental health agency. With its focus on understanding reality and taking action on problems, it is fully compatible with the functions of social workers in public assistance agencies, child-placing organizations, psychiatric clinics, hospitals, schools, probation departments, family casework agencies and social action programs.

Although cognitive theory is mainly a clinical theory, it also provides a rationale for social action. Consciousness is held to be the primary determinant of behavior, but consciousness itself is formed by the larger society, the immediate environment, interpersonal relationships and individual experiences. To the extent that social action changes the external happenings in people's lives, their consciousness changes and produces alterations in emotions, goals and behavior. Positive environmental modifications make possible better human lives, in regard to both physical health and personal happiness. It is implicit in the theory that the worker should make accessible to the client, either directly or by referral, those concrete services needed to relieve any external stresses which have a destructive effect on the inner life. Counseling plus concrete services is a higher level of treatment than counseling alone.

Implications for various treatment modalities

Because cognitive theory is reality-oriented, it can serve as a guide to all forms of treatment: individual, family, group or community. Every treatment modality is concerned with people-in-situations, with the interplay between reality and perception, and with the resolution of problems through taking action. Not only individuals, but small groups and large groups are most clearly understood in terms of their perceptions, goals and basic patterns (life styles). Perceptions, goals and patterns are the principal concerns of the theory.

Counterindications for use of theory

A cognitive approach is not applicable to the treatment of phobias, addictions or psychoses.

A phobia is a specific fear which a person knows is irrational but cannot control. A phobia of elevators may have developed out of a traumatic incident in which the individual was trapped between floors for many hours under frightening conditions. Although the person now recognizes that incident to have been an atypical one not likely to recur, the phobia has become entrenched and is not subject to removal by reasoning. Realistic thinking does not produce realistic behavior, because the phobic reaction bypasses the higher cortical centers, the thinking parts of the brain. It has become an automatic

physiological phenomenon, a conditioned reflex built into the nervous system. This concept was summarized by Gerz as follows:

> Since the nervous system in itself is well known for its repetitious qualities, and since our feelings are carried and expressed through nerve tissue, namely, the autonomic nervous system, a once-established neurotic feeling pattern will tend to repeat itself and become a sort of reflex, even when the causes of the neurotic systems have been resolved and removed. (15, p. 207)

Phobias are best treated by a behavior modification approach. This writer once treated a client with an elevator phobia by gradually desensitizing him, at first accompanying the client in an elevator, then later having him ride alone on increasingly longer trips.

Wortis noted that "a rational psychotherapy . . . can be successfully applied to those psychic disorders which do not have prominent physiological components" (50, p. 181). The strong organic factors in drug, alcohol, overeating and smoking addictions place them outside the scope of cognitive treatment because the body's physical needs are too powerful. They first need to be brought under control by medical, pharmaceutical or behavior modification means. Likewise, the organic component in the schizophrenias and other psychoses and the separation of the person from reality render cognitive theory ineffective for these conditions.

Implications for social work research

Cognitive theory has definite implications for social work research, especially the efforts to compare the effectiveness of different treatment approaches and the attempts to measure client change after treatment.

The theory maintains that a person can be understood accurately in terms of his stated thoughts, goals, emotions and experiences, and in terms of his manifest behavior. From the research point of view, these are objective items, because different observers are bound to record them in essentially the same way. They leave little room for personal judgment or guesswork by the observer. If these items are the ones that are utilized to match sets of controls and sets of experimental subjects, we avoid the hazards of matching which is done on the basis of presumed unconscious dynamics. If these items are the ones that are used for studying the same client before and after treatment, we are again on solid research ground. We make no guesses about unconscious phenomena, but compare the client as he is now with the way he used to be, in relation to certain objective items.

Because of its reality orientation, cognitive theory contains many guidelines for objective research.

Gaps in knowledge from social work viewpoint

It has been stated elsewhere that there is general agreement in social work on the following: casework should promote mutual adjustment between individuals and their environment; each person is unique; the difficulties of our clients are psychosocial problems; individuals cannot be understood in isolation but only in relationship to society; and helping people requires both art and science (46, p. 16). It is our contention that cognitive theory provides the knowledge and the concepts necessary to understand these principles and put them into practice.

This theory points out the crucial influence of environment on thought and the primary effect of thought on emotions and behavior. Nevertheless, many people living under healthy and desirable social conditions exhibit emotional and behavioral difficulties. This is not necessarily indicative of a gap in the theory. As Gronfein suggested:

Regardless of what societal alterations take place, some persons in all classes will continue to have problems of interpersonal relations and faulty self-management. This is in the nature of the human condition. There are no utopias! (19, p. 655)

Case vignettes exemplifying treatment

Helen

Helen, a married woman with children, entered treatment still maintaining the inaccurate perception of herself which began in childhood. Constantly criticized and rejected by her parents, she came to feel that she had no value as a person and was not entitled to have any wants of her own. In her marriage, she was dominated by an insensitive husband who insisted she confine herself exclusively to the roles of housekeeper and always available sex partner. As the years passed, Helen began to feel trapped by this constricted existence and wanted to satisfy some of her cultural and intellectual interests. However, her husband had no such interests himself and opposed her joining any community group, not wishing to lose any of his control over her.

In treatment she was depressed and anxious. She needed to enrich her life, but had doubts about her right to assert herself. She could not tolerate the current situation, yet her goal was to continue the marriage. The worker's approach was to try to understand Helen in terms of her reality perceptions and her goal: she inaccurately saw herself as having no worth and no right to fulfill her own needs. She wanted relief from the depression and anxiety associated with her marital relationship, yet did not want to solve the problem by leaving her husband.

Helen was helped to achieve the treatment

objective she herself formulated: overcoming her depression and anxiety. This was accomplished by challenging her inaccurate evaluation of herself both in individual and then in group treatment. She was finally able to stand up to her husband and gradually acquired the freedom to attend various cultural activities in the community, in which her husband later began to join her. At the end of treatment she was demonstrating courage and confidence in handling her situation. She had no expectations that her husband would change very much, but he no longer controlled her life. The satisfactions from outside activities gave her the strength to cope with the incompatibilities existing between herself and her husband.

Arnold

Arnold was a young man who asked for professional help with his sexual problem. He had been engaging in overt homosexual acts, but at the same time was repelled by this kind of life and wanted very much to move in the other direction. He expressed a strong wish to become heterosexually oriented so that he could have a wife, family life and children, yet he feared he was doomed to be a permanent homosexual.

Cognitive theory holds that the worker's task is not deep exploration of the client's drives. Rather, the focus should be on helping the client acquire accurate perceptions and constructive goals. The client can and will control his drives if his goals require it. (An obvious example is the celibacy of men who enter the priesthood.)

In Arnold's case, the worker, after consultation with a psychiatrist, assured him he was not doomed to be a homosexual if he was willing to struggle against these tendencies. Such a struggle would involve self-control and avoidance of homosexual contacts, combined with seeking out relationships with women. If he could find physically and emotionally satisfying relationships with the opposite sex and continue them, he might be able to weaken the tenden-

cies he wished to abandon. Fortunately, Arnold met a girl with whom a close relationship developed quickly, and he began to report satisfaction from their growing physical intimacies. He stated that he gained the confidence to approach this girl only after his worker had told him that he was not necessarily destined to remain homosexually oriented. Later, Arnold and his girlfriend started to talk about marriage and the kind of life they wanted together.

Sandra

Sandra, a young adult, came for help with a problem of compulsive-obsessive behavior which had begun to interfere with getting to her job on time and doing her work properly. Brought up in a family with a phobic mother who was hospitalized twice for mental breakdowns, she was strongly conditioned to view the world as a dangerous and insecure place. Because the world was so full of hazards, she took great pains to make no mistakes.

In treatment, she talked about her compulsions to triple-check household appliances to be sure they were turned off; to try the front door over and over as she left for work for fear it might not be locked; and to wash her hands many times during the day at the office as a precaution against germ infection.

Treatment was based on Salzman's concept of the compulsive-obsessive person as someone with excessive feelings of insecurity who requires absolute guarantees of safety (37, pp. 1139-1146). The problem was considered to be a consequence of Sandra's particular perception of reality, in contrast to the psychoanalytic view that behavior such as compulsive handwashing is a ritual to deal with unconscious sexual guilt and unconscious feelings of dirtiness. The cognitive worker saw Sandra's extreme insecurity as a result of all kinds of life experiences, possibly but not necessarily including sexual ones. In her case, by performing her rituals,

Sandra believed she was following a proven, automatic procedure which would eliminate possible dangers.

The cognitive worker had to teach Sandra that there are no absolute guarantees in life, that we have to live with a small element of risk in everything we do. A cognitive approach to treatment is not considered successful unless the client is enabled to take action on the stated problem. Therefore, the worker, through a warm and supporting relationship, helped her to find the courage to live normally by accepting the small risks in her daily life.

Buddy

Buddy, a twelve-year-old boy, was a good student who had no difficulties with his academic work. He spoke up in class, conversed easily with his school peers, and had no trouble keeping up with them in sports or other types of play. In his neighborhood he kept busy with many friends. At home, he was engaged in a fierce rivalry with his brother and was often punished by his parents for fighting and minor misconduct. His parents brought him for help with a problem of speech blocking, which occurred only in the home during clashes with his brother or in the presence of his parents.

On the premise of cognitive theory that perception determines functioning, the worker hypothesized that Buddy's view of the significance of speech had a great deal to do with his blocking. He further hypothesized that Buddy regarded his spoken words at home as a danger to himself, since quarreling with his brother or talking back to his parents usually resulted in harsh punishments. The parents were therefore asked to discontinue punishing Buddy for any spoken word. They could continue to penalize him for his behavior, but not for anything he said. The new arrangement at home was then explained to the boy.

Almost immediately, there was a marked decrease at home in Buddy's stuttering and blocking. A great deal of work was done with the parents to encourage them to avoid punishing or hitting Buddy when he spoke disrespectfully, and they were able to maintain their self-discipline. Meanwhile, the worker pointed out to Buddy the need for self-control on his part to avoid the parents' returning to stern punishments for what he said. The boy was finally able to meet this responsibility, aided greatly by the father's becoming less critical of him and recognizing that sometimes his brother was the real instigator of the fights between them. At the termination of treatment, Buddy's speech at home was still continuing to improve.

Summary

The approach of these cases discards the concept of an "unconscious" as the primary determinant of the psychic life. It illustrates the basic premise of cognitive theory: emotions, motives, goals and behavior are conscious phenomena that are usually the consequences of thought.

References

1. Alland, Alexander Jr. *The Human Imperative*. New York: Columbia, 1972.
2. Ansbacher, Heinz L. "Alfred Adler: A Historical Perspective," *American Journal of Psychiatry*, CXXVII, No. 6, December, 1970.
3. ———. "Ego Psychology and Alfred Adler," *Social Casework*, XLV, No. 5, May, 1964. Published by Family Service Association of America.
4. ———, and Rowena Ansbacher. *The Individual Psychology of Alfred Adler*. New York: Basic Books, 1956.

5. Arnold, Magda B. *Emotion and Personality*. 2 vols. New York: Columbia, 1960.

6. Beck, Aaron T. *Cognitive Therapy and the Emotional Disorders*. New York: International Universities Press, 1976.

7. Borenzweig, Herman. "Social Work and Psychoanalytic Theory: A Historical Analysis," *Social Work*, XVI, No. 1, January, 1971.

8. Brenner, Charles. *An Elementary Textbook of Psychoanalysis*. Garden City, N.Y.: Doubleday, 1957.

9. Dewey, Edith A. "Family Atmosphere," in Arthur G. Nikelly (ed.) *Techniques for Behavior Change*. Springfield, Ill.: Thomas, 1971.

10. Directors of the Robbins Insitute. "An Integrated Psychotherapeutic Program," *Psychotherapy*, I, No. 1, Fall, 1955.

11. Ellis, Albert. "Rational Psychotherapy," *The Journal of General Psychology*, LIX (1958).

12. ———. *Reason and Emotion in Psychotherapy*. New York: Stuart, 1962.

13. Epstein, Norman. "Brief Group Therapy in a Child Guidance Clinic," *Social Work*, XV, No. 3, July, 1970.

14. Furst, Joseph B. *The Neurotic—His Inner and Outer Worlds*. New York: Citadel Press, 1954.

15. Gerz, Hans O. "The Treatment of the Phobic and the Obsessive—Compulsive Patient Using Paradoxical Intention Sec. Viktor E. Frankl," in Viktor E. Frankl (ed.) *Psychotherapy and Existentialism: Selected Papers on Logotherapy*. New York: Simon and Schuster, 1968.

16. Glasser, William. *Reality Therapy: A New Approach to Psychiatry*. New York: Harper and Row, 1965.

17. Goble, Frank G. *The Third Force: The Psychology of Abraham Maslow*. New York: Grossman, 1970.

18. Gottlieb, Werner, and Joe H. Stanley. "Mutual Goals and Goal-Setting in Casework," *Social Casework*, XLVIII, No. 8, October, 1967. Published by Family Service Association of America.

19. Gronfein, Berthe. "Should Casework Be on the Defensive?" *Social Casework*, XLVII, No. 10, December, 1966. Published by Family Service Association of America.

20. Hallowitz, David, Ralph Bierman, Grace P. Harrison and Burta Stulberg. "The Assertive Counseling Component of Therapy," *Social Casework*, XLVIII, No. 9, November, 1967. Published by Family Service Association of America.

21. Hilgard, Ernest R. "Hypnosis and Consciousness," *Human Nature*, I, No. 1, January, 1978.

22. Hora, Thomas. "Existential Psychotherapy," in *Current Psychiatric Therapies*, Vol. II. New York: Grune and Stratton, 1962.

23. Krauss, Herbert H. "Anxiety: The Dread of a Future Event," *Journal of Individual Psychology*, XXIII, No. 1, May, 1967.

24. Krill, Donald F. "Existential Psychotherapy and the Problem of Anomie," *Social Work*, XIV, No. 2, April, 1969.

25. Lazarus, Arnold A. "Has Behavior Therapy Outlived Its Usefulness?", *American Psychologist*, XXXII, No. 7, July, 1977.

26. ———. *Multimodal Behavior Therapy*. New York: Springer, 1976.

27. Maslow, Abraham H. *Motivation and Personality*, 2nd ed. New York: Harper and Row, 1970.

28. Maultsby, Maxie C., Jr. *Help Yourself to Happiness*. New York: Institute for Rational Living, 1975.
29. May, Rollo. "Existential Bases of Psychotherapy," *American Journal of Orthopsychiatry*, XXX, No. 4, October, 1960.
30. ———. *The Meaning of Anxiety*. New York: Ronald, 1950.
31. Mayer, John E., and Noel Timms. "Clash in Perspective Between Worker and Client," *Social Casework*, L, No. 1, January, 1969. Published by Family Service Association of America.
32. Nikelly, Arthur G. "Basic Processes in Psychotherapy," in Arthur G. Nikelly (ed.) *Techniques for Behavior Change*. Springfield, Ill.: Thomas, 1971.
33. ———, and Don Verger. "Early Recollections," in Arthur G. Nikelly (ed.) *Techniques for Behavior Change*. Springfield, Ill.: Thomas, 1971.
34. Rado, Sandor. *Psychoanalysis of Behavior*. New York: Grune and Stratton, 1956.
35. Rank, Otto. *Will Therapy*. New York: Knopf, 1936.
36. Reynolds, Bertha C. "The Social Casework of an Uncharted Journey," *Social Work*, IX, No. 4, October, 1964.
37. Salzman, Leon. "Therapy of Obsessional States," *American Journal of Psychiatry*, CXXII, No. 10, April, 1966.
38. Sarbin, Theodore R. "Anxiety: Reification of a Metaphor," *Archives of General Psychiatry*, X, No. 6, June, 1964.
39. Scarbrough, H. E. "The Hypothesis of Hidden Health in the Treatment of Severe Neuroses," *Social Casework*, XLIX, No. 5, May, 1968. Published by Family Service Association of America.
40. Shepard, Martin, and Marjorie Lee. *Games Analysts Play*. New York: Putnam's, 1970.
41. Siporin, Max. "Situational Assessment and Intervention." *Social Casework*, LIII, No. 2, February, 1972. Published by Family Service Association of America.
42. Smalley, Ruth. *Theory for Social Work Practice*. New York: Columbia, 1967.
43. Sunley, Robert. "New Dimensions in Reaching-out Casework," *Social Work*, XIII, No. 2, April, 1968.
44. Ullman, Montague. "The Dream Process," *Psychotherapy*, I, No. 1, Fall, 1955.
45. Van Kaam, Adrian, *The Art of Existential Counseling*. Wilkes-Barre, Pa.: Dimension Books, 1966.
46. Werner, Harold D. "Adler, Freud, and American Social Work," *Journal of Individual Psychology*, XXIII, No. 1, May, 1967.
47. ———. *A Rational Approach to Social Casework*. New York: Association Press, 1965.
48. ———. *New Understandings of Human Behavior*. New York: Association Press, 1970.
49. White, Colby L. "Untangling Knots in Casework with the Experiential Approach," *Social Casework*, LI, No. 10, December, 1970. Published by Family Service Association of America.
50. Wortis, Joseph. "Comments and Conclusions," in Joseph Wortis (ed.) *Basic Problems in Psychiatry*. New York: Grune and Stratton, 1953.

Annotated listing of key references

BECK, Aaron T. *Cognitive Therapy and the Emotional Disorders.* New York: International Universities Press, 1976.
> *A definitive formulation of the principles of cognitive theory, with emphasis on their practical application to the treatment of the major emotional disorders. Many case illustrations are provided and specific treatment techniques are spelled out.*

ELLIS, Albert. *Reason and Emotion in Psychotherapy.* New York: Stuart, 1962.
> *A complete discussion of the theory and practice of the writer's "rational-emotive psychotherapy."*

GLASSER, William. *Reality Therapy: A New Approach to Psychiatry.* New York: Harper and Row, 1965.
> *The concepts and techniques of "reality therapy," an approach which views human problems as irresponsibility rather than illness.*

NIKELLY, Arthur G. *Techniques for Behavior Change.* Springfield, Ill.: Thomas, 1971.
> *The author has edited thirty papers, some written by himself, which succinctly outline Alfred Adler's principal ideas and practical treatment techniques derived from Adlerian theory. Included are assessment methods, individual and group treatment techniques, ways of treating specific problems and educational techniques.*

WERNER, Harold D. *A Rational Approach to Social Casework.* New York: Association Press, 1965.
> *Theory and technique for a type of casework treatment which views the client as fully understandable in terms of consciousness.*

WERNER, Harold D. *New Understandings of Human Behavior.* New York: Association Press, 1970.
> *A collection of twenty-five articles by psychiatrists and psychologists explaining behavior in non-Freudian terms. In addition to serving as editor, the author has supplied an introduction and a final chapter dealing with non-Freudian treatment methods, most of them cognitive.*

10

Contributions of Gestalt Theory to Social Work Treatment

by

MICHAEL BLUGERMAN

Introduction

While there has not been a great deal written about the gestalt approach in social work treatment, many social workers are becoming familiar with this point of view. There are some idiosyncratic parts of the system of Gestalt Therapy that make this state of affairs no accident.

Fritz Perls, the major proponent of the gestalt approach, once wrote:

What I do next year, I cannot tell. . . . I shall be very happy indeed if my paper has encouraged you to be benevolently sceptical towards both your own and my present convictions, and to make the transition from any compulsive dogmatism to the experimental, insecure, but creative pioneering attitude for which I can find no better example than the courage of Sigmund Freud. (28, p. 55 and p. 68)

These words, written two years after his arrival in New York from South Africa, very much understated Perls' relentless struggle to understand himself, therapy and the human personality.

The colorful contours of this development have been well described by Perls himself (15) and others (21). Even if these works had not been written, Perls' reputation has spread through the professional community; through his innumerable workshops, lecture tours, films and almost three generations of therapists whom he trained or influenced.

Perls grew suspicious of the value of concepts and "intellectual understanding." As we shall see, his view of human growth was predicated on principles antithetical to written work and the professional establishment. He attempted always to get beyond the false knowing of intellectualism and strived for understanding on a much more complete and organismic plane.

This kind of knowing emerges from a complete contact with our subject material—the human condition. It is an integration of cognitive, kinaesthetic and emotional material.

Historic origins

Although Perls frequently dropped names of major theorists and philosophers, very little of his writing was intended to trace the roots of his thinking. Several authors have since tried to establish these important connections: Polster (19), Wallen (29, p. 8), Smith (26) and Kogan (7), to name a few. Some threads will be presented here.

Smith (26) describes five main influences on Perls' thought: Psychoanalysis, Reichian Character Analysis, Existential Philosophy, Gestalt Psychology and Eastern Religion. Polster (19) adds the name of Otto Rank to this list.

Perls' early work, *Ego, Hunger and Aggression,* (13), demonstrates the importance of his classical analytic training. In this work, Perls makes some major contributions which will continue to be the cornerstone of his development. According to Smith (26, p. 5):

> In terms of his revision of the psychoanalytic position, Perls (1947) set forth three criticisms of Freud: (1) The treatment of psychological facts as if they exist in isolation from the organism as a whole, (2) the use of a linear association psychology as a basis for a four dimensional system, (3) the neglect of the phenomena of differentiation. . . .
> As a result, Perls offered the following revisions: (1) replacement of the psychological by the holistic organismic content, (2) replacement of association psychology by the field theory of gestalt psychology and (3) application of a differential thinking based on Friedlander's notion of creative indifference.

In developing a perspective on human devel-

opment based on *hunger* in contrast to Freud's *sexuality,* Perls laid the way for an integration between organismic assimilation of food and psychological symbolism and meaning.

These and other influences will be developed below as we discuss components and techniques flowing from this theory: particularly, the disturbances of function at the contact boundary.

Smith describes Reich's influence on Perls, and their differences, in these ways: (1) remembrances must be accompanied by the appropriate affect; (2) it is essential to bring into therapy the body of the client through the understanding of retroflection, or turning back onto the self (often through the use of musculature); (3) there must be a frustrating and confronting style of the therapist in order to strike a balance between support and frustration; (4) it must be understood that the character resistance is revealed in the "how" of the patient's communication instead of the "what"; (5) Perls' description of the layer notion of working with the impasse has some correlation to the idea of the breaking down of "secondary narcissism"; (6) Reich maintains that there is only one technique for a patient at any time, that which flows from the uniqueness of the individual's circumstances, while Perls maintains that the role of the therapist is to promote growth of the individual and not to follow a formula or technical model; (7) there must be an appreciation of the political dimension of the life of the therapist in society; and (8) while Reich feels that the freeing up of character armor puts the patient into a better stance vis à vis the world, in which he can go beyond addressing particular symptoms, Perls sees the development of self—support of the individual through awareness and responsibility—as a path to a more creative interaction with the environment (26, pp. 7-13).

From Existentialism, Perls developed the notion that one must take personal responsibility for one's own existence. Smith cites Perls' statement to the effect that no one can be different from what they are at that moment. "The model which Perls chose for the therapeutic relationship is one delineated by Buber as the 'I-Thou' relationship. . . . Gestalt therapy is based on the coming together of two persons in an atmosphere where the therapist respects the personhood of his patient" (26, p. 16).

As he continues to trace the roots of Gestalt therapy, Smith describes the contribution of the Gestalt psychologists to Perls:

> From the writings of Goldstein, Angyal, Lecky and Maslow, a coherent position of organismic theory evolved. These are the major facets of that position: (1) The normal personality is characterized by unity, integration, consistency and coherence. Pathology is defined as the converse. (2) Analysis of the person begins with the whole and proceeds by a differentiation of that whole into its aspects. (3) The individual is unified and motivated by a sovereign drive—self-actualization or self-realization. (4) The influence of inherent potentialities is emphasized, while the influence of external forces is minimized. (5) The vocabulary and principles of Gestalt psychology are used. (6) The emphasis in research is idiographic (the comprehensive study of a single case). (26, p. 31)

Finally, the principle of organismic self-regulation emerges from this rubric. The principle is that the need-motivation system of the individual determines the most relevant figure and its background formation, merging into a meaningful gestalt at that point in time.

Perl's interest in Zen and other eastern religious philosophy shows prominently in his work. Smith describes the paradox of the "likeness of the not alike." From eastern thought and the work of S. Friedlander, there is a suggestion that if one slows down contact and increases experience with a primarily undifferentiated object and then progressively differentiates the feeling until both poles are recognized, one can learn that opposites within a context are more related

than either of the opposites is to any other concept. For example, love and hate are opposite polarities on one level. At the same time, they have more in common (involvement with the object) than with another polarity of each of them—indifference or apathy (no involvement with the object).

In working with these polarities, it is important that the poles be experienced and teased apart, so that each aspect can be seen for what it is and integrated into the personality.

Another central paradox is that of change (2). The notion here is that change is occurring all the time. We are often engaged in a process to manage change in ways that we can handle. In *Future Shock,* Toffler has described the effect of social change on the individual and the ways through which we try to maintain constancy in our lives. We often succeed in slowing down our experience of life's flow to the point that we think it is stuck, and then we try to get it going again. The paradox here is that change begins to flow when we allow ourselves to be where we are at that moment. From this identity, we can once again track the impulse and momentum of a natural tendency toward movement. Acceptance of oneself in the here and now is a first step toward allowing the organism to break up a stagnant process.

Polster (19, p. 314) adds this reference to the influence of the work of Otto Rank:

> The *constructive* view of resistance and its role in the resolution of disparate parts of oneself is a major theme in gestalt therapy. Gestalt therapy realizes the *power of creative resistance* mobilizing it into a major force moving beyond the mere resolution of contradiction and into a new personal composition.
>
> Finally, Rank's interest in the developing sense of individual identity led to a change of focus in the interaction between patient and therapist. Acknowledgement of the human aspects of this interaction make

him one of the major influences toward a harmonistic orientation in psychotherapy—an important inheritance for gestalt therapy [italics mine].

Principal proponents

Shortly after his arrival in New York, Perls and his wife Laura developed an intellectual circle of colleagues and participated in some writing and teaching. Paul Goodman was a key figure in the development of this circle. He wrote much of "Gestalt Therapy: Excitement and Growth in the Human Personality (part 2)," and was part of the inner circle that developed the central ideas of the gestalt approach into sound thought and practice. However, the massive explosion of gestalt therapy as an influence in the helping professions did not really occur until Perls went to California. Shepard (21) describes this conversation:

> "If you write a book about Fritz," said Wilson Van Dusen, a west coast phenomenologist who brought Fritz to California in 1959, "you must emphasize what things were like when he turned up on the scene. We were all imbued with psychoanalysis, we must get an extensive history of the person. We were all basically retrospective, strongly retrospective, in both our analysis and our therapies. We couldn't conceive of understanding a patient without an extensive history. And for a man to just walk into a room and describe people's behaviour so accurately added a whole new dimension. This is where I considered Fritz very great. His incomparable capacity to observe. He could see all that he needed to see in the present. He often said, 'I'm only trying to see the obvious....' It was dealing right here on the surface, the skin, the obvious. Yet all you needed to know was right there. The patient's history would only elaborate—repeat again—what you are seeing now.

> This was illuminating. At the time I was well into existential analysis. I was drifting in the general direction of the *here and now.* We had gobs of Binswanger, Minkowski, Heidegger. But here was a man who could put into practice a rather tortured theory. So naturally, I studied and learned as much as I could from him."

Perls broke into the professional system through the back door. He had a tremendous flair for drama, loved to be the center of attention and delighted in illustrating his genius. The kicker was that he could do what he claimed his theory promised. Time after time, all manner of credentialed, "successful" but dissatisfied professionals, tired of the thin comfort of their well-learned dogma, saw in the work of Perls some hope for a different quality to *their* work with their clients: face to face and person to person.

Smith (26, p. 3) describes the growth of Gestalt therapy "to the extent that the *Directory* of the American Academy of Psychotherapists lists it as the sixth most common affiliation." This development occurred in spite of the fact that there were very few formal courses in professional schools teaching this system.

Impact on social work practice

With philosophical roots in phenomenology and existentialism, Gestalt therapy can offer a great deal to social work. Beginning where the client is at is often a difficult task, because of the difficulty in locating where the client is really at. Do we pay attention to the content that the client brings? Do we notice that he is holding his breath now? Do we accept the tremor in the chin as indicating the holding back of tears? Do we consider the fact of this client's being a man or a woman?

The most effective answer lies in the understanding of the client's point of view or situation as it is experienced. Often, a worker may listen to a client disclose painful detail after painful detail in his life situation. Asking the client what he is experiencing, what he wants and what he feels at this moment may offer many of us quite a surprise. In many cases, we have been hearing the story from our own heads, with our own agendas and embellishing this with our imagined pain.

Gestalt therapy offers a different map to the client's territory. It encourages acceptance in the fullest sense of the I-thou relationship. It demands our participation as another human being in order to keep from performing robot-like with a bag of cliché interventions and tricks.

Much of social work practice involves dealing with people as they experience difficulty in their environment. While some question the clinical value of dealing with intrapsychic difficulties, and suggest that the profession's responsibility is with the environmental end of this continuum, it will be seen that this artificial boundary makes less sense. If one deals competently with the environment, in a contactful way, personality integration and self-growth may be a large part of the outcome. This is especially the situation in the larger amount of relating to the environment that we do through the mechanism of projection. Social work has the opportunity to thaw out the process of movement from environmental support to self-support, interdependence and dignity. Much of this facilitation can occur through the *how* of the helping process. In later sections, we can examine these ideas further.

General therapeutic concepts

We have looked at some of the assumptive roots of the gestalt approach. Developed from these basic thoughts, we can identify several organizing principles to prepare for our work with clients.

First, we may consider the awareness continuum. Central to the work of Gestalt therapy is the use of the flow of conscious contact with the environment. The individual may be in touch with the inner zone, or how he experiences himself; the outer zone, or what he experiences as an object in the environment; or the middle zone, the thoughts and illusions modifying the clarity of contact with either the outer or inner zones. It should be clear that the problematic use of the middle zone doesn't allow contact between self and object or self and self.

Perls has said that the essence of gestalt is the awareness process.

> Everything is in flux. Only after we have been stunned by the infinite diversity of processes constituting the universe, can we understand the importance of the organizing principle that creates order from chaos; namely the figure, background formation. Whatever is the organism's foremost need makes reality appear as it does. It makes such objects stand out as figures which correspond to diverse needs. It evokes our interest, attention, cathexis or whatever you choose to call it. (28, p. 51)

Further, in the same article, he states:

> The most important fact about the figure-background formation is that if a need is genuinely satisfied, the situation changes. The reality becomes a different one from what it was as long as the situation was unfinished. . . .
> The healthy organism rallies with all its potentialities to the gratification of the foreground needs. Immediately as one task is finished, it recedes into the background and allows the one which in the meantime has become the most important to come to the foreground. This is the principle of organismic self-regulation. (28, pp. 51–52)

A second organizing principle is the value of the here and now. Whether the client remembers *now* what happened in the past, or anticipates *now* what may happen in a little while, or experiences his contact with the environment *now*, at this moment, the richness of experience is occuring here and now. This is not a metaphysical statement of truth as much as a workable reality. While we are striving to bring about integration of alienated parts of our clients, or address their apparent duplicity, it is most helpful to utilize the concerting function of the here and now. While we encounter them and engage at the contact boundary, the here and now remains the point of maximum contact possible.

A third assumption is that growth occurs at the contact boundary of systems. As difficult as it is, there is no more powerful level of analysis or focus of attention than the obvious or surface. Perls remarked that a neurotic is someone who cannot see the obvious. It may be that both the client and the worker have been avoiding the obvious, and instead dealing with much more "meaningful material": the client through his middle zone of cluttered self-doubt and the worker through his middle zone of "professional diagnosis or politeness."

The nature of disturbance between the organism and the environment can be observed and identified in definite ways. Let us consider these: confluence, introjection, projection and retroflection.

Confluence is an agreement to maintain the status quo, to pretend that there are no differences, to avoid making waves, to emphasize the similarity or identification between two individuals or two systems. If you place your hand on the table in front of you, your experience in the first instance will probably be something like a feeling of temperature difference, a feeling of texture, a sense of pressure. If you let your hand move a little, some of these experiences may intensify. If, however, you leave your hand there for some time, much of your experience may diminish. You may feel some pressure and it may not be immediately clear where your hand stops and where the table surface starts and stops. If you stay with this notion a little longer, you may experience some restlessness and boredom.

This process happens just as easily between

people, often marriage partners. Polster describes this scene:

> Indeed, someone can be involved in a confluence contact without ever having been consulted or having even negotiated its terms. One may buy into such an arrangement through indolence or ignorance and discover that such a contract existed to his surprise only by breaking or disturbing it. Even if vaguely sensed differences may never have erupted into overt argument, there are signs of disturbance in confluent relationships between husband and wife, parent and child, boss and underling, when one of them, knowingly or otherwise, breaches the contract terms. (19, p. 93)

The remedy is the reactivation of difference, through contact and awareness. Polster continues:

> Questions like, "What do you feel now?", "What do you want now?", or "What are you doing now?" can help him focus on his own directions.... Stating his expectations aloud, first to the therapist, perhaps, and finally to the person from whom these satisfactions are demanded can be the first steps in sorting out covert attempts at confluent relationships. (19, p. 95)

Let us consider the other three. *Introjection* is the incomplete assimilation of what the environment has to offer. This may be due to the avoidance of meeting the material head on and breaking it down into digestible pieces. This may refer to physical or symbolic material. It is usually identifiable with language such as "I should . . .", "I ought to . . .", "I have to . . .", and so on. One source of much introjection material is parental messages. As a result of this type of disturbance at the contact boundary, growth is limited through incomplete digestion of the differential information. The antidote or action plan for this disturbance is the "spitting up" and "rechewing" of the introjected material. If, for example, one is carrying the voice of a parent around with them, and it is not yet clear how much of this voice is parent and how much is client, the client may be asked to become the voice and express it until some identification occurs with the voice. At that point the client can confront the speaker of the voice and meet him head on in a contactful battle.

Many students have reported that the book *Gestalt Therapy* (12) is a difficult one to read. There is a popular story currently, that the authors purposefully did not want to make the material too easy to swallow. They hoped that readers would have to struggle to digest the information in a form that enhanced their learning, not simply to reproduce the information back on an exam.

Although the risk is one of frustration and possible rejection, out of hand, by potential students, if one's goal is in fact the serious study of the subject, there must be this active interchange between the teacher and the student. This idea is actively promoted in the pragmatism of John Dewey: the notion of learning by doing, with a high quality of engagement in the process.

Perhaps it was a good thing that material such as the gestalt approach to human growth wasn't taught in professional schools. In the struggle to digest material that I have outlined above, some heat is generated, and further, this kind of learning cannot be crammed or put on schedule. The demand is on the parties to provide some honest engagement. It may be that this kind of learning is better done in a setting compatible with these goals—a professional institute, for example.

Another style of disturbance at the contact boundary is *projection*. This approach is characterized by a disowning of some aspect of the personality, pleasant or unpleasant, and spotting it outwards in the environment. This approach results in a personal depletion of energy,

insofar as the talent or power of the disowned aspect disappears from the psychic economy. Further, it is added to the supply of the environment in a way that the environment gains more influence and control over the individual's life. Because of the fact that projections often find appropriate screens, the individual may operate with some successful intuition.

The task in dealing with projection is to facilitate the reclaiming of the disowned aspect of the individual. Somewhere in the mechanism of the projection is some element of an introject directing the giving away of the projector's attributes. Sometimes a helpful route may be to assist the identification of the projected material and the client. If the client can appreciate *how* he gives away his capability and power, he may choose to use it in a different way.

The fourth of these patterns of disturbance of contact at the boundary of systems is *retroflection*. This may take the form of the self using itself as object or environment—either to avoid doing something to someone else or to replace that outside object and do something to the self that the self wishes the outside object to do.

This pattern is usually anchored in muscular activity. Consequently, some mobilization of physical energy may be necessary before redirection to the more appropriate environment may be possible. As in the previously described patterns, each of these in itself is not necessarily problematic. It is only when the pattern becomes fixed and preferred by the organism that a deceleration of growth occurs. Thinking and planning are a form of retroflection. There is no doubt that most of the time this is a healthy and helpful function. If, however, the individual didn't move to the environment now and then for nourishment and refueling, stagnation would be quickly evident.

Each of these patterns occurs often in combination with some of the others. In each there is often some central introjection that must be dealt with. The advantage of this conceptual map is that it offers a direction for action as well as a diagnostic aid, at the same time. They are *process*-oriented labels rather than *event*-oriented labels. More clarification of this distinction will be made below.

Implications for history taking and diagnosis

In just the same way as we have been looking at principles for growth at the contact boundary between the individual and the environment, the same patterns hold true at the contact boundary between worker and client. In the interview, the worker becomes an active part of the environment, acting and challenging the client within a framework of support and frustration.

The material that is being obtained then may be seen as material from the client to the worker. What is the style of contact at this point? What would describe the quality of exchange occurring?

Instead of a diagnosis—usually in the form of a statement like "He is an X," where the X stands for a label, e.g., neurotic, single parent, character disorder, welfare mother and so on—we are looking for a description of process; that is, a pattern.

This would take the form, "When L, then M" or "When I want him to come home on time he dawdles," for example.

The advantage of this difference is the emphasis on "how" and "what" instead of on the more linearly causal "why." This allows movement from a theory of explanation to a theory of action, where the pattern suggests an action plan for intervention.

In describing the tasks of the therapist, Fagan gives us this description:

Of course, past events of much importance do arise from the process of exploring posture, gestures and dreams. However, the Gestalt therapist is not interested in the historical reconstruction of the patient's life, nor in focusing upon one specific behavior such as communication style. Rather, he is interested in a global way in the point of contact between the various systems available for observation. The interactions between a person and his body, between his words and his tone of voice, between his posture and the person he is talking to, between himself and the group he is a member of, are the focal points. The Gestalt therapist does not hypothesize nor make inferences about other systems that he cannot observe, though he may ask the patient to reenact *his* perceptions of them, as in a dialogue with his father, for example. Most Gestalt procedures are designed to bear upon the point of intersection, and the nature of the other system is viewed as less important than how the patient perceives or reacts to it. (4, p. 91)

This is not to say that there is no room for educated hunches which could expand the possibilities surrounding the patterns that are discovered. In the same way that a figure and ground create a demand for understanding, the figure of a client in front of you demands some background to make the image or gestalt sensible and complete. Often, the little missing pieces which come to mind as the worker sorts through his own process of understanding the client lay the groundwork for further intervention. This understanding need not be only intellectual or cognitive. It may be on any level of experience.

Part of the rationale for moving to patterns and here-and-now material as the basis for work is the notion that intervention begins at the first moment of contact with the client. The honest interaction between the two parties is the beginning of fostering a growth-producing relationship.

The concept of organismic self-regulation and the notion that the most valuable contact occurs at the surface of systems help support this point of view. The client is bringing you the most pressing material in his social system at that moment. He is, as well, showing you where to start work.

It is in the relation to work that a diagnostic statement is helpful. Current social work practice develops good assessments that are unrelated differentially to the provision of service. In the gestalt view, the process of diagnosis (patterning) is already the beginning of the work. As a viable hypothesis, the pattern serves to close the gap between client and worker, rather than creating professional distance through "knowing about."

Treatment methods and techniques

Later in his life, Perls was convinced of the value of the workshop, commune and multimedia approach to getting across his world view. Consequently, while some may miss a solid academic book from Perls, there is no shortage of transcripts, episodes and fragments of his work with clients (14, 16, 17).

In addition to these, other workers have tried to share their integration of gestalt theory and themselves(4), and statements on personal philosophy of practice (20). Gestalt therapy has developed a great number of "rules," "games," etc. These have been documented in several places (4, 5, 26, 27).

It must be remembered that many of these techniques were developed as much to illustrate the process of growth to an audience as to facilitate something for the client. Take Perls' use of drama—the hot seat was clearly more a way to show the audience the internal process of the client.

The only valid technique is one that grows out of the full I-Thou contact with the client in the here and now, and that is emerging from sound gestalt principles.

Two points must be made here: the first is the value of the gestalt approach as an orienting principle to the work, and the second is the notion of the experiment.

As an orienting principle, the gestalt ap-

proach allows the worker to use himself in unique ways. The worker focuses on *how* the client makes contact with him as part of the environment. He looks for patterns. These data are available whether the client is filling out a housing application with the worker or is engaged in relating a heavily charged emotional incident in his life.

Zinker (31, p. 97) states that the Gestalt therapist is particularly interested in bridging blockages of the awareness-excitement-contact cycle within the individual.

As the worker monitors the client's contact with the environment, including himself, he may see where in this rhythm of contact and withdrawal there is an interruption of flow. As well, the *how* of that disturbance of contact may be seen (e.g., confluence, retroflection, etc.). In utilizing this paradigm, Zinker moves into a nice piece of integration between gestalt theory and psychoanalytic theory (31, pp. 98 ff.).

The point of interest for us here is that the worker can use himself to monitor the nature of disturbance of contact boundary work. He can see where the flow of experience is being broken and can attend to an active bridging of that avoidance.

Jonh Enright (4, p. 108) states: "The task of the therapist is to help the patient overcome the barriers that block awareness and to let nature take its course (that is, to let awareness develop), so that he can function with all his abilities. Note that the therapist in this view does not help directly with the transaction—he does not help solve the problem—but helps reestablish the conditions under which the patient can best use ·his own problem-solving abilities.

Fagan and Sheperd (4, p.82) describe how Gestalt deals with inconsistencies between theory and technique:

> However, in Gestalt therapy the theory that people's problems arise from their lack of awareness and from the ways in which they block awareness leads

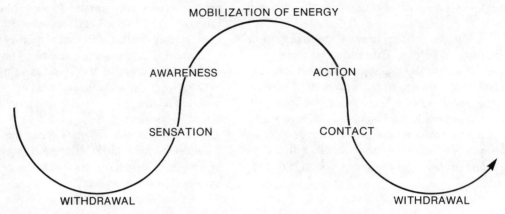

Figure 10-1.   THE AWARENESS-EXCITEMENT-CONTACT CYCLE

directly to the therapist's focusing attention on this area and offering suggestions, tasks, exercises designed either to promote awareness in general or to assist an individual with his specific avoidances. (4. p. 108)

Both Polster and Zinker have developed the notion of the value of the experiment in Gestalt work. Perls stated (28, p. 14) that in the safe emergency of the therapeutic situation, the neurotic discovers that the world does not fall to pieces if he gets angry, sexy, joyous, mournful.

The translation of the idea of a safe emergency into action leads us to the investigation of the experiment as a medium for growth. Polster states (19, p. 234 ff.):

The experiment in gestalt therapy is an attempt to counter the aboutist deadlock by bringing the individual's action system right into the room. Through experiment the individual is mobilized to confront the emergencies of his life by playing out his aborted feelings and actions in relative safety. A safe emergency is thus created where venturesome exploration can be supported. Furthermore both ends of the safety-to-emergency continuum can be explored, emphasizing first the support and then the risk-taking, whichever seems salient at the time.

Zinker (31, p. 122 ff.) states that "Gestalt

therapy bridges the gap between cognitive therapies and behaviour modification." He further states:

Gestalt therapy is an integrated version of phenomenology and behaviourism. Our orientation is similar to phenomenology because we respect the individual's internal experience: Therapeutic work is rooted in the client's own perspective. At the same time, we modify concrete behaviour in a graded and carefully timed manner. Thus, a unique quality of Gestalt therapy is its emphasis on modifying a person's behaviour in the therapy situation itself. This systematic behaviour modification, when it grows out of the experience of the client, is called an experiment. The experiment is the cornerstone of experiential learning.

Zinker (31, p. 128 ff.) has identified and outlined a way of understanding and coming to terms with the development of the helpful experiment. The purposes of the experiment are to increase awareness and social competence. Specifically, Zinker addresses these goals:

1. to expand the individual's repertoire of behaviour;
2. to create conditions under which the person can see his life as his own creation (take ownership of therapy);
3. to stimulate the individual's

experiential learning and the evolution of new self-concepts from behavioural creations;

4. to complete unfinished situations and overcome blockages in the awareness/excitement/contact cycle;
5. to integrate cortical understandings with motoric expressions;
6. to discover polarizations which are not in awareness;
7. to stimulate the integration of conflictual forces in the personality;
8. to dislodge and re-integrate introjects and generally place "misplaced" feelings, ideas, and actions where they belong in the personality;
9. to stimulate circumstances under which the person can feel and act stronger, more competent, more self-supported, more explorative and actively responsible to himself. (31, p. 126)

With these goals in mind, Zinker goes on to describe the process by which an experiment evolves.

1. Laying the Groundwork.
It is important to develop an honest and contactful appreciation of where the client is at that moment. This requires the reconnecting of the relationship with the client at the beginning of the interview—a "warming-up process of re-establishing contact again and again."

As the interview progresses, themes emerge—some stronger than others. Through staying in contact with the client, the worker begins to visualize a unifying theme. Zinker states that for every learning process, there is the matter of preparation and timing. If one cannot take the time to establish a field within which the experiment can be done properly, the client will not learn very much, nor will he remember the substantive outcome of the experience.

Equally as important is the genuine curiosity and interest in the client as another human being. Without this aspect, a great amount of material will not enter the worker's experience. For that matter, the client requires this interest in

order to share some cognitive and, more important, some feeling material.

2. Negotiating a Consensus Between Client and Therapist.
The worker addresses the responsibility and choice of the client and negotiates a common task for the next part of the interview.

3. Grading.
An experiment is successful if it is within the client's ability to perform it successfully. Zinker states that considerable skill and experience in human understanding are necessary to tailor-make a situation that provides the proper balance of support and frustration. The goal is not explosion or breakthrough, it is incremental learning. Consequently, experiments must be graded up or down to challenge the client's experienced difficulty.

4. Surfacing the Client's Awareness.
The awareness the client experiences is preceded by an increase in sensation. As the worker monitors the client's process, he can check for incongruence or confusion. A successful intervention is continued through this experiment by close tracking of the client's movement experientially as indicated by his awareness.

5. Locating the Client's Energy.
This process involves staying aware of changes in movement, breathing and color of skin in order to track the building or diminishing of energy. In the next step, as we find support, this energy may be engaged in work.

6. Generating Self-Support for Both Client and Therapist.
The client needs enough support to continue to contact the environment. Failure of establishing this support will draw attention away from the experiment and toward a search for this needed support. The worker can be helpful by attending to the client's usual support system, breathing, posture or other muscular activity.

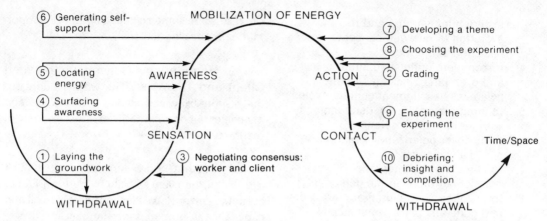

Figure 10-2. TRACING THE DEVELOPMENT OF AN EXPERIMENT ALONG THE AWARENESS-EXCITEMENT-CONTACT CYCLE.

7. Generation of a Theme. Zinker describes the "focus" in the experiment as an indicator of the process and direction of the session. The theme is related to the content. There may be several themes which become material for possbile synthesis. After the experiment, the client can often articulate how he understands or perceives the theme at another level.

8. Choice of Experiment. The client brings forth some themes. The worker develops some through his own process and through staying with the client's process. The particular experiment chosen will be a blending of these factors. The clearer a worker is, the more free he is to use what he feels, knows or intuits with the client

9. Enacting the Experiment. The experiment itself may address any of the goals listed above. It is a careful balance of ego-alien and ego-syntonic material, carefully graded up or down to challenge the client at his experienced level of support.

10. Insight and Completion. The important point here is that the learning takes place for the client. It is true that the worker may have learned a great deal from remaining in contact with the client and the work. His learning, however, is separate from the learning of the

client. The client may be asked to comment on his experience at this point. He may be directed to continue some form of the experiment on his own, outside the session, in order to enhance the integration of this new material.

Zinker summarizes this process by describing the experiment as a work of art, having elegance in the sense that it is easily observed or assimilated by the client. The flow of energy may follow the paradigm shown in Figure 10-1, above. In Figure 10-2, we can follow the course of an experiment through the "awareness-excitement-contact" cycle (with apologies to Zinker!). The reader is directed to Zinker for further elaboration of this conceptualization of the experiment and case examples (31).

Considerations in the application of methods

The gestalt approach is as much a way of viewing the helping process as a body of methods. It is difficult to imagine a situation where the gestalt perspective would not lend itself to social work.

Following its phenomenological roots, the gestalt approach values the personal experience and existence of the client. Many of the techniques developed thus far may not be applicable to *this* client, *this* worker or *this* agency setting. The essence of the gestalt approach lies in the faithful attending to the emerging situation: client; agency or worker. From this process a relevant technique or method may be developed. If one wonders, however, how a particular technique that he has just seen at a conference, seminar or workshop can be useful to him, we have a different question.

Passons (10, p. 28) states that a large part of the gestalt method is addressed to develop self-knowledge and self-exploration on behalf of the client. He points out that self-awareness is a core ingredient in any theoretical approach. He states that it is in the enhancement of awareness that counselors from many schools of thought may borrow gestalt techniques. He then identifies different theoretical frameworks and how they might benefit from this added perspective.

Utilization of the gestalt approach makes different demands on client and worker. While some humanistic workers believe that growth can occur in any person regardless of how dysfunctional he is at that point in time, many of us have neither the patience, skill nor personality to work in this way.

Demands of agency mandate, caseload and client population may militate against working where the client is at. In many of these situations alternate conceptual frameworks are necessary.

In order to develop the working conditions that support the use of gestalt methods, some good will between client, worker and agency is essential. Polster (19) has stated that Gestalt therapy may be too good for sick people. In some way, his statement reflects on the fact that much of the early work in this approach is geared to (a) mobilizing awareness of the client's experience, (b) encouraging a sense of his personal responsibility for the growth process, and (c) backing acceptance of the self of the client by himself.

Not only is good will necessary to support this challenging process, but it may be seen there is a geometric increase in benefit the more

this early work is developed and the more the client is mobilized.

In some ways, Gestalt theory offers a method of discovering method. Based on the *how* of the helping process, it orients the worker to developing a technology that constantly stays in contact with the work. True adherence to the gestalt approach may allow theory and practice to evolve unrecognizably past what we consider the method today. This can clearly be seen in the revisions over time in Perls' work. We can track his focus from the individual to the group, to the workshop and finally to the commune or kibbutz.

Implications for practice

Due to the organismic nature of Gestalt theory, there is a close connection with systems theory. We can consider the language of the gestalt approach to be translatable across the range of macro- or microsystems. General systems theory suggests that there is an organismic tendency of systems to complicate themselves. This process of growth occurs at systems' boundaries. Consider the popular saying, "You are what you eat," or the title of Edmund Carpenter's book, *They Became What They Beheld.*

If we observe the nature of contact at the boundaries of systems, we can observe patterns of disturbance or enhancement of this contact. Some of these patterns have been described. In many situations, it is just as important to interfere in this growth process as to facilitate it. The important consideration here is whether this interference is done with awareness and a sense of responsibility, and whether we are willing to pay the necessary costs.

An example of interference with a growth process is the case of racial intermarriage. For the sake of cultural identity and values, contact between racial systems may be limited or even curtailed. The hidden emotional costs of this curtailment may never be fully known. The majority of people, however, may never realize the costs and, consequently, may not make this choice in full awareness.

In working with individuals, our goal is often the reowning of disowned parts of the personality. In our attempts to strengthen the client's sense of competence and responsibility, we work with disturbances at the contact boundary between him and his environment. In the interview situation we are a large part of the environment. What is this client's pattern of making a disturbing contact with us? In dealing with the integration of projected parts or aspects of his personality, does the client utilize the cast of characters in his own repertory company or does he overuse one or two "stars," causing discontent in the others in the dressing room or wings of the theatre of his mind?

When we work with a family (6) the level of abstraction changes. We observe how the family subsystems make contact with each other at their boundaries. We may consider the parent-child system, the couple system or the intergenerational system. Our task is to design experiments that will allow for the discovery of new possibilities of relating: replacing learned limitations of experience and action.

As we stay in contact with the family, we obtain some hunch or hypothesis about the operating patterns between individuals or subsystems. The family is acting "as if" an unwritten script were being enacted. In the design of the helping experiment, we challenge the "unwritten script" and allow more contactful sequences to develop.

In working with groups, we are also faced with another collection of subsystems. We can examine what is going on between the leader and member(s). How is contact disturbed at this boundary? We can also look at intermember boundaries, or look at contact between subgroupings or cliques. Much of Perls' work was done in a group format. We can see this as the interaction of a subsystem (leader-member) in front of the remainder of the group. Several authors have examined this and other uses of groups (3, 10, 31). It is also of interest to consider the boundary between the group and the host agency or wider parts of the environment.

This type of analysis can also be made at larger levels of abstraction. If our concern is organizational development in an agency, we may notice how the board of directors subsystem is kept, or keeping itself, from full contact with either the staff or the client subsystem. We can notice how line workers, middle management and the agency director have designed their interactions to limit or prevent healthy contact.

In the professional school, we can examine the contact between the teacher and student subsystems. We can deal with the subsystems of theory and field practice and how they are in contact. Is there a flow across the boundary of theory and practice data, or are there two unrelated activities?

The community affords a look at interaction between subsystems organized on socioeconomic, cultural, racial or other variables. In all these situations growth occurs at the boundary between systems. Our task as social workers addressing these situations is to produce the same kind of safe emergency and constructive experimentation that we have arranged in aiding individual growth. Techniques, strategies and methods will vary greatly, and are limited by the creativity of the worker.

The gestalt perspective may be used to develop these techniques, provided the worker is available to enter the target system and develop the necessary groundwork and contract to work.

Counter indications for the use of theory

Shepherd (22, p. 728) describes the limitations and cautions in the gestalt approach. Some of these are:

1. The therapist's capacity for I-thou, here and now relationships is a basic requisite and is developed through

extensive integration of learning and experience. Probably the most effective application of Gestalt techniques comes with personal therapeutic experiences gained in professional training workshops and work with competent supervisors and therapists.

2. Gestalt therapy is most effective with oversocialized, restrained, constricted individuals—often described as neurotic, phobic, perfectionistic, ineffective, depressed, etc.—whose function is limited or inconsistent.

3. Work with less organized, more severely disturbed or psychotic individuals is more problematic and requires caution, sensitivity and patience. Such work should not be undertaken where long term commitment to the patient is not feasible.

4. Individuals whose problems center in lack of impulse control—acting out, delinquency, sociopathy, etc.—require a different approach.

5. Because Gestalt techniques, in general, facilitate the discovery, facing and resolution of the patient's major conflicts in often dramatically short time, the inexperienced therapist, observer or patient may assume the Gestalt therapy offers "instant cure."

Gestalt techniques were developed out of work with particular client groups. Many of the groups with which social work deals are different from these. It remains to be seen whether the principles of Gestalt theory can generate some methods to deal with these groups. Many of the current techniques have developed from Gestalt principles and contact with specific client populations. With the same principles of Gestalt theory and different client groups the question

becomes: What techniques can flow from interaction between workers and clients in these categories as they are involved in the helping process?

Implications for social work research

It has been indicated that some of the contributions from phenomenology and Gestalt psychology have influenced the development of this approach. In considering the connection between this approach and social work research, we need to discuss two of these contributions. The first is the focus on ideographic study of single cases, and the second is the replacement of stimulus response learning with field theory.

The study of single cases is important in focusing on how this client, with his experienced difficulty, can be helped by this worker through this method.

It is not enough to ask: Does aspirin cure a headache? At this time, science has identified over two hundred types of headaches. It is important to know how this headache is functional and meaningful in this client's life. Consider programs to provide service dealing with social concerns such as truancy, delinquency and alcoholism. It may be demonstrated that at this level of abstraction we have created an event or noun that replaces a more complicated sequence of behavior or process. The gestalt approach operates by reversing this abstracting process, once again finding the functional groundwork of events that led up to this labeling of an event.

In this process, truancy becomes more of an operational description than a label. We may find that the truancy is based on a mother who prefers the child at home; a family that requires the child to work; a peer group that demands allegiance in misdeeds; a sense of physical embarrassment at the thought of entering the common showers; and so on. In each of these examples the details of the helping technique might be different. What is important is the personal meaning of the problem behavior and the reestablishment of a personal solution to this concern. This does not mean that we cannot generalize treatment methods. It does mean that through the detailed study of single cases we can answer the differential demand situation of a specific problem, a specific worker, a specific approach.

In just the same way as valid theory is that which is anchored in practice skills, meaningful research is most useful when it is grounded in the experienced phenomena that are being studied rather than in grand levels of abstraction.

The shift from stimulus response approaches to gestalt field theory learning allows a shift from *why* to *how* as an operating principle. Our thinking on causality is best done when we can move from "A causes B" statements to statements describing the range of experienced vector forces brought to bear on a situation, together with the client's experienced perception of the meaning of these vectors.

Summary

Gestalt theory orients the worker toward encouraging the fullest expression of the client as a person. Application of gestalt methods must go beyond techniques and gimmicks into the development of a safe emergency situation within which experiments designed to enhance functioning can be undertaken. Considerable skill on the part of the worker is one prerequisite. Another is the willingness of the worker to engage himself fully as a human being in the helping process.

This I-thou connection with the client is at the center of our work. In accepting the client where he is at, the worker sees in the client's difficulty a positive and creative adaptation to the environment as he experiences it. The task is to restore the awareness-excitement-contact cycle in a way that mobilizes the client's creative resources.

If one is faithful to gestalt principles, one's techniques will continue to develop along lines based on client need and potential. Applications in social work will continue to need to be formally tested. Currently, some formal teaching of this approach may be just beginning in professional schools. It is quite encouraging to consider the number of people in the helping professions who have discovered the gestalt approach as a perspective that "fits" and is helpful. It is particularly encouraging because of the grounding of the work in a natural, organismic approach to an interpersonal enterprise in human service.

References

1. Appelbaum, A. A. "A Psychoanalyst Looks at Gestalt Therapy," in C. Hatcher and P. Himelstein (eds.) *Handbook of Gestalt Therapy*. New York: Aronson, 1976, pp. 753-778.
2. Beisser, A. "The Paradoxical Theory of Change," in J. Fagan and I. L. Shepherd (eds.) *Gestalt Therapy Now: Theory, Techniques, Applications*. Palo Alto, Calif.: Science and Behavior Books, 1970, pp. 77-87.
3. Cohn, R. C. "Therapy in Groups: Psychoanalytic, Experiential and Gestalt," in J. Fagan and I. L. Shepherd (eds.) *Gestalt Therapy Now: Theory, Techniques, Applications*. Palo Alto, Calif.: Science and Behavior Books, 1970, pp. 130-139.
4. Fagan, J., and I. L. Shepherd (eds.) *Gestalt Therapy Now: Theory, Techniques, Applications*. Palo Alto, Calif.: Science and Behavior Books, 1970.
5. Hatcher, C., and P. Himelstein (eds.) *Handbook of Gestalt Therapy*. New York: Aronson, 1976.

6. Kempler, W. *Principles of Gestalt Family Therapy: A Gestalt-Experiential Handbook.* Salt Lake City: Deseret Press, 1974.

7. Kogan, J. "The Genesis of Gestalt Therapy," in C. Hatcher and P. Himelstein (eds.) *The Handbook of Gestalt Therapy.* New York: Aronson, 1976, pp. 235-258.

8. Levitsky, A., and F. S. Perls. "The Rules and Games of Gestalt Therapy," in J. Fagan and I. L. Shepherd (eds.) *Gestalt Therapy Now: Theory, Techniques, Applications.* Palo Alto, Calif.: Science and Behavior Books, 1970, pp. 140-149.

9. Naranjo, Claudio. "Expressive Techniques," in C. Hatcher and P. Himelstein (eds.) *Handbook of Gestalt Therapy.* New York: Aronson, 1976, pp. 281-305.

10. Passons, W. R. *Gestalt Approaches in Counselling.* New York: Holt, Rinehart and Winston, 1975.

11. Perls, Frederick S. *Legacy from Fritz,* and Baumgardner, P. *Gifts from Lake Cowichan.* Palo Alto, Calif.: Science and Behavior Books, 1975.

12. ———, R. F. Hefferline and P. Goodman. *Gestalt Therapy: Excitement and Growth in the Human Personality.* New York: Dell, 1951.

13. ———. *Ego, Hunger and Aggression.* New York: Vintage Books (Random House), 1969 (a). London: Allen and Unwin, 1947.

14. ———. *Gestalt Therapy Verbatim.* Lafayette, Calif.: Real People Press, 1969 (b).

15. ———. *In and Out the Garbage Pail.* Lafayette, Calif.: Real People Press, 1969 (c).

16. ———. "Theory and Technique of Personality Integration," in John O. Stevens (ed.) *Gestalt Is.* Moab, Utah: Real People Press, 1975.

17. ———. *The Gestalt Approach and Eye Witness to Therapy.* Palo Alto, Calif.: Science and Behavior Books, 1973.

18. Perls, L. "One Gestalt Therapist's Approach," in J. Fagan and I. L. Shepherd (eds.) *Gestalt Therapy Now: Theory, Techniques, Applications.* Palo Alto, Calif.: Science and Behavior Books, 1970, pp. 125-129.

19. Polster, E., and M. Polster. *Gestalt Therapy Integrated: Contours of Theory and Practice.* New York: Vintage Press, 1974. (Brunner/Mazel, 1973.)

20. Rosenblatt, D. *Opening Doors: What Happens in Gestalt Therapy.* New York: Harper and Row, 1975.

21. Shepard, Martin. *Fritz, An Intimate Portrait of Fritz Perls and Gestalt Therapy.* New York: Saturday Review Press, Dutton, 1975.

22. Shepherd, I. L. "Limitations and Cautions in the Gestalt Approach," in C. Hatcher and P. Himelstein (eds.) *Handbook of Gestalt Therapy.* New York: Aronson, 1976, pp. 725-731. (Also in J. Fagan and I. L. Shepherd [eds.] *Gestalt Therapy Now.* Palo Alto, Calif.: Science and Behavior Books, 1970.)

23. Simkin, J. S. "Mary, A. Session with a Passive Patient," in J. Fagan and I. L. Shepherd (eds.) *Gestalt Therapy Now: Theory, Techniques, Applications.* Palo Alto, Calif.: Science and Behavior Books, 1970, pp. 162-168.

24. ———. "The Use of Dreams in Gestalt Therapy," in C. Sager and H. S. Kaplan (eds.) *Progress in Group and Family Therapy.* New York: Brunner/Mazel, 1972.

25.   ———. "The Development of Gestalt Therapy," in C. Hatcher and P. Himelstein (eds.) *The Handbook of Gestalt Therapy*. New York: Aronson, 1976, pp. 223-234.

26.   Smith, E. W. L. (ed.) *The Growing Edge of Gestalt Therapy*. New York: Brunner/Mazel, 1975.

27.   Stevens, J. O. *Awareness: Exploring, Experimenting, Experiencing*. Lafayette, Calif.: Real People Press, 1971.

28.   ———. *Gestalt Is*. Moab, Utah: Real People Press, 1975.

29.   Wallen, R. "Gestalt Therapy and Gestalt Psychology," in J. Fagan and I. L. Shepherd (eds.) *Gestalt Therapy Now: Theory, Techniques, Applications*. Palo Alto, Calif.: Science and Behavior Books, 1970, pp. 8-13.

30.   Yontef, G. M. "The Theory of Gestalt Therapy," in C. Hatcher and P. Himelstein (eds.) *The Handbook of Gestalt Therapy*. New York: Aronson, 1976, pp. 213-222.

31.   Zinker, J. *Creative Process in Gestalt Therapy*. New York: Brunner/Mazel, 1977.

Annotated listing of key references

FAGAN, J., and I. L. SHEPHERD (eds.) *Gestalt Therapy Now: Theory, Techniques, Applications.* Palo Alto, Calif.: Science and Behavior Books, 1970.

This book developed from second-generation Gestalt therapists who saw a need to address the professional community and to do so in writing. Very little had been written in the area for some time, due to the distrust of the "computer" (mind) in favor of experience. This book contains some very valuable work spelling out principles and applications in gestalt work. At the same time it is faithful to feeling and experience.

HATCHER, C., and P. HIMELSTEIN (eds.) *Handbook of Gestalt Therapy.* New York: Aronson, 1976.

This large anthology contains several articles that are not available or published elsewhere. Many different therapists describe their personal integration of gestalt in their work. There are several papers discussing the gestalt approach in comparison with other theoretical frameworks.

PERLS, F. S., R. F. HEFFERLINE, and P. GOODMAN. *Gestalt Therapy: Excitement and Growth in the Human Personality.* New York: Dell, 1951.

Although this is a volume to be worked through slowly, it is a valuable piece. Paul Goodman wrote the second part from a manuscript by Perls. Many Gestalt therapists consider the first part a historic curiosity. This work is derivative of a great deal of serious philosophical, social and political discussions among the first generation of Gestalt therapists surrounding Fritz and Laura Perls in New York. It was seen as an attempt to go beyond psychoanalysis toward a radically new approach.

PERLS, F. S. *Ego, Hunger and Aggression.* New York: Vintage Books (Random House), 1969. London: Allen and Unwin, 1947.

This book is of great historic interest. It is possible to trace the movement toward an alternative system of therapy from classical psychoanalysis. Perls thought much of this material was obsolete; however, there are many valuable ideas presented here and this makes exciting reading for anyone wanting to follow Perls' development over the next period of his life's work.

PERLS, F. S. *The Gestalt Approach and Eye Witness to Therapy.* Palo Alto, Calif.: Science and Behavior Books, 1973.

Published after his death, this book presents a short synthesis of Perls' thinking about Gestalt therapy. In addition to a theoretical presentation in The Gestalt Approach, *the second part of the book,* Eye Witness to Therapy, *is a transcription of films of some of Perls' seminars. The original films are available elsewhere, making this book a handy teaching aid.*

POLSTER, E., and M. POLSTER. *Gestalt Therapy Integrated: Contours of Theory and Practice.* New York: Vintage Press, 1974. (New York: Brunner/Mazel, 1973.)

Of particular interest to the helping professional, this book makes a valuable contribution to gestalt therapy. The development of the concept of the contact boundary gives insight into the development of process in the gestalt approach. The book presents a good integration of theory and practice and, in addition, offers some clinical examples.

SMITH, E. W. L. (ed.) *The Growing Edge of Gestalt Therapy.* New York: Brunner/Mazel, 1976.

This collection of articles traces many of the historic roots and parallel paths of gestalt therapy. Connections are made with a wide range of philosophical thought, including eastern religions. Gestalt practice and thought are the takeoff point into many other directions. This is a good collection of papers for a serious study of gestalt therapy.

ZINKER, J. *Creative Process in Gestalt Therapy.* New York: Brunner/Mazel, 1977.

This is a first-rate exposition of Gestalt therapy from someone who understands creativity and the human process. Zinker offers a refreshing formulation of some key ideas in therapy. This work moves a long way from the medical model of helping. Zinker's description of the creative experiment is clear and valuable.

11

Transactional Analysis—
A Social Treatment Model

by

DENISE CAPPS COBURN

A refreshing, optimistic theory of social treatment and change, Transactional Analysis brings strong support for the value of human beings. A primary assumption of this theory is that people are OK, which means that people can think, act spontaneously, and get close to other people in intimacy that is beneficial for all concerned. Further, the concepts of Transactional Analysis stress that people can and deserve to feel good both physically and mentally most of the time, and that we have awesome power to decide whether we will get this kind of life for ourselves and whether we have social systems that foster autonomy. These ideas are in close harmony with the ethics and values of professional social work.

Eric Berne, M.D., the founder of Transactional Analysis, lived from 1910 to 1970. He began his work constructing the concepts for his theory in the nineteen-forties when he was training to become a psychoanalyst. The beginnings of his work actually began long before this when

he was a little boy and he had a dream about helping people to be well and happy (44). His beloved physician father, a dedicated country doctor, died when Eric was ten years old (44); evidently Eric was then more determined than ever to fulfill his "little boy dream."

Dr. Eugene Kahn, Professor of Psychiatry at the Yale School of Medicine, and Dr. Paul Federn of the New York Psychoanalytic Institute were Berne's intimate teachers, influencing much of his early thought and work. He was an analysand of Erik Erikson who, no doubt, also had a profound influence on his thinking.

Sigmund Freud's work was an important part of Berne's basic ideas. A. A. Brill in the preface to Berne's first book, *The Mind in Action*, written in 1947, revised in 1957 and called *A Layman's Guide to Psychiatry and Psychoanalysis* (3), said:

> Berne is a young Freudian who like the new generation of Egyptians did not

know Joseph and hence would follow a new path and expound the new psychology without the affectivity of the older Freudians. The psychoanalytic theories were well established when Dr. Berne mastered them; that is why he could complacently survey the whole field of psychoanalysis, the fons et origo, as well as all the deviations from it, and then easily separate the kernels from the sheaf.

Berne himself, in the Author's Foreword of the same book (3), said:

> It is taken for granted that most of the ideas, like the ideas of every dynamic psychiatrist today, are based on the work of Sigmund Freud.

The San Francisco Social Psychiatry Seminars was a nonprofit educational corporation started by Berne in 1958. It was initially a small group of professionals interested in social treatment who met every Tuesday evening in San Francisco. The group included psychiatrists, social workers, psychologists, nurses, and other mental health professionals and students in these fields; anyone with a degree in medicine or the social sciences engaged in work or enrolled in advance study at a recognized university, and certain well qualified undergraduate students were welcome. Various approaches to psychotherapy were discussed, including Berne's developing Transactional Analysis theory. Berne encouraged questions about theory and practice and presentations by seminar members about new ideas in treatment. Berne learned from these seminars and included ideas from students in his own theory of treatment. The size of the seminars grew until it was not unusual to have people attending on Tuesday nights from states all over the nation. In 1960, these seminars were granted a charter by the State of California. Also in 1960, the name was changed to San Francisco Transactional Analysis Seminars. Then, in 1970, the name

was changed again to Eric Berne Seminars of San Francisco in honor of their founder.

In 1965, the International Transactional Analysis Association was founded to promote understanding and knowledge of Transactional Analysis and to provide training standards and appropriate training and certification of therapists. The membership has grown to nearly ten thousand, with members in thirty-five countries (2, Introduction).

Training standards have been a major concern of the Association. Serious ethical leaders in the Association have developed excellent training requirements. Certification is possible in two areas:

Clinical Certification. Required mastery of the theory and its clinical application is evaluated by a written test prepared by the Educational Testing Service at Princeton University and by meeting with a board to take an oral examination.

Special Fields Certification. The examination process is similar to the clinical one, except that these candidates do not prepare for clinical practice but for application of Transactional Analysis is special systems and areas such as Education, Business and Industry, Health Care Delivery, Social Services, and International Relations. This is a newly developing area of Transactional Analysis and promises leadership toward humanistic, socially sound institutions and worldwide cooperation. This is the hope and dream of many members of the International Transactional Analysis Association; it fits the ethics, goals, and standards of social work for advocacy, policy, and systems change toward social justice and personal fulfillment for all people.

Basic assumptions of transactional analysis

1. People are born OK. I'm OK, you're OK position is a point of view about people (49, In-

troduction, p. 1) which Berne says is not only good but true (49, Introduction, p. 3).

2. People in social/emotional difficulty are intelligent and capable of understanding their stress and the liberating process of change; they want, and need, to be part of the treatment process. They must be involved in the healing process; if they are to solve their problems, this involvement is essential. Social work treatment supports client participation in an effective change process.

3. All social/emotional difficulties are curable, given adequate knowledge and a proper approach (49, Introduction, p. 2). People who may be called schizophrenic, alcoholic, delinquent, or deviant are basically good and capable of leading satisfying, healthy lives that do not interfere with the lives of others.

Theoretical concepts of transactional analysis

Strokes

Strokes are defined as units of social recognition that are essential to survival. Berne based this idea on the classic work of Rene Spitz (43) with infants who were failing to thrive. Physical and social stimulation (strokes) brought remarkable improvement to the infants in a short time. Berne maintained, then, that stroking is necessary for human survival; he extended stroking to include verbal transactions.

People spend their time in life seeking strokes. There are four kinds of strokes (51, p. 16): negative, positive, conditional, and unconditional. *Negative* strokes deny the reality of the spontaneity, rationality, and ability of people to be socially intimate. *Positive* strokes recognize, openly, the value, awareness, and spontaneity in people. If a person does not get positive strokes, he will settle for negative ones, since negative strokes are better than none at all. *Conditional* strokes must be earned; a person has to do something to get them. For example:

"You did a good job!" *Unconditional* strokes do not require earning. You do not have to do anything special to get them, and your existence is enough. An example of an unconditional positive stroke is: "I like to be with you."

Strokes can be given in three ways: verbally, nonverbally (such as by gestures, facial expression, and body movements—a wink—a smile—a frown), and physically (by body contact such as hugging, slapping, touching, or pushing).

Knowing your own and your client's stroke economy helps develop information on how you can problem solve together. Knowing your own stroking patterns as a therapist will help develop your professional potency. Social work clients deserve positive verbal and nonverbal strokes for seeking help, for being willing to change, for changing, and for problem solving for themselves. Modeling positive stroke-giving is an important and powerful part of effective social work practice. People can learn how to stroke freely and how to receive strokes which will help them find intimacy and avoid loneliness. One good approach to becoming stroke conscious is to use a stroke-awareness grid to record most liked and least liked strokes in all categories. Many people are taught not to stroke, especially not to stroke themselves positively. It is frequently thought of as "bragging" or "selfish."

In many families, children are taught to be critical of their own behavior and to give themselves internal negative strokes. A resulting inner dialogue may be: "You never do anything right" or "When are you going to get it together?" This is a good way to stay depressed, helpless, and passive. Positive internal stroking is a powerful way to maintain high self-esteem. In addition to family systems, welfare, health care, and educational systems are sometimes so rigid and inflexible that individuals cannot get their needs met no matter what they do and, as Martin Seligman says, they learn helplessness, which fosters feelings of hopelessness, depression, and passivity (42).

Time structuring is defined in six ways by

STROKE—AWARENESS GRID (WITH EXAMPLES WRITTEN IN)

| | Types of Strokes | | | |
| | POSITIVE | | NEGATIVE | |
Methods of Stroking	Conditional	Unconditional	Conditional	Unconditional
1. Verbal	"You did a good job"	"I like you"	"I don't like your cooking"	"Drop dead"
2. Nonverbal	Smile when child obeys	Sitting with someone, feeling close and silent	Pointing finger and shaking it angrily	Turning away
3. Physical	Pat on back for job done	Backrub	A kick to stop daydreaming	Push downstairs— Hitting to hurt— Abuse—Rough pushing

Berne (10, pp. 188-205), with accompanying advantages and disadvantages. * They are listed in the table on page 297.

In Transactional Analysis, the use of time is seen as important since appropriate time structuring is a way to stay socially healthy. The way a person structures time is a major factor in whether she† is coping with life, problem solving, and feeling as though there are good reasons to live. The individual has considerable control over how time is spent. Transactional Analysis encourages time spent for creative, spontaneous work and play.

Existential Positions

Transactional analysis defines four basic life positions:

1. I'm OK—you're OK.
2. I'm OK—you're not OK.
3. I'm not OK—you're OK.
4. I'm not OK—you're not OK.

Franklin Ernst invented a diagram for gaining awareness of existential positions to lead to contracts for change to get to the OK-OK position (20, p. 33) (see Figure 11-1).

Structural analysis is defined by Berne as the first step in treatment (3, p. 267). The personality is defined as being "made of three ego states each with a set of coherent systems of thought and feeling manifested by corresponding patterns of behavior." The three ego states are Parent, Adult, and Child.

Berne's structural diagram of the ego states looks like Figure 11-2 (6, p. 12).

The Parent ego state is like a tape recorder containing recorded messages about how to get along in life, messages like study, work, please others, from adults who tended us such as parents, teachers, friends, etc. The Adult ego state is like a computer; it gathers facts and makes decisions based on information. There are no feelings in the Adult state. The Child ego state contains natural feelings, sensations, and urges present since the beginning of life (archaic), and includes all of the body, skin, brain, lungs, heart, etc.

An appropriate flow of energy from one ego state to another is essential to satisfying social interaction. The importance of stuctural analysis lies in the control and power involved in conscious, appropriate use of ego states. A winner is described as a person who maintains a

---

* Specific advantages and disadvantages are author's.
† Male and female pronouns are used interchangeably and alternately throughtout the chapter when referring to a nonspecfic person.

	SOCIAL ADVANTAGE	SOCIAL DISADVANTAGE
Withdrawal	Refreshment	Isolation
Ritual	Security	Social distance
Pastimes	Source of strokes	Avoidance of intimacy
Activities (includes daily work job)	Creative self-fulfillment	Conditional strokes only based on doing something
Games	Structures time with some strokes	Avoids intimacy
Intimacy	warmth and security; unconditional strokes from all categories; deep sense of well-being	Risk of loss

basic self-confidence (27, p. 2); she uses her ego states consciously to get what she wants and needs. The Adult ego state can be in charge— asking questions, assessing and making decisions that will allow the full development and expression of the Child ego state, which can be described as the center of creativity, joy, curiosity, and spontaneity, and thus the center of social being. The Parent ego state can also be used to assure protection and self-actualization for the

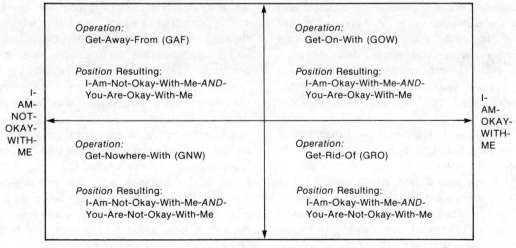

YOU-ARE-OKAY-WITH-ME

Operation:
Get-Away-From (GAF)

Position Resulting:
I-Am-Not-Okay-With-Me-AND-
You-Are-Okay-With-Me

Operation:
Get-On-With (GOW)

Position Resulting:
I-Am-Okay-With-Me-AND-
You-Are-Okay-With-Me

I-AM-NOT-OKAY-WITH-ME

I-AM-OKAY-WITH-ME

Operation:
Get-Nowhere-With (GNW)

Position Resulting:
I-Am-Not-Okay-With-Me-AND-
You-Are-Not-Okay-With-Me

Operation:
Get-Rid-Of (GRO)

Position Resulting:
I-Am-Okay-With-Me-AND-
You-Are-Not-Okay-With-Me

YOU-ARE-NOT-OKAY-WITH-ME

Figure 11-1.

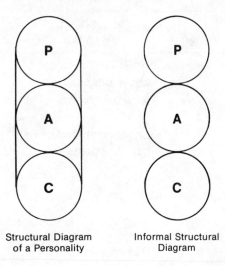

Structural Diagram   Informal Structural
of a Personality   Diagram

Figure 11-2.

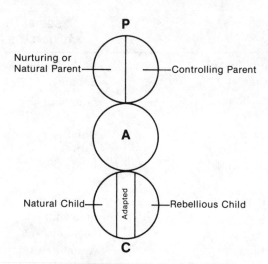

Figure 11-3. DESCRIPTIVE ASPECTS OF THE PERSONALITY

Child so that a winner is described as a person who keeps the appropriate ego state available and ready for use at all times. When a thinking, nonfeeling position is needed in a therapist, for instance, she can cathect (energize) her Adult ego state and figure out what is needed; she can consciously program herself: "Stay in your adult now. Keep control of your feelings right now. It is important for you to think clearly right now."

Berne gives four ways to identify or diagnose ego states (10, pp. 177-178): behavioral, social, phenomenological, and historical. Gesture, voice, and vocabulary are typical in each ego state for *behavioral* diagnosis. For instance, some Adult words are *how, when, where, what*—words that assess and discover facts; feelings are not reflected behaviorally in the Adult ego state. A *social* diagnosis of an ego state involves how people react to you, a *phenomenological* diagnosis is experiencing old feelings from the past in the present—for instance, a person is probably in her Child ego state if she is crying like she did as a child when her dog died. *Historically,* diagnosing an ego state means looking at the past reflected in the present. For instance, a person may be using a gesture typical of his father and will discover he is in his Parent ego state.

The next Adult question, then, can be in this instance: "Do I want to be in my Parent state right now?" This process of deciding how one wants to be socially with others or internally with self at a particular time is an exciting and provocative approach to autonomous control of life. Social work theory and practice strongly support this idea.

The functional diagram further delineates the ego states as to functions. The Parent ego state functions in a nurturing or controlling manner, the Adult has no change from the way it is in the structural diagram, and the Child is divided into the Natural Child and the Adapted Child. Berne describes the functional diagram as descriptive (6, p. 13) (see Figure 11-3). Woollams, Brown, and Huige note further delineation of the functions of the Parent ego state as negative or positive nurturing and negative or positive controlling (51, p. 2). These are helpful theoretical refinements since it allows closer diagnosis of the kind of Parenting that is going on. For instance, a mother in a negative nurturing Parent will overprotect her child and inhibit his growth, spontaneity, and social and intellectual development. This information will be helpful in diagnosis and treatment.

Contaminations occur when the ego state

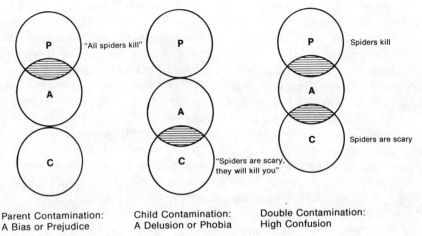

Parent Contamination: Child Contamination: Double Contamination:
A Bias or Prejudice   A Delusion or Phobia   High Confusion

Figure 11-4.

boundaries of the Child and/or Parent permeate the Adult, and Child delusions or Parental bias are seen as fact (Adult) (see Figure 11-4).

Exclusions occur when one or more ego states dominate a personality or when one ego state is not energized and functional. An unhealthy unresolved symbiosis may be present and two people may be interacting as though they have only three ego states between them; this interferes with the development of spontaneity, awareness, and intimacy (40, p. 6) (see Figure 11-5).

Jack Dusay's Egogram, defined as a "bar graph showing the relationship of the parts of the personality to each other and the amount of energy emanating outward" (15, pp. 3 and 5) is an important diagram for diagnosis and treatment. A person's Egogram may vary in different social situations (see Figure 11-6).

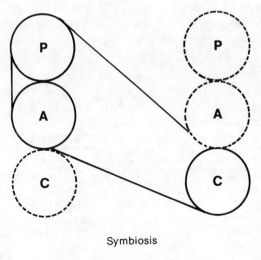

Symbiosis

⟲ = Energy not cathected
in these ego states.

Figure 11-5.

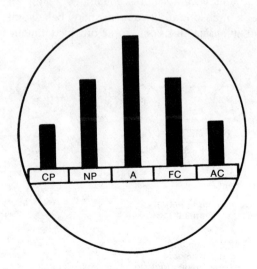

Figure 11-6.   AN EGOGRAM

Transactional Analysis—Analysis of Interaction Between People

This part of Transactional Analysis theory describes a transaction as a unit of social interaction (6) made up of a stimulus and a response, the stimulus being sent from an ego state in one person to an ego state in another person. If the response to the stimulus comes from the expected ego state, the lines are parallel. This is called a complementary transaction and the accompanying communication rule is that communication can go on indefinitely as long as the lines (vectors) are parallel. A crossed transaction occurs when the response comes from an unexpected ego state and the lines (vectors) are crossed. Then the rule is that communication will stop abruptly, and to resume, a switch in ego states will be necessary by one or both people (30, p. 79). Sometimes messages will be sent at a social level and also at a psychological level. The psychological level is hidden; the communication rule in this case is that the response given will be to the psychological message. This is adapted from Berne (6, pp. 15-19) (see Figure 11-7).

Script analysis is a significant concept for treatment since a script is defined as a life plan made in childhood; it contains many behavioral and attitudinal decisions, some of which may be interfering with satisfactory social adjustments in adult life and should be changed. Claude Steiner received the first Eric Berne Memorial in 1971 for his diagram of a script, the script matrix. The script matrix is a drawing that shows the messages a child receives when he is little (under seven years) from parents or primary caretakers (45, p. 48) (see Figure 11-8). Awareness of these messages and decisions and feelings based on the messages is part of script analysis and can provide a basis for change if change is indicated for more satisfying social interactions.

Game Analysis

A game is described by Berne as a set of ulterior transactions, repetitive in nature, with a well-defined psychological payoff (6, p. 23).

Rackets

The payoff in a game is a familiar bad feeling such as sadness, guilt, or inferiority and it is called a *racket*; the feeling has usually been with the client since childhood. Games are played to keep the racket going, structure time, get strokes, implement the script decision, and make people predictable.

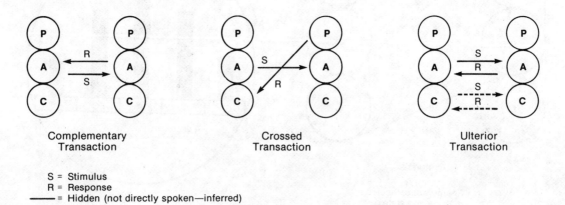

Complementary Transaction
Crossed Transaction
Ulterior Transaction

S = Stimulus
R = Response
——— = Hidden (not directly spoken—inferred)

Figure 11-7.

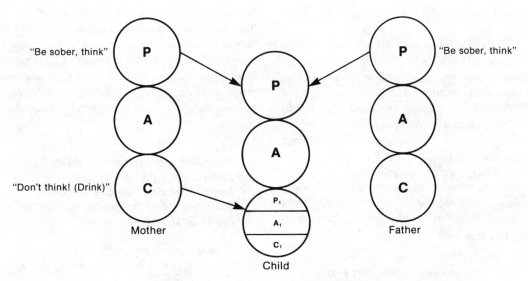

Figure 11-8.   SCRIPT MATRIX: AN ALCOHOLIC

Stamps

Some people collect bad feelings like trading stamps and, when they have saved enough, they trade their bad feelings or brown stamps in for a larger payoff. For instance, anger stamps are collected; when a person has enough, she can justify a drunken spree, a divorce, or an attempted suicide. Gold stamps are collected for good deeds. When a person saves enough gold stamps, she feels justified in taking a vacation.

Discounts

A discount is a denial of reality. Jacqui Schiff delineates three areas of discounting: self, others, and situation (41, p. 14). Games start with a discount of one of these areas. A passive, helpless-acting client is discounting self unless he is in an immediate reality crisis such as injury, loss, or abrupt change in life. Becoming aware of bad feelings and the racket system, discounting, and transacting that keeps the bad feeling present is called game analysis. Winners do not play games.

Social treatment techniques

Identification of ego states and their appropriate use brings awareness and coping power to clients. For instance, some clients worry (Adapted Child) instead of enjoy (Free Child).

A woman with a worry racket (pattern) from childhood became aware that when she had nothing to worry about in her own life, she worried about other people's problems or world problems. One day while going to work on a bus, she saw a woman and her little boy who looked "poor and unhappy"; she "couldn't forget them." On the bus, she thought of their problems, what they might be and on and on. She spent about two hours thinking. When she realized the time she spent doing this she said, "I can't believe I did that; I will never see them again probably."

Her awareness through treatment continued and she contracted to stay in her Free Child and away from pointless worry or adaptation which she learned as a little girl.

Decontaminating and Degaming

Awareness of parental bias and childish fears that interfere with clear thinking is encouraged through expression of thoughts and feelings, social discomfort, and contracting for a well-thought-out change to allow the Adult, Child, and Nuturing Parent ego states to control social functioning. Awareness of bad feelings and support of bad feelings by games can be gained through script analysis.

Script analysis is learning what early messages were received by the Child ego state and what decisions were made by the client when she was little.

> A 30 year old man whose father died suddenly and unexpectedly when he was 10 years old decided never to be committed to anything again. When he became aware of his decision using a script matrix to diagram his messages, decisions, bad feelings, games, time structuring patterns, and existential position, he contracted to start commitment again by expressing his feelings openly. This was the beginning of change and new joy for him.

Contracting

Transactional Analysis is a contractual and decisional model for change. The treatment contract is based on awareness and decision to change. The Adult ego state contracts for a change that makes sense and a change that the Child in the client wants; it is important in contracting to bring the Child of the client into the treatment plan; otherwise the plans may be sabotaged. Social workers, in family therapy especially, will appreciate the value of the client's cooperation in contracting and will enjoy the awareness that script analysis brings the client, awareness that energizes desire for change. Contracting entails work by the therapist and work by the client and considera-

tions of time competency by the therapist and time and commitment to treatment and change by the client.

The following are contracts based on awareness gained through structural analysis, script analysis, time structuring consideration, decontaminating, and analysis of stroke economy.

> "My Child (ego state) isn't dead; for awhile I thought he was, but now I can feel him moving way down under everything, and *I'm gonna dig him out*" (burst of energy with awareness).

Contracts to gain control of life and find social fulfillment or contracts to thrill a therapist:

"I'm going to start brushing my teeth."

"I'm going to live" (not kill self).

"I'm going to stay sober."

"I'm going to spend more time with Janie (wife)."

"I'm going to tell Jim how I feel."

"I'm going to smile more."

"I'm going to dance more and eat less."

Change is exciting, scary, and sometimes painful.

> Jim, who had been in weekly group treatment for about three months, decided one evening (after analyzing his script) to contract to smile more. His background was Mennonite and he had learned at home to "mask" (not to trust or get close to outsiders) his feelings and to keep them from showing in his face. He was actually (underneath) a warm, sensitive, responsive man who felt sad, socially alienated and lonely so he decided to show his warmth by smiling when it fit his feelings (Child ego state). This, of course, was risky to him since it meant going against his learned family

"protective" behavior; he did it anyway. When he returned to group the following week, he reported with a big smile that he fulfilled his contract but for the first three days, his face was so sore that it hurt to touch it. "Talk about rusty, those muscles were really out of shape," he said. "Now I feel a lot happier and like I belong!"

Redecision Therapy

Familiar bad feelings, behavior, and attitudes (rackets) such as guilt, fear, sadness, anger, pouting, yelling, discounting, cruelty, and dependency are brought to awareness by use of Gestalt techniques discussion and/or group interaction. Since decisions are made in the Child early in life, redecision work done by the Child ego state in the client is more likely to be lasting than that done from the Adult ego state (21, pp. 46-48).

The Gouldings (21, pp. 43-46) in their intensive clinical work have identified and named ten injunctions that people received from their parents and may decide to live their lives by:

1. Don't be—don't exist
2. Don't be you
3. Don't be a child
4. Don't grow
5. Don't make it
6. Don't
7. Don't be important
8. Don't belong
9. Don't be close or don't trust or don't love
10. Don't be well (sane)

Also

Don't think
Don't feel
} separate

A 48-year-old woman whose husband died nine years previous to treatment was still talking about her husband as though he were alive: "George always does that" and "I'm used to asking George" and remaining in a depressed,

stuck position. She had not separated herself from him. Working back with her sadness to early childhood allowed her to break her early symbiosis with her father, then say goodbye to her husband and begin to live again, probably for the first time fully. In the work, this woman became aware through script and structural analysis of her father's message to her: "don't grow"; she became aware that she decided not to leave her dad when she was little, and she was stuck also in not leaving her dead husband. In a piece of Gestalt double chair work, she talked with her dad when she was little and redecided to grow. She said "goodbye" to her husband, again using gestalt techniques, and decided to begin to live fully and autonomously for the first time in her life. She experienced significant relief and liberation (Child ego state).

Checking out time structuring using the six time structures often brings important awareness to a client of opportunities for needed change for better social functioning.

Permission and protection are treatment techniques that encourage and facilitate change. A therapist can give permission from all three ego states such as giving a depressed suicidal client permission to live:

Therapist:

N. Parenting: You deserve to live and enjoy yourself

Adult: It makes sense that you stay alive and then I can treat you.

Child: I want you around.

Steve Karpman would call this a bull's-eye because it reaches the client's three ego states all at once (30, p. 83).

A redecision to live or express feelings or take care of herself on the part of a client requires that the therapist offer protection for the Child ego state of the client while the change is being made. Permissions are appropriate for each childhood decision and redecision. For instance:

Decision	Permission Needed to Redecide
Don't think	OK to think
Don't feel	OK to feel
Don't get close	OK to enjoy others

Atmosphere for change

Transactional Analysis is usually done with a one-on-one approach in a group; usually less attention is paid to group interaction than in most group therapy. Group members report that through other people's work they gain awareness for change as well as when they themselves work directly with the therapist. The support and presence of the group are powerful for protection, permission, and reality testing. Transactional analysis groups, as most groups do, offer a place to try out new behavior in a supportive atmosphere.

The Child ego state of the group members is made as comfortable as possible by offering snacks, pillows, warmth, humor, and time for physical activity and relaxation (breaks). Bob Goulding at the Western Institute for Group and Family Therapy says cookies in jars, delicious fruit, and relaxing meals provide an atmosphere for the Child in the client that is like what a loving grandmother would provide, encouraging change through an energized Child ego state.

Transactional Analysis is also used with individual clients.

Versatility of transactional analysis as a social treatment method

Some Transactional Analysis therapists "think Transactional Analysis" (2, p. 351), but their clients may or may not know the theory and vocabulary. For example:

John, a 27-year-old construction worker, came for help with depression and drinking. Hearing from him about his discomfort and his daily life made it clear to me that John had felt "bossed around" when he was a child by a domineering and directive mother. His anger was old, justified anger, over not being allowed to be a child, but interfering with his life now. John contracted to express his anger as he goes in the present and to deal with the old feelings toward his mother through treatment in the group. The primary permission John needed was "do it your way" and "it's OK for you to think not drink." Thinking and spontaneity were stroked by group members and the therapist. After several months of treatment, John terminated with a plan to check back at six month intervals. He doesn't know Transactional Analysis, but the theory and techniques were used in treating him. At the end of two years, he was still without a drinking problem and was no longer depressed.

Use of transactional analysis in social work practice

Frequently clients in social work practice are confused by complex social systems that are dehumanizing. Transactional Analysis offers an approach to client advocacy and policy planning and change by "thinking Transactional Analysis" or by teaching basic Transactional Analysis theory to administrators, legislators, and executives. Policy planners can ask themselves what about the Child ego state of poverty clients, hospitalized children, or particular oppressed groups such as Blacks, Chicanos, women, men, children. What do they need? Have they had a part in planning their own system (Adult)? Everyone deserves security, joy, and a chance to impact on their world (Nurturing Parent). What is their stroke economy? Often the client will give diagnosis and a plan of action/treatment if he is heard (Nurturing Parent/Adult). Also, an important point in all social work practice is that the worker enjoys his work and finds satisfaction in it; primarily because the worker deserves it, and also because the all-too-common problem of worker "burnout" can be avoided if the workers are nurtured/stroked in the system. This way clients can have more consistency of service at less cost, and everyone benefits.

In planning a program for hospitalized children to ameliorate social/emotional stress, I used all three of my own ego states to consider what would be beneficial for all three ego states of the children. Study of research about effects of hospitalization, other programs, talking with parents and children, and knowing basic needs of children (Adult) allowed plans to go forward to nurture and support the Child (Nurturing Parent) through the following new policies:

1. Open parental visiting and parents' living-in option.
2. Play—bedside and in a special activity room for the children.
3. Learning—school and group interaction with a teacher at appropriate grade level.
4. Expression of feelings of fear, anger, separation through therapeutic play and talk.

The problem was established and my Child ego state felt good because many children would benefit and leave the hospital emotionally OK as well as physically OK.

Transactional analysis and work with confused, psychotic clients

Jacqui Schiff, a social worker and Director of the Cathexis Institiute in California, cures schizophrenia and other confusions using a Transactional Analysis approach. Her basically optimistic approach, combined with providing a protected live-in environment for change, has produced impressive and significant results for these clients (2, pp. 58-61). Basically, the work involves caring and encouraging thinking in the client to develop ways to take care of himself and to get what he needs to exist: stroking, information, basic physical needs, and permission to change. These ideas are transferable to general social treatment except for regressive techniques used at Cathexis which require a protected, live-in arrangement.

Considerable work using Transactional Analysis has been done with children, including adolescents who can learn to think and feel and ask. Delinquent adolescents have been treated (2, pp. 134-136) by Transactional Analysis with some success. Research is developing on how to do more with this.

Transactional Analysis in the public schools has grown by leaps and bounds in the last five years. Encouraging stroking in the classroom, plus expression of feelings and consideration of the teacher's Child's ego state as well as that of the student, has been a contribution of Transactional Analysis, through social workers and others trained in Transactional Analysis in the schools.

Eric Berne related body function and social emotional problems early in his work. Work on redecision in heart, cancer, asthma, and other patients is growing. Jacqui Schiff and her staff are doing research on effects of social treatment by Transactional Analysis on body function. It is becoming clearer that Flanders Dunbar was right when she related feelings to decision to live, die, go crazy, or get sick (14). Social treatment with clients like these can encourage redecision to live, be sane (think), and stay well.

Ruth McClendon and Mary Goulding of the Western Insititute for Group and Family Therapy, both social workers, have done impressive work in family therapy using Transactional Analysis concepts. Virginia Satir has also worked with the Gouldings and uses many basic Transactional Analysis tenets in her outstanding work with families.

Transactional analysis in training therapists

A unique and effective use of Transactional Analysis is in education or training of therapists. Bob and Mary Goulding, directors of the Western Institute for Group and Family Therapy, have trained hundreds of therapists using Transactional Analysis and Gestalt, combined for cognitive and affective work.

Others are using Transactional Analysis to train human service workers in agencies and universities; the clear concepts, logical cognitive approach, lucid language, and nonpathological assumptions of Transactional Analysis lend themselves to gaining self-awareness and changing while learning a potent treatment method. Students express exhilaration and excitement in this new learning experience which combines personal growth and professional development through experiential learning. This is an effective way for schools that train professionals to assume educational responsibility for providing ways for students to "know themselves" and be "self-aware."

Limitations of the effectiveness of transactional analysis

Present limitations of social treatment with Transactional Analysis are not known. There may be some limitation of effectiveness with brain damaged, mentally retarded, and character-disordered clients since the theory is highly cognitive. Even with these clients, however, effective work has been reported—notably, work with delinquents and prisoners. It remains for future research to delineate advantages and disadvantages further.

Social research and transactional analysis

Transactional analysis is being used more and more in research. Script analysis, ego-grams, and structural analysis are predictors of attitude and behavior which can provide excellent research information. Two doctoral students with whom I work at present are using Transactional Analysis in research designed to predict Parenting behavior. An interview with parents will be the basis for analysis of script issues, rackets, parental decisions, and game behavior to predict Parenting style; abusive parents and parents who have a positive, caring style will be studied.

The literature is beginning to reflect some research results with Transactional Analysis as a treatment method (55).

I have done social treatment using Transactional Analysis with asthmatic children and their families. The results were significant and exciting since the children learned to manage both wheezing and social life and the parents began to break their protective symbiotic relationship with them. This was an exploratory research. All the children missed less school, had less hospitalization, and in 80 percent of the cases used less medication after treatment. All parents reported more cooperative attitudes in the family.

Most Transactional Analysis research has involved small projects reported but not carried out long enough or broadly enough to produce conclusive findings. At the anecdotal level, many clients that I know are reporting, "I changed my life using *Transactional Analysis!*"

Transactional Analysis encourages self-management and responsibility for the quality of life; it will be important in future research to see if this social treatment method produces more self-actualization for clients.

References

1. Allen, Brian. "Liberating the Manchild," *Transactional Analysis Journal,* 2:2 (April, 1972), pp. 68-71.
2. Barnes, Graham, ed. *Transactional Analysis After Eric Berne.* New York: Harper's College Press, 1977.
3. Berne, Eric. *A Layman's Guide to Psychiatry and Psychoanalysis.* New York: Ballantine Books, 1947-1957.
4. ———. *Games People Play.* New York: Grove Press, 1964.
5. ———. *Transactional Analysis in Psychotherapy.* Palo Alto, Calif.: Science and Behavior Books, 1970.
6. ———. *What Do You Say After You Say Hello?* New York: Grove Press, 1972.
7. ———. *Sex in Human Loving.* New York: Simon and Schuster, 1970.
8. ———. "Evolution of a Script," *Transactional Analysis Bulletin,* 3:12 (October, 1964), p. 160.
9. ———. "Pathological Significance of Games," *Transactional Analysis Bulletin,* 3:12 (October, 1964), p. 160.
10. ———. *The Structure and Dynamics of Organizations and Groups.* New York: Grove Press, 1963.
11. Concannon, Joseph P. "An Adult Therapeutic Contract on a Psychiatric Ward," *Transactional Analysis Bulletin,* 5:17 (January, 1966), pp. 102-103.
12. Crossman, Patricia. "Permission and Protection," *Transactional Analysis Bulletin,* 5:19 (July, 1966), pp. 152-154.
13. Drye, Robert, Robert Goulding, and Mary E. Goulding. "No Suicide Decisions: Patient Monitoring of Suicidal Risk," *American Journal of Psychiatry,* 130:2 (February, 1973), pp. 171-175.
14. Dunbar, Flanders. *Mind and Body.* New York: Random House, 1947.
15. Dusay, John M. *Egograms—How I See You and You See Me.* New York: Harper and Row, 1977.
16. ———. "Egograms and the Constancy Hypothesis," *Transactional Analysis Journal,* 2:3 (July, 1972), pp. 37-38.
17. ———. "Eric Berne's Studies of Interaction 1949-1962," *Transactional Analysis Journal,* 1:1 (January, 1971), pp. 34-46.
18. Edwards, Mary. "The Two Parents," *Transactional Analysis Bulletin,* 7:26 (April, 1968), pp. 37-39.
19. English, Fanita. "Episcript and the Hot Potato Game," *Transactional Analysis Bulletin,* 8:32 (October, 1969), p. 77.
20. Ernst, Franklin. "The O.K. Corral," *Transactional Analysis Journal,* 1:4 (October, 1971), pp. 33-41.
21. Goulding, Robert L. and Mary E. Goulding. "Injunctions, Decisions, and Redecisions," *Transactional Analysis Journal,* 6:1 (January, 1976), pp. 41-48.
22. Goulding, Robert L. "New Directions in Transactional Analysis, Creating an Environment for Change," in Sager and Kaplan, *Progress in Group and Family Therapy.* New York: Brunner/Mazel, 1972, pp. 105-134.
23. ———. "Thinking and Feeling in Transactional Analysis: Three Empasses," *Voices: The Art and Science of Psychotherapy,* 2:1 (1975), issue 39.
24. ———. "Decisions in Script Formation," *Transactional Analysis Journal,* April, 1972, p. 91.

25. Harris, Amy. "Good Guys and Sweethearts," *Transactional Analysis Journal,* 2:1 (January, 1972), pp. 59-61.
26. Holloway, William. "The Crazy Child in the Parent," *Transactional Analysis Journal,* 2:3 (July, 1972), pp. 32-34.
27. James, Muriel and Dorothy Jongeward. *Born To Win.* Reading, Mass.: Addison-Wesley, 1971.
28. James, Muriel. "The Down-Scripting of Women for 115 Generations: A Historical Kaleidoscope," *Transactional Analysis Journal,* 4:1 (January, 1973), pp. 15-22.
29. Kahler, Taibi and Hedges Capers. "The Miniscript," *Transactional Analysis Journal,* 4:1 (January, 1974), pp. 26-42.
30. Karpman, Stephen, M.D. "Options," *Transactional Analysis Journal,* 1:1 (January, 1971), pp. 79-87.
31. ———. "Fairy Tales and Script Drama Analysis," *Transactional Analysis Journal,* 7:26 (April, 1968). pp. 39-44.
32. Kupfer, D. "Social Dynamics on Stroking," *Transactional Analysis Bulletin,* 1:2 (April, 1962), p. 9.
33. Lynch, James J. *The Broken Heart.* New York: Basic Books, 1977.
34. Maslow, Abraham H. *The Farther Reaches of Human Nature.* New York: Viking Press, 1971.
35. May, Rollo. *The Courage to Create.* New York: Norton, 1975.
36. Montagu, Ashley. *Touching: The Human Significance of the Skin.* New York: Harper and Row, 1971.
37. Perls, Frederick S. *Gestalt Therapy Verbatim.* Utah: Real People Press, 1959.
38. Polster, Irving and Miriam. *Gestalt Therapy: Integrated Contours of Theory and Practice.* New York: Brunner/Mazel, 1973.
39. Schiff, Aaron and Jacqui. "Passivity," *Transactional Analysis Journal,* 1:1 (January, 1971), pp. 71-78.
40. Schiff, Jacqui. "Reparenting in Schizophrenia," *Transactional Analysis Bulletin,* 8:31 (September, 1969), pp. 45-71.
41. ———. *Cathexis Reader.* New York: Harper and Row, 1975.
42. Seligman, Martin, ed. *Helplessness—On Depression, Development and Death.* San Francisco: Freeman, 1975.
43. Spitz, Rene. "Hospitalism, Genesis of Psychiatric Conditions in Early Childhood," *Psychoanalytic Study of the Child* (1945), pp. 53-74.
44. Steiner, Claude. "A Little Boy's Dream," *Transactional Analysis Journal,* 1:1 (January, 1971), pp. 49-60.
45. ———. *Games Alcoholics Play.* New York: Grove Press, 1971.
46. ———. "The Stroke Economy," *Transactional Analysis Journal,* 1:3 (July, 1971), pp. 9-15.
47. ———. "A Script Checklist," *Transactional Analysis Bulletin,* 6:22 (April, 1967), pp. 38-40, 56.
48. ———. "Script and Counterscript," *Transactional Analysis Bulletin,* 2:6 (April, 1966), pp. 133-135.
49. ———. *Scripts People Live.* New York: Grove Press, 1974.
50. Twomey, John F. "A Transactional Theory for the Treatment of 'Hardcore' Social Offenders," *Transactional Analysis Bulletin,* 7:28 (October, 1968), pp. 96-97.
51. Woollams, Stanley, Michael Brown, and Kristyn Huige. *Transactional Analysis in Brief.* Ann Arbor, Mich.: Huron Valley Institute, 1974.

52. Woollams, Stanley J., M.D. "Formation of the Script," *Transactional Analysis Journal,* 3:1 (January, 1973), pp. 31-37.
53. Wyckoff, Hogie. "The Stroke Economy in Women's Scripts," *Transactional Analysis Journal,* 1:3 (July, 1971), pp. 16-20.
54. Yalom, Irving D. *The Theory and Practice of Group Psychotherapy,* 2nd ed. New York: Basic Books, 1975.
55. ——, Morton Lieberman, and Matthew B. Miles. *Encounter Groups: First Facts.* New York: Basic Books, 1973.

Annotated listing of key references

BARNES, Graham (Editor). *Transactional Analysis After Eric Berne.* New York: Harper's College Press, 1977.

> *This is an impressive collection of expressive writings reflecting the heart of the work of many students of Eric Berne who are leaders in Transactional Analysis now and who are also creative, potent therapists. Many of the writers are old friends of Eric's who spent time with him at the early Carmel and San Francisco seminars as he was developing and refining his Transactional Analysis concepts. The work of four Transactional Analysis leaders, Robert Goulding, Mary Goulding, Jacqui Schiff, and Jack Dusay, with their respectively developed schools of Transactional Analysis, is featured. The work of other vibrant, creative therapists such as Ruth McClenden, Fanita English, Stan Woollams, Bill Holloway, and others presents Transactional Analysis and family therapy, script work, various therapeutic styles, and clinical and historical information about Transactional Analysis.*

BERNE, Eric. *What Do You Say After You Say Hello?* New York: Grove Press, 1972.

> *This is an exciting, intellectually provocative presentation of Berne's major Transactional Analysis concepts—games, rackets, strokes, time structuring, Three Basic Hungers, and scripts—in his thoughtful and fun-loving way. Some detailed description of theory development and additions are presented, such as adding the "crossup" in the game formula and calling it "Formula G." He discusses the beginnings of games when children are young and formulating their script and life plan. Considerable material is presented on scripts.*

BERNE, Eric. *Structure and Dynamics of Organizations and Groups.* New York: Grove Press, 1963.

> *This book contains extensive information on Berne's game theory, time structuring in groups related to games and rackets, and early life scripts reflected in behavior attitude and feelings of members of treatment groups. He presents diagrams of groups: seating, authority, organizational, group process diagnosis, and transactional diagrams. He discusses "ailing" groups and a new word group "image," or how individuals will relate to peers and authority persons based on early childhood decisions.*

JONGEWARD, Dorothy and Muriel James. *Born to Win.* Reading, Mass.: Addison-Wesley, 1971.

> *This is a warm, sensitive, positive, and optimistic book about many social truths that Transactional Analysis supports, such as that persons are OK and that awareness can lead to change. Information about stroking, scripts, structural analysis, games, and all significant concepts are presented with exercises after the chapters for experiential experiments on application of the*

theory. A very popular and well received introduction to Transactional Analysis.

WOOLLAMS, Stanley, Micheal Bown, and Kristyn Huige. *Transactional Analysis in Brief*. Ann Arbor, Mich.: Huron Valley Institute, 1974. *The authors present a clear, succinct creative review of basic Transactional Analysis theory with illuminating diagrams and examples. A significant and useful contribution to Transactional Analysis literature for therapist and client.*

12
Meditation and Social Work Treatment

by

THOMAS KEEFE

Meditation is an ancient discipline wedded to several major psychophilosophical systems arising from diverse cultures. Among others, American Indian, Central Asian Sufi, Hindu, Chinese Taoist, widespread Buddhist, and some Christian traditions have cultivated forms of meditation as a source of spiritual enrichment and personal growth. Now meditation has begun its marriage to the rational-empirical tradition of western science. In this most recent alliance it will be tested, objectified, stripped of its mystical trappings, and enriched with empirical understanding. And, with its beauty still intact, at last accepted as valuable to the human endeavor.

Meditation, therefore, is still experimental. Although testing is under way and final acceptance is some time away, the potential of meditation in psychotherapy and social work treatment has been recognized by some. Meditation is a method that is adjunctive to

social work treatment. Its potential in treating a variety of problems and persons is becoming clear. Yet meditation as a method will demand much from, and occasionally will challenge, the theories underlying social work treatment for its full description and explanation.

Description and explanation: the mind as an open hand

Meditation is a set of behaviors. Some of the consequences of meditation are directly observable; others can be indirectly inferred. Meditation here does not refer to the mind's wandering and floating in fantasy or to the mind's laboring along a tight line of logic toward a solution. In contradistinction to these common western notions, meditation is the deliberate cultivation of a state of mind exclusive of both fantasy and logic. While there are several varieties of meditation, they share some common characteristics which shall be described in detail to provide an overview of the method.

In essence, meditation is the development—or discovery, depending on your orientation—of consciousness independent of visual and verbal symbols that constitute what we call thought. It is the deliberate cultivation of a mental state conducive to intuition. Meditation usually pairs a relaxed state of the body with an attentive focus of the mind. A brief description of this common process in meditation will help orient us to the method.

One meditates by focusing attention upon a single thing. This may be a sound, *mantra,* a design, *mandala* (17), an object, a part of the body, a mental image, or a prayer. This ostensibly simple task is in fact extremely difficult for most people. Internal dialogues, monologues, images, and emotions constantly interrupt the task to break one's attention. Meditation then becomes a task of (1) continually noticing the intrusion of a thought, (2) recognizing or naming the loss of attention, e.g., "thinking," "feeling," "remembering," etc., and (3) letting go of the chain of associations to return to the meditation object. This task of refocusing attention and cultivating an attitude of noninvolvement to the distracting chains of association that would pull the meditator from his object of attention constitutes meditation for the beginner. *The mind becomes like an open hand. Nothing is clung to, nothing is pushed away.*

While meditating, distractions by the stream of thought seem to present themselves in a hierarchy of personal importance. Those incidents of the recent past evoking the most anxiety or anger seem to intrude first. These are followed by memories or anticipations of increasingly remote concern. Thoughts, images, and feelings well up, momentarily distract, and if not clung to or elaborated upon, burn themselves out. When paired with the relaxed state of the body and followed by refocus upon the pleasantness of the meditation object, a *global desensitization (12)* of cathected thoughts

and images occurs. Increasing equanimity and objectivity secure the meditator in an attitude of observation of the symbolic self and ego and constituent concerns.

The meditation behaviors of focusing attention, recognizing when attention is interrupted, sometimes naming the nature of the interruption—e.g., "thinking," "feeling," "remembering," etc.—and deliberately refocusing attention are readily recognized as forms of discrimination learning (14). Perceptions, thoughts, and feelings are discriminated from the meditation object. Slowly, the capacity to discriminate thoughts and feelings from any focus of attention is developed. The meditator discriminates memory and anticipation, fear and guilt from the immediate focus of attention. He cultivates a present centeredness. As this learning to discriminate the ingredients of consciousness or contents of mind becomes easier an *observer self*, also called *watcher self* (6, p. 135) or *witness* (28, p. 178), emerges. The observer self is helpful in a variety of areas of functioning.

We must be very clear that the observer self is not an alienated, depersonalized, or neurotic self sustained by dissociative processes or suppression of thought and emotion. It is, instead, a secure subjectivity that allows full experience without judgment, defense, or elaboration. In the cultivation of this observer self of meditation there emerge several psychofunctional capacities to be taken up below and elaborated further as we examine meditation as a technique in personality change.

Capacities learned in meditation

For us who are involved in social work treatment, examining the learnings transferred from meditation practice into the psychosocial functioning of the meditator may prove valuable. This is one of our own cultural mechanisms for integrating meditation behavior within our own psychophilosophical traditions.

The learnings transferred from meditation are best termed "capacities," and there are several of them.

The *capacity to focus attention on a single thing or task* is enhanced. This is called *one-pointedness-of-mind.* When carried over into everyday life, tasks undertaken with this state of mind are completed with less distraction and with the expenditure of less wasted energy. The Buddhists call this state of mind, carried into everyday life, *right mindfulness* (4, p. 30).

The *capacity to discriminate among internal stimuli,* such as memories, fears, anger, etc., provides a measure of enhanced self-awareness useful in empathic relating and communicating of one's responses in social situations. The capacity to view with a degree of objectivity and nonattached concern these internal processes allows enhanced performance in complex behaviors. Consider the snow skier. Skiing requires concentration. As speed increases and the slope becomes more steep and varied in surface, concentration must intensify. If the skier becomes suddenly preoccupied with a distant dropoff, or with an intruding and distracting fear of falling, his concentration is broken and falling is more likely. The clutched athlete, the self-conscious speaker, the ego-involved attorney are all momentarily off their present time center—far from their observer self.

Finally, an *altered mode of perception* is cultivated in the meditation process. The passive-receptive phase of perception, wherein one allows the senses to be stimulated delaying cognitive structuring and allowing the things perceived to speak for themselves, is enhanced in meditation. Psychologists Sidney Jourard (16) and Abraham Maslow (11) both described this form of perception as necessary to supplement the more active, structured, need-oriented perception typical of western consciousness. Thera described the Buddhist view of this perceptual mode generated in meditation as *bare attention.* Thera elaborated:

It cleans the object of investigation from the impurities of prejudice and passion; it frees it from alien admixtures and from points of view most pertaining to it; it holds it firmly before the eye of wisdom, by slowing down the transition from the receptive to the active phase of the perceptual or cognitive process, thus giving a vastly improved chance for close and dispassionate investigation. (36, pp. 34-35)

In sum, we see the results of meditation behaviors as including such global capacities as relaxation, desensitization of changed stimuli, enhanced discrimination, concentration of attention, self-awareness, intentional present centeredness, development of a secure observer self, and augmented perceptual modes. Each of these factors has implications for enhanced personal and interpersonal functioning. Moreover, meditation behaviors are used to counter specific behaviors seen as symptomatic or problematic for clients. These include anxiety, some forms of depression, phobic reactions, interpersonal difficulties, and others. Generally arising from traditions that are unhampered by notions of health and illness in relation to human behavior, meditation has been used in the personal growth and consciousness development of the normal person or the select initiates of particular orders. Meditation, therefore, has been used as a tool to extend the potential of practitioners, and it has been oriented toward the possible rather than the merely adequate or healthy in human functioning. Consequently, there are several ramifications for social work treatment. Meditation has, as shall be seen later, potential for the social work practitioner as well as for the client. It requires no predisposing diagnosis for its use—although there are definite contraindicators—and it has potential for use with individuals, families, groups, and in community settings. The foregoing suggests that an appreciation of the origins of meditation in the psychophilosophical traditions of other cultures and a tracing of its path into the helping professions will supplement our understanding of its potential as a tool in social work treatment.

Origins and paths into social work treatment

The origins of meditation are paradoxical. It comes to us from diverse cultures and traditions. Yet meditation forms, whatever their source, express a common origin in man's intuitive modes of thought. As an example, the zazen meditation of Zen Buddhism has its origin with the intuitive enlightenment of Siddhartha Gautama, Buddha in about 544 B.C. (4, p. 21). Siddhartha was said to have led a life of wealth and indulgence and then a life of asceticism in his spiritual quest to find the cause of suffering in the world. After relinquishing these extremes of self-preoccupation his answer and enlightenment came. His *Four Noble Truths* together with his Eightfold Path served as transmission and intuitive insight into his wisdom for centuries. The Buddha's noble Eightfold Path includes meditation as one of the paths to spiritual freedom from suffering (4, p. 30). Thus, it is a central practice in all branches of Buddhism, although characteristic variations have developed in each different tradition.

Buddhism is thought to have been carried from the northern India of Siddhartha to China in 520 A.D. by Bodhidharma(22, p. 302). There the Indian *dhyana* became the Chinese *Ch'an.* Influenced by Taoism in China, meditation was transmitted to medieval Japan, where it is referred to as *Zen,* which literally means "meditation." Zen found its way to the West by several routes and has been popularized by D. T. Suzuki (35), Allen Watts (38), and others.

But Zen is only one form of meditation that has ancient and divergent cultural origins. In fact, meditation has been an important practice in the major world religions: Hinduism, Confucianism, Taoism, Buddhism, Judaism, Islam, and Christianity.

For centuries in India, meditation was taught in the oral traditions of the Hindu Vedas. Then, sometime before 300 B.C., some of these traditions of meditation were written in the *Yoga Sutras* of Patanjali (40). The techniques used in yoga include mantras, visualizations, breath control, and concentration on various postures or parts of the body. The purpose of yoga meditation is to unify the body, mind, and spirit allowing an individual to become whole, integrated, and functioning as *Atman,* a godlike higher self (29). Ultimately, union with Brahman, or God, is achieved. The *Bhagavad-Gita* (c. 200 B.C.) suggests meditation as one of three main ways to achieve freedom from *Karma* (29) or the world of cause and effect.

In China, Confucius recommended meditation as a part of personal cultivation. Later it became the central feature of the Lu Chiu-Yuan school of Neo-Confucianism. Taoists during the same period in China also used meditation to facilitate mystical harmony with the Tao (41).

Some types of Jewish mysticism incorporate meditation to achieve metaphysical insights. Philo of Alexandria (c. 15 B.C.–40 A.D.) and other Jewish scholars in the Middle Ages used this type of meditation (7, p. 183).

From the twelfth century A.D., Sufism, a popular folk Islam, has encouraged various types of meditation as well as other techniques such as whirling to induce trance. Meditation is considered to be an important remembrance of God. It is also used to facilitate perceptions of inner reality (1).

Christianity, too, is rich in traditions using a variety of meditative techniques, from the early Christian Gnostics to the medieval monasteries to eighteenth-century Greek Orthodox teachings. In fact, some of the clearest original training manuals include *The Philokalia* (Greek Orthodox) and *The Way of Perfection* by St. Theresa of Avila (25, p. 26).

Interestingly, the philosophies of the Yogic and Buddhist meditators are reflected in their contrasting meditation behaviors. For example, most Yogic meditators seem to cultivate a *habituation effect* (28, pp. 52-56, 178) to the object of meditation and experience a loss of perception of the object or a "blending" with it. This subjective experience of habituation corresponds with productivity of alpha waves that accompany relaxed awareness. These Yogic meditators reduce awareness of outside stimuli and experience a blissful indifference sometimes called *samadhi*. For the Yogi, *samadhi* is a high state of self-transcendent consciousness, a link with the godhead or universal consciousness to be attained through rigor and single-minded devotion.

Like the Yogic meditators, advanced Zen meditators undergo the habituation effect and record increased alpha wave productivity. However, when exposed to outside stimuli while meditating, they respond with sharp, momentary attention as evidenced by corresponding short bursts of beta wave productivity. These meditators seem to be able to respond repeatedly to external stimuli without habituating to them. Psychologist Robert Ornstein suggests that they are responding without constructing a visual model or verbal label for the intruding stimulus, perceiving it clearly each time (28, p. 179). For the Buddhist, the state of *nirvana*, analogous to *samadhi*, is attained but rejected by the protagonist in favor of an act of compassion. This act is to enter the world in a state of wisdom, or *prajna*, there to undertake the work of bringing other sentient beings—or aspects of the larger consciousness—to enlightenment. In interesting ways, then, the responses of meditators parallel the doctrines of their traditions. Given these parallels found in other traditions, it seems natural that meditation should become a part of western therapeutic traditions. The reciprocal influences between meditation and social work should be exciting.

While meditation comes to the West by many paths, it has far from penetrated to all parts of our industrial culture. Professional social work, a byproduct of the industrial market system, is itself relatively new in man's endeavors. The path of meditation is a new trail in social work. It comes to the profession at a time when variety and eclecticism are the norm. As the instability, contradictions, and stresses of the socioeconomic structure create a frenetic search for relevant modes of treatment, medita-

tion will perhaps be another technique to be taken up in the interest of more effective practice.

This vision of the reasons for the profession's interest in meditation is not meant to be derogatory. Basically because of the contradictions and instability of the economic system, we live in an age of anxiety. Meditation may fill a symbolic and practical need in our personal and professional psyches. To face the fragmentation and contradictions of our lives, a safe and quiet place to recollect, sort out, and relax is a natural balm. Moreover, if meditation is more than a clinical adjunct technique but is also a facilitator of other social work skills and a precursor to action as well, it has relevance for the profession as a whole.

Meditation is used or discussed by various psychologists and psychiatrists. Psychologists using biofeedback apparatus are naturally drawn to meditative techniques and their work influences social work colleagues.

Meditation as an aid for the psychotherapist (19) and in the development of empathic skill (18) has been proposed and examined. Both endeavors have generated interest among clinical social workers and social work educators. The author's interest was spurred by his own experience with meditation. By the time of this writing some other workers must have had experience with meditation, especially Transcendental Meditation (3), and incorporated it into their work. While a good fix upon the extent of its use is difficult without a study, one can assume that as more findings are reported in the literature, more interest will be generated in the social work profession.

As noted in the historical origins of meditation, the technique has been refined for personal growth and positive behavior change in several cultural traditions. In each of these traditions meditation is linked to conceptualizations that explain the subjective experiences of meditation and the behavioral and psychosocial outcomes for practitioners. Each culture has placed meditation within its own context. To use meditation as an adjunct to psychotherapy and social work treatment is to place it within a western rational, technological, cultural context. In so doing, we can refine and extend meditation technique and at the same time enrich our own tradition.

Assessing meditation in western terms links the technique and its experience and outcomes to those major theories of personality and treatment used in the assessment.

Meditation, the personality, and personality change

The experience and outcomes of meditation related to the organization of the personality extend western psychodynamic conceptualizations. We will be concerned with those areas relevant to psychodynamically oriented social work treatment where modifications or extensions of theory are suggested.

The ego or symbolic self in traditional Freudian theory is thought to form in the necessity of symbolizing real objects that meet our needs. Our capacity to symbolize allows deferred gratification in keeping with social reality. Thus, symbol formulation is seen as necessary to creation of meaning and social interaction. Meditation experience does not refute these perspectives, but it does challenge certain assumptions underlying them.

First, the symbolic self or ego is experienced as a network of verbal and visual symbols linked to emotional or physiological responses. However, as already described, the meditator can develop a capacity to observe the symbolic self as if from a vantage point of equanimity. In meditation the emotions, internal dialogue, and visualizations are recognized, experienced vividly, and sometimes labeled, but they do not become self-perpetuating. As suggested earlier, the advanced meditator generalizes certain capacities learned in meditation to daily functioning. These are the capacities to (1) *discriminate* memory, fantasy, worry, the ac-

companying emotional content and present time perceptions, (2) *decide* which cognitive or emotional responses will become stimuli to further responses and which will not. In learning these two faculties, the meditator cultivates the observer self. In describing a form of Zen breath meditation useful in psychotherapy, psychologist Gary Deatherage suggests:

> If a patient is taught over time to note interruptions in breath observation and to label each interruption with neutral terms such as "remembering," "fantasizing," "hearing," "thinking," or "touching," he will quickly discover a rather complicated, but comforting, situation where there is one aspect of his mental "self" which is calm and psychologically strong, and which can watch, label, and see the melodramas of other "selves" which get so involved in painful memories of the past or beautiful and escapist fantasies of the future. By helping the patient to identify for a time with a strong and neutral "watcher self" there begins to develop within him the strength, motivation, and ability to fully participate in, and benefit from, whatever other forms of psychotherapy are being provided to him. (6, p. 136)

For the meditator, then, the ego or symbolic self is not the only locus of experience. There is an undifferentiated or unconditioned awareness upon which the symbols and felt physiological responses play—like a drama before a mirror.

The process of meditation occupies the focal attention of the rational, linear, verbal (usually left hemisphere) function of the personality. Meanwhile a diffuse, nonlinear awareness emerges before the observer self. The meditator experiences the larger linkages of his symbolically constructed self with the past, present, and future world. This experience of the "larger self" has again and again been described as ineffable, uncommunicable. This is because our verbal, logical self must focus on single components of what is a panorama of perception and experience undifferentiated in time—past, present, or future—and space—here, elsewhere, etc. Because only portions of our more diffuse, intuitive (usually right lobe) awareness can be the focus of the narrow beam of our focal attention, only portions of our larger consciousness are immediately accessible to our verbal-logical, verbal-conscious self. This notion of a larger self separate from what we have called our conscious self has recently provoked much interest.

In 1977, in "Meditation and the Unconscious: A New Perspective," John Welwood hypothesized that the *unconscious* of traditional Freudian and Jungian theory limited our understanding of human functioning. In essence, Welwood postulated that the phenomena defined as evidence of an unconscious—forgetting, slips of the tongue, laughter, habit, neurotic symptoms, and dreams—are evidence that we function outside our ordinary focal attention (39). Rather than postulate an internal, unknowable psychic region inhabited by instincts, Welwood suggested that we might envision a focal attention that defines the *figure* in a universal *ground* of perception and awareness. For Welwood, the ground is not simply an internal structure. Instead, the ground is comprised of felt meanings, patterns of personal meanings, ways the organism is attuned to patterns and currents of the universe, and the immediate presence.

While Welwood's particular definition of ground is very different from traditional concepts of the unconscious, the conceptualization of ground is descriptive of the way in which the meditator experiences those aspects of awareness not labeled conscious in traditional psychodynamic terms. In meditation, the ego or symbolic self does not dissolve. The meditator does not become "egoless."

Meditation, instead, facilitates the realization of the *socially conditioned* nature of the self. That each person has a history of conditioning by the interpersonal context of his world, that he can attend to or be conscious of only a small part of his own social programming at a given time, and that meditation is a means for liberating him from social conditioning are the fruits gained in meditation. These are the sources of personality change in meditation.

In light of meditation, then, the personality is not structured into conscious-unconscious components. Rather, it is a web of interlacing symbolic meanings, each rooted in the social world. The self is like an eddy in a stream. In a sense, it is illusory.

In cultivating an observer self, the meditator grasps the illusory nature of the symbolically constructed self. Conflicts, anxiety arousing ideas, and repetition compulsions are the experienced components of this symbolic self. Seen from the vantage of an observer self, their power and control of response are rendered impotent. Hence, the advanced meditator discriminates the sources of problems and decides with a degree of objectivity alternative lines of action. As the anxiety or anger related to particular incidents or situations is desensitized in the relaxed state of meditation, their power and control are further diminished as the capacity for intentional decision about behavior and responses is increased. Treatment is facilitated when these behaviors are a component of the treatment endeavor. As psychotherapist Gary Deatherage puts it:

> By becoming aware of the intentional process, one can then intercept and cancel unwanted words or deeds before they are manifested in behavior—something many patients find useful since it places control of their own behavior back at the conscious level. (6, p. 136)

These experiences and outcomes of meditation, therefore, extend and modify traditional psychodynamic perspectives, particularly with regard to the nature and function of the unconscious.

The traditional cultural contexts of meditation universally interject their own myths to supplant critical observation of what exactly comprises the conditioning of the psychosocial self. Communication science, social psychology, symbolic interactionism, sociology, and other western sciences fill the void of the processes that actually condition the self. However, even western psychologists and therapists who have taken up the practice and systematic study of meditation fall back to philosophical musings when the parameters of the interpersonal ground are defined. Some use the language of mysticism and speak of the larger self or cosmic consciousness, to which each small ego is linked and of which each person is a small manifestation. This language is very global and a more precise and critical view of the social realities should not be abandoned for a blind belief or mystification of social realities.

Social work, with its particularly broad orientation toward human behavior and the social environment, has a particular contribution to make toward an understanding of this larger ground of the self. Social workers are cognizant of the extent to which social conditions interact with the individual psyche and condition its nature, prospects, and levels of awareness. Briefly extending this orientation, Marx postulated that the economic organization or structure of society conditions the social and ideological life of a society (26, p. 159). We might caution, then, that the global language of mystical traditions must not supplant critical analysis of the experiences of meditation, for they are behaviors that may carry over into daily functioning with positive benefit to the practitioner's personality and social functioning.

Personality exchange

Physical relaxation, concentration of attention, desensitization of anxiety-arousing thoughts, discrimination of thoughts from other stimuli, insight into behaviors and events, and cultivation of an observer self are outcomes of meditation that enhance psychosocial functioning.

First, learning to be more self-aware—aware of feelings and motivations—can inform one's responses to interpersonal situations. As we shall learn later, the self-awareness of meditation facilitates sensing and then communicating one's responses to others—both behaviors conducive to empathy. Glueck and Stroebel, in their study of the effects of meditation and biofeedback in treatment of psychotherapy patients, made detailed observations of the physiological changes occurring during meditation. They found that Transcendental Meditation generated recordable electroencephalographic changes in the brain that parallel relaxation. They think that the repeated sound, mantra, is the direction of relaxation which eventually involves both the dominant and nondominant hemispheres of the brain. This response is functional to self-understanding and psychotherapy by allowing "repressed" material to come into consciousness more quickly, permitting more rapid recovery of patients than therapeutic treatment (10).

Second, learning to relax through meditation is conducive to managing anxiety-related problems. For example, Shapiro found Zen meditation combined with behavioral self-control techniques effective in reducing anxiety and stress in a client experiencing generalized anxiety and a feeling of being controlled by external forces (34). In overcoming insomnia in patients, Woolfolk et al. found that meditation derived attention-focusing techniques as effective as progressive relaxation exercises in reducing the onset of sleep. Both meditation and relaxation were effective in improving patients beyond controls on six-month follow-up (41).

Third, combining self-awareness and the capacity intentionally to relax permits an individual to transfer behaviors learned in meditation to other realms of life where there is undue stress or excessive stimulation that would hamper objective or reasoned functioning. Two studies suggest that meditation may be useful for alcohol abusers and addicts to reduce anxiety, discriminate stimuli that evoke the problematic habits, and cultivate an "internal locus of control" (8, p. 2). One might also reason that anxiety-arousing stimuli are less likely to become self-perpetuating in the symbolic system if they are discriminated and desensitized in the meditative process. For example, some individuals have associated worry over coming events with positive outcomes of those events. Worry, intermittently rewarded, is likely to persist, complete with fantasized negative outcomes, anxiety, and preoccupation (5, p. 94). Meditation enables the individual to discriminate worrisome fantasy and to observe its impact upon the body and overall functioning. Desensitization and a secure observer self enable the individual to recognize worry, minimize its effects, and allow worrisome thoughts to burn themselves out without negative consequences. As the observer self is cultivated, the normal state of consciousness of modern westerners, complete with split attention, worry, preoccupation, and anxiety can be sharpened to a mindfulness in which attention is voluntarily riveted to the action at hand. Preoccupation with oneself and how one is performing, worry over consequences, and wandering attention interfere less in the tasks one has decided to do. In a sense, the self is lost in the activity.

Fourth, observation and discrimination of one's thoughts in meditation enable the meditator to use thoughts and images more as tools to represent reality, to communicate, and to serve as intentional guides to action than as illusory and unintentional substitutes for real circumstances. Symbols and cognitive constructs no longer interfere with clear present-time perceptions.

Finally, meditation as discrimination training may have specific usefulness in managing depression. In her article, "Learned Helplessness," social worker Carol Hooker reviewed literature suggesting that reactive depression is dynamically similar to experimentally induced states of learned helplessness in ex-

perimental animals (15). The work of Seligman and others (31, 32) suggests that one may learn in effect not to learn when repeatedly subjected to noxious circumstances over which one can find no mastery or control. Under such conditions one learns that there is no escape, no solution other than an unresponsive withdrawal with little or no mobility, eye contact, or normal need-fulfilling behaviors. Hooker, drawing on the work of Beck (2), sees this learned helplessness as having cognitive components in humans wherein all known avenues of mastery and solution have been tried or rehearsed to no effect. Action and effort have no effect on circumstances. Beliefs about one's ineffectiveness sustain a depressive reaction. Loss of a loved one to death, for example, is an insoluble trauma. Repetition of guilt-evoking thoughts, self-deprecation, and beliefs that there is no future without the deceased may in some cases sustain depression for extended periods. Meditation may help the depressed person to regain a sense of self separate from the dilemma, partially sustained in the symbol system. Traumatic thoughts associated with the event are desensitized and one learns increasing mastery over the contents of one's depression sustaining ruminations. Eventually, thoughts that constitute new tasks and new opportunities for mastery and rehearsal of new roles to play can be sustained intentionally and used as guides for action and mastery. Similar processes used with cautions, elaborated below, may be therapeutic for persons with thought disorders. In other words, observation of thinking, not building upon associations and becoming "lost in thought," is the intent of meditation for enhanced discrimination.

In summary, meditation is an adjunct to treatment of a potentially wide variety of problems. There are, as suggested in the discussion of depression, certain problems that should not be approached with meditation except with intense supervision by workers skilled in treatment of both the problem and meditation. While much needed definitive studies that show direct contraindications for the use of meditation are not available at this time, some guidelines are emerging.

Cautions and contraindications

In the author's experience, some people find meditation more suited to their temperament than others. Also , certain severe disorders make the correct practice of meditation difficult or impossible.

Anxious but organized persons seem to take to meditation quickly. Relaxation and learning control over focal attention is rewarding and rather immediate. With very anxious, driven people, however, a caution is in order. Meditation of the Zen type, which requires a continued refocusing to the breath of another object of attention, or of those Yogic types that require strict postures and attention can become a do-or-die endeavor. Individuals may incorrectly feel compelled to suppress thoughts and emotions. Or they may force their breath in an unnatural way rather than following their natural breathing systems. Often this response is not unlike their life style, in which they constantly push themselves to perform or conform without attention to their own desires and physical needs. The attitude of wakeful awareness is misinterpreted as rigid attention where all interruptions are excluded before their full perception. Sometimes the body is not held relaxed, but rigid and tense. With such persons the point must be made clear that they are to let go of interrupting thoughts, not push them away and not compulsively follow them. The analogy of the mind as an open hand, neither pushing away nor grasping, is useful in interpreting the correct attitude. In any case, the worker or therapist must make sure that the client is meditating and not magnifying anxiety, building anxiety-provoking images, or obsessing an improbable chain of associations about hypothetical destructive interpersonal events or outcomes.

Depressed persons may potentially benefit a great deal or they may stand to magnify their depressions if not correctly instructed or supervised. As indicated above, some therapists see cognitive processes as giving rise to the affective components and other responses in reactive depression. Learned helplessness or belief in one's inability to have any effect upon noxious situations is in keeping with this perspective. As suggested, meditation may be useful in the individual's learning to discriminate beliefs about his own ineffectiveness or hopelessness from beliefs about mastery, coping, and constructive response rehearsal. This use of meditation in depression allows the self nurturing or constructive ideas to be identified and used as guides to action and recovery. But the potential is present in the depressed person to use meditation time as a period of rumination on destructive, suicidal, or self-effacing thoughts without an effort to discriminate notions, giving them more and more power. Discussion of each meditation session with guidance about the mental contents and processes is a necessity in using meditation in treatment of depression. For example, helping the client to communicate the feelings that have emerged, to sort out personally destructive or effacing thoughts, and to construct images and ideas as guides for action is the appropriate post-meditation-session procedure for depressed persons.

Two authors have discussed use of meditation by persons who suffer severe mental problems or who are labeled psychotic or schizophrenic. Gary Deatherage, in discussing limitations on the use of Buddhist mindfulness meditation in psychotherapy, cautions, "While this psychotherapeutic approach is extremely effective when employed with patients suffering from depression, anxiety, and a wide variety of neurotic symptoms, a caution should be issued regarding its use with patients experiencing actively psychotic symptoms such as hallucinations, delusions, thinking disorders, and severe withdrawal" (6, p. 142). Deatherage goes on to note that the particular meditation technique for self-observation requires "an intact and functional rational component of mind, as well as sufficient motivation on the part of the patient to cause him to put forth the effort to do that observation" (6, p. 142). Arnold Lazarus, discussing psychiatric problems possibly precipitated by Transcendental Meditation, cautions that his clinical observations have led him to hypothesize that T.M. does not seem to be effective with people classified as hysterical reactions or strong depressive reactions. He speculates that "some 'schizophrenic' individuals might experience an increase in 'depersonalization' and self preoccupation" (24).

In general, then, clients or patients with severe disorders, whose reality testing, perception, and logical thinking are such that they cannot fully understand meditation instructions or follow through with actual meditation under supervision, are poor candidates for its successful use in treatment. Just as the anxious client may build upon anxiety-arousing associations or the depressed client may ruminate on ineffectiveness and despair instead of actually meditating, clients with severe thought disorders and problems with reality testing may substitute hallucinations, delusions, withdrawal, depersonalization, and catatonic responses for meditation, thereby aggravating their problems. Glueck and Stroebel (10, however, found Transcendental Meditation effective as adjunctive treatment with a sample of 96 psychiatric patients who would have been expected to have the kind of difficulties outlined here. Preliminary investigation indicated that the higher the level of psychopathology, the greater the difficulty patients had producing alpha waves. Testing transcendental meditation against autogenic relaxation and electroencephalogram (EEG) alpha wave biofeedback training, Glueck and Stroebel found T.M. to be the only one of the three experimental conditions that patients could persistently practice. Consequently, the authors match-paired their meditation sample with a comparison group and found their meditating patients to have higher levels of recovery than both their twins and the general

patient population. Controls for "halo" effect and other factors render the research strictly preliminary. But the research does suggest that testing varieties of meditation with the severely disturbed is in order if the supervisory precautions outlined earlier—and noted by Glueck and Stroebel (10, p. 307)—are followed. Treatment of the severely depressed and psychotic patients with meditation without close supervision and immediate post-meditation checks is contraindicated until further research is done.

Psychosocial history and diagnosis

One remarkable phenomenon occurring in most forms of meditation is the intrusion of the memory of events in the meditator's life into the meditative state. Meditators employing Zen and similar concentration techniques usually experience mental images of significant and emotionally intense events replayed before their relaxed mind. Desensitization of these memories has been discussed. But intentional use of meditation to allow significant facts and events of the psychosocial history is possible. Requesting the client to record these memories following meditation, for use in the context of treatment and for rounding out a more complete psychosocial history, may be helpful to workers with psychodynamic and psychoanalytic orientations.

The diagnostic value of meditation, implicit in earlier discussions, lies in the nature of the difficulty that the client has in meditating correctly. Elsewhere, the author has discussed optimal psychosocial functioning based upon eastern conceptualizations related to and developed from meditation (20). Briefly stated, the capacity to attend to activities one is about without interference by irrelevant ideation, worry, and guilt suggests a positive level of functioning. Meditation evokes memories and worries that intrude upon the meditation task. Repetitive anxiety-, anger-, or guilt-associated thoughts will indicate to the meditator and the worker or therapist those areas of conflict or unfinished business that hinder the client's functioning. Repetitive self-destructive images will indicate disturbed role rehearsal or depression. Conflicts from pushing or driving oneself will manifest themselves in forced breath or lack of relaxation in meditation.

The therapeutic relationship

There are several behaviors learned in meditation which would theoretically contribute to enhance empathic functioning on the part of the meditating social worker. Some preliminary study suggests that this notion should be researched further (18). First, learning increased voluntary control over one's attention permits one to shift from attending to the various verbal and nonverbal communications of the client to one's own emotional responses to the client. This ability to sense one's own emotional reactions from moment to moment facilitates sensing and verbalizing feelings that parallel those of the client. Accurate reflection of these feelings to the client, of course, is a major component in therapeutic empathy (30), a worker skill conducive to positive behavior change for the client.

Second, learning to discriminate internal or cognitive stimuli from perceptual stimuli in meditation and learning to gain a measure of voluntary control over cognitive processes can enhance empathic functioning in another way. The worker can hold complex cognitive elaboration in abeyance and allow himself to perceive the client as he is without premature diagnosing or other cognitive elaboration coloring his bare attention to the client as he is. This intentional slowing of the perceptual process that allows the client to speak for himself holds the worker in the present time—where emotions are felt, where the worker can be fully with the client, and where behaviors are changed.

Third, the meditating worker is likely to have cultivated a strong centeredness or observer self not easily rattled by the stresses of intense emotional interaction. Therefore, staying with the client in his deepest feelings, as Carl

Rogers described high-level empathy (30), becomes more likely. And because such a worker has a perspective on his own reactions, countertransference responses may be more accessible.

Meditation as an adjunctive technique to treatment has a virtue common to all profound and shared experiences. It is an experience a worker can impart and then share with the client that may serve as a basis for communication, trust, and mutual discovery when other bases for relationships are less productive. In this sense, meditation can be a common ground of mutual experience that can strengthen a therapeutic relationship.

Teaching meditation: one technique

There are several techniques for meditation useful as adjuncts for treatment. Among the more prominent are Yogic mantra techniques, Benson's relaxation technique (10, p. 314), Transcendental Meditation (3), and Zen techniques. The technique to be briefly detailed here is a form of Zen meditation. The general instructions are readily found in a variety of texts. Expert instruction and a good period of time meditating are recommended for workers considering meditation as an addition to their repertoire of techniques.

The client is instructed that the meditation technique is for therapeutic purposes and does not carry any religious connotations. He is helped to see the technique as conducive to insight, relaxation, and the development of here-and-now awareness of feelings of oneself and others.

The client is instructed to meditate one half hour each day in a quiet place where he is unlikely to be interrupted. The client is asked to record briefly meditation experiences on a log for later discussion with the worker. The meditation posture is as follows:

1. A sitting position with the back straight.
2. Sitting cross-legged on a pillow is ideal.
3. If uncomfortable, sit in a straight wooden

chair without allowing the back to come to rest against the back of the chair.

4. The hands should be folded in the lap.
5. The eyes may be open or closed; if open, they are not to focus on any particular thing.
6. The back must be straight for comfort since slumping causes cramping.
7. Loose clothing around the waist is suggested.

The client is instructed to focus on the breath and to begin the first three sessions by counting each exhalation up to 10 and beginning again. In the fourth session and thereafter the client may simply follow the natural—unforced, uncontrolled—breath for the duration of each session. The attention should be focused on the surface of the center of the body about an inch below the navel.

The client is told that there will be frequent intrusions of thoughts, feelings, sounds, and physical responses during his concentration. The response to these is in every case an easy recognition that attention has wandered and refocusing to the breath.

Repressed material will usually emerge as insights. These are automatically paired with a relaxed state. The client should be instructed that, if the meditation becomes upsetting or frustrating, he or she should stop for the day and resume the next day or until the next appointment with the therapist. Particular cautions with special clients were enumerated above. Generally, if the experience is not pleasant and rewarding this may be evidence that the client is pushing rather than allowing mental content to flow in; it should be recognized and released to refocus upon the breath.

Settings and levels of intervention

Meditation is a worldwide phenomenon. It is practiced in settings as varied as Japanese corporate offices, quiet monasteries, downtown apartments, and mental health centers. Most physical settings where social workers practice would be conducive to meditation. While each agency has its own major theoretical orientation or admixture of orientations, few would preclude meditation as an appropriate technique if thoughtfully and systematically introduced. While a psychodynamically oriented worker would define and describe meditation behavior and results differently than a behaviorist or an existentialist, the technique is not tied to single systems. Therefore, agency acceptance hinges more upon properties of tolerance for innovation, interest in research, and openness to new ideas. Meditation as a social work technique was thought to be well out of the mainstream and esoteric a few years ago, but it has gained wide acceptance in related disciplines and promises to become a more common technique in work with individuals, families, and groups.

Because meditation is thought of as an individual activity, it is naturally thought of as a treatment mode for individual treatment only. However, in addition to its use and ramifications for individual treatment addressed above, meditation is of use for certain kinds of groups, including families.

Group meditation can enhance group processes. Beginning and ending a group with a meditation session can enhance group feeling and mellow out intense feelings enough to allow their sharing, analysis, and discussion. A unison group chant of a mantra such as *Om,* pronounced "aum," evokes a sense of group unity and feeling with a lessening of feelings of isolation and egocentrism by individual members. A group meditation sets the atmosphere for constructive interaction. Meditation to end a group meeting has similar effects and supports solidarity and identity within the group.

Receptivity to meditation a few years ago was largely restricted to young people and the religiously or spiritually oriented. One form, Transcendental Meditation, has crossed many class and age barriers and is widely practiced (3). Increasingly, meditation can be introduced into group work with a variety of people. The author has used individual meditation to begin and group chants to end treatment groups for college-age youth and for sex-role-consciousness–raising groups for married persons ranging from 22 to 45 years old. Meditation for family treatment may help to reduce conflict and allow the family a positive, common experience to share and discuss.

Claims of increased harmony and lower crime rates have been made resulting from certain percentages of meditation in given communities (3, pp. 283-284). Obviously, if meditation does contribute to personal functioning, certain aspects of community life will be enhanced.

But much research must be done to determine the long-term effects of the various forms of meditation on individuals, groups, and families. Optimal personal and group functioning does not lead directly to more harmonious community life if the social order is fundamentally exploitive and contradictory. As with many forms of treatment and techniques, the gaps in our knowledge about meditation, as an adjunct to treatment at whatever level of intervention, are many, and considerable research is in order.

Implications for research

Meditation is a widely studied behavior. Nevertheless, our understanding is still far from complete. As a treatment technique, meditation has been found valuable in a variety of situations. However, there is little knowledge of the most appropriate forms of meditation, precise contraindications, the relative value of meditation and other relaxation techniques, and even the effects of meditation upon the nervous system, psyche, and social life.

Transcendental Meditation has in recent years inspired much research. As more of these findings are reported in referenced professional journals, the research base related to this particular technique will become more familiar to social workers and allied professionals. Much

research is in order for assessing other techniques, including Zen meditation, also in increasing use as a treatment adjunct. Well controlled outcome studies comparing meditation with autogenic relaxation, biofeedback, and similar techniques following the work of Glueck and Stroebel is in order.

Although there is much clinical evidence and intuitive exploration, the research concerning subset meditation phenomena is sparse. These include the desensitization, discrimination, and observer self mentioned earlier. Use of meditation with groups and families has been little studied. Researchers also have rich opportunities to follow the differential effects of meditation used with various clinical problems and various personalities.

Being a technique of potentially great value for social work, meditation must be examined empirically. Hopefully, it will not be picked up "whole hog" and incorporated into practice without critical evaluation. This would render it, like some other techniques, a passing fancy, soon discarded in favor of new approaches. Nor should meditation be disregarded as the esoteric product of foreign and bygone cultures. Despite barriers that exclude the wisdom of other cultures and other lands from our consideration, a critical openness is in order. We must try out, test, and incorporate meditation as an adjunct to treatment where it benefits our clients, our practice, and ourselves.

Conclusion

Meditation is, of course, more than just an adjunct to social work treatment. Meditation must flourish in our culture independent of the helping professions and their practice. If we in social work and others in related professions find it a powerful adjunct to treatment, we should not attempt to subsume it as ours alone. Meditation is unique because it is a vehicle of consciousness. We must not pretend to bring what is a powerful vehicle under our hegemony to enhance our own power and prestige. Most forms of meditation are public domain. They must remain so in our society. This is all the more important precisely because meditation is a vehicle of consciousness. It can be used to liberate, to extend individual functioning, to help create social change in the democratic interest. It could also be used to mystify, to distract people from their social concerns related to their personal problems. How the technique will be used is related to the conscience, wisdom, and position of the profession in the years of profound social change ahead. This author hopes that what has been presented here will be used in the development of critical consciousness, and that it will encourage and facilitate constructive involvement in the world by workers and clients alike.

A brief case example

The Use of Meditation in the Treatment of Functional Bowel Disease *

A 36 year old, married, mother of three children ages 3, 7, and 12 living in California was referred from her doctor with abdominal pain. Extensive physical examinations and tests had all been negative, though she recently had an increase in pain when she was under stress. She wanted to understand why she was having these troubles and how she could control them.

She had been experiencing an increase in her pains over the past year. She had gone on special diets, consulted several

* This case was provided by Dr. Ronald J. Lechnyr, D.S.W., A.C.S.W. Dr. Lechnyr is a psychiatric social worker in private practice in association with 48 physicians at The Eugene Hospital and Clinic, 1162 Willamette, Eugene, Oregon 97401. He operates a psychotherapy, biofeedback, and pain-therapy program and uses meditation techniques in the treatment of selected clients.

health care professionals, and taken many different medications, but there was no change in her distress which was becoming overwhelming. She said she was becoming increasingly depressed, anxious, and overly self-critical as her symptoms continued and there seemed no hope for any change in them. Psychological tests completed at the time of the initial evaluation confirmed that she was indeed severely depressed, with little energy. There seemed to be an emotional overlay to her pains.

The client was quick to agree to short-term out-patient treatment of eight weekly sessions. The goals would include developing some understanding of her emotions, the stresses in her life, her coping skills and difficulties, and learning various types of relaxation techniques. It was also agreed that the results of the psychological tests would be fully reviewed with her in the third session. In addition, she was helped to work through some related unresolved feelings from earlier years related to her parents' divorce and the death of her first husband. She explored how she could utilize some of her past coping skills with some of her present difficulties.

The client was experiencing many stressful and unstable living conditions at the present time while her husband was building their new home. This necessitated their living in a series of different friends' homes. Her husband had been so involved in building their dream home that he had not involved her in the process. Her husband was included in one of the out-patient sessions in order to increase communication between the two and to help the two of them to reinstitute their previous level of positive interactions that had been present in the year previous to all of these changes.

In the second treatment session the client was taught a passive, modified hypnotic, relaxation technique which was tape recorded for her daily use at home.

She was quite pleased with her ability to immediately relax and experienced a definite decrease in her abdominal pains. She was instructed to listen to the tape recording of the relaxation four times a day and to record her responses to this on a "Relaxation Log" which she was to bring with her to each session. In the following week the patient had several days without any pains until she would forget to use the technique because she would be feeling "so good." The patient continued with the passive–therapist directed relaxation techniques by listening to the tape recording daily. The worker was very directive with this technique. She was slowly encouraged to try the relaxation technique on her own and at times without using the "tape." She quite quickly became more able to do this.

After the fourth treatment session the client was introduced to a new technique designed to help her relax on her own, to become more comfortable with her own body, and to learn how she could help herself on an on-going basis. It was introduced as a new coping-skill which she could continue to utilize after the termination of treatment. Since the client was now feeling much better, she was eager to continue to increase her skills in this area. She was therefore given oral and written instructions for meditation. She was asked to take the instructions home and read them and to try and implement them into her daily routine. Initially she found some difficulty in being totally comfortable with the technique, so she would continue listening also once a day to the relaxation tape. However, she found less need to rely on the tape recording as she increased her ability to relax with the meditation. By the end of the first week, the client found that she was able to relax just as fully as she had with the tape recording. Further, she felt quite proud of her ability to do it on her own. By the last session she reported that she was able to relax without any reliance on the tape. She found that if she would meditate once a day, she would have no pains and could reduce any stresses that may arise by short relaxation techniques she would go over by herself in her mind. At that point she had been totally pain free for three weeks. Follow-up contacts with the patient one month after formal termination of treatment contacts showed that she continued to do her daily meditation, was pain free, felt much more self-confident in her abilities and coping skills, and felt that all aspects of psychotherapy, relaxation, and finally meditation had been quite beneficial to her. She recognized the benefits to her of continuing to practice what she had learned, and her family was quite supportive.

References

1. Al-Ghazzali (Bankey Behari, trans.). *The Revival of Religious Sciences.* Farnham, Surrey, Eng.: Sufi, 1971.
2. Beck, Aaron T. *Depression: Clinical Experimental and Theoretical Aspects.* New York: Harper and Row, 1967.
3. Bloomfield, Harold H. and Robert B. Kory. *Happiness.* New York: Pocket Books, Simon and Schuster, 1977.
4. Burt, E. A., ed. *The Teachings of the Compassionate Buddha.* New York: New American Library, 1955.
5. Challman, Alan. "The Self-Inflicted Suffering of Worry," cited in "Newsline," *Psychology Today,* Vol. 8, No. 8 (January 1975), p. 94.

6. Deatherage, Gary. "The Clinical Use of 'Mindfulness' Meditation Techniques in Short-Term Psychotherapy," *Journal of Transpersonal Psychology*, Vol. 7, No. 2 (1975), pp. 133-143.

7. *Encyclopaedia Britannica*, Macropoedia. Vol. 10 (London: Benton, 1974), p. 183.

8. Ferguson, Marilyn, ed. "Valuable Adjuncts to Therapy: Meditation, Relaxation Help Alcoholics Cope," *Brain-Minded Bulletin*, Vol. e, No. 7 (February 20, 1978), p. 2.

9. Fromm, E., D. T. Suzuki, and Richard DeMartino. *Zen Buddhism and Psychoanalysis*. New York: Harper and Row, 1970.

10. Glueck, Bernard C. and Charles F. Stroebel. "Biofeedback and Meditation in the treatment of Psychiatric Illness," *Comprehensive Psychiatry*, Vol. 16, No. 4 (1975), p. 316.

11. Goble, Frank. *The Third Force*. New York: Pocket Books, 1970.

12. Goleman, Daniel. "Meditation and Consciousness: An Asian Approach to Mental Health," *American Journal of Psychotherapy*, Vol. 30, No. 1 (January 1976), pp. 41-54.

13. ——. "Mental Health in Classical Buddhist Psychology," *Journal of Transpersonal Psychology*, Vol. 7, No. 2 (1975), pp. 176-183.

14. Hendricks, C. G. "Meditation as Discrimination Training: A Theoretical Note," *Journal of Transpersonal Psychology*, Vol. 7, No. 2 (1975), pp. 144-146.

15. Hooker, Carol E. "Learned Helplessness," *Social Work*, Vol. 21, No. 3 (May 1976), pp. 194-198.

16. Jourard, Sidney. "Psychology of Transcendent Perception," in Otto, H., ed., *Exploration in Human Potential*. Springfield, Ill.: Thomas, 1966.

17. Kapleau, Philip. *Three Pillars of Zen*. Boston: Beacon Press, 1967.

18. Keefe, Thomas W. "Empathy: The Critical Skill," *Social Work*, Vol. 21, No. 1 (January 1976), pp. 10-15.
——. "The Development of Empathic Skill: A Study," *Journal of Education for Social Work*, in press.

19. ——. "Meditation and the Psychotherapist," *American Journal of Orthopsychiatry*, Vol. 45, No. 3 (April 1975), pp. 484-489.

20. ——. "Optimal Functioning: The Eastern Ideal in Psychotherapy," *Journal of Contemporary Psychotherapy*, in press.

21. ——. "A Zen Perspective on Social Casework," *Social Casework*, Vol. 56, No. 3 (March 1975), pp. 140-144.

22. Kennett, Jiyu. *Selling Water by the River: A Manual of Zen Training*. New York: Vintage Books, 1972, p. 302.

23. Kohr, Richard L. "Dimensionality in Meditative Experience: A Replication," *Journal of Transpersonal Psychology*, Vol. 9, No. 2 (1977), pp. 193-203.

24. Lazarus, Arnold A. "Psychiatric Problems Precipitated by Transcendental Meditation," *Psychological Reports*, Vol. 39 (1976), pp. 601-602.

25. LeShan, Lawrence. "The Case for Meditation," *Saturday Review*, Vol. 2, No. 11 (February 22, 1975), pp. 25-27.

26. Marx, Karl. *Preface to Contribution to the Critique of Political Economy*, as cited in Allen, Edgar, *From Plato to Nietzsche*. New York: Fawcett, 1966, p. 159.

27. Miller, William R. and Martin E. P. Seligman. "Depression and the Perception of Reinforcement," *Journal of Abnormal Psychology,* Vol. 82 (1973), pp. 62-73.

28. Ornstein, Robert E. *The Psychology of Consciousness,* 2nd ed. New York: Harcourt Brace Jovanovich, 1977.

29. Prabhupada, Swami A. C. B. *Bhagavad Gita As It Is.* New York: Bhaktivedanta Book Trust, 1972.

30. Rogers, Carl R. "The Necessary and Sufficient Conditions for Therapeutic Personality Change," *Journal of Consulting Psychology,* Vol. 21, No. 2 (1957), pp. 95-103.

31. Seligman, Martin E. P. *Helplessness: On Depression, Development, and Death.* San Francisco: Freeman, 1975.

32. ———. "Depression and Learned Helplessness," in Friedman, Raymond J. and Katz, Martin M., eds., *The Psychology of Depression: Contemporary Theory and Research.* New York: Halstead Press, 1974, pp. 83-107.

33. Shapiro, Deane H. and Steven M. Zifferblatt. "Zen Meditation and Behavioral Self-Control; Similarities, Differences, and Clinical Applications," *American Psychologist,* Vol. 31, No. 7 (July 1976), pp. 519-532.

34. Shapiro, Deane H. "Zen Meditation and Behavioral Self Control Strategies Applied to a Case of Generalized Anxiety," *Psychologia: An International Journal of Psychology in the Orient,* Vol. 19, No. 3 (September 1976), pp. 134-138.

35. Suzuki, D. T. *An Introduction to Zen Buddhism.* New York: Grove Press, 1964.

36. Thera, Nyanaponika. *The Heart of Buddhist Meditation.* New York: Weiser, 1970.

37. Walsh, Roger. "Initial Meditative Experiences: Part I," *Journal of Transpersonal Psychology,* Vol. 9, No. 2 (1977), p. 161.

38. Watts, Allen. *Psychotherapy East and West.* New York: Ballantine Books, 1961.

39. Welwood, John, "Meditation and the Unconscious: A New Perspective," *Journal of Transpersonal Psychology,* Vol. 9, No. 1 (Spring 1977), pp. 1-26.

40. Wood, Ernest. *Yoga.* Baltimore: Penguin Books, 1959.

41. Woolfolk, Robert L., Lucille Carr-Kaffashan, Terrence McNulty, and Paul Lehrer. "Meditation as a Training Treatment for Insomnia," *Behavior Therapy,* Vol. 7, No. 3 (May, 1976), pp. 359-365.

42. Yu, Lu K'ann (Charles Luk, trans.). *The Secrets of Chinese Meditation.* New York: Weiser, 1972.

Annotated listing of key references

DEATHERAGE, Gary. "The Clinical Use of 'Mindfulness' Meditation Techniques in Short-Term Psychotherapy," *Journal of Transpersonal Psychology,* Vol. 7, No. 2 (1975), pp. 133–143.

Deatherage provides five interesting and useful case examples in his lucid description of the use and limitations of "mindfulness meditation" in short-term psychotherapy. This article is of value to workers and therapists who are using or considering using meditation as an adjunct to treatment.

GLUECK, Bernard C. and Stroebel, Charles F. "Biofeedback and Meditation in the Treatment of Psychiatric Illness," *Comprehensive Psychiatry,* Vol. 16, No. 4 (1975), p. 316.

This article is an important pioneering study that compared meditation and similar treatments for psychotherapy patients. In addition to the study's partially successful major thrust, other insights, including the function of meditation in mental health and indications for its use, are provided.

KEEFE, Thomas W. "Meditation and the Psychotherapist," *American Journal of Orthopsychiatry,* Vol. 45, No. 3 (April 1975), pp. 484–489.

This article describes a form of meditation and hypothesizes ways in which behavior learned in meditation can enhance the skill of the psychotherapist in the therapeutic relationship.

SHAPIRO, Deane H. and Steven M Zifferblatt. "Zen Meditation and Behavioral Self-Control, Similarities, Differences and Clinical Applications," *American Psychologist,* Vol. 31, No. 7 (July 1976), pp. 519–532.

A systematic description of Zen meditation and its effects upon functioning as followed by a comparison with the behavioral self-control approach. The article represents a useful advance for behaviorally oriented therapists interested in meditation.

WELWOOD, John. "Meditation and the Unconscious: A New Perspective," *Journal of Transpersonal Psychology,* Vol. 9, No. 1 (Spring 1977), pp. 1–26.

Welwood's article is a provocative critique of traditional western perspectives of the conception of the unconscious. The article provides the foundation for a theoretical understanding of human consciousness based upon meditation.

13

General Systems Theory and Social Work

by

GORDON HEARN

Encounter

In 1955 James G. Miller (43) was informing his fellow psychologists that

> general systems theory is a series of related definition, assumptions, and postulates about all levels of systems from atomic particles through atoms, molecules, crystals, viruses, cells, organs, individuals, small groups, societies, planets, solar systems and galaxies. General behavior systems theory is a subcategory of such theory, dealing with living systems, extending roughly from viruses through societies. Perhaps the most significant fact about living systems is that they are open systems, with important inputs and outputs. Laws which apply to them differ from those applying to relatively closed systems.

These words, when I read them then,

seemed literally to jump from the page, capturing my attention and fancy in a vise-like grip that has persisted to the present time. From that day forward it is fair to say that I have been addicted to general systems theory and the general systems approach to theory building. It seemed to have such an enormous potential for advancing theory, particularly in a profession such as social work. I thought so then, and the intervening years have only served to enhance this enthusiasm.

I was really ready for James Miller's article when, quite by chance, I encountered it, in Toronto, in 1955. But an appreciation of why this was so requires the tracing of some experiences in the period immediately preceding the memorable year I spent as Cassidy Visiting Research Professor at the School of Social Work, University of Toronto.

In 1948, after completing doctoral work with the Lewinian group at MIT I had joined the faculty of the School of Social Welfare at the

University of California, Berkeley, where my assignment was to develop a new specialization in social group work and to undergird it with a solid scientific base.

Group work and casework were sharply differentiated in those days and a student was required, when entering school, to make a choice as to whether to specialize in work with individuals or work with groups. The idea that one could be trained for both or that one could do both in subsequent practice was strongly denied and discouraged.

But while this was what the elders of the day were contending, it is interesting that student interest and actual practice were beginning to challenge the validity and practicality of this kind of specialization. My colleagues and I found ourselves, as we developed the group work program, "introducing" the group workers to the casework process, and we had an elective course in group aspects of professional practice, offered every term and taken by practically all the caseworkers. Throughout this period and despite the fact that my responsibility with my colleagues was to develop a specialized program in social group work at the school, we were becoming more and more troubled by the separation of group work and casework. It did not seem to fit the realities of practice. It was foreign to the way clients lived their lives, and it seemed like an unnatural way to provide social service. This was my frame of mind when the sabbatical year began in Toronto, a truly remarkable year for me. What made the experience especially rich was the fact that I was given a year "just to think," free to follow my nose wherever it might lead. I didn't have to produce anything in particular, although my own natural compulsiveness could not really free me of this obligation. *Theory Building in Social Work* (26) was the tangible product of the Toronto year.

In referring at the outset to the Miller article, I was moving a little ahead of the story. Actually the first six weeks in Toronto were quite frustrating and somewhat discouraging. When I went I thought that I wanted to search the grow-

ing social science literature for what insights it might suggest concerning the social group work process. The first thing I realized, however, was that I was now more interested in the social work process, in general, than in the more limited group work aspect. Apparently, my determination to see social work as a whole was already well established.

While this shift rekindled my interest, it was still quite bewildering and overwhelming not to know where or how to start the quest. Undoubtedly, this state of mind contributed substantially to the impact of the Miller article when it was encountered.

The article was saying that there are living systems at the level of human individuals, groups, organizations, and communities, those entities with which social workers do their work, and that as systems they have certain characteristics in common. I began to reflect. If this is so, is it possible that a universal theory of human behavior might be developed which would serve us at all levels when we are attempting to understand individuals, groups, organizations or communities? If so, it would be a great help to us in practice in those instances when we find ourselves shifting from level to level. And if we could develop a universal theory of human systems behavior, might this also serve as a base for the development of a general theory of social work intervention? A very exciting prospect.

And so I was off on the quest, reading everything I could find on general systems theory, reading in journals and sources that were completely new to me and exploring the work of biologists, physicists, chemists, mathematicians as well as of psychologists and sociologists, with which I was considerably more familiar. For some reason there was a special excitement about acquiring a new insight concerning social work from physics and chemistry, particularly when, at that time, commerce of this kind between the disciplines was strongly discouraged. Now, to be moving so freely among them seemed just a little mischievous—but very appealing and satisfying. It made one a confirmed interdisciplinarian. I realize, too, that I was encouraged in this by Kurt Lewin, who was never reluctant to cross discipline lines in his own work.

As the year progressed not only was there an exploration of general systems theory, but also the emergence of a somewhat clearer conception of the theory-building process, and particularly how theory is built in a profession such as social work. Much more will be said about this later, but suffice it to note here that I came to see theory building as a cyclical process of repeating phases. One such phase was conceptualizing, in which one postulates certain concepts and constructs which enable one to organize and relate a number of generalizations drawn from experience or practice. System was seen as one such central construct.

System: A Central Construct

The systems construct as I understood it in Toronto is presented as Chapter V in the theory-building monograph (26, pp. 38-51). What is attempted here is a brief resumé of that chapter, enumerating the several concepts discussed, but stressing the ideas about social work that many of the concepts suggest. In this revision of the original material, I have also included some additional concepts that social workers have indicated they have found useful.

The monograph, after describing the nature of general systems theory along the lines suggested by the Miller article, discusses the nature and variety of systems. A *system* is defined as a set of objects together with relationships between the objects and between their attributes. There are conceptual systems—the mathematical type; there are real systems, the kinds of living and nonliving systems that can be observed; and there are abstracted systems, classes of behavior and relationships that can be inferred about real systems.

Systems vary in terms of the *models* they employ for purposes of symbolization, and they vary in terms of their inherent openness and closedness. Individuals, groups, organizations and communities, the entities with which we deal in social work, are best represented as complex adaptive systems (11). They are also living systems.

The phenomenon of *openness* and *closedness* has been of great interest, and I have found myself using it frequently in pondering human nature and in probing the nature of social work intervention. Systems at all levels seem to vary from time to time in terms of their openness and closedness. The client systems with which we work at times seem too closed or too open for their own good or that of others. And they seem to go through cycles of opening and closing according to their perception of the potential security or threat in the impinging environment. Much of social work is devoted to helping the client achieve an optimum degree of openness for the conditions of the moment and the capacity to change this state as conditions change. The concepts of openness and closedness also call attention to the boundary region of the system. (More about boundaries in a later section.)

One cannot discuss the difference between open and closed systems without introducing the concept of *entropy*. The operation of a closed system is described by Newton's Second Law of Thermodynamics, which holds that a certain quantity called entropy, or degree of deorganization in the system, tends to increase to a maximum until eventually the process ends at a state of equilibrium. Entropy is present in all systems, but in open systems the opposite process, which general systems theorists have called *negative entropy,* * is also present. This is so because open systems have access to free energy with which they can organize and build.

One of the articles read at a recent seminar observed that in a living system both positive

---

* In a recent seminar it was pointed out to me that the concept *negative entropy* is a mathematical impossibility. The phenomenon was not being challenged, only the designation. A new and better designation for this concept is needed.

and negative entropy are present until the point of death, when entropy assumes full reign. This led me to ponder the nature of the life cycle from birth to death. Is it possible that in the early period of life, when growth is rapid, negative entropy far outweighs positive entropy, that in middle age they are somewhat in balance and in old age positive entropy has the balance of power?

Both open and closed systems attain stationary states. In closed systems it is a state of *equilibrium* or rest; in open systems it is a dynamic interplay of forces giving the appearance of rest but being in reality a dynamic *steady state*, a quasi-stationary equilibrium (37), to use one of Kurt Lewin's concepts, or a complex adaptive system, to use Buckley's phrase.

There are other properties which are to be found in all systems, open or closed.

Every order of system with the exception of the smallest has *subsystems,** and all but the largest are part of a suprasystem consisting of the system in its environment.

Anderson and Carter (1) have drawn our attention to the holon, a concept introduced by Arthur Koestler (34, 35). A *holon* is an entity which is simultaneously both a part and a whole. "The unit is made up of parts to which it is the whole, the supra-system; and at the same time, is part of some larger whole of which it is a component, or (general purpose) subsystem." What is central is that any system is by definition both part and whole.

Anderson and Carter note that there are certain corollaries to Koestler's whole–part proposition. The systems approach requires the designation of a *focal* system, the system which

sets the perspective and is the system of primary attention at the moment. "Holon requires the examiner to then attend to the component parts (the subsystems) of that focal system *and* to simultaneously attend to the significant environment (the suprasystems) of which the focal system is a part, or to which it is related." As an example, they note that a family may be identified as a focal system. If viewed as a holon, attention must be given both to its members and to its significant environments such as schools, community, work organizations, other families and the neighborhood. Merely to look at the interactions among family members (the family as a whole) ignores the functions of the family as part. The environment of a system is everything that is external to its boundary. Higher orders of systems, consequently, are always parts of the environment of lower orders. And for each system there may be both a *proximal* and *distal* environment, the proximal being that part of which the system is aware and the distal being that part which is beyond awareness.

Open systems have certain additional features which distinguish them from closed systems. We have already noted that open systems exchange energy and information with their environment, that they have important inputs and outputs and that they tend to maintain themselves in a steady state.

Bertalanffy (5) has pointed out that the characteristics of steady states are exactly that of organic metabolism. Given a continuous flow of materials, a constant ratio among the components of the system is maintained. The composition of the system is independent of, and maintained constant in, a varying import of materials. Presumably, poverty could be regarded as a state in which the necessary input requirement to maintain a steady state is unavailable to the system.

After any disturbance, a system tends to reestablish a steady state, and a system can also establish another steady state if and when the disturbing external condition is prolonged. Another property of open systems, then, is the pro-

---

* The general systems theorists now recognize two kinds of subsystems: general purpose and special purpose. A *general purpose* subsystem is a separately operating system within a larger system which does not play a specialized role in the larger system. A *special purpose* subsystem is an element or functional component of a larger subsystem which fulfills the conditions of a system in itself but which also plays a specialized role in the operation of the larger system.

cess of *self-regulation*, a characteristic with important implications for social work theory and for social work education.

Another concept closely related to steady state is that of *equifinality*, which simply means the achieving of identical results from different initial conditions. When this concept was first encountered, I found myself relating it immediately to the process of professional education. It suggests that professionally competent social workers may be produced from many different beginnings. We have tended to think in the past, and to some extent we may still think, that the development of professional competence requires a particular level of competence to begin professional education, and that one must be subjected to a particular curriculum. The concept of equifinality suggests that students may begin at different levels, take various routes "up the mountain," at several speeds, and still reach the peak. It tends to direct attention away from what is taught toward what is learned. It tends to support the principle of individualization in professional education. At least this is where my reflections about equifinality have taken me.

There are two additional properties of open systems deserving special attention. One is the *dynamic interplay of subsystems operating as functional processes*, and the other is the phenomenon of *feedback*. The former is the condition in living systems called *functional unity* in which all the parts of the system work together with a sufficient degree of harmony to maintain the system in a steady state. Feedback is the particular way in which living systems, as open systems, may be maintained in or near a steady state. Feedback has been defined as a property of being able to adjust future conduct by past performance (60). A certain portion of the system output or behavior is fed back to the input to affect succeeding outputs (24). Thermoregulation in warm-blooded animals is one of the best examples of this process in living organisms. Cooling of the blood stimulates certain centers in the brain which "turn on" heat-producing mechanisms of the body, and the

body temperature is monitored back to the center so that temperature is maintained at a constant level.

There is a certain relation between feedback and the dynamic interplay of processes which is worth noting. Feedback mechanisms are seen as secondary and superimposed on the dynamically related processes which are primary. Feedback mechanisms are relatively fixed arrangements operating as a consequence of a principle of organization which may be called *progressive mechanization*. Bertalanffy (6, p. 44) points out that at first living systems are governed by dynamic interaction of their components, but that later on fixed arrangements and conditions of constraint are established which render the system and its parts more efficient, but also gradually diminish and eventually abolish its equipotentiality.

And Bertalanffy notes that there is also the process of *progressive segregation* (6, p. 68) which, along with progressive mechanization, imposes limitations upon the natural regulatory processes in systems. In progressive segregation, the system divides into a hierarchical order of subordinate systems which gain a certain independence of each other.

Magaroh Maruyama has added greatly to our understanding of phenomena such as feedback and the dynamic interplay of processes, by the introduction of the concept of *mutual causal processes* and the several forms they may take. All mutual causal processes are forms of feedback but there can be those which are *deviation-counteracting*, tending to return the system to a state from which it has deviated, and those which are *differentiation-amplifying*, which are heterogeneity increasing, leading to change. He thinks that there may yet be a third type which is *diversity-symbiotizing*. Furthermore, deviation-counteracting equilibrating mutual causal processes are sometimes called *morphostatic* processes, and differentiation-amplifying heterogenizing mutual causal processes are called *morphogenetic* processes.

In morphogenesis there is always an "initial

kick" in some direction, followed by progressive and continuing amplification of that direction. A rocket speeding to the moon is a familiar current example, but the old adage that "the rich get richer and the poor get poorer" is also an example of deviation-amplification or morphogenesis.

Maruyama has added another concept which is proving useful in social work theory. He has pointed out that morphogenetic processes suggest that there is an opposite principle to equifinality which might be called *multifinality*, wherein similar initial conditions may lead to dissimilar end-states (10).

General systems
in historical perspective

Ludwig von Bertalanffy is generally acknowledged to be the father of general systems theory, and a paper published in 1945 is regarded as the point and the means by which this new perspective entered the public domain (22). Not that it was conceived all at once. Actually, it was the product of a fairly long gestation period and represented the synthesis of many views, including two concepts which may be regarded as the precursors of general systems theory. These were (1) the theory of organismic biology about which Bertalanffy wrote in 1928 (4), and (2) his theory of open systems, presented in 1932 (5).

The concept of general systems theory was published in 1945 (22), although the idea had been presented much earlier, in 1937, in a Charles Morris Philosophy Lecture at the University of Chicago. It is interesting that the reason it lay dormant so long was Bertalanffy's fear that it would have been overwhelmingly criticized by the classical and orthodox biologists of that time.

It was about a decade later, in 1954, while at the Center for the Advanced Study in the Behavioral Sciences at Palo Alto, that he found some kindred spirits in Kenneth Boulding, Anatol Rapoport and Ralph Gerard, and together they formed the Society for General Systems Research. Beginning in 1951, Roy Grinker had also assembled a distinguished group of behavioral scientists in a series of ten semiannual conferences in a search for a Unified Theory of Human Behavior (23).

Like all important new ideas, general systems had its roots in a number of antecedents developed in a variety of disciplines. Irma Stein (54) notes for us that the new organismic conception was reflected in the works of Cassirer (the philosophy of symbolic forms), Piaget (language and learning) and Goldstein (biology and neurophysiology). It is clear, too, that the organismic idea, holding that for full comprehension one must comprehend a system as a whole, derives from the "physical gestalten" of Wolfgang Kohler (6). And how well I remember that my own teacher, Kurt Lewin, was constantly reminding us, in the forties, that the whole is different from the sum or its parts—the concept of nonsummativity.

The idea of living systems as open systems was also a concept whose time had come. It enabled us to consider the process of system-environment exchange, the hierarchical order of systems, the relations within and between subsystems, systems and suprasystems and the utilization of intersystem generalizations. It finally laid to rest the persistent but outworn concept of vitalism and it resolved the apparent contradiction between *entropy* (the relentless movement toward disorder) and *evolution* (the tendency toward higher levels of order).

General systems theory in social work education dates back to the middle fifties. As noted at the outset, it all began for me in 1955 with the reading of an article by James G. Miller in which he had introduced general systems to his fellow psychologists (43). Blessed by a sabbatical year in 1955-1956 I was able to explore, in some depth, the possible applications of general systems to social work. As noted, that resulted in my monograph on theory building (26), a work that lay dormant for several years until it began to be used in social work doctoral programs in the mid-sixties.

In 1966 Irma Stein presented a paper at the Annual Program Meeting on "The Application of Systems Theory to Social Work Practice and Education" (55) and the following year, in Minneapolis, several papers were presented which were later published by the council under the title *The General Systems Approach: Contributions Toward an Holistic Conception of Social Work* (29).

During the seventies there has been a marked acceleration in the application of general systems theory to our field and appearance of the first original contributions, by social workers, to the body of general systems theory. Some of our number—notably, Pincus and Minahan, Anderson and Carter, Stein, Whittaker, Siporin, Bloom, Kahn, and Turner— have written books employing a systems perspective.* Papers have been presented annually at our program meetings, and there are numerous articles in our journals. In the latter category I think particularly of Ann Hartman's article entitled, "To Think About the Unthinkable," in *Social Casework* (25), and Gerald K. Rubin's "General Systems Theory: An Organismic Conception for Teaching Modalities in Social Work Intervention" (48), part of a volume of Smith College papers.

---

* Allen Pincus and Anne Minahan, *Social Work Practice* (Itasca, Ill.: Peacock, 1973); R. E. Anderson and I. Carter, *Human Behavior in the Social Environment* (Chicago: Aldine, 1974); Irma L. Stein, *Systems Theory, Science, and Social Work* (Metuchen, N.J.: Scarecrow Press, 1974); James K. Whittaker, *Social Treatment* (Chicago: Aldine, 1974); Max Siporin, *An Introduction to Social Work Practice* (New York: Macmillan, 1975); Martin Bloom, *The Paradox of Helping* (New York: Wiley, 1975); Alfred J. Kahn, *Shaping the New Social Work* (New York: Columbia University Press, 1974); Francis J. Turner, *Social Work Treatment* (New York: Free Press, 1979); James E. Herrick, *Theory Building for Basic Institutional Change* (San Francisco: R. & E. Research Assoc., 1977.

The social work experience with general systems theory

In preparation for a paper presented in 1976 at the Philadelphia meeting of the Council on Social Work Education, I employed a procedure similar to one which had been used almost a decade earlier in preparation for the Minneapolis meeting of the Council. In both cases a simple questionnaire was sent to social work educators asking them what they were doing with general systems in their teaching and writing. This time the questionnaire was sent to 142 accredited undergraduate as well as the 87 graduate programs. There were responses from 64 graduate programs (74%) and 31 undergraduate programs (22%). In all, 94 individuals reported, but there are undoubtedly more because several spoke generally for their colleagues. We heard from 68 different schools.

As I read the responses it occurred to me that many, about three-fourths, might best be characterized as consumers of general systems theory, while somewhat fewer, about one-fourth, could be thought of as producers or generators of theory.

Where Used

The general systems perspective has been used in literally every aspect of the curriculum, although not with equal emphasis. In descending order of frequency, it is being used in practice/methods; human behavior and the social environment; the "core" (micro/mezzo/macro/); social welfare policy and services/ social work as a social institution; marital and family therapy; administration/organizational theory; and field work.

How Used

When we consider how general systems has been used in social work, perhaps the most important observation that can be made is that we have come to realize that it is more a way of thinking, a way of viewing the world, than it is a theory.

The principal ways we have used general systems, again in descending order of frequency, are (1) to organize and reduce complexity (integrating, reducing, coordinating, bridging); (2) to build theory (provide a theoretical base, a framework and an umbrella); (3) to show relationships (comparing, analyzing); (4) to teach (showing, illustrating, describing and orienting); (5) to develop and plan; and (6) to seek understanding.

Concepts Used

Literally all of the concepts contained in any lexicon of general systems terms are being used by social work educators today. Many of the respondents indicated that they have developed glossaries as a ready reference for their students.

The most commonly used concepts, again in descending order of frequency, are: boundary definition and maintenance; feedback; open system; entropy; input/throughout/output; steady state; equifinality; interdependence; homeostasis; wholeness/holism; interrelatedness; holon; synergy and environment.

Other concepts, although less frequently mentioned, are beginning to be utilized. They include: negentropy, linkages, multifinality, nonsummativity, transaction, interface, suprasystem/system/subsystem, and morphostasis/morphogenesis. I must also note that many have found useful the Pincus and Minahan differentiation of change agent, client, target and action systems.

Potential Uses

As might be expected, many see as potentialities some of the uses already realized in the teaching and practice of others and reported above. I want to identify only those uses which

might be regarded as relatively new applications of the general systems approach.

Foremost, I think, is the prospect that is seen for developing an ecological conception of social work. Related to this is the prospect of an image of man that truly sees man-in-nature, that sees life in process, that pays attention to the environment.

It is also seen as useful in focusing on the social dimension in practice and supporting a social problem orientation. It is useful in policy analysis; it is useful for looking at self; and it is useful for looking at wholes. Some see as a potentiality what others have found most difficult, namely, the learning conjointly of skills and concepts.

Building theory within a general systems framework

The remainder of this chapter is an account of this author's experience in building theory within a general systems framework. It begins with some general comments about theory building in a profession and follows with a description of some of the insights suggested by general systems theory and how these have influenced my thinking and my practice, primarily as a social work education administrator.

Theory Building in a Profession*

The Toronto year had a double focus. Not only was there an encountering of general systems theory, but there was also the

---

* The principal publications in which this area of concern was addressed were: G. Hearn, *Theory Building in Social Work* (Toronto: University of Toronto Press, 1958); "Phases in the Theory Building Cycle," *Education for Social Work: Proceedings of Annual Program Meeting,* Council on Social Work Education (Oklahoma City, 1960), pp. 38–49; "The General Systems Approach to the Understanding of Groups," *Health Education Monographs,* No. 14 (1962), pp. 12–26.

emergence of a preoccupation with the manner in which theory is built in a profession. The two combined led to the realization that there is a general systems approach to theory building which is particularly applicable in the development of social work theory.

The Pursuit of Knowledge and the Refinement of Practice

One of the consequences of encountering and exploring general systems theory was the development of a conviction that the pursuit of knowledge and the refinement of practice are inseparably connected.

I tend to think visually. I have always found it natural and helpful as ideas are developing in my mind to represent them graphically, to get them out where I could see them. As I read and thought about theory building in a profession, the image as shown in Figure 13-1 gradually emerged.

Theory building was seen as a repeating cycle of experiencing, generalizing, conceptualizing, testing and operationalizing—all held together by communication. This figure also serves to demonstrate the power of graphic representation, because once the basic figure had been drawn certain additional ideas were seen in it and deduced from it.

As one moves from experiencing to generalizing to conceptualizing, one is becoming progressively more abstract, and as one moves from conceptualizing to testing to experiencing, one becomes progressively more concrete. It is clear, too, that if one is to pursue knowledge and build theory, and if one is to refine practice, one must go around the entire cycle and do so continuously.

Indeed, there are certain consequences which accrue from failing to go around the entire cycle, by choosing to experience, exclusively, or to conceptualize, exclusively. The person who does nothing but have more and more experience, without trying to understand it, goes

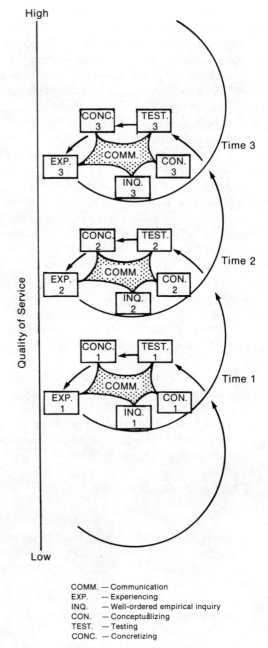

COMM. — Communication
EXP. — Experiencing
INQ. — Well-ordered empirical inquiry
CON. — Conceptualizing
TEST. — Testing
CONC. — Concretizing

Figure 13-1. PURSUIT OF KNOWLEDGE AND REFINEMENT OF PRACTICE

around in circles, and the quality of his practice remains relatively unchanged. The one who chooses to specialize exclusively in conceptualization spins off into "cloud nine." His theories may become purer, but their relevance and usefulness in practice is often remote.

There was a time when social workers saw others as the producers and themselves as the appliers of theory. Hopefully, this dysfunctional kind of specialization is diminishing. The true professional does both. He is a theory builder who practices or a practitioner who also builds theory.

This conviction or realization led us in building a professional school faculty to search for people who were interested in both theory building and practice, and to make it possible for them to continue to do both. In the methods area, at least, the better teacher is the one who continues to practice concurrently. I expect that this is also true in every area of the curriculum.

In short, the pursuit of knowledge and the refinement of practice are interdependent processes. The only way to extend knowledge is to test it in practice, and the only way to improve practice is to reflect upon it theoretically. It follows, too, I believe, that we cannot rely upon others to develop theory for the practice of our profession; we must do it ourselves, or at least be active participants in the process. Unless we do, we are not fully professional.

Phases in Theory Building

A short time after the publication of the Toronto monograph, the opportunity arose to think more specifically and more operationally about the phases or sequence of steps in theory building (27).

A first approximation suggested that there is an orientation phase, a developmental phase and a utilization phase in theory building, and that these three phases are a repeating cycle, as shown in Figure 13-2. And, further, when these are examined more closely, theory building emerges as a sequence of steps or a series of fairly discrete activities. They are delineated in Figure 13-3. One notes, again, the representa-

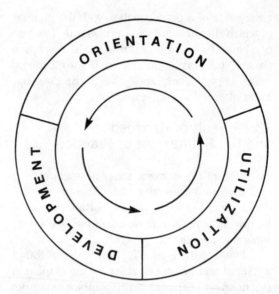

Figure 13-2.   PHASES IN THEORY BUILDING

tion of theory building as a continuous repeating cycle of steps. Operationalizing and pretesting are seen as part of both the developmental and utilization phases.

"Making explicit one's value orientation" in the orientation phase warrants special comment. No theory is ever entirely value-free, and no theory builder is ever completely free of bias. For this reason it is important for the theory builder to make explicit the values he holds with reference to the domain in which he is working. Doing so helps, first, to reveal possible inconsistencies in one's positions. Second, it alerts one to his own blind spots—things which may be missed because one is looking for something else. Third, it helps the consumer of the theory to evaluate it for his own purposes. And, fourth, it helps in being more objective when the research phase is undertaken.

The General Systems Approach to Theory Building

General systems can be regarded as both a product and a process. The product is a unified body of theory about systems at all levels; the process is an approach to building of theory

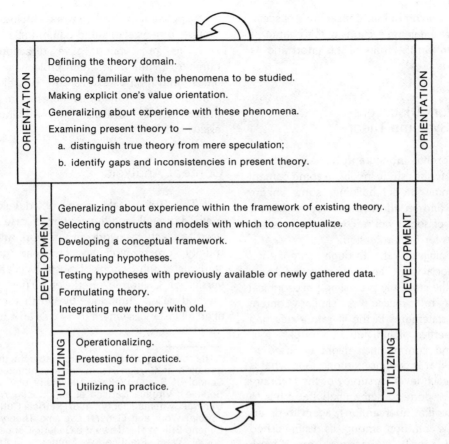

ORIENTATION

Defining the theory domain.

Becoming familiar with the phenomena to be studied.

Making explicit one's value orientation.

Generalizing about experience with these phenomena.

Examining present theory to —

    a. distinguish true theory from mere speculation;

    b. identify gaps and inconsistencies in present theory.

DEVELOPMENT

Generalizing about experience within the framework of existing theory.

Selecting constructs and models with which to conceptualize.

Developing a conceptual framework.

Formulating hypotheses.

Testing hypotheses with previously available or newly gathered data.

Formulating theory.

Integrating new theory with old.

UTILIZING

Operationalizing.

Pretesting for practice.

Utilizing in practice.

Figure 13–3.   SEQUENTIAL STEPS IN THEORY BUILDING

about systems. The 1962 Dorothy Nyswander Lecture at the School of Public Health, University of California at Berkeley (28), afforded me the opportunity to think more definitively about the latter.

I had noted that the general systems approach to theory building takes two forms, the analogistic and the generic. When you use the *analogistic* method, you begin with a system at any given level, observe it and find that it has certain properties or that its parts bear a certain relationship to one another. Moving, then, to a system at some other level, you test to determine whether the same properties or the same relationships are present. Thus, a fact or phenomenon that is observed at one level suggests a hypothesis to be tested at all other levels.

Shulman's article (51), cited later, shows the power and the practicality of analogistic theorizing.

The *generic* form of the general systems approach is somewhat similar in that it also uses the analogistic method, but it is superior in that it attempts to produce master models. Instead of focusing on a system at one particular level, such as a group, it may take several levels, including the individual, the group, the organization and the community and attempt to construct a master model or theory capable of describing each one separately or all of them together.

It was this recognition, that there is a generic form of the general systems approach, that stimulated and activated a subsequent interest in developing holistic conceptions of social work. In the remaining sections of this chapter, I will comment on the fruits of this effort and its current status.

Social Work Discovers General Systems Theory

The Toronto monograph had suggested a program of further study involving some content analysis, some model building, some theory elaboration and an effort to develop an holistic conception of social work. These were seen as urgent tasks for the profession.

It was suggested that through content analysis of the social work literature one might derive a sense of the currently prevailing philosophical orientations to practice. A similar content analysis of statements in the literature referring to the properties of individuals, groups, organizations and communities might be used to determine what is common among, and what is unique at, each level. A survey of the literature might also be done to determine what it has to say about worker interventions, again to determine what is common among, as distinguished from what is specific to, casework, group work and community organization.

Model building was to be directed toward the refinement of the complex adaptive systems model, the identification of the functional subsystems common to living systems at all levels, the development of a model of the systems universe and of living systems.

Theory building was to be directed toward the elaboration of the properties of the subsystems of living systems, the enunciation of behavioral propositions through a process of cross-level hypothesizing and analysis, and studies of various phenomena such as homeostasis, feedback, boundary maintenance and entropy.

In the effort to develop an holistic conception of social work, one would be trying to describe intervention prescriptions in such a way as to apply equally well to work with individuals, groups, organizations and communities.

This prescription gave direction to a number of student research projects in the late fifties and early sixties at Berkeley and Portland.* It also made us more aware and appreciative of particular work being done elsewhere.†

Content Analysis

The Brill et al. group (9) developed a method of analyzing the content of case records used to teach casework, group work and community organization to first-year graduate students at the School of Social Welfare, University of California, Berkeley. They used a method called "unitizing" by which they identified all instances where there was an encounter

---

* The following student research projects, under the direction of Gordon Hearn, were completed at the School of Social Welfare, University of California, Berkeley: Virginia Carlson et al., "Social Work and General Systems Theory," 1957; Patricia Cutler et al., "Social Work and General Systems Theory," 1958; Eugene Brill et al., "Toward a Generic Conception of Social Work Practice, A Method of Analyzing Teaching Records," 1960; Agnes Bolter et al., "Toward a Generic Conceptualization of Human Systems," 1962. Later, at the School of Social Work, Portland State University, Frank Miles directed two studies in the series: Richard L. DeCristoforo et al., "Development of a Tool to Measure Applicability of Social Systems Theory to General Social Work," 1965; and Patricia M. Armstrong et al., "Constructing a Tool for Measuring Common Social Work Activities," 1966. The most recent in the series, directed by Florence Clemenger at Portland, was: George A. Fisher et al., "The Use of Self-Determination and Confidentiality in Casework and Group Work Practice: An Exploratory Study," 1967.

† The following were particularly pertinent to the tasks enumerated above. J. G. Miller, "Living Systems: Basic Concepts," *Behavioral Science,* 10 (1965), 193–237. Also "Living Systems: Structure and Process," and "Living Systems: Cross-Level Hypotheses," *Behavioral Science,* 10 (1965), 337–411; R. Lippitt, J. Watson and B. Westley, *The Dynamics of Planned Change: A Comparative Study of Principles and Techniques* (New York: Harcourt, Brace, 1957); Frank Montalvo, "Homeostasis in Functional and

between the social worker and a client system. Once the units were identified an attempt was made to designate the type of client system, the setting, the auspices, the type of worker and the locus of the interaction.

The purpose of the DeCristoforo et al. project (17) was to test the applicability of general systems theory to the traditionally held concept of generic social work. General systems theory was extended to include the properties of organismic human group systems. There were twenty-one categories at this level of abstraction.

Internal consistency of general systems theory and social work treatment concepts were then tested. This was done by isolating a total of 427 concepts describing social work actions and found in traditional social work literature, and its three methods of practice.

The group demonstrated that all of the action categories could be classified into the general systems theory categories, although not yet with a high degree of reliability. Social work action concepts were found to be vague, not discrete, and of uncertain levels of abstraction. They concluded that before general systems theory and social work practice theory could be reconciled, the latter would have to be reconceptualized in more accurate terms.

The purpose of the Armstrong et al. project (2) was to develop a questionnaire to test the generic quality of the actions performed in the three traditional specialties of social work— casework, group work and community organization. They were able to demonstrate that a panel of student social workers and professional social workers could make judgments about the clarity of meaning, the frequency of use and the importance of social work practice of the 427 action concepts noted by the previous group. Their analysis showed, further, that there were a considerable number of concepts generic to the

field—that is, that they were applicable to all three practice methods.

The Fisher et al. study (20) explored the use of the concepts of self-determination and confidentiality in casework and group work practice. One of the principal contributions of this study was the development of a method of operationalizing abstract concepts such as self-determination and confidentiality in terms of practice principles. They found that there was a statistically significant difference in the worker's judgment of the use of self-determination in casework and group work practice, but that no such difference existed in the use of the concept of confidentiality. They also observed that practice principles are not used exclusively of one another but, rather, that they have overlapping referents, indicating that ideas and concepts in practice do not appear as self-contained entities but, rather, as complex interdependent ideas that combine to form the body of social work theory.

Model Building

Agnes Bolter et al. (8) applied themselves to model building.* They developed two models—one of the system universe and the other of "The Human System, Its Internal Resources and Their Relationships." The models, once developed, were tested to see whether they could be readily and usefully employed in social work.

The model of the system universe was represented as shown in Figure 13-4. The system is represented as the area within the triangle and it has two subdivisions: the area outside the circle, that part of which the system is aware; and the area inside the circle, that part which is unknown to it. Similarly, there are two regions

---

Dysfunctional Family Systems," *US Army Social Work '64,* Social Service Consultant, Office of Surgeon General, Department of Army, Washington, D.C.

*A fuller account of this project is contained in a paper which I presented at a Conference on Health Research and the Systems Approach, Wayne State University, Detroit, March 1-4, 1971, and published in H. H. Werley *et al., Health Research: The Systems Approach* (New York: Springer, 1976), Chap. 3.

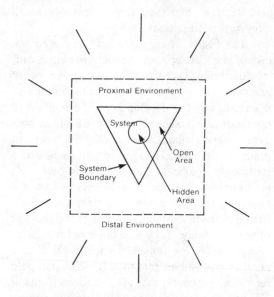

Figure 13-4. THE SYSTEMS UNIVERSE

in the environment: the distal environment outside the square and the proximal environment inside the square. The *proximal* environment may be defined as that part of the environment of which the system is aware, whereas the *distal* environment affects the behavior of the system but is beyond the awareness of the system.

The appeal of the model is that it applies equally well, regardless of the level of human system to which it is referred, be that an individual, a group, an organization or a community.

The Berkeley group found the work of Lippitt, Watson and Westley (39) particularly useful. Using a general systems approach, the latter group had described the process of planned change as directed toward individuals, groups, organizations and communities. The Lippitt group used the concepts "client-system" and "change agent" and developed a generalizable seven-phase model of the change process. But possibly the aspect of this work which proved most useful to the Berkeley group was the Lippitt, Watson and Westley typology of systemic problems.

According to them, a system, in order to

maintain viability, copes with problems, some of which are internal to the systems and others which are external. The internal problems are: (1) the distribution of energy; (2) the mobilization of energy; and (3) communication within the system. The external problems are: (1) achieving correspondence between internal and external reality; (2) setting goals and values for action; and (3) developing skills and strategies for action.

It seems obvious that in the social professions we assist our clients by helping them deal with any and all of these systems problems. The Berkeley group was particularly interested in the first of the external problems, *achieving correspondence between internal and external reality,* and subsequently focused their attention on how the change agent might help with this problem.

As they thought about their work as professional change agents in relation to their model of the system universe, they concluded that the Lippitt, Watson and Westley formulation might be paraphrased "to achieving correspondence between the *pairs of regions* in the System Universe." Because there are four regions, there are the following six pairs of regions: (1) conscious and unconscious regions of the system (○ and △); (2) the conscious region of the system and the proximal environment, (△ and □); (3) the proximal and the distal regions of the evironment (□ and ●); (4) the unconscious region of the system and the proximal environment (○ and □); (5) the unconscious region of the system and the distal environment (○ and ●) and (6) the conscious part of the system and the distal environment (△ and ●). Their attention was drawn also to the boundary between any pair of regions and particularly to the degree of openness and closedness for input from one region to another and output to one region from another.

The openness or closedness of the boundary between any two regions is controlled from both sides, as is the case of a door between adjoining hotel rooms which can be either locked or unlocked on each side. Only when there is

Matter-Energy Processing Subsystems	Subsystems Processing Both Matter-Energy and Information	Information Processing Subsystems
	REPRODUCER	
	BOUNDARY	
Ingestor Distributor Decomposer Producer Matter-Energy Storage Extruder Motor Supporter		Input Transducer Channel and Net Decoder Associator Memory Decider Encoder Output Transducer

Figure 13–5.   THE CRITICAL SUBSYSTEMS

correspondence between conditions on both sides of the boundary will it be fully closed or fully open. Openness on one side and closedness on the other describes a condition of conflict or lack of correspondence between the two regions with reference to boundary conditions.

The second model was an attempt of the Berkeley group to develop a means of representing the human system which would serve at all levels of human organization. They entitled it "The Human System, Its Internal Resources and Their Relationships." It is not developed here because it has not been used extensively in practice and has been superseded by a new and more sophisticated model developed by Miller (43).

For the past two decades, Miller has been developing, refining and testing a universal model of living systems (43). It has been a monumental undertaking in which he has identified a set of functional subsystems and demonstrated their applicability at the levels of the cell, organ, organism (individual), group organization, society and supranational system.

His model is based on the assumption that all living systems are engaged in the processing of matter-energy and information. Certain processes are necessary for life and must be carried out by all living systems that survive or be performed for them by some other system. They are carried out by the critical subsystems listed in Figure 13-5. In order to facilitate cross-level analysis and in order to keep the scientist familiar with one level but comparatively unfamiliar with others, Miller has used the one outline with similar numbered sections to analyze the present knowledge about each of the seven levels of living systems.

So far as I know, the Miller model has not yet been used by social workers. But clearly it could be. An obvious initial undertaking would be to take a collection of social work intervention descriptions and translate them into the Miller framework. One could, for example, using the unitizing method described in Brill et al. (9) to study case records, and then for each unit or each instance in which the worker is reported as having done something with respect to a client system, identify the critical subsystems involved in the intervention. A more advanced stage in such an investigation would be to identify the method of intervention involved in work on different subsystems with the ultimate aim of discovering the similarities and differences when the object of the intervention is a different level of system. Such would be a giant step forward toward the evolution of a generic theory of social work practice.

Theory Building

The several research groups to whom we have been referring made notable contributions to theory. Another of the contributions of the Bolter et al. (8) group was to draw attention to the importance of openness–closedness in systems. They were able to show that many of the "psychoanalytic" problems which social workers encounter in their work with client systems at all levels occur at the boundary and take the form of dysfunctional degrees of openness and closedness.

The Carlson, et al. (13) group, which was the first group with whom I worked at Berkeley after the Toronto year, elaborated in important ways on the concept of feedback. A correctional school for girls in which there had been a recent riot was diagnosed as a system with inadequate feedback mechanisms.

Frank Montalvo (45) used the concept of homeostasis in distinguishing functional from dysfunctional families. There is a kind of homeostasis which is stultifying and a kind which is growth-producing for its members. The importance for social workers is to know the difference and to know how the latter can be induced.

Conceiving Social Work Holistically

A number of the studies referred to set the stage for viewing social work holistically. Lippitt, Watson and Westley gave us concepts such as planned change, change agent and client system; they suggested a typology of systemic problems, as we have noted, and they sketched a model of the process of planned change. The Bolter et al. group (8), as we saw, contributed a model of the systems universe which can be applied at all levels; they drew attention to the boundary region and showed its importance in social work. Other studies have demonstrated that a number of concepts currently in use are common to casework, group work and community organization. And, finally, Miller has provided us with a generic model of living systems with which we can build.

The Profession Responds

It is perhaps instructive to note in what manner and how quickly a profession incorporates and utilizes a new perspective. For about five years after the publication of *Theory Building in Social Work*, there was relatively little general response. It was a lonely period in which one wondered why one's own enthusiasm for general systems theory and its application to social work did not appear to be more widely shared.

Probably because of their preoccupation with theory analysis and development, the first to use the monograph tended to be faculty and students in the various social work doctoral programs. The other principal users were curriculum builders.

Eventually, there were inquiries from colleagues around the country. Many wrote to describe what they were doing with general systems theory; many sent papers. This prompted me, in 1966, to do the first simple survey to determine who, among the faculties of the Canadian and American schools of social work, were making any kind of use of general systems theory or the general systems approach to theory building.

There were 68 responses from 35 different schools. About half reported use of the general systems approach in one form or another and the remainder had used system as a concept in their work. Use had been made in literally all aspects of the curriculum, but principally in the human behavior sequence and in social work methods.

On the strength of this interest, an all-day seminar was organized at the Annual Program Meeting of the Council on Social Work Education in Minneapolis in 1968. About 250 attended, hearing and discussing five papers* by social work educators who had made impressive use of the general systems approach. The papers were subsequently published by the Council under the title *The General Systems Approach: Contributions Toward an Holistic Conception of Social Work* (29).

Teaching General Systems Theory

Is general systems theory too abstract to be of value to the social work practitioner? This is a question that has often been asked and a criticism that has often been made. It was something of a challenge, therefore, to see if general systems theory could be presented in such a way as to gain the attention of the practitioner and to interest him sufficiently to stimulate the use of general systems concepts or the general systems approach as a guide to practice.

Several attempts† to teach general systems theory have convinced me that the key to success is to engage the practitioner in a process in which he relates general systems concepts and theory to situations that are familiar to him in practice.

---

* Contributors to the symposium were: William E. Gordon, "Basic Constructs for an Integrative and Generative Conception of Social Work"; Howard Polsky, "System as Patient: Client Needs and System Function"; Carl M. Shafer, "Teaching Social Work Practice in an Integrated Course: A General Systems Approach"; Lawrence Shulman, "Social Systems Theory in Field Instruction: A Case Example"; and Donald E. Lathrope, "The General Systems Approach in Social Work Practice."

† The author has presented general systems theory in workshops in Iowa City, Baton Rouge, Oklahoma City, Miami, Denver, East Lansing and Portland.

Typically, in the workshops I have conducted, the participants are asked to think of an individual, group, organization or community with which they have worked in practice, and they are asked first to test whether it meets the definition of a system and whether it has the properties of systems, e.g., general purpose subsystems, an environment and a boundary. They are assisted in identifying the functional subsystems that are critical to the system's continued existence. They learn at this stage that what they thought of as the system may be a collection of many subsystems, each of which can also be regarded as a system in its own right.

They learn that in many practice situations the worker may be dealing with systems at several levels, and this affords the opportunity to demonstrate the utility of theory that can be used interchangeably at different levels.

The practice examples can be used further to provide examples of input and output processing and the phenomenon of feedback in its many forms. They search for examples of the processing of matter-energy in contrast with the processing of information, and are encouraged to recognize the functional subsystems through which this processing is accomplished. Usually it is possible to show the presence of the same subsystem at different levels and to show the form that it assumes in each.

Because social workers typically encounter systems under conditions of stress, the analysis inevitably turns to a focus on the malfunctioning of systems. Sometimes the effort is to identify what is wrong with the system, what is preventing it from functioning well or from realizing its full potential. One looks for systemic pathology.

But very often when one uses a process of systemic analysis one finds that what might have been regarded as pathological within another frame of reference is seen as more normal and functional within the general systems framework. An example is reported by Helen E. Durkin (18), a group psychotherapist trained in the psychoanalytic tradition, but also an ardent general systems theorist. In a recent paper, she has examined the phenomenon of patient resistance within the two orientations. In analytic group therapy, she says, the primary task is to overcome resistance with the therapist either analyzing it, breaking through it violently or using the influence of his authority to change it. She describes the analytic group method for dealing with resistance, but does so within the framework of general systems theory employing such concepts as boundary porosity, openness-closedness, central functions or Miller's "decider" subsystem and steady state. Her conclusion is that the broader, more objective general systems view diminishes the therapist's tendency to view the patient's resistance in a personal way, which brings about serious counterresistance in the therapist, diminishing the effectiveness of the analytic group technique.

Usually, in the teaching workshops, this kind of systemic analysis has been done in the total group at first to introduce the concepts and to demonstrate the method of analysis. This has been followed by work in smaller groups where more examples could be explored. It was only after this exposure to and experience with the theory that any formal papers, usually extending the theory, were read.

This approach seemed to take the mystery and strangeness out of general systems theory and to convince many practitioners that they can apply it quite readily, and that doing so often leads to some new insights. In each group there were always some who showed an interest in and a talent for building theory. When such theory building occurred spontaneously in any of the workshops, I was always quick to point out that we had just witnessed an example of the theory-building cycle in which the pursuit of knowledge and the refinement of practice had come together.

A holistic viewpoint

In my judgment, one of the profession's most important tasks in theory development is the formulation of a way or ways of thinking about social work as a whole. It has always seemed strange to me and somewhat unfortunate that while we have had theory about casework, group work and community organization we have had little, until recently, about social work itself. The serious consequence of this deficiency in the theory of social work is that it has led us to practice as specialists more than as generalists and without a generalist base to anchor our specialties.

In this final section of the chapter a holistic conception of social work is presented, partly as an example of what is meant as a holistic conception and partly for its inherent value.

This formulation derives from the work of William E. Gordon, a fact which should not be surprising to those who know how hard he has worked to define and conceptualize the social work process. The formulation suggests that social work does three different kinds of work, one of the most important of which is boundary work.

Social Work as Boundary Work

The point of departure is the article by William Gordon (21) in the Minneapolis monograph. For me, this very seminal article is built around seven basic ideas. Gordon holds that:

1. Social work has a *simultaneous dual focus*. It focuses at once upon the person and his situation, upon the system and its environment.

2. It *occurs at the interface* between the human system and its environment.

3. The phenomenon which occurs at the interface is a *transaction* between system and environment.

4. The transaction is a *matching effort*, whose focus is the coping behavior of the organism on the system side, and the qualities of the impinging environment on the environment side.

5. An encounter between an organism and the environment *leaves both changed*.

6. This next point is of special importance

because it raises the crucial question of how we judge the outcome of an encounter. How do we know how good an outcome it is? Gordon's answer is that the best transactions are those which *promote the growth and development of the organism while at the same time being ameliorative to the environment,* that is, making it a better place for all systems depending upon this environment for their sustenance.

7. The seventh point addresses itself to how this is done. Gordon suggest that *entropy is the key.* The answer, he says, is found in the second law of thermodynamics, which holds that unattended systems proceed relentlessly toward disorder, evenness, high probability, disorganization, randomness and continuity, or what is technically called a positive increase in entropy.

We know, too, that entropy is a constant in the universe. It cannot be destroyed; it can only be distributed differently. Thus, for growth and development to occur, there has to be a continuous redistribution of entropy between organism and environment.

On the organism side, entropy has to be reduced or extracted. On the evironment side, the entropy extracted from the organism has to be deployed in such a way that the entropy level of the impinging environment is not itself increased—it has to be distributed to the environment in a nondestructive way. Energy which cannot be used by the system has to be transformed so that it is available to other systems that depend on this environment for their growth and development. This is the process that ecologists refer to as *recycling.* That which is useless to one organism is extracted into this system's environment in a form that is useful to other systems in the same environment. They, in turn, in using it, convert the extracted matter into a form that may be reused by the organism that originally exported it.

Every feature of this formulation suggests that social work *occurs at the boundary* between the system and its environment and that, in this sense, social work is boundary work. This being so, it is logical, then, to consider the kind of work that occurs at the boundary.

When we speak, thus, of boundary work it is important to remember that we refer not only to work which may occur at the boundary between the system and its environment, but also at the boundary between one system and another, or at the boundary between subsystems of a total system.

One of the things that social workers do is to help the system *locate where its boundary is.* It may be a matter of defining a boundary if none is clearly perceived, or it may be a matter of reconciling the system's perception of its boundary with the way others see it, if there happens to be a discrepancy between the two.

Social workers help the human systems with which they work to regulate *their degree of boundary openness and closedness.* Systems can be so open that their integrity as a system is endangered. Or they can be so closed that they are denied sustenance in the form of materials and ideas that they need for their growth and development. There is an optimum degree of openness and closedness for each organism. Systems may vary in what that optimum degree may be. And the degree of openness that is optimal for any given moment may not be suitable for succeeding situations. Social workers help systems to regulate the opening and closing of client boundaries as circumstances require.

Social workers help the human systems with which they work to regulate *how much comes in and how much goes out* of the system. There can be either an overload or a deficiency of matter, energy or information and this applies both to input and output. Social workers help systems to develop mechanisms for regulating the flow.

Social workers help the systems with which they work to regulate *what comes in and what goes out.* This is essentially a filtering or censoring process, although I hasten to note that I am not suggesting that social workers should serve as censors. What we do, I think, is to facilitate the development and operation of self-filtering and self-censoring processes. I expect this is what we mean by ego development. It is the process by which the organism determines what is beneficial and what is harmful to either the organism or the environment.

Social workers help the systems with which they work or of which they are a part to regulate *the form* in which matter and ideas are exported from the system to the environment or imported into it. In what form do people emerge from our welfare system? Are they permanently crippled and dependent? Undoubtedly many of them are and will of necessity continue to be, in a physical sense, because of the nature of their infirmity or disability. But is it not possible that many can be helped to recycle themselves, at least in spirit, into the growth-inducing processes of society? This is clearly the thrust of *reeducation* and of *new careers for the poor.* And how do we export the physical and social wastes of human existence into the environment? Somehow we must find ways of doing it so that instead of polluting the environment, unusable material and energy are made available for other systems that rely on that environment for their sustenance.

Social workers help the systems with which they work to determine *how sharply their boundary should be defined.* This, too, is a matter of degree, depending upon the condition of the organism and the surrounding environment. When the organism feels threatened, it is probably more natural and more functional for the boundary to be rather clearly defined so that it is easier to determine what is in and what is out. On the other hand, when the system feels secure and the environment is experienced as relatively benign, it is more likely and more desirable for the boundary to be less clearly defined. I like the boundaries of our schools of social work and our social agencies to be somewhat vague so that it is relatively easy for other kindred systems to be a part of us—to intermingle freely and collaborate.

Finally, social workers help the systems with which they work to determine how narrow or expansive they will be. They help to determine *how much is to be included within their boundary.* One way to think of growth and development is to see the territory within the boundary as expanding. It seems likely that there will be great variation in the rate of expansion among systems, and also that the rate may vary during successive phases in the life cycle of any given system. I wonder if it is not likely toward the end of the system's life cycle, when positive entropy is tending to overcome the rate of production of growth-inducing negative entropy, that this process will be reversed, that the boundaries will be contracted, that the territory will be diminished. It may be more functional for the aging system to pull in the boundary than to expand it. As the energy level decreases the system may wish to be more fully a part of less than less fully a part of more.

The Social Work Domain

As I see it now, boundary work is one of three kinds of social work, the others being system work and environment work. In my view boundary work is probably the most crucial because it is where social work is, or ought to be, centered.

I have tried to represent this view of social work in Figure 13-6. One notes that there are three regions, each with two subregions. The subregions of the system are the unknown (unconscious) and the known; there is that part of the boundary region which is inside the system and that part of the boundary region which is in the environment—the two interface; and, finally, there are the proximal and distal subregions of the environment. These can be summarized as follows:

System Regions
a. Unknown
b. Known
Boundary Regions
c. In the system
d. In the environment

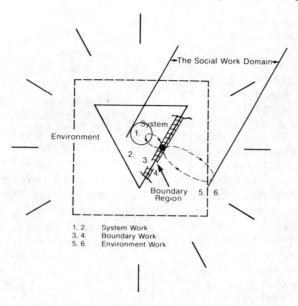

Figure 13-6.   THE SOCIAL WORK DOMAIN

Environment Regions
e.   Proximal
f.   Distal (remote)

Work is done in all of these subregions and they are sufficiently clear, I believe, as not to require further elaboration or illustration from our practice. The holistic view of social work that I am proposing regards boundary work, not as the whole of social work but as that aspect which may be its principal and most unique function. It is the function which *focuses and centers* social work. As Figure 13-6 indicates, we may often venture into system work and environment work, but when we do we should always return to the boundary to check the degree of correspondence between the system and its environment that has resulted.

If we are to think of ourselves as specialists among the helping professions, we should think of ourselves as specialists in work with wholes or holons and we should be especially skilled in boundary work. As such, we will be seen as the experts in such functions as linking, coordinating, relating, negotiating, mediating and encountering. This conception, I think, gives

social work a distinct and fairly unique function. Few, if any, other professionals think of themselves as boundary workers.

Toward a new world view

I find myself approaching the last section of this chapter with tentativeness and uncertainty, but with the conviction that it is a realm we must actively enter. What I refer to is the delineation of a new world view that is radically different from that which has guided inquiry of the past.

Outlines are beginning to emerge of a new conception of living systems, of the environment, of how to contemplate an uncertain and unstable future, and of how best to undertake the process of inquiry itself. My comments are sketchy and brief, intended merely to suggest some of the parameters of a new perspective.

Living Systems

One of our critical needs is for a new way of conceiving living systems. Buckley has made one such attempt, and he states the rationale for it as follows:

We have argued at some length in another place that the mechanical equilibrium model and the organismic homeostasis models of society that have underlain most modern sociological theory have outlived their usefulness. A more viable model, one much more faithful to the *kind* of system that society is more and more recognized to be, is in process of developing out of, or is in keeping with, the modern systems perspective (which we use loosely here to refer to general systems research, cybernetics, information and communication theory, and related fields). Society or the socio-cultural system is not, then, principally an equilibrium system or a homeostatic system, but what we shall simply refer to as a complex adaptive system. (10)

He notes that a well-functioning complex adaptive system will be characterized by (1) greater and greater flexibility of structure (2) ever more refined, accurate and systematic mapping, decoding and encoding of the external environment and the system's own internal milieu, and (3) the greater elaboration of self-regulating substructures (10). As we have noted, Miller (43) has approached the task in a different, but no less useful, way, in providing a paradigm for analyzing and describing living systems at all levels. He has identified the functional subsystems which are required to maintain the viability of living systems at each level. We might think of these as the universal properties of living systems.

Burian and Flynn (12) have identified other parameters in the new and emerging view of living systems of the types with which we work.

They suggest that we ought to think of *life in process* rather than of life in structure. We should take a holistic approach based on the principle of nonsummativity (the whole is different from the sum of its parts) rather than a reductionistic approach to understanding. We should search for isomorphisms in our theory building (although I must note that I ran into a criticism by Thomas Simon in the current General Systems Yearbook questioning the utility of isomorphism) (52). We should acknowledge the indeterminativeness of living systems. We should recognize morphogenesis as well as morphostasis, and we should be aware of the stochastic process which sees the events of life as not random but shaped by the events of prior process. So as not to be misunderstood, they elaborate on this latter point by asserting that life process is neither determined nor random. Prior life processes shape the probability of future events or, stated another way, prior life process shapes the probable range of future patterns of interaction. Stochastic process refers to the flow of human interaction subject to continual change, within a range of probability of future process. A very useful concept.

The Environment

Another part of the realm which ought to be explored in much greater depth is the environment. For the most part it has been neglected until very recently. We have known it is out there, but have paid very little attention to its form and substance.

The principal work on the environment, of which I am aware, was that done by Emery and Trist (19). Most of their work has been done in an industrial setting and concerns the organizational level of living systems. In an article about the causal texture of organizational environments, they identify four kinds of causal texture, each of which creates a different organizational environment:

1. The *placid, randomized* environment in which goods and bads are relatively unchanging and randomly distributed.
2. The *placid, clustered* environment in which goods and bads are not randomly distributed but hang together in certain ways.
3. The *disturbed, reactive* environment in which there are a number of systems competing for the same turf.
4. The *turbulent field* in which the dynamic

properties of systems in that environment arise not simply from the interaction of the component systems but also from the field itself.

While all four types are important, the *turbulent* type of environment would seem to have special significance for use in social work. It should also be noted that Shirley Terreberry, one of our own social work educators, has done some important theoretical work on turbulent environments (57).

The Uncertain Future

Another aspect of our new world view must, of necessity, deal with how to contemplate and fathom an uncertain and unstable future.

Harold Linstone (38), a systems scientist and a futures theorist, suggests that there are four ways to approach the future, each with different consequences.

The Surprise-Free Future. This is an approach to the future that acts as if and does everything it can to assure that the future will have all of the characteristics of the present. There will be no surprises. The conservative approach.

Internal Reconstruction or Reform. This second orientation believes that the surprise-free extension of the present is doomed to disaster and that the needed changes in the system can be understood, planned and implemented without dismantling the basic framework. The liberal approach.

The New Society. The third alternative, the new society, advocates a more revolutionary, though not necessarily violent, change. It believes that the system and its institutions are unworkable and must be restructured with a humanistic focus. The radical approach.

Authoritarianism. His fourth alternative is authoritarianism. Failure in any of the other three can easily drive a society toward an authoritarian or totalitarian regime.

A Fifth Perspective. Harold Linstone has still another alternative which he regards as superior to any of the previous four. As yet it doesn't have a name because it is only an idea awaiting embodiment. It is a "good risk" approach which increases the likelihood of a satisfactory future in view of its uncertainties. In this approach the formulation of better questions is regarded as more valuable than the statement of answers. The aim is to lessen the counterintuitive aspect of system behavior, to recognize threats to homeostasis, to disclose options which *increase system resilience and thereby avoid catastrophic occurrences.*

It requires new kinds of thinking and new kinds of mathematics such as topology and graph theory. It requires a sophistication in the modeling and gaming of complex systems. It involves extensive use of the computer.

The Process of Inquiry

These observations by Linstone lead us to a consideration of the process of *inquiry* itself. I shall confine myself to a quote from another systems scientist, John Sutherland, who states it well when he says:

We find the general systems theorist arguing for an end to academic parochialism and for adoption of an interdisciplinary attack; arguing against simple statistical–mathematical models . . . and asking for more elegant and relevant formulations . . . ; arguing against unwarrantedly deterministic paradigms and for paradigms which reflect the inherent complexity of most phenomena of any sociobehavioral significance.

The general systems theorist can argue in these ways because his commitment is not to any discipline or school, but to a philosophy; ... As such, he is free to exercise his dedication to the subjects he studies and to which he owes a responsibility; free from the ritualistic defense of his predecessors' positions ... free from the necessity to pay homage to any academic abstractions such as Freudian psychology, functionalist anthropology, or Parsonian sociology. ... He is an autonomous man, free to attack his *own* discipline and free to advance the cause of science. For when one is captured by a disciplinary dogma, one ceases to be scientist and becomes evangelist, ceases to be investigator and becomes concept-monger. (56)

This is advice that is well worth pondering.

And, now, a final plea of my own to the social work profession. May I suggest that what is greatly needed are more social work professionals with well-developed *metaphoric* minds. Along with the ability to think rationally, logically and analytically we need persons who can also integrate and synthesize, who can think creatively, and who can invent new ideas and new structures. We need persons who can see and work with wholes as well as parts.

There has been a great deal of interest in recent years in alternative states of consciousness. Andrew Weil writes of *The Natural Mind;* Carlos Castaneda (14) has given us a graphic account of his own experience with altered states of consciousness; and most recently Bob Samples has written about *The Metaphoric Mind: A Celebration of Creative Consciousness* (49).

Closely related to this line of thinking is the research being done on the two hemispheres of the brain showing that the left hemisphere controls logical, rational and analytical thinking whereas the right hemisphere, which Samples calls the metaphoric mind, governs our intuition, our emotions and our creative consciousness. It is the part of the brain which enables us to see things whole, to synthesize and to invent.

Samples believes that the rational mind is much more developed and much more widely used than the metaphoric mind. From birth on, culture supersedes the natural processes and tends to develop and encourage the use of the rational mind to the neglect of the metaphoric mind.

Clearly, what is needed are persons capable of rational and metaphoric thinking. This is absolutely essential if we should choose to think and practice within a holistic and generalist perspective.

It is a great challenge for social work education to find ways of activating and developing the metaphoric mind. I expect that if this is to happen much more of our teaching will need to be done experientially. I believe, too, that we will need to rely on other media for interaction than merely the verbal. We will need to develop our ability to communicate and interact through art, music, poetry, dance, drama and play because it is often through these that we experience the alternative states of consciousness that are necessary for metaphoric thinking.

Need I say that general systems theory, along with Wolfgang Kohler's "physical gestalten" and Kurt Lewin's Field Theory, are especially well adapted to the metaphoric mode?

References

1. Anderson, R. E. and I. E. Carter, *Human Behavior in the Social Environment.* Chicago: Aldine, 1974.
2. Armstrong, P. M. et al., "Constructing a Tool for Measuring Common Social Work Activities," School of Social Work, Portland State University, 1966.

3. Berrien, F. K., *General and Social Systems*. New Brunswick, N.J.: Rutgers University Press, 1968.

4. Bertalanffy, L. von, *Kritische Theorie der Forbildung*. Berlin, 1928.

5. ———. "The Theory of Open Systems in Physics and Biology," *Science*, Vol. 3, 1950.

6. ———, *General Systems Theory*. New York: Braziller, 1968.

7. Bloom, M., *The Paradox of Helping*. New York: Wiley, 1975.

8. Bolter, A. et al., "Toward a Generic Conceptualization of Human Systems," School of Social Welfare, University of California, Berkeley, 1962.

9. Brill, E. et al., "Toward a Generic Conception of Human Systems: A Method of Analyzing Teaching Records," School of Social Welfare, University of California, Berkeley, 1960.

10. Buckley, W., *Sociology and Modern Systems Theory*. Englewood Cliffs, N.J.: Prentice-Hall, 1967.

11. ———, *Modern Systems Research for the Behavioral Scientist*. Chicago: Aldine, 1968.

12. Burian, W. A. and J. P. Flynn, "The Systems Approach as Philosophy and Framework for Social Work," School of Social Work, Western Michigan University, Unpublished Paper.

13. Carlson, V. et al., "Social Work and General Systems Theory," School of Social Welfare, University of California, Berkeley, 1957.

14. Castaneda, C., *The Teachings of Don Juan: A Yaqui Way of Knowledge; A Separate Reality; Journey to Ixtlan: The Lessons of Don Juan; and Tales of Power*. New York: Simon and Schuster.

15. Chin, R., "The Utility of Systems Models for Practitioners," in W. G. Bennis et al., eds., *The Planning of Change: Readings in the Applied Behavioral Sciences*. New York: Holt, Rinehart and Winston, 1961.

16. Cutler, P. et al., "Social Work and General Systems Theory," School of Social Welfare, University of California, Berkeley, 1958.

17. DeCristoforo et al., "Development of a Tool to Measure Applicability of Social Systems Theory to General Social Work," School of Social Work, Portland State University, 1965.

18. Durkin, Helen E., "General Systems Theory and Group Psychotherapy: Resistance," Unpublished Paper.

19. Emery, F. E. and E. L. Trist, "The Causal Texture of Organizational Environments," *Human Relations*, Vol. 18, 1965, pp. 21-32.

20. Fisher, G. A. et al., "The Use of Self-Determination and Confidentiality in Casework and Group Work Practice: An Exploratory Study," School of Social Work, Portland State University, 1967.

21. Gordon, William E., "Basic Constructs for an Integrative and Generative Conception of Social Work," in Gordon Hearn, ed., *The General Systems Approach: Contributions Toward an Holistic Conception of Social Work*. New York: Council on Social Work Education, 1969.

22. Gray, W., F. J. Duhl, and N. D. Rizzo, *General Systems Theory and Psychiatry*. Boston: Little, Brown, 1969.

23. Grinker, R. R., *Toward a Unified Theory of Human Behavior*. New York: Basic Books, 1956.

24. Hall, A. D. and R. E. Fagan, "Definition of System," *General Systems*, Vol. 1, 1956, pp. 18-29.

25. Hartman, Ann, "To Think About the Unthinkable," *Social Casework,* October, 1970.

26. Hearn, G., *Theory Building in Social Work.* Toronto: University of Toronto Press, 1958.

27. ———, "Phases in Theory Building," in *Education for Social Work.* New York: Council on Social Work Education, 1960.

28. ———, "The General Systems Approach to the Understanding of Groups," *Health Education Monographs,* No. 14, 1962, pp. 12-26.

29. ———, *The General Systems Approach: Contributions Toward an Holistic Conception of Social Work.* New York: Council on Social Work Education, 1969.

30. ———, "Social Work as Boundary Work," *Iowa Journal of Social Work,* Vol. 3, No. 2, 1970, pp. 60-64.

31. ———, "The Client as Focal Subsystem," and "Social Work as an Intervention Subsystem," Chaps. 3 and 6 in H. H. Werley et al., *Health Research: The Systems Approach.* New York: Springer, 1976.

32. Herrick, J. E., *Theory Building for Basic Institutional Change.* San Francisco: R. & E. Research Assoc., 1977.

33. Kahn, A. J., *Shaping the New Social Work.* New York: Columbia University Press, 1974.

34. Koestler, A., *The Ghost in the Machine.* London: Hutchinson, 1967.

35. Koestler, A. and J. R. Symthies, eds., *Beyond Reductionism: New Perspectives in the Life Sciences.* Boston: Beacon Press, 1971.

36. Lathrope, Donald E., "A General Systems Approach in Social Work Practice," in Gordon Hearn, ed., *General Systems Approach: Contributions Toward an Holistic Conception of Social Work.* New York: Council on Social Work Education, 1969.

37 Lewin, K., "Frontiers in Group Dynamics: Concept, Method and Reality in Social Science: Social Equilibria and Social Change," *Human Relations,* Vol. 1, No. 1, 1947, pp. 13-31.

38. Linstone, H. A., "Four American Futures: Reflections on the Role of Planning," *Technological Forecasting and Social Change,* Vol. 4, 1972, pp. 41-60.

39. Lippitt, R., J. Watson and B. Westley, *Dynamics of Planned Change.* New York: Harcourt Brace, 1958.

40. Lloyd, G. A., "Current Trends in Social Work Practice and Knowledge," Graduate School of Social Work, University of Texas at Austin.

41. Maruyama, Magaroh, "The Second Cybernetics: Deviation-Amplifying Mutual Causal Processes," *American Scientist,* Vol. 51, 1963.

42. ———, "Paradigmatology and Its Application to Cross Disciplinary, Cross Professional and Cross Cultural Communication," *Cybernetics* (Namur), Vol. 17, No. 2, 1974, pp. 149-151.

43. Miller, J. G., "Toward a General Theory of the Behavioral Sciences," *American Psychologist,* Vol. 10, 1955, pp. 513-531.

44. ———, *Living Systems.* New York: McGraw-Hill, 1978.

45. Montavlo, F., "Homeostasis in Functional and Dysfunctional Family Systems," *U.S. Army Social Work, 1964.* Social Service Consultant, Office of Surgeon General, Department of Army, Washington, D.C.

46. Pincus, A. and A. Minahan, *Social Work Practice.* Itasca, N.Y.: Peacock, 1973.

47. Polsky, H., "System as Patient: Client Needs and Systems Functions," in Gordon Hearn, ed., *General Systems Approach: Contributions Toward an Holistic Conception of Social Work*. New York: Council on Social Work Education, 1969.

48. Rubin, Gerald K., "General Systems Theory: An Organismic Conception for Teaching Modalities in Social Work Intervention," *Smith College Studies in Social Work*, Vol. 43, No. 3, 1973, pp. 206-219.

49. Samples, Bob, *The Metaphoric Mind: A Celebration of Creative Consciousness*. Reading, Mass.: Addison-Wesley, 1976.

50. Shafer, Carl M., "Teaching Social Work Practice in an Integrated Course: A General Systems Approach," in Gordon Hearn, ed., *The General Systems: Contributions Toward an Holistic Conception of Social Work*. New York: Council on Social Work Education, 1969.

51. Shulman, L., "Social Systems Theory in Field Instruction: A Case Example," in Gordon Hearn, ed., *The General Systems Approach: Contributions Toward an Holistic Conception of Social Work*. New York: Council on Social Work Education, 1969.

52. Simon, T. W., "Toward an Empiricist Systems Theory," *General Systems*, Vol. 20, 1975, pp. 209-211.

53. Siporin, M., *An Introduction to Social Work Practice*. New York: Macmillan, 1975.

54. Stein, I., *Systems Theory, Science and Social Work*. Metuchen, N.J.: Scarecrow Press, 1974.

55. ——, "The Application of Systems Theory to Social Work Practice and Education," Paper presented at the annual Program Meeting of the Council on Social Work Education, New York, January, 1966.

56. Sutherland, J. W., *A General Systems Philosophy for the Social and Behavioral Sciences*. New York: Braziller, 1973, pp. 189-190.

57. Terreberry, S., "The Evolution of Organizational Environments," Unpublished Paper, 1967.

58. Turner, F. J., *Social Work Treatment: Interlocking Theoretical Approaches*. Second Edition. New York: Free Press, 1979.

59. Weil, A., *The Natural Mind*. Boston: Houghton Mifflin, 1972.

60. Weiner, N., *The Human Use of Human Beings*. New York: Doubleday, Anchor Books, 1954.

61. Werley, H. H. et al., *Health Research: The Systems Approach*. New York: Springer, 1976.

14
The Life Model
of Social Work Practice

by

CAREL GERMAIN and ALEX GITTERMAN

The science and humanism of ecology have been gaining ground in the behavioral sciences and the helping professions since the mid-1960s when Earth Day celebrated a growing concern for the well-being of all organisms and environments. Among academic disciplines, sociology drew upon ecology even earlier.[1] It has now been joined by anthropology, psychology, geography, and history.[2] Psychiatry, clinical psychology, guidance counseling, and social work are developing applications of ecological ideas.[3] One reason for the widening interest is that ecological ideas offer diverse disciplines and professions a conceptual means of viewing the intricate complexities of human life. Social workers, for example, have been hard pressed historically by continuing debates concerning social change efforts versus efforts to change people. The practice commitment to person-situation has been difficult to implement; most often, it has been the situation that is given short shrift, perhaps because it seems intractable.

Ecological ideas, used metaphorically as an orientation to human phenomena, can help social work reach toward a complementarity between its two essential functions of individualized services to individuals, groups, and families, *and* social action to improve environments. The ideas can also help repair the unintended severance between person and situation so that practice will be more effective in dealing with human needs and problems in the complicated world of the 1980s. We believe that social work has a dual, simultaneous function to promote natural growth and development of people and to influence the environment to be supportive of such growth and development. The focus of practice, then, is on the interface where the coping patterns and adaptive potential of the person and the qualities of the impinging environment come together. This means that the practitioner's and client's efforts are directed to the patterns and potential of the client, the qualities of the environment, or both in order to improve the transactions between them.[4]

Ecological concepts

The ecological perspective and its evolutionary, adaptive view of people and their environments lead quite naturally to an emerging approach to practice, now being referred to in the literature as the Life Model of practice.[5] Before examining the dimensions of the Life Model, however, we will present the particular theoretical concepts, derived from ecology, that are pertinent to the dual function of social work practice, and on which the Life Model rests. One set of concepts refers to the transactions that take place between people and environments. These include adaptation, reciprocity, mutuality, goodness-of-fit, stress, coping, and pollution. The second set of ideas refers to particular human attributes achieved in growth and development through interaction with environments. These include the sense of identity, competence, autonomy, and relatedness. The third set refers to environmental qualities and are not yet as well developed in the literature as the first two sets. The major concept is the nutritive environment of stimuli and properties that foster human growth and development, which we discuss within the concept of environmental layers and textures. It is important to note that within the three sets of ideas, some concepts refer to outcomes when things go well, and some to outcomes when organism-environment relations do not go well.

Transaction Between People and Environments

Ecology is a science concerned with the relations between living organisms—in this case, human beings—and all the elements of their environments. It is concerned with how organisms and environments achieve a goodness-of-fit or adaptive balance and, equally important, how and why they sometimes fail to do so. As a humanistic world view, ecology is concerned with what is good for human beings and how to keep their environments safe for human growth and development biologically, cognitively, socially, and psychologically. Thus the ecological perspective embraces both knowledge, or theory, and values.

All forms of life strive toward a goodness-of-fit with their environment—over evolutionary time in the case of the species, and over the developmental life span in the case of the individual. At times the fit may be achieved at the expense of other organisms, thus reflecting issues of conflict and differential power. Living forms need to receive from the environment the stimuli and resources needed for development and survival. Reciprocally, the environment becomes more and more differentiated through the products of its life forms and thus capable of supporting more, and increasingly diverse, forms of life.

These reciprocal processes do not always go well. The environment constantly changes, not only because of the activities of living organisms, but because of weather, erosion, earthquake, etc. Organisms must adapt to such changes, making use of random genetic mutations which are selected by the environment for their survival value. Living forms also change the environment to make it conform to their needs, as in the nest-building of birds or the dam-building of beavers, and must adapt to these changes as well. If organisms damage the environment too severely, it may no longer be able to support them or other life forms. Reciprocally, if the environment fails to provide what the organism or the species requires, it may damage or threaten the survival of the organism or the species. Some species develop migratory patterns as adaptations to seasonally depriving environments.

In human beings, all of this is considerably more complex. The adaptive processes are not solely biological but are also psychological, social, and cultural. Dubos suggests that human beings have undergone little genetic change in the past one hundred thousand years.[6] Through language, symbolization, knowledge and belief systems, and technology human beings have changed both themselves and their environments, and then have had to adapt to those changes. The remakable human adaptability, due to a large brain and to the diversity of the gene pool for recombination, enables human beings to continue adapting to physical and social environments they have created and often damaged to the point where the quality of human life may decline. Many of these adaptations may, in fact, be in violation of human biological and psychological equipment that developed over aeons of time in response to the evolutionary environment of hunter-gatherer groups. Thus, modern, urbanized, and industrialized life poses adaptive demands of a biological, psychological, and social nature that may exceed the adaptive limits of many or most human beings. Any genetic change through random mutation and natural selection, in order to accommodate to present environments, will, of course, require further aeons of time, while human technology continues to change the environment with greater and greater rapidity. Because genetic change cannot keep up with technological change, it would seem that human beings must continue to rely on cultural and social processes to change both themselves and their environments to achieve an adaptive balance. Such a balance is a constantly changing one since human needs and goals are constantly changing, in addition to the constant changes in the environment.

The excessive adaptive demands are clear in the case of chemically polluted environments, but it is also becoming clearer in the case of socially polluted environments such as public housing projects, designed without sufficient attention to the basic human need for privacy and security, on the one hand, and intimacy and social relations, on the other. Even such a highly regarded man-made environment as the obstetrical service of a technically advanced medical center may violate innate or biologically based needs of mother and infant for intimate contact immediately following birth, or for the social need of father for role induction.[7] Similarly, urban environments such as schools and work sites often violate deep-seated biological rhythms that evolved over the millennia and have remained essentially unchanged. These and a host of other adaptive challenges may account for some forms of disorganized behavior, interpersonal distress, and certain physical disorders that have resisted medical control.[8] Moreover, we not only pollute our physical environments by technological processes and social neglect, but we also pollute our social environments by such social and cultural processes as poverty, racism, sexism, and ageism. Such processes are created by human beings as they strive to reach a goodness-of-fit with their environments. Yet they make human development and functioning—i.e., adaptation—more difficult and sometimes impossible.

Upsets in the usual or desired fit can be conceptualized as stress. Either internal or external stimuli may provoke stress because of their presence or their absence. They are termed stressors, while the personal or social response is viewed as a state of stress. The response is mediated by age, sex, culture, past experience, genetic endowment, particular vulnerabilities, and present physical state. As a natural, recurring life process, stress is not always problematic. It may even be sought after to relieve tedium, and can be experienced as pleasurable or be derived from pleasurable events. Where it is problematic, however, stress may still be manageable as people call upon their usual coping repertoire for eliminating, reducing, or accommodating to stress. Stress is considered unmanageable when the usual coping strategies fail to accomplish their purpose, or when people perceive coping demands to be beyond their capabilities. As an upset in the usual fit or balance between persons and environments, stress occurs in the interface where coping patterns and environmental qualities touch.

Coping is mediated, in part, by personality

variables that are in reciprocal relation to the environment. For example, the personality variables include motivation, a degree of self-esteem and psychic comfort, problem-solving skills, and the autonomy to make decisions and take effective action. Mechanic points out, however, that motivation depends upon the incentives and rewards provided by the environment.[9] Self-esteem and at least minimal control of anxiety or depression depend upon social supports and emotional sustainment provided by the environment. Problem-solving abilities depend upon adequate training by the family, school, and other institutions in the social environment. Adequate time and space, literally and figuratively, for the exercise of autonomous action must be provided by the physical and social environments. In other words, coping, too, is a transactional phenomenon located in the interface.

In concluding this section on transactions, we wish to emphasize, first, that the human being must receive appropriate environmental nutriments at the appropriate time if genetic potential is to be released and biological, cognitive, sensory-perceptual, physical, emotional, and social development is to proceed. The ecological perspective abjures notions of genetic, psychic, or environmental determinism. Modern biological theory has made it increasingly clear that human development and functioning (phenotype) is the outcome of complex interaction between polygenetic potential (genotype) and environmental releasers, stimuli, or nutriments.[10] Theories of adult socialization and competence suggest that, contrary to the tenets of psychic determinism, human personality continues to develop and even to change over the life cycle as the result of life events and processes.[11] Thus it would seem that human beings achieve degrees of freedom from biological and environmental limits by virtue of their culture. They achieve degrees of freedom from their own histories (psychic limits) by their genetic potential for growth, development, and the acquisition of adaptive abilities through learning.

Second, we wish to emphasize that, in contrast to popular usage, biological and personality theorists refer to adaptation as an active, creative process by which human beings change their environments to conform to their needs and aspirations, and by which they actively change themselves to conform to acceptable, or unchangeable, environmental requirements.

A third form of adaptation is migration to a new environment.[12] adaptive maneuvers may, of course, also represent passive adjustment—sometimes as the result of an active process of decision making[13]—but sometimes as the result of a passive orientation to life. The latter is an attempt at adaptation, but in Western cultures it may be essentially maladaptive since it leads to relinquishment of autonomy, submergence of competence, and weakening of identity. It is frequently manifested in apathy, alienation, and physical or psychological symptomatology.

Identity, Competence, Autonomy, and Human Relatedness

These concepts are clearly related. The sense of *identity* arises from the interaction with other human beings, beginning in the intimacy of the first relationship[14] and later attachments within the family, and then moving outward in ever widening circles of social experience. The infant has innate, genetically programmed capacities that assure his connectedness to the environment, including sucking, clinging, and rooting reflexes. Mother brings her own qualities and experiences to the interaction. But, in addition, the infant's appearance, his postural responses to being held, his spontaneous crying, his ability to soothe himself, and his sensitivity to sensory stimuli evoke particular behaviors in the mother, to which the infant then responds. His responses evoke responses in the mother in a mutually regulated series of interactions.[15] In these interactions, the baby's image of himself develops and his early store of self-esteem is laid down. Much depends, too, on the appropriate provision of sensory-perceptual stimuli.[16]

As the child grows, social experiences continue to shape her sense of identity, self-image, and self-esteem. The perceptions and evaluations made by others of herself and of her family will have a profound impact, particularly as gender, race, and social class factors are incorporated into her identity. For Erikson, the achievement of identity is the major task of adolescence in which past experiences, present realities, and future aspirations must coalesce into a sense of self that meshes well with the perceptions of significant others and the role definitions of the culture.[17] Nevertheless, identity remains an issue across the life cycle, worked and reworked many times over through interactions with the social and physical environments and in the course of life events.

Competence is tied to the sense of identity, autonomy, and relatedness. In White's view, it is the sum of the person's successful experiences in the environment.[18] As an innate motivation, it is gratified when the baby experiences his effects on the environment. If he has the opportunity to learn that his cries bring food or soothing or comfort in response to his signals, or that his smile and gaze bring interesting and pleasurable social interaction with mother and other caretakers, then he experiences a sense of competence. Curiosity, explorative behavior, and learning are related to competence motivation. Subsequent experiences of having an effect on the social and physical environments, of influencing them to meet one's need and to stimulate one, can contribute to the sense of competence in childhood and adulthood, or stifle it. In Erikson's terms, competence is the major developmental task of the school child. In order for the child to achieve a sense of industriousness and competence, however, the family, school, and community must provide the conditions that will maintain curiosity and exploration and be responsive to the individual needs of the child for successful learning experiences within his unique capacities, interests, and life style.[19] Further, the outer world must provide the resources necessary for the school

to be a place where teachers are free to teach and children are free to learn. Competence is actually a lifelong issue, with opportunities for successful action in the environment strengthening the sense of competence so that future action is also likely to be successful. People who have had little or no opportunities for taking successful action, who have been deprived of social respect and power, are caught too often in cycles of failure which dampen or obscure the motivation for competence.[20]

Autonomy, or the capacity for self-regulation, reflects a relative inner freedom and a relative outer freedom. The autonomous individual is relatively free from bondage to internal demands through her ties to other human beings and to the world of nature, maintained by innate and acquired adaptive capacities. The autonomous individual is relatively free from bondage to the demands of the external world through her ability to remain in touch with internal biological and psychological needs and demands.[21] The two areas of autonomy are reciprocal and each maintains the other. If either becomes total, then the other is lost.[22] For example, if defenses are so strong that one is no longer in touch with inner needs, one is in danger of losing one's autonomy to the environment, passively conforming to environmental demands. If, on the other hand, one fails to maintain one's ties to the environment for any reason, or fails to receive adequate sensory-perceptual stimuli, one is in danger of losing one's autonomy to the inner world, enslaved by biological and autistic preoccupations. Hence the achievement of autonomy derives from human relatedness, competent action in the environment, a clear sense of identity—and contributes to them.

While Erikson suggests that autonomy is a major developmental task of the preschool child along with initiative, the struggle to establish and maintain autonomy clearly continues throughout life. Indeed, in the Eriksonian framework, the developing individual at each stage is dependent upon both internal and external stimuli for development to take place, yet she achieves more and more relative autonomy from both the inner and outer worlds as each stage is successfully traversed.

Human relatedness is a major biological and social imperative for the human being over the life cycle. Without relationships, the human infant could not survive, and without a sense of relatedness to others, the human being would scarcely be human.[23] While the infant comes into the world preadapted for survival through equipment provided by evolution, she needs to undertake a long and complex period of learning and socialization into her society and particular cultural group. Such learning and socialization can take place only within the context of human relationships, first within the family and later among peers, and in the social world of school, recreation, religious, health, work, and other institutional systems.

The young child, who is deprived for whatever reason of a continuing primary relationship with a consistent care-giver, may remain unrelated, trusting neither himself nor others. The infant without love, without attachment, however hygienic his care, fails to thrive. The loss of a loved person, either in childhood or adulthood, is perhaps the most difficult experience for a human being to undergo, and particularly excruciating in the case of a primary attachment such as parent, child, or spouse. These deeply painful experiences of emotional isolation, derived from loss and separation, are distinguishable from the pain of social isolation felt by the person who lacks a network of human relationships, such as the newcomer or migrant, and the person who has learned to fear relationships because of their potential for loss and pain.[24] Often the aged person—and, indeed, other individuals as well—suffers a double burden of both emotional and social isolation when, having lost a spouse, he is also without a network of caring others. To care and be cared for are among the most treasured of human experiences, and such experiences underscore the connection between dependence and indepen-

dence. The appropriateness of each, in the varying circumstances of life, may best be expressed as interdependence, which is maintained across the life span by reciprocal processes of respect and caring in mutually valued relationships.

Part of the adaptive achievements in the human attribute of relatedness includes attachments to treasured objects and to the sense of kinship with the world of nature. The sense of identity is tied not only to primary and other human relationships, but is also frequently associated with a sense of place—a country, a region, a town—the place of one's origin. A move away from one's roots and from a place to which one is attached can be painful. The loss of one's home or any treasured possession may also be stressful, for such objects often represent attachments that have become incorporated as part of one's identity. Those who are uprooted from their neighborhoods by urban development sometimes respond to the loss with depression.[25] The loss is felt not only with respect to the network of human relationships within the neighborhood, but is also derived from attachment to the layout, design, structure—the ambience—of the neighborhood itself, which has become part of the sense of relatedness and belonging.

Dubos, a biologist, and Searles, a psychiatrist, have each written eloquently of the need of human beings for a sense of kinship with nature, arising out of their evolutionary heritage.[26] The joy in pets, plants and gardening, and the pleasures of experiences in parks, countryside, and seashore attest to this kinship. Adults and children who are imprisoned in urban slum environments are deprived of natural resources for psychological well-being, spiritual refreshment, and an enriched sense of identity, competence, autonomy, and relatedness. Searles takes the position that human beings throughout life struggle to differentiate themselves in increasing measure, not only from the human environment, but from the "nonhuman" environment as well. To the degree that the individual succeeds in these differentiations, he or she develops increasingly meaningful relatedness with other human beings and with the natural world.[27]

Erikson suggests that intimacy and generativity—the caring for others—are the major developmental tasks of young and middle adulthood. Integrity, as the fruit of having taken care of people and things, is the major task of the ending years. The principle of epigenesis, on which Erikson's framework is based, postulates that the successful resolution of these tasks in human relatedness flows out of earlier, age-appropriate adaptive achievements of trust, autonomy, initiative, industry and competence, and identity in the transactions between person and environment. Issues of human relatedness and involvement with others are therefore critical across the life cycle, and crucial to the achievement of integrity at the end of life: "Death itself is a human experience of relatedness, its interpersonal quality often being distorted as greatly by the withdrawal of the living as of the dying."[28]

The Environment

The environment may be considered as consisting of layers and textures. The layers are the social environment and the physical environment, while the textures are time and space. The social environment is the human environment of other people at many levels of organization, ranging from a dyadic relationship to society itself. Our principal interest in the social environment will be in social networks and bureaucratic organizations since they touch closely on social work practice. The physical environment comprises the world of nature and the built world constructed by human beings. The physical and social environments interact in complex ways, each shaping the other. Their interaction is still more complex by virtue of the relation between them and the culture. Values, norms, knowledge and belief systems, the polity and the economy influence the ways in which

people use and respond to the physical environment, and they also shape the patterns of social relationships and the functions of social structures. Thus the interactions among the physical and social environments and the culture influence people's behavior. Reciprocally, people's behaviors affect and often change the physical or social environments, influencing the development and direction of cultural norms and values. The scientific and technological development (culture) of oral contraception, for example, affected social behavior in the realm of sexuality by changing the norms for that behavior. It contributed to the emergence of new family forms and changes in the traditional roles of men and women, and created new social structures within the health care system. These effects, in turn, have had profound and unanticipated influences in other realms of life.

Cultural values and social forces influence the construction, location, and design of public mental hospitals, housing projects, and welfare offices, which then have an impact on the self-image and sense of identity of those dependent upon the services, shaping the nature of their social interaction. One need only view the exterior and interior differences between a welfare office and a private family agency, between a ghetto school and a suburban school, between a state hospital and a private psychiatric facility, or between a public housing project and a private apartment complex to see the interdependence of culture, the social environment, and the physical environment. In each paired example, it is probably safe to say that one member of the pair represents a non-nutritive environment while the other represents a nutritive environment, from the standpoint of their differing impact on the sense of identity, autonomy, competence, and human relatedness of those functioning within them.

Bureaucratic organizations are a salient feature of the social environment. Within the institutions of social welfare, health and mental health, and education, in particular, bureaucratically organized structures are established in response to a need, and in order to meet that need efficiently and fairly by division of labor, policies and rules, and authority and decision-making structures. Sometimes, however, such organizations gradually become more oriented toward system maintenance. Such an orientation displaces the original goals; the service function and the needs of the users of the service are subordinated to organizational needs and interests. Many hospital procedures, for example, appear to serve the convenience of the medical or nursing staffs rather than the comfort and dignity of the patient. Long waiting lists or the lack of evening hours in a social work agency sometimes serve the professional and personal preferences of staff, rather than the needs or life styles of potential clients. The latent function of such phenomena is to screen out groups considered not amenable to the agency's particular service approach.

In some organizations, power flows increasingly upward as they become larger and larger. This often means such structures are less and less able to individualize people. They depend instead on rules, computers, formal and informal labeling processes, and inflexible and dehumanizing policies. Thus it is that hospitals sometimes make people sicker, welfare organizations sometimes create generational cycles of poverty, schools may fail to teach children how to learn, and social agencies may fail to respond appropriately to human need.[29] In each such situation, the organizational environment is non-nutritive for clients, and probably for staff as well.

Social networks, by definition, are different from a mere collection of relationships. They represent a system of relationships in which the linkages between and among the members are considered influential in behavior.[30] The client need not have contact with, or even know, someone a little farther out in the network to be influenced by that person's linkages to other members of the network either positively or negatively. How that person views applying to a social agency for help with a family problem, for example, may influence whether the potential client even makes an application, or, if she does, whether she maintains contact with the agency.[31] Or that person farther out in the network may be a source of material or informational help to the client through the linkages connecting him and the client.

Networks may be natural, occurring within the life space of the person or family as the result of real-life relationships and interests. Thus they may be composed of kin, friends, neighbors, work mates, and/or others.[32] Other networks may be of an artificial or constructed nature, such as self-help groups of all kinds that come together with or without the assistance of a professional to deal with a shared problem, need, or goal.[33] A somewhat related concept is that of the natural helper and the natural helping networks.[34] The natural helper is someone in the neighborhood, single-room occupancy hotel,[35] or housing project[36] to whom others in the ecological context turn for help, guidance, and support. These helpers may also be found in certain occupations, including bartenders, hairdressers, taxi drivers, druggists, and, among Hispanic groups, spiritualists and the botanica.[37]

In general, social networks serve instrumental and affective functions. They are often mutual aid systems for the exchange of resources, the provision of information, and the teaching of coping skills.[38] Affectively, they can provide emotional sustenance, contribute to self-esteem and feelings of worth, and provide experience in mutual caring. Social networks, when they fulfill these functions, may be described as nutritive environments for the nourishment of identity, autonomy, competence, and human relatedness. Other networks, such as some adolescent peer networks, particularly within the drug culture, and an occasional kin, neighbor, or workmate network, may be non-nutritive, or even noxious, components of the social environment. They may undermine self-esteem, withhold resources, demand unreasoned conformity, exploit one member or scapegoat another, exert unrealistic or nonsocial expectations, and interfere with members' growth and development.

Related to the social and physical environments are the textures of time and space, and people's temporal and spatial behaviors, which reflect their responses to and uses of time and space. People's experiences of time and space are mediated by age, sex, culture, experience, and physical condition.[39] Culturally, people differ in their orientations to time and in whether they place greater value on past, present, or future time. Socially, much of our lives is governed by temporal cycles established by the social institutions and organizations of modern urban life. Such social cycles may or may not fit either our culturally derived orientations to time and its pacing, tempo, and duration, or the biological, temporal rhythms entrained in our genes by evolution. In addition to the biological rhythms of which we are aware, such as respiration and heartbeat, there are many others outside our awareness. We are only now learning of the physiological and emotional stress created by violations of deeply embedded temporal aspects of our being, and the possible connections between out-of-phase biological rhythms and such phenomena as depressive states. Familiar examples of temporally related stress are observed in long-distance jet travel, night and swing work shifts, and the lack of fit between individual or familial temporal rhythms and the social cycles of school and workplace. In family life, members regulate distance and closeness among themselves, and between themselves and the outside world, through their use of time and space.[40] This brings us to a consideration of space as an environmental texture and of people's spatial behaviors.

A social-psychological framework for understanding people's spatial behaviors, organized around concepts of privacy, personal distance, territoriality, and crowding has been developed by Altman.[41] The framework focuses on the interaction between internal phenomena of perception, cognition, and emotion, on the one hand, and the spatial features of the physical environment as mediated by the social environment and the culture, on the other. Privacy is viewed as a process that regulates social interaction at the interpersonal boundary. The desired amount of social interaction is achieved through spatial behaviors related to personal distance (body buffer zone) and territoriality. If less social interaction is achieved than is desired, there is too much space between self and others, and the person experiences an unpleasant state of social isolation. If the amount of social interaction achieved is greater than what is desired so that one's need for space exceeds the supply, then the person experiences an unpleasant state of crowding. Crowding is distinguished from density, in which the number of people present in a given space may not be experienced as unpleasant and stressful.

The actual physical space available, how it is designed, and the way in which objects are arranged within it affect how distancing mechanisms work. For example, the arrangement of furniture in hospitals, treatment cottages, and geriatric facilities influences the amount of social interaction that occurs. Chairs placed side by side along the walls of a common room discourage interaction, whereas seating arrangements around small tables encourage interaction.[42]

Territoriality in animals appears to be an innate mechanism that maintains patterns of social dominance related to access to food, nesting sites, and mates. Whether such behavior is innate in human beings is controversial, but the behavior itself is observable. In dwellings and offices, people use signs, screens, locks, fences, verbal and nonverbal communication, and even weapons to mark their control over space. Such props and behaviors serve the functions of protection, distance regulation, and clarification of role relationships. Territorial behaviors are also observed in mental hospitals and other total institutions as newcomers seek to establish a niche, and others cling to "their" chairs.[43] In family life, the child must learn early which spaces are open and closed to him and which objects are accessible to his parents but not to him. Closed doors, locked doors, and spaces designated as shared or private are used to regulate interaction in family life and also in institutional life.

Personal distance is a much smaller unit of space than territory, and has been discribed as a bubble of space carried around by the human being.[44] It is especially influenced by culture, but also by emotional states, sex, and age. The size of the bubble is different across cultures and thus carries the potential for distorted communication and relationships. Schizophrenic patients have a large personal distance and often react with flight if approached too closely, even by eye contact. Violent prisoners have also been found to have large personal distances, and misperceive intrusions into that bubble of space as hostile. They tend to react with fight responses.[45] Aged persons, because of declining acuity in sense perceptions, often have very small pesonal distances, seeking to maintain physical nearness to people and objects. This, too, may result in conflicted or distorted interpersonal relations. Young staff may react to what they perceive as intrusiveness by withdrawing, or young family members may react to what they perceive as sloppiness or disorder in the spatial arrangement of treasured objects.[46]

Crowding has been found to be destructive of established social patterns in animals.[47] Mating activities, mother-infant interaction, and dominance hierarchies appear to be undermined by crowding. Whether the effects of crowding on humans is similar is still controversial. Dubos notes, however, that human beings evolved in small bands, and it is likely that the crowded conditions of urban life, coupled with the need to relate in an impersonal way with many people, is a likely source of stress. What is even more likely is that the violation of the human need for privacy and for regulating the time and amount of interaction occurring in crowded, substandard slum housing is a source of physiological, psychological, and social stress. At the very least, adaptation, growth, and development become exceedingly difficult in such environments.

In considering the qualities of the environment, it is clear that the textures of time and space may be nutritive or non-nutritive elements of both the social and physical environments, depending on whether they support and foster the sense of identity, competence, autonomy, and human relatedness or inhibit and stifle these human attributes.

The life model of practice

In a sense, the foregoing sections have set forth the theory and value bases of the Life Model of practice. By this we mean that practice principles are derived from the concepts presented; and ecology's humanistic world view and its evolutionary, adaptive view of people and environments are consistent with what social work prefers for people, i.e., its value system. For the Life Model, the ecological perspective represents a philosophical conception of the human being as active, purposeful, and having the potential for growth, development, and learning throughout life. Such a conception lies in both the theory and value realms of the practice model. It results in a shift from an illness to a health orientation, and it reflects an emphasis on progressive rather than regressive forces.[48] The theoretical and value premises affect the following aspects of practice: the definition of needs or problems and the unit of attention; client and worker roles and the view of the professional relationship; and the nature of the helping process and its objectives. We will examine each in turn, and will end with a practice example.[49]

The Definition of Need/Problem and the Unit of Attention

In the ecological perspective, people and their environments are viewed as interdependent, complementary parts of a whole in which each is constantly changing and each is reciprocally shaping the other. In the Life Model, therefore, human problems and needs are conceptualized as outcomes of transactions between the parts of that whole. Thus they are defined as problems in living which have created stress and taxed coping abilities. Within the interface where person and environment touch, the problem or need reflects a disjunction between coping needs and environmental nutriments. Thus the unit of attention is the person(s) and the life space: the individual, family, or group *and* the ecological context become the "case" or the unit of service.

The domain of practice—the interface—is conceptualized as comprising three related areas of the life space, each with its associated life tasks, and each with a potential for stress if the goodness-of-fit between the life tasks, needs, and goals *and* the necessary environmental stimuli and resources is not present or is interrupted. The first area refers to natural life transitions as they occur in a particular culture. The second refers to the tasks that people face as they attempt to use, change, or otherwise influence their social and physical environments to be more responsive to their needs and goals. And the third area refers to the interpersonal relationships and communication patterns in families and groups that affect how individual, family, or group needs, goals, and tasks are met.

Life transitions include developmental changes across the life cycle; changes in status that present new or conflicting role demands; and crisis events—all with reciprocal tasks for the individual, family, or group and the environment. Erikson, for example, suggests that the life cycle can be viewed as a series of stages marked by an inner biologically based push toward growth and development.[50] This maturational impetus interacts with expectations and requirements exerted by the society and the culture. The interaction results in phase-specific tasks for the developing individual, and reciprocal tasks for the social and physical environments according to the given culture and historical era. The successful resolution of these reciprocal tasks depends, in part, on what the individual brings to them by virtue of her physical, mental, emotional, and social capacities as these emerged from earlier task resolution. It also depends, in part, on the qualities of the social and physical environments. When all goes well, innate adaptive capacities such as cognition, sensory perception, motor abilities, and language structures are released, acquired adaptive capacities are developed through learning and other interactions with the environment, and societal benefits accrue.

Families, as families, also go through developmental stages with associated adaptive tasks that may or may not mesh with the developmental tasks of the individual members. Family stages refer to the changes in family life that occur as the composition of the family, the ages of its members, and the nature of its interactions with its environment change over time and space.[51] The family faces different sets of adaptive tasks related to internal and external demands at each stage. Groups also go through developmental stages with associated tasks, although of a somewhat different character from those of individuals and families.[52] An "ostomy" group, for example, must not only deal with common life tasks connected to the disability; its members must also resolve group tasks as they proceed through stages of approach and avoidance, power and control, intimacy, differentiation, and separation. Should they be unable to handle a stage and its tasks successfully, they may not be able to achieve a mutual support system through which they help one another cope with shared concerns about their physical condition, social relationships, self-image, etc.

Various changes in status occur across the life cycle, resulting in new and sometimes conflicting role demands. These life transitions may or may not coincide with developmental stages. Occasionally, they may even upset or distort a developmental stage, as in teen-age motherhood. Certain statuses in our society carry particularly difficult role demands, including the statuses of mental patient, foster child, and AFDC mother.

As a life transition, crisis differs from other kinds of stress in its suddenness, its time-limited character, and the enormity of its impact on the individual, family, or group. Natural disasters, bereavement and other losses, grave illness or injury are among the expectable and unexpectable events in life that are experienced by most people as crises. Their successful resolution often leads to growth, while unsuccessful resolution may lead to prolonged stress and maladaptive functioning. Like other life transitions, crisis states pose adaptive tasks for both person(s) and environment. For many different reasons, all life transitions can be stressful, and people seek help with them or are referred for help.

People may also experience problematic and even unmanageable stress as they seek to use, modify, or influence their environment to be more responsive. They may be dealing with, or failing to deal with, a non-nutritive organization, social network, some other aspect of the social environment, or the physical environment. They may be seeking, or failing to seek, resources, support, information, or affirmation from an organization, social network, or another aspect of the social or physical environment. They themselves may be defeating the environment's efforts to be responsive. Issues of time or space may be contributing to the stress. Individuals, families, and groups often need social work help in pursuing these and other environmentally related tasks.

Interpersonal relationships and communication patterns affect all spheres of family and group life, including the ways in which the entity deals with life transitions and environmental issues. Family or group processes may be adaptive or maladaptive for the entity as a whole, or they may be adaptive for the entity but maladaptive for one member. Thus, scapegoating may stave off disorganization in the family or group while promoting it in the scapegoated member. When maladaptive relationships and communi-

cation patterns create problematic and unmanageable stress, families and groups may seek help or look to the social worker for help with the coping tasks involved.[53] Related to this third area are the maladaptive processes that can arise between worker and client(s) in the form of inappropriate perceptions, expectations, and responses—and which require attention by both the client(s) and the worker.[54]

The Life Model, then, is a model of service to individuals, families, and groups dealing with the stresses that arise from problems in living. It is not defined by traditional methodological distinctions, but uses individual, family, or group approaches differentially in response to clients' needs and objectives. While the practice domain has been conceived as comprising three areas for the purpose of analysis, the reality of practice (and of life) is such that the social worker and client(s) are almost always involved in two areas, and frequently in all three. This practice reality is consistent with a dual, simultaneous function to enhance adaptive capacities and improve environments.

Client and Worker Roles

This dimension of the practice model arises from the ecological emphasis on autonomy, competence, and reciprocity. Mutuality and authenticity, therefore, characterize the relationship of worker and client as a way of promoting the competence of the client(s) and reducing social distance and power differentials between them. The worker is responsible, however, for protecting the vulnerability of the person(s) being helped, and for seeing that client(s)' needs and not worker needs are the basis of their work together. What is being described is not an egalitarian relationship, although ideally characterized by openness and mutuality. The worker brings professional knowledge and skill to the encounter, while the client(s) brings experiential knowledge of his situation or predicament and what might be helpful, and his own skills and capacities. The two sets of knowledge and skill are of differing orders. Studt has suggested that the client has primary responsibility for work toward his goals, while the worker has secondary responsibility for providing the conditions that will help assure the success of the client's work on his goals and tasks.[55]

Contracting with respect to problem definition, objectives, planning, and action sustains mutuality in the relationship. It also engages the client's decision making and cognition, enhancing the sense of autonomy, identity, and competence. Here we must give attention to the ways in which people take on the client role. It is usually at the point where stress becomes problematic or unmanageable that people are propelled into social work service—either out of their own quest for help in managing the stress or by their environments, which find intolerable the stress created by the client's need, problem, or behavior. Thus people seek social work services of their own accord, or they may be referred by a person or social institution in the environment, often the court or school. There is still a third group of potential social work clients, to whom the agency itself proffers a service which the potential clients may either accept or decline.[56] Such offers are often made by social workers in hospitals, housing projects, or whatever the social work department or agency seeks to reach out to a population at risk, or to persons viewed as in need even though they may not themselves recognize the need or even see the agency as a source of help.

Engaging clients in a relationship and in contracting is a very different process across these three groups. Suffice it to say that with the person who defines her needs and objectives, the worker's responsibility is to find the common ground where client definition and professional definition meet. With clients on whom services are imposed and who often disclaim any need for help, the worker's responsibility is to locate areas of personal discomfort that may or may not coincide with the environment's discomfort, which precipitated the referral. The responses of such clients are usually defined as resistance and

lack of motivation, but with patience, empathy, and skill the worker may find what it is the client would like to see changed, usually in the environment. By conveying realistic hope that together they can change it, the worker may succeed in engaging the client in a relationship and in the contracting process. In proffering a service, the worker's task lies in establishing a balance between persistence and respect for a person's right to refuse a service. There are value dilemmas and knowledge issues involved, particularly as the profession seeks to move toward primary prevention programs, but discussion of them is beyond the scope of this chapter.

The relationship itself is viewed as a transactional system in which the worker and client(s) each serves as environment to the other. Each shapes the other. They learn and grow together, and the sense of human relatedness is enhanced in both. An action orientation for both worker and client is paramount, but must be geared to the client's own life style, capacities, interests, sense of time, and use of space.

The Helping Process

In the Life Model, activity is conceived as taking place in the initial phase of engagement, exploration, and contracting; the ongoing phase; and the ending phase of termination, which also includes evaluation in order to understand what was helpful and not helpful, and why. As in any systematic approach to practice, intervention in the Life Model is continually guided by assessment of the interplay of dynamic forces within the life space, including the influence of the agency as a presence in the client's ecological context. Together, worker and client seek to understand the meaning and impact of the pertinent forces on the person(s) and the problem/need in order to set objectives and to devise action that will engage positive forces in the person(s) and in the environment, remove environmental obstacles, and change negative transactions. Assessment, as a habit of mind throughout the contact, focuses on the manifest and latent functions of what is going on rather than searching for linear chains of cause and effect.

In the area of techniques or helping procedures, the Life Model is not prescriptive since most practice skills are common to most models. What may be different are the ends toward which the procedures are directed, as well as the areas of the ecological context where action takes place. By education and experience, social workers are highly skilled in helping people deal with stress. In their services to individuals, groups, and families social workers help build self-esteem and strengthen defenses against disabling anxiety and depression so that coping can proceed, while gradually encouraging the more accurate perception of reality so that coping can continue. Social workers mobilize and support motivation through skilled use of incentives, rewards, and the balancing of hope and discomfort.[57] They provide needed information and teach problem-solving skills on which cognitive mastery of the stress often depends. They mobilize and strengthen social supports through the client's real-life relationships and her linkages to social networks. If the client is without a network, she and the worker may consider joining an existing, or establishing a new, self-help group. Role rehearsal, games, puzzles, and simulations such as family sculpting, genograms, and ecomaps are often used for cognitive, perceptual, and emotional mastery of what might otherwise be a hopelessly chaotic situation.[58]

Help directed to the person(s) is coupled with providing opportunities for action and mastery in the life space, through the use of tasks, "homework," and action that the client herself can take in her own life space.[59] Action by client and worker can be directed to the physical environment, in reorganizing the use of space and time and in providing options for interaction and privacy in family life or in institutional life. It may involve the provision of more or less sensory stimuli, or of opportunities for ex-

ploration of the urban or natural environment or the care of a pet or a plant. Introducing such environmental props as calendars, clocks, signs, and labels can strengthen the orientation to space and time among institutional residents.

Action directed toward increasing the responsiveness of an organization, especially our own agency, requires the use of practice skills which are different from those utilized with the users of the service. It hinges on the differences between helping and influencing,[60] and requires skills of a political nature. These include the use of knowledge and skill in locating organizational barriers to service, identifying the forces likely to support or to resist change in policy or procedure, developing bases of support and devising means for neutralizing opposition in both the formal and informal systems. Knowledge and skill are required, also, for analyzing the power and decision-making structures and devising strategies for introducing, implementing, and institutionalizing the proposed change.[61]

Most social workers are skilled in individual case advocacy, with their own or another agency, securing entitlements for a particular individual, family, or group, or obtaining an exception to a policy or procedure. This very important activity must continue, of course, but an additional responsibility is suggested by the dual focus on person and environment, and thus by the Life Model. This is the responsibility to maintain vigilance regarding the impact of agency policies, personnel, and practices on all those whom the organization serves or is expected to serve; and, where needed, to take well-planned, knowledgeable, and skilled action in feasible efforts to influence the organization to change those structures and practices which have an adverse effect or fail to meet a need.

The practitioner who is highly regarded for his or her competence, knowledge, and practice skill is in a position to propose needed innovations in services and programs, such as introducing group services to replace long waiting lists, proposing arrangements for helping people before stress arises or becomes problematic, developing team models of service, or assisting in designing organizational roles for service users, perhaps even as team members. If clients are to achieve a strengthened sense of identity, autonomy, and competence they must be regarded as users of services who have the right to participate in shaping the services that shape their own destinies. If services are to be more responsive to needs and life styles, basic research is needed in such environmental areas as social networks, impact of physical environments on adaptation, coping styles of various population groups, and differential responses to particular kinds of stress. There are also gaps in our knowledge about the connections between interventions and outcomes—of what works when, with whom, and in what situations, with what kinds of needs, and under what kinds of organizational arrangements.

In any field of social work practice, the ecological perspective suggests that the social worker's professional competence must go beyond the level of technical knowledge and skill in the service context. It must also encompass a breadth of knowledge about the interacting forces impinging on that field of practice, including fiscal and political forces, demographic trends, issues of social policy, changing needs, research findings and technological developments, and changing cultural values, all of which affect the nature of practice in that field. Obviously, the demands of ecologically oriented practice require not only a high level of professional competence, but a strong sense of professional identity as well. Such practice also requires an agency that is willing to commit its resources to meeting client need according to how and where it is experienced, and to grant its staff the degree of professional autonomy needed to carry out the commitment. Social workers will then be professionally accountable not only to the agency and its funding sources, but also to the users of its services. While all of this may sound like a large order, it may also represent the minima by which the social work

practitioner may become a proactive force in social change. It may also distinguish the graduate social worker from other practitioner levels.

Practice Illustration

Mrs. Smith (white) was referred to the family agency after she called a hot line because Jane and Linda, aged 15 and 13, had stopped going to school. The agency's clientele comprises low-income families who face a variety of predicaments. Because Mrs. Smith was unable to come into the office, home visits were arranged. In the initial contact, the worker was struck by the physical appearance of the small apartment, which reflected a sense of isolation. Even the curtains were drawn shut as though the family felt itself under siege.

In this and subsequent sessions, the worker learned that Mrs. Smith blamed the children's school problems on her husband's drinking. She said Mr. Smith has been an alcoholic, in and out of treatment programs for years. He is a poor provider, and Mrs. Smith had recently asked him to leave because his drinking was disrupting the family. He continues to visit daily, which is all right with Mrs. Smith. About a month after service began, Mr. Smith was hospitalized with a serious ulcer condition, and this was a crisis for the family.

In addition to Jane and Linda, there is a son, Tim, age 16, who has not attended school in two years and is heavily involved with drugs. Jane told the worker she had stopped going to school because the kids teased her about an abortion. Linda said she quit too because she wants nothing to do with high school kids, lipstick, smoking, drinking, and boys, and she criticized Jane for her interest in these things.

Mrs. Smith said the family is supported by public assistance. She does all the household chores by herself. She has no relatives or friends, and has had no skills training. She explained there is no household routine, because no one has to be anywhere at any particular time. Finally members do not retire or arise at the same time. They do not eat meals together or share activities, except for constant quarreling over TV programs. The TV set is the focal point in the family and is apparently the major contact with the outside world. On the one hand, the family's use of time serves to keep them apart. Yet, on the other, their space is so cramped that when they interact it is almost always in very angry ways, as though to maintain some sense of spatial distance or separateness. Helpless and hopeless feelings seemed to pervade the family, and they were especially marked in Mrs. Smith.

The family's lack of connectedness with environmental institutions such as school, the world of work, and supportive social networks, plus their poor housing, insufficient income, and the devalued statuses related to welfare, alcoholism, and drugs had made family and individual life tasks exceedingly difficult. Clearly, the problems and needs in living experienced by the Smiths went far beyond the school problems of Jane and Linda.

Based on her assessment, the worker offered extensive outreach including home visits, telephone contacts, transportation, and help with environmental pressures and inadequacies. Once some of the environmentally induced stress was relieved, it became possible to engage the family in weekly family sessions on interpersonal discomforts identified by the family, individual sessions with the girls on the mutually defined goal of returning to school, and help to the family in negotiating welfare, health, and school systems on a more sustained basis. It was not possible to engage Tim, although he did attend some family sessions.

Environmental Stress and Intervention. As might be expected, massive intervention in the environment was required from the outset, along with the family and individual session. The severe winter presented a series of emergencies, and the worker used her skill as advocate and her professional contacts to help Mrs. Smith contest fuel bills and to secure special oil allowances and other entitlements for the family. Increasingly, Mrs. Smith was able to do some of this by herself, especially with arranging for better housing. Work was also done with the school in order to stave off legal action and its threat of foster placement for Jane and Linda. This included a tutoring program to capitalize on their own concern about falling behind, and helping them negotiate "individualized" programs to help ease the transition back to school. The worker also helped to expand the girls' social world. She took them on museum and library visits and shopping trips, and to recreational facilities, attempting to fit some of the activities to the girls' fantasies about wanting to act, travel, and do things they had never done before.

Stresses in Life Transitions and Interventions. In the individual sessions with the girls, the worker purposefully used herself as a role model. They had no alternative models in addition to their mother, and the worker made use of every life space event that occurred to aid in the process of identity formation. Jeering comments by boys on the street, an unpleasant gynecological examination experienced by Jane, and some episodes from family sessions were used to help the girls move toward greater acceptance of their approaching womanhood, more positive attitudes toward ethnic groups different from their own, more tolerance of their mother's passivity and of their own need to be both dependent and independent. These efforts were successful with Jane and less so with Linda, not only because of Linda's age, but because she was quite fragile, untrusting, negativistic, and unhappy. The worker supported Jane's attempts to achieve appropriate autonomy and distance from her mother. At the same time, family sessions were used to support Mrs. Smith's parental role and to help her see that Jane's need to grow up was not a rejection of herself.

Interpersonal Stresses and Intervention. The family sessions were directed to various issues, including individual differences, weekly reports on respective worker and client tasks in getting members moving again, and working on communication and relationship patterns. In one early session, for example, the worker helped Mr. and Mrs. Smith see their roles as parents and what this means for them individually and as partners and family members:

> I pointed out how Mrs. Smith could be seen as the "good" parent because of her over-sensitivity to the children's feelings (e.g., how hard it is to go back to school), and how Mr. Smith is seen as the "bad" parent because of his strong need for rules and discipline in the family. Mrs. Smith said she didn't see herself as trying to be the good parent, but as weak because she didn't discipline the children. She always felt sorry for them, having an alcoholic father. Mr. Smith said his wife cares too much about every little thing about her kids, which drives him crazy. As the tension rose between them, Jane, who had been mumbling under her breath, announced that she wanted to be somewhere else—a foster home. She hates this house—it's no fun. Her anger and unhappiness triggered a burst of tears from Mrs. Smith and many words of hopelessness and guilt. I commented on how alone Mr. and Mrs. Smith feel in their respective persons and roles within the family. They expressed anxiety about whether they are still a couple. They talked of how they hadn't lived as man and wife during many of Mr. Smith's drinking years, how the kids seem to try to divide the parents, and how Mr. Smith feels he is in competition with them for his wife. They looked at options, whether to come back together, to stay separated temporarily or permanently. When we ended, I said that Mrs. Smith had cried a lot today, and wondered if she cries during the coming week, could Mr. Smith help her with whatever is bothering her? He thought he could do this.

Many family sessions centered on communication patterns. For example:

> There was some silence, and then Jane said she wished Tim were here today because he would talk, and could speak for everyone. I commented that happens a lot in this family. People talk for other people which makes it easy for people never to have to say how they feel, because someone else will do it for them. The rest of the session then dealt with how people can talk about problems and issues without falling apart, so that feelings can be dealt with and issues can get resolved.

Frequently there were recriminations and name-calling, and the worker tried to move the family members away from blaming the TV for their fights to looking at the hurt and anger they felt for each other, especially from the name-calling.

Six months after service began, Mrs. Smith entered the hospital for a week for surgery, and Mr. Smith moved into the home to look after the family. For Mrs. Smith's return home, the worker, Jane, and Linda planned a special dinner that involved all the family members in its preparation. This was in line with the worker's aim to make use of natural life situations to the greatest extent possible. Although earlier efforts to engage the Smiths in family activities had not been successful, this plan worked. Mrs. Smith's temporary inability to perform her usual chores seemed to provide the lever for real change. Since her return, Mrs. Smith has been saying that if it weren't for their conflict over the children, she and her husband could be happy together, especially since her husband has been on the wagon since his illness. They have now asked to be seen alone for marital counseling. A new phase of the work is about to begin.

Summary. At the time of the initial contact, this family seemed to be on the verge of entropy as a result of lack of interchange with their environment and disorganized relations within.

All members were suffering stress associated with life transitions, interpersonal discomforts, and a harsh environment. The familial tasks did not mesh well with individual tasks, partly because earlier developmental stages of the family had not been successfully handled, and partly because of a non-nutritive environment. Out of their early and current deprivations, neither parent had achieved a sense of identity as a worthwhile person, or a sense of competence arising from successful actions in the environment. They had little autonomy or self-regulation, as Mrs. Smith was essentially passive, allowing the events of life to wash over her. Mr. Smith, enslaved by his impulses, was even less able than his wife to assume control of his life and to guide his family. Mr. Smith's years of alcoholism, while probably fulfilling functions for the marriage, and perhaps even for the family, had also contributed to Mrs. Smith's overinvestment in her children, and her inability to view their "growing up" and their struggles with separation as positive. Mutuality, respect, and caring within the family, and between the family and others, had never been established. Indeed, the family had had a "bad name" in the neighborhood, which caused them to isolate themselves and withdraw even more.

Family interpersonal stress and apparent inability to locate supports in school and with peers meant that all three children found it hard to achieve a sense of identity, to exert effects upon their environment that would contribute to their own growth, development, and learning. Thus they were unable to reach an age-appropriate balance between dependence and independence; and, above all, they lacked the nourishment of human relatedness inside and outside the family.

The worker, by conveying hope, respect, and concern for concrete needs, was able to reinstate competence and motivation. Self-esteem was partially restored in the parents through providing opportunities for successful action in the environment. All members were helped to reach toward some separateness and intimacy, toward some interdependence and reciprocity. The likely outcomes are still uncertain. Whether Jane and Linda can tolerate remaining in school and whether Mrs. Smith can tolerate their being there remains to be seen. Whether Mr. and Mrs. Smith can rebuild their marriage so their children will be free to move outward; whether Mr. Smith can abstain from alcohol, and regain his health and his role as provider is not yet known. The worker herself points out, "The multiplicity of needs and problems, the myriad of possible intervention points, and the well-established patterns make for slow progress and frustration at times—for the Smiths and for me."

But a successful beginning has been made.

Notes

1. See, for example, Hawley, Amos, *Human Ecology*, New York: Ronald Press, 1950; Park, R., "Human Ecology," *American Journal of Sociology*, 1936, *42*, 1-15.
2. Bennett, John W., *The Ecological Transition: Cultural Anthropology and Human Adaptation*, New York: Pergamon Press Inc., 1976; Moos, Rudolf H. *The Human Context*, New York: John Wiley & Sons, 1976; English, Paul W., and Mayfield, Robert C. (eds.), *Man, Space, and Environment, Concepts in Contemporary Human Geography*, New York: Oxford University Press, 1972; Spring, David and Eileen (eds.), *Ecology and Religion in History*, New York: Harper Torchbooks, Harper & Row, 1974.
3. Auerswald, Edgar, "Interdisciplinary vs. the Ecological Approach," *Family*

Process, 1968, *7,* 202-215; Kelly, James G., "Ecological Constraints on Mental Health Services," *American Psychologist,* 1966, *21,* No. 6; Blocher, Donald H., "Toward an Ecology of Student Development," *Personnel and Guidance Journal,* 1974, *52,* 360-365; Germain, Carel B., "An Ecological Perspective on Casework Practice," *Social Casework,* 1973, *54,* 323-330.

4. This conception of the profession's social purpose is drawn from Gordon, William E., "Basic Constructs for an Integrative and Generative Conception of Social Work," in Hearn, Gordon (ed.), *The General Systems Approach: Contributions Toward an Holistic Conception of Social Work,* New York: Council on Social Work Education, 1969.

5. See, for example, Bandler, Bernard, "The Concept of Ego-Supportive Psychotherapy," in Parad, Howard, and Miller, Roger (eds.), *Ego Oriented Casework,* New York: Family Service Association of America, 1963, pp. 27-44. To the best of our knowledge, the first use of the concept of a life model appeared in Dr. Bandler's article. See also Oxley, Genevieve, "A Life-Model Approach to Change," *Social Casework,* 1971, *52,* 627-633; Strean, Herbert S., "Application of the 'Life Model' to Casework," *Social Work,* 1972, *17,* 46-53; Gitterman, Alex, and Germain, Carel B., "Social Work Practice: A Life Model," *Social Service Review,* 1976, *50,* 601-610.

6. Dubos, Rene, *So Human an Animal,* New York: Charles Scribner's Sons, 1968.

7. See, for example, Klaus, Marshall H., and Kennell, John H., *Maternal-Infant Bonding,* St, Louis: The C. V. Mosby Co., 1976.

8. Dubos, *op. cit.,* p. 56.

9. Mechanic, David, "Social Structure and Personal Adaptation: Some Neglected Dimensions," in Coelho, George V., Hamburg, David A., and Adams, John E. (eds.), *Coping and Adaptation,* New York: Basic Books, Inc., 1974, pp. 32-44.

10. Dobzhansky, Theodosius, "The Genetic Predestination and Tabula Rasa Myths," *Perspectives in Biology and Medicine, 19,* No. 2, Chicago: University of Chicago Press, 1976.

11. Brim, Orville G., Jr., "Adult Socialization," in Clausen, John A. (ed.), *Socialization and Society,* Boston: Little, Brown & Co., 1968, pp. 182-226; Smith, M. Brewster, "Competence and Socialization," in Clausen, *ibid.* pp. 270-320.

12. See, for example, Dubos, Rene, *Man Adapting,* New Haven: Yale University Press, 1965, and Hartmann, Heinz, *Ego Psychology and the Problem of Adaptation,* New York: International Universities Press, Inc., 1958.

13. Bettelheim makes this point with respect to prisoners in concentration camps. See Bettelheim, Bruno, *The Informed Heart,* New York: The Free Press, 1960, Chaps. 3, 4, and 5.

14. Stern, Daniel, *The First Relationship,* Cambridge, Mass.: Harvard University Press, 1977.

15. Korner, Anneliese, "Individual Differences at Birth: Implications for Early Experiences and Later Development," *American Journal of Orthopsychiatry,* 1971, *41,* 608-619.

16. Schaffer, Rudolph, *Mothering,* Cambridge, Mass.: Harvard University Press, 1977.

17. Erikson, Erik, "Growth and Crises of the Healthy Personality," in Erikson, Erik (ed.), *Identity and the Life Cycle,* Psychological Issues, *1* No. 1, New York: International Universities Press, Inc., 1959, pp. 50-100.

18. White, Robert, "Strategies of Adaptation: An Attempt at Systematic Description," in Coelho et al., *op. cit.,* pp. 47-68; White, Robert, "Motivation Reconsidered: The Concept of Competence," *Psychological Review,* 1959, *66,* 297-333.

19. Gitterman, Alex, "Social Work in the Public Schools," *Social Casework,* 1977, *58,* 111-118; Gitterman, Alex, "Group Work in the Public Schools," in Schwartz, William, and Zalba, S. (eds.), *The Practice of Group Work,* New York: Columbia University Press, 1971.

20. Smith, M. Brewster, *op. cit.*

21. Rapaport, David, "The Theory of Ego Autonomy," *Bulletin of the Menninger Clinic, 1958, 22,* No. 1.

22. Miller, Stuart C., "Ego-Autonomy in Sensory Deprivation, Isolation and Stress," *The International Journal of Psychoanalysis,* 1962, *43,* Part I, 1-19.

23. See, for example, Will, Otto, "Human Relatedness and the Schizophrenic Reaction," *Psychiatry, 1959, 22,* No. 3.

24. This is a useful distinction made by Weiss. See Weiss, Robert, *Loneliness, The Experience of Emotional and Social Isolation,* Cambridge, Mass.: The MIT Press, 1973.

25. Fried, Marc, "Grieving for a Lost Home," in Duhl, Leonard J. (ed.), *The Urban Condition,* New York: Simon & Schuster, Clarion Book, 1969, pp. 151-171.

26. Dubos, Rene, *A God Within,* New York: Charles Scribner's Sons, 1972; Searles, Harold F., *The Nonhuman Environment,* New York: International Universities Press, Inc., 1960.

27. Searles, *ibid.,* p. 30.

28. Will, *op. cit.*

29. Miller, Irving, speech before the Alumni Conference of The Columbia University School of Social Work, November 3, 1973 (mimeographed).

30. Swenson, Carol, "Social Networks, Mutual Aid, and the Life Model of Practice," in Carel B. Germain, ed., *Social Work Practice: People and Environments,* New York: Columbia University Press, 1979.

31. Mayer, John, and Rosenblatt, Aaron, "The Client's Social Context," *Social Casework,* 1964, *45,* No. 9.

32. Litwak and Szelenyi identity differential functions for these groups. See Litwak, Eugene, and Szelenyi, Ivan, "Primary Group Structures and Their Functions: Kin, Neighbors, and Friends," *American Sociological Review,* 1969, *34,* 465-481.

33. See, for example, Katz, Alfred H., and Bender, Eugene I., *The Strength Within Us: Self-Help Groups in the Modern World,* New York: New Viewpoints, A Division of Franklin Watts, 1976.

34. Collins, Alice H., and Pancoast, Diane L., *Natural Helping Networks,* Washington: National Association of Social Workers, 1976.

35. Shapiro, Joan, *Communities of the Alone,* New York: Association Press, 1970.

36. Lee, Judith, and Swenson, Carol, "A Community Social Service Agency: Theory in Action," to be published in *Social Casework.*

37. See, for example, Fisch, Stanley, "Botanicas and Spiritualism in a Metropolis," *Milbank Memorial Fund Quarterly,* 1968, *46,* 377-388.

38. For one such example, see Stack, Carol B., *All Our Kin: Strategies for Survival in a Black Community*, New York: Harper Colophon Books, Harper & Row, 1974.

39. For more detailed discussion, see Germain, Carel B., "Time, an Ecological Variable in Social Work Practice," *Social Casework*, 1976, *57*, 419-426.

40. Kantor, David, and Lehr, William, *Inside the Family*, San Francisco: Jossey-Bass, 1975.

41. Altman, Irwin, *The Environment and Social Behavior*, Monterey: Brooks/Cole Publishing Co., 1975.

42. Sommer, Robert, *Personal Space*, Englewod Cliffs, N.J. Prentice-Hall, Inc., 1969

43. For studies of territorial relations among disturbed boys, see Esser, Aristide H., "Cottage Fourteen: Dominance and Territoriality in a Group of Institutionalized Boys," *Small Group Behavior*, 1973, *4*, 131-146.

44. These ideas have been developed by Hall. See Hall, Edward T., *The Hidden Dimension*, New York: Doubleday & Co., Inc., 1966.

45. Kinzel, Augustus, "Body-Buffer Zone in Violent Prisoners," *American Journal of Psychiatry*, 1970, *127*, 59-64; Hildreth, A., "Body-Buffer Zone and Violence: Reassessment and Confirmation," *American Journal of Psychiatry*, 1971, *127*, 1641-1645.

46. De Long, Alton J., "The Micro-Spatial Structure of the Older Person: Some Implications of Planning the Social and Spatial Environment," in Pastalan, Leon A., and Carson, Daniel H. (eds.), *Spatial Behavior of Older People*, Ann Arbor: The University of Michigan-Wayne State University Institute of Gerontology, 1970, pp. 68-87.

47. Calhoun, John, "Population Density and Social Pathology," *Scientific American*, 1962, *206*, 139-146.

48. Bandler, *op. cit.*

49. For a detailed analysis of the model, with illustrations, see Gitterman, Alex, and Germain, Carel B., *The Life Model of Social Work Practice*, New York: Columbia University Press (forthcoming).

50. Erikson, *op. cit.*

51. See, for example, Rhodes, Sonya, "A Developmental Approach to the Life Cycle of the Family," *Social Casework*, 1977, *58*, 301-311.

52. Garland, James A., Jones, Hubert E., and Kolodny, Ralph L., "A Model for Stages of Development in Social Work Groups," in Bernstein, Saul (ed.), *Explorations in Group work*, Boston: Boston University School of Social Work, 1968, pp. 12-58; Bennis, W., and Sheppard, H., "A Theory of Group Development," *Human Relations*, 1956, *9*, 415-537.

53. See, for example, Hoffman, Lynn, "Breaking the Homeostatic Cycle," in Guerin, Philip J., Jr. (ed.), *Family Therapy, Theory and Practice*, New York: Gardner Press, Inc., 1975, pp. 501-519; Aponte, Harry, "The Family-School Interview: An Eco-Structural Approach," *Family Process*, 1976, *15*, 303-312; and Shulman, Lawrence, "Scapegoats, Group Workers, and Preemptive Intervention," *Social Work*, 1967, *12*, 37-43.

54. See, for example, Gitterman, Alex, and Schaeffer, Alice, "The White Professional and the Black Client," *Social Casework*, 1972, *53*, 280-291.

55. Studt, Eliot, "Social Work Theory and Implications for the Practice of Methods," *Social Work Education Reporter*, 1968, *16*, 22-24, 42-46.

56. We are indebted to Professor Irving Miller for this distinction between imposed and proffered services.

57. Ripple, Lillian, and Alexander, Ernestina, *Motivation, Capacity and Opportunity,* Chicago: University of Chicago Press, 1964.

58. On the use of genograms, see Hartman, Ann, "The Extended Family as a Resource for Change," in Germain and Associates, *op. cit.* On the use of network maps, see Attneave, Carolyn, "Social Networks as the Unit of Intervention," in Guerin, *op. cit.,* pp. 220-231. On the use of family sculpting, see Papp, Peggy, "Family Choreography," in Guerin, *ibid.* pp. 465-479; Duhl, Frederick, Duhl, Bunny, and Kantor, David, "Learning, Space and Action in Family Therapy: A Primer of Sculpture," in Bloch, Donald (ed.), *Techniques of Family Psychotherapy,* New York: Grune and Stratton, 1973. On the use of puzzles and other activities, see Lance, Evelyn, "Intensive Work with a Deprived Family," *Social Casework,* 1969, *50,* 454-460.

59. Maluccio, Anthony N., "Action as a Tool in Casework Practice," *Social Casework,* 1974, *55,* 30-35.

60. Brager, George, "Helping vs. Influencing: Some Political Elements of Organizational Change," paper presented at the National Conference on Social Welfare, San Francisco, May, 1975 (mimeographed).

61. See, for example, Brager, George, and Holloway, Stephen, *Changing Human Organizations: Politics and Practice,* New York: The Free Press, 1978; Gitterman and Germain, *The Life Model of Social Work Practice, op. cit.*

Annotated listing of key references

The Ecological Perspective

COELHO, George V., Hamburg, David A., and Adams, John E. (eds.), *Coping and Adaptation*, New York: Basic Books, 1974.
Thirteen articles examine theoretical, practical, and research issues in coping and adaptation, with the emphasis on biological and social frames of reference. Each author is a highly regarded behavioral scientist.

DUBOS, Rene, *So Human an Animal*, New York: Scribner's, 1968.
Written by a microbiologist, who is also a humanist, this book presents an evolutionary perspective on human beings, and discusses the impact of modern physical and social environments on the development of human potentialities. The author suggests some components of the "good" environment.

GERMAIN, Carel B. and Associates, *The Ecological Perspective in Social Work Practice*, New York: Columbia University Press (in press).
Social work practitioners and educators, whose thinking and work are rooted in ecological ideas, present their conceptions and their practice. The articles range across fields of practice and individual, family, and group modalities. Attention is given to underdeveloped areas of practice, including the use of social networks, the therapeutic potential of life experiences, the ecology of Black language, social prevention, and citizen participation.

The Function of Social Work

GORDON, William E., "Basic Constructs for an Integrative and Generative Conception of Social Work," in Gordon Hearn (ed.), *The General Systems Approach: Contributions Toward an Holistic Conception of Social Work*, New York: Council on Social Work Education, 1969.
The author connects the two historical traditions of social work—a concern for people and a concern for environments that will promote the well-being of people—by drawing upon the constructs of general systems theory. The article represents the culmination of many years' effort to develop a working definition of practice, undertaken by the author and Harriett Bartlett on behalf of NASW.

SCHWARTZ, William, "Social Group Work: Interactionist Approaches," *Social Work Encyclopedia*, New York: National Association of Social Workers, 1971
Schwartz has long advocated a mediating function for social work, and a generic practice, based upon reciprocal relations between people and environments. This article analyzes and

describes how the social worker carries out the mediating function, with particular reference to the worker's function in small groups. The worker's focus is on the transactions between people and the systems of society.

Social Work Practice

BRAGER, George and Holloway, Stephen, *Changing Human Organizations: Politics and Practice,* New York: Free Press, 1978.
The authors present the theory base and the specialized practice skills necessary for understanding how organizations work and for making them work better for clients. The book is particularly helpful for social workers at lower levels in the organization's hierarchy who may feel they lack the power to effect change.

GITTERMAN, Alex and Germain, Carel B., *The Life Model of Social Work Practice,* New York: Columbia University Press (forthcoming).
Designed as a textbook, this volume presents the theories, values, and practice skills incorporated within the Life Model. Illustrations are presented of services to families, groups, and individuals in which the worker focuses on the transactions between people and environments, in a dual effort to release adaptive potential and improve environments.

MINUCHIN, Salvador, *Families and Family Therapy,* Cambridge, Mass.: Harvard University Press, 1974.
The literature on family therapy is prodigious, and the schools of thought diverse. We have found the writings of Minuchin and his colleagues, including the social workers Harry Aponte and Lynn Hoffman, congenial. Minuchin's ecostructural approach views the family as facing adaptive challenges in response to the stress of internal and external changes. He presents strategies for entering the family structure and influencing its internal and external relations.

15
Role Theory

by

HERBERT S. STREAN

Definitions of "Role"

The concept "role" has been variously defined in and out of social work. Its implications have been many and "role," particularly "social role," has been applied to an array of social and interpersonal situations. Most scholars and practitioners utilize the "role" concept to denote behavior prescribed for an individual occupying a designated status. Role or role behavior usually refers to how the status occupant should act toward an individual or individuals with whom his status rights and obligations put him in contact. Every individual occupies positions or statuses within a number of status systems, and a status system may be conceived of as a map that locates different statuses in relation to one another and demonstrates how they are interconnected. A person's status is represented by his location on such a map (16).

Status generally implies a relationship to another person; it characterizes an individual in terms of a set of rights and obligations that regulate his transactions with individuals of other statuses. For example, the status of "mother" implies certain rights (respect and obedience) and certain obligations (physical and emotional nurturing). A "middle-class" status locates an individual on a socioeconomic map and affords the individual certain prestige and a rank in his community for which he is obligated to behave in a certain manner if he wishes to maintain his position (80).

A status involves interaction and transactions with many individuals (16). The social worker in a social agency may interact and transact with clients, supervisors, administrators, other social workers, and a board of directors; with each group his or her status rights and obligations differ. By occupying a designated social status, the individual is inevitably confronted with a complement of role relationships which the sociologist, Merton, has termed the "role set" (45). "Role set" or "role" usually applies to situations in which the prescriptions for interaction and transaction are culturally defined and independent of the particular personal relationships that may otherwise exist between persons occupying the positions or statuses, as between an applicant wishing welfare assistance and a social worker. While there will, of course, be differences in behavior in social worker-client dyads depending on the individuals involved and the social context of the agency, much of the behavior that transpires between those in need and those occupying the status of dispenser of social services is culturally prescribed (76).

In a survey of the literature in many fields in which the concept "role" appeared in books and articles during the period from 1900 to 1950, Neiman and Hughes discovered that "role" appeared, at first, to be "a hopeless mass of different definitions, usages, and implications" (50). Upon careful analysis, the definitions yielded several categories into which most definitions of "role" could be lodged.

The categories that evolved from the Neiman and Hughes analysis are as follows:

1. *Role as the Basic Factor in the Process of Socialization.* Many texts use such a definition of "role" when they refer to personality as the sum and organization of all the roles one enacts in all the groups to which one belongs (54). For example, Cottrell advised, "Personality, or the most significant part of it, is the organization of the roles the person plays in group life" (14).

2. *Role as a Cultural Pattern.* As an example of using "role" as a cultural pattern, Sutherland and Woodward have stated: "Roles are culturally determined patterns of behavior; culture sets the limits of variation of roles, but alternative roles may be available in a given culture" (78).

Linton advised: "The patterns of organization of all societies begin with the division of the entire group into certain age—sex categories and the assigning of particular activities (roles) to

each. . . . The members of each society perpetuate the culture by training each succeeding generation to its behavior patterns (roles) and values" (41).

Znaniecki has used the concept similarly: "Members' roles and groups are cultural products, systems of values, and activities regulated in accordance with definite historical patterns" (82).

3. *Role as a Social Norm.* Many authors have defined "role" as implying culturally defined social norms which dictate reciprocal action. Komarovsky, for example, has distinguished two mutually exclusive, contradictory sex roles presented by the environment of the college woman: (1) a feminine role, and (2) a modern role (38). Ruth Benedict has also used a social norm definition of role. "Contradictory roles can be played in series, and in sequence, if required by society." She has discussed breaks between social roles of the male child and of the adult in American society as compared with other societies and has pointed out that the nature of the transition varies with the society (6).

4. *Role as a Synonym for Behavior.* "Role" is frequently used as a synonym for "behavior," as in the following statements: "Personality is a role in a social situation" or "Role is a pattern of behavior" or "The adolescent is an individual with a status and role in society" (18, 59, 77).

5. *Role Defined as Participation in a Specific Group.* "Role" has also been used in the literal, dictionary sense and refers to the individual's assumption of or assignment to the performance of "a part" in a specific situation. Moreno, for example, has used the term "role playing" or "role practice" to refer to assuming a role in a social situation constructed for the purpose of training the person for some occupational status or for gaining insight into his behavior (48).

Upon subsequent reexamination of the definitions that they analyzed, Neiman and Hughes concluded that the use of "role" in association with "status" is "one of the most concise and most frequently used in the literature." They further pointed out:

1. In all the definitions of the concept there is involved either an individual definition of a specific situation or an individual acceptance of a group's definition of a specific situation; and

2. Role behavior involves interaction and communication as prerequisites which lead to the generalization that man is the only role-playing animal and that this is one of the characteristics which distinguishes man from other animals. (50)

"Role" Definitions in Social Work

Those who have utilized the "role" concept in social work (4, 11, 47, 58, 76) have emphasized features of the definition which focus on the social determinants of patterned behavior of individuals and the social positions of which they are members. "Role" carries a considerable freightage of meaning in social work (57) because it implies a means of individual expression as well as dimension of social behavior. As Carol Meyer (47) and others (57, 72) have pointed out, there are both social and individual determinants of role behavior and both must be taken into consideration. "Role," as Ackerman has stated, can be conceived as "a bridge" between psychological and social processes (1).

Helen Perlman, in her definition of "role" for social workers, has viewed the concept as "a person's organized pattern or modes of behaving, fashioned by the status or functions he carries in relation to one or more persons. Such a behavior pattern is selected, shaped and colored by several dynamic factors: (1) the person's needs and drives—what he wants, consciously and unconsciously; (2) the person's ideas of the mutual obligations and expectations that have been invested (by custom, tradition, convention) in the particular status and functions he undertakes; and (3) the compatibility or conflict between the person's conceptions of obligations and expectations and those held by the other person(s) with whom he is in reciprocation" (57, p. 167).

"Role" provides a basic script for behavior which at the same time allows the individual person wide play for "ad libbing." From childhood on, they are not only the forms in which the personality is expressed; they are also the means through which object relationships are experienced and through which ego capacities develop. Certain ground rules are prescribed for all major roles and each person elaborates upon them or modifies them according to personal needs and drives, what the role requires and according to agreements between him and his role partner (58).

Perlman's definition of role (57) seems to parallel those used most frequently in social work parlance and will be the definition used in this chapter as we discuss the concepts and constructs of role theory and their application to social work.

Concepts and constructs of role theory

Deutsch has stated: "Of all the scientific theories, role theory is farthest from the ideal scientific theory. . . . It consists mainly of a set of constructs with little in the way of an interrelational calculus or rules of correspondence. It is often difficult to find consensus on the nature of the concepts themselves. On the other hand, the constructs of role theory are exceptionally rich in their empirical referents and provide an approach to the analysis of social behavior which is missing from many other theories" (16, p. 244).

Role theory, while still a relatively new field of study and far from the ideal scientific theory, already possesses an identifiable domain of study, perspective, and language. Role analysts have chosen as their domain of study real-life behavior as it is displayed in genuine ongoing social situations. Role theorists and role analysts have examined such problems as the processes of socialization, interdependencies among individuals, the organization and characteristics of social positions, processes of conformity and sanctioning, specialization of performance and the division of labor, and others (10).

A major tenet of role theory is that the real-life behavior which it studies is determined socially—much, although not all, of the variance of behavior is ascribed to the operation of immediate or past external influences. Such influences include the demands and prescriptions of others, the behavior of others as it rewards or punishes the person, and the individual's understanding of these factors. As such, role behavior is in large measure learned behavior. What is known about the learning of role behavior derives largely from the concept called "socialization," which is concerned particularly with the learning of socially relevant behavior at various stages of the life cycle (10).

Learning of Roles

George Herbert Mead was the first writer to focus on the learning of socially relevant roles. He delineated two stages in the development of the self-play and games (43). In play, the child takes on a set of dual roles: his own and that of some other person, e.g., teacher, mother, grocer. Such activity affords the child an opportunity to explore the attitudes held by others toward himself. By taking the role of the other, the child learns to regard himself from an external point of view. At this early stage of development, a person's self is constituted by an organization of the specific attitudes held by other persons toward himself and toward one another in the contexts of those social acts he has explored in his play. It is through this process that the child eventually learns the generalized attitudes of the community of which he is a part.

Utilizing Mead's formulation, a means of evaluating the individual's capacity for interpersonal relations is provided. A limited capacity or ability to extend the range of introjected roles implies an inability to "put oneself in the other guy's place" and therefore limits the range of possibilities in interpersonal interaction. Asch, for example has demonstrated that tension in interpersonal relationships may be ascribed to an inability or resistance to introjecting appropriate roles (3).

Role Vigor

The more rigorously roles are defined, the more stringently are their prescriptions enforced and the more difficult it is for a person to resolve conflict by deviating from them. "Role vigor" as developed by Getzels and Guba refers to the amount of deviation that is permitted from the role's prescriptions (25). In contrast to our rural society in America, where roles were clearly demarcated and little deviance from them was permitted, our contemporary social structure permits a great deal of role vigor. Consequently, many individuals are uncertain about which roles to enact and have experienced doubt concerning the appropriate ingredients of their role-sets (73). As a result, contemporary man has been described as in search of an identity. In his essay, *The Quest for Identity,* Wheelis concluded that the quest for an identity is a search for meaningful social roles (81).

Role Ambiguity

Role ambiguity refers to those roles for "which no place has been made in the social system, no formal recognition given that the particular status exists, that it is judged 'good' or 'bad' or that it lacks regularized expectations for what and how its occupants are to operate" (58, p. 151). Helen Perlman, who has devoted much study to "role ambiguity," considers the aged as foremost among those who suffer from role ambiguity. Another example she has offered is the foster parent who is sought for his or her capacity to love and nurture but is not supposed to care too much or love the child too much. Still another example of role ambiguity is that of applicant to a social agency when help is sought for a problem that is neither tangible nor visible (58).

The Role-Set

Merton (46) and Newcomb's investigations have illustrated the many different roles most individuals enact (52). Implicit in the fact that one's status set involves a wide variety of role relations is the possibility that one will find oneself occupying positions with incompatible role requirements. For example, a social worker employed in a school or hospital may feel different obligations to the administrators of the institution, on the one hand, and to his clients, on the other. A parent may feel pressure to nurture his or her children, but simultaneously may wish to maintain an active role in communal or professional activity (72, 76).

The person, it can be said, assumes various types of roles with many different individuals at various times for different purposes. Role theory, therefore, provides a means of studying and describing the interaction of two members of a social group as they adjust to each other within a social system. Spiegel has stated: "A role is a goal-directed pattern or sequence of acts tailored by the cultural process for the transactions a person may carry out in a social group or situation" (67).

Role Complementarity and Discomplementarity

Any small social group, such as the family, achieves some level of stability or equilibrium. Each actor (or person) in the group has his allocated roles in relation to each other member of the group. Complementarity, or the fit of the roles of ego and alter, is desirable. For every speaker there should be a listener, for every writer a reader, for every parent a child, and for every social worker a client (29). Complementarity exists when the reciprocal role of a role partner is carried out automatically without difficulty, and in the expected way. Strains in the equilibrium of the system may occur because of an unstable role structure, ambiguous role definitions and expectations, or the failure of role complementarity between role partners (67).

Spiegel has specified five main causes for failure in role complementarity. The first is a "cognitive discrepancy" in which one or both parties are not familiar with the roles which they are expected to assume, and thus miss their cues. The second cause for failure is a discrepancy of roles—when ego or alter require roles that the other does not possess. Third, there is an "allocative discrepancy" which indicates that roles are not accepted by at least one of the role partners. The fourth reason for failure of role complementarity is the absence of "instrumental means." For example, a person who is expected to be generous may be unable to be so because of the lack of money. A teacher may not be able to satisfy a student's expectations because he does not possess the necessary knowledge, or a social worker may not have the knowledge or ability to handle a particular situation or problem. The fifth reason for failure in role complementarity offered by Spiegel is "a discrepancy in cultural value orientations," as in mixed marriages (67).

Roles are allocated in a variety of ways. They may be "ascribed" automatically by age, sex, etc. They may be "achieved" by virtue of occupation or they may be "adopted" because they satisfy some need of the individual. Finally, roles may be "assumed" in a playful, "let's pretend" attitude (42).

Reequilibration

As mentioned, when there is an allocative discrepancy in roles, there is a failure of complementarity or disequilibrium. After disequilibrium has occurred, there is usually an effort to establish equilibrium again which is called "reequilibration." Reequilibration may be established by ego, who attempts to "induce" alter into an appropriate role by such means as coercing, coaxing, evaluating, masking, and postponing. Alter has a series of defenses that he can utilize in order to avoid being inducted into the role which ego desires. Thus, he may defy, refuse, deny, unmask the pretensiveness, or provoke ego. Another means of reequilibration may be established through "mutual modification" of roles. The two participants may resort to joking, referring the matter to a third party, exploring or reexploring the issue, compromising, and consolidating their positions in their transactions (67).

Explicit and Implicit Roles

Roles may be "explicit" or "implicit." Explicit roles are conscious, exposed to observation, and both participants in a transacting system are aware of them. An individual who comes to a social agency as a client and states that he is a client and enacts the role of client is enacting an "explicit" role. Implicit roles are those of which the person may not be aware and of which he is usually unconscious (67). Therefore, the client by virtue of his *explicit* role may enter the agency in order to understand his situation better but may implicitly enact the role of a dependent child who is not really interested in self- or situational understanding but in having the caseworker satisfy his demands (29).

Role Conflict

Significant to the notion of role is the concept of role conflict. The experiencing of role conflict is distinguished from a role conflict situation which occurs when a system member is exposed to conflicting sets of legitimized expectations such that complete fulfillment of both is realistically impossible (55). Role conflict, as a concept, has been enlarged by Gross, Mason, and McEachern to include legitimate and illegitimate incompatible expectations and refers to both intra- and inter-role conflict; that is, when the conflicting expectations refer to the perceived legitimacy or illegitimacy and the in-

dividual's incumbency in a single position and his incumbency in two or more positions. The authors state, therefore, that "any situation in which the incumbent of a focal position perceives that he is confronted with incompatible expectations will be called role conflict" (30).

A number of role conflict situations have been analyzed by social scientists. One occurs when the generalized status of the member is defined differently by two reference groups, such as when a social worker's role in a school system is defined by the administration as "keeping order" and by his colleagues as enhancing the social functioning of the students. Another exists when each of two reference groups perceives a generalized status in terms of its own status-role system, so that the individual is perceived as occupying a different status with its role counterparts by each of two different reference groups. For example, a social worker in a military mental hygiene clinic who is an enlisted man has a different status in the clinic than he does in his company. Still another type occurs when there are incompatible sets of role expectations with respect to two or more statuses of the individual (52). Role inadequacy is cited as a source of role complementarity failure (the absence of "instrumental means") and occurs when the individual lacks the capacities to fulfill role expectations for reasons such as lack of education, training, or other limitations (as when a poverty-stricken client is labeled "resistant" by his middle-class social worker) (67). Role incongruency is a stress situation in which one's perception of his own role is different from the expectations of "significant others" in the role system. An agency administrator may conceive of his role as "father figure," while staff may wish him to be an "enabler."

Cited earlier was Ruth Benedict, who referred to those situations in which the successive roles that the individual occupies are not prepared for by the preceding roles as "role discontinuities" (6).

The most comprehensive examination of

role theory has been performed by Biddle and Thomas. They found that the basic concepts and constructs for behavior used by most role analysts could be classified as prescription, description, sanction, action, and evaluation. For each of these "partitions" there is a "descriptive similarity among the behaviors falling within a classification," and this is apparently what distinguishes basic behavioral concepts from one another (10).

Prescription

Many of the terms used in role theory apply to prescriptive behavior. The term "role" itself is often used prescriptively as referring to behaviors that "should" or "ought to" be performed; "expectations," "standards," and "norms" are others. Much of social behavior is affected by prescriptions, and many social situations are dominated by the expression of overt demands. Demands appear, for example, in parent-child communications, work, politics, education, and social worker–client interactions (10).

By defining the rights and obligations of individuals, prescriptions appear to be among the most potent factors in the control of human behavior, either by "directly triggering conformity behavior or through a system of positive and negative sanctions that accompany them" (10, p. 103). Prescriptions are important also because they emerge from the interaction of individuals and groups and thus, to some extent, are themselves controlled by some of the same behavior which they are presumed to govern. Prescriptions may be formal and informal, expressed and implicit, individual and shared. They may vary in permissiveness, completeness, complexity, and in the degree to which they are universal.

The notion of role prescription has been used extensively in social casework treatment. In "Role Theory, Role Models, and Casework: Review of the Literature and Practice Applications," the present writer suggested that every client in casework treatment is induced by the worker to enact a specific role in order to receive casework help. If the role prescribed is not congruent with the client's expectations, strain occurs between the two actors (72). In another paper, the writer suggested that rather than prescribed roles for clients, particularly for those who are quite resistive to enacting classical client roles, the client should be used as a consultant, prescribing what roles the two actors should enact (74). This type of role reversal has been followed up and used by Schwitzgebel in *Street Corner Research,* where delinquents were not only used as consultants in treatment but were paid for doing so (64). In casework with the poor, many writers have felt that impoverished clients have not responded successfully to treatment, because the workers involved have prescribed roles which have been incompatible with the client's modal forms of socialization (60).

Psychoanalysts Meerloo and Nelson in their book *Transference and Trial Adaptation* contend that if analysts wish to take into fuller account the concepts of transference and countertransference, certain problems of role reciprocity that permeate the therapeutic relationship must be considered. One example given by them is that the patient's resistances overtly manifest themselves as a sequence of presented roles which he mobilizes to influence or compel the analyst to modify his role. By implication, the fundamental tenet of analytic neutrality is questioned by the authors' assertion that the patient's efforts to induce the analyst to abandon his therapeutic role and actualize a different role (e.g., parent, sibling, lover) are matched by the analyst's efforts to induce the patient to enact a prescribed role despite the latter's resistances. Thus, analyst and patient alike engage in efforts to induce one another to enact the role or roles which each deems necessary to maintain the interpersonal situation (44).

In a study conducted by the writer, it was concluded that students' success in field work in a graduate school of social work depended to a large extent on whether student and field-work instructor prescribed mutually acceptable role prescriptions. If instructor and student both prescribed similar role prescriptions for themselves and each other, the student's success was essentially assured (71).

Virtually all methods in social work—casework, group work, and community organization—are always dealing with role prescriptions. Whether an individual, family, group, or community becomes a focus of social work attention rests to a large extent on whether certain culturally sanctioned role prescriptions are being met. If they are, the individual, family, etc. is less likely to be a client or client system. Deviant or socially undesirable behavior is labeled as such in accordance with the enactment or violation of normative prescriptions.

Description

Behavior in which persons represent events, processes, and phenomena without affective or evaluative accompaniment is designated as descriptive. In role-theory literature terms such as "concept," "anticipation," "expectation" refer to descriptions.

Descriptions may be overt or covert, distorted or nondistorted; they are the individual's representation of aspects of the real world as he experiences it. They are also shaped by the individual's experience—by the positions to which he belongs, by the role behavior engaged in while a member of positions and by the ways in which he is interdependent with others (10).

Descriptive role expectations have been researched in psychotherapy and social work. In *The Anatomy of Psychotherapy*, Lennard and Bernstein studied role expectations in the therapeutic situation. They viewed therapy as a social system involving two subsystems, those of role expectations and communication. Their research documented the hypothesis that asymmetry in the system of role expectations is reflected in asymmetry in the system of communication. If therapist and patient differ in the

expectations each holds for one another, strains will appear, and the participants will attempt certain strategies to resolve the strains (39). Overall and Aronson demonstrated that when clients of lower socioeconomic groups hold expectations for treatment at variance with the actual behaviors of the therapist, a higher dropout rate follows than with clients holding more accurate expectations (53). Further research by the same authors revealed differential treatment expectations of clients in different socioeconomic classes (2). Treatment expectations among clients in casework as a function of reference-group expectations have been documented by Rosenblatt (61). The incongruity of expectations between caseworker and client, particularly in the intake situation, has received attention from Perlman. Like Rosenblatt, she attributed client dropout to the divergency of role expectations between client and worker (57). The relationship between role expectations and performance was the subject of a study by Dinitz et al., who reported on the relationship between the role expectations of family members and the performance of female mental patients following their discharge from a mental hospital. Their findings demonstrated a direct relationship between the expectations held for the patient's role performance, that is, the higher the expectations held for the patient's role performance, the higher the level of the patient's actual performance (17).

Sanctioning

Sanctioning is behavior engaged in by individuals with the intent of achieving a modification in another's behavior; this modification is usually toward greater conformity. Sanctions may or may not be effective in achieving an actual alteration of the behavior in question and conformity may occur without any sanctioning whatsoever (10). Sanctioning is not only necessary to enforce role conformity, but acts of sanctioning become the obligations, and hence, the role of others (26).

A friend's sanction may be different from

that of some representative of society and, therefore, the concept of consensus is very much inherent in role theory, particularly in the "partition" of sanctioning. The degree of consensus can vary from near maximum disagreement, through polarization or conflict, to unanimous agreement or consensus (10).

Jacobson's research related to consensus and conflict of marital partners. The study indicated that divorced couples exhibited greater disparities than did married couples in their attitudes towards the roles of husband and wife in marriage (36). Considering the same phenomenon, Ingersoll has stated: "Each young man who marries brings with him his idea of the part to be played by himself as husband and the part to be played by his wife as wife. Similarly, the young woman enters marriage with a preconceived notion of the roles of husband and wife. . . . If the conceptions of both are reasonably fulfilled, we can expect a satisfactory adjustment. We should remember, however, that we enter marriage with definite expectations, and if reality falls short of them, dissatisfaction follows" (35, p. 316).

Related to consensus on particular roles is Merton's notion of "anticipatory socialization." Individuals may acquire new characteristics of a position of which they are not currently a member, but into which they are about to move through anticipating what these new behaviors are. When there is some degree of consensus on a role, through anticipatory socialization the individual becomes prepared for a new position and thereby eases his movement into it (46).

Patients and clients, as do all individuals, behave differently depending on which individuals and social contexts sanction which behavior. Lennard and Bernstein in *Patterns in Human Interaction* (40) discuss Freud's "Schreber Case." They point out that the patient's paranoid illness and delusional system appeared only in certain social situations when sanctioned by certain individuals. Freud has quoted the following remarks of Schreber's physician, Dr. Weber:

Since for the last nine months Herr President Schreber has taken his meals at my family board, I have had the most ample opportunity of conversing with him. . . . In his lighter talk with the ladies of the party, he was both courteous and affable . . . never once during these talks did he introduce subjects which should more properly have been raised at a medical consultation. (23)

Action

Action is behavior distinguished on the basis of its having been learned previously, its goal directedness, and its apparent voluntariness. Much of the behavior of the child at play, the employee at work, and the individual at home is "performance." Role analysts are concerned with such aspects of performance as its complexity, uniformity, adequacy, the bias with which it is presented, and the extent to which individuals are organismically engaged (10, p. 193).

Most persons are interdependent with others in their performance, and, as a consequence, an individual may incur rewards and costs and have his performance facilitated or hindered by the performance of others. Performance is also related to the personality characteristics of those performing, to the positions of which they are members, to the prescriptions for their behavior, among many other factors. Sarbin's notion of "role enactment" (62) impinges on the concept of action or performance. Elaborating on several of the dimensions of his notion, Sarbin, like Newcomb (52), has referred to the number of roles simultaneously enacted by the individual associated with the individual's social adjustment.

Role enactment has received attention in the therapeutic area. In *Roles and Paradigms in Psychotherapy,* Nelson et al. have taken the position that each individual is a group with a blend of introjected and internalized roles. In helping the patient to strengthen his equipment and function at a greater capacity in his life situations, the writers advised that comprehensive treatment necessitates the adoption of multiple roles by the therapist. These roles vary according to the dynamic unfolding of each individual case. The therapist, therefore, acts as a paradigm of the world in which the patient must learn to move (51). Enacting the role of the helpless and naive child can help self-destructive clients verbalize aggression (69). Enacting the narcissistic, self-indulgent role can involve rebellious adolescents in treatment (70) and enacting a role which is a mirror image of the highly defended client can prevent further acting out and the compounding of resistances (75).

Evaluation

Behavior is partitioned as evaluative as it relates primarily to approval or disapproval. "Preference," "value," "affect," and "esteem" are terms which generally pertain to evaluative behavior. Evaluations are pervasive in social life. The mother who rejoices over her child's performance, the audience member who claps or boos, the teacher who grades a paper are expressing overt assessments of the performance of others (10, p. 27).

Closely linked to evaluation is a role concept, namely "position." In no society are the members entirely alike or are the individual differences among members random and unordered (10). Leader, follower, black, client, patient, neurotic, relief recipient, are among a host of positions in American society and all of these positions contain evaluative implications.

Murray Sherman has addressed the evaluative implications of "role" and uses the concept "role title." He points to the phenomenon wherein certain behavior is rewarded under one title but condemned under another. Thus, taking drugs may be approved under the title of "patient" but condemned under the title of "addict." Homicide may be approved when performed by "a soldier" but repudiated by "employees." Temper tantrums may be acceptable from a supervisor but less so from a supervisee (65).

Application of role theory to social work

All social workers, in working with individuals, families, groups, and communities, follow a prescribed process. While other terms have been used, the client or client system is *studied, diagnosed, or assessed,* and *treated* with and by the social worker. In this section, we shall attempt to demonstrate the applicability of role theory to each of the phases of the social work process, social study, diagnosis, and intervention or treatment.

Social study

The application of role theory may be used in the two essential parts of the study phase, namely, inducing the person or persons to move from readiness to ask for help to a readiness to use it and in understanding the person or persons with the problem as well as the problem itself (32).

Several writers have alluded to the phenomenon of client dropout, i.e., the client leaves the social worker prematurely (57, 61, 66, 68). One of the reasons offered for this is that the applicant's understanding and expectations of the agency were not clear to the social worker and the worker's understanding and expectations of the applicant were not clear to the applicant (57). Therefore, the barriers that can be created between client and worker in the study phase may be considered within a role theory context—the two actors can be viewed as having incongruent role expectations regarding their respective roles. For example, if the client views his role as an actor who will receive financial help as soon as possible, while the worker perceives the situation as one in which he will help the applicant understand the etiology of his joblessness, we have a failure in complementarity of roles and the client may very well withdraw from the agency (57).

The study phase usually does create role strains. Most frequently, the worker expects the applicant to provide data (tell the story of his life, get to the root causes behind his request, etc.), while the client frequently expects initially to be given to rather than to provide. This role incongruency has been cited as one of the failures of social work, particularly in working with clients of lower socioeconomic groups. Many of the latter do not view the putting into words of feelings, thoughts, memories, and facts as a legitimate or prescribed part of any role-set. Consequently, the more action-oriented client who wants the worker "to act rather than talk" can be baffled by the worker's reluctance to act and provide for him and may interpret the worker's behavior as disinterest or rejection. The middle-class verbally oriented caseworker can be equally baffled by the applicant's "reluctance to verbalize" and may interpret his client's behavior as pathological acting out or resistance. The social situation just described may end by the applicant asking, "When are you going to start helping me?" and the worker inquiring of the client, "When are you going to get involved with me and the agency?" (2, 57, 76).

The role theorist, therefore, would advise the social worker that one of his fundamental tasks during the study phase would be to clarify the respective role expectations of the two actors, client and worker, so that both may be able to have some consensus regarding their respective positions and tasks. As Perlman has stated, "The aim of the beginning phase of casework is to help an 'applicant' undertake the role of 'client.' " Thus, certain understandings must evolve between worker and applicant before the latter becomes a client. What an applicant will do in the study phase is conditioned by his conception of what is expected of him and what he may expect in return from the caseworker and the agency—in short "by his conception of his and the caseworker's roles in relation to the

problem he brings" (57). It may be confidently hypothesized that if the applicant wishes to discuss his physical aches and pains while the worker wishes to discuss the client's psychological dynamics, dropouts will occur (2). Until the social worker and applicant have come to some tentative or rudimentary agreements about their present and future transactions, the social worker does not have a client (57).

The role and status-set of client as prescribed by many social workers for the study phase is probably acceptable to only a very small percentage of casework's clientele. The worker expects that his future client should attempt to "involve himself in a relationship," attend "regularly scheduled appointments," "take some responsibility for his role in the psychosocial difficulty," "reveal secrets from his present and past," and "listen to the worker's supportive and clarifying remarks." However, a client may not be able to form the relationship that the worker may demand (72, 76) because of the causes we have alluded to for failure in role complementarity—cognitive discrepancy (the applicant is not familiar with the role he is expected to assume); discrepancy of roles (he may not possess the necessary ingredients for the role he is required to enact); he may refuse to accept the role because the worker's prescribed role clashes with his subjective role with the social worker (allocative discrepancy); there may be an absence of "instrumental means" (the applicant does not have the verbal facility or motivation to "involve himself"); and there may be a discrepancy in the cultural value orientations between worker and client (67).

Becoming a client can interfere with an existing status- or role-set when the applicant adds the status of client to it—a host of conflicts may then be generated (61). In addition to the potential discomfort of enacting a dependent role in a culture which champions independence, many members of the client's current role network may not sanction his receiving professional assistance. As several writers have reiterated, it appears quite conclusive that for the social work relationship to be sustained, the applicant's reference groups must support the idea. An unsupportive social environment does not foster the client's continuance with a social agency (57, 61, 66, 68).

In attempting to understand the person and his situation (the other objective of social study) the contribution of role theory is quite clear. By studying the client's role-set and status-set, the worker may be able to note a wider ramification of the presented problems of the client. As his reciprocal role relationships are studied, different members of his family or his job situation may emerge as more strategic, i.e., where is there role complementarity and where is there complementarity failure in the family, job, etc.? The utilization of role theory in the study phase would inevitably induce the worker to investigate what demands for social performance are being made on the client, by whom, and in what social contexts. The worker would be more sensitized to the client's subjective view of his psychosocial difficulties as he focused on the client's and his reference groups' social standards with their prescriptions, sanctions, evaluation, etc. (11).

Each role is composed of a number of activities, a few of which seem to be so essential that impaired performance or failure to perform certain roles may be considered an indication of social dysfunctioning. For example, a husband is expected to work for a living and to provide economic support—alone or together with a wife. He is expected to share in family decisions and other activities and his wife is expected to engage in reciprocal activities in many of the same areas. The role concept makes it possible to identify crucial tasks which, if not performed or if inadequately performed, may make for individual or family stress and may lead to specific types of social dysfunctioning. As the role concept is used in the study phase, the specific stresses of the client may emerge as his role expectations are investigated. Frequently, there may be a lack of consensus on these expectations between the client and significant others.

There may be differences in definition of the same role on the part of different members of the family or job, differences in perception of the role performances, or of disagreement about the role rigor (degree of freedom) each member of the family has to perform his roles (9, 25).

Because the social study is a psychosocial process in which the worker must achieve a social level of perception as he correlates socioeconomic, cultural, and psychological data (32), the role concept can facilitate an understanding of these phenomena in light of the interaction of psychic, social, somatic, and cultural factors as they impinge on the client's role and status-set (11).

In gathering information during the social-study phase, a role analysis is an efficient manner in locating the person-situation strengths as well as deficiencies, because as the worker focuses on role expectations, role reciprocity, and role complementarity, he avoids the danger of an exclusive concern with clinical pathology. In studying the role interaction of two people, e.g., a marital pair, he learns that a "good" marriage with congruent reciprocal role expectations may very well be two neurotic individuals who meet many of each other's needs and wishes. The dominant-wife–passive–husband constellation has been offered as a prime etiological factor in virtually every psychosocial disturbance, but it also consists of two role partners who are enacting implicit roles that each partner implicitly prescribes and sanctions. The constellation may not be congruent with the worker's role prescriptions for husband and wife, but this is not sufficient to label it "a sick relationship" and throw it into disequilibrium by questioning it (1).

Diagnosis

As the worker attempts to draw inferences from the facts gathered during the social study and organize these inferences in a systematic manner so that a comprehensive psychosocial diagnosis may evolve, role theory and role analysis may enrich the diagnostic formulations.

As the worker attempts to understand the client's subjective interpretation of the latter's expectations of his various roles and role relationships and as the worker sensitizes himself to the way individuals in the client's role network view the client's and their own role obligations, a more individualized diagnosis may be the result. The utilization of role theory with its emphasis on interaction and transaction and its respect for the client's and "significant others' " *own definitions* of appropriate role behavior, truly meets the client where he is and accepts him as he is. The worker's own biases may be exposed and need not interfere with his diagnostic objectivity as he compares and contrasts his own role expectations with those of his client and his client's "significant others."

The utilization of role theory will require the worker to draw inferences from the facts gathered in relation to the "norms" that impinge on the client. The diagnostic interpretation will take into consideration the way the client's ethnic group, religion, and social class view certain behavior and what the role prescriptions are for the client. What the worker may view as pathological might very well be "normal" for a specific role network and, therefore, might yield a different treatment prescription if cultural and subcultural norms are considered.

Hellenbrand has advised that values are the major agent in a client's role commitments and therefore are a necessary part of the data that go to make up a diagnosis. The cultural norms or values determine to a large extent parent–child, marital, school, and work relationships. Therefore, in formulating a diagnosis, the worker must ask, "What has priority—the individual's wishes or cultural imperatives?" A conflict between them pinpoints, in part, the locus for therapeutic intervention (33).

The application of role theory for purposes of organizing data enlarges the diagnostic picture in another way. As the worker diagnoses a mother, he will take into consideration that the latter is not only a mother but a wife, daughter, daughter-in-law, and possibly a wage earner.

These roles may or may not be in conflict with each other and may conflict with some and may not conflict with others in the role-set (47).

Boehm has used role theory for the purposes of a comprehensive diagnostic classification. By classifying role performances and viewing all clients as role carriers, diagnosis can be more comprehensive and point to a clearer direction for intervention according to Boehm. He classifies role performance at various levels.

Level I—Role performance violates minimum societal standards and may cause stress to individuals and groups in the client's role network.
Level II—Role performance meets minimum societal standards but causes stress to individuals and groups in the role network.
Level III—Role performance meets minimum societal standards for members of the role network but is not commensurate with role performance potential.
Level IV—Role performance meets minimum societal standards and is commensurate with role performance potential.

Clients classified at the first level (Level I) would come to social workers from courts and similar institutions. At Level II, the impetus for help comes from the person whose role performance is impaired. Public health measures are required for clients at Level III and no services seem to be required for clients at the last level (11, pp. 118–124).

Family Diagnosis and Family Treatment

The role concept, with its emphasis on social interaction, has enriched social work's ability in diagnosing and treating families in conflict. Rather than viewing the referred client merely as a diseased entity, family therapists have tended to view him as a reflection of a family system in which roles are not congruent. The child with a school phobia, for example, may not only be considered a patient suffering from separation anxiety, but also as the displayed expression of conflict in the role relationships of several subsystems: parent-parent, parent-child, husband-wife, and sibling (40, 67). Furthermore, the presence or lack of role reciprocity between child and parent with the school and neighborhood would be considered in any comprehensive diagnosis and treatment planning.

Family treatment can be considered as an attempt to modify and clarify role expectations and enhance role complementarity between members. Implicit would be an enhancing of each of the family members' role repertoire. Thus, the concept of role can be used for making more explicit the interworkings of the family's functioning and for understanding of individual and group behavior within the family setting. It should be mentioned that, from the family's point of view, the family will assign the therapist a role and incorporate him within the family's functioning system. The role assigned to the therapist will include many prescribed role expectations, some of which will be accepted by the therapist and some not (19).

Role theory, when applied to the family, considers "the problem" as a dysfunction of a role network that needs modification, and hence, there is shared responsibility for "the problem" and its resolution.

Group Work and Community Organization

Similar to its pertinence to work with families, role theory has been helpful in the assessment of groups and communities. In both initiating a group experience or in intervening in a group, expectations of members can be reviewed by client and worker so that unrealistic expectations of members and worker can be modified, particularly when these expectations interfere with the client's or other people's interpersonal functioning. Like interpersonal problems in families, so too in small groups and communities, as role relationships are examined, and prescriptions, descriptions, and sanctions reviewed, problems become shared responsibilities and their resolution is also a group or community task.

Theorists and practitioners who have explored crisis situations in families, small groups, and communities view a crisis as a disruption of a steady state or a disruption of role equilibrium. A crisis such as a tornado, unemployment, death of a family member, modifies the unit system. Hence, assumption of new and modified roles by all of the actors is frequently necessary before equilibrium is restored (19, 67).

Group workers and community organizers not only have been addressing themselves to the role expectations of group members and significant actors of the community, but have increasingly recognized that for groups and communities to be enhanced, role assignments of members might have to be modified. For example, in the recent attempts to diminish racial and other types of interpersonal tension in groups and communities, members of minorities (blacks, women, etc.) have been assigned roles that carry more status. It has been felt that with increased status in his new role the minority member will afford himself and be afforded by others more esteem and worth.

Social workers who have been involved in group and community work have recognized that to negotiate successfully for and with groups and communities the role of the social worker has to be carefully scrutinized. Depending on the needs of the group or the community, the worker will decide the most appropriate role for him to enact—catalyst, neutralizer, advocate, stimulator, etc.

Locating Points for Intervention

Part of a diagnostic assessment in any social work activity is determining where in the client system or in the client's life, the worker will intervene (32). Atherton, Mitchell, and Schien, in an attempt to locate a focus for intervention, have made considerable use of role theory in their attempt to classify problems of clients. Three major categories that they developed are (1) problems related to performance of legitimate and acceptable roles, (2) problematical roles, and (3) problems in the structure of social systems that affect the behavior of individuals (4).

Some of the examples of problems related to role performance that Atherton et al. offer are: impairment of role performance because of illness, incapacity for role performance, lack of motivation in role performance, intra- and inter-role conflict and frustrating role expectations. Illustrations of problematical roles are rolelessness (the role that lacks a definition), inadequate role modeling, illicit role, and deviant role (4).

In a continuation of their examination, Atherton et al. have prescribed various worker roles for different role problems of clients. Worker roles that they prescribe depending on the role conflicts of clients are broker, mediator, educator, crisis intervenor, advocate, and others (5).

Intervention

No formula exists for determining the specific weight of factors in the etiology or resolution of psychosocial disorders. An approach predicated on the assumption that psychosocial factors are inherent in both the etiology and intervention of problems that confront the social worker and that use role theory in intervention would proceed from a number of linked postulates: (1) roles that individuals in the client's environment assume (past and present) have a critical influence on his past and present socialization, (2) faulty learning and dysfunctional role habituation are critical sources of emotional and social disorder, and (3) the worker-client relationship constitutes an opportunity for new learning (13, 51, 72, 76).

In considering the relationship of social worker and client as a system of interaction and transaction between ego and alter, we may ap-

ply what has been learned from role theory. Intervention or treatment can be visualized as a system consisting of an individual enacting the role of client who is interacting with a role partner, his social worker. Complementarity of these roles is conducive to the worker's obtaining the data that he needs to understand the client and to the client's incorporating the worker's suggestions and other prescriptions. Disequilibrium, due to noncomplementarity (but eventually resulting in reequilibrium), represents the disruption of an old repetitive process and the establishment of a new system. This can produce learning, change, and therapeutic results.

Role Induction in Treatment

In order to feel comfortable in any interpersonal situation, the individual attempts to *induce* his role partner to enact roles which will maintain the feeling of comfort. In a treatment relationship the client will mobilize changing role patterns of cooperation and resistance that will be designed to influence the worker to modify *his* role. The worker is also minimally obliged to induce the client to enact a role because the cooperative effort required of the client may be felt by the latter as purely formal and ego dystonic. Therefore, it can be postulated that worker and client will engage in efforts to induce one another to enact the role or roles which each deems necessary to maintain and promote the interpersonal situation (51, 70, 72, 76).

It would appear that the psychoanalytic concepts "transference," "countertransference," and "resistance" can be fused into one role construct, "role induction," and in adapting these concepts for role theory, their meaning may be enriched. Transference may be seen as the client's efforts to induce the worker to abandon his chosen role of either helper, explorer, or environmental manipulator and instead project roles of parent, sibling, etc.; resistance may be viewed as the client's noncompliance with the worker's role prescription for either himself or the client (39, 44, 51, 72, 76). Because the client's efforts at role induction are paralleled by those of the worker, we may consider as countertransference those efforts of the worker to persuade the client to enact prescribed roles when the latter resists them (44).

Any person who has been engaged in the practice of casework or psychotherapy has recognized that, in the face of all logic and reason, the client can often behave in a most obstinate and uncomprehending manner. To try to convince a suspicious client that his spouse is well-meaning or a self-hating client that he is competent in certain areas usually intensifies the client's self-doubts. Consequently, social workers have long held that no client is so completely rational and no worker so sufficiently wise that a dialogue could ensue in which the worker could interpret the client's problems so that the client, having arrived at a reasonable understanding, would embark on a new course of action based on the new insights he has acquired from the worker (9, 51).

Role Enactment

Recognizing the above phenomenon, it was Freud who first considered the application of role theory (although not labeling it as such) when he was faced with the "negative therapeutic reaction" (22). Realizing that certain patients repudiated every interpretation and suggestion that he had made, in "The Outline of Psychoanalysis," Freud virtually suggested role-playing or role enactment (24). In this essay, the founder of psychoanalysis advocated that presenting role prescriptions to the patient should be part of the role-set of the psychoanalyst. He stated that in every individual case of analysis, the psychoanalyst is obliged to use a mixed panel of authorities to back up his direct or indirect therapeutic demands. Depending on the factors that will influence the patient at the moment, he shifts from one to the other. Freud stated that the analyst has to enact many different roles—the analyst will be a teacher, a parental figure; he will instruct, give guidance,

and impose rules of conduct; he will praise or condemn, depending on the degree of narcissism of the patient (24).

The statements of Freud may be viewed as a suggestion to the analyst that by his enacting roles of teacher, parent, etc., he may enable the patient through role induction to cooperate with his analyst and eventually assimilate the latter's interpretations. Other analysts and therapists have used role theory in relating to similar therapeutic problems. Greenson has referred to "reeducation," in which the therapist offers himself as a role model for introjection and identification, enabling the client to emulate the therapist's more mature role behavior. Nelson et al. have used "paradigmatic treatment" in which the treatment situation "becomes a model of the world, a stage on which all possible dramas and roles may be played out" (51). The consistent theme in all of the literature in which role theory has been applied to treatment situations has been that for an individual with defective ego functioning to learn again is similar to problems of learning in children. To be effective in the treatment situation, it has been suggested, the worker must realize that comprehensive treatment necessitates throughout the adoption of multiple stances and roles determined by the dynamic unfolding of each individual case. By adopting various roles, Coleman and Nelson have pointed out, the therapist serves a complex of functions:

> He helps correct faulty perceptions of reality and demonstrates to the patient those ego functions which the latter does not have or misuses; he assists in giving the patient needed practice in coping with life situations. The therapist thus acts as a paradigm of the world in which the patient must learn to move. (13, p. 41)

Equilibrium and Disequilibrium in Treatment

In applying the concepts and constructs of role theory to intervention in social work, one may view the interventive decisions that the worker has to make as always involving a choice in either promoting equilibrium or disequilibrium in the interaction. It has already been suggested that during the study phase, when the worker is gathering information and attempting to induce the client to move from the applicant role to the client role, some role complementarity is necessary; otherwise, there is the danger of the client leaving the situation prematurely. Therefore, for the action-oriented client, some form of worker action would probably be indicated; and for the verbal client, some form of verbal interaction would appear to be the procedure of choice. Therefore, as Varley has stated in "The Use of Role Theory in the Treatment of Disturbed Adolescents" (79), the worker in the early interviews should first state how he views his own role and how he and the client can work together. Second, he should discuss with the client what is expected of him during treatment—the client's role. Also, the client's involvement in the evaluation process is considered crucial so as to avoid early discomfort and confusion.

While role complementarity and equilibrium will preserve the interaction, most social workers would concur that the old, repetitive, self-defeating processes that the client will inevitably bring to the encounter cannot be eternally left unattended by the worker. It would appear, therefore, that certain role prescriptions that the client offers must be frustrated; otherwise, learning of new and healthier rules by him will not be achieved. For example, to gratify the wishes of a demanding, self-destructive client and obey his role prescriptions is, in effect, joining him in his self-destructiveness. Although this client may enact an explicit role which seems logical to the worker, such as consistently asking for advice and guidance from the expert, acquiescence to the induced role by the worker may, in fact, further weaken the client's sense of self and autonomy. If the role of the worker is that of frequent giver, the frustration tolerance of the client will be limited instead of his being

able to sustain a sense of conflict, so important for the socialization process (15, 49). The client will find it difficult to express disagreement or deal with external reality, since his learning experience with the worker will at best result in an egocentric identification (49, 72, 76).

There are certain situations where the client's prescription can be complied with and it can be to the client's eventual benefit. These are situations in which the client's prescribed roles have never been complied with by previous workers or other significant people in authority, and no amount of persuasion or appeal to the client's logic on their part seems to have distracted the client from his pleas. The clients are usually individuals who have suffered a great deal of deprivation—either psychological, social, or economic. In many ways they are trying to prove that "no one cares," and they are convinced of this when the worker refuses to consider their prescriptions, which may on the surface appear absurd.

Regardless of the social work method used, the role theorist would seek to offer clients new experiences which are designed to enhance psychosocial functioning. One of his major tools for this is his own role repertoire as a professional. He gives to those who need giving, he frustrates those who need frustration, he is broker, advocate, leader, follower, expert, or neophyte depending on the dynamic unfolding of the case situation. The social worker attempts to offer a corrective experience with a new and different role partner that did not or does not exist in the client's previous or current socialization experiences. The social worker, in sum, enacts those roles that will assist his client or clients to assume and strengthen those social roles which have to do with individual growth and development (31).

Summary and conclusions

Role theory is beginning to have more influence on social work practice, particularly as the profession has focused its lens more on deprived groups and ethnic minorities. The role expectations of these clients, as they emerge in work with families, parent-child, and marital relations, and all of psychosocial functioning, are grist for the diagnostic mill (2). Furthermore, different socioeconomic and ethnic groups have different expectations about the role of the helper and the helped, and the social worker must take these expectations into account as he relates to a more and more diverse clientele (53). Role theory has also been making its contribution in conceptualizing the role repertoire of the practitioner as he provides help to clients—the social-broker role, the advocate role, the mediator role, the parental role, etc. (4, 5).

More social agencies are beginning to use role theory as they consider the role requirements for clients and workers and attempt to understand how complementarity might be achieved between them. Certain agencies, for example, require their clients to enact a role-set which necessitates their verbalizing intrapsychic problems, introspecting on them, etc., while other agencies may require a role-set that is very different—a nonverbal expression of physical and tangible needs with no desire to be involved in a one-to-one professional relationship. As social workers have focused on the role requirements they have held for clients, they have been forced to examine their role requirements for themselves and have frequently modified both when the expectations were incongruent (72).

While the role concept embodies psychological, biological, and social considerations, its major emphasis is on the task-oriented aspects of social functioning. Consequently, one of the weaknesses of "role" for social work is that it does not always bring into full focus the unique inner mental processes in the individual that work for adaptation. While the term "social functioning" is very compatible with the "role" concept, when we study, diagnose, and treat the unique individual and his situation, we still

have to ascertain how an externally induced conflict leads to idiosyncratic and specific forms of behavior in a designated role.

A common observation of social workers is that the same external stimulus can activate a host of different behaviors in different individuals. The "role" concept can contribute toward an understanding of the individual's response, but it may only partially explain the particular individual's very specific motives behind his behavior. If the "role" concept is used exclusively in diagnosis and treatment, there is the inherent danger of what Fraiberg has called attention to, namely, we can be led into the position of manipulators of social roles which calls for a wisdom beyond the scope of any person (20). Although there is nothing in role theory which negates psychoanalytic theory or other orientations, by focusing exclusively on the client's role, one might unwittingly fail to individualize the client as completely as possible (20, 76).

Role theory has been used largely in conjunction with social system theory. To understand how the actors in any system, e.g., family system, are interacting and transacting, it is incumbent on the system analyst to examine the role expectations and role prescriptions of the actors, particularly when imbalances and dysfunctions of the system are apparent (1). Role theory has also been used by those engaging in behavior modification therapy, when certain behaviors are reinforced to help the client achieve a more successful enactment of more socially acceptable roles (10).

Role theory will continue to be used in the diagnosis and treatment. It will also be considered helpful in researching family dysfunctioning, small group processes, educational problems as they emerge in school social work, and elsewhere. As with other incomplete scientific theories, role theory should be used in conjunction with other orientations and with the practice wisdom that is part of every social worker's role repertoire.

References

1. Ackerman, Nathan. *The Psychodynamics of Family Life.* New York: Basic Books, 1954.

2. Aronson, Harriet and Betty Overall. "Treatment Expectations of Patients in Two Social Classes," *Social Work,* Vol. 11, No. 1, January, 1966, pp. 35-42.

3. Asch, Solomon E. "Forming Impressions of Personality," *Journal of Abnormal and Social Psychology,* Vol. 38, No. 1, January, 1943, pp. 225-249.

4. Atherton, Charles R., Sandra T. Mitchell and Edna Biehl Schien. "Locating Points for Intervention," *Social Casework,* Vol. 52, No. 3, March, 1971, pp. 131-141.

5. ——. "Using Points for Intervention," *Social Casework,* Vol. 52, No. 4, April, 1971, pp. 223-233.

6. Benedict, Ruth. "Continuities and Discontinuities in Cultural Conditioning," *Psychiatry,* Vol. 1, May, 1938, pp. 161-167.

7. Bern, Wesley. "An Expansion and Test of a Role Theory of Marital Satisfaction," *Journal of Marriage and the Family,* Vol. 33, May, 1971, pp. 368-372.

8. ——. "Role Transitions: A Reformulation of Theory," *Journal of Marriage and the Family,* Vol. 34, August, 1972, pp. 407-416.

9. Bernstein, Arnold. *On the Nature of Psychotherapy.* New York: Random House, 1954.

10. Biddle, Bruce J. and Edwin Thomas. *Role Theory.* New York: Wiley, 1966.

11. Boehm, Werner W. "The Social Work Curriculum Study and Its Implications for Family Casework," *Social Casework,* Vol. 40, No. 8, October, 1959, pp. 428-436.

12. ——. "The Social Casework Method in Social Work Education," Vol. 10. New York: Council on Social Work Education, 1959.

13. Coleman, Marie and Benjamin Nelson. "Paradigmatic Psychotherapy in Borderline Cases," *Psychoanalysis,* Vol. 5, No. 3, Fall, 1957, pp. 28-44.

14. Cottrell, Leonard S. "Roles and Marital Adjustment," *Publications of the American Sociological Society,* Vol. 27, May, 1933, pp. 107-112.

15. Davis, Kingsley. "Adolescence and the Social Structure," *Annals of the American Academy of Political and Social Science,* Vol. 26, No. 5, November, 1944, pp. 11-12.

16. Deutsch, Morton and Robert H. Krauss. *Theories in Social Psychology.* New York: Basic Books, 1965.

17. Dinitz, Simon, Shirley Angrist, Mark Lefton and Benjamin Pasamanick. "Instrumental Role Expectations and Posthospital Performance of Female Mental Patients," *Social Forces,* Vol. 40, 1962, pp. 248-254.

18. Faris, Ellsworth. "The Social Psychology of George Mead," *American Journal of Social Psychology,* Vol. 43, November, 1937, pp. 391-402.

19. Fisher, Lawrence and Robert C. Warren. "The Concept of Role Assignment in Family Therapy," *International Journal of Group Psychotherapy,* Vol. 22, No. 1, January, 1972, pp. 60-75.

20. Fraiberg, Selma. "Psychoanalysis and the Education of Case Workers," in

Howard J. Parad and Roger R. Miller (eds.) *Ego-Oriented Casework: Problems and Perspectives*. New York: Family Service Association of America, 1963, pp. 236-258.

21. Fraley, Yvonne L., "A Role Model for Practice," *Social Service Review*, Vol. 43, 1969, pp. 145-154.

22. Freud, Sigmund. "Freud's Psychoanalytic Method," in *Collected Papers*, Vol. 1, London: Hogarth, 1953, pp. 236-258.

23. ———. "Psychoanalytic Notes Upon an Autobiographical Account of a Case of Paranoia," in *Collected Papers*, Vol. 3, London: Hogarth, 1959, p. 394.

24. ———. "On Psychotherapy," ibid., pp. 249-263.

25. Getzels, J. W. and E. G. Guba. "Role, Role Conflict and Effectiveness," *American Sociological Review*, Vol. 19, No. 1, February, 1954, pp. 164-175.

26. Goode, William J. "Norm Commitment and Conformity to Role-Status Obligations," *American Journal of Sociology*, Vol. 61, 1960, pp. 246-258.

27. Gouldner, Alvin W. "The Norm of Reciprocity: A Preliminary Statement," *American Sociological Review*, Vol. 25, 1960, pp. 161-178.

28. Greenson, Ralph. "The Borderline Case," *Journal of the American Psychoanalytic Association*, Vol. 3, No. 2, April, 1955, pp. 295-297.

29. Grinker, Roy, Helen MacGregor, Kate Selan, Annette Klein and Janet Kohrman. *Psychiatric Social Work: A Transactional Case Book*. New York: Basic Books, 1961.

30. Gross, Neal, Ward S. Mason and Alexander W. McEachern. *Explorations in Role Analysis*. New York: Wiley, 1958.

31. Gyarfas, Mary. "Social Science, Technology, and Social Work," *Social Service Review*, Vol. 43, No. 3, 1969.

32. Hamilton, Gordon. *Theory and Practice of Social Casework*. New York: Columbia University Press, 1951.

33. Hellenbrand, Shirley. "Client Value Orientations: Implications for Diagnosis and Treatment," *Social Casework*, Vol. 42, April, 1961, pp. 163-169.

34. Hurvitz, Nathan. "The Marital Roles Inventory as a Counseling Instrument," *Journal of Marriage and the Family*, Vol. 27, 1965, pp. 492-501.

35. Ingersoll, Hazel L. "Transmission in Authority Patterns in the Family," *Marriage and Family Living*, Vol. 10, 1948, p. 316.

36. Jacobson, Allvar Hilding. "Conflict of Attitudes Toward the Roles of the Husband and Wife in Marriage," *American Sociological Review*, Vol. 17, 1952, pp. 146-150.

37. Kammeyer, Kenneth, "Sibling Position and the Feminine Role," *Journal of Marriage and the Family*, Vol. 29, 1967, pp. 494-499.

38. Komarovsky, Mirra. "Cultural Contradictions and Sex Roles," *American Journal of Sociology*, Vol. 52, November, 1946, pp. 193-203.

39. Lennard, Henry L. and Arnold Bernstein. *The Anatomy of Psychotherapy*. New York: Columbia University Press, 1960.

40. ———. *Patterns in Human Interaction*. San Francisco: Jossey-Bass, 1969.

41. Linton, Ralph. "Culture, Society, and the Individual," *Journal of Abnormal and Social Psychology*, Vol. 33, October, 1938, pp. 425-436.

42. ———. *The Study of Man*. New York: Appleton-Century, 1936.

43. Mead, George Herbert. *Mind, Self and Society,* Charles W. Morris (ed.). Chicago: University of Chicago Press, 1934.

44. Meerloo, Joost A. M. and Marie Coleman Nelson. *Transference and Trial Adaptation.* Springfield, Ill.: Thomas, 1965.

45. Merton, Robert K., George Reader and Patricia L. Kendall. *The Student Physician.* Cambridge, Mass.: Harvard, 1957.

46. ———. *Social Theory and Social Structure.* Glencoe, Ill.: Free Press, 1957.

47. Meyer, Carol. "Quest for a Broader Base for Family Diagnosis," *Social Casework,* Vol. 40, July, 1959, pp. 370-376.

48. Moreno, Joseph L. *Who Shall Survive?* Washington, D.C.: Beacon Hill, 1934.

49. Nagelberg, Leo. "The Meaning of Help in Psychotherapy," *Psychoanalysis and the Psychoanalytic Review,* Vol. 46, No. 4, 1959, pp. 50-63.

50. Neiman, Lionel J. and James W. Hughes. "The Problem of the Concept of Role—A Resurvey of the Literature," *Social Forces,* December, 1951, pp. 141-149.

51. Nelson, Marie, Benjamin Nelson, Murray Sherman and Herbert S. Strean. *Roles and Paradigms in Psychotherapy.* New York: Grune and Stratton, 1968.

52. Newcombe, Theodore and Eugene L. Hartley. *Readings in Social Psychology.* New York: Holt, 1967.

53. Overall, Betty and Harriet Aronson. "Expectations of Psychotherapy in Patients of Lower Socioeconomic Class," *American Journal of Orthopsychiatry,* Vol. 31, pp. 421-430.

54. Park, Robert E. and Ernest W. Burgess. *An Introduction to the Science of Sociology.* Chicago: University of Chicago Press, 1921.

55. Parsons, Talcott. *The Social System.* Glencoe, Ill.: Free Press, 1951.

56. Peal, Ethel. " 'Normal' Sex Roles: An Historical Analysis," *Family Process,* Vol. 14, September, 1975, pp. 389-409.

57. Perlman, Helen Harris. "Intake and Some Role Considerations," in Cora Kassius (ed.) *Social Casework in the Fifties.* New York: Family Service Association of America, 1962, pp. 163-174.

58. ———. *Persona: Social Role and Personality.* Chicago: University of Chicago Press, 1968.

59. Reuter, Edward B. "Sociological Research in Adolescence," *American Journal of Sociology,* Vol. 42, July, 1936, pp. 81-94.

60. Riessman, Frank, Jerome Cohen and Arthur Pearl. *Mental Health of the Poor.* New York: Free Press, 1964.

61. Rosenblatt, Aaron. "Application of Role Concepts to the Intake Process," *Social Casework,* Vol. 43, 1962, pp. 8-14.

62. Sarbin, Theodore. "Role Theory," in G. Lindzey (ed.) *Handbook of Social Psychology,* Vol. 1. Cambridge, Mass.: Addison-Wesley, 1954, pp. 223-258.

63. Schafer, Walter E. "Deviance in the Public School: An Interactional View," in Edwin T. Thomas (ed.) *Behavioral Sciences for Social Workers.* New York: Free Press, 1964.

64. Schwitzgebel, Ralph. *Street Corner Research.* Cambridge, Mass.: Harvard University Press, 1964.

65. Sherman, Murray H. "Role Titles, Vocations and Psychotherapy," *Psychoanalytical Review,* Vol. 58, No. 4, Spring, 1971, pp. 511-528.

66. Shyne, Anne W. "What Research Tells Us About Short-Term Cases in Family Agencies," *Social Casework,* Vol. 38, No. 5, 1957, pp. 223-231.

67. Spiegel, John P. "The Resolution of Role Conflict Within the Family," in Norman W. Bell and Ezra F. Vogel (eds.) *The Family.* Glencoe, Ill.: Free Press, 1960, pp. 361-380.

68. Stark, Frances B. "Barriers to Client-Worker Communication at Intake," *Social Casework,* Vol. 40, No. 4, 1959, pp. 177-183.

69. Sternbach, Oscar and Leon Nagelberg. "On the Patient-Therapist Relationship in Some Untreatable Cases," *Psychoanalysis and the Psychoanalytic Review,* Vol. 5, 1957, pp. 63-71.

70. Strean, Herbert S. "The Contribution of Paradigmatic Psychotherapy to Psychoanalysis," *The Psychoanalytic Review,* Vol. 51, No. 3, Fall, 1964, pp. 29-45.

71. ——. "Role Expectations of Students and Teachers in a Graduate School of Social Work: Their Relationship to the Students' Performance," *Applied Social Studies,* Vol. 3, 1971, pp. 117-122.

72. ——. "Role Theory, Role Models, and Casework: Review of the Literature and Practice Applications," *Social Work,* Vol. 12, No. 2, April, 1967, pp. 77-88.

73. ——. "Social Change and the Proliferation of Regressive Therapies," *Psychoanalytic Review,* Vol. 58, No. 4, Spring, 1971, pp. 581-594.

74. ——. "The Use of the Patient as Consultant," *Psychoanalysis and the Psychoanalytic Review,* Vol. 45, No. 4, 1959, pp. 36-44.

75. ——. "Treatment of Mothers and Sons in the Absence of the Father," *Social Work,* Vol. 6, No. 3, 1961, pp. 29-35.

76. ——. "The Application of Role Theory to Social Casework," in H. Strean (ed.) *Social Casework: Theories in Action.* Metuchen, N.J.: Scarecrow Press, 1971.

77. Sullivan, Harry Stack. "A Note on Formulating the Relationship of the Individual and the Group," *American Journal of Sociology,* Vol. 44, May, 1939, pp. 922-937.

78. Sutherland, Robert L. and Julian L. Woodward. *Introductory Sociology.* New York: Lippincott, 1940, pp. 250-253.

79. Varley, Barbara K. "The Use of Role Theory in the Treatment of Disturbed Adolescent," *Social Casework,* Vol. 49, No. 6, June, 1968, pp. 362-368.

80. Warner, W. Lloyd. *Social Class in America.* Chicago: Science Research Associates, 1949.

81. Wheelis, Allen. *The Quest for Identity.* New York: Norton, 1958.

82. Znaniecki, Florian. "Social Groups as Products of Participating Individuals," *American Journal of Sociology,* May, 1939, pp. 799-812.

Annotated listing of key references

BIDDLE, Bruce J. and Edwin Thomas. *Role Theory.* New York: Wiley, 1966.

The most comprehensive text on role theory, it offers the major concepts of role theory and in short papers many rich examples of role prescriptions, role descriptions, role sanctioning, role enactment, and role evaluation.

GROSS, Neal, Ward S. Mason and Alexander W. McEachern. *Explorations in Role Analysis.* New York: Wiley, 1958.

A pioneering study in role theory with a focus on role conflict. The role conflicts of a superintendent of schools are analyzed.

LENNARD, Henry L. and Arnold Bernstein. *The Anatomy of Psychotherapy.* New York: Columbia University Press, 1960.

A research study on the role-sets of patient and therapist in psychotherapy and an analysis of complementarity and discomplementarity in several therapeutic relationships.

NELSON, Marie, Benjamin Nelson, Murray Sherman and Herbert S. Strean. *Roles and Paradigms in Psychotherapy.* New York: Grune and Stratton, 1968.

An explication of various types of role enactment in psychotherapy with several therapeutic sessions reproduced.

PERLMAN, Helen Harris. *Persona: Social Role and Personality.* Chicago: University of Chicago Press, 1968.

A colorful and clear application of role theory to problems of family, parent–child, and work life as they emerge in the social agency.

STREAN, Herbert S. "The Application of Role Theory to Social Casework," in H. Strean (ed.) *Social Casework: Theories in Action.* Metuchen, N.J.: Scarecrow Press, 1971.

Reviews some of the concepts in role theory and demonstrates their applicability to diagnosis and treatment in social casework.

16

Communication Concepts and Principles

by

LOTTE MARCUS

Communication between people, one of man's most basic needs, has also become one of the most complex civilized activities. The term itself has been assigned a variety of different meanings by different writers. Definitions range from the monadic concept of a response to a stimulus to a global view of communication, equivalent to a system which transcends acts of individuals. In rather general terms, communication can be viewed as human interaction and social relatedness. Examined more closely, each communication act will be conceived as consisting of a multiplicity of messages traveling in several channels, enveloped in many contexts, with constant interaction between them. It is the writer's intention to illuminate this complexity and reach out to a variety of disciplines engaged in the pursuit of knowledge in this field. By attempting to do justice to the great wealth of material, a more detailed analysis of particular aspects of communication could not be undertaken. A comprehensive, rather than intensive,

treatment of the subject was the result. The reader may find that much of the knowledge described in this chapter has direct application to social work practice, while some of the observations and research data derived from various fields can best be viewed as tools for a richer and more refined understanding of human interactions.

Theories influential in furthering knowledge of human communication

Many discrepancies can be found in the descriptions of the theories and the use of terminology in the communication sciences. Some writers, mostly American, under criticism from others, mostly British, use the term "information theory" and "communication theory" interchangeably. Some authors trace the development of a communication science from its early beginnings, in the thirteenth century, to a highly

complex mathematical and statistical conceptualization termed "information theory" (8, pp.
30-65). The French are said to employ the
word "la cybernétique" as equivalent to information theory, whereas in England the term
"control systems" is used rather than cybernetics. When the physical scientists cannot
agree about the boundaries of the knowledge
developed in their realm, it is not surprising that
the social scientists, greatly influenced by some
of the stimulating ideas, have frequently
adopted them with little regard to their origins
and logical derivations.

Following Cherry's admonition that communication theory, which rests on a solid foundation of mathematics, cannot be understood by
those who want to avoid the mathematics (8, p.
168), no attempt will be made to apply communication theory to human communication.
However, although the theory with all its
assumptions cannot truly be popularized, its
concepts are certainly basic to the study of
human communication. A very brief description
of some of the scientific formulations are
presented as a backdrop to the more detailed
analysis of the individual concepts and their application to social work thinking and practice.

Cybernetics

Cybernetics, derived from the Greek word
for "a steersman," is the science of government
and control (63). Its most basic concept is that of
feedback, discussed more fully later on. The latter implies the control of a machine (or
organism) on the basis of its past performance,
i.e., the operation of a furnace as regulated by
"information" supplied by a thermostat. The
name of Norbert Wiener is usually associated
with this theory, and he and his coworkers have
called attention to the great generality of the
concept of feedback which has since been
employed widely in the physical, biological and
social sciences. Its usefulness for the understanding of human communication lies in the
principle that all information, transmitted and re-

ceived, can be redirected in a circular process to
its source and has the potential of modifying,
correcting errors and changing subsequent information. A common misuse of the term feedback
is to regard it as an end in itself ("We must have
feedback"), rather than as a means toward an
end ("We must correct our behavior on the basis
of feedback"). The perspective of cybernetics is
on the operation and structuring of the system,
rather than on its elements. In this respect it is
closely linked to general systems theory, which
is described in another chapter.

Communication Theory

Communication theory served initially as "a
model which enabled the engineer to structure
his conceptions of the changes through which
an electrical system passes, beginning as input
and ending as output" (43, p. 228). The
elements of the system are an information
source which produces the message, a transmit-
ter which renders it suitable for transmission, a
channel as a medium, a receiver where the
message is reconstructed and a destination
where the message leaves the system as output.
With the development of telecommunication the
really hard core of mathematical theory was introduced with its direct application to the
technical equipment itself.

Information Theory,* the Mathematical Theory of Communication

Shannon and Weaver are usually seen as
the creative fathers of what we now know as information theory (8), a statistical or probability
theory which has been defined as a
"mathematical technique for measuring the effectiveness of sign transmission in a man-made
system" (43, p. 229). Effectiveness includes the
speed and economy with which information can
be brought about. "Information" in this context

---

*American usage of term.

implies a quantity, rather than content or meaning, and serves to reduce uncertainty, rather than convey a message. The quantity depends on the set of circumstances, or amount of uncertainty. The more uncertainty in the system, the more information is required. Another basic tenet of the theory is "noise," or any disturbance affecting the signals which interferes with their error-free transmission. Thus information can be measured, as can the loss of information, in terms of what could have been communicated under certain circumstances, rather than what is actually communicated at a particular moment. Furthermore, the concept of information, in its mathematical context, concerns not merely the signals themselves, but rather their potential, the probability of their selection and the patterned relationship between them.

The theories of communication are not substantive theories; they do not tell us why information is transmitted, what meaning it contains or what constitutes an interference. While not adequate in explaining human communication, the conceptualizations serve as a guide in structuring the communication process and in analyzing its individual components.

Model of Human Communication

Figure 16-1 illustrates the communication process. The terms borrowed from the communication theories are shown in juxtaposition to those employed in human communication.

Context of Communication

Every behavior occurs in a context, a social situation, and is shaped by it. This is almost a truism for social workers. We "set the scene" when we decide to visit a client at home, rather than interview him in our office; we note well the cultural background in which he was socialized; we select an appropriate medium for reaching him; we are alert to timing; we are aware of our position as professionals, agency representatives, members of a socioeconomic

group, and the effect of these on our interactions. It would therefore seem obvious that context and content are a unified whole, a gestalt, and that interventions are ineffective unless one takes cognizance of this fact. Context to the social worker is not Goffman's "neglected situation" (22, pp. 61-66), nor is it the psychologist's "independent, extraneous factor." (18, p. 181)

Less well known may be the study approach called "context analysis," which was formulated in 1956 by the Palo Alto group and developed further by Birdwhistell and Scheflen (54, pp. 263-91). Context analysis stems from the natural history method used in anthropology where subjects are studied in their natural surroundings. Communication in this approach is seen as a social system where structural units are organized in patterns along different levels of complexity (maneuvers, tactics, strategies, programs) and are related to each other and to outside systems in the total cultural context (54). Training in context analysis involves repeated viewings of films and videotapes and observation and analysis of communicative behavioral sequences, i.e., the entry of a new member into a group, in the context of the total interactive process. Although complex and time-consuming, such training would seem feasible for social workers, especially as part of an educational experience at a school of social work or in staff development sessions, preferably of an interdisciplinary nature.

Communicator A

As can be seen from the diagram, the designations Communicator A and Communicator B were chosen, instead of the more usual "speaker" and "listener," to emphasize the mutuality of the roles. The starting point of a communication is frequently indeterminate, and the "speaker" who appeared to have initiated it may have responded to cues sent, perhaps out of awareness, by the "listener." This situation has been described as a difficulty in punctuation of a sequence (60, pp. 54-59). Each participant

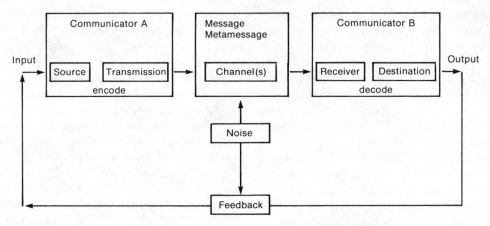

Figure 16–1.   CONTEXT OF COMMUNICATION

labels the other as the active initiator of the sequence and assigns to himself the role of passive recipient. Thus both Communicator A and Communicator B may see themselves as only reacting to, but not determining, the other's behavior. The terms "source," "transmission" and "encode" in the diagram can refer both to a machine and a living organism. In human communication the source will be the brain, where the impulse to communicate originates. The transmission would thus respond to the specific organ, i.e., larynx, vocal cords, etc., for speech; body and limbs for gestures, and so on.

Communicator A, in his role of sending a message, can be seen to possess certain potentials. The credibility of the communicator, a term used in mass communication, is said to depend on his expertise, intention and trustworthiness (27). It would seem logical that the communicator's knowledge and experience has an effect on his communications. This is true up to a point. For an individual in a crisis, a community stricken by disaster, factual information and an experienced helper will be important, to avoid disorganization and confusion. In many situations, however, expertise is less important than personal characteristics. Expert leaders are often less effective in community organization than trusted leaders; the social work student is

frequently more successful than the experienced social worker.

Group dynamics has taught us to look at the intention of the communicator in a very specific way. Low-status persons who want to improve their status but have no opportunity to do so are said to use communication as "substitute upward locomotion," directed at high-status persons, whereas the high-status person who is still building up his power may communicate more freely with low-status persons to gain their support (9, pp. 166–87). Group workers are very sensitive to the power struggles among group members which often create obstacles to interaction. Observation of communication exchanges and the direction in which messages are sent may give an indication of such a situation.

Trustworthiness, the social approval the communicator masters and the personal regard given to him by others, is a very important element in any change effort. Studies have shown that opinion change depends heavily on this, at least for a limited time. When the effect of the personality factor wears off, the content of the communication begins to assume greater importance again. This is referred to as the "sleeper effect." However, the salience of the source can be reinstated when attention is drawn to it (27).

The quality of trustworthiness assumes special significance in community change efforts, in the context of a bargaining or mediation process. To channel information to trusted opinion leaders and informed people in the community, which personalizes the communication, has been tried with good results. This method is referred to as "two-step flow of communication" (2).

Probably the most important characteristic of the communicator is his skill in encoding and transmitting messages. Fanshel developed a "capacity-to-communicate" scale for casework clients. Scores on this scale showed a relationship to the clients' ability to make use of casework help, as judged by caseworkers, and to their continuance in treatment when the latter was fairly intensive. The author suggested—as has also been pointed out by others—that casework may favor the client who is able to express himself verbally. This would imply that the capacity-to-communicate scale measures mainly verbal capacity (17).

This variable was also studied by Polansky under the term "verbal accessibility," which he believes is the product of the client's readiness to communicate verbally and the skill with which he is met (46, p. 185). The author regards verbal accessibility as an aspect of ego functioning, found to be stable across time and social situations. He emphasizes the healing properties of verbal communication and the deleterious effects of the failure to learn how to use words or to mistrust them.

Closely related to Polansky's stress on the therapeutic quality of words are Bruch's observations that the form of verbal communication, as distinct from its content, may make psychotherapy effective or defeat its goal (5). She believes that the wording and sentence formation frequently used by psychotherapists convey the concept of an active, omniscient helper and a passive, inert patient. An example of this may be the question: "Did I make myself clear?" rather than "Do you understand me?"; or the report that the patient "has been given insight," rather than "has gained insight." Bruch strongly urges therapists to use wording which conveys to the patient that he is seen as capable of experiencing and reporting on his own thoughts, feelings and sensations. Such an exhortation may seem unnecessary for the social worker of today, but are we also innocent of the mind-reading type of behavior Bruch describes, where the helper assumes to know what the other thinks? Who could not be humbled by hearing someone say: "I know you believe you understand what you think I have said, but I'm not sure you realize that what you heard is not what I said."*

The skill of the communicator has been analyzed most ably by Satir (52). Her descriptions of the functional communicator who sends messages clearly and directly; restates, clarifies and modifies them when necessary; is receptive and tuned in to feedback and checks out his own perceptions; asks for clarification, for examples; acknowledges feelings and generally acts as a model of communication—these descriptions are undoubtedly very familiar to social workers, as they are required readings for all social work students. Likewise, Satir's examples of dysfunctional communicators who send unclear or masked messages; leave out connections; ignore questions; switch sentences and do not complete them; respond out of context and inappropriately—cannot be equaled for poignancy and dramatic impact.

Satir's distinctions between functional and dysfunctional communicators apply to clients and helpers alike. Furthermore, verbal and nonverbal behavior are considered equally in her delineation of the communicative ability. This factor cannot be emphasized enough. The communicator's repertoire should extend flexibly to all media of communication.

The Channel

The channel of communication can be equated with the medium used to transmit

---

* Inscription in Main Conference Room at the University of Waterloo, Ontario, Canada.

messages. This applies to the machine as well as to man. The two aspects which must be considered are the channel capacity with its communication load and the type of medium, or sensory pathways, selected for the transmission of messages. Every person has a certain capacity to receive and absorb information which varies with age, health, training, motivation, the situation and many other factors. Both an overload and an underload can be harmful. Social workers are familiar with persons who have been removed from sources of stimulation with other humans during lengthy periods of hospitalization, in solitary confinement, due to language barriers and other circumstances, and who have lost some of their communication skills or became uncertain of them and consequently withdrew, became apathetic, depressed or even paranoid and hallucinatory. Likewise, an overload, an exposure to many verbal demands, poorly timed and perhaps conflicting, may lead to passive compliance or the shutting out of stimuli and ignoral of messages, and perhaps mistrust of communication and of people.

The distribution of communication loads, or the "fit of overall patterns and constituent parts," as Ruesch calls it (49, p. 35), is an important criterion for successful communication and good mental health. In a group, when one member monopolizes the discussion; in family therapy, when a child is made the spokesman or scapegoat by other family members, while others remain uncommitted and uninvolved, there exists an uneven distribution. The traffic density is greater in one part of the network than in another. A functional communicator would draw the members' attention to this situation and may elicit the feelings of the person(s) contributing to the overload and those affected by it.

Epstein found that in a sample of families communication was most effective and most conducive to mental health when it contained a high collective pattern, when each member communicated with every other, rather than when the flow of communication was central-ized in one person (15). This finding may not be generalizable to all cultures, as the researcher points out. It is obviously not accepted in Greek Stoic philosophy: "Nature has given man one tongue, but two ears, that we may hear from others twice as much as we speak" (Epictetus). *

"The medium is the message" (36) is one of the most famous McLuhanisms. Like all clever aphorisms, it contains much truth, while at the same time it oversimplifies its statement. In face-to-face human contacts, communication is a multichannel affair and involves all sensory modalities simultaneously. This does not mean that we do not deliberately select one medium, e.g., speech, to convey an idea and are unaware of communicating our uncertainty through the tone of voice; our pleas for acceptance by a look; our wish to dominate by means of the distance we establish between ourselves and the other; our cultural affinity by the clothes we wear, and so on. Furthermore, Communicator B may only perceive part of the message, perhaps the one we consciously intended for him, perhaps the one he wants to apprehend.

Social workers are constantly struggling to hear, see, feel and understand what others are trying to express or to conceal and are often painfully aware of the complexity of this task. The studies described in the following pages deal with the analysis of verbal and nonverbal content, in auditory and visual media. This search for a more precise and meaningful understanding of communicative behavior is not only an interesting and intriguing intellectual pursuit, but can be of great practical value in the diagnostic, therapeutic and evaluative process of any human interaction. The imagination and ingenuity required to adapt some of these methods to social work activities have not been lacking, as can be seen. A fuller acquaintance with this material may serve as a further stimulus.

---

*Cited by George A. Miller (38, p. 47).

Content Analysis

The systematic ordering of the content of communication processes is a research technique which involves the division of the content into units. These units are then assigned categories, counted, described and analyzed. Content analysis of interviews or groups can give information about clients' emotional states and attitudes, about therapist characteristics and interventive techniques, about interactional systems and relationships between variables (35).

Perhaps the earliest application of content analysis in social work involved the Distress-Relief Quotient of Dollard and Mowrer (12), which was used by the Community Service Society of New York as part of the Movement Scale to measure changes in clients after social work treatment. The Distress-Relief Quotient was later abandoned when it was found to have a low correlation with workers' judgments of movement in treatment.

Among the many other content analyses developed is the type token ratio (TTR), which shows the relationship of "different words" (types) to "total number of words" (tokens), and is thus a measure of verbal diversification. A low ratio, or little verbal diversification, is characteristic of disturbed affect, anxiety and confusion in the speaker (29). A well-known method of analyzing group processes is Bales' interaction process analysis, which permits a scrutiny of the problem-solving activities and changes in interaction within the group (1). This measure has been used widely in family therapy research. A very comprehensive content-analysis investigation by Strupp taps the behavior of the therapist, the degree of inference and warmth in his communication, and makes possible a comparison of therapists of different orientations (57).

Analysis of therapist behavior was also the object of Hollis' typology, which classifies both client and worker communications according to types of casework techniques and client reactions (26). Originally used in single-client interviews, the technique was subsequently adapted to joint interviews. Stimulated by the above analyses, Dalibard (in her Master's research at McGill University) applied the TTR, as well as Hollis' typology, to two excerpts of a casework interview. Contrary to expectations, the TTRs remained the same in both extracts, while the profiles obtained on Hollis' typology differed. Dalibard concluded that the extracts were not long enough for increasing client discomfort to manifest itself through repetition of words. However, an examination of the tape revealed a number of nonverbal features indicative of anxiety, which concurred with Hollis' findings. Dalibard concluded with a recommendation that content analysis should be taught to social work students and could profitably be used as guidelines to a more uniform type of social work recording (10).

Paralinguistic Research

Paralanguage or paralinguistics refers to the nonverbal vocalizations which co-occur with verbal behavior and are commonly referred to as "tone of voice." Examples of paralinguistic components are: pitch, loudness, tempo, laughs, sighs, pauses and others. Clinicians of a variety of disciplines are concerned with the role of these vocal cues in clinical interviews. In their study of fifteen taped psychotherapy sessions, Eldred and Price found durable alterations in the patient's normal speaking voice when angry or depressed and noticeable changes in vocal patterns from the beginning to the later stages of therapy (14). Duncan established that paralinguistic phenomena were closely correlated to the judgments made by therapists of their own work. Interviews rated as particularly good or particularly poor by them were also distinguished by different paralinguistic patterns (13). Similarly, Mahl and his coworkers, in a series of carefully designed studies, isolated seven distinct vocal features which proved to be highly correlated to fluctuations in the speaker's anxiety level (32). It was Mahl's research which prompted this writer to examine the ability of social workers of different levels of training to perceive anxiety from taped interviews (33).

One of the most thorough applications of microscopic linguistic analyses to clinical material is provided by the book *The First Five Minutes* (44). It shows how the linguist specifies signals, item by item, and the psychiatrist identifies states which are in the form of a gestalt and how the two can be coordinated—a very fruitful interdisciplinary enterprise. Lastly, an exciting discovery was made by Milmoe et al., who examined the speech of physicians who were urging alcoholics to accept treatment for alcoholism. They employed an electroacoustic method which filters out verbal content and leaves vocal features—which contain affect—undisturbed. They found that judges who were quite unable to postdict the success of a physician in referring his patient by listening to his words were, however, able to do so, with great accuracy, from his filtered speech. The latter contained a high degree of hostility (40).

As can be seen, paralinguistic analysis leads to an objective evaluation of those aspects of speech which are usually considered vague and elusive. Social workers need not shy away from these endeavors, which may sound complex and formidable. Awareness of and sensitivity to these phenomena can be cultivated by careful listening to one's own and others' taped speech. The writer had the experience of training volunteer social workers for a few weeks only and was amazed at the progress they made in this short time.

Kinesic Research

Kinesic analysis is a method of studying and analyzing body-motion communication and is most closely associated with the name of Ray Birdwhistell. The latter emphasizes that there are no body motions, facial expressions or gestures which are universal and convey the same message the world over.

A body can be bowed in grief, in humility, in laughter, or in readiness for aggression. A "smile" in one society portrays friendliness, in another embarrassment, and, in still another may contain a warning that unless tension is reduced, hostility and attack will follow. (3, p. 34)

Kinesics must be viewed as behavior learned and patterned within a culture and understood together with its context. Unlike an earlier belief that verbal content carries meaning and paralanguage and kinesics qualify, modify, add emphasis and emotional elaboration, it has been found that a message is carried in all media and that any one of them can assume priority at any given moment. However, it must be understood that behavior, while being communicative on one level, can also be, on another level, instrumental (I move my arm because it has gone to sleep) or reflex motion (I sneeze because my nasal passages are irritated).

Kinesic analysis, applied rigorously, is very time-consuming, but useful studies can be carried out relatively simply, still applying the concepts developed by Birdwhistell and others but using a wider net of observation. Krim, for instance, explored the relationship between movement patterns and verbal content of social work interviews, using only a one-way screen. She stresses the value of this exercise in sharpening diagnostic ability and stimulating sensitivity (30). Findley and Gervais examined excerpts of a videotaped interview which yielded interesting speculations about the client-worker interactions (20).

Proxemics

This is the term coined by E. T. Hall for "the theories and observations of man's use of space," or "spatial accents" (24). Some of his findings would seem to be of great importance to social work. All channels of communication, all sensory modes, are involved in the sending of spatial messages which can be interpreted only within the context of a particular culture. Three types of space can be distinguished.

Fixed-feature space, or territory. Man creates an environment around him which in turn creates opportunities and restraints to his way of life and social interactions: as Churchill remarked when the rebuilding of the House of Commons was planned: "We shape our buildings and they shape us" (24, p. 100). It is a well known fact that many animals exhibit different behavior while in home territory and foreign territory. This applies to humans also. Social workers are familiar with clients who do not appear as the same people during home visits—on home turf—as in offices, hospitals, waiting rooms, at mass meetings, rallies and so on. Not only can we observe territorial behavior and elicit information from our clients about their feelings concerning their living and working space (59), but some of us may, if cognizant of this knowledge, make significant contributions backed by research, to the design of hospitals, nursing homes, subsidized housing projects and in participating on planning commissions.

Semifixed-feature space. This involves the arrangement of movable objects, such as chairs, tables, desks, to create living and working areas. Humphrey Osmond, a Saskatchewan physician, noticed in his health center that some spaces keep people apart, while others tend to bring them together. The former, which he labeled "sociofugal," can be seen in waiting rooms, lecture halls and in some hospital wards, where chairs are placed in rows and patients become, rather like the furniture, "permanently and silently glued to the walls at regular intervals between beds" (24, p. 102). Spatial arrangements which facilitate contacts, called "sociopetal," characterize sidewalk cafes, restaurant booths and others. In a hospital cafeteria, cross-corner conversations were noticed to occur twice as frequently as side-by-side ones (24).

These and similar observations are well known to social workers who automatically arrange chairs in semicircles for group meetings, move from behind their desks when interviewing clients and try to fit spatial arrangements to specific needs. Perhaps it has even become necessary to sound a warning against the overuse of sociopetal space and the tendency to underestimate the beneficial effects of permitting, and even encouraging, temporary spatial isolation for some persons, at some times.

Informal Space. This includes the distance maintained by people in encounters with others. These vary with the culture, the specific circumstances and with regard to the different senses. During periods of stress, crowding will be experienced more acutely than at times of relaxation; feelings about being seen, heard, touched, vary greatly in different cultures. Hall differentiates four main distances: (1) the intimate distance when the sensory involvement with the other is intense—if undesired, defensive devices are applied, as the tensing of one's muscles and the averted look in a crowded subway; (2) the personal distance, when the individual builds a small protective sphere around him which signals the relationship; (3) the social distance, usually maintained in working relationships or casual encounters, and (4) the public distance, where gestures become more important than facial expressions and the voice has to be projected (24, pp. 110-22).

Social work relationships encompass mainly social and personal distances, and the advantages of one over the other have been the subject of many disputes. Ardent advocates can be found among those who believe that physical closeness, as in sensitivity or encounter groups, and the personal touch in the literal sense of the word, are remedies for many of man's ills, while others maintain that objectivity and preservation of distance from the problems we try to alleviate are an essential factor in any helping process. An acquaintance with some of the knowledge about the communication media, as they involve the various sensory channels and cultural complexities, may help to avoid generalizations. Lastly, an interesting study must be mentioned of the behavior of participants of a conference (37). By means of still photographs, Byers analyzed movements and spatial relationships as they manifested themselves and developed in the course of the conference meetings, another example of a relatively simple technological procedure which, combined with extensive knowledge of communication, can yield most useful results.

The Message

As mentioned earlier, information, in the context of the mathematical theory of communication, does not deal with content but with the potential of signs to reduce uncertainty. When the term "information" is used in this section it refers to "content information," and the particular meanings and shades of meaning are the subject of attention. Content information is connotative, which implies that it expresses not only the explicit and denoted meaning, but the implicit, suggested and affective properties. Connotative meaning is an individual matter, conditioned by prior experience and associations and thus liable to give rise to ambiguity, as the meanings may differ among communicators. The message sent may not be the message received. Thus content information, rather than remove uncertainty, may increase it. Furthermore, uncertainty in human interactions involves the information already acquired but unsatisfactorily absorbed, and absence of uncertainty does not preclude the acquisition of information, as it does in information theory (43, pp. 45-47). Problems of meaning are the concern of semanticists and philosophers, and much research has resulted from the development of the semantic differential, the measure which attempts to subject meaning to quantitative measurement (42).

A clear distinction must be made between language and speech. The latter is the observable behavior, the visible and audible signals, whereas language refers to the cultural system, the code which is inferred from the behavioral variations of speech. Two opposing forces are said to govern language. One force is evoked by the desire to be understood, the "social force," which tries to counteract the disturbances from the environment and the inadequacies of language. It achieves this end, or attempts to do so, by means of redundancy, or the addition of signs, repetition of words, expansion of sentences and the use of several channels. Too much redundancy leads to boredom in the individual and red tape in an organization. The other force is governed by the desire to minimize effort, the "individual force," or the "force of personal laziness," which leads to brevity and simplification of expression. The latter, also termed "principle of least effort" (8, p. 100), was substantiated by experimental evidence from statistical studies of language which revealed that the most frequently used words in all languages are also the shortest (8, p. 35)—an interesting, though not surprising, finding.

Clients, in their efforts to be understood, frequently communicate with redundancy and, in turn, demand a similar response from the social worker, who may feel he sounds like a broken record, but merely acts as a functional communicator. The "individual force" may lead the communicator to an oversimplification and a telegraphic type of message, sometimes observed in language used by schizophrenics or very angry individuals. Furthermore, the social worker would have to determine whether a message was meant to fulfill an instrumental need for the client—if it was a means to an end—or whether it was a consummatory type of communication, a need to express himself, an end in itself (19).

Group dynamics offers some guidelines about different communications and their effectiveness. It has been shown, for instance, that a message which fosters awareness of the norms of the reference group has a better chance of acceptance than one which stands on its own merits, supported only by its own internal consistency or logic. This is an important point for the community organizer. He must use his knowledge of group norms in trying to introduce change and in suggesting innovations.

Another source of useful knowledge is the study of linguistic codes, the forms of speech used by different groups. Whether speakers of different languages, by virtue of the language they speak, dissect nature along lines laid down by the structure of the language and perceive the world in this way, as Whorf asserted (64), has evoked a great deal of discussion. Even though this "linguistic Weltanschauung," as it has been called (7, p. 106), has not received full support by linguists and other scientists, it cannot be denied that a person learning to speak and even speaking with fluency a language other than his mother tongue, is forced to express his ideas differently, which may, in turn, exert an influence on his view of the world and those around him. This consideration could be of value in interactions with clients of different ethnic origins.

Not only between languages, but within them, interesting variations can be observed. Bernstein, in a series of studies in England, found radically different modes of speech among persons of the lower working class compared with those from the middle class. The *restricted* code of the former, according to Bernstein, is a function of the social arrangements and social relationships of lower working class families who share common interests and life styles. It is a condensed, concrete, descriptive and emotive type of speech which is closely tied to its context and often cannot be understood without it. It signals the speaker's social, rather than personal, identity and sustains solidarity with the group. The *elaborated* code, on the other hand, specifies and articulates meanings which are freer of the context in which they are embedded and can be understood apart from it (34, p. 17). The codes, furthermore, bear the influence of different role structures, not necessarily tied to social class. Bernstein distinguishes between "positional" families, in whom status boundaries are strong and territorial rights clearly delineated, and "person-centered" families, where roles are carved out rather than stepped into by the individual.

The restricted code also characterizes other groups who possess a common way of life, such as families, army companions or prison inmates, where unspoken assumptions, sign language and metaphors take the place of explicit meanings and verbal elaborations. Bernstein stresses that a restricted code which can be very rich and colorful is in no way inferior to an elaborated one, nor can it be equated with linguistic deprivation or deficiency. However, switching from one code to another is easier when an elaborated code is the more usual way of communication. It is this difficulty of translating the restricted code into an elaborated one which makes school activities—which are predicated upon the latter—more arduous for the child of a lower socioeconomic group (21, 64). The following is an example of five-year-old children telling a story about a series of pictures which they were shown and asked to describe.

1. Three boys are playing football and one boy kicks the ball   and it goes through the   window   and the boys are looking at it   and a man comes out and shouts at them because they've broken the window   so they run away. . . .
2. They're playing football   and he kicks it and it goes through there it breaks the window and they're looking at it   and he comes out and shouts at them   because they've broken it   so they run away. . . .*

As can be seen, the first story, using an elaborated code, does not require an examination of the pictures by the reader. The meaning is explicit, whereas the second story, in a restricted code, contains the implicit assumption that the reader knows the context.

"Accusations have been levelled against social workers for failing to establish meaningful

* Basil Bernstein, "Social Class, Language and Socialization" (21, p. 167). (In his earlier writings, the author used the terms "public" language and "formal" language for the restricted and elaborated code, respectively.)

communication with the 'poor'. Although the suspicion and mistrust of this group against social workers could be mainly due to inadequate, inappropriate and frequently demoralizing services provided for them, the possibility that their messages are misunderstood and misinterpreted cannot be ignored" (34, p. 17).

It is probably true to say that many of our messages are misunderstood, or only partially understood. Some of the origins of this problem have already been described. The context of the communication may contain an impediment for the message, through poor timing and an inappropriate setting; the communicator may be at fault in his function of encoding and transmitting; the difficulty may lie with the channel, if there is an overload or underload; the media may have been poorly chosen, or the code itself may create complications. Examples of messages characterized by a high potential for being misunderstood are thus numerous. There is the message containing the unstated assumption, which relies on implicit knowledge and involves a considerable risk of being distorted. McLuhan's definition of a "cool medium" which suggests, rather than explains and invites interpretations, as well as many art forms, are messages with unstated assumptions. Another high-risk message would be an incomplete one, when the speaker proceeds without filling in the missing part or pauses without indicating whether he plans to continue. Indirect messages will create uncertainty and often elicit undesired responses such as the following:

Wife: Would you like to go to the movies?

Husband: No.

(10 minutes later)

Wife: You never take me out. Why did you refuse?

Husband: You never asked me.

Wife: I asked you 10 minutes ago. You never listen, you don't care.

Husband: (She may be right. I don't remember her asking. So maybe I don't listen, don't want to hear.) (47, p. 11)

Messages may be quantitatively inappropriate when the communicator responds excessively or too tersely. Likewise, the quality of the message may be inappropriate if the context is overlooked, as the ill-timed joke, or when the intent and the feeling of the sender are disregarded. This happens frequently when several contradictory messages are sent concurrently through different channels. Misunderstandings will almost certainly arise in such situations unless the interpreter is particularly sensitive, or uncommonly lucky. Many more examples could be brought to illustrate the vagaries of content information. However, human communication contains an invaluable compensatory device in the form of the metamessage.

Metamessage. As language has its counterpart in metalanguage, or the language of the observer who studies it, so can a message be complemented by a metamessage. Whereas the message reports on the content, the metamessage explains and clarifies it, informs about the speaker's intentions and feelings and the relationship between himself and the recipient of the communication. The metamessage can be sent verbally or use any of the nonverbal media, but usually involves a multilevel structure. When a client asks "Can you help me?" and the social worker replies truthfully "I do not know," he can add, "I would have to know more about you and about your difficulty before I can answer this," or "I do not know, but I will certainly try." The social worker may also convey by his smile that he is friendly and well disposed toward the client; his eyes may command trust and confidence; his handshake may relate his strength and determination and the tone of his voice his appreciation of the client's fear and anxiety. This description exemplifies congruity between message and metamessage. This is frequently not the case. The person who says "Thank you so much; you have helped me a lot" and sounds or looks as if he were about to attack; the words of criticism accompanied by a satisfied smile, and many similar incongruities can be observed in numerous contexts.

What has been described above is no doubt very familiar to every social worker, and the reader may well remark, like M. Jourdain in the *Bourgeois Gentilhomme,* "For more than——— years I have been talking prose [metamessages] without knowing it."*

Noise

In telecommunication, noise has been classified as any disturbances which are not part of the messages coming from a specific source. All signals are subject to interferences which enter the channel and which neither the source nor the destination can predict (8). Crackling or atmospherics on the radio, flickering or dots on the television screen, crosstalk on telephone lines, all can constitute noise. In physical systems, it appears as if there were a second source which introduces signals into the same channel and thereby produces errors in the original message (8).

Analogically, in the human system, "noise" is referred to as any interference with a message, whether this is undesired sound or any other distraction for the listener. There is a basic difference, however. When a person's speech becomes unintelligible because he begins to cry, the cry itself may become the message, communicating his feelings and complementing or substituting for his words. Likewise, communication traveling through one channel may interfere with the reception of a message sent through another. If I gesticulate wildly while talking, the listener may be unable to follow my words, being distracted by my movements. However, my body language may be a more

significant signal about my motivations or intentions than the content of my words. I may want to influence him with persuasive gestures or hide my ignorance behind them, and I might not be aware of either. Noise in human communication is very relative and depends heavily on the meaning assigned to it as destroyer or creator of messages.

Reference was made earlier to the concept of redundancy, the superfluity of rules in a language, the repetitions, elaborations and emphases which are designed to counteract the interference with a message and in this manner facilitate communication. Multichannel communication can build in redundancy. One can turn off the sound of the television and still follow the story, sometimes even better. The sound may have acted as noise. In a helping relationship we may choose to "switch off," for a few seconds, the client's words, label them as noise, and listen to the tone of his voice, or watch the movements of his eyes and understand more clearly what he is trying to tell us, or attempting to conceal from us.

Another type of noise, found in the language system, has been termed "code noise" or "semantic noise." It refers to differences between languages or codes which are the cause of misunderstandings between communicators. Semantic noise, however, can be predicted and controlled. As soon as the social worker learns the client's "language," or vice versa, semantic noise will subside or disappear altogether and misunderstandings dissolve. If semantic noise is the cause of wrong interpretations of messages, the engineer's noise the cause of wrong receptions of signals (8, p. 240), noise for the "human engineer" can be seen as ambiguity of meaning and yet another complexity of human communication.

Communicator B

Communicator B has several roles to play. He is the recipient of messages, including noise,

---

* Molière, *Bourgeois Gentilhomme,* Act 2, Scene 6, in *Oxford Dictionary of Quotations,* 2nd ed. (London: Oxford University Press, 1954), p. 353.

which he must interpret, incorporate into his field of experience, store in his memory and, most important in terms of communication, acknowledge its receipt to Communicator A, making the first step in the feedback cycle. As can be seen, all the characteristics and skills necessary for Communicator A also apply to his function as sender of feedback.

It is a well-known fact that thousands of sensory impressions bombard us every second of our waking day, and that all but a few must be screened out. There are marked individual differences in this screening process and every person's perceptual world is unique. An interesting observation was made concerning overlapping stimuli. As often happens in human interactions, several messages may reach us at the same moment and, provided these messages are not too similar, we are able to attend to more than one, until a critical moment is reached and our information space becomes overcrowded. If the signals are too much alike, perception is lowered (4). Furthermore, we are able to attend to one of the messages in preference to another, an ability no tape recorder possesses. The latter is referred to as the "cocktail party" problem (8).

Selective attention, or the selective readiness to react, depends on one's past experience, present needs and attitudes, as well as future expectations. We hear and see what we are trained to hear and see and what we want to perceive. This fact is of great importance to the understanding of human communications. In crisis situations, when the needs of the moment are uppermost, pertinent information is frequently screened out by the crisis victim, and the helper must be prepared to report it many times and in many different ways. Furthermore, every social worker knows clients whose early experiences have been so damaging that all subsequent messages are perceived as potentially threatening. Likewise, the client's expectations about the future affect his interpretation of current interactions. Several studies directed at an exploration of clients' perceptions of the "poten-

tially helpful person" have proved this point (58).

How, then, can Communicator B improve his ability to attend to signals and to interpret messages in such a way that communication is flexible and functional? A number of research and educational projects have been designed to answer this question. Based on Reik's concepts of "listening with the Third Ear," and "free-floating attention," which makes use of preconscious perception (48), Roger Miller designed the now well-known experimental study of the observational process in casework (39). His three groups of students who watched the film of an interview were given three different instructions on how to observe and listen. Marked differences in the assessment of the interview resulted, favoring the two groups who had utilized passive, or free-floating, attention.

In a study of factors involved in listening to taped recordings of therapists' own interviews, Ruesch and Prestwood found that all therapists became anxious on first hearing themselves, and that this anxiety lessened on repeated listening. The authors suggest that the participant role in the interview makes self-observation difficult because of the stereotypes we hold about our own behavior. In listening back, the therapist for the first time becomes an observer, and anxiety arises over his perception of himself. This anxiety, in turn, distorts his view of the client. On repeated listening the therapist again focuses on the patient rather than on himself, and his anxiety lessens (51).

Many social workers today tape their interviews and groups and have no doubt experienced this anxiety. Repeated listening may involve an investment of time in excess of the expected benefit from such an endeavor. However, the opportunity to stand back from one's own performance and to reach a consistent and more objective opinion of one's contribution to an interaction process, would seem of great value and lead to the type of self-awareness which Erikson labeled "disciplined subjectivity" (16).

In describing the message, mention was made of some of the ways in which its reception and interpretation can be disturbed. Devious acknowledgements were referred to, as was the tangential response and poor timing, making the reception of the message hazardous. Communicator B may also be guilty of partializing his response, replying to one aspect of the communication, ignoring the others. His interpretations may oversimplify the message and overlook some of its complexity. It often happens that we come away from an encounter, satisfied that we were understood, but after further reflection, come to the conclusion that the other's acknowledgement has distorted the meaning we had intended to convey and what had seemed obvious to us had been overlooked. The following is an example of a common response which oversimplifies and partializes.

Client: (after detailed account of her child's illness) Do you think I should take Jimmy back to the doctor? He does not seem well at all. Or should I wait and see?

S.W.: You must be worried about him.

Client: (long silence)

S.W.: I understand how you must feel.

Client: (angrily) You have not answered my question.*

The client has a valid reason for being angry. The social worker responded to the feeling he inferred rather than to the information requested of him. The feeling may be very important and many nonverbal signs may have portrayed them, but the question nevertheless required an answer. As a functional communicator, the social worker has to respond to what is said as well as to what he inferred.

Feedback

As mentioned in discussing the cybernetic model, feedback characterizes the property of

---

* Fictional example.

being able to adjust future behavior on the basis of past performance (65). In the communication situation, information about the impact of a message on its interpreter becomes incorporated in successive messages and determines its direction and quality. Effective behavior should be informed by feedback, which can be either positive or negative. It is rather unfortunate that in the context of behavioral psychology, positive feedback signifies reward and continuance of the rewarded behavior, whereas in cybernetics, positive feedback leads to change and frequently loss of stability and equilibrium. The term "positive" in cybernetics does not imply a value judgment, but merely explains that the information contained in the response is continued and amplified. Negative feedback, in behavioral psychology, means punishment and extinction of the punished behavior. In the cybernetic model, negative feedback leads to homeostasis and stability and corrects or decreases errors (63).

In the meeting of a citizens' group where dissension was rampant, the community organizer supports the proposal, made by one faction, to hold a peaceful demonstration. On the basis of strong opposition from another faction that favored confrontation, he suggests that the group discuss the matter further in order to reach consensus. Without this corrective (negative) feedback, internal strife may have led to a complete breakdown of communication and a freeze of all activity in the group. As can be seen, the effectiveness of feedback is in direct proportion to the ability of the communicator to perceive it and correct his actions accordingly.

Major principles of communication

Having examined the elements of the communication process and illustrated one of its cycles, a brief description follows of some of the major principles underlying human communication.

One Cannot Not Communicate, or Nothing Never Happens

A number of students of human communication (3, 49, 60) have asserted that in an interactional situation it is impossible not to communicate. Whether we speak or remain silent, whether we move or remain motionless, whether we use a conventional code or talk gibberish, if we are in the presence of another who is conscious and awake, we exert an influence. The other cannot not respond, even if he ignores the message. His response or failure to respond will act as feedback and steer our next move. Birdwhistell draws attention to two distinct ways of looking at communication. If one regards man as possessing the psychological ability to communicate, it follows that he also has the ability not to communicate. If one looks upon communication acts as units of action and reaction, misunderstandings can be seen as breakdown in communication. If, on the other hand, one regards communication as intrinsic to man, who engages in it as a member of his culture, one perceives communication as a system which transcends individual behavior, in which every message has transactional qualities in transforming its surroundings. In this context there would be no breakdown, but a different order of communication (3, p. 251).

Watzlawick offers a clinical example of the schizophrenic who appears not to communicate but, in remaining withdrawn, immobile, silent, etc., nevertheless communicates his denial, while he may, at the same time, deny his denial verbally (61). Silence may serve as self-protection or as provocation; it may convey understanding or mistrust; express anger or emptiness and apathy—but it will convey a message to the perceptive communicator and will undoubtedly evoke a reaction in him. Neither can the different kinds of nonverbal behavior be ignored as message bearers, and frequently as substitutes for verbal communication which seemed ineffective or failed to express true feelings (55). Somatic symptoms,

likewise, may be seen as signals alerting the sensitive physician to his patient's "efforts" to express himself.

> For him who has eyes to see and ears to hear no mortal can hide his secret; he whose lips are silent chatters with his fingertips and betrays himself through all his pores.*

To Understand What Is Communicated, We Must Understand What Is Not Communicated

In trying to solve a problem, whether mathematical or human, it is often useful to begin by excluding the impossible or unlikely solutions. Certain conventions and rules help us to decide. When a topic is chosen by a client, the social worker may ask himself—or ask the client—why this rather than another matter was brought up at this particular time and in this particular context. The range of alternatives could be large, but some are more reasonable and more likely to occur than others. Furthermore, to speculate about the topics which were not mentioned, the words which were not spoken, can be a very informative preoccupation. When one considers one aspect of the message, i.e., its emotional content, it is important to recognize that the voice was raised and shrill, rather than lowered and monotonous, that the hands were clenched and shaking, rather than limp and motionless, that the patient moved his chair closer rather than pulled away and that he began to perspire and wipe his brow, rather than shiver and pull his coat around himself. These signals (perhaps differentiating anxiety from depression) may be seen as standing in contrast to their alternatives and provide useful information to the interpreter. In the communication context, the latter should ask himself, "What does this behavior

---

* Cited by Robert E. Pittenger and Henry Lee Smith (45, p. 61).

say to me?" rather than "What does it mean?" The principle of "contrast or reasonable alternatives" (44) is analogous to information theory and the selection of signals by the receiver, where the occurrence of one out of a set of alternative stimuli signifies information and the amount of information increases as a function of the number of alternatives.

Every Communication Signals Both Content and a Relationship

The relationship aspect of communication has already been discussed under the heading of the metamessage, or the message about the message. It is frequently pointed out that one of the significant differences between communication in humans and that of animals lies in the ability of the former to communicate about matters which are not in their immediate sensory environment, as for instance the past or the future and abstract concepts. However, this characteristic of "immanent reference" which characterizes animal communication is also of importance in human communication (44, p. 228). Often the topic is a means of establishing a relationship, as are the remarks made at the beginning of an interview or a group session. But even when the subject matter is of prime importance, the wish to inform, to instruct, to influence or to persuade will find expression, together with the formal content. Some of the monitoring behavior which can be observed in interactions—for example, the raised eyebrow of disbelief—may be directed at the relationship between the communicators. It could be interpreted as "You want me to believe this? I cannot take you seriously," as well as "The information seems wrong."

Summary

The reader who has reached the end of this chapter, has covered much ground rather rapidly. After a cursory acquaintance with the communication theories of the physical sciences, a more detailed examination followed of the elements of the human communication process and the context in which it occurs. Communicator A and Communicator B were viewed as both senders and receivers of messages, possessing functional and dysfunctional characteristics, differential skills and capacity. The communication channel was described from the point of view of its load, as well as of its sensory selection. Examples of research of verbal and nonverbal content were quoted in order to show the usefulness of such endeavors for a fuller and finer understanding of the media and their effect on the communication. The message and the metamessage were examined with their potential for conveying understanding or creating chaos. Attention was drawn to the relativity of "noise" and the function of feedback.

Of the many principles of human communication, three were singled out as particularly pertinent to social work interactions. The assumptions were made that one cannot not communicate; furthermore, that it is as important to understand what is communicated as what is not; and lastly, that every message contains both content and a relationship.

Much has remained unsaid. The writer undoubtedly left unsatisfied those who had expected to hear about the mass media and their relevance to social work; about the communication hardware, videotapes, films, feedback loops and others, and their usefulness to the profession. No guidance has been given to those who had hoped to learn about ways to improve communication with the disadvantaged, the alienated and the disenchanted. Little has been said about the "games people play" in their interactions and the paradoxes which arise from them. Furthermore, no value issues were raised about the principle of freedom of speech or the danger of "information pollution." The writer hopes that perhaps some of the knowledge described in this chapter might be extended to the areas left uncovered and to those sparsely covered.

References

1. Bales, R. F. *Interaction Process Analysis.* Cambridge, Mass.: Addison-Wesley, 1950.
2. Berelson, Bernard, and Gary A. Steiner. *Human Behavior.* New York: Harcourt, Brace and World, 1964.
3. Birdwhistell, Ray L. *Kinesics and Context: Essays on Body Motion Communication.* Philadelphia: University of Pennsylvania Press, 1970.
4. Broadbent, D. E. *Perception and Communication.* New York: Pergamon Press, 1958.
5. Bruch, Hilde. "Some Comments on Talking and Listening in Psychotherapy," *Psychiatry,* XXIV, No. 3, August, 1961, 269-72.
6. Carpenter, Edmund, and Marshall McLuhan. *Explorations in Communication.* Boston: Beacon Press, 1960.
7. Carrol, John B. *Language and Thought.* Englewood Cliffs, N.J.: Prentice-Hall, 1964.
8. Cherry, Colin. *On Human Communication.* New York: Science Editions, 1961.
9. Collius, Barry E., and Harold Guetzkow. *A Social Psychology of Group Processes for Decision Making.* New York: Wiley, 1964.
10. Dalibard, Jill E. "Content Analysis of Verbal Aspects of Therapeutic Interviews." Unpublished Master's research report, School of Social Work, McGill University, 1969.
11. Davitz, Joel R. *The Communication of Emotional Meaning.* New York: McGraw-Hill, 1964.
12. Dollard, J., and O. H. Mowrer. "A Method of Measuring Tension in Written Documents," *Journal of Abnormal and Social Psychology,* XLII, 1947, 3-32.
13. Duncan, Starkey D., Jr. "Paralinguistic Behaviors in Client-Therapist Communication in Psychotherapy." Unpublished doctoral dissertation, University of Chicago, 1965.
14. Eldred, Stanley H., and Douglas B. Price. "A Linguistic Evaluation of Feeling States in Psychiatry," *Psychiatry,* XXI, 1958, 115-21.
15. Epstein, Nathan B., and William A. Westley. *Patterns of Intra-familial Communication.* Psychiatric Research Reports, II American Psychiatric Association, December, 1959.
16. Erikson, Erik H. "The Nature of Clinical Evidence," *Evidence and Inference,* D. Lerner (ed.) New York: Free Press, 1959.
17. Fanshel, David. "A Study of Caseworkers' Perception of Their Clients," *Journal of Social Casework,* XXXIX, December, 1958, 543-51.
18. Fearing, Franklin. "Toward a Psychological Theory of Human Communication," *The Human Dialogue,* Floyd W. Matson and Ashley Montagu (eds.) New York: Free Press, 1967.
19. Festinger, Leon. "Informal Social Communication," *Group Dynamics,* D. Cartwright and A. Zander (eds.) Evanston, Ill.: Row, Peterson, 1953.
20. Findlay, Barbara, and Jacquelyn M Gervais. "Kinesics and Communication—An Examination of the Role of Body Motion in the Communication Process during a Clinical Interview." Unpublished Master's research report, School of Social Work, McGill University, 1971.

21. Giglioli, Pier P. *Language and Social Context*. Harmondsworth: Penguin, 1972.

22. Goffman, Erving. *Strategic Interaction*. Philadelphia: University of Pennsylvania Press, 1969.

23. Gottschalk, Louis A., and Arthur H. Auerbach. *Methods of Research in Psychotherapy*. New York: Appleton-Century-Crofts, 1966.

24. Hall, Edward T. *The Hidden Dimension*. New York: Doubleday, 1966.

25. ———, and William F. Whyte. "Intercultural Communication: A Guide to Men of Action," *Human Organization*, XIX, Spring, 1960, 5-12.

26. Hollis, Florence. "Exploration in the Development of a Typology of Casework Treatment," *Journal of Social Casework*, XLVIII, June, 1967, 335-41.

27. Hovland, Carl I., Irving L. Janis, and Harold H. Kelly. *Communication and Persuasion*. New Haven: Yale University Press, 1953.

28. Jackson, Don D., Jules Riskin, and Virginia Satir. "A Method of Analysis of a Family Interview," *Archives of General Psychiatry*, V, 1961, 321-39.

29. Jaffe, J. "Dyadic Analysis of Two Psychotherapeutic Interviews," *Comparative Psycholinguistic Analyses of Two Psychotherapeutic Interviews*, Louis A. Gottschalk (ed.) New York: International Universities Press, 1961.

30. Krim, Alaine. "A Study of Nonverbal Communication—Expressive Movements During Interviews," *Smith College Studies in Social Work*, XXIV, October, 1953, 41-80.

31. Lyman, Stanford M., and Marvin B. Scott. "Territoriality: A Neglected Social Dimension," *Social Problems*, XV, No. 2, Fall, 1967, 236-49.

32. Mahl, George F. "Disturbances and Silences in the Patient's Speech in Psychotherapy," *Journal of Abnormal and Social Psychology*, LIII, July, 1956, 1-15.

33. Marcus, Lotte. "The Effect of Extralinguistic Phenomena on the Judgment of Anxiety." Unpublished doctoral dissertation, School of Social Work, Columbia University, 1969.

34. ———. "Emotional Perceptivity in Social Work," *Intervention*, XXVIII, Winter, 1970, 15-19.

35. Marsden, Gerald. "Content Analysis Studies of Therapeutic Interviews: 1954-64," *Psychological Bulletin*, LXIII, May, 1965, 298-321.

36. McLuhan, Marshall. *Understanding Media: The Extensions of Man*. New York: McGraw-Hill, 1964.

37. Mead, Margaret, and Paul Byers. *The Small Conference*. The Hague: Mouton, 1968.

38. Miller, George A. *Language and Communication*. New York: McGraw-Hill, 1963.

39. Miller, Roger. "An Experimental Study of the Observational Process in Casework," *Social Work*, III, April, 1958, 96-102.

40. Milmoe, Susan et al. "The Doctor's Voice: Postdictor of Successful Referral of Alcoholic Patients," *Journal of Abnormal and Social Psychology*, LXXII, No. 1, 1967, 78-84.

41. Moeller, Clifford B. *Architectural Environment and Our Mental Health*. New York: Horizon Press, 1968.

42. Osgood, Charles E., George J. Suci, and Percy H. Tannenbaum. *The Measurement of Meaning.* Urbana: University of Illinois Press, 1957.

43. Parry, John. *The Psychology of Human Communication.* New York: American Elsevier, 1968.

44. Pittenger, Robert E., Charles F. Hockett, and John J. Danehy. *The First Five Minutes: A Sample of Microscopic Interview Analysis.* Ithaca, N.Y.: Martineau, 1960.

45. ———, and Henry Lee Smith. "A Basis for Some Contributions of Linguistics to Psychiatry," *Psychiatry,* XX, No. 1, February, 1957, 61-78.

46. Polansky, Norman A. *Ego Psychology and Communication.* New York: Atherton, 1971.

47. Rabkin, Richard. "Uncoordinated Communication Between Marriage Partners," *Family Process,* VI, No. 1, March, 1967, 10-15.

48. Reik, Theodore. *Listening With the Third Ear.* New York: Garden City Books, 1951.

49. Ruesch, Jurgen. *Disturbed Communication.* New York: Norton, 1957.

50. ———, and W. Kees. *Non-Verbal Communication.* Berkeley and Los Angeles: University of California Press, 1956.

51. ———, and Rodney Prestwood, "Anxiety, Its Initiation, Communication and Interpersonal Management," *Archives of Neurology and Psychiatry,* LXII, November, 1949, 527-50.

52. Satir, Virginia. *Conjoint Family Therapy.* Palo Alto, Calif.: Science and Behavior Books, 1964.

53. Scheflen, Albert E. "Communication and Regulation in Psychotherapy," *Psychiatry,* XXVI, No. 2, May, 1963, 126-36.

54. ———. "Natural History Method in Psychotherapy: Communicational Research," *Methods of Research in Psychotherapy,* L. A. Gottschalk and A. H. Auerbach (eds.) New York: Appleton-Century-Crofts, 1966.

55. Sherman, Murray H. et al. "Non-verbal Cues and Re-enactment of Conflict in Family Therapy," *Family Process,* IV, No. 1, March, 1965, 133-62.

56. Soskin, William F., and Paul E. Kauffman. "Judgment of Emotion in Word-Free Voice Samples," *Journal of Communication,* XI, No. 2, June, 1961, 73-80.

57. Strupp, Hans H. "A Multidimensional System for Analyzing Psychotherapy Techniques," *Psychiatry,* XX, 1957, 293-306.

58. Thomas, Edwin J., Norman A. Polansky, and Jacob Kounin. "The Expected Behavior of a Potentially Helpful Person," *Behavioral Science for Social Workers,* E. T. Thomas (ed.) New York: Free Press, 1967.

59. Voitkus, Ilze V. "The Use of Territorial Instinct in Human Beings." Unpublished Master's research report, School of Social Work, McGill University, 1969.

60. Watzlawick, Paul. *An Anthology of Human Communication.* Palo Alto, Calif.: Science and Behavior Books, 1964.

61. ———, Janet H. Beavin, and Don D. Jackson. *Pragmatics of Human Communication.* New York: Norton, 1967.

62. Weblin, John. "Communication and Schizophrenic Behavior," *Family Process,* L, No. 1, March, 1962, 5-14.

63. Weinstock, Carol. "Cybernetics and Information: Application to Social Work." Unpublished Master's research report, School of Social Work, McGill University, 1970.

64. Whorf, Benjamin Lee. *Language, Thought and Reality*. Cambridge, Mass.: The Technology Press of M.I.T., and New York: Wiley, 1956.

65. Wiener, Norbert. *Cybernetics*. New York: Wiley, 1949.

66. ——. *The Human Use of Human Beings*. New York: Doubleday, 1954.

67. Williams, Frederick (ed.). *Language and Poverty: Perspectives on a Theme*. Chicago: Markham, 1970.

Annotated listing of key references

BIRDWHISTELL, Ray L. *Kinesics and Context: Essays on Body Motion Communication.* Philadelphia: University of Pennsylvania Press, 1970.
> *This book contains a collection of twenty-eight of Birdwhistell's essays on body movement and human communication. Essay 11 summarizes in some depth the author's theoretical viewpoint, while Chapter 14 gives an interesting perspective on redundancy in multichannel systems and Chapter 15 stresses the importance of the social context. Part 5 presents a detailed analysis of an interview, in terms of body motion behavior. Although rather technical, the author's careful scrutiny of particular movements in their social context will stimulate the reader to reach greater precision in his own observations.*

CHERRY, Colin. *On Human Communication.* New York: Science Editions, 1961.
> *The author, a reader in telecommunication at the University of London, England, describes his book as a review, survey and criticism. It introduces the reader to the field of linguistics, phonetics, communication theory, semantics, psychology and mathematics, and tries to extract from these sciences the common related concepts and ideas concerning communication, in such a way as to show the historical development and growth of the subject. The first chapter gives a lively and clear overview of the subject matter covered in this book.*

HALL, Edward T. *The Hidden Dimension.* New York: Doubleday, 1966.
> *The central theme of this book is social and personal space and man's perception of it. The author begins with observations and studies of distance regulation and social behavior, under conditions of overcrowding, in animals. He then analyzes space as it is experienced differentially by our senses. The most important observations for the social worker are contained in Chapter 9, termed "The Anthropology of Space: An Organizing Model," and Chapter 10, "Distance in Man," as well as in the last chapter, "Proxemics and the Future of Man."*

LYMAN, Stanford M., and Marvin B. Scott. "Territoriality: A Neglected Social Dimension." *Social Problems,* XV, No. 2, Fall, 1967, 236-49.
> *This article adds a sociological and interactional dimension to the concept of territoriality. Four types of territory (public, home, interactional and body territory), three types of territorial encroachment (violation, invasion and contamination), as well as three types of reactions to such encroachment (turf defense, insulation and linguistic collusion) are analyzed. The absence of "free space" by spatially deprived groups, such as urban ghetto dwellers, and their responses to this deprivation, are described; an important article for the social worker concerned with grass-roots organizations.*

PITTENGER, Robert E., Charles F. Hockett, and John J. Danehy. *The*

First Five Minutes: A Sample of Microscopic Interview Analysis. Ithaca, N.Y.: Martineau, 1960.

This book is the outcome of an interdisciplinary study of the linguistic and paralinguistic transcription and analysis of a five-minute interactional sequence of an initial interview. Of particular interest are chapters 4, 5 and 6, which describe the research techniques, findings and practical applications.

RUESCH, J., and W. Kees. *Non-Verbal Communication.* Berkeley and Los Angeles: University of California Press, 1956.

This book deals with visually perceivable, nonverbal communication and delineates biology and culture as its two determinants. Examples are brought of the use of gesture of several cultural groups. Descriptions, illustrated by photographs, of the informational value and sociocultural significance of action and object language are of particular interest to the social worker.

SCHEFLEN, Albert E. "Natural History Method in Psychotherapy: Communicational Research," L. A. Gottschalk and A. H. Auerbach (eds.) *Methods of Research in Psychotherapy.* New York: Appleton-Century-Crofts, 1966.

The author outlines his approach to communication from a systems view in which one can distinguish an organization of structural units, shared by members of the same culture. His methodology, termed context analysis, is described and explained, using illustrations from a psychotherapy film.

SHERMAN, Murray H. et al. "Non-verbal Cues and Re-enactment of Conflict in Family Therapy," *Family Process,* IV, No. 1, March, 1965, 133–62.

The relationship between nonverbal cues and the psychodynamics of family conflict are demonstrated in this article, which includes the typescript of a videotaped segment of a family therapy session. The analysis of verbal and nonverbal behavior led to the main conclusion that family members who suppress their opinions tend to give vent to more nonverbal forms of expression, and these, in turn, act as cues for a reenactment of emotional conflicts between them.

WATZLAWICK, Paul. *An Anthology of Human Communication.* Palo Alto, Calif.: Science and Behavior Books, 1964.

This booklet is the transcript of an audiotape of the same title. It is intended as an introduction to some basic concepts of human communication. The author's orientation is biased toward pathology and disturbed communication. The text may be used alone, but the experience of listening while reading the typescript provides a more comprehensive and meaningful experience.

WILLIAMS, Frederick (ed.). *Language and Poverty: Perspectives on a Theme.* Chicago: Markham, 1970.

This book is a collection of articles by linguists, psychologists, sociologists, educators and others which represent a range of perspectives and varying definitions of language, language behavior and poverty. The first chapter gives an excellent overview of different theories and contrasting viewpoints. The chapter by Bernstein is one of the most up-to-date analyses of this author's theories of linguistic codes and their relationship to sociological structures.

17

Behavior Modification: A Technology of Social Change

by

RICHARD B. STUART

For a great many centuries, humankind has gone about the business of solving its problems by becoming aware of some need for change, assessing the obstacles to that change, and striving to overcome those obstacles. There may be incidental speculations about why obstacles arose in the first place or how they developed their strength, but these luxuries have traditionally been the province of philosophers and historians. This level-headed, direct approach to the remediation of focal problems has been termed "action therapy" by Perry London (9), who views it as the basis of modern-day behavior modification. Approximately a century and a quarter ago, however, a different approach to the remediation of human distress gained currency. This approach starts from the assumption by so-called "information" therapies that the client "suffers from illusions that must dissipate when once he knows himself. Chief among them, and most illusory of all—he thinks that what he thinks really is his trouble really is his

trouble" (9, p. 75). Therefore, information therapists neither accept the client's description of his own problems nor offer the type of prescriptive remedies sought by the client. Instead, information therapists seek to overcome the client's despair by helping the client to understand its origin, its dynamics, and, in some instances, its role in his current conundrum.

Interestingly enough, the action and information therapists share several sets of assumptions which are of very great importance. Both, for instance, subscribe to the same model of human behavior, one which posits a sequence of thoughts and feelings which give rise to behavior which, in turn, leads to a set of intended or unintended social consequences (see Figure 17-1). Thoughts and feelings, which comprise the phenomenology of our "inner lives" and are subject to a myriad of physiological and experimental influences, serve as an important set of cues for behavior. An individual who feels happy and thinks that he can achieve his heart's desire is likely to act very differently from one who feels depressed and thinks that all behaviors lead to the same unhappy end. By the same token, one who acts in a friendly manner toward associates is likely to experience a much warmer response from them than another who acts with diffidence toward others. And finally, the one who has positive experiences with others has cause for feeling more satisfied with his lot in life than the one who is rejected or ignored. Virtually all social and psychological systems accept this model and differences come into play only at the point at which decisions are made to attempt to change behavior.

Information therapists tend to initiate the behavioral change process by seeking to change thoughts and feelings first, with changes in behavior and social experience following. The success of this effort hinges upon a number of factors including: (1) the accuracy with which the therapist understands the client's thoughts and feelings; (2) the persuasiveness with which the therapist suggests changes in these processes; (3) the willingness and ability of the client to translate this information into altered patterns of action; and (4) the willingness of key people in the client's social environment to accept or strengthen these changes. The chain leading from the therapist's efforts to influence the client to the maintenance of changes in the client's behavior is thus a long one in which a number of barriers must be overcome.

The action therapist, on the other hand, seeks either to promote changes in the client's behavior directly (eliminating the necessity to make accurate inferences about the client's thoughts and feelings) or to "reprogram" key people in the client's environment to act differently toward the client (eliminating the problem of translating therapeutic information into action). For the action therapist, then, the chain of actions culminating in modified client behavior is shortened considerably, eliminating several potential obstacles to change. Thus, success or failure occurs more promptly and hopefully more reliably than is true for information therapies (17).

In addition to sharing a model of behavior, action and information therapists also share a reliance upon critically essential processes of social influence (6, 12, 24). While their goals in managing interactions with clients differ substantially, both recognize the importance of increasing the attractiveness of the therapeutic situation as a means of optimizing the therapist's influence. Both also recognize the importance of offering the client a cogent framework for planning the change of his own behavior as well as recognizing the need to create within the therapeutic situation an environment which will essentially neutralize anxiety and facilitate the client's expression of goals, resources, and reactions to the ongoing intervention process (5).

But the approaches also have very important differences which set them apart in a myriad of ways. Whereas the explicit goals of the client are rejected by the information therapist, they are accepted by the action therapist. Whereas the goal of the information therapist tends to be the reduction of the pathology of the client, which is seen to rebound in his problematic dispositions, the goal of the action therapist is to build upon the client's existing resources. Whereas the information therapist assesses and attempts to change the person, the action therapist assesses and attempts to change the interaction between the client's behavior and the environment which produces and sustains it. Finally, whereas the information therapist tends to rely upon the direct influence of the therapist

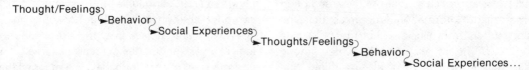

Figure 17-1.

upon the client as a means of invoking change, the action therapist uses therapist-client interaction merely as an expedient to promote more meaningful changes in the client's social environment.

An illustration may help to clarify these important differences. For many years information therapists have assumed that overeaters' requests for help in the control of consumatory behavior were to be set aside in favor of efforts to produce understanding of the history and intrapersonal dynamics of eating problems. Action therapists, on the other hand, recognized that overeaters are often quite articulate about the origins and dynamics of their problem, an understanding which by definition has not led to the amelioration of the difficulty (20). Action therapists, then, accept the goal of eating change. While information therapists have tended to describe the overeater as "an orally fixated person," action therapists have tended to regard overeating behavior as the logical response to an environment which is relatively rich in cues for problematic eating and weak in support for alternative behavior. Finally, while the information therapist has traditionally sought to use the therapeutic situation as an arena in which the client might develop both new insights and new emotional reactions, the action therapist has sought to promote experiential changes for the client in his natural, social environment, the arena in which his life is normally carried out.

As a result of these differences, the two therapeutic approaches take very different forms in practice. Information therapists tend to use rather standardized procedures across clients. Action therapists, on the other hand, use techniques as different as their clients are unique. Information therapists tend to regard their clients as failing in treatment, while action therapists consider unsuccessful intervention to be a therapist weakness. Therefore, information therapists tend to require that the client dominate the therapeutic session, while action therapists assume responsibility for offering a very highly structured therapeutic encounter. Furthermore,

because the information therapist regards the individual client as being both the bane and hope of his own mental health, the activities of the information therapist are relegated to transactions with his individual client. In contrast, the action therapist might seek to promote changes directly in the behavior of the client, in interactions between the client and key figures in the microsocial (face-to-face) environment, or even changes in the macrosocial environment, recognizing that events which are quite remote can impinge upon the activities of every individual.

The remainder of this chapter will be concerned with explicating various aspects of the logic of behavior modification—perhaps the quintessential action therapy. An explanation of the processes of behavioral assessment will be followed by a discussion of therapeutic structuring and behavioral engineering. This chapter will present a model for behavioral assessment and a taxonomy of techniques for promoting behavioral change.

Behavioral assessment

Behavioral assessment is concerned with identifying a target behavior and its controlling and antecedent conditions. It is conceived as a plan for clinical action, and therefore, it is limited to these observations which can be readily translated into clinical maneuvers. There are three major steps in the assessment process.

Step 1: The Selection of Target Behaviors

For the purposes of behavioral assessment, "behavior" is defined as any class of responses which is socially monitorable. A class of responses is any number of specific actions which "are correlated with the same stimulus" (13, p. 158). For example, the phrase "expressing an affectionate greeting" actually refers to a response class originated by the presence of a spouse, friend, or relative, etc. and includes approaching close to, sustaining eye contact with, leaning toward, smiling at, and speaking certain words to the other person. Social actions are thus classes of interrelated behaviors which occur under the same conditions. Further, response classes are monitorable if their occurrence can be determined by an independent observer. For example, the way in which a client thinks or feels might be classified as behaviors if they were measured through the somewhat imprecise means of EEG or polygraphic instrumentation. It is more common for therapists, however, to monitor what people say about the way they think or feel, and in those instances it is the speaking about thoughts or feelings which serves as the data, not the deeply personal experiences themselves.

Descriptions of each behavioral class have two important dimensions. The first is the topographic dimension which includes all that would be included in a static description of the behavior—e.g., leaning toward, smiling at, and speaking with a friend. The second is the rate of the response—its frequency over time. Some behaviors are identified as problems because of the topography of the response. Exhibitionism, criminal acts, and child abuse are illustrations of behavioral problems associated with the topographic dimension. Other behaviors are identified as problems because of the rate of responding. For example, truancy is defined as a low rate of school attendance, impotence as a low rate of sexual arousal, and overeating as an excessive rate of food consumption. It is important to realize however, that all of these definitions are socioculturally determined (25). Behavior which is defined as overly aggressive in one context might be defined as too passive in another. For example, a husband whose faithfulness is valued by his wife may be the object of teasing by his cronies.

Because behavioral assessment must be closely related to the process of behavioral change and because, as will be demonstrated shortly, behavioral change techniques have more power for strengthening as opposed to weakening responses, it is important to identify as target behaviors responses which are posi-

tively valued. For example, if the identified problem behaviors are school truancy, marital infidelity, overeating, or child abuse, then target behaviors should be construed as school attendance, faithfulness to the spouse, the emission of prudent eating behaviors, and the exercise of positive child management practices. For any behavior which is identified as a problem, it is absolutely essential to identify its reciprocal—a response which can be strengthened, the occurrence of which will preclude the occurrence of the problem behavior. One cannot both attend and skip school at the same time any more than one can have sexual contact only with a spouse and yet have contact with others, overeat and eat prudently, or beat and be kind to a child.

In the above illustrations, the targets are specific actions. When clients present very generalized problems, exactly the same process must be followed. For example, when a client complains that anxiety and a general sense of uneasiness is a problem, the task of the therapist is to find out what the client would be doing if anxiety were not a problem, and then strengthen these behaviors. When a client complains of depression, the therapist must find out what the client would be doing if he were not depressed, and these become the behavioral targets. Or, when a client complains of low self-esteem, the therapist is faced with the task of identifying what the client might do to produce personal pride and strengthen these behaviors. A client who is anxious about social encounters and subsequently has successful encounters will (must) feel less anxious just as a client who receives strong reinforcement for behaviors which compete with depression or self-devaluation will (must) experience less depression or self-abnegation.

Once the target behavior is identified, the remaining task is to determine the rate and the conditions under which it is expected to occur. Bearing in mind the fact that for every behavior which is to be weakened, another behavior must be strengthened in its place, the processes of decelerating or decreasing the rate and accelerating or increasing the rate of responding are primary rate change goals. For instance, one might wish to accelerate the number of correct responses through decelerating the number of error responses. Once these accelerations or decelerations occur, they must be maintained. While not a change, in the absolute sense, maintenance, which is often wholly neglected in treatment planning, requires a set of procedures which are related to, yet distinct from, those which are needed to promote the rate change in the first instance. For example, while highly routinized procedures may be needed to modify marital interaction initially, focused attention to the process between spouses may be all that is necessary to sustain the positive changes (16).

The two other rate changes are closely tied to the controlling conditions of behavior. The first of these is fluctuation. This goal is employed when a behavior occurs at a stable rate under all conditions, and the therapist would like it to occur at different rates and under various conditions. For example, it is very useful for an individual to reveal certain facts about himself when his goal is to build intimacy in a relationship, but this same behavior can become quite troublesome if it occurs across business situations as well. In this instance, the goal would be to train the client in discriminating situations in which he will from those in which he will not engage in self-revelatory behavior. Stabilization is a rate change goal on the other side of the fluctuation coin. When behaviors which could optimally occur across situations instead occur only sporadically, the therapist may wish to promote generalization of these responses through the process of stabilization. For example, the lonely, depressed single woman who has an effective social repertoire with her relatives who live in distant cities, but who is withdrawn and aloof from peers in more proximate work situations, might be encouraged to generalize her social self-expressiveness. Taken together, fluctuation and stabilization account for much of the process of socialization in which behaviors are variously brought under the control of social

situations by accelerating behaviors in some circumstances and decelerating them under other circumstances.

Step 2: Identifying the Antecedents of Behavior

Some of the conditions which control the occurrence of a class of behaviors precede the responses and others follow. The conditions, events, or stimuli which precede responses are their antecedents, and these fall into four classes. The first class of antecedents consists of those materials or tools without which the behavior cannot occur and those skills upon which the behavior depends. For example, if a parent wished to accelerate the rate at which an adolescent completes his algebra homework, it is neccessary to supply him with a quiet place in which to work, a text in which to work, and pencil and paper to complete the task. It is also necessary to make certain that he has the basic arithmetic skills which are the foundation of algebra. These materials and skills are the facilitating antecedents of behavior.

A second class of events which precondition the occurrence of behavior are instructional antecedents. These are the rules under which the individual is expected to operate—e.g., the algebra assignment and the prescription that the work should be undertaken independently. Parents are often irritated that their children fail to do things which they were not instructed to do, just as teachers are frustrated by the failure of students to follow rules which have not been stated. Needless to say, both suffer from displaced annoyance because one cannot realistically hold another accountable for the failure to meet requests which were not expressed.

The next two classes of antecedents are less obvious than the provision of the materials, skills, and instructions of behavior. The first of these can be termed "potentiating" antecedents. These are efforts made before a response to strengthen the value of the consequences which will follow the response. There are three ways to potentiate a consequence. If the opportunity to watch television is to be used as a consequence for doing homework, then access to television must be restricted to those occasions when it has been earned. This is one potentiation technique. Conversely, if a mental patient has not experienced the stimulation of a walk in the country, giving him an opportunity to sample the consequence can create it as a reinforcer, a second technique (1). Finally, since all people are not pleased by the same things at all times, individualizing the selection of consequences can increase their value. For instance, in a classroom situation, some children may enjoy free time artwork, while others may enjoy reading. Allowing children to choose individually the consequences of their work from a "menu" of such consequences can increase their value.

The final class of antecedents can be categorized as signal cues. Some of these, termed "discriminative stimuli," are cues which have been associated with particular consequences in the past. As an example, for a husband who has shared many positive experiences with his wife, the presence of his spouse can be a discriminative cue for social approach; that is, because positive experiences have been associated with her in the past, her presence cues her husband's positive expectations and behavior. Conversely, if the marital interaction has not been a positive one in the past, the wife's appearance on the scene in the present can be a "stimulus delta" or neutral cue which does not lead to approach behavior.

Since target behaviors always imply goals for acceleration, every instance of behavior modification must include, if not be limited to, efforts to accelerate behavior. This implies that, upon the initiation of intervention, certain desired behaviors occur at rates judged to be insufficient. These low rates of action can be attributed to any or all of several factors related to antecedent or consequent conditions. Those relating to antecedent conditions generally involve the absence of cues necessary to facilitate, instruct, potentiate, or signal the occurrence of the

desired behavior, and/or the presence of such cues for the occurrence of problematic behaviors which interfere with the emission of the desired behavior. For example, John would like to have more satisfying conversations with his wife, Nancy. (1) At present, he and Nancy do very few things together and so do not have common experiences (the tools or facilitative antecedents for conversation), nor has John told her of his wish to have more conversation with her (instructional antecedent). In addition, he has offered her little incentive to attend to his descriptions of things of interest to him (lack of potentiation) so that their conversations promise little satisfaction to Nancy (serving as a stimulus delta). (2) Both John and Nancy have very close friends with whom they bare their souls (facilitating conversation with others). They have also made an agreement to spend as much time with their friends as either wishes (an instructional antecedent). When they have disagreements, they know that they can seek the solace of their respective friends (potentiating disagreement), so that unpleasant encounters with each other are actually signals (discriminative stimuli) for seeking the company of others. In order to help them to achieve their goal, changes must be taken in both sets of antecedents: those listed under the first heading must be strengthened, while those listed under the second heading must be weakened. That is, they must share sufficient experience to enable them to have the basic tools of conversation—topics of mutual interest—just as they must set new rules for their encounters and must each attend to what the other has to say, building a history of satisfactory conversation upon which to base expectations of more of the same. To make this possible, they must agree to limit their contact with their friends (reducing the facilitative cues and arriving at a new, mutually agreed-upon set of guidelines), must agree to have contacts with others only after positive encounters with each other so as to potentiate agreements rather than disagreements, and on the basis of this changed experience, they can change their expectancies relative to each other and to their friends. The cues for constructive encounters with each other are thus to be strengthened as the antecedents of behaviors which might weaken their bond are either eliminated or suppressed (19).

Step 3: Identifying the Consequences of Behavior

The consequences of a class of behaviors determines the probability of the future occurrences of the actions. Some consequences strengthen a behavior or increase the likelihood of its occurrence, while others weaken a behavior or decrease the likelihood of its occurrence. The four types of consequences which are available are rarely used singly, but the combinations of consequences must always be guided by the necessity to have at least one set of accelerating consequences for each set of decelerating events.

The first type of consequence and the one which is by far the most important tool in the hands of behavior modifiers, is positive reinforcement. A positively reinforcing event or stimulus is one which strengthens the likelihood that a response will occur. Whenever it is produced by a response—e.g., whenever a teacher attends to a student's raised hand—the response producing the consequence will be strengthened. Therefore, positive reinforcers must be offered "response contingently"—that is, they must be used only as consequences for target behaviors. Thus a teacher wishing to increase the rate at which her students raise their hands before contributing to a class discussion must make certain that only the contributions of those who have raised their hands are recognized. If students who "talk out" are as likely to gain a hearing as those who raise their hands, then talking out will be inadvertently strengthened (18).

A great many events may be positive reinforcers for an individual; these definitely do vary over time, and positive reinforcers do not necessarily have to be experienced or viewed as positive. For example, a teacher who repeatedly asks her class to "sit down" might appear to be reprimanding the class. But for children who do not otherwise earn attention, these commands may actually strengthen standing-up behavior. Conversely, chocolate ice cream might be a powerfully positive reinforcement for a child's behavior during the middle of the afternoon, but the requirement that he eat a third bowlful of ice cream for dessert could well be experienced as quite painful by him. Therefore, it is important that behavior modifiers observe the effects of consequences which are intended to serve as positive reinforcements rather than simply assuming them to be positive.

Finally, it is important to note that there are four broad categories of positive reinforcements. The first is "program," which means that a behavior modifier may reinforce one class of behaviors by providing an opportunity for the individual to emit a related class of actions. For example, a teacher may reinforce reading by the students in the class with an opportunity for them to work on mathematics. The value of using programmatic reinforcers is that related classes of behavior are accelerated at the same time that the value of program itself is strengthened.

The problem to be overcome in successfully applying programmatic reinforcers is the selection of programs as consequences which have sufficient appeal to serve as accelerators. One way to do this is to look for high-probability behaviors (15)—behaviors which are relatively likely to occur when there are no significant constraints upon the choices to be made—which are programmatically related. For instance, a teacher who finds that students make free choices of an opportunity to work on mathematics can have some assurance that this will serve as an effective reinforcer for reading. In areas unrelated to program, high-probability behaviors can also be extremely potent consequences. A therapist who uses a chance to smoke a cigarette (a high-probability behavior) to reinforce the writing of case summaries (low-probability behavior) or the parent who allows adolescents to telephone friends (a high-probability behavior) following completion of designated homework assignments (low-probability behavior) are both using well this set of consequences.

The third class of positive reinforcements is social, and it is by far the most universal and ubiquitous. Attention and approval are almost the inevitable consequences of any actions which are socially monitored. They are the sought-after consequences of almost the entire range of human behavior, including virtually all prosocial and antisocial responses.

The final class of positive consequences is material reinforcers, which might be the natural consequences of a class of behaviors (e.g., the harvest for the farmer) or synthetic consequences (e.g., the wages of laborers or the tokens earned by mental patients or offenders living in programmed environments). Material reinforcers are often the first consequences suggested as accelerators of behavior, but they are also the least valuable over time for several reasons. First, it is not always practical to deliver material consequences over extended periods. Second, the value of material consequences is likely to overlook the requirements of making the task itself interesting and arranging for social controls. And finally, the use of material reinforcers is very likely to be regarded as "bribery"—particularly among those who have grown accustomed to receiving the positive behaviors of others gratis (18). On the other side of the coin, however, the use of material reinforcement, which can be immediately effective, is often a very desirable technique for initiating change in behavior slowly (i.e., "fading in" new behavior controls) with the material reinforcers being slowly removed or "faded out" as their functions are taken over by social and/or programmatic consequences.

The second class of consequences is familiarly known as punishment, events which describe the rate of the response which pro-

duces them. As with positive consequences, it is important to realize that an event does not function as punishment simply because it is labeled as such. Fights between spouses, for example, may appear to be punishing events for both. But the persistence of the fights clearly indicates that rather than decelerating offensive behaviors, the likelihood of these behaviors is strengthened.

When a truly aversive (decelerating) consequence is available, it is programmed to occur following the occurrence of the problematic behavior. The behavior is then expected to be stopped in the future to permit avoidance of the aversive event. However, there are fourteen conditions which must be met if punishment is to be used effectively (2), and it is rarely possible to meet these conditions. Even if it were possible to do so, however, punishment is associated with a sufficient number of problems to make its use unwise. First, it can lead to the development of very negative responses to the person who metes out the punishment. The punished person may then seek to avoid the presence of the punisher, and the opportunity for behavioral influence is lost. Second, punishment can lead to attacks upon innocent bystanders—termed "reflexive aggression." Jokes about the boss punishing the father and the father punishing his son and the son kicking the sleeping dog are quite familiar examples of reflexive aggression. Finally, punishment is also likely to engender counteraggression against the punisher, and if this person is a parent, spouse, or teacher, such aggression is extremely problematic. For these reasons—the difficulty in using punishment effectively and its unpleasant concomitants—its use should be very much restricted.

The third class of consequences is negative reinforcement or the removal of an aversive consequence following the occurrence of a positive behavior. Four steps are involved in this process: (1) a problematic behavior takes place; (2) it is followed by an aversive consequence which continues until: (3) a positive behavior occurs; at which point (4) the aversive consequence is removed (hence, "negative" reinforcement). Thus, the husband who nags his wife to iron his shirts puts relentless pressure upon her until the job is done. Unfortunately, the consequences of negative reinforcement are likely to be the same as those produced by punishment, and therefore it is as much to be avoided as is punishment.

A final class of consequences has been termed extinction. This involves following a problematic behavior with consequences which are essentially neutral with respect to that behavior. Since it is not reinforced, it is expected that the rate of the response will decelerate. There are several problems associated with the use of extinction. First, it is necessary to gain a very high level of control of the environment in order to eliminate positive consequences of problematic behavior. For instance, a teacher is hard pressed to ignore insults howled by one student when these insults are attended to by others. Second, certain problematic behaviors are very noxious (e.g., disrupting a classroom) or very dangerous (e.g., driving at high speed), and they cannot be ignored. Third, when extinction is undertaken and some reinforcement has been removed, it is common to find the behavior increasing in intensity in an effort to regain the lost reinforcement. Finally, the removal of reinforcement from one class of responses without rescheduling it as a consequence for others weakens the attractiveness of the environment by subtracting pleasures; thus, as with punishment and negative reinforcment, the opportunity for social influence may be lost.

It should be clear from this discussion that the use of positive reinforcement offers considerable advantage over the use of the other three classes of consequences. As a general rule: NO DECELERATION TECHNIQUE SHOULD EVER BE USED UNLESS ALTERNATIVE BEHAVIORS ARE POSITIVELY REINFORCED. This principle is often applied in the normal course of human interaction. One tends to respond positively to the preferred actions of others, and to ignore those which are less favored. If the less favored actions were merely ignored, punished, or made the objects of negative reinforcement, without a counterbalancing use of positive influence techniques, it is obvious that the relationship would soon lose its value and be dissolved.

When combining positive reinforcement with decelerating strategies, complex paradigms of behavioral control emerge. For example, parents of a predelinquent might: (1) establish that driving privileges are a strong reinforcer for an adolescent; (2) provide access to the use of the car as a consequence for acceptable schoolwork; (3) restrict access to the car when the quality of schoolwork falls; and (4) restore access to the car when work improves. This is termed "time out," and it is a strategy used almost universally in social interaction. The effectiveness of this procedure depends upon the selection of a sufficiently powerful reinforcer, using this consequence response contingently, monitoring behavior during time out to make certain that experiences during this time are not reinforcements for problematic behaviors, and promptly restoring the positive reinforcement when positive behavior recurs.

In applying these concepts to an analysis of the occurrence of behaviors, procedures similar to those employed in the assessment of antecedents are used. First, it is necessary to identify the positive consequences which can be used to strengthen the target behavior, followed by efforts to make certain that these positive consequences reliably follow upon the occurrence of positive behaviors. Sometimes it will be found that positive behavior may be punished (e.g., the parent who greets a child who has come home promptly from school by saying, "What's wrong? Wouldn't anyone play with you today?"); sometimes it will be found that consequences are made available for negative behavior as well as positive (e.g., the parent who provides his child with an allowance despite extremely antisocial behavior), or sometimes positive responses are simply ignored (e.g., the parent who does not ask to see the "A" grades on a child's report card). The process of behavioral change is designed to correct these deficiencies as well as those noted in the assessment of antecedents.

Process of behavior change

The Structure of Intervention

While behavior modification shares with the information therapies a profound reliance upon the tactics of social influence, it tends to be more highly structured than the information-oriented approaches. The first structure-related decision which the behavior modifier makes is the selection of the people with whom to work. The therapist might work directly with the focal client. For example, the therapist might work directly with the adult seeking relief from repression or with the teacher interested in having help in bringing an unruly class under control. The therapist could also choose to work through a mediator or important agent of social control in the social environment. In instances in which the therapist counsels with parents or teachers in order to overcome the behavioral problems of the children in their case, the adults are the mediators and the children the targets. This therapist-mediator-target configuration has been termed the "triadic model" of intervention (23). Finally, the therapist could combine both approaches and, as is traditional in family therapy, have contact with mediators and targets conjointly. When this happens, however, it is more correct to consider the mediators (whose behavior must be changed in order to change the behavior of the targets) to be targets as well as mediators—that is, they have dual roles in the intervention.

In deciding which format to use, the therapist should be guided by the realization that the level of success in achieving each behavior-change goal will be directly proportional to the success of efforts to reprogram the environment relevant to that goal (14). Thus, more positive outcomes can be anticipated as the precision of the therapist's environment change efforts rises. When the case is structured to include only one person, whether single or married, child, adolescent or adult, the therapist must influence the target to change his or her behavior toward forces in the environment, working "second hand" with these forces because he depends upon the target as a social engineer in his own behalf and as a source of data for evaluating the success of his own efforts. On the other hand, when the case is structured to include the agents of social control, the therapist is in a position to use his influence directly with mediators and is in a much stronger position to change and to evaluate the consequences of change in their behavior. Furthermore, inclusion of mediators within the treatment situation helps to increase the likelihood that they will accept responsibility for changing their behavior as a precondition for change in the target's behavior. For example, Stuart and Davis (20) have found that including the spouse of overweight women in the treatment helps to overcome stereotyped condemnation of the overeater as "self-indulgent and immature," redirecting the focus to attention to social interaction as a pathogen.

Once the decision is made to see targets, mediators, or both, it is next necessary to decide whether to focus intervention procedures indirectly or directly upon behavior in the natural environment. The focus is indirect when the therapist attempts to rely upon interaction with the client as a form of "deutero learning" (4), or when the therapist seeks to follow the replication therapy paradigm and produce within the treatment situation analogs to troubling aspects of the client's natural environment (7). For example, if the therapist attempts to train the client in social interaction techniques through their experiences together, or if the therapist endeavors to help the client to relax while imagining successive approximations of fear-evoking situations (termed "systematic desensitization") (27), the therapist-client interaction is the direct focus and the client's interactions with others the indirect focus. On the other hand, if the therapist seeks to instigate the client to change his behavior in the extratherapeutic environment, or if the therapist engages in so-called "intervention therapy" and takes over the external environment directly, the primary focus is upon change in the external environment with the therapist-client transactions relegated to the status of important expedients.

These four forms of intervention—interaction, replication, instigation, and intervention—are typically used in combination with each other. For example, a therapist seeking to instigate greater social assertiveness with a depressed client might first seek to build the trust of his client through management of the interaction; and then he might use role play as practice in a replication of social situations before instigating changes in the client's extratherapeutic behavior. Conversely, a therapist who uses shock-avoidance conditioning—administration of an electric shock until the client changes stimuli under his control, such as moving from viewing slides of homosexual contact to slides of heterosexual contact (11)—in a replication paradigm would necessarily instigate changes in the client's sexual behavior outside of the therapeutic situation in an effort to measure the validity of changes observed within the sessions.

Following the structural decisions relating to who will be included in the treatment and whether the focus will be on intra- or extratherapeutic behavior, several other structuring maneuvers typify behavior modification. First, the focus of treatment is narrowed as closely as possible to an evaluation of present behavior. While every presenting behavior has a history, these precipitating events are by definition no longer operative, so they are perforce beyond therapeutic influence, and they are rarely recalled accurately. Thus, they are essentially irrelevant to the intervention. Second, the client is fully trained in the logic of the intervention in order to equip him to be as effective as possible as an accomplice in planning for changes in his own behavior. Third, provision is

made for the systematic evaluation of the effectiveness of each step in the therapeutic process. Each therapeutic suggestion is a "microexperiment" in which the therapist and client plan together to promote adaptive change in the client's interest and then collect data adequate to the task of measuring the outcome of each experiment. Both are thereby in a position to know whether continuation, modification, or cessation of any given procedure is in order. Finally, the intervention represents a planned sequence of strategies designed to move progressively toward behavior change in small steps—a process termed "behavioral shaping." For example, in promoting marital change, Stuart (22) has suggested a five-module approach beginning with efforts to modify the vocabulary which spouses used to describe their interaction through steps designed to build behavioral reciprocity, effective communication, and reliable means of decision making to the acceptance of techniques which will maintain these various changes. Each of these modules, in turn, can be broken down into component parts. For example, couples must first be trained to express their messages unambiguously, then trained to understand these messages, and finally trained in the techniques of reaching agreement. It would be absurd to expect couples to reach valid agreements if they neither expressed nor understood messages accurately.

Several criteria can be used in selecting the starting targets of intervention. First, the target must be positive—that is, it must be possible to produce the desired behavior change through the reliance upon positive influence techniques. Such an approach is both more likely to be successful and likely to build the client's investment in treatment. For example, the treatment of homosexuality might best be undertaken by increasing heterosexual approach behavior than by attempting to punish homosexual behavior. Second, the initial target should be one which will preclude occurrence of as many other targets as possible when it is achieved. For example, the abusive parent who is trained to provide a child with sufficient stimulation to reduce the level of crying will need little training in curbing destructive behaviors which are cued by a crying infant. In the same vein, a teacher who is trained in stating and enforcing explicit rules for social behavior will probably overcome the disruptive behavior of several problematic children in the class by virtue of the effect of these rules in reducing uncertainty about acceptable social behavior. Third, the targets selected should lead to prompt change. For example, a suicidal adult who complains of problems in work, social life, and in virtually all areas of life might best be helped by promoting changes in a work situation which could be promptly arranged. Not only would such change modify his social experience during long segments of his day, but the efficiency with which improvements could be made might instill hope for change in other areas as well.

Overriding these three criteria are two caveats which have obvious importance. The first is that behaviors which might result in harm to the client or to others must be the objects of initial attention. Second, the client must have an opportunity to agree to all goals which do not involve minimally socially necessary behaviors— e.g., behaviors which are necessary in order to conform to the law (21). In these situations clients may be the objects of involuntary treatment, as in correctional or certain mental health settings. In all other treatment encounters, however, involving efforts to achieve "optional" goals, client consent to the focus of intervention is an ethical necessity.

Therapeutic contracts which are written, highly explicit agreements specifying the responsibilities of both clients and therapists are one means of summarizing the structure of treatment and assuring that the clients have properly agreed to the goals and methods to be used in their own treatment. A contract might include the identification of who will participate in treatment sessions, which behaviors are to be the focus of these sessions, and the techniques to be employed in promoting behavior change. Con-

tracts can further specify such administrative details as the duration of service, spacing of sessions, fees, availability of the therapist, and the like (22).

Environmental Engineering

It is a strange paradox that in the action therapies, the technology for engineering environmental change is secondary to the techniques of behavioral assessment and the structuring of treatment. The nature of efforts made to modify the conditions of behavior is clearly a logical extension of the results of the assessment process and of the structure of the intervention situation which is acceptable to the client. The changes to be made must occur in one of four areas: the antecedents and consequences of desirable behavior must be strengthened and the antecedents and consequences of problematic behaviors must be weakened. In some instances, antecedents which fail to control certain behaviors must be "conditioned" to produce these reactions, while in other instances antecedents which give rise to problematic behaviors must be "deconditioned." For example, a drug user who is indifferent to opportunities for constructive social experience such as school might be conditioned to react positively to educational opportunities by being offered the positive reinforcement of success in such programs. As the value of these experiences increases relative to the value of drug mediated experiences, the value of the latter can be expected to diminish through deconditioning. In the same vein, when the delivery of social approval, a strongly reinforcing consequence, is reprogrammed to occur following prosocial behavior, the emission of the acts which lead to approval can gain ascendance over behaviors which are likely to lead to neutral or aversive experiences.

The manipulation at these controlling conditions can occur at three levels (21). As noted earlier, the therapist can attempt to modify the individual's behavior directly. For example, a so-called "frigid" woman might be offered treatment designed to recondition her sexual reactions. In treating the same individual, however, the therapist may attempt to reprogram the sexual behavior of the husband in an effort to increase the effectiveness of his approach to encounters with his wife. In this writer's experience, every problem of frigidity in a woman yields to change in the sexual behavior of the mate. This focus of intervention upon the microsocial environment is thus a second level of intervention. The third level of intervention would involve an effort to reprogram the sexual expectancies and/or tolerances of the society as a whole. This macrosocial change occurs continually, although generally without planning. For example, as changes in the role of women occur and women are freed from the bondage of denying their sexual interests, support for assertiveness can obviate many of the conditions of frigidity which are the outgrowth of the hesitance of wives to make known their desires.

In choosing to focus upon individual, microsocial, or macrosocial change, the major criteria to be considered is pragmatic. What is the highest level of intervention to which a therapist can gain entrance? The wisdom of this criteria was recognized many years ago by child therapists who learned with dismay that their efforts to modify the behavior of children directly in institutions typically led to short-range changes when the child was returned to problematic parents. Parents were then included in the intervention unit, and there is growing awareness that the child can be let out of the therapeutic situation as change in parental behavior is also both a necessary and sufficient condition for change in the behavior of children. Moving one step higher, the promotion of cues and social support for modified interactions within families can go a long way toward making lasting change in family life. While mass education is certainly an imperfect means of modifying parental behavior, history has shown that shifts in scheduled as opposed to demand feeding could be accomplished (although not necessarily

with positive effects) through efforts to reprogram an entire community.

In choosing behavior-change techniques within each level, the first criterion must be simplicity. The more complex a procedure is, the greater the likelihood that it will not be cleanly executed, and the lower the likelihood of maintaining the change over the long run. For example, using microsocial intervention, a teacher would be better advised to begin by offering programmatic reinforcement for the study behavior of a class than to begin by offering a banquet for each assignment completed by all pupils in the room. Should social approval fail, it is always possible to offer banquets later. The second criterion is that the procedures used should offer further opportunities for growth rather than engendering negative side effects. For example, the teacher who uses praise models constructive social behavior for students, while the teacher using punishment models aggressiveness which is likely to be imitated. Finally, the strategy used must "build in" toward the target behavior. For example, if the parents of a poverty-level family depend upon the economic contribution of an adolescent and therefore encourage him to be truant from school in order to search for odd jobs, a strong counterpressure exists to reduce the likelihood that efforts to encourage school attendance will be successful. Therefore, the individual influence effort must realistically be preceded by efforts to meet the material needs of the family.

Within the limits of these considerations, the range of techniques available to the action therapist is vast, and a review of the surveys of techniques in the better textbooks on behavior modification (3, 8, 26) reveals the full sweep of an approach to change in the behavior of units ranging from individuals to the society as a whole. Perhaps no time in history has witnessed the rapidity with which the technology of behavior control has developed. The general community could afford to be relatively indifferent to the development of information therapies because their successes have fallen far short of their promises. Action therapies, on the other hand, have met with astounding success within a few decades, and the community is justifiably alarmed about the potential of the technology. Because the techniques of behavior control are essentially as contentless as are the canons of logic—that is, behavior modification is a method of analysis above all else, a form of social logic—it can be used to achieve great strides in relieving human misery or it can be used as a vile source of suppression. Because the technology exists and because it will continue to grow, it is therefore essential that its uses be openly discussed in the public forum to insure its constructive application (10).

References

1. Ayllon, Teodoro and Nathan Azrin. *The Token Economy: A Motivational System for Therapy and Rehabilitation.* New York: Appleton-Century-Crofts, 1968

2. Azrin, Nathan H. and William C. Holz. "Punishment," W. K. Honig (ed.) *Operant Behavior: Areas of Research and Application.* New York: Appleton-Century-Crofts, 1966, pp. 380-447.

3. Bandura, Albert. *Principles of Behavior Modification.* New York: Holt, 1969.

4. Bateson, Gregory. "Social Planning and the Concept of Deutero Learning," Gregory Bateson (ed.) *Steps to an Ecology of Mind.* New York: Ballantine, 1972, pp. 159-176.

5. Frank, Jerome D. "The Role of Cognitions in Illness and Healing," Hans H. Strupp and Lester Luborsky (eds.) *Research in Psychotherapy.* Washington, D.C.: American Psychological Association, 1962, pp. 1-12.

6. Gergen, Kenneth J. *The Psychology of Behavior Exchange.* Reading, Mass.: Addison-Wesley, 1969.

7. Kanfer, Frederick and Jeanne S. Phillips. "A Survey of Current Behavior Therapies and a Proposal for Classification," Cyril M. Franks (ed.) *Behavior Therapy: Appraisal and Status.* New York: McGraw-Hill, 1969, pp. 445-475.

8. ——— and ———. *Learning Foundations of Behavior Therapy.* New York: Wiley, 1970.

9. London, Perry. *The Modes and Morals of Psychotherapy.* New York: Holt, 1964.

10. ———. *Behavior Control.* New York: Harper and Row, 1969.

11. MacCulloch, M. J., M. P. Feldman, and J. M. Pinshof. "The Application of Anticipatory Avoidance Learning to the Treatment of Homosexuality," *Behavior and Research and Therapy,* Vol. 3, 1965, pp. 21-44.

12. McGinnies, Elliott. *Social Behavior: A Functional Analysis.* Boston: Houghton Mifflin, 1970.

13. Millenson, J. R. *Principles of Behavioral Analysis.* New York: Macmillan, 1967.

14. Patterson, Gerald R., S. McNeal, N. Hawkins, and R. Phelps. "Reprogramming the Social Environment," *Journal of Child Psychology and Psychiatry,* Vol. 8, 1967, pp. 181-195.

15. Premack, David. "Reinforcement Theory." David Levine (ed.) *Nebraska*

Symposium on Motivation: 1965. Lincoln: University of Nebraska Press, 1965, pp. 123-180.

16. Stuart, Richard B. "Operant-Interpersonal Treatment of Marital Discord," *Journal of Consulting and Clinical Psychology,* Vol. 33, 1969, pp. 675-682.

17. ——. *Trick or Treatment: How and When Psychotherapy Fails.* Champaign, Ill.: Research Press, 1970.

18. ——. "Behavior Modification Techniques for the Education Technologist," Rosemary Sarri and Frank F. Maple (eds.) *The School in the Community.* Washington, D.C.: National Association of Social Workers, 1972, pp. 88-135.

19. ——. "Situational versus Self-Control," Richard D. Rubin (ed.) *Advances in Behavior Therapy: 1970.* New York: Academic Press, 1972, pp. 129-146.

20. —— and Barbara Davis. *Slim Chance in a Fat World.* Champaign, Ill.: Research Press, 1972.

21. ——. "The Role of Social Work Education in Innovative Human Services," F. W. Clark, D. R. Evans, and L. A. Hamerlynck (eds.) *Implementing Behavior Programs for Schools and Clinics.* Champaign, Ill.: Research Press, 1972, pp. 3-40.

22. ——. "Behavioral Remedies for Marital Ills: A Guide to the Use of Operant-Interpersonal Techniques," Travis Thompson (ed.) *International Symposium on Behavior Modification.* New York: Appleton-Century-Crofts, in press.

23. Tharp, Roland G. and Ralph J. Wetzel. *Behavior Modification in the Natural Environment.* New York: Academic Press, 1969.

24. Truax, Charles B. "Reinforcement and Non-reinforcement in Rogerian Psychotherapy," *Journal of Abnormal Psychology,* Vol. 71, No. 1, 1966, pp. 1-9.

25. Ullmann, Leonard P. and Leonard Krasner. *A Psychological Approach to Abnormal Behavior.* Englewood Cliffs, N.J.: Prentice-Hall, 1969.

26. Whaley, Donald L. and Richard W. Malott. *Elementary Principles of Behavior.* Kalamazoo, Mich.: Behaviordelia, 1969.

27. Wolpe, Joseph. *The Practice of Behavior Therapy.* New York: Pergamon Press, 1969.

Annotated listing of key references

AYLLON, Teodoro and Nathan H. Azrin. *The Token Economy.* New York: Appleton-Century-Crofts, 1968.

> *By far the best and most explicit work on token management of complex behavior, serving as a model of behavioral investigation and control.*

KANFER, Frederick H. and Jean Phillips. *Principles of Behavioral Analysis.* New York: Wiley, 1970.

> *An excellent and scholarly analysis of behavior modification designed to meet the needs of the student and professional seeking deeper knowledge in the area.*

REESE, Ellen P. *The Analysis of Human Operant Behavior.* Dubuque, Iowa: Brown, 1966.

> *A short (73-page) introduction to the principles of operant and respondent behavior modification.*

SKINNER, B. F. *Science and Human Behavior.* New York: Macmillan, 1953.

> *The "essential" Skinner—a volume which provides much of the philosophical basis for the presently evolving practice of behavior modification.*

WATSON, David and Roland Tharp. *Self-Directed Behavior.* Monterey, Calif.: Brooks/Cole, 1972.

> *A primer in the functional analysis and control of one's own behavior which provides a good, in vive introduction to behavior modification.*

18
Family Therapy

by

SANFORD N. SHERMAN

Social and historical content

Family therapy has by now gained wide acceptance in mental health and social service circles—and even among the more informed laymen. There is something most compelling about the concepts that link the individual person and family system in health and in sickness or dysfunction. This is not to say, however, that there is an approach universally accepted by family therapists any more than it can be said for practitioners of individual therapy. The closer one gets to the particulars of practice, the more differentiated the field of family therapy becomes.

The general ripeness of movements within the different helping professions for family therapy has not been fortuitous, it has been a function of internal dynamic changes within those professions and their ideologies and reflexive to changing social conditions.

The rapidly accelerating *rate* of change in

our society has been altering and even transforming many social institutions. It has often been noted that the effect of these social changes on at least one social institution—the family—has been so profound that it has become a matter of some concern whether the family will survive at all. To satisfy socioeconomic functions, the postindustrial society mandates a kind of fragmentation of the family (13). We are only at the beginning of identifying what these alterations in the family are going to mean for individual personality, since the family is such an important matrix for the psychosexual development and socialization of its individual members. Moreover, there is a problem in the disparateness between *the rate at which changes in the family structure function and role organization are "demanded"* and effected by our society and the rate at which individual persons can *adapt psychologically and emotionally* to the changing expectations of them. People and families may conform in their external behavior

449

but at greater emotional and psychological costs. The dialectics of change processes are such that accommodation to the pulls of society tends to be overdone by many. Family ties are *prematurely* fractured, young *prematurely* discharged, neighborhood residence *too easily* abandoned, and so forth.

All around us we see signs of people being "out of sync" with ecological phenomena that are manmade; that are wrought by the very society of which the people are part. Technological and social "progress" has a "fallout" in the form of polluted atmosphere and seas, ravaged landscapes, and so forth (37). Less obvious than the contamination of our physical environment but of great import in the ecology of human relations is the possibility that *emotional* needs of people are increasingly frustrated by the changes in human relations "forced" by societal changes. The emotional and psychological needs are increasingly out of sync with the intergenerational discontinuity, the early discharge of the young and the old from the family bower, the gender confusion in the nuclear family, the farming out of what were once family functions to other social institutions, or, worse, to limbo, and other profound changes in the family.

These changes have had consequences in widespread personal maladaptation and, even for those who are "making it," more static or "flak" in their personal lives. We see around us social anomie; alienation of the youth generation; avoidance of intimacy in personal or family relationships; inconstancy of marriages; deviant behaviors that seek vainly to fill or give meaning to empty lives; obsessions with violence, in fantasy if not in overt behavior.

It would be naive to attribute linearly all these phenomena to the erosion of the family, but a mistake not to read the evidence that there is some significant connection. The clinical worker can adduce the many times he encounters the young parents or marital partners conflicted in marital and parental roles because they still feel partly as dependent children to their own parents, or other individuals who in

late adolescence or early adulthood have presumably left their homes to be socially "independent" but for whom separation from their families, though cognitively desired, was emotionally more a rupture than a resolution. The examples from clinical work are numerous, lending empirical specificity to the general observation on the lag in personal adaptation to the changes in the family wrought by the larger society.

Our general society can be conceptualized in systems terms* as calibrating and feeding back correctives or needed modifiers of any of its processes. In other words, it might be said that our society, in its inevitable flux, develops new institutions or makes changes in existing ones to meet newer or changed needs, but its imperfect and inexact course produces side effects, even dangerous pendulum swings, that threaten the homeostatic balance of the society. Therefore the society develops additional forces or processes to counter, neutralize, or control these side effects or excesses. This is a rather simplistic view of the transactional character of social process, but it serves to point up the basic societal sources of social work and mental health services and their relation to the homeostatic needs of society. These services have as *one* of their important overall functions, even as *raison d'être*, that of social control and they have been "created," prosper, or atrophy as society needs them for this purpose. As society changes over time, so does its homeostatic need to summon forth callings and professions (or changes within old ones) to make them relevant to its changing needs (2, p. 3).

In this context we can see family therapy today as social work's adaptation to the summons of social need. The family is undergoing traumatic change, even disruption. No adequate nurturant substitute exists, yet the postindustrial society undermines the traditional family willy-nilly. If it cannot reverse itself, it can at least encourage countering or reparative processes, of

---

* See Chapter 13.

which family therapy is one, to heal the lacerations caused by too easy jettisoning of kinship values, familial nest, and anchorage. This evocation of family therapy in our present social order can be likened to the sudden upsurge of environmentalists, urban planners, and all manner of callings and service enterprises which has occurred in reflexive response to the growing awareness of the dangerous excesses of our industrial technology.

This historical and large societal perspective is important if we are to grasp the relevance of family therapy to our times. This has nothing to do with being faddist or fashionable or aboard a bandwagon. It has to do with the fact that family therapy as a modality (but, far more important than modality, as a broad treatment orientation) is crucial for comprehending, and more effectively intervening in, the human predicaments abounding in our contemporary way of life.

Edgar A. Levenson, in *The Fallacy of Understanding,* says:

> We are living in a period of tremendous flux. What we tend to think of as eternal verities are in reality time- and place-bound. We, our patients, their complaints, our very concepts of treatment and cure are all manifestations of the particular epoch in which we live and ultimately of each other. We are as imbedded in our time and place as bugs in amber. The therapist who expects his theoretical and clinical perspectives to remain long relevant will find himself in the position of the little boy who is astounded to find that the train, not the platform, just moved out. (23, p. 7)

How family therapy views behavior

Family therapy, in its conceptual framework, raises its clinical eye level one notch in the social organizational continuum, moving from the atomized level of individuals to the nuclear level of the family. Family therapy stakes out this level as a focal concern (35). There are orientations or schools of thought in family therapy that abandon any focus on the individual person, in order to stay unrelievedly related to the *whole* family system. This chapter presents rather an "integrational" approach, in which the focus on the family as a unitary organism is additional to, and interlinked with, the concurrent individual focus (39).

"Integrational" family therapy does not view the family as simply a congeries of significant others in the life of the individual client. It sees the family as a whole, unitary organism. The relationship of individual person and family is a version of the universal phenomena of part-whole concentric relationships, in which every whole is also a part of a larger whole, and so must be fully comprehended in both its discrete and its relational natures. Thus every individual person, and of course the index client, is ideally perceived by the family therapist, as by the individual therapist, in his wholeness, singularity, separateness—seen, felt, experienced, touched. Where the family therapist takes off from the more traditional individual caseworker or therapist is that at the same time he also perceives the persons in their relational aspects (as *members,* or parts, of a larger whole), interdependent on each other and together forming a larger system, the family, that in good measure determines their collective and individual destinies and identities.

Necessarily concomitant with the foregoing is a third level of perception: the simultaneous clinical eye on the family in its wholeness, having a specific and unique identity and continuity and thus "requiring" or "tugging" at its component parts—family members (and subparts of family members as well as larger alignments of dyads, triads, etc., of family members)—to mesh with each other, and separately as well as together functioning also in extrafamilial roles to serve the homeostatic needs of the family.

Then, finally, there is the dimension of the family as a component or part of the larger community, the reciprocity between family and social institutions and culture—less immediately in the perception of the clinical therapist and yet vital contextually in understanding. In summary, family therapy has four tiers of focus: the family as part of the community; the family as a whole; each individual as part, or member; and each individual as discrete. The long-term challenge to family therapy is to synthesize these several foci (1). Their synthesis is as yet incomplete in clinical work as it is in the theory of social and behavioral sciences and, of course, for the same reasons.

When the family therapist approaches the problems of an individual person, he always respects the individuality of the problem and of the pain, and he also interprets them as symptomatic expressions of a problem, a distortion, a disability in the family, and seeks to comprehend and to decide on intervening also on that level. A child's rebellious behavior or poor school achievement, an adult's dissatisfaction with his marriage, a middle-aged woman's depressiveness *are* problems or dysfunctions of each of the individual persons. But they are *also* to be viewed as symptoms of something askew in the larger unit, the family, of which these people are members.

Recognizing the deficiencies in analogy, we may compare this with physical medicine. A chronic abdominal ache in a patient is certainly an abdominal problem and tells the diagnostician that there is difficulty in the functioning of a particular abdominal organ, but the diagnostician is also always alert to it as a symptom of something else that may be wrong with the whole organism. The ache is only the beginning point of the physician's effort to understand what is really wrong. It is not optimal for him to make it immediately the focus of treatment or of palliative efforts before he determines what part it is playing in the larger bodily system. It is in a somewhat parallel way that family therapy looks at the individual complainant or individual object of complaints and assumes that it is not optimal in practice to see this individual as *the* problem, but rather to see him as an aching limb

or member of a family "body" whose functioning and balance have gone awry, whose problems may not be straightforwardly expressed in these symptoms (the individual complaint) and may even be cloaked by the symptoms.

Schools of thought, eclectics, and integration in family therapy

Such a focus on the family enlarges (and broadens) our view of individual man. We do not get straitjacketed into an exclusively psychological approach to the individual. The very terms of the focus on the family—a social unit—centers attention on the social-psychological linkage. It leavens the psychological with the social determinant of behavior; *it joins social therapy with psychological therapy* (1). This joining has resulted in family work becoming a kind of meeting ground for all the helping professions. Social work comes to family therapy naturally out of a long history of work with families and with social functioning. Psychiatrists and psychologists turn to family therapy out of their increasing awareness of the need to break away from the false dichotomy between what goes on inside the mind of a person and what goes on between the minds of people.

Of course, social work's revitalized interest in the family through family therapy has not meant a *return* to the older forms of family work. Rather, it has meant older, traditional family concepts, and infusing them with more recent findings. Social work, as have the other professions, has projected a model of family therapy that has been heavily influenced by general systems theory and cybernetics (16), social science contributions such as those of social role theory and small group theory (12, 34), communications theory (18),* linguistics and, actually, elements large or small as the case may be, from most social and behavioral scien-

---

* See Chapters 3, 5, 6, 7, 8.

tific theoretical developments. Contributions have come even from the most rigorous individual-centered psychologies and psychoanalysis, at least some of whose practitioners have tried to break away from the "medical model" that overemphasizes single patient autonomy, seasoning the instinctual personality theories with concepts of socialization and adaptation. For example, the reformulation in neo-Freudian psychology that all ego energy does not originate only as id energy but also from the wellsprings of social experience is part of the seepage into psychoanalytic theory of social contexts and social influences. It exemplifies the expansive view that recognizes significant growth and change in persons beyond the early development childhood years.* With personality and behavior seen in ever more plastic terms even in the adult years, it is apparent that such modified psychoanalytic theory leaves more room for concepts of meaningful feedback and reciprocity of influence among persons (and especially within the family—including not only children but adults as well).

Though different professions have in some measure been turning to family therapy, by its very nature it lends itself more readily to practice by groups or teams of practitioners than by the lone practitioner. Not uncommon, and having many interesting and effective results, is the practice of co-therapy—that is, two therapists acting as a team in joint responsibility for the total family therapy, and together conducting the family sessions. The most usual co-therapy practice is for the two therapists to sit in family group sessions, sharing therapeutic responsibility there, and when parts (individual or couple) of the family need to be seen separately and concurrently one of the therapists carries that as a continuing responsibility. The practice of co-therapy tends to occur more within agencies and institutions than in private offices, often with multi- or interdisciplinary personnel (15, pp. 572-580).

---

* See Chapter 3.

Coupling these essentially logistical factors with the historical interest in the family by social work, and with social work's long familiarity with the social dimensions of the family, we see it as no accident that social work is perhaps the most fertile ground of all the helping professions for the seeding and growth of family therapy. This is borne out, for example, by the findings of the Group for the Advancement of Psychiatry. A G.A.P. committee, composed primarily of psychiatrists and with only one social worker serving as "consultant," found in the responses to a 1970 survey that social workers composed the largest single group of practitioners of family therapy (about 40 percent) (15).

If we conceptualize a family as a vital psychosocial field and as a definable organism with boundaries (though permeable), and if we see it on a continuum of social organization between the individual person and forms of larger social organization like the neighborhood or the community, then, at the risk of seeming too compartmentalized, we can descry certain functions that this organism (the family) fulfills for society (e.g., providing a convenient unit of consumption of the economy's production, inculcating societal values in its members). On another level of construct, moving to the interior of the family, we can formulate functions that the family performs in the *psychosocial* service of its members: provision of material necessities, affectional bonding and mutual support, sexual differentiation, encouragement of individual autonomy, and cultivation of personal creativity in adaptation.

To carry out these functions, complicated role-sets are necessitated within the family, determinative attitudes and behaviors on the parts of individuals and combinations of individuals. The point here is that the necessity for the fulfillment of family functions choreographs the individual members within the family, their relationships with each other and with life, their joinings, unions, separations. With due regard for individual constitutional factors and biological vicissitudes, the family "choreography" helps to spell out personal individual identities as well as mutual interpersonal, intermember experiences and relationships.

We have referred to the contribution to family therapy of social role theory. Family role patterning as just described requires in effect our "psychologizing" social role concepts (34); that is, within the operational concept, integrating the subjective experience of each person with the objective assignment to his roles by society and culture.

It should also be apparent to the reader the significant contribution that has been made to family therapy by communications theory, which emphasizes the "programming" of individual behavior by cultural and social systems and subsystems.* As indicated earlier in this chapter, there are some schools of thought and practice in family therapy that are so committed to these determinants of behavior that they espouse working exclusively with the family group and only with the overt communications and interactions within the family (18, 24). They may counsel against or even prohibit any reference in family sessions to the subjective states, emotions, or thinking of individual members and stay focused only on the exchanges among the family members, attempting to alter these communications by dint of the authority of the therapist or by the use of conditioning or reinforcement. The family therapist of this persuasion feels that by *exclusive* focus on the communication pattern in the family he is dealing with that which is directly perceivable, knowable, and alterable, and that if alteration of the communication pattern is achieved, there will be feedback from improved communications to the individual emotional state of each family member without the therapy having to deal directly with the latter. To get directly related to the emotional state or psychic conflict of any individual family member in the family group is by this standard a departure from family therapy and an ensnarement into individual therapy,

which is different from traditional individual therapy only in that it is conducted in the compresence of other family members. For similar reasons, some family therapists go to the extreme of refusing to see individual family members at any time or even refusing to see the family group if one of the members has failed to appear with the others, the therapist seeing the request for an individual interview or the "absent member maneuver" as probably being ploys to defeat the direction taken by the family therapist.

Family therapy "schools" or approaches that are based predominantly on communication theory have been given instructive names, such as "*structural* family therapy" (2), "*strategic* family therapy," or "*systems* therapy," and the like (16).

It is useful to contrast so exclusive a reliance on communication theory with an integrational approach to family therapy. Although in practice these sharp distinctions break down and are not so parochially applied, some discussion here of the contrast at the concentual extremes can clarify an integrational or eclectic approach. To the integrationist, the purist systems or communication approach has elements of clinical verity, but it is as one-sided in its way as has been the psychoanalytically influenced prejudice that a therapeutic relationship must be one-to-one and uncorrupted by the presence or even the recognition, by the therapist, of other family members. These two extremes each in turn relate to one part of the total person to the virtual exclusion of the other: the one-to-one therapist relates operationally to behavior as though it is totally a function of the person's psychological and emotional state, and therefore the only effective approach to behavioral change is to the affective-psychic inner life; at the other extreme the purist communications therapist acts on the assumption, seemingly, that all emotional and psychic life are functions of an individual's behavior, which is programmed by culture and society—alter the client's patterned behavior within the concentrated subculture of therapy or

---

* See Chapter 16.

in his life space in the family, and you will also have effected emotional change without "dipping" into the client's psyche.

We recognize here several essential issues. We meet again the underlying riddle of part-whole relationships. Is a particular existential person *only* a part, a component, of a larger complexity: a family organization, a community, a culture? Is he then, at bottom, *entirely* programmed by the whole process of which he is a part? Or is he also a creator, fashioning, in as yet incompletely fathomable ways, notions, feelings, ideas, behaviors, and responses, and does he not reciprocally influence other individuals and families and polities of which he is a part? (11) Communications and systems ideas can become so beguiling because they *do* introduce valid and hitherto quite neglected considerations, but a *caveat* against one-sidedness in their application must accompany them.

Nathan Ackerman's oft-repeated commentary on these issues, when they arose in debate on approaches to family therapy, was that family therapy must follow nature, respecting both the autonomy as well as the component status of the person (2). Man is both an individual and a member of the family; neither part of the self can be sacrificed to the other, and a clinical view that does so risks being partializing and fragmenting. In life the family is a very complex pattern of privacies, autonomies, and interdependences. Every person in the family experiences the ontological loneliness or aloneness; inevitably, he has his private world or individual existence, no matter how much he openly shares with other family members. Subsystems within the family also have their private worlds. The marital couple obviously does, as symbolized by the sexual intimacy and the shared adult responsibility. Each parent-and-child dyad and both-parents-and-child triad also have their private warrens, usually unspoken and perhaps even tucked away out of awareness. Similarly, the sibling group has its fence that separates it from the parents, as do even parts of the sibling group, such as those of a particular gender.

Even beyond this there are the private liaisons of parents with grandparents, and so on. *When these "natural" alignments are distorted or rigidified, they become pathogenic splits.* (41).

Integrating the elements of family therapy

An integrational family therapy thus focuses on the family system and family process, subsystems and subprocesses in which various individuals and members are aligned, and, at the same time, relates to each individual member as a particular and different human being rather than as part of an undifferentiated mass. It is quite a challenge for the therapist in his thinking and in his activity to *perceive* the family as a whole: its values, dominant threads or themes of aspiration, behavior, and defense; to do similarly with significant subsystems within the family—dyads and triads; and, concurrently, to be trying to grasp something of the inner experience of each of the family members. A further challenge to the family therapist is that, even while he responds to larger-than-individual themes in the family interaction, he must be touched by and be able to touch significantly individual members of the family (4, 25).

As an illustration of this challenge, let us briefly abstract one bit of interaction in a client family. The family therapist takes note of the repeated occurrence in sessions with the Brown family of mother's sharp criticism of the adolescent son, usually accompanied by a warmer nod, by word or gesture, in her daughter's direction, not discouraged and even sometimes encouraged by daughter. Father stays out of range of this little sequence of behaviors, says nothing, and a few times even repositions his chair inches backward while mother is talking.

This repetitious sequence of behavior imparts a great deal of information about the Browns, confirmed by much other data that have emerged in the earlier therapeutic contact.

We are discussing the little exchange just described as a representative interaction in this family, its meaning amplified and validated by other data. On a communication level, mother's harsh "messages" to her son are abetted by father's silence (his default and failure to intervene); daughter's competitiveness encourages mother's prejudicial attack on son; and even the boy, by tacitly "accepting" the role of victim, reinforces and fixes this pattern of communication. The overt criticisms by mother, father's withdrawal, daughter's competitiveness, and son's collusive passivity are each, severally and all together as a synthesized interaction, dysfunctional for the family and each of its members, reducing levels of gratification and feelings of support, and draining the family energies from fulfilling more developmental tasks.

On a communications level, the therapist might confront the question of how to interrupt, alter, or break into this fixed pattern of overt behaviors. Should he intervene directly on mother's verbal assaults, call attention to them and challenge her to change them, call attention to daughter's sly maneuver that encourages mother not to desist; challenge father not to edge *away* but to edge *in,* to try in his way to change the pattern; support dissent or resistance by the son? Any one or all of these interventions would touch on the communications system, and by repeating such interventions (having both aversive and positively reinforcing elements) there could conceivably be effected a break in this rigid pattern of responses in this family and a shift toward a more wholesome interaction.

A psychodynamically oriented therapist might agree in part but might want to ask additional questions, for example: how plastic is mother's internal conflict whence in part comes this strong attack; does it also have a sexual warp (antimale), and is it a defensive identification with the aggressor; is mother attacking out of a sense of loss and helplessness, and would, therefore, a therapist's challenge to her to inhibit

her destructive outburst be beyond her emotional competence, reinforcing her helplessness and confirming that the therapist is "against" her? These are just a few of the psychological possibilities to which the "psychodynamicist" might be cued about mother and, in a parallel way, other psychological possibilities might be seen in the others. Assessment of the psychological states of each of the members would be determinative in shaping the kind and quality of therapeutic intervention.

The integrational approach attempts to put together the behavioral and psychodynamic dimensions of the communications system. Though no such unitary theory of behavior exists, what we do know presents the therapist with additional considerations for comprehension and thus with potential interventions in the Brown family. In addition to the above suggested exclusive concerns with the family as whole system, or alternatively with the individual psychodynamics, family therapy also adds the dimension of *interpersonality,* or *relational behavior* (44, p. 58). For example: Is mother's sense of deprivation and lack of nurture not only an incremental deposit from childhood and adolescent trauma, but are they being continuously reinforced by her husband's withdrawal from her? Does she hit out at her son as though he were a stand-in for her husband? Is her striking out at the boy a distorted call for affection or support from her husband? Is the father threatened by the demands for closeness by his wife (because of both developmental and contemporary interpersonal factors) and, fearing for his own skin, does he draw back even more, though by this act the son becomes a kind of sacrificial goat? Has daughter felt abandoned in affection by father, especially since her pubescence, and in frustration "thrown in her lot" onesidedly with mother in an alignment against father and, by extension, brother? Is the son accepting or even inviting by his provocation the role of scapegoat, because subliminally he gets the message that his action will keep the family "together," an action that will substitute for and cloak a more violent or potentially disruptive confrontation between his parents? Is there a gender split developing or developed in this family between its males and females in relation to the giving and receiving of emotional nurture; the exercise of authority; and the distribution of power—a split that tends to warp the sexual differentiation of the family members?

Only a few representative questions have been suggested as occurring to each of the hypothetical therapists who might have encountered the Browns. The integrational family therapist is both systemic and individual; his "geiger counter" is attuned to sensations from the family as a whole and the reciprocity of processes that go on inside the family—between the individual family members and within their minds. His interventions will be governed by those perceptions. What he specifically *does* at any point, if viewed discretely, may seem to be only on a communications level or, at another point, may seem directed solely at the feelings of one person, but these acts are *different* because they come out of a different context of immediate and ultimate aims and goals and are links in a chain of different earlier and later-to-come interventive acts—forming different gestalts. For example, in a Brown family session, a family therapist (momentarily appearing remarkably like one exclusively concerned with communications) might challenge father actively to come between, and interrupt, the destructive exchange between mother and son. However, the context for this challenge might already have been defined in an earlier therapeutic exchange as not only relating to father's interrupting a destructive cycle involving all of the family members, but also by the same act of his confronting again his own exaggerated dread of the internalized punishing mother, and countering it. Thus the contexts defined in integrational family therapy weld together the family interactive and individual psychological elements.

In parallel fashion, Mrs. Brown might be interrupted by a therapist in her attack on her son in one context that carried the message "stop hurting your son." A therapeutic interruption that appeared overtly identical, in a different context, might carry a very different therapeutic intent and message; that is, the therapist, viewing mother's use of attack as also personal defense, might interrupt in order to reach mother's tender or vulnerable side. There would, of course, have been some groundwork laid earlier to carry this meaning for mother, and the interruption might be followed up by the therapist's expression of how helpless and frustrated mother felt at that very moment of her attack. Even more, the family therapist might extend this opening to touch on mother's chronic fear that she cannot, or will not, receive any nurture from father. In this snippet of a possible response from the family therapist, psychological and interpersonal elements are tied together, in a contextual (metacommunicational) sense.

Boundaries of the family

There was a reference earlier in this chapter to relativity in the definition of functions of a family—depending on who was doing the defining, and with what purpose quite different sets of functions could be postulated. A family therapist, being interested in a different order of vital processes and starting from a different vantage point from, say, a sociologist, would therefore opt for constructs of family functions that would tend to be in the psychosocial arena. Then would follow the question: Whom do you include as members? In its actual family life style, whom the family includes within its boundaries varies considerably cross-culturally, or across ethnicities (13). The definition of family boundaries varies even *within* specific cultures or ethnicities, depending on many variables such as class, habitat, even occupation. A rural family is far more inclusive of linear (grandparents, grandchildren) and collateral (uncles, aunts) figures within its primary circle than is the conjugal family, usually found in the city. Italian-American or Jewish-American families also tend to have more inclusive self-images than the Yankee-American family (3, p. 40).

Family therapy moves in a psychosocial universe, and its concept of structure follows psychosocial function. Not only the nuclear family, but those in lineal or collateral relationship to the nuclear family and those others who have important roles or part-roles in carrying out the family's psychosocial functions can be conceptualized as part of the family by the therapist. Such relevant individuals are often grandparents, sometimes uncles, aunts, siblings of the parents, married sons and daughters and their spouses, and so forth (6). As clinical workers know, there is a great variety of kinds of relatives or even non-kin who can have determinative influences on the inner family unit. Physical separation or geographic distance of these persons may not weigh in the balance. Separation or divorce of a spouse may not be contraindicative of his entry into family process, particularly when the therapeutic "business" at hand involves the children (21). Whether or not these persons can be included in the interview sessions themselves—the conjoint meeting with them having many additional advantages—they need at least to enter into the *comprehension* of the family therapist because they may be integral parts of the whole psychosocial field or system. Their omission from the therapist's ken results in partial and defective comprehension of the family phenomena and less effective intervention.

In the beginning of this chapter there was reference to marital partners or parents who felt inadequate in their roles in the conjugal family because they were emotionally fixated in some significant measure in their families of origin. Such conflict is often encountered in our contemporary society which, in its kaleidoscopic changes, creates an obstacle course to the achievement of adulthood and imposes a need for a stretched-out adolescence as a vestibule to adulthood. But contrarily, other processes in our society act to extrude the sons and daughters from families at an earlier age than

even a generation ago. In clinical practice we encounter many nuclear families which are rudderless and deficient in leadership. Children in these families are often drawn into filling the vacuum by what looks like a precocious, but is really a pseudo, leadership that they exercise. Or there may be deficiencies in nurturance in the family for which restitutional efforts (e.g., using money as a substitute) do not fill the void but, to the contrary, add further complications. Such deficiencies lead us to inquire after missing links, links that never existed, or that once were there and were prematurely broken, or that can no longer be effective in the present circumstances of the family. Such links we frequently find to be father, mother, sibling from the family of origin, or a more distant relative. One or both of the adult clients have unfinished business with one or both of their own parents. Their dependence on parents is for support and nurture or because they cannot end an angry railing for the support and nurture that never were—either extreme resulting in as tight a bondage as the other.

In systems terms, we would look for (and probably find) that the parents' parents in these instances were and are collusive in maintaining the bondage, in which event we may have positive indications for including them within the clinically defined family boundaries, where we have a better, more direct possibility of touching their need to hang on to their adult children's coattails. Repeatedly, in the discussion of family therapy, we will come back to such reciprocals or complements between persons. It is almost of the status of psychosocial "law" that hardly any behavior exists discretely in a family, but rather will have reciprocals in other family members. This points to why, in *appraisal,* we try to encompass the whole field of interaction (interaction in the psychosocial sense that is not limited to physically present members or physically evident behavior) and why we may incline toward whole family sessions in *treatment,* because then we have "in hand," so to speak, the several points of reciprocity of attitude and behavior (25).

There are family therapists in children's services who operationally define the unit of therapy as limited to the triad of the presenting problem child and his parents. Others may include siblings in family sessions, but not those younger than seven or eight, on the premise that family sessions are talk sessions and the youngsters are not verbal (7). A truly holistic orientation toward therapy must move beyond these imposed barriers to an expansive inclusiveness in defining family boundaries. *All* members of the family, and, as indicated, often including kin, are inextricably parts of the family system or field to which the therapist's attention is to be directed. If the family interaction is perceived as occurring on many levels including, most decisively, the nonverbal, and if the therapist conceives his transactions with the family as being directed on these different levels, obviously he would want to include even preverbal youngsters in at least some of the therapy sessions.

It is a truism that the "whole" system in which the individual person is embedded goes far beyond the family, as bounded above, and includes ever larger concentric interdependent subsystems of neighborhood, community, ethnic subculture, and so on (8). However, family therapy, being a clinical practice, is necessarily limited in its operational sphere to that which it can *directly* deal with and influence, and it leaves to epidemiology, mental hygiene, and public mental health education (and other fields) the larger concentricities. The family therapist who includes in his interviewing compass the individual person all the way to the intergenerational family or kinship group may be going just about as far as possible in inclusiveness in *direct clinical work*. This is not to say that he is not enhanced in his work if he *understands* the societal and cultural contexts of his practice. Nor, in fact, does it mean that direct intervention into social institutions, communities, and polities is without therapeutic consequence for people. Quite the contrary. Such intervention, however, has not only its consonances with, but also its very vital differences in method, process, and knowledge base from, the direct work with families and requires its own expertise.

Social interventionists can learn from and be enriched in their work by family therapists. Therapists who have steeped themselves in working with family groups develop almost a visceral sensitivity as well as a cognitive response to the exquisite nuances and multiple facets of the individual's linkage with the larger biosocial group, the family. In some respects these dynamics can be seen as paradigmatic of the complex ways in which individual persons and families are reciprocally linked with other, even larger social organizations of persons—neighborhoods; communities of ethnicity, of occupation, even of class; and so on. The extrapolations from family therapy, as they continue to be made, may provide some needed lower-ordered conceptualizations of social process in communities and in the larger society, and of the processes of individual integration within them (1).

Family process: helpful constructs

A family begins when an adult man and woman, each having a distinct personal identity forged in a developmental experience in a family of origin, join their identities in marriage to form the nucleus of a new family. The tasks undertaken at this point—and of course in the premarital association—are in effect to create a joint marital identity that is made up of parts of their separate individual identities, but it is also more than and different from a composite (13).

The family, therefore, begins with the gratifications of union mixed with the confrontation of critical tasks. The sense of fulfillment for a family and its members is always mixed with the resolution of developmental crises, beginning with this very first one and extending throughout its life cycle. Phases of growth and expansion follow the family's beginning and then decline, leading toward an ending—all of which is punctuated throughout by turning points and crises, minor beginnings and endings within the larger continuity (31).

Every family develops its own rules of behavior, its codes and metaphors of communication, its strengths and vulnerabilities in meeting or failing to master inner and outer stresses, all the while maintaining its balance, integrity, wholeness, adaptability—its identity. The vital dynamism that fuels a family in this way can be captured by our minds only in metaphors. "It" has been called a "steering mechanism" (20), "a gyroscope," the process of "equilibration" or "balance" (35), even the family "ethos" (16). "It" can be likened to the creative something that ethologists are now hypothesizing as a kind of life force in all animals—including man—that is beyond, and compels a revision of, the laws of natural selection. Homeostasis is a loose and general hypothesis to blanket these multifaceted processes, to explain the centripetal force the family exerts on its members and the self-stabilizing and adaptational energies it develops (18, 19).

The foregoing describes healthy homeostatic process. The families we see in therapy usually have some homeostatic disturbance. This is another way of saying that whether one or several family members are carrying the manifest symptoms of disturbance or dysfunction, the family as a whole is faltering in fulfilling all of its psychosocial functions, and in some way the whole family is experiencing a "tilt"—if not a more violent threat—to its integrity. The index client, or member with the presenting problem, "the family symptom," is one overt expression of the distortion that has developed—or was never absent, but simply deepened or broadened—in the family. This much we have discussed earlier.

However, pursuing the metaphor of "symptom" a little further, (1) a symptom is the overt evidence for some more or less hidden pathological or noxious process within the organism; and (2) by virtue of deferral, displacement, and other intermediate process, the symptom also often obscures the connections between itself and the underlying pathogenic process; but (3) a symptom is also created by *the organism's effort to correct or neutralize the underlying affliction.* A symptom or syndrome is the resultant of both the existence of disease and the organism's attempt to recover; and we know that often the self-healing or restitutional efforts of the organism are only temporarily effective, and the relative comfort or freedom from pain is often uncertain and unstable. Sometimes the organism's autonomically evoked remedy is worse than the disease itself.

In parallel fashion, the distressed or dysfunctional individual may be a symptomatic expression of a warp or inequilibrium of the family; he—or, rather, his complaint—may *at the same time be the effect of the family's restitutional, reequilibrating efforts,* the only option the family seems to have in its repertoire for trying to ward off threats to its wholeness, balance, even continued existence—all, needless to say, occurring in good measure below the level of awareness. The presenting individual problem is both evidence of underlying family *difficulties* and the family's imperfect, unstable way of *trying to cope with the difficulties.*

We can refer, by way of illustration, to some of the problems frequently presented to helping agencies:

1. The application for foster placement of a child. His behavior is so difficult for his family to bear, it is almost by itself demanding of separation from the family, even though on another level the child, and perhaps the family, deplore and resist the idea of placement. Appraisal of the whole family process will often disclose evidence that the proposed placement of the child is *in part* an extrusion of him to preserve the intactness or balance of the remainder or fragment of the family (33). He is the family sacrifice. His misbehavior, *in part,* is the child's collusion with the signals from parent or parents to prove that he *should* be exiled. For some reason, his presence had been perceived as threatening to the continuity of the family (not enough affection to go around? male sexuality a threat? etc.). Again the reader must be reminded that exploration of the family dynamics, as in this illustration, is not an attempt at exclusive explanation. It is presented here, as throughout this chapter, as one important dimension in the complexity of behavior.

2. The young adolescent who is behaving promiscuously (or the one who is truanting from school, or the one who is having brushes with the law, etc.) may through that social symptom be calling attention to underlying hypocritical, dishonest social conformity in the parents by which means their own anti- or asocial impulses are barely kept in check. The youngster's deviant behavior may be a cloaked expression of the superego lacunae of one or both parents, and he "misbehaves" so that the parent doesn't. He is delegated not only "to sow the wild oats" but to reap the consequences, including the parent's disapproval and even rejection. Dynamically, in such a situation the child and his behavior are buttresses on the perimeter of the parents' uncertain defenses against their own "wildness." The parent or parents "blame" the child for his excesses of behavior, contrast it with the more compliant behavior of his siblings, and quite sincerely see it as "the problem" needing change; suppressed are the underlying inter-and intrapersonal, and value conflicts within the family, touching all the members, of which the presented child's behavior is symptomatic. Their collective gaze is averted from the "secret" that, by having him to blame, they do not have the more discomfiting blame of themselves. His behavior is *needed* as the lesser threat in the family's psychosocial economy, so the behavior was "helped to happen."

3. As final examples, there is the father who is driving the others in the family crazy to "preserve" his own sanity (and they collude with him even while complaining about him). Or the mother who incites the family to push her to the brink of complete helplessness, so that all in desperation would agree to the recall of the banished grandmother (mother's mother) to

whom mother inwardly feels bonded. And so on.

Needless to say, families are infinitely variable: every family is idiosyncratic; no two families are exactly alike. The paradox holds for families as it does for any other organism or area of inquiry: the appreciation of the unique features of the specific requires that there be knowledge of the general. Without generalizations at our command, we are helpless in the face of variability to perceive the singularity of each subject. A number of constructs of a middle or lower order of generality than homeostasis have been proposed by family researchers or clinicians in the recent past. They have been proposed with unusual tentativeness and with the expectation that they will be received tentatively and certainly not invested with intrinsic validity. They are validated if to a degree they can help explain what otherwise appears inexplicable or order what otherwise appears random or anarchic; if they can be predictive of what will likely follow or be found in association with certain phenomena; if they can direct a clinician's attention, clarify his perception, hone his aims.

Given the newness of family therapy, it is to be expected that such taxonomic efforts would still be rudimentary. There is hardly even a language to name family psychosocial phenomena—of health or disturbance and dysfunction—and there is a consequent necessary resort to the language and metaphors of individual psychology or those of small group processes, with some losses in exactness of meaning. We will identify some of the better known concepts. Their choice also stems from what the author has found helpful, which may be of similar value to the reader, although the chief utility in discussing them at all is in the sensitization of the reader to the ferment among family theorists and therapists out of which will come more and more clinically useful generalizations or extrapolations.

Homeostasis, or the process of adaptation and stabilization, of a family is based on and regulated by interpersonal mechanisms. Gregory Bateson divides these mechanisms between those that are symmetrical and those that are asymmetrical, or complementary (5). The symmetrical mechanisms are much more commonly encountered in the literature or in clinical discussions. Imitation, modeling, positive identification, competitiveness, or the like exemplify the symmetrical mechanisms among family members, emphasizing *likeness* and equality—vital to development of joined, shared values and unity of a family.

Equally vital, equally the stuff of life itself, is complementarity of roles and identities among family members (1, p. 85). Complementarity is the fit of difference, the synthesis of components to make a whole. We recognize complementarity in biological, as in social or psychological, phenomena. Sexual differentiation is an obvious example of complementarity in higher ordered animal life. Where in simpler organisms all sexual, reproductive process and "role," if we wish, are contained in each organism, in more complex animal life they are split into component parts, male and female, each different from the other, and each of which is not the "whole" sex but a complement of the other, so that together they form the whole of sex, for reproduction, pleasure, and mature fulfillment, biologically, socially, and psychologically.

Complementarity is a ubiquitous process in life. "Wife" or "husband," "marital partner" are obvious relational and complementary *social* terms and roles, the whole being marriage. A "child" implies a complement, the parent, for neither in social status nor in fulfillment of his primitive needs can the youngster be a "whole child" by himself. Complementation of emotional growth needs and fulfillments exists throughout a family. The child's emotional growth and the mother's (or father's or parents')—yes, emotional growth as an adult—are complements of each other.

Complementarity is of various orders, the most general and the most specific, of family life. The exercise of authority and the giving of nurture are complementary functions, each one of which by itself is not healthful parenting; rather, they are inextricably interdependent and, as components, fit together in fulfilling parental functioning. Dependency in a family implies someone who is dependent and, the complement, someone who is depended upon. Such a dependency axis might exist as rather stable role relations in a family, or it can exist momentarily among two or more family members in a given situation, to be succeeded by even an exchange of roles of the dependent and the depended upon. Both fixed and transitory kinds of complements in dependency and other exchanges are part of the ebbs and flows of relationship within a family.

Ivan Boszormenyi-Nagy discusses processes like complementation in a larger context which he calls "dialectical psychology," a self-defining, self–other relational system:

> In dialectical psychology the self becomes a self only by virtue of its being a center of something else; moment by moment it is grounded in the existence of an Other. This is not a new concept, but the real puzzle is this: What happens to the Other the moment I make him the ground of my existence? This formulation is based on a Sartrean kind of thinking. (2, p. 91)

We have been discussing complementarity that spells out health and growth and creative adaptability in families. There are also the complementarities that reflect the fit and jelling of component tendencies which are compromises, incompletely gratifying and even pathogenic for the individuals and the family (1, p. 86). The healthful complementation on dependency just described can be supplanted by a fixed relationship of overdependency in one member complemented by overbearing behavior in another. Here is a fit of component behaviors, of individual maladaptive patterns, in which each extreme seems to satisfy and complete the other.

But the total effect is lopsided; neither person's autonomy or socially adaptive potential is being served. The relationship itself in these circumtances is not a growing, expanding, fulfilling entity. It is fixed, rigid, constricted, and even unstable, especially in the face of any inner or outer changes. Thus the lopsided negative or pathogenic complementarity of a family (e.g., overdependent-overbearing; timid-brash; passive-aggressive; indecisive-overcertain pairings) may not adjust to events like the death or absence of a significant parent, the birth of a child (or of a second child), and the loss of income, or to inner changes like the deepening of a phobic response in one member or even the subjective symbolism of the approaching thirtieth? fortieth? fiftieth? etc. birthday of a parent.

Appraising the identifications and unions as well as positive and negative complementarities among family members is an essential part of the diagnostic process. The family therapist learns to tune in to complements, reciprocals, resonances within families, so that, perceiving aggression in one individual, he immediately looks for the probable complement in the family—someone or "someones" who, by their submission, may be forming the completed circle of aggressor and aggressed, *each partner to the act reinforcing the other's behavior.* Similarly with the whole panoply of individual maladaptive or adaptive behaviors. In this, there is not the suggestion that such family interaction is always the *cause* of the behavior. It is enough for us to see that out of the complementary cycling, there is a reinforcement, a superimposed whole additional layer that intensifies, deepens, and qualitatively alters behavioral tendencies in each family member, that may also have other developmental or even constitutional origins or reinforcements (3, p. 3).

Of helpful constructs to understanding families we have summarized *homeostasis, positive and negative complementarity, and symmetrical processes.* There are other general constructs about families that have been borrowed from such apparently remote epistemologies as cybernetics or thermodynamics. Always, in borrowing notions from other than human systems or fields of dynamic interaction, we must remain alert to the limitations or dangers in reducing creative human relations to mechanical formulae.

Constructs of a lower order, of greater particularity, have been discussed in the literature or in forums on family therapy. The *double-bind* is perhaps one of the best known. It was originally conceptualized by Gregory Bateson and his associates as a process tending to appear in association with schizophrenia in a family member (5), but subsequently it was acknowledged to be a distortion in the communication process of families whose member(s) evince many different kinds of individual pathology (18). One is "double-bound" when he has been given at the same time such contradictory messages from another person that he is left no course to pursue or reply to give that cannot be faulted, so that he cannot escape an equivocal, if not mystified, state. *Scapegoating* is the process by which a family member becomes the object of displacement of conflict or destructive affect from others in the family, and with his complicity (a negative complementarity existing between scapegoater[s] and scapegoat). The scapegoat experiences the dangers or rebuffs as surrogate for others and is thus a sacrifice to "protect" them. The vignette of the Brown youngster presented earlier* is an example of scapegoating (8, 48).

Birdwhistell and Scheflen, among others, have contributed ideas about *kinesics* and channels of communication other than the linguistic (9, 30); Lyman Wynne and others on *splits* and *alignments* in family process (41) and on *pseudomutuality* and *pseudohostility* (42), and Zuk on *triangulation* (44). These are only tokens of the vast outpouring of empirically developed or researched concepts that we can expect inevitably to occur, because they are so needed as

---

* See pp. 455–457.

instruments of diagnosis and appraisal of families and of sharpening family therapies.

When family group sessions? Issues of therapeutic focus

Earlier, reference was made to family therapy not only as a modality (i.e., family group or conjoint sessions) but also as a more encompassing conception of personality, dysfunction, and therapy. The modality of the family group session is prominent in family therapy, this following naturally from the orientation toward the whole family. Most family therapists would agree that at least one or several sessions with the whole family are essential in arriving at an appraisal of the dynamic place of the individual symptom in the family matrix of relationships.

A continuous process of appraisal of the client family and the therapeutic indications could result in the family group sessions being the exclusive modality in some cases, or it could take the family therapist to other modalities: triadic, dyadic, or individual sessions, either concurrent with family sessions or in sequential phases of the treatment process. Of course, this discussion subsumes the family's participation in choices of who is to be seen, but is directed at the professional's aims and to the basis of his decisions. The determination of modality is a part of the determination of therapeutic focus, which in turn is a continuous questing for mutuality between client family and therapist and for reducing the perceptual gap between them.

There is an advantage in sessions with the whole family group coming as close as possible to the beginning of the therapy process, because in the presence of the whole family the presenting problem (usually perceived in *individual* terms) can be dynamically traced, *with the participation and comprehension of all members,* to the *family* phenomena. Consequently, if only a part of the family is subsequently to be the focal

subject of interviews (e.g., parental couple or individual member), the connection between the choice of participants in these subsequent sessions and the family task in treatment will have been traced and will have some clarity for all the family members.

For example, the presenting problem of the runaway adolescent may be traced in the whole family sessions to the anxious cleaving of the parents to each other in a way that literally provides no "breathing space" for the child between them, so that he collusively responds to the signal from the parents and leaves the scene. The therapeutic focus in the whole family sessions turns to the undifferentiated relationship of the parents, to which the symptom—the son's running away—has been traced. Recognizing his collusion and the need for him to work on that, nevertheless, for the next phase, the therapist decides with the family on the couple coming in without their son to work on the lack of separateness in their relationship. They and the boy understand that a critical interactional conflict of the *whole* family is being treated by a phase of concentration on a *part* of the triadic conflict. During this phase the boy may be seen in concurrent individual sessions or in a concurrent adolescent therapy group or temporarily in no treatment modality at all until a next phase in which the whole family is again involved in sessions. Any combination of these possibilities could result, all depending on the changing therapeutic focus.

Many family therapists, including the writer, prefer to start right off with family sessions, if at all possible, because even if one later turns to individual sessions, it means going from whole to part, rather than from part to whole (36). This is a most important distinction. A family's "choice" of who among its members first contacts the helping agency and offers to come in, or of whom is to be brought in, is an expression of how they perceive the problem, and, in a sense, how and with whom they want the helping agency to begin its intervention. This initial self-presentation, then, is of the symptom and of the joined family defense; their keeping out of sight the whole family involvement in the conflict or disturbance is commonplace and to be expected. However, by falling in with it, the therapist unwittingly allows himself to get programmed by the family defense and distortion and to reinforce them by his compliance, so that it becomes more difficult for the therapist to extricate himself from the position he has helped himself into, if indeed he is even aware that he has been pulled into the family distortion. It is surprising to those workers less initiated in family modalities to see how many families respond easily and willingly to the intake worker's invitation on the telephone or during the initial session to have the whole family come in for the first or next session. Certain other applicants may respond with some awkwardness to the invitation: "it only involves my husband and me" or "only my son and not the other children." In the writer's and his agency's experience, a quiet, firm invitation, "We would like to meet all the people you (and your husband, your son, etc.) live with," makes sense to many of these other callers. Of course there are some applicants who will not be persuaded and the agency needs to bend to begin with less than the entire family, but the client's selection of those family members who were left at home or "couldn't come in" has diagnostic import and bears further consideration in the contacts that follow.

The opening contact of applicant and agency is worth this much detailed discussion because the kind of beginnings made in a process has such substantial influence on what follows, and because there is so much misunderstanding of the slogan "one begins where the client is." This truism actually defines a *dialogic* kind of beginning, a two-party system, a "one," the therapist or collective agency, and a client (an "other"). The "one" (the agency), just as the "other," must have some breath of identity or there can be no dialogue—or, in fact there is no "one," harking back to the wisdom of Boszormenyi-Nagy's "dialectical psychology" (10). The agency—even in the open-

ing telephone call—needs to differentiate itself, not inflexibly or challengingly, but with some self-definition. The average applicant is defining the agency in his own terms, which are a conglomerate not only, as earlier stated, of the fragmented way in which he sees (and expects the agency to see) his problem, but also of how the mental health and social welfare institutions and their representations in popular media have for many years emphasized the *individual* approach to mental health and social dysfunction. The agency can do no less than the client in explaining itself and how it proposes to make a beginning with the client family. If this results in the joining of an issue—that is, the client's need to fragment the *family* problem versus the agency's inclination toward beginning with the whole of it—it is a therapeutic issue and the joining of it can be a good start in the therapy.

Seeing the family at the outset is no guarantee to the therapist against his being unwittingly sucked into becoming part of the family's distorted relations, but it can provide a most helpful baseline for avoiding this and for finding a helpful line of approach. Thus, Mr. Bauer, a father, telephones to seek help with a rebellious daughter and wants to arrange for daughter and mother to come in. On the telephone, the therapist says that the appointment will be for the whole family, including not only daughter and mother, but father and the two other children. Mr. Bauer says he is willing but too pressured on time "right now" to make it; anyway, it is a problem mostly of mother and daughter, so his presence isn't necessary—and, even more, "Why drag the other kids in? They're doing okay." The therapist, by emphasizing the importance the agency attaches to it, gains the reluctant agreement of father to all members of the family coming in.

The actual session quickly demonstrates the father's role as spokesman in the family and mother's timid acceptance of his explanation that it is her mildness and inability to back up father's authority or to exercise her own authority that have caused daughter's refractory behavior. Daughter herself suggests her chief problem is with father's harsh and perfectionistic demands.

It is apparent now that had the agency agreed to see only mother and daughter for a first session, even though the therapist might have inferred the parental collusion in displacing father-daughter conflict to the mother-daughter relationship, the therapist's compliance with the father's proposed absenting himself would have been tacit conformance with father's defense. To the contrary, the effect of verbal responses of the therapist in the interview with mother and daughter would have been preempted and partially vitiated by the implicit opposite message conveyed by the agency's having begun on the father's terms—i.e., his assertions that the problem centered on mother and daughter. Even beyond this, in the family session that actually took place, it began to emerge that the "well" siblings were even more subversive of parental authority than their sister, but in muted and undercover ways, having a kind of pact with sister that she would be their protector and the one who was "out front" in battling father.

Had the therapist not put forward his firm suggestion that all the family come in, and had he selflessly responded to "where the client was" by not including the siblings in the session, he would have implicitly reinforced the scapegoat role of daughter. Though the worker might respond to the daughter *in the interview* with verbal appreciation of her scapegoat role, in *form* (that is, in the *act* of agreeing to see her alone of all the children), he would be tacitly complying with the notion that she was the index client, of all the children, the focal point of infection. Obviously whom we choose or agree to see has as potent, often more potent, an effect as the insightful other things that we do or say. Having begun with a part of the family—in this instance, the scapegoated daughter and parent—we enter, and in a sense become part of, a fragmented view by the family of themselves and their problem from which it becomes difficult to extricate the therapy.

Premises that underlie family sessions

If, as indicated earlier, family sessions are not necessarily the sole modality to be used throughout the therapy of a family, they are certainly essential at various points in the therapy process, because they bring into *live* and *simultaneous* clinical focus individual person subjectivity and interpersonal behavior of the family members and the shape of the family as a whole, with the following results (2, 10, 17, 25, 32, 35, 38):

1. That which in individual interviews may (but also may not even) have been *reported* of attitudes, feelings, behaviors between family members, is actually *enacted,* witnessed, and experienced at the same time by all—family and therapist.

By way of illustration, in the case just cited, if Mr. Bauer had not come in with his wife and daughter, the therapist would probably have at least inferred, or mother might even have discussed, father's aggressive role and her own compliance in the family. It would have been a discussion *about* this relationship. With father in the session, almost immediate enactments of father's forward push and mother's compliance took place, in mother's deferential manner and father's literally shouldering her aside, and in the disparity between them in vigor and resoluteness of vocal delivery. These behaviors contrasted with the content of father's verbal assertions and mother's confirmation that they both perceived daughter's misconduct similarly. Daughter's silence "said nothing" in words, but her *moves* and the rolling of her eyes punctuated skeptically her parents' references to their agreement. She sat between them as though she were the offering presented to the agency by the parents who flanked her; the siblings' seats stretched out to the side—as though they and the others did not wish to detract from the spotlighted sister. Were the word messages completely garbled, a therapist could still decode the sounds and the unfolding tableaux toward a more accurate comprehension of the interaction than the family's word content conveyed. This scene illustrates additional aspects of family sessions:

2. *Interpersonal behavior and attitudes are not only described in a family session, they are acted out.*

3. *Nonverbal behaviors between people are eloquently communicative—very often closer to the marrow of true feeling and intention than are words* (30). It suggests the paraphrase: "More by their deeds than by the words shall ye know them" (and can they get to know themselves).

4. The perception of incongruence between what is being told in words and what is being enacted below the level of words is full of *clues to the nature of the psychological conflict* of the individual persons *and of the interpersonal conflict* among the people in the family. It is as though the word messages are defensive or cloaking in function because of the anxiety attendant to the sensitive areas underneath. The incongruence of word and deed being often spontaneously enacted in the session, there is afforded a here-and-now means of therapeutic entry into the family conflict (29, 31).

5. If the interpersonal behavior in the session adds to the breadth and accuracy of the *comprehension* by the therapist, it affords live, white-hot opportunity for meaningful *therapeutic response*. In the Bauer family episode, the therapist's light sally that mother's voice was getting drowned out and her shoulders seemed literally to be bending inward proved to be a more effective entry into the negative complementarity between the parents than would the exchange of many words during a *discussion* about the parental relationship with either parent alone. Here again there is illustrated the additional impact of an intervention into an occurrence between people in the live present, in contrast to clarifying discussion *about* occurrences of the recent or older past (25, 35).

6. The here and now of the clinical session affords a *lively present-tense entry into both the interactive processes of the family and the sub-jective experience of individual members.* It is not, however, to be construed at the expense of, or to the exclusion of, discussion of past events or historical antecedents to the interpersonal and personal behavior. Picking up on the here and now vitalizes the past in the clinical discussion, and the "use" of the past reciprocally frames and deepens the meanings extracted from the here and now (25, 35).

7. We conceptualize that the subjective experience of an individual person and his behavior toward and with others are intimately related—in fact, might profitably be viewed as sides of the same coin. Thus, an inner experience of fright is usually accompanied by some form of frightened behavior, or its correlate: if there is actual danger emanating from another, a person will experience fear and react in some way—fight or flight, perhaps—to the other person. If the danger is not actual but is indirectly prompted or imaginary or fantasied, the individual experiences neurotic fright, or anxiety, and his behavior (let us say some form of flight) toward other persons may be as *though* they are actual sources of danger and thus be puzzling or problematic to himself and to others. In fact, his impulse to respond as though endangered may so puzzle the person as to cause him to suppress his flight and act with apparent bravado.

In the instance of actual danger, the connection between subjective experience and interpersonal behavior is quite clear; in the instance of fantasied, etc., danger, the response has followed more intricate and obscure pathways. However, connection of response to stimulus is there even though there may be such dynamic permutations of it as to require sensitive and finely honed tracing of its course if it is to be descried.

The empirical premise on which the family therapist works in the family session is that *neurotic distortion is usually more susceptible to therapeutic entry and change when it is approached in its interpersonal expression*, rather than as a discrete individual psychological phenomenon. As stated above, neurotic distortion has not only its *intra-* but its *interpersonal* face. Family members are in a continuous interaction in which there are both healthy and pathogenic elements. Each individual member presents to the others, in a variety of ways, the interpersonal faces of his own inner subjective self, and *their responses serve to alter, weaken, or reinforce* his own. Responses to responses form a complex transactional web. The actors and the acted upon, the several poles of a multiparty system, all are present in the family session. The reciprocal responses among them that reinforce neurotic distortion can be reached and interrupted by the therapist, just as those responses which serve health and are growth-inducing can be supported and strengthened. The therapist also uses the interpersonal phenomena in the family as a point of entry to the subjective experience of each member: the interaction in the family provides a forum for the reality testing of the individual's neurotic fright (the *imagined* external danger), as it does for bringing to the surface *actual* endangering drives. The therapist can shuttle back and forth from individual subjectivity to family interpersonality. The therapist is thus not a selective reactor who is ever alert to the individual and system meanings of the interpersonal messages in the family session; he *actively evokes explication between the family members* of stifled feelings, diverted or displaced behavior, and so forth (4).

8. *The role of the family therapist requires entry into the family system rather than a standoffish, clinically antiseptic distance* from the family. The family in trouble will seek help by tending to cast the therapist in roles determined by their own images of need and succor. The therapist cannot really stay out of the family system; even if he attempts to stay out, he is pulled in by the family willy-nilly. In his standoffishness or neutrality, and thus by his omission, he may be unhelpfully endowed by them with the lineaments of the emotionally absentee father, the parent or spouse who was too self-interested, and so forth. Or the therapist's attempt at emotional

distance can provide openings for transference of idealized images. He can unwittingly lend himself to being cast as the omnipotent or omniscient or magical parent. By volitionally and actively entering the family's psychosocial field, the therapist becomes more sensitive to the images being inscribed upon him by the family and to the family conflicts, lack, deficits, aspirations that lie underneath and result in these expectations of the therapist. Not only does he have this diagnostic purpose served, but simultaneously the family therapist can use himself in a way that is not in total defeat of the family's expectations while winnowing out the negative or pathogenic aspects.

Concretely, as illustration, the family therapist may meet the implicit pull of a leaderless family, whose children are being allowed to run roughshod over any and all, by acting the role of a strong grandparent—not in a complete takeover fashion, as the parents seem to desire, and which would be aborting of their own (and the children's) growth, but as an intervener into the chaos while supportively challenging the parent or parents not to play dead. It may even be necessary for the therapist, as "grandparent," himself to act in some way to control directly the anxiety which underlies the family's anarchic behavior, but he does it even while he is dealing with the parents in *their* roles. His direct intervention with the children is as a surrogate leader and is on a kind of lend-lease basis, not allowing the family to institutionalize it permanently; his leadership role in the family is apportioned, offered, or withheld in step with his efforts to help the parents assume this role.

The foregoing details one instance of how the therapist enters the family, not on the family's terms, yet not out of touch with their terms, and with the purpose of responding to the nucleus of positive need. Thus when one family may seem to want decision making, authority, nurture, or whatever from the therapist as a permanent fixture in their lives, the therapist perceives the implied threat of a permanent freezing of the client's liabilities, and the therapist's "offer" of himself, his "ego," will rather carry transitional implications; or in another situation, he may perceive the pull of the family for magical or *deus-ex-machina* solutions from him as self-infantilizing, and he may offer counsel, opinion, or whatever, but within the context of his own fallibility and the need for some assumption of self-responsibility by the family or by some of its members (3, 35).

9. There are families who lack the potential for achieving satisfying levels of functioning through their own resources, no matter how extensive or intensive the direct therapeutic effort. There may be constitutional limitations or quite irreversible pathological conditions or deficits of the individual members and the family as a whole, so that there cannot be developed sufficient nurture, authority, decisiveness, or separateness (even sometimes cognitive awareness) for supporting the psychosocial growth of the children or the social relatedness of an adult member. Short of confirming the need for the family to break up, or for children to be placed in foster care, or similar other drastic, but sometimes necessary, conclusions, the family therapist tries to enlarge the canvas on which he or the family themselves view their psychosocial field. Are there collateral relatives whose interest can be activated, whose ties to the *family* can be strengthened? Are there neighborhood or community individuals who can be recruited to serve complementary or surrogate functions? A homemaker or other paid personnel may prove to be a decisive addition to the household (21, 24, 28).

Thus, family therapy can sometimes quite naturally lead to social network, or a kind of kinship network, therapy. Of course there is much more to these broader therapies than can be discussed here. In passing on to other aspects of family therapy, however, we do take special note of the increasing number of times that an apparently remote uncle, aunt, cousin, if not grandparent (even in more singular instances as, for example, the second wife of a divorced father or the husband or parents-in-law of a newly married daughter), are helped to surface and to become firmly helpful complements or surrogates in vulnerably weakened families *as the therapists broaden their perceptions of their actual and potential* psychosocial field.

Aims of family therapy

The ultimate aim in family therapy is no different from the goal of all therapies and helping processes, that is, to improve the lot (better social functioning, restore equilibrium, strengthen adaptation, etc.) of individual persons. To achieve this goal, the family therapist tries to take full cognizance of the connective tissue binding the individual's and his family's destinies, the powerful linkages among the subsystems (individuals, pairs, triads, etc.) and between them and the family as a whole. Thus, he may make (as the case may be) (1) his only, (2) his principal, or (3) his auxiliary goal an alteration in the family interactive pattern, having formulated and continuously reformulated the strands of reverberation between the family patterns and the individual members' predicaments and growth needs. So it is not inaccurate to refer to goals for the family in therapy; they are proximate goals, their raison d'être, selection, and achievement measured also by the degree of their congruence with goals for the individual family members.

Family "interaction" is not intended to refer simply to overt acts or message transmissions; it also implies states of being, the sheer interdependent existence of persons whose bonds are biological, psychological, social, and cultural. Interaction is subliminal as well as palpable; in fact, most of the interaction in a family is, like an iceberg, below the water line of awareness. By no means does this mean that the aware family strivings, conflicts, struggles, and unions are slight and discountable—they need, however, to be comprehended by the therapist both as real in themselves and as symbols or indices of much else that is less perceived, and certainly not formulated, of essential processes and events in the life of the family. The network of these elements is almost infinite for any family. Thus it is grandiose to aim at "cure" or "reorganization" of the family interaction. The therapist must have focused on some threads of family interaction that are reciprocally linked etiologically or in reinforcement to the dysfunction or symptomatic picture of individuals or couples and that are within the compass of achievable therapeutic change. These changes become the therapeutic goal—imprecise, approximate, and tentative, as all goals in human change processes must be. There are, of course, degrees of particularism and thoroughness that are possible for a therapist to achieve in diagnosing and treating a family, but a great mass of unpredictability accompanies the most expert delineations. The major reparative changes are always in the family's "hands," and the therapist's role is largely to trigger these changes. To discharge this important purpose, the therapist needs both to respect fully the homeostatic surges toward health and functioning and to appraise areas of needed and *possible* change, as well as the potential, and limits to the potential, for change.

What may seem, when stated, as modest goals can have far-reaching reverberations in the experience of the family and each member. Husbands and wives, for example, who have sexual or gender roles that are fairly firmly fixed cannot be expected to achieve—with or without therapy—a metamorphosis of their individual characters or of their union. But we have seen far-reaching ripple effects for them and their endangered children as the polarized prototypes of male-female values in the family are even slightly modified—for instance, with evocation of the latent hunger for tenderness in the apparently crusty or tomboyish woman and an effective challenge to the man to dare even tentatively to flex his moral muscles.

Or in the family that is beset by unending debate and conflict, with the children in open conflict with other adults in school and elsewhere, the wellsprings of discord may be perceived by the therapist to tap so deeply irreplaceable emotional deficits in the parents, that the goal becomes not the end of contention, but the shared commitment by all to stay together for better or worse, resulting, in turn, in a partial dissolution of the terror of abandonment that had been a constant companion of parents and children alike, and the general acceptance of "family healer" or partially supportive roles for one or several children.

Or in other families the therapeutic purpose might be, as already described, to modify their structure psychosocially if not physically by stimulating latent ties of potentially supportive kin or by bringing in vital additions or, contrarily, to separate out an overbearing, strength-sapping or otherwise destructive grandparent or in-law, and so forth.

A literature has grown up around the concepts of precipitating factors in the disequilibrium of families and the goal of therapy at reequilibration, requiring an appraisal of the precipitants, their dynamic impact, and the reparative needs (14, 32). These concepts are especially to be found in the literature on crisis intervention (26), but their impact is not confined to crisis interventive work alone. They have generic usefulness, and particular applicability to family work. The eddying effect of an upset to the equilibrium in a family—resulting, let us say, from as specific and concrete a trauma as father's loss of job or the remarriage of a grandparent—can permeate much of the circuitry of family process and of individual well-being without any awareness by anyone in the family of the cause-effect linkages, the chain of reactions can be so rapid and extensive.

The reparative efforts that are limited to replacement of the precipitant—a job, a surrogate grandparent, or whatever—may not be enough in themselves. Too much tissue may have been lacerated for so simple a remedy but, on the other hand, even less may be achieved by efforts to treat that overlook the precipitants to emphasize the loss of equilibrium, even though the therapy is "intensive" and aimed at uncovering "deep" developmental fixations and conflicts.

In parallel fashion, efforts at treating individual dysfunctions may fail entirely because insufficient weighting was given the counterthrusts of family systems or subsystems that serve as stubborn reinforcements of the individual dysfunction. The reinforcing layer of family process and the precipitants to loss of equilibrium may need to be dealt with first, or at least simultaneously with whatever other interventions may be part of the therapeutic effort. Otherwise the therapist can, unaware, be tampering with a system, with the unwitting result of quickening its defense against change and further locking the family members into their skewed role patterns, dysfunction and all.

Intervention in, and modification of, the family interaction may be all that is needed from formal therapy to liberate further natural reparative, reequilibrating, and adaptive forces and to set in motion an auspicious cycle that goes quite beyond the direct therapeutic process in extent and time. Thus, the goal in family therapy can be limited to the mere "dent" or even shift made in the part of the family role organization that has been appraised as linked with the dysfunction, and this can be quite enough of a goal. Or, in some instances, the modification of family behavior may still require therapeutic sequelae, such as further individual help for a member. However, in the event that more treatment is called for, the family interaction, being altered, may be more an ally to the individual's further growth than the inhibiting force it had previously been.

Indications and contraindications to family therapy

In a period of hardly more than fifteen years, a number of efforts have appeared in the literature, empirically based, listing positive and negative indications for family therapy (10, 15, 32, 39). In every instance, these premises, sometimes offered with conviction and conclusiveness, have had later to be revised or jettisoned as more clinical evidence became available. A good example of this is in the writer's own experience: his earliest premise that family therapy or family session were contraindicated for certain kinds of nonverbal acting-out families was, with later experience, completely reversed, family sessions emerging as a modality of *choice* for these families. The difference over time no doubt lay not only in a changing ideology, but, with experience, in the author's growing self-confidence and strength in exercising therapeutic control over the anarchy and ever present latent violence that threaten to burst out in these families. The alteration in the therapist's mood could help to set up quite a different total interactive pattern and thus a different family response, the chain of experiences having the consequence that a type of family previously considered not only untreatable but unmanageable in family sessions, could now be viewed as requiring them.

The lesson in this is that in family therapy, as is especially true for all enterprises that are formative and in swaddling clothes, there are far too many variables unassessed and not empirically validated to arrive at hard, fast conclusions. The range of experience and convictions of those practicing family therapy has far too wide a scatter. This fact alone militates against conclusions or contraindications, as the role and impact of the therapist are all too determinative. Similarly, the ideological differences weigh heavily in the balance. Obviously, a family therapist who relies primarily on lexical communication will tend to find contraindications to seeing conjointly a young family with several young children. The therapist who usually actively enters the family interaction will have a very different pecking order from that of the more detached therapist as to which families he can or should work with conjointly and which not. All meet and proper, but neither can serve as generalizations for the field as a whole.

Examples of contraindications for family therapy or family sessions that we encounter in the literature are: (1) almost complete "absence" of a sense of family ties or of affectional supports; (2) severe paranoia of a family member; or (3) "impenetrable" hostility or "overwhelming" personal narcissistic needs of a family member. These, as most, "criteria" that we encounter are obviously not absolute and are usually best established in family sessions by the particular therapist. In other words, rather than generally accepted *a priori* contraindications, choice of family therapy may in a nutshell depend on a *particular* therapist's decision (often with a liberal assist from the family) *out of his experience in attempts* at family sessions with a particular family. The writer has too many times witnessed the radical difference in workability of a family as a unit when a second therapist has entered the therapy process, either by virtue of a difference in this therapist's approach, role, or even sheer personality. Above all, the field of family therapy is far too "young" for anything so inhibiting as generalizations on contraindications.

In conclusion: family therapy *as an orientation* (i.e., the holistic inclusiveness in diagnostic appraisal and in treatment of the relational aspect of behavior, of the potency of what happens between as within people in families, and between families and society) is *always* valid, because it is close to nature (35). This orientation must underlie all therapies, whatever the modality. Whole family or part family sessions are a central and powerful *mode* for family therapists—not possible or desirable all the time or for all families, but at this stage of development of the field of family therapy, the preferred way of determining contraindications is not *a priori*, by some handed-down criteria, but by the experience of an attempted initial convening of the whole family in therapy session, a near replication of how they are living naturally (17).

Present and future perspectives

Family therapy is in the stage of differentiation not uncommon to all developmental processes. It is better that there be so many "schools of thought" and differences in practice and that both zealots and eclectics have their day, rather than for some unnatural or forced synthesis to be imposed at this time. One can be confident that there will be, with time, more commonalities as well as emergents that will flow naturally from the dynamic interplay of creative thinking, extensive practice, and research.

One important direction for the future is that of the development of a typology of disabling family conditions, not a static diagnostic classification but one that is dynamically associated with therapy. Some of the attempts that have already been made at classification are worthwhile beginnings (3, 15, 27, 32, 40), but their limitation is that the referents for the family typology are individual typologies. The differentiation of classes, or types, of families employs "variables" borrowed from classifications of individuals (whether in some instances psychiatric variables, in another social situational variables, etc.). The wholeness of the family identity is not captured.

Thus, the rubric, "acting-out family" is a family that is being described simply by the behavior of each or several of its members, not in its wholeness. A "chaotic family" changes the nomenclature, but is still more indicative of individual members' behavior than it is of the warp and woof of the family unit. There is also little in these categories that is suggestive of the treatment course to follow. It is not clear now, whether the diagnostic classificatory system of the future will be syndromal or functional—or some transcendent form of structuralism—but if and when it is taken to the bosom of practicing family therapists, it will have been because of its relevance to and enhancement of clinical work.

There are dissidents in all of the helping professions who are "against" diagnosis and "labeling," but it seems evident that their objections are to the vulgarization and stereotypy of diagnostic typologies. If all diagnostic classification systems were hypothetically excommunicated by edict, there would still have to be "shorthand" ways of recognizing and exchanging information about generalizations and extrapolations from hard data.

The family processes named and discussed earlier may be some of the components that will enter into the formulations of types. These processes are on the molecular, typologies on the molar, level of a systematic diagnostic scheme.

Any diagnostic scheme worth its salt will need both to be turned inward, to the family psychosocial interior, and outward, to the family's relationships to other families, social institutions, communities, and so forth. As little as family clinicians can encompass of the internal processes of families, it is far more than they know *and can work with* of the families' external hookups. At this point of the psychological-societal spectrum, at the interface of family to community, there can be enlightenment shed simultaneously from two directions: by family clinicians "anchored" within the individual family and looking outward to community and society, and by social scientists whose perspective starts with the community and looks toward the idiosyncratic family. The family may yet prove to be the keystone for a true unitary psychosocial construct of behavior (3, p. 20).

References

1. Ackerman, Nathan W. *The Psychodynamics of Family Life.* New York: Basic Books, 1958.
2. Ackerman, N., Frances L. Beatman, and Sanford N. Sherman (eds.) *Exploring the Base for Family Therapy.* New York: Family Service Association, 1961.
3. ——, ——, and ——. *Expanding Theory and Practice of Family Therapy.* New York: Family Service Association, 1967.
4. Aponte, H. and L. Hoffman. "The Open Door: A Structural Approach to a Family with an Anorectic Child," *Family Process,* 12:1-44, 1973.
5. Bateson, Gregory. "Schizophrenic Distortion and Communication," in Carl Whitaker (ed.) *Psychotherapy of Chronic Schizophrenic Patients.* Boston: Little, Brown, 1958.
6. Beatman, Frances L. "Intergenerational Aspects of Family Therapy," in *Expanding Theory and Practice of Family Therapy, op. cit.*
7. Bell, John. *Family Group Therapy,* U.S. Public Health Service Monograph, No. 24. Washington, D.C.: U.S. Government Printing Office, 1961.
8. Bell, Norman W. and Ezra F. Vogel (eds.) *A Modern Introduction to the Family.* Glencoe, Ill.: Free Press, 1960.
9. Birdwhistell, R. *Essays on Body Motion Communication.* Philadelphia: University of Pennsylvania Press, 1970.
10. Boszormenyi-Nagy, Ivan and James L. Framo (eds.) *Intensive Family Therapy.* New York: Harper and Row, 1965.
11. Boszormenyi-Nagy, Ivan. "Communication Versus Internal Programming of Relational Attitudes," in *Expanding Theory and Practice of Family Therapy, op. cit.*

12. Coser, Rose L. (ed.) *The Family: Its Structure and Functions.* New York: St. Martin's Press, 1964.
13. Goode, William J. *The Family.* Englewood Cliffs, N.J.: Prentice-Hall, 1964.
14. Green, Sidney L. and Jeanette Regensburg. "Casework Diagnosis of Marital Problems," in Victor W. Eisenstein (ed.) *Neurotic Interaction in Marriage.* New York: Basic Books, 1956.
15. Group for the Advancement of Psychiatry. *The Field of Family Therapy.* New York: GAP, 1970.
16. Haley, Jay. "Approaches to Family Therapy," *International Journal of Psychiatry,* 9:233-242, 1970.
17. ———. "Family Therapy," in Clifford J. Sager and Helen S. Kaplan (eds.) *Progress in Group and Family Therapy.* New York: Brunner/Mazel, 1972.
18. Jackson, Don D. (ed.) *Communication, Family, and Marriage,* Vols. 1 and 2. Palo Alto, Calif.: Science and Behavior Books, 1967.
19. ———, and Irving Yalom. "Family Homeostasis and Patient Change," in Jules Masserman (ed.) *Current Psychiatric Therapies.* New York: Grune and Stratton, 1964.
20. Josselyn, Irene M. "The Family as a Psychological Unit," *Social Casework,* October, 1953.
21. King, Charles H. "Family Therapy with the Deprived Family," *Social Casework,* April, 1967.
22. Leader, Arthur. "Family Therapy for Divorced Fathers and Others Out of the Home," *Social Casework,* January, 1973.
23. Levenson, Edgar A. *The Fallacy of Understanding.* New York: Basic Books, 1972.
24. Minuchin, S. "Family Therapy: Theory or Technique?", in J. Masserman (ed.) *Science and Psychoanalysis,* Vol. 14. New York: Grune and Stratton, 1969.
25. Mitchell, Celia B. "The Therapeutic Field in the Treatment of Families in Conflict," in *New Directions in Public Health.* New York: Grune and Stratton, 1968.
26. Parad, Howard J. (ed.) *Crisis Intervention: Selected Readings.* New York: Family Service Association of America, 1958.
27. Pollak, Otto. "Developmental Difficulties and the Family System," in Otto Pollak and Alfred Friedman (eds.) *Family Dynamics and Female Sexual Delinquency.* Palo Alto, Calif.: Science and Behavior Books, 1969.
28. Rabinowitz, Clara. "Therapy for Underprivileged Delinquent Families," in *Family Dynamics and Female Sexual Delinquency, op. cit.*
29. Satir, Virginia M. *Conjoint Family Therapy,* rev. ed., Palo Alto, Calif.: Science and Behavior Books, 1967.
30. Scheflen, Albert E. *Body Language and the Social Order.* Englewood Cliffs, N.J.: Prentice-Hall, 1972.
31. Scherz, Frances H. "Theory and Practice of Family Therapy," in Robert W. Roberts and Robert H. Nee (eds.) *Theories of Social Casework.* Chicago: University of Chicago Press, 1970.
32. ———. "Family Treatment Concepts," *Social Casework,* April, 1966.
33. Schulman, Gerda and Elsa Leichter. "The Prevention of Family Breakup," *Social Casework,* March, 1968.

34. Sherman, Sanford N. "The Concept of the Family in Casework Theory," in *Exploring the Base for Family Therapy, op. cit.*

35. ———, "The Sociological Character of Family Treatment," *Social Casework,* April, 1964.

36. ———. "Family Treatment: An Approach to Children's Problems," *Social Casework,* June, 1966.

37. ———. "Intergenerational Discontinuity and Therapy of the Family," *Social Casework,* April, 1967.

38. ———. "Relevance of Family Interviewing for Psychoanalysis," *Contemporary Psychoanalysis,* January, 1971.

39. Stein, Joan W. *The Family as a Unit of Study and Treatment.* Seattle: University of Washington School of Social Work, 1970.

40. Vorland, Alice L. et al. *Family Casework Diagnosis.* New York: Columbia University Press, 1962.

41. Wynne, Lyman. "The Study of Intrafamilial Alignments and Splits in Exploratory Family Therapy," in *Exploring the Base for Family Therapy, op. cit.*

42. ——— et al. "Pseudo Mutuality in the Family Relationships of Schizophrenics," *Psychiatry,* May, 1958.

43. ———. "Some Indications and Contra-Indications for Exploratory Family Therapy," in *Intensive Family Therapy, op. cit.*

44. Zuk, Gerald H. and Ivan Boszormenyi-Nagy. *Family Therapy and Disturbed Families.* Palo Alto, Calif.: Science and Behavior Books, 1967.

Annotated listing of key references

ACKERMAN, Nathan W. *The Psychodynamics of Family Life.* New York: Basic Books, 1958.

If there is a basic "text" on family therapy, in thoroughness and in its integration of contributions from the behavioral and social sciences, coming chronologically early in the development of family therapy, it is this book. Even those who are at the farthest extreme reaches of the range of orientations to family therapy define their thinking in terms of its borrowing as well as its differentiation from Nathan Ackerman's work.

BOSZORMENYI–NAGY, Ivan and James L. Framo (eds.) *Intensive Family Therapy.* New York: Harper and Row, 1965.

This compendium has a wealth of contributions from a variety of authors, all in one form or another integrational of psychodynamic as well as social theories. It contains the best historical view of the development of family therapy as well as chapters by Boszormenyi-Nagy, Searles, and others that add depth to the perspective on family therapy.

BOSZORMENYI–NAGY, Ivan and Geraldine M. Spark. *Invisible Loyalties.* Hagerstown, Md.: Harper and Row, 1973.

This work comes closest to capturing that ineffable bond that makes families rather than mere groups of individuals—a bond one clinical lexicon does not touch.

GROUP for the Advancement of Psychiatry. *The Field of Family Therapy.* New York: GAP, 1970.

This work comes the closest to an objective survey of theories and practices in family therapy: an objective perspective that tries to report rather than advocate and which has polled family therapists of different persuasions, disciplines, and geographical locations for what their actual principles and practices are today.

MINUCHIN, Salvador. *Families and Family Therapy.* Cambridge, Mass.: Harvard University Press, 1974.

Dr. Minuchin's ideas about structured family therapy are compelling, particularly for social workers whose training and experience center on the social functioning of their clients.

SATIR, Virginia M. *Conjoint Family Therapy.* Palo Alto, Calif.: Science and Behavior Books, 1964.

Mrs. Satir is far and away the widest traveled and most active expositor of family therapy concepts, as well as demonstrator of methods directly to professional groups. She has been the most influential social worker with social workers. Her work and Ackerman's, above, are very different but important complements of a whole perspective on family therapy today.

STIERLIN, Helm, M.D. *Psychoanalysis and Family Therapy.* New York: Aronson, 1977.

Dr. Stierlin posits a psychoanalytically oriented model of family therapy. As he puts it, to truly reconcile psychoanalysis (read:

individual psychotherapies) and family therapy, "we have to take into account that family theory implies a system rather than an individual (or at best a dyadic) approach, that observable transactions often have primacy over inferable intrapsychic processes, and that therapeutic activism may be more effective than a passive furtherance of insight."

19

Task-Centered Treatment

by

WILLIAM J. REID

Task-centered treatment evolved from a model of brief, time-limited casework tested in the mid-sixties at the Community Service Society of New York. The results of this test suggested that brief psychosocial casework might provide a more efficient means of helping individuals and families with problems in family relations than conventional, long-term forms of psychosocial practice (24). Using that brief service approach as a starting point the author, in collaboration with Laura Epstein, attempted to develop a more comprehensive, systematic, and effective model of short-term treatment (23). In its initial conception the task-centered approach utilized the time-limited structure and techniques of short-term psychosocial casework as a means of helping clients devise and carry out actions or tasks to alleviate their problems. Perlman's view of casework as a problem-solving process (17, 18) and Studt's (31) notion of the client's task as a focus of service were particularly influential in this beginning formulation.

During the past decade, there has been a continuing research effort to refine, expand, and improve this system of practice. A good deal of this work has been conducted at the School of Social Service Administration, the University of Chicago, in conjunction with the education of graduate social work students. As a part of their training in task-centered treatment, students have applied the model to more than one thousand cases in school, psychiatric, and other settings. A smaller number of these cases (two hundred) has been part of formal research projects, including controlled experiments, in which systematic data have been collected on treatment processes and outcomes (19, 20, 22, 23). Additional projects relating to aspects of the model have been conducted by doctoral students at the school (5, 7, 25).

In addition, contributions to the theoretical and empirical foundations of the model have been made by social work practitioners, researchers, and educators through numerous projects in this country and abroad. These undertakings, usually carried out in consultation with the author and his colleagues but in some cases done independently, have ranged from clinical trials of the model with a small number of cases to large-scale implementations of the approach in state public welfare agencies (4, 27). Finally, insights gained from formal tests of the model or through its application under ordinary practice conditions have been combined with knowledge emerging from the social sciences and from developments in related treatment approaches.

As a result of these efforts, the task-centered system has continued to grow and change. This is as it should be. In fact, our intent was to create an approach to practice that would keep evolving in response to continuing research, and to developments in knowledge and technology consonant with its basic principles. Generally, modifications have been in the form of extensions and elaborations of the original formulation: the more significant include the development of interventions related to task planning and implementation; the incorporation of compatible behavioral techniques; the creation of adaptions of the model for conjoint work with families and with formed groups; and the restructuring and enlargement of its theoretical framework. Some of these developments have been reported on separately. All of them appear as part of a recent reformulation of the task-centered system as a whole (21).

In this chapter a review of the task-centered system of practice will be presented. The review will encompass the major theoretical formulations that underlie the treatment model; the treatment model itself, that is, the strategy and methods that guide work with clients; and research evidence relating to the efficacy of the treatment model. The chapter will conclude with a brief consideration of the range of application of task-centered treatment.

Theoretical foundations

Both our initial and subsequent theoretical work have been based on the premise that the essential function of task-centered treatment is to help clients move forward with solutions to psychosocial problems that they define and hope to solve. The primary agent of change is not the social worker, but the client. The worker's role is to help the client bring about changes that the client wishes and for which he is willing to work.

The initial theoretical base of the model consisted largely of formulations concerning the nature, origins, and duration of psychosocial problems so conceived. A problem classification was devised in which the range of difficulties considered to be targets of the model was defined. Problems in family and interpersonal relations, in carrying out social roles, in effecting social transitions, in securing resources, and emotional distress reactive to situational factors constituted the major categories. We suggested that these problems generally reflected temporary breakdowns in problem coping that set in motion forces for change. These forces, principally the client's own motivation to alleviate his distress, operate rapidly in most cases to reduce the problem to a tolerance level, at which point the possibility of further change lessens. If so, clients might be expected to benefit as much from short-term treatment as from more extended periods of service. Placing time limits on the brief service might be expected to enhance effectiveness by mobilizing efforts of both practitioner and client. Effectiveness would be further augmented by concentrated attention on delimited problems in which practitioners would help clients formulate and carry out problem-solving actions.

The planned brevity of the model was then based on the proposition that effectiveness of interpersonal treatment is relatively short-lived—that is, that the most benefit clients will derive from such treatment will be derived within a relatively few sessions and a relatively brief period of time. The proposition has been supported by a large amount of research evidence that suggests the following: (1) recipients of brief, time-limited treatment show at least as much durable improvement as recipients of long-term, open-ended treatment (3, 6, 12, 13, 24); (2) most of the improvement associated with long-term treatment occurs relatively soon after treatment has begun (14, 30); (3) regardless of their intended length, most courses of voluntary treatment turn out to be relatively brief—the great majority of such treatment courses probably last no longer than a dozen sessions or a three-month time span—a generalization which suggests that most people may exhaust the benefits of treatment rather quickly (2, 8,); (4) finally, the modest evidence we have from controlled studies which suggests that interpersonal treatment as a whole can be effective rests largely on studies of relatively brief treatment programs—those of six months or less duration; that is, the typical study showing that clients or patients receiving treatment did better than those in no treatment groups is a study of a relatively brief program (14, 28).

This theoretical base has been considerably enlarged by the development of formulations for understanding the nature and dynamics of psychosocial problems and the role of human action in their alleviation. These formulations, which have been inspired by the work of Goldman, a philosopher, will be summarized (11).

It is assumed that such psychosocial problems are always the expression of something the client wants that he does not have, whether he desires something as concrete and humble as a warm coat or as complex and elegant as self-actualization. The usual and most effective way to obtain what one wants is to take action to get it. Since the client is a human being, his action is guided by a sophisticated set of beliefs about himself and his world, beliefs that help him form and implement plans about what he should do and how he should do it. Since his problem is psychosocial, his plans and actions will usually involve others—the individuals, groups, and organizations that make up his social system. These actions, in turn, will be shaped by his evaluation of the responses of this system.

This theory does not attempt to deal with remote or historical origins of a problem, but rather with those factors that are currently causing it. Attention is further focused on those factors that the client or practitioner can act to change. These factors become, in effect, obstacles to problem resolution that can be modified through the collaborative efforts of client and practitioner. Such obstacles are found in the same matrix of forces that bring about problem resolution—in the client's actions, beliefs, and social system. Dysfunctional patterns of action and belief and deficient or uncooperative social systems provide the usual barriers to problem alleviation. In this view, problems are created by the same elements through which they are solved. Both problem causation and remediation can then be understood in terms of a common set of concepts.

These formulations, more than some others that guide social work practice, stress man's autonomous problem-solving capacities—his ability to initiate and carry through intelligent action to obtain what he wants. In this conception, man is seen as less a prisoner of unconscious drives than he is in the theories of the psychoanalyst and less a prisoner of enironmental contingencies than he is in the views of the behaviorist. Rather, he is viewed as having a mind and a will of his own that are reactive but not subordinate to internal and external influences. We think those human problem-solving capacities—complex, ingenious, and, in the main, quite effective—deserve more prominence than they have received in theories of helping. We have tried to build our theory accordingly.

The treatment model

The basic strategy and selected methods of the task-centered model will be presented as they are used in work with individual clients—the usual form of the application of the model to date. Adaptations for conjoint and group treatment will then be taken up.

Strategy

Guided by the foregoing theory, the practitioner helps the client identify specific problems that arise from unrealized wants, and that are defined in terms of specific conditions to be changed. Work proceeds within the structure of contracts in which the client's problems and goals, and the nature and duration of service are explicitly stated and agreed on by both practitioner and client. Analysis of a problem leads to consideration of the kinds of actions needed to solve it, what might facilitate those actions, and obstacles standing in the way of their implementation.

Change is effected primarily through problem-solving actions or tasks that the client and practitioner undertake outside the interview. The practitioner helps the client select tasks to realize his wants. He facilitates task work through assisting the client in planning task implementation and establishing his motivation for carrying out the plan. He helps him rehearse and practice the task and analyze obstacles to its achievement. Reviews of the client's accomplishments on each task allow the practitioner to provide corrective feedback on the client's actions and serve as the basis for developing new tasks.

To supplement the client's problem-solving efforts, the practitioner may carry out tasks within the client's social system. These tasks are usually designed to assist others in facilitating the client's task or to secure resources from the system that the client cannot readily obtain on his own. Although a client's problem may be resolved exclusively through practitioner tasks, the theory and methodology of the system are obviously oriented toward problems in which at least some client initiative is indicated and will be of most value when such problems are at issue.

The central and distinctive strategy of the present system is found in its reliance upon tasks as a means of problem resolution. The client's and the practitioner's efforts are devoted primarily to the construction, implementation, and review of tasks. The success of these tasks largely determines whatever benefit results from application of the model.

The stress on tasks is an attempt to build upon the considerable capacity of human beings to take constructive action in response to difficulty. In effect, we have modeled our intervention strategy after the way most people resolve most of their problems—by doing something about them.

To be sure, the problems brought to the attention of social workers have usually not yielded to the client's problem-solving initiatives. Nevertheless, we assume that a capacity for problem-solving action is present. It is the social worker's responsibility to help the client put this capacity to work.

The strategy that we advocate leads to a parsimonious form of intervention that respects the client's right to manage his own affairs. If the client is clear about what is troubling him and has a reasonable plan for resolving the difficulty, the practitioner's role may be limited largely to providing encouragement and structure for the client's problem-solving efforts. If more is needed, more is supplied, to the extent necessary to help the client resolve his difficulties. Even when the practitioner's involvement is great, his purpose is to develop and augment the client's own actions. Thus the practitioner may need to help the client determine what he wants, and in the process may need to challenge wants that are unrealizable. He may need to help the client identify and modify action and interaction sequences contributing to the difficulty, to provide corrective feedback on the client's action, to teach him necessary skills, to work with him to alter beliefs that are interfering with problem solving, to bring about changes in the social system and to secure resources from it, and even to suggest specific tasks for him to carry out. But whatever is done is done collaboratively and leads to actions that must be agreed to by the client. The decisive actions in most cases are those that the client himself performs in his own way and on his own behalf.

Enabling the client to take constructive and responsible action in his own interest has an important corollary: the action so taken is likely to be incorporated as part of his strategy for continued coping with the problem. Since he has participated in its planning, has an understanding of its rationale, agreed to carry it out, actually implemented it and reviewed its results, one can assume that the action is more a part of him and, if successful, is more likely to be used again with appropriate variations, than if he were simply following the practitioner's instructions or unwittingly responding to contingencies arranged by others.

While the distinctive strategy of the model flows from its task structure, other elements are needed if the approach is to work successfully. Two merit discussion at this point: the practitioner-client relationship and the social agency.

The relationship between the practitioner and client provides a means of stimulating and promoting problem-solving action. Their sessions together do not provide the essential ingredients of change; rather, they serve to set in motion and guide subsequent actions through which change will be effected. It is assumed, nevertheless, that this purpose will be facilitated through a relationship in which the client feels accepted, respected, liked, and understood. This kind of relationship is considered fundamental in most forms of interpersonal practice, although it has been difficult to define and measure the various qualities it is supposed to contain. Perhaps the most promising work in this regard has consisted of efforts to isolate and study what have been called the "core conditions" of an optimal therapeutic relationship: empathy, nonpossessive warmth, and genuineness (34). While research on the core conditions has usually lacked adequate controls and has produced mixed results, the evidence on the whole suggests that these conditions do contribute to successful treatment outcomes (15).

The strategy of the task-centered model calls for the actualization of these conditions within the context of a treatment relationship that is problem focused, task centered, and highly structured. This means that the expression of these conditions must be fitted to the requirements of the model. It is assumed that this fit can be made without unduly sacrificing either these relationship qualities or the essential structure of the treatment program. But in so doing it may not be feasible, or desirable, to push the core conditions to the limits possible in less structured forms of treatment. Thus, the task-centered practitioner may bring a client back to focus on an agreed-upon problem rather than simply responding at a high level of empathy to a tangential communication. Nevertheless, ways can be found, I think, to maintain a reasonably high level of the core conditions and keep at the business of the contract.

Perlman has described a good treatment relationship as containing both support and expectancy (17). Its supportive elements, which assume specific expression in the core conditions, have perhaps been given the greater weight in social work practice theory. Within the task-centered system, the expectations that the practitioner conveys to the client are viewed as a therapeutic force of at least equal importance. The practitioner expects the client to work on agreed-upon problems and tasks and communicates these expectations to the client both explicitly and implicitly. While he respects the client's decision to reject his services, he also holds the client accountable for following through once a contract has been established. These positions are not inconsistent: they both reflect an acceptance of the client as a person who can make responsible decisions. Expectations, if clearly communicated, serve to influence the client's actions, since the client is likely to regard the practitioner as an authority who can be trusted to advance his interest and whose approval is important. The practitioner's reaction, which is likely to be more approving if the client makes an effort to resolve his problem than if he does not, serves to strengthen the force of these expectations. This is as it should be if the practitioner-client relationship is to be used to full advantage on the client's behalf. But if clients are to be helped to resolve problems, qualities of the relationship must be fused with specific problem-solving methods. The relationship provides the raw material but not the finished product.

Behind any social work practice model stands a social agency. The intervention strategy of a model can be seen, in fact, as an expression of the agency's purposes. One often gets the impression from the social treatment literature that the main function of the agency is to provide office space and salary for the practitioner and a sanction for his clinical work. Too little attention has been paid to the agency's contribution to the potency of a treatment approach.

The agency's role in the task-centered approach is twofold. First, it provides a variety of resources, including supervision (particularly for inexperienced workers), staff training programs, and tangible services. Second, the agency confers on the practitioner an "authority of office" critical to the helping process. In order to be helped, a client must be willing to place himself under the influence of a helper. The client must then perceive the practitioner as someone who has the capacity to help him and is worthy of his trust. In well-established professions, like law or medicine, the practitioner relies on the image of his profession to provide this aura of authority and competence. The social worker, whose profession still lacks a clear-cut image, must usually rely on the agency to perform this function. The client is likely to see him as qualified to help, not because he is a social worker, but because he is an employee of an agency. Similarly, the practitioner's agency status exerts more influence than his professional identification with other persons and with organizations in the client's social system.

The immediate purpose of the model is to help the client resolve problems through enabling him to plan and execute necessary problem-solving actions. This objective should be attained in such a way as to provide the client with what might be called a constructive problem-solving experience—that is, an experience that, regardless of the specific problem worked on and the amount of resolution achieved, should hold the client in good stead in his future problem-solving activities.

The experience should benefit the client in two ways. First, his attitude toward potential helpers should be enhanced, so that he will be receptive to using another if the need arises. This result is most likely to be obtained if the practitioner respects what the client himself wants. Should the practitioner think the client is misguided, then he should so inform the client and tell him why he thinks so, rather than trying to impose his own goals in a devious way. In general, the practitioner should present himself as the client's agent. In this role he may counsel the client about his problems, but in the final analysis he should be subservient to the client's informed wishes. In addition, the practitioner needs to demonstrate competence in helping the client define his problem and take action to solve it. It is crucial that he follow through with his part of whatever plans he and the client have developed.

If the social worker can act in this manner, he has, perhaps, done more than help the client with his immediate problem. He has given him the sense that turning to another for help can be a rewarding (or at least not degrading) experience, one that he may wish to repeat in the future.

The second kind of extra benefit should consist in enhancement of the client's ability to alleviate psychosocial problems on his own. I assume that skills in solving personal problems can be learned. Although learning problem-solving skills per se is not the major objective of our model, we expect that the client will be able to apply to other situations what he has learned from his problem-solving experience. In particular, this application should take place with problems similar to those he has dealt with in treatment. The practitioner does certain things to help this process along. During the course of treatment, he makes the various problem-solving steps explicit so that the client can comprehend the logic and process of the approach. He tries to stimulate and utilize the client's own strategies for working on the problem, thus giving him practice in independent problem solving. At the close of treatment, as we shall see, he goes over the client's problem-solving experience in a systematic manner. The client is helped to see how he might apply the methods he has used to problems that may remain or that may arise after treatment.

Practitioner–Client Activities

The central strategy of the model is effected through a series of activities carried out in a collaborative manner by the practitioner and client. Although specific practitioner techniques, such as encouragement, advice giving, role playing, and exploration are important in this process, stress is placed upon the practitioner's and the client's joint problem-solving efforts. The major activities are outlined briefly below.

Problem Specification. Problems are explored and clarified by the social worker and the client in initial interview. As suggested, the focus is on what the client wants and not on what the practitioner thinks the client may need. The practitioner may point out, however, potential difficulties the client has not acknowledged or the consequences that may result if these difficulties are allowed to go unattended. In other words, the target problem is not necessarily defined by what the client says he wants initially, but rather by what he wants after a process of deliberation to which the practitioner contributes his own knowledge and point of view. As a result, the client may alter his conception of his problem or in the case of an "involuntary client" may realize he does have difficulties he may wish to work on. But at the end of this process, normally at the close of the first or second interview, the practitioner and client must come to an explicit agreement on the problems to be dealt with. These problems are de-

fined as discrete, numerable entities and are specified in terms of definite conditions to be changed. The problem is generally summarized in a single sentence (the problem statement) and then specified.

For example, the case of Mrs. N., who was seen concerning difficulties in caring for her two-year-old daughter, Ann, produced the following problem statement and specification.

Problem: Mrs. N. constantly loses her temper with Ann, frequently shouting at her and slapping or shaking her.

Mrs. N. becomes quickly irritated whenever Ann "gets into things," spills food, cries or won't obey. Mrs. N. generally starts shouting at her when these things happen. If Ann then persists in the behavior or starts to cry, Mrs. N. usually will scream at her and then slap her or shake her. During the past week, Mrs. N. lost her temper with Ann on the average of about five times a day and slapped her at least once a day.

As the above example illustrates, problems are spelled out in concrete terms and in language the client can understand. Estimated frequencies of problem occurrence over a specified period add additional precision to the problem description and provide a baseline against which change in the problem can be measured. The problem of most concern to the client normally becomes the primary focus in treatment, although usually more than one problem is defined and worked on. Analysis of the problem is concentrated upon identifying the manipulable causes that are contributing to it. What are the immediate causative factors in the client's beliefs, actions, or environment that we or the client can do something about? We are interested in causal analysis only as a means of arriving at possible solutions.

Contracting. We insist on an oral or written contract in which the client agrees to work with the practitioner on one or more explicitly stated, acknowledged problems. The contract may also include a statement of the client's goals in relation to the problem—that is, what kind of solution of the problem does he want to achieve? The client need not even be highly motivated to solve his problems, but he must at least agree to work on them with us. Once the contract is formed, we try to hold to its terms. We try to avoid the kind of practice in which the client has agreed to see the social worker for one kind of problem but the social worker attempts covertly to treat him for another.

The contract then states at least one problem on which the practitioner and client will begin to work. The contract also includes an estimation of the limits of treatment, usually expressed in terms of an approximate number of sessions and length of time. We normally limit treatment to eight to twelve interviews, weekly or twice weekly, with a one- to three-month time span. The contract is open to renegotiation at any point, to include new problems or longer periods of service, but we insist that this process be carried out explicitly with the client and that his explicit agreement to any revisions be secured.

Task Planning. Once agreement has been reached on the targets and duration of treatment, tasks are formulated and selected in collaboration with the client and their implementation is planned. A task defines what the client is to do to alleviate his problem. The task may be cast in relatively general terms, giving the client a direction for action but no specific program of behavior to follow. We call these general tasks. For example, Mrs. B. is to develop a firmer, more consistent approach to handling her child's behavior; Mr. C. or Mrs. C. is to develop a plan for the care of their mentally retarded daughter. Or a task may be very specific, what we term "operational." Operational tasks call for specific action that the client is to undertake. Mr. A. is to apply for a job at X employment agency within the next week, or Johnny is to volunteer to recite in class on Mon-

day. The push in the model is toward task specificity. Thus, an effort is made to spell out broadly defined tasks in terms of specific operational tasks. In order that a proposed course of action be considered as a task, the client must agree that he will try to carry it out. The client's express commitment to try to achieve the task is crucial.

In some cases the nature of the problem and the client's circumstances may point to a particular course of action, which can then be developed. In others, alternative actions need to be considered and appraised. The process works best if both the practitioner and the client can freely suggest alternatives as they come to mind, without too much consideration initially as to their appropriateness. Research on problem solving indicates that this kind of "brainstorming" is an effective means of devising solutions, perhaps because it stimulates imaginative thinking about a wide range of approaches to a difficulty (16). The best alternatives can then be selected for more serious consideration. In addition to suggesting alternatives, the practitioner tries to encourage the client to generate his own. At this stage, practitioner criticism of particular client proposals is kept to a minimum.

Often the practitioner is the primary generator of alternatives. The client may not be able to produce much on his own. Moreover, the practitioner may have special knowledge about kinds of tasks that generally work well for particular problems. Our research, to date, does not indicate a relationship between who originated the idea for the task and task accomplishment. Tasks initially proposed by practitioners tend to show about the same amount of progress as those suggested by clients. It should be kept in mind, however, that the practitioner proposes *ideas* for tasks that are then gone over with the client. The client's contributions normally become a part of the task plan. He does not "assign" the task to the client.

An agreement between practitioner and client on the client's task—that is, on what he is to do—may occur after alternatives have been sorted out and the best selected. Generally, an agreement at this point concerns the global nature of the client's proposed action, and not the detail, which is developed subsequently. In some cases the practitioner may prefer to explore in some depth the stategies and tactics of carrying out a possible task before reaching agreement on it with the client. This option may be used when extensive planning of a possible task may be necessary before a judgment can be made about its usefulness. In any event, a final agreement on the task is made at the end of the planning process, after it is determined what the execution of the task will involve.

Once an action alternative has been selected for consideration as a task, the practitioner and client work on the plan for its execution. Most tasks involve hierarchies or sequences of operations, or subtasks. A task can be carried out in an endless variety of ways, depending on which operations are selected and how they are ordered and executed. Generally, planning proceeds by breaking down the task into sequences of operations that may be required to carry it out. Suppose the client's proposed task is to look for a job. The question then becomes: How can he proceed to do this? As this question is answered, a number of immediate steps become apparent. He may need to decide what kind of work he wants to look for; he may want to consult the want ads, contact friends or acquaintances who might be able to inform him about job openings, look up employment agencies, make arrangements to visit one, and so on. The question of how to proceed may be meaningful for some of these steps. For example, the client may have a friend who might be able to give him a job. He may want to approach the friend but may be uncertain about how to do so without jeopardizing the friendship. Even tasks that are specific to begin with can profitably be broken down in this manner. A client's task may be to initiate a conversation with a coworker. Whom should he select? What might he say? How? When?

Whatever the level of client action under consideration, the process proceeds until a plan is developed that the client *can begin to execute prior* to his next visit with the social worker. The plan may consist chiefly of a general task (to look for a job) together with one or more operational tasks that he can carry out in the interim (to contact an employment agency). Or it may be built around one or more operational tasks. The plan always contains at least one operational task. In addition, it generally includes some guidelines for the execution of the operational task(s).

Regardless of the form of the plan, the practitioner attempts to make sure it calls for initial actions that the client will be able to carry out. We have found that it is better to err on the side of having the first task be too easy rather than too difficult, since it is important, we think, that the client experience initial success in his work on the problem. There is empirical evidence to support this position. It has been found, for example, that subjects in laboratory experiments will do better on a second task if advised their completion of the first was successful (29). The impression that one has performed successfully can create a sense of mastery and self-confidence that can augment problem-solving efforts. The actual experience of success is perhaps the best way to acquire this impression.

For the plan to work, it is essential that the client emerge with a clear notion of what he is to do. To insure that he does, the practitioner and client go over the plan in summary fashion, normally at the end of the interview. This final wrapup may be preceded by summarization of parts of the plan during the process of its formulation. An important part of this procedure is to elicit from the client the essentials of the plan. The client is asked to present the plan as he sees it. The practitioner can then underscore the essential elements of it or add parts that the client has left out. Summarizing the plan gives the practitioner the opportunity to convey to the client his expectation that it will be carried out and that his efforts will be reviewed. "So you will try to do——. We'll see how it worked out next time we meet."

The same principles are applied to planning of practitioner tasks or to actions that the practitioner will take outside the session in an attempt to bring about desired changes in the client's social system. Although such actions may not be planned in detail with the client, their consideration as tasks not only enables the client to understand and perhaps help shape the worker's environmental interventions but makes the worker accountable, as is the client, for task performance.

Establishing Incentives and Rationale. The worker and client develop a rationale, or purpose for carrying out the task, if it is not already clear. Either the worker or the client might first consider the potential benefit to be gained from completing the task. What good will come of it? The practitioner reinforces the client's perception of realistic benefits, or points out positive consequences that the client may not have perceived.

Analyzing and Resolving Obstacles. After a task is first formulated but not yet attempted, the worker and the client clarify the obstacles—i.e., the problems that may be encountered in carrying out the task. If the client sees none, the practitioner may raise possible problems in the form of likely contingencies. What if this or that happens, how will you handle it? After the task has been attempted but not completed, the actual obstacles encountered are examined. These obstacles may be either psychological or environmental or some combination of both.

The client's beliefs about himself and his world are seen as constituting a major source of psychological obstacles. A client may be unable to initiate a friendship because of his belief that others will reject him. Or he may be unable to undergo a medical examination because of his belief that a fatal illness will be discovered. Efforts are made to resolve psychological obstacles

through bringing to the client's awareness distortions or inaccuracies in the beliefs that influence his actions and through helping him develop more realistic and functional beliefs. In this process use is made of the methods of cognitive treatment (1). Environmental obstacles usually involve actions (or inactions) of individuals or organizations that are a part of the client's social system. Thus, a mother who wants her child returned from foster care may be thwarted in her task of fixing up her apartment by an uncooperative landlord and an inefficient welfare department. The practitioner and client attempt to clarify ways in which such obstacles are interfering with task achievement. The result may be development of client or practitioner tasks addressed to removing the obstacle or revision of the original task.

Simulation and Guided Practice. The practitioner may model possible task behavior or ask the client to rehearse what he is going to say or do. Modeling and rehearsal may be carried out through role play, where appropriate. For example, if the client's task was to speak up in a group, the practitioner may take the role of group leader and the client could rehearse what he might say if called on. Or the roles could be reversed, with the worker modeling what the client might say. Guided practice is the performance of the actual (as opposed to simulated) task behavior by the client during the interview; thus, a child may practice reading or a marital pair more constructive forms of communication, with the worker taking a coaching or teaching role. Guided practice can also be extended to real-life situations. For example, a practitioner might accompany a client (with a fear of going to doctors) to a medical clinic.

Task Review. The client's progress on his tasks is routinely reviewed at the beginning of each session. The review covers what the client has and has not accomplished, and what he has tried to do. Practitioner tasks are reviewed in a similar manner. What the practitioner does next depends on the results of the task review. If the task has been substantially accomplished or completed, he may formulate another task with the client on the same problem or a different problem. If the task has not been carried out or only partially achieved, the practitioner and client may take up obstacles, devise a different plan for carrying out the task, or apply other task implementation activities. The task itself may be revised or replaced by another.

Terminating. The process of terminating is begun in the initial phase when the duration of treatment is set. In the last interview, the practitioner and the client review progress on his problems. The client is helped to plan how he will continue work on his tasks or to develop new ones that he might undertake on his own. What the client has achieved is given particular stress. Extensions beyond agreed-upon limits are normally made if the client requests additional service. Extensions, which usually involve a small number of additional sessions, occur in only a minority of cases, less that 20 percent in most settings.

Work with Families and Formed Groups

The strategy that has been outlined for treatment of the individual client is applied, with certain modifications, to work with clients in groups. Specific adaptations have been developed for two types of groups: families (or individuals who live together) and groups assembled expressly for the purpose of helping members work on individual problems.

With respect to treatment of families or family equivalents, our position has been that problems involving the interaction among family members are most effectively addressed through conjoint sessions with the family members involved in the problem. Since the target of intervention is an interacting system, it makes sense to work with the system as a unit. In so doing, it has proved helpful to supplement our

theoretical framework with concepts drawn from theories of family interaction (35). In general, relational problems usually presented by family members are viewed as expressions of patterns or rules of interaction that at least one family member has found undesirable. These unwanted rules appear to be deviations from general norms, or metarules, that govern family life. Thus, departures from the metarule of reciprocity, or giving value for value received, is assumed to be of central importance in marital discord; conflicts between parents and children tend to represent breakdowns of metarules concerning parental authority. These notions suggest a strategy of helping family members resolve problems through tasks designed to bring about better fits between their actual interactions and their conceptions of the norms of family life.

At a technical level, the model follows roughly the same sequence of steps as in work with the individual client: problems acknowledged by the clients are specified and problem-solving tasks are formulated, planned, carried out, and reviewed. Differences result from the interactive nature of the problems and tasks. Thus, emphasis is placed upon helping clients define problems in common or interactive terms ("Mr. and Mrs. J. cannot agree on how to discipline their son"). Use is made of shared tasks in which two or more family members cooperate on the same task (Mr. and Mrs. S. will take the children to the beach on Saturday) and reciprocal tasks in which family members carry out different tasks in quid pro quo fashion (Mr. C. will not drive over 55 miles per hour on the C.s' weekend trip; Mrs. C. will refrain from criticizing Mr. C.'s driving the trip). Since family members are seen together, tasks involving communication and decision making may be practiced within the session with the practitioner taking on a coaching role (32).

Thus far, applications of the model in treatment of problems of family relationships have been limited largely to marital and parent-child dyads. One reason has been the dearth of intact families among the populations served in most task-centered projects. Another has been the model's focus on relatively specific problems of interaction as perceived by family members, rather than on more general interactional difficulties are perceived by the practitioner.

The principles of conjoint treatment that have been presented can be applied to any situation in which target problems involve interaction of members of natural groups—that is, groups that have a life apart from the treatment session. Somewhat different principles apply when clients are treated for individual problems within the context of a formed group—that is, a group created to help individuals with their own concerns. The ultimate change target against which success is measured is not interaction of group members outside the session but, rather, resolution of the separate problems of each. Within the task-centered framework, the term "group treatment" is used to describe this form of intervention. The strategies and methods of task-centered group treatment have been presented elsewhere in detail (9, 10, 25).

In task-centered group treatment, the group process is used to further the basic activities of the model. Group members, guided by the leader, help one another to specify problems, plans tasks, rehearse and practice behavior, analyze obstacles to task achievement, review task progress, and so on. The leader's role is to make effective use of this process through orchestrating his own interventions with the contributions of the members.

In order that the contribution of members can be used to best advantage, groups are made relatively homogeneous in respect to target problems. Thus, a group may be formed around problems of academic achievement or posthospitalization adjustment. As a result, group members have firsthand knowledge of the kind of problems that others are experiencing and are thus in a good position to provide support and guidance. Moreover, members can more readily apply lessons learned from the task work of others to their own situations.

While it does not permit the kind of sustained, focused attention on individual problems and tasks possible in one-to-one treatment, the group mode has certain distinct advantages. Group members in the aggregate may possess more detailed knowledge than the leader about intricacies of the target problems. Given this experiential knowledge base, the group can often suggest task possibilities that may not have occurred to either the leader or the member being helped at the moment. Gaining recognition from a group provides an incentive for task accomplishment not available in individual treatment; in particular, a member who carries out a task successfully can serve as a model to others. These advantages are not always realized, however. Groups may become unfocused and discordant. Members may become competitive and overly critical. Certain participants may become objects of group hostility—the well-known "scapegoating" phenomenon. In order to exploit the potentials of this medium and to avoid its pitfalls, the group leader needs to exert a constructive influence on the dynamics of the group. The purpose of the group—generally, to help individual members with their target problems—needs to be clarified and kept in view. The communications of the participants must be channeled in relation to this purpose.

Beliefs that members have about one another and about appropriate behavior in the group influence the sociometric and normative structures of the group. The practitioner attempts to encourage beliefs that are functional for the group's purpose: for example, that each participant is a worthwhile person who deserves help in working out his problems; that each has to find a solution that is right for him; that each has a right to his fair share of attention and assistance from the leader and the group. Shared beliefs about how the group should conduct itself become the basis for group control of the behavior of its members. The practitioner attempts to foster group control efforts that will maintain focus on problems and tasks; that will facilitate sharing of relevant information (but discourage prying into aspects of the members' lives not germane to work on their problems); and that will stress positive reactions to task accomplishment over negative responses to task failure.

Leadership within the group is an additional facet that needs to be attended to and used constructively. Although the practitioner normally assumes the primary leadership role in task-centered groups, he may use members as coleaders for particular purposes—one member may be particularly adept at reducing tension in the group; another at keeping the group focused on the business at hand.

While procedures for forming and conducting groups vary, the following format is typical. Preliminary individual interviews are held with prospective group members to determine primarily if the applicant has at least one problem that would fall within the potential focus of the group, and to orient him to the general structure and purpose of the group treatment model. In the initial group meeting, clients are asked to state the problems they wish to work on and to assist one another in problem exploration and specification. A contractual agreement is reached on the purpose of the group and its duration (which is planned short term as in the individual treatment). In subsequent sessions each member, in turn, formulates, plans, practices, and reviews tasks with the help of the practitioner and other group members. In addition, the practitioner may undertake tasks outside the session on behalf of a single client or the group as a whole, or group members may perform extrasession tasks to help one another with their problems.

Studies of the task-centered approach

Over a dozen uncontrolled studies of the task-centered model have been conducted in a variety of sites, including medical, family, child guidance, psychiatric, school, corrections, and public welfare settings. In these studies data have been collected on such factors as characteristics of clients and problems treated, types of tasks attempted, task progress, problem change, and client satisfaction with the model (22, 23). The results have suggested that task-centered methods have a broad range of application and are generally well received by clients. Outcome data in the form of measures of task progress and of problem change have suggested that the great majority of clients studied received some benefit from the approach.

Since controls were not used in these studies, it was not possible to determine the extent to which the task-centered model was responsible for the outcomes observed; other factors, that might have produced change, such as tendencies for problems to dissipate with the passage of time, could not be ruled out. Some recent studies in which controls were employed have provided more definitive evidence on the impact of the model.

The first of these studies suggested that the use of methods to help clients plan and implement tasks resulted in more task progress than occurred when clients were not given such help (19). A single case study, using a multiple baseline design, indicated that these methods were effective in reducing specific communication problems of a couple with marital difficulties (33).

A more ambitious controlled study was then undertaken to evaluate the effectiveness of the model (20, 21). The study consisted of an experimental test of the activities related to task planning, implementation, and review, as described in the preceding section (23). The test was primarily conducted in two settings: a public school system and a psychiatric clinic, both located in an inner-city area on the south side of Chicago. Eighty-seven families referred for social work help were assigned to project workers. The families were predominantly black and low-income. The project practitioners, 44 in number, were first-year graduate students enrolled in the task-centered program at the School of Social Service Administration.

Following procedures set forth in the

model, problems were specified with relevant family members who became the actual clients of the project. Problems relating to school adjustment of children and interpersonal difficulties of adults were the most common. When the problem specification phase was completed, clients were randomly divided into two comparable groups. One group (the experimental group) received three weeks of intensive task-centered treatment, consisting of six interviews per case plus related environmental work. The other group (the control group) was given three weeks of "placebo" treatment in which there was client–practitioner contact but no use was made of task-centered or other forms of problem-solving intervention. The amount of problem alleviation that occurred in each group during this period was measured and compared by independent judges who did not know which cases had received the task-centered intervention and which had received the placebo treatment.

The control group then received the three-week, task-centered intervention package that had previously been used to treat the clients in the experimental group. A second comparison was then made: the amount of problem alleviation shown by the clients in the control group during the period in which they received the placebo treatment was compared with the amount of problem alleviation they experienced during the period in which they received the task-centered treatment.

Follow-up interviews were conducted with the clients in both groups, from one to three months after termination of treatment. Structured recordings completed by practitioners and tape recordings of their interviews with clients were used as a basis for analyzing the characteristics of the task-centered services.

The findings revealed that the amount of problem alleviation experienced by clients in the experimental group during task-centered intervention was significantly greater than the amount experienced by clients in the control group while they were receiving the placebo treatment. Moreover, problem alleviation for clients in the control group showed a significant acceleration when they received task-centered service. Data obtained at follow-up suggested that gains achieved by clients in both groups had been maintained following termination of service. There was no evidence that these gains had been affected by the emergence of problems in other areas. We were not able to identify from the data particular characteristics of clients, problems, or workers that strongly affected the apparent effectiveness of the model, although task-centered intervention seemed to be somewhat more effective with adults than with children.

Findings on service characteristics suggested that the model was implemented as planned in most respects. The amount of time devoted to continuing specification and monitoring of the clients' target problems proved much greater than had been anticipated, however. Also certain interventions, such as helping clients rehearse tasks, were used less than expected. Although there were few clues as to which types or combinations of interventions might be particularly effective, the findings did suggest that the use of client tasks was an important ingredient in helping clients resolve problems. The majority of tasks that clients agreed to carry out were in fact achieved, at least to a substantial degree. A positive correlation between task progress and problem change suggested that the clients' task work did contribute to the alleviation of their problems.

Range of application

A question inevitably asked of any treatment system, in one form or another, is, "For what kind of case is, and is not, the system applicable?" In answering this question, it is important to distinguish between use of the system as a whole and use of activities for task planning, implementation, and review. The latter, of course, have a much wider range of application than the former. In fact, sequences of task-centered activities can be used in almost any form of treatment to enable clients to define and carry through particular plans of action. Thus, a practitioner might use task-centered methods during the course of long-term psychosocial treatment to help the client translate into action some aspect of insight into his problems.

An illustration of this partial use of the model was provided by work with Cheryl, an adolescent girl in a residential treatment center. The youngster had been under long-term care for problems of extreme aggressive behavior. The treatment program consisted of a combination of milieu therapy and psychoanalytically oriented casework. One of the issues in her individual treatment was her relationship with her mother. Their visits at the institution had become increasingly upsetting to Cheryl because her mother dwelt on problems at home, particularly her difficulties with Cheryl's father. Matters came to a head when Cheryl refused either to see her mother or to talk to her on the phone. Since her caseworker thought it was essential for Cheryl to resume contact with the mother, she identified the breakdown in communication as a specific problem that Cheryl and her mother needed to work on. Somewhat reluctantly, Cheryl agreed; she would give her mother another chance. A plan of action was devised. Cheryl's task was to call her mother and have a five-minute phone conversation about her own recent activities. Her mother's task (worked out with another caseworker) was to participate in the conversation without making any reference to problems at home. Both tasks were planned in detail, rehearsed with mother and daughter in separate sessions, and carried out. Problem-task sequences of this kind have been used in a variety of contexts, ranging from very brief (one or two sessions) crisis-oriented intervention to long-term psychodynamic approaches.

The use of full, time-limited sequences of task-centered treatment within the context of long-term, personal-care arrangements has been previously described (25). In brief, the model is employed to work on specific problems that arise in the course of cases for which the practitioner may have legally mandated responsibilities that may extend beyond the limits of a brief service design. In one recent application of this strategy, cases accepted for foster placement were referred to a unit of task-centered practitioners who worked with natural and foster parents and children on a range of specific problems, including aspects of the child's adjustment to foster care and obstacles preventing return to natural parents (26). In some cases, it was possible to effect a return of the child to his natural parents at the conclusion of the brief treatment program. When this outcome was not possible, an effort was made to work out visiting arrangements with natural parents, set a plan for them to follow in order to have the child returned, and resolve problems that the child might be having in foster care. These cases were then transferred to other staff for continued supervision.

When the task-centered system is used in full as the sole or primary method of treatment, its range of application is narrower. Nevertheless, the range is broad enough, I think, to serve as a basic approach for the majority of clients served by clinical social workers. This conclusion has received support from a large number of demonstrations of the model in most settings in which social workers practice (18). But the majority is not all. It is possible to identify certain types of clients for whom the model in full may not provide the optimal mode of practice. Such types would include the following: (1) clients who are not interested in taking action to solve specific problems in their life situations, but who want help in exploring existential issues, such as concerns about life goals or identity, or wish to talk about stressful experiences, such as loss of a loved one, with an accepting, empathic person; (2) clients who are unwilling or unable to utilize the structure of the model—for example, clients who prefer a more casual, informal mode of helping or those faced with highly turbulent situations in which it is not possible to isolate and follow through on specific problems; (3) clients who wish to alter conditions, such as certain psychogenic and motor difficulties, for which it is not possible to identify problem-solving tasks that they are able to carry out; (4) clients who wish no help but may need to be seen for "protective reasons."

Although all these categories merit elaboration, the last in particular requires additional comment because of frequent misunderstandings concerning the use of the model with involuntary clients. The task-centered approach can be used with many persons who may not have sought the social worker's help or who may be initially reluctant to accept it since the social worker, as noted, does have the opportunity to influence the conception of their problems. There are situations, however, in which the practitioner's efforts to engage the person in collaborative problem solving are unequivocally rejected, but the practitioner must remain on the scene for "protective" reasons. His role, then, is not to provide "help" for the person on his terms, as prescribed by the task-centered model, but to "protect" others, such as children; the interests of society, as in the case of offenders; or the person himself, as may be required with some mentally retarded or impaired individuals.

While elements of helping approaches, including the present model, can be employed in such situations, there is need for alternative models of practice clearly based on the social worker's protective or social control function. Efforts to develop such approaches have perhaps been retarded by the narrow view that social workers must always be helpful or therapeutic in their work with deviant persons.

Summary

Task-centered treatment is a system of brief, time-limited practice that emphasizes helping clients with specific problems of their own choosing through discrete client and practitioner actions or tasks. Service interviews are devoted largely to the specification of problems, and to the identification and planning of appropriate tasks, which are then carried out between sessions. Although there are limits on its range of application, it is offered as a basic service for the majority of clients dealt with by clinical social workers. The core methods of the approach, notably activities designed to help clients plan and implement problem-solving tasks, can be used within most practice frameworks.

References

1. Beck, Aaron T. *Cognitive Therapy and the Emotional Disorders.* New York: International Universities Press, 1976.
2. Beck, Dorothy Fahs and Mary Ann Jones. *Progress of Family Problems: A Nationwide Study of Clients' and Counselors, Views on Family Agency Services.* New York: Family Service Agency of America, 1973.
3. Bergin, Allen E. and Michael J. Lambert. "The Evaluation of Therapeutic Outcomes," in S. L. Garfield and A. E. Bergin (eds.) *Handbook of Psychotherapy and Behavior Change,* 2nd ed. New York: Wiley, 1971.
4. Bogatay, Alan and Frank Farrow. *An Assessment of the Management Impact of the Task-Centered Model in Public Welfare Agencies.* Washington, D.C.: Lewin and Associates, 1975.
5. Brown, Lester B. "Client Problem Solving Learning in Task-Centered Social Treatment," Dissertation research in progress, University of Chicago, School of Social Service Administration, 1977.
6. Butcher, Allen E. and Michael J. Lambert. "The Evaluation of Therapeutic

Outcomes," in S. L. Garfield and A. E. Bergin (eds.) *Handbook of Psychotherapy and Behavior Change*, 2nd ed. New York: Wiley, 1971.

7. Fortune, Anne E. "Practitioner Communication in Task-Centered Treatment," Dissertation research in progress, University of Chicago, School of Social Service Administration, 1977.

8. Garfield, S. L. "Research on Client Variables in Psychotherapy," in S. L. Garfield and A. E. Bergin (eds.) *Handbook of Psychotherapy and Behavior Change*. New York: Wiley, 1971, pp. 271-99.

9. Garvin, Charles D. "Strategies for Group Work with Adolescents," in W. J. Reid and Laura Epstein (eds.) *Task-Centered Practice*. New York: Columbia University Press, 1977.

10. ———, W. J. Reid and L. Epstein. "Task-Centered Group Work," in R. Roberts and H. Northen (eds.) *Theoretical Approaches to Social Work with Small Groups*. New York: Columbia University Press, 1976.

11. Goldman, Alvin I. *A Theory of Human Action*. Englewood Cliffs, N.J.: Prentice-Hall, 1970.

12. Gurman, Alan S. and David P. Kniskern. "Research on Marital and Family Therapy," in S. L. Garfield and A. E. Bergin (eds.) *Handbook of Psychotherapy and Behavior Change*, 2nd ed. New York: Wiley, 1971.

13. Luborsky, Lester, Barton Singer, and Lise Luborsky. "Comparative Studies of Psychotherapy," *Archives of General Psychiatry*, Vol. 32, pp. 995-1008.

14. Meltzoff, J. and M. Kornreich. *Research in Psychotherapy*. New York: Atherton Press, 1970.

15. Mitchell, Kevin M., Jerold D. Bozarth, and Conrad C. Krauft. "A Reappraisal of the Therapeutic Effectiveness of Accurate Empathy, Nonpossessive Warmth and Genuineness," in A. S. Gurman and A. M. Razin (eds.) *Effective Psychotherapy: A Handbook of Research*. New York: Pergamon Press, 1977.

16. Osborn, Alfred F. *Applied Imagination: Principles and Procedures of Creative Problem Solving*, 3rd ed. New York: Scribner's, 1963.

17. Perlman, Helen Harris. *Social Casework: A Problem-Solving Process*. Chicago: University of Chicago Press, 1957.

18. ———. "The Problem-Solving Model in Social Casework," in R. Roberts and R. Nee (eds.) *Theories of Social Casework*. Chicago: University of Chicago Press, 1970.

19. Reid, William J. "A Test of a Task-Centered Approach," *Social Work*, Vol. 20, 1975, pp. 3-9.

20. ———. *The Characteristics and Effectiveness of Task-Centered Methods*. Report of the Task-Centered Services Project, vol. 2. Chicago: School of Social Service Administration, 1977.

21. ———. *The Task-Centered System*. New York: Columbia University Press, 1978.

22. ——— and L. Epstein. *Task-Centered Practice*. New York: Columbia University Press, 1977.

23. ——— and L. Epstein. *Task-Centered Casework*. New York: Columbia University Press, 1972.

24. ——— and Ann Shyne. *Brief and Extended Casework*. New York: Columbia University Press, 1969.

25. Rooney, Ronald H. "Adolescent Groups in Public Schools," in W. J. Reid

and L. Epstein (eds.) *Task-Centered Practice*. New York: Columbia University Press, 1977.

26. ———. "Separation Through Foster Care: Toward a Problem-Oriented Practice Model Based on Task-Centered Casework," Dissertation research in progress, University of Chicago, School of Social Service Administration, 1978.

27. Salmon, Wilma. "A Service Program in a State Public Welfare Agency," in W. J. Reid and L. Epstein (eds.) *Task-Centered Practice*. New York: Columbia University Press, 1977.

28. Sloane, R. Bruce, Fred R. Staples, Allen H. Cristol, Neil J. Yorkston, and Katherine Whipple. *Psychotherapy versus Behavior Therapy*. Cambridge, Mass.: Harvard University Press, 1975.

29. Stoland, Ezra. *The Psychology of Hope*. San Francisco: Jossey-Bass, 1969.

30. Strupp, H. H., R. E. Fox, and K. Lessler. *Patients View Their Psychotherapy*. Baltimore: Johns Hopkins Press, 1969.

31. Studt, Eliot. "Social Work Theory and Implications for the Practice of Methods," *Social Work Education Reporter*, vol. 16 (1968), pp. 22–46.

32. Thomas, Edwin J. *Marital Communication and Decision Making: Analysis, Assessment, and Change*. New York: Free Press, 1976.

33. Tolson, Eleanor. "Alleviating Marital Communication Problems," in W. J. Reid and L. Epstein (eds.) *Task-Centered Practice*. New York: Columbia University Press, 1977.

34. Truax, Charles B. and Kevin M. Mitchell. "Research on Certain Therapist Interpersonal Skills in Relation to Precess and Outcome," in A. E. Bergin and S. L. Garfield (eds.) *Handbook of Psychotherapy and Behavior Change*. New York: Wiley, 1971.

35. Watzlawick, Paul, Janet Helmick Beavin, and Don D. Jackson. *Pragmatics of Human Communication*. New York: Norton, 1967.

Annotated listing of key references

REID, William J. and Laura Epstein. *Task-Centered Casework.* New York: Columbia University Press, 1972.
   The original formulation of the task-centered system of practice is presented together with studies of preliminary trials of the model.

REID, William J. and Laura Epstein. *Task-Centered Practice.* New York: Columbia University Press, 1977.
   This volume reports on applications of the task-centered model with children, families, and adults in a variety of contexts, including child guidance, mental health, medical, school, public welfare, family service, and correctional settings. The contributors—nineteen in all—provide data on the employment of the model as well as illustrative case materials.

REID, William J. *The Task-Centered System.* Columbia University Press, 1978.
   Developments in the task-centered system since its original formulation are set forth. The theory underlying the system is enlarged and new methods of intervention are described. Adaptations of the model for use in conjoint treatment of families and formed groups are presented. The book also includes a report of a two-year experiment in which the operation and effectiveness of the model were studied.

20
Crisis Theory

by

NAOMI GOLAN

Summary of theory

Over the past thirty years, a number of theoretical formulations, reports of therapeutic innovations, and research studies have been loosely drawn together under the rubric of "crisis theory." The parameters are probably too broad and too amorphous to grant it recognition as a systematic theory in the sense of its being an internally consistent body of verified hypotheses, as discussed by Turner in Chapter 1. Nevertheless, enough generalizations and conclusions have coalesced to recognize the emergence of a discernible framework within which to examine stressful situations and to offer a body of guidelines and techniques for intervention at such times.

The crisis approach is rooted in several disparate bodies of theory and practice, some of which developed quite independently and others which have converged, fused, and sometimes separated again to go off in diverse directions. No one particular discipline can lay claim to ownership, although the Harvard Schools of Psychiatry and Public Health have probably been most active in pioneering the theoretical framework, while the Benjamin Rush Center of Los Angeles has undoubtedly developed the practice application most fully, at least within the mental health field. However, for the last ten years, its usage has broadened until today it is widely accepted by a broad range of helping professions. A prolific body of professional literature accumulated around two foci: the nature and process of crisis and stress situations and the utilization of these formulations to deal with a broad spectrum of psychosocial difficulties.

Although crisis theory is essentially eclectic in nature, certain basic assumptions, hypotheses, and concepts appear to form the core approach. These can be summarized in a set of statements gleaned initially from the work of Erich Lindemann and Gerald Caplan and developed and expanded by Lydia Rapoport, Howard Parad, David Kaplan, Gerald Jacobson, Martin Strickler, Peter Sifneos, and others:

1. An individual (or family, group, or community) is subjected to periods of increased internal and external stress throughout his normal life span which disturb his customary state of equilibrium with his surrounding environment. Such episodes are usually initiated by some *hazardous event* which may be a finite external blow or a less bounded internal pressure that has built up over time. The event may be a single catastrophic occurrence or a series of lesser mishaps which have a cumulative effect.

2. The impact of the hazardous effect disturbs the individual's homeostatic balance and puts him into a *vulnerable state,* marked by heightened tension and anxiety. To regain his equilibrium, he goes through a series of predictable phases. First, he tries to use his customary repertoire of problem-solving mechanisms to deal with the situation. If this is not successful, his upset increases and he mobilizes heretofore untried emergency methods of coping. However, if the problem continues and can neither be resolved, avoided, nor redefined, tension continues to rise to a peak.

3. At this point, a *precipitating factor* can bring about a turning point, during which self-righting devices no longer operate and the individual enters a state of *active crisis,* marked by disequilibrium and disorganization. This is followed by a period of gradual *reorganization* until a new state of equilibrium is reached.

4. As the crisis situation develops, the individual may perceive the initial and subsequent stressful events primarily as a *threat,* either to his instinctual needs or to his sense of autonomy and well-being; as a *loss* of a person, an attribute (status or role), or a capacity; or as a *challenge* to survival, growth, or mastery.

5. Each of these perceptions calls forth a characteristic emotional reaction that reflects the subjective meaning of the event to the individual: threat elicits a heightened level of anxiety; loss brings about feelings of depression, deprivation, and mourning; challenge stimulates a moderate increase in anxiety plus a kindling of hope and expectation, releasing new energy for problem solving.

6. Although a crisis situation is neither an illness nor a pathological experience and reflects a realistic struggle to deal with the individual's current life situation, it may become linked with earlier unresolved or partially resolved conflicts. This may result in an inappropriate or exaggerated response. Crisis intervention in such situations may provide a multiple opportunity: to resolve the present difficulty, to rework the previous difficulties, and/or to break the linkage between them.

7. The total length of time between the initial blow and final resolution of the crisis situation varies widely, depending on the severity of the hazardous event, the characteristic reactions of the person, the nature and complexity of the tasks that have to be accomplished, and the situational supports available. The actual state of active disequilibrium, however, is time-limited, usually lasting up to four to six weeks.

8. Each particular class of crisis situation (such as the death of a close relative or the experience of being raped) seems to follow a specific sequence of stages which can be predicted and mapped out. Emotional reactions and behavioral responses at each phase can often be anticipated. Fixation and disequilibrium at a particular point may provide the clue as to where the person is "stuck" and what lies behind his inability to do his "crisis work" and master the situation.

9. During the unraveling of the crisis situation, the individual tends to be particularly amenable to help. Customary defense mechanisms have become weakened, usual coping patterns have proved inadequate, and the ego has become more open to outside influence and change. A minimal effort at such time can produce a maximal effect; a small amount of help, appropriately focused, can prove more effective than extensive help at a period of less emotional accessibility.

10.   During the reintegration phase, new ego sets may emerge and new adaptive styles may evolve, enabling the person to cope more effectively with other situations in the future. However, if appropriate help is not available during this critical interval, inadequate or maladaptive patterns may be adopted which can result in weakened ability to function adequately later on.

After the first flush of controversy, during which proponents of the crisis approach seemed to advocate its usage as a universal panacea and opponents damned it as ineffective symptom removal, the theory and its application have entered the mainstream of social work knowledge. Currently it is being used discriminately by practice theoreticians to explain certain types of phenomena encountered throughout the life span of individuals, families, and groups during periods of enhanced stress. It has become an important transitional theory, binding traditional casework practice to new developments in ego psychology, learning theory, and the role and systems approaches.

For practitioners, it provides the conceptual frame of reference for brief, focused intervention in a wide range of pressureful situations and is being offered as the treatment of choice for a considerable part of the activities within family agencies, public welfare offices, medical facilities, mental health clinics, school services, and community development programs, among others. Social workers in traditional primary agencies, in complex secondary settings, and in special crisis and emergency management outposts now tailor their practice toward helping clients deal with problems generated by anticipated and unanticipated stress, according to guidelines set down by crisis theory.

Historical origins

Present-day crisis theory can be viewed as the merging of two mainstreams of developments since World War II: psychological and sociological theory and experimentation, on the one hand, and social work practice theory, on the other.

Psychological Developments

In the field of psychodynamic theory, while classical psychoanalytic theoreticians continued to concentrate on unconscious processess and the psychopathology of patients, significant segment of second- and third-generation metapsychologists, such as Heinz Hartmann, Ernst Kris, Rudolf Loewenstein, Ives Hendrick, Abraham Kardiner, Bela Mittelmann, David Rapaport, Sandor Rado, Franz Alexander, and Abraham Maslow, turned their attention to the executive, conflict-free areas of the ego. Hartmann's concept of ego autonomy (75), amplified and developed by Rapaport (58), spurred interest in the autonomous role of the ego in personality formation. Functions such as cognition, perception, intention, motility, motivation, and mastery began to be studied in detail and a far more optimistic view of personality growth and development started to supplant the earlier, more deterministic id psychology.

Meanwhile, Erik Erikson, working independently, developed his eight-stage epigenetic approach to the life cycle (45). He postulated that, as the person passes through the various stages in his life span, he faces key problems ("psychosocial crisis") in reorientation. His ability to solve each successive crisis either enhances or weakens his ability to master problems in subsequent stages. At this same time, child psychologist Jean Piaget was examining minutely children's intellectual and motor processes to determine at which levels they developed their cognitive capacities to organize and incorporate new experiences and to solve problems (137).

Sibylle Escalona investigated the normal developmental patterns of infants (47) and Lois Murphy mapped the unfolding abilities of children and adolescents to evolve coping and master patterns (121). The new field of life-span developmental psychology began to view the individual's normative life span from the dual perspective of his unfolding personality and his socialization to his environment (10), with special attention paid to the transitional phases between developmental stages (39, 150).

Parallel to this, laboratory experimenters were studying stress from quite a different point of view. Using Cannon's concept of homeostasis and Herrick's theory of systemic equilibration as a starting point, Hans Selye (161) began in the 1950s to observe the individual's performance under various stress-inducing conditions. He proposed a series of three stages: first, an *alarm reaction*, consisting of successive shock and countershock phases; then, *resistance*, during which maximal adaptation is attempted; and finally, *exhaustion*, when adaptive mechanisms collapse.

Experimental psychologists examined reactions under naturally stressful conditions such as isolation in the Antarctic or in prison camps, or through laboratory studies during which stress-producing variables were systematically introjected (34). Of particular interest are Richard Lazarus' studies on cognitive factors underlying stress (101, 102) in which he emphasizes the need to appraise both the threatening condition and the potential avenues for solution and mastery. Irving Janis' original interest in patients' response to high-threat situations such as impending surgery (89) has more recently broadened to the decisions individuals make under stressful conditions (90). He sees such dicision making as involving appraisal of the challenge posed by the stress situation, evaluation of recommended alternatives, reaching a tentative decision as to the best available policy, commitment to the new policy, and adherence to it despite challenge.

Learning theorists were also looking at coping and decision making, using a cognitive approach with its emphasis on information processing. Thus Taplin (180) sees the person experiencing a crisis as having his processes of perception, cognition, and decision making in-terrupted as the result of some physical or psychological "overload"; he now needs new information to build new cognitive maps and to develop his capacity to design and select new coping strategies. Even after the crisis peak is passed, these can stand him in good stead in the future.

Behavioral modification advocates stress the need, during periods of crisis, to unlearn old, unsuccessful, or damaging patterns of interaction and to learn new, constructive ones. Emphasis is placed on teaching the person how to change and to recognize how others perceive him. Behavior is shaped toward helping him to engage in more socially acceptable and less pain-producing activities and learn more productive ways to deal with problems (30).

Sociological Studies

Sociologists have been studying crises in two main areas: family stress situations and reactions to community disasters.

Pioneer work on family responses was carried out by Reuben Hill and his associates (71), who investigated stress reactions of family members during various stages in the family life cycle. He found three interacting elements that appeared to determine whether a given event would bring about a family crisis: the external hardship or crisis-precipitating event ("stressor"), the internal organization of the family, and the family's definition of the event as stress-inducing. Customary adequacy in family functioning was contrasted with crisis proneness in multiproblem families (79). Ernest Burgess (22) noted that sudden changes in family status and conflict among family members as to their roles added to family crises, while Vogel and Bell (187) found that the family's designation of an emotionally disturbed child as the scapegoat often served as a tension-reducing device that allowed the family to maintain its internal equilibrium.

Other researchers examined the impact of various types of family developmental and transitional crises such as marriage (143), parenthood (155), and old age (105), as well as viewing the entire process of change and development within the life cycle (107). The effect of stressful life events such as physical and emotional illnesses (40) and poverty, deprivation, and alienation (132) on both individual and family functioning were also studied.

Extensive attention has been paid by sociologists and "disasterologists" to large-scale disasters (9, 31) and field studies have been carried out on community behavior during tornadoes (181), floods (182), mine collapses (108), etc. James Tyhurst (186) noted that community disasters produced three overlapping phases: *impact, recoil,* and *post-trauma.* Other researchers found that, while each disaster followed its own unique pattern, seven common stages could be discerned: *warning, threat, impact, inventory, rescue, remedy,* and *recovery* (162). Much of the current work on emergency and disaster management (129, 172) has been built upon this foundation.

Psychiatric Developments

Since the mid-forties, military psychiatrists, as the result of experiences in the armed forces during and after World War II (66), the Korean conflict (73), and the Vietnam war (67), attempted to predict the performance of soldiers who might later break under field pressures. Early theories of a "stress personality profile" turned out to be unpredictive under subsequent tests and were eventually revised to include current situational factors that could mitigate underlying pathology. Jaffe (88) found the need for self-preservation, libidinal ties with friends in the army, identification with his nation's ideals, an intact body image, and ego-controlled aggression were predominant characteristics of Israeli soldiers in the Six-Day War, while Merbaum and Hefez (114) were able to isolate common personality characteristics of Israeli and American soldiers who broke under extreme stress.

As an offshoot of the Vietnamese war and its aftermath, the plight of families of prisoners of war and servicemen missing in action began, in the late 1960s, to receive particular attention for the first time (110). Special counseling services were set up to discuss with families problems arising out of the incipient and subsequent reunion with their long-separated husbands and fathers.

In Erich Lindemann's seminal study on grief reactions to the Cocoanut Grove nightclub fire in Boston in 1943 (106), he found that the duration and severity of bereavement depended upon the extent to which each survivor or relative could successfully carry out his "grief work," i.e., the degree to which he was able to achieve emancipation from his bondage to the deceased, to readjust to an environment in which the deceased was missing, and to be able to form new relationships over time.

Lindemann noted that certain inevitable events in the individual's life cycle generate emotional stress and strain, which are countered by a series of adaptive mechanisms that can either lead to mastery of the new situation or failure, with impairment of functioning. While some situations may be stressful to all persons, they become crises for those who are particularly vulnerable because of personality factors or whose emotional resources are unduly taxed. This theoretical formulation led to the establishment, in 1948, of the Wellesley Human Relations Service, a community-based project aimed at preventive intervention in typical hazardous family situations (97).

Parallel to and interwoven with Lindemann's work, Gerald Caplan, whose early interest in crisis situations grew out of his work with immigrant mothers and children in Israel after World War II (26), began to develop his own approach, which was set in the public health format of primary, secondary, and tertiary levels of intervention (27). He defined a crisis as occurring when a person faces an obstacle to important life goals that is, for a time, insurmountable by means of customary methods of problem solving. He identified two types of crisis situations: those precipitated by changes in the normal course of living, such as entry into school, birth of a sibling, marriage, retirement, and death; and those occasioned by accidental hazardous events such as acute or chronic illness, accidents, or family dislocation.

During the 1950s and early 1960s, a series of investigations was carried out by the Harvard School of Public Health, under Caplan's direction, at the Family Guidance Center and elsewhere in the Boston area on various types of situational and maturational crisis such as the premature birth of a child (29) and adjustment to marriage (142). Much of the core theory on crisis intervention was developed within this framework.

The public health model questioned use of the traditional treatment model of sickness and cure and offered, as an alternative, the concept of the "acute situational disorder," in which crises are seen as similar to infectious disease states, which are usually self-limiting and are often superimposed upon healthy personalities or on long-term chronic conditions (92). Intervention in such cases becomes limited to alleviation of the acute reactive condition without dealing with the underlying pathology.

More recently, Caplan and his colleagues at the Harvard Department of Psychiatry's Laboratory of Community Psychiatry carried out studies on widowhood (169) and reactions to death (90). In the past several years, Caplan has focused his attention upon the natural and mutual support systems in the community that can be used to prevent and/or ameliorate the destructive aspects of crisis situations (28).

On the west coast, Gerald Jacobson and his colleagues opened the Benjamin Rush Center for Problems of Living as part of the Los Angeles Psychiatric Service, using Caplan's framework to offer brief, immediate crisis intervention in a wide range of social and emotional problems (2, 87). As their contribution to crisis theory, they differentiated between two approaches, the *generic*, which emphasizes classes of situational and maturational crises that

occur to significant population groups and can be dealt with by paraprofessionals and volunteers as well as professionals, and the *individual*, which stresses the patient's specific intrapsychic and interpersonal processes and requires more intensive treatment (86).

As a special development within the mental health field, the suicide prevention movement, largely in the hands of clinical psychologists, developed with astonishing rapidity in the late 1950s and in the 1960s (111). Much of the pioneering work was carried out, first by Louis Dublin (41) and then by Edwin Shneidman, Norman Farberow, and Robert Litman (165), who contributed the concept of the "psychological autopsy." In recent years, suicide prevention centers have broadened their scope to cover other types of crisis and emergency situations, such as alcohol and drug abuse and psychiatric difficulties.

Path into social work

Social workers have been confronted with clients seeking help because of acute, stress-generated problems since the early days of the "friendly visitor." Bertha Reynolds recalled that the first summer course in psychiatric social work at Smith college in the summer of 1918 was set up "to contribute to the war effort by training workes for the rehabilitation of shell-shocked soldiers" (149).

Involvement on a broad scale, however, probably started during the Great Depression of the 1930s with its widespread economic and social dislocations that forced numerous individuals and families, for the first time, to turn to public and private social agencies for help. Gordon Hamilton (70) noted that caseworkers, drawn from private and voluntary services, were initially bewildered and overwhelmed by the staggering caseloads. Under the pressure of necessity, however, they learned to combine mass assistance with "reasonable individualization."

It was during this period that the Travelers Aid, which primarily operated in railway stations and bus terminals, developed its special approach, backed by intuitive and skillful practice, for dealing with frightened, upset, disheartened clients:

A crisis which has just developed is far easier to resolve than one less abrupt in development.... The sudden crisis presents a challenge to the client; friends and family recognize the need to rally to his reinforcement. But the problem which has been slowly developing over a period of months or years requires a different attack. While the latest point of difficulty may be treated in the short contact, the more fundamental problem may have to remain untouched. (192, p. 64)

Trained caseworkers were purposely placed within easy reach of the public under the agency's firm conviction that it was possible to provide fundamental help in one or several interviews (185).

World War II, following closely after the Depression, eased some of the economic pressures but brought other family disruptions, separations, and difficulties. This resulted in both increased pressures and new opportunities for family agencies that undertook to help mothers take necessary jobs in defense industries and to develop child-care services for their children. Agencies also became concerned with men rejected for service for physical and emotional reasons. Family breakup as the aftermath of separation, war tensions and anxieties, and hasty war marriages called for quick, skilled casework services (151). Within the armed forces, psychiatric social workers, rapidly trained to meet the burgeoning needs, focused on short-term treatment of service-connected problems (35).

During this period, social work theoreticians were attempting to reconcile two divergent viewpoints: the *diagnostic* approach, which emphasized the importance of a careful, all-encompassing evaluation of the total person-in-his-social-situation, and the *functionalist* outlook, which emphasized the special needs of the client under pressure and the importance of time as a factor in the casework relationship (95).

Charlotte Towle (183) was one of the first to bring out the rehabilitative goal in helping people in periods of trouble as a way of meeting their common human needs. During the Korean conflict, she observed:

Social work has always served families whose individual worlds have been stressful. The noteworthy features today are the totality of life's uncertainty and the facts that parents and children have grown up during precarious times—war, inflation, depression, war, inflation, and now a defense economy. Many are vulnerable by reason of long-standing strain.... Stresses become traumatic through repetition. (151, p. 163)

Helen Perlman described the client coming to a social agency as being under a twofold stress: the problem itself is felt as a threat or actual attack and his inability to cope with it increases his tension. She also pointed out that

the greater the client's sense of duress and tension, the more overwhelmed and helpless he may feel. The problem-solving functions of his ego are likely to be at least temporarily disabled or constricted.... Relief from stress in one aspect of living may lighten the burden in another (134, pp. 25–26).

She pointed out that, while not every problem brought to an agency may be an actual crisis, at the point of calling or walking in, the applicant feels that it is. Thus the chance to provide the "little help at the strategic time" is lost if the applicant is asked to wait (135).

By the early 1960s, social workers were becoming increasingly concerned over lengthening waiting lists and staff shortages, on the one hand, and frequent dropouts and unplanned terminations, on the other. Research studies brought out the startling information that one out of three cases did not return to family agencies after the first interview (12) and four out of five discontinued by the fifth (152). A series of research investigations at the Community Service Society of New York (147) and at the University of Chicago (145) led to the development of a short-term, time-limited model of focused treatment, which was subsequently tested in a wide range of settings (146).

Much of the traditional dichotomy between "treatment aimed at maintaining adaptive patterns" and "treatment aimed at modifying adaptive patterns" (50) had broken down by this time and a far more eclectic approach to clients in acute stress was emerging. The prevalent social work position on dealing with such situations has probably been stated most clearly by Max Siporin:

> When faced with excessive stress and crisis and when needed resources are inadequate to the requirements of the tasks involved, people have difficulty in social functioning and problems in social living; their coping abilities break down or are impaired. . . . (They) are believed to be able to regain equilibrium, to recover from their demoralization, and to resume optimal functioning, when their competence is restored or strengthened and when requisite social resources and welfare services are provided. . . . In the assessment process there is a focus on identifying the immediate, specific difficulties in social functioning that people are having in their current life situations. There is an examination of current coping capacities of individuals and groups, of situational hazards, obstacles, opportunities, and resources; and of the meanings and consequences of crisis-precipitating events. . . . The interventive process in this approach emphasizes brief, prompt, intensive helping activity in the immediate crisis

situation, so as to restore functional equilibrium for individuals and groups. (171, pp. 147–148)

Principal social work proponents

Social Work Theory in Crisis Intervention

Much of the early adaptation of crisis theory to social work practice was developed by Parad (125), Rapoport (140), and Kaplan (93) through their participation in the School of Public Health program at Harvard, and by Strickler and his colleagues at the Rush Center in Los Angeles (177). More recently, Golan (62), Lukton (109), and Parad (127) have attempted to place the theory in the context of current approaches to practice.

In evaluating the current status of crisis theory in social work, we note that its development has passed through three stages. First, a number of theoretical, experiential, and research formulations on crises and the related areas of stress, disasters, and emergencies were gathered together. Next these ideas were woven into a theoretical framework that was applied, tested, and modified to meet the specific conditions and needs of a wide variety of clients, workers, and settings. Finally, selected elements from both theory and practice were integrated into a series of models that became integrated into the matrix of practice and accepted as part of the armamentarium of strategies and techniques which practitioners could call upon. (These will be developed in detail later on.)

Strickler and Bonnefil (179) see similarities between crisis intervention and traditional casework as it is currently being practiced. Treatment goals in both instances are aimed at enhancing the client's ability to cope with current problems in living. Treatment is focused on specific problems of interpersonal conflict and role dysfunction; it is concentrated on the problem to be solved and is largely geared to the conscious and near-conscious levels of emotional conflicts. The practitioner recognizes transference aspects but moves to replace them with analogous feelings related to the client's current situation and significant relationships. The worker in both types of treatment must be able to make a diagnostic evaluation based on the client's position in his intrafamilial and extended social relationships.

Nevertheless, they find significant differences between the two approaches. In the traditional psychosocial viewpoint, the practitioner seeks to help the client gradually to sort out and clarify his feelings; in the crisis approach, he works at an intense pace, sharing the client's sense of urgency as they work together to resolve the problem at hand. Treatment is based on the client's readiness to risk himself in order to gain a sense of mastery, of being once more in control of his life, and on the worker's alertness to forestall or minimize the client's dependent or regressive fantasies. The need to make quick, independent decisions and to take an activist stance makes many caseworkers uneasy and uncomfortable.

Social Work Practice in Crisis Situations

Even before crisis theory reached its present level of extrapolation, social work practitioners were beginning to use elements inherent in the theory to resolve some of the unresolved difficulties encountered in their ongoing practice. Starting in the late 1950s, reports began to appear at national and regional conferences and in the professional literature, ranging from simple experiential accounts on the "we-did-it-and-it-worked" level to highly sophisticated evaluations, complete with research components, of crisis-oriented service programs.

As might be anticipated, much of the innovation initially developed in the mental health field. In some instances, special programs, such as the Benjamin Rush Center described above,

were set up where walk-in patients were helped to regain psychic equilibrium by reducing their anxiety over a particular difficulty in their current life situation. In pilot projects, such as the Emergency Psychiatric Service experiment at Massachusetts General Hospital in Boston, alcoholics and other types of patients were offered immediate, round-the-clock help with social and emotional problems as part of an intensification of admissions arrangements (33). In traditional psychiatric clinics, such as the Madeline Borg Child Guidance Institute of the Jewish Board of Guardians in New York City (163) and the Langley-Porter Neuropsychiatric Institute in San Francisco (91), theoretical frameworks of practice were modified to pave the way for the use of the crisis approach. In psychiatric hospitals, crisis intervention with patients' families was used profitably as an alternative to admission (100).

Since the mid-sixties, these innovative programs have increased and proliferated, with social workers often acting as prime movers in offering direct service to patients and their families, individually and in groups. The Crisis Clinic of the Youth Guidance Center in Framingham, Massachusetts (48), and the Siblings Group Project at the York Woods Center of the Ypsilanti, Michigan, State Hospital (32) are current examples of new modes of practice in stressful situations.

Some of the early projects in family service agencies were simply modest efforts to modify the ways in which traditional help was offered (42). It took the national survey of family services and psychiatric clinics for children in 1965–1966 to bring widespread attention to the extent and relative success of crisis-oriented programs in this area (128). This project, as well as the Reid research studies mentioned earlier, were undoubtedly instrumental in encouraging the shift in practice to short-term, focused intervention, often with a crisis orientation. Family agencies began to hold staff development seminars to update workers' orientation (43), and in recent years crisis intervention has become the treatment of choice for many cases seen in family agencies (13, 99).

Services for the aged, in children's courts, and in legal conciliation programs were all accustomed to dealing with clients at points of high urgency; they now adopted the crisis approach as a theoretical justification for what they had already been doing on a *de facto* basis. Even public welfare agencies began to shift to the crisis intervention framework for part of their services. Basing their practice on the premise that a family's request for financial assistance often implies other needs as well, workers in a special counseling project at the New York Bureau of Child Welfare used reaching-out techniques to help clients restore coping capacities temporarily impaired by stress situations (118).

Child welfare workers have become active in using the crisis approach, both in foster home placements (170) and in providing services to children in their own homes (80). Denominational child placement facilities, usually very conservative, were helped to modify their placement procedures to make full use of the maturational crises in adolescence (96). The stress inherent in the pregnancy of unwed college students was used to teach them new, growth-producing coping skills (157).

Since medical situations, by their very nature, tend to generate crises, hospital social workers have always spent a major part of their practice in dealing with them (116). Recent reports of work in a neonatal intensive-care nursery service (164) and with families of patients undergoing kidney transplants (24) reflect efforts to deal with the stress induced by diagnosis of the illness or defect. In cases of terminal illness, helping parents anticipate the death of their child (94) or working to keep communication open between patient and spouse (103) demonstrate the sensitive, crisis-oriented practice taking place in these highly traumatic situations. Social workers on continous call in emergency services make immediate psychosocial assessments and rapid dispositions of nonmedical problems as part of admission service staffs (14, 68).

Rape victims are being seen in a special program in a community mental health center and are helped, through crisis intervention techniques, to pass through the sequential phases of acute reaction, outward adjustment, and final resolution of the experience (53). Sometimes several agencies band together to provide comprehensive service for rape victims (72). Sometimes social workers and police form special teams to deal with these and other violent situations in which crisis intervention is deemed necessary (23, 194). In other instances, new structures of services have been set up, such as a special runaway center to provide emergency service for youngsters unwilling to use established service (195).

Assistance during and after periods of community and social disasters had formerly been given in an informal, unplanned, spontaneous way. Within the past few years, following implementing federal legislation, disaster aid has become an established form of social intervention. Siporin (171) points out that at these times individuals and their social systems become disequilibrated and dysfunctional. A pattern of disaster service has emerged in which public and voluntary programs combine in a delicate balance. Short-term ameliorative help, often carried out by social workers "on the front line", is provided on a crisis-intervention basis while longer range prevention and amelioration programs are being developed on the administrative and policy-making level within governmental frameworks.

Despite the wide variations in structure, clientele, and service affiliation, all these recent programs show a common orientation rooted, to a greater or lesser degree, in crisis theory.

Today crisis intervention has become an accepted approach, both for new situations with clients struggling with anticipated or unanticipated changes in their life patterns and in long-term cases where sudden deepening—or heightening—of clients' stress enables the practitioner to take advantage of the opportune moment to centralize his focus and intensify the pace of treatment. Much of the current interest in crisis intervention has become merged into experimentation with task-centered models of practice (64).

Social workers have become ardent advocates of the crisis approach, probably because much of the theory is in general agreement with their own value system and because it tends to supplement and flesh out their own practice experience. Rapoport (141) points out that this theory incorporates a great deal of familiar and accepted knowledge and clinical notions, as well as relevant principles and techniques. Nevertheless, actual application is at times *pro forma* and somewhat halfhearted. From personal observation, it was found that the extent to which crisis intervention is being applied successfully in practice appears to be positively associated with individual workers' enthusiasm and personal commitment to this approach.

Connection with other theories

Crisis theory as presently formulated has its primary roots in psychodynamic personality theory, in stress theory, and in learning theory, with sideshoots reaching into systems theory, role theory, and communications theory. While much of recent thinking in ego psychology has fundamental pertinence, several concepts have proved particularly useful.

In his later writings, Freud (56) suggested, but did not develop, the concept of *signal anxiety*. He noted that the young child, in the course of growing up, learns to anticipate a traumatic situation and to react to it with anxiety before it becomes traumatic; its production in a situation of actual or anticipated danger is an ego function which serves to mobilize the forces at the ego's command to meet or avoid the impending peril. Hartmann (76) adds that signal anxiety is paramount among those forms of anticipation which makes organized action possible, helping to master an inner danger before it becomes an external threat. Erikson (45) differentiates between *fears*, which are states of apprehension that focus on isolated and

recognizable dangers so that they may be judiciously appraised and realistically countered, and *anxieties,* which are diffuse states of tension that magnify and even cause the illusion of an outer danger, without pointing to any avenue of defense or mastery. White, however, sees the avoidance of anxiety as equivalent to effectance, an independent ego energy. He uses it to explain the transformation of rigid defensive arrangements into more flexible ones (191, pp. 155-156).

In discussing the *mechanisms of defense,* Anna Freud (55) points out that, when persons are subject to the same real danger, those who have had no opportunity to master their tension by fulfilling some overt task are more likely to react with panic. Hartmann (75) points out that not every adaptation to the environment or every learning or maturation experience is a conflict; defense mechanisms can have a positive, reality-adaptive component. With change in function, the activity can become pleasurable in its own right.

White feels that one should pay careful attention to the way in which defenses adopted at time of crisis lead to "actions of an efficacious sort which work well upon the particular environment and thus become the basis for the continuing growth of competence and confidence" (191, p. 193). It is this temporary weakening of the defense mechanisms during the crisis situation which led Caplan to suggest that this period offers a time-limited opportunity to intervene effectively.

The third concept has been variously called "coping devices," "problem-solving activities," or "grappling patterns"; this refers to the way in which individuals learn to adapt and master internal and/or external pressures. Lois Murphy distinguishes between two kinds of coping: "the capacity to make use of the opportunities, challenges, and resources of the environment and to manage the pain, frustration, difficulties, and failures with which he (the child) is confronted" and "the capacity to maintain internal integration along with the resilience or potential to recover after a period of disintegrative response to stress" (120, p. 222). The development of these coping patterns as ways of dealing with anxiety and reducing tensions are highly individual and related to the child's or family's basic lifestyle.

As noted earlier, learning to cope more successfully with stressful situations is one of the keystones of crisis theory. Caplan (27) outlines three general patterns for healthy crisis resolution: correct cognitive perception of the situation, management of affect through awareness of feelings and appropriate verbalization leading to tension discharge and mastery, and development of patterns of seeking and using help with actual tasks and feelings by using interpersonal and institutional resources.

Other psychodynamic concepts that connect with crisis theory are the three components, the *sense of basic trust,* the *sense of autonomous will,* and the *sense of initiative,* which Erikson feels are crucial to the development of the individual, though they are each ascendant at different phases of development. Each stage of the life cycle becomes a crisis because the incipient growth and awareness go together with a shift in instinctual energy and, at the same time, cause a specific vulnerability in that sphere of the personality. Crisis, he points out, denotes, not a threat or catastrophe, but a turning point, a crucial period of increased vulnerability yet heightened potential (46, pp. 95-96).

Finally, John and Elaine Cumming maintain that the ego develops through a series of disequilibrations and subsequent reequilibrations between the person and his environment. Successful crisis resolution promotes ego growth by increasing the repertoire of ego sets available and the ability of the individual to cope with future crises. Thus crisis becomes an opportunity for growth and change. While ordinary problem solving demands new uses or combinations of existing ego sets, a crisis requires the learning of new sets and their integration into the personality (38, pp. 54-57).

Many of the concepts taken from stress theory have already been described. The term

"stress" itself has been used variously to describe three kinds of phenomena: (1) the noxious, stimulating condition, the stressful event or situation—sometimes called the "stressor"; (2) the state of the individual who responds to the stressful event (he is considered to be "in stress"); and (3) the relation between the stressful event, the individual's reaction to it, and the events to which it leads (141, pp. 273-274).

In its original engineering usage, the term "stress" was often given a negative connotation and linked with "strain"; this has carried over into the psychological research in this area. (This is in contrast to the term "crisis," which has been given a positive, challenging connotation. Babcock points out that stress is handled by the ego. Its determinants, like those of ego strength, can be found in the person's biological matrix, in his environmental structures, and—in the case of illness or disability—in the scope and ramifications of the particular disease process (5, p. 47). Evaluating these structures later led to the building of an ecologic model for the assessment and design of services in stress situations (74, p. 280).

The attempt to establish a relationship between stressful events and their consequences spurred efforts by Thomas Holmes, Richard Rahe, and their associates to build scales to measure *susceptibility to stress* at various points in the life cycle (83). A long series of studies attempted to apply this type of classification to a wide range of stressful life events (40). While such a summation of values attached to various incidents can appear to have an arithemetic summation leading up to a danger point (in one study, of 300 points in one year), Dohrenwend points out that distinctions must be made between objective and subjective events, gain and loss events, and events for which the individual may or may not be responsible. Differentiation needs to be made between physiological, psychological, and social processes that mediate the individual's response to stressful situations.

Recent developments in learning theory have been concerned with cognitive process and functioning. Much of the recent thinking on motivation and ego autonomy in psychodynamic theory has been paralleled and overlapped by that in learning theory (84). Alexander (4), for example, suggests that the therapeutic process contains two components: the motivational factor and the acquiring of new patterns of behavior. Every change in the total situation requires the unlearning of old patterns and the learning of new and more adequate responses. Cognitive and learning elements in actual life experiences (and in the therapeutic interaction) result in "emotional insight," which is motivated by some kind of urge for mastery and accompanied by tension resolution as a reward.

This is very similar to the position of behavioral modification theorists who say that treatment consists of unlearning old, unsuccessful, or damaging patterns of interaction and learning new, constructive ones. Emphasis is placed on the cognitive aspects of experience, on learning how to change and how others perceive the individual who needs to change. By stressing the cause–effect aspects of behavior, the worker gets the client to see that, if he modifies what he does, others too will change in response. His shaping or relearning of behavior is directed toward helping him engage in more socially acceptable and less pain-producing activity and in learning more productive ways of dealing with the problem situation (30). This is very close to what appears to take place in the resolution phase of crisis intervention.

Taplin (180) advocates the use of a cognitive perspective in crisis situations, with the emphasis on information processing. He advocates the acquisition of new information, the building of cognitive maps, and the learning of new means of adaptation in order to develop his capacity to design and select among competing strategies. Successful crisis resolvers are those who have learned to call upon such strategies to solve problems at times of disequilibrium and which can stand him in good stead in the future.

Crisis, in this approach, is defined as a breakdown in thinking through a physical or psychological overload. At the peak of the crisis, too much dissonant information prevents the usual planning and executive processes from functioning normally. Once the peak is passed, all strategies, both those leading to good and those leading to bad outcomes, result in the restoration (adaptation) process, with a consequent decreased sensitivity to intervention.

Recent experiments by behavioral modification proponents suggest that coping behaviors reinforced at the time of crisis tend to be stronger and those extinguished weaker at times of subsequent crisis (36). It is suggested that family caseworkers who work with parents train them to expose their children to a series of varied, real-life crises, systematically graduated in difficulty, to help them develop flexible coping repertoires which will be resistant to extinction. Alevizos and Liberman (3) find that, in family crisis intervention, instruction and feedback can be used to point out confused or discrepant communication and to show the family, as a unit, how to solve their problems more effectively.

General therapeutic concepts

The basic precepts of crisis theory have been listed in the first part of this chapter and need not be recapitulated. We might emphasize again that intervention in a crisis situation is predicated, not on the traditional psychiatric or surgical model of sickness and cure, but, to a large extent, on the public health approach to "populations at risk." The practitioner may attempt to intervene at several levels: on the primary prevention level to keep a potential situation from developing into a crisis; on the secondary level, once the client has experienced the hazardous blow and while the acute stage is developing, to minimize the effects of the impending disequilibrium; or on the tertiary level, once the client has "fallen apart" and after maladaptive or even destructive adjustment to the situation has occurred, to halt further deterioration and deal with the debilitating aftereffects of the active crisis.

Crisis theory operates, not according to a normalcy-abnormalcy dichotomy, but on the presumption that all persons tend to be subjected to various internal and external stresses at various stages in their life cycle. As part of their ego development, they assemble a repertoire of coping devices and problem-solving techniques. While these may suffice for the usual tasks of daily living, sometimes, because of an increase in pressure, both internal and external, or of a decrease in their ability to handle such pressure, their self-righting homeostatic devices fail and disequilibrium results. Korner (98) points out that two different etiological processes can precipitate the crisis. In the *exhaustion crisis,* the individual may have coped effectively under prolonged conditions of stress but suddenly reaches the point where he no longer has enough strength to continue to cope. In the *shock crisis,* a sudden change in the social environment creates an explosive release of emotions that overwhelms his available coping mechanisms. Without forewarning, which would have given him time to prepare for the impact, he goes into emotional shock.

At the point of disequilibrium, if help is offered within the time-limited period when anxiety is high and motivation great, when defense structures have been weakened or shaken, "a little help, rationally directed and purposefully focused . . . is more effective than more extensive help given at a period of less emotional accessibility" (140, p. 38).

Two therapeutic concepts closely allied to this last idea have been receiving increasing attention in recent examinations of the outcome of short-term treatment: *hope* and *expectation.* Ezra Stotland (176) emphasizes that hopefulness is a necessary condition for action; the motivation to achieve a particular goal is partly a function of the perceived probability that the goal can be achieved and the importance attached to it (pp. 7-27). Research on the role of hope in psychotherapy showed that aspects of

the treatment that aroused and strengthened the patient's hope of relief were found to be positively correlated with short-term improvement. The essential ingredient was the therapist's ability to stimulate the patient's expectation of relief and to convey confidence in his ability to help (54).

Expectations, both on the part of the client and of the practitioner, emphasize the power of the present and the future to mold, influence, and modify behavior, and they can become a significant force in determining the outcome of treatment. It was found that successful crisis intervention not only helped to solve persons' current situations but altered some of their negative expectations of what the future would hold. Brief treatment, with its focus on realistic, time-limited goals, affirms some expectations of what can be accomplished in treatment and removes others that are unrealistic and fantasy-linked (173, pp. 36-46).

The aspect of hope is also tied to the practitioner's degree of therapeutic enthusiasm, notes Rapoport. Both are necessary, particularly in the initial stage, to produce the desired therapeutic climate. To effect rapid reintegration, the worker needs to play an active role, both in conveying the expectation that things can be changed and in creating confidence in his own active investment in the process. Maluccio (112) points out that crisis intervention (as well as behavior modification, gestalt therapy, family treatment, and milieu therapy) emphasizes experiential learning and the use of action in the here-and-now situation.

The nature of the worker-client relationship assumes a different dimension in crisis intervention. By definition, Naomi Brill points out, a helping relationship is purposeful and goal directed; otherwise there is no reason for its existence. It is aimed at enabling one of the participants—the client—to achieve a more satisfactory degree of functioning. When the purpose is served and the goal achieved, the specific relationship is terminated (20, p. 50).

In crisis intervention, as in other forms of

brief treatment, the worker needs to establish quick rapport in order to elicit needed information quickly and to inspire confidence that he can help. The traditional concept of a "meaningful relationship," based largely on a leisurely exploration and testing over time and which often deepens into regressive transference, has little place in this form of intervention. It may very well be that emphasis on active involvement of both the client and the worker, rather than passive attachment, is the significant factor here. The worker's authority, based on professional competence and expertise, can be enlisted to capitalize on the client's readiness to trust him during this period of confusion, helplessness, and high anxiety. Thus his ability to engage the client in taking an active role in resolving his current impasse is a crucial step in involving him in crisis work.

One final casework concept which takes on a different aspect in crisis intervention is that of *insight based on self-understanding,* considered to be a prerequisite to significant change in traditional practice. Rapoport shrewdly points out that sometimes insight is no more than hindsight, of little relevance to the current situation. Except insofar as it breaks the links to the present conflict, she sees crisis-oriented brief treatment, which seeks to deemphasize the past, as requiring a more appropriate goal—that of *foresight.* This she defines as the enhancement of anticipatory awareness of what can be expected in the future and how stress can be handled more adequately (140, pp. 42-43).

Implications for practice

Within the past several years, serious attempts have been made to apply crisis theory to the field of practice by developing various types of models for intervention in different settings. Some have been tailored to the training of crisis counselors who operate as part of mixed professional-semiprofessional teams in community crisis centers (57) or in emergency rooms of general hospitals (148). Often these services are geared to a special type of clientele, such as rape victims or battered wives, where definition of the situation as a crisis is taken for granted. In other situations, the service is structured to offer aid within the crisis format, as at the Rush Center in Los Angeles (87) or the Crisis Hostel in Denver (21).

The selection of the crisis approach as the treatment of choice, in juxtaposition to other practice modalities, as part of the service offered by social workers in multifaceted settings, is more complex. It calls for an early determination of whether, in fact, a crisis situation exists, and at what stage the individual or family is being seen. Since different persons faced with the same circumstances, or the same person at different stages of life or in other circumstances, may react differently, a careful, individualized evaluation of the total field of social forces is needed. The traditional phases of the casework process—study, diagnosis treatment planning, treatment, and evaluation—tend to be inapplicable since the sometimes extreme nature of the situation, the client's * high level of anxiety, and the strong involvement of interested others provides an atmosphere of urgency and requires immediate action.

Parad, Selby, and Quinlan have offered a "patterned approach" based on four basic steps (130, pp. 320-321):

I.   The search for the precipitating event and its meaning to the client.
II. The search for coping means utilized by the client.
III. The search for alternate ways of coping that might better fit the current situation.
IV. Review and support of client's efforts to cope in new ways; evaluation of results.

---

* The term "client" may be taken to refer to an individual, family, group, or even community as the situation demands.

Golan (65, pp. 80-95), using somewhat the same frame of reference, offers a basic treatment model for use by practitioners in a range of primary and secondary settings. It is rooted in the problem-solving theory of casework and was developed as part of the short-term, task-centered approach to practice. Intervention is divided into three phases. The beginning phase aims at *formulation* and assessment of the present situation, with determination of whether a crisis exists and what its current status is, and with setting up a working arrangement. The middle phase concentrates on *implementation,* on the identification and execution of tasks designed to solve specific problems in the current situation, to modify previous inadequate or inappropriate ways of functioning, and to learn new coping patterns. The ending phase deals with *termination* and building new ties with persons and resources in the community. Although couched in quite a different framework, this model bears some similarity, at least in its general format and progression of steps, to the "focused problem resolution" model of family therapy developed at the Brief Therapy Center in Palo Alto (189).

Assessment of the Situation

Five components of a client's situation must be evaluated at the outset to determine the nature and extent of the crisis: the hazardous event, the vulnerable state, the precipitating factor, the state of active crisis, and the extent of reintegration. While these are diagnostic abstractions, sometimes hard to isolate or describe, their determination is a necessary precondition to effective intervention.

The *hazardous event* is a specific, stress-producing occurrence, either an external blow or internal change, which occurs to an individual or family in a state of relative stability in terms of biopsychosocial situation, initiating a chain of reverberating actions and reactions. Such events can be classified as anticipated and predictable, or as unanticipated and accidental.

Anticipated events are generally of two kinds, the normal developmental critical periods, such as adolescence or middle adulthood, when a person is particularly vulnerable, and transitional stages, such as getting married or moving to a new place, when the person passes from "one condition of certainty through uncertainty to another condition of certainty" and has to take on new roles, learn new tasks, and adjust to new circumstances (115, pp. 72-74).

Unanticipated events are the unpredictable changes that can occur to anyone, at any stage in life, with little or no advance warning. They usually involve some actual or threatened loss (to the person or a significant other) of a person, a capacity, or a function, such as the sudden loss of a spouse or a debilitating heart attack; conversely, they may entail the sudden introduction of a new person into the social orbit, such as the premature birth of a child or the unexpected repatriation of a war prisoner. These may be totally unexpected or merely not anticipated at this particular time; they may happen to one person or family or involve entire communities and populations as in the case of natural disasters, like tornadoes and floods, sociopolitical events such as civil wars or atomic bombings, or economic-environmental catastrophes such as the wiping out of a community by an urban renewal program or the gutting of a neighborhood by fire.

Although a client seen for the first time may not be able to pinpoint "when it all started," this information is important in determining the baseline for subsequent changes in the person and the situation.

The *vulnerable* or upset *state* refers to the subjective reaction of the individual or family to the initial blow, both at the time it occurs and subsequently. Rapoport has noted that each person tends to respond in his own way, depending on whether he perceives the event as a *threat* to instinctual needs or to emotional or physical integrity, as a *loss* of a person or an ability, or as a *challenge* to survival, growth, mastery, or self-expression (141). Each reaction calls forth a primary characteristic affect: threat is usually accompanied by a high level of anxiety; loss brings out feelings of depression and mourning; challenge stimulates a moderate degree of anxiety plus elements of hope, excitement, and expectation. We also find elements of shame, guilt, anger, and hostility, with some cognitive and perceptual confusion.

Questioning about the vulnerable state also includes queries as to how the individual attempted to grapple with the difficulties posed by the hazardous event prior to coming, and the extent to which such efforts were effective.

The *precipitating factor* or event is the link in the chain of stress-provoking happenings that brings tension to a peak and converts the vulnerable state into one of crisis. It may coincide with the initial hazardous event or it may be a negligible incident not even directly or consciously linked to it. It becomes, however, the "straw that breaks the camel's back," the final push that overloads the system and serves to tip the balance. It is often viewed as the presenting problem and thus becomes the immediate focus for engagement of the client, since it has motivated him to seek some form of help (168, pp. 34-35).

Some practitioners feel there is little need to go beyond working on the precipitating event and the thoughts and feelings behind it in order to restore equilibrium (91). Hoffman and Remmel (81) call these thoughts and feelings the *precipitant* and see them as connected with some earlier unresolved core conflict, which becomes the focus of treatment.

The *state of active crisis* refers to the individual's subjective condition, once tension has stopped, his homeostatic mechanisms no longer operate, and disequilibrium has set in. It is the key element in crisis theory and the criterion for determining whether or not to use the crisis intervention approach. During this time-limited period, often only four to six weeks, Caplan describes the person as passing through a predictable series of reactions: psychological

and physical turmoil, including aimless activity or even mobilization, disturbances in body functions, mood, mental content, and intellectual functioning. This is followed by a painful preoccupation with events leading up to the state of crisis. Finally comes a time of readjustment and remobilization (27, pp. 39-44).

The stage of *reintegration* or reorganization occurs gradually and is an extension of the previous one. As the disequilibrium gradually subsides, some form of adjustment, either adaptive and integrative or maladaptive and destructive, takes place. Pasewark and Albers (131) find that initially the problem is maintained at a conscious thinking level, with cognitive perceptions corrected. Next, affect is managed through awareness of feelings and an appropriate acceptance and release of emotions associated with the crisis, such as remorse, guilt, and hostility. Finally, the client develops new behavioral patterns of coping as he begins to deal constructively with the problems that arise and to utilize other persons and organizations to help him carry out prescribed tasks.

This period of learning to cope has become the focus, in recent years, for some of the most creative thinking on how to help clients (136). Perlman calls it the "person's effort to deal with some new, and often problematic, situation or encounter or to deal in some new way with an old problem." She sees partialization, the carving out of some piece that can be coped with, as the way to deal with such stress. In crisis intervention, the problems-to-be-worked-through in the formulation and implementation stages become tied in with the psychological tasks described by Kaplan (93) and by Scherz (159).

Operationally, in terms of the intake process, the initial interview becomes crucial. Armed with his knowledge of the nature and process of the crisis situation, the worker focuses immediately on the "here and the now," finding out the essential details of the precipitating event, its scope and severity, and the persons involved. He does a preliminary sweep of the applicant's current condition, both subjectively as reported by the client and/or collaterals, and objectively as observed in the interview: his dysfunctions in feelings, thoughts, behavior, and physical condition. He checks out the significant role networks to determine how widespread the disturbance is, and its main effects are, and what previous efforts have been made to deal with the situation.

He then attempts to identify the original hazardous event and to trace the subsequent blows that may have aggravated the effects of the initial impact. He encourages the client to ventilate his feelings of loss, guilt, fear, anxiety, sadness, etc. He probes the particular significance of the crisis to the client and what links, actual or symbolic, have been made to previous unresolved conflicts. Once the emotional tone is lowered and the client's anxiety has been somewhat abated, he and the worker get down to discuss resolution of the crisis situation.

Setting Up Treatment Goals

The goals in crisis intervention are primarily aimed, says Parad, to cushion the impact of the stressful event by offering immediate emotional first aid and by strengthening the person in his coping and integrative struggles through on-the-spot therapeutic clarification and guidance (127, p. 237).

More specifically, Rapoport lists six goals for this kind of treatment. Four of them may be considered minimal: (1) relief of symptoms; (2) restoration to the optimal precrisis level of functioning; (3) understanding of the relevant precipitating events that contributed to the state of disequilibrium; and (4) identification of remedial measures that can be taken by the client and his family or that are available through community resources. In addition, where the individual's personality and the social situation are favorable and the opportunity presents itself or can be created, work can be done on (5) recognition of the connection between the current stress and past life experiences and con-

flicts, and (6) initiation of new models of perceiving, thinking, and feeling and development of new adaptive and coping reponses that can be useful beyond the immediate crisis situation (141, pp. 297-298).

In planning treatment, Jacobson and his associates (86) suggest two treatment approaches. The *generic* approach emphasizes specific situational and maturational crises occurring to significant population groups, with no attempt made to assess the particular psychodynamics of the individuals involved. Intervention is often carried out by a paraprofessional, a non-mental health professional, or a community care-giver, focusing on the characteristic course that the crisis situation will probably take. It concentrates on the acute crisis episode and treatment consists of specific interventive measures aimed at the target group as a whole.

The *individual* approach, designed to be used by mental health professionals, emphasizes assessment of the interpersonal and intrapsychic process of each person in crisis, with particular attention paid to the unique aspects of the particular situation and the solution specifically tailored to help the client return to a new steady state.

Langsley and Kaplan (100) suggest two models for crisis treatment: the *recompensation* model, which sees the person as "falling apart" and in need of treatment geared to helping him pull himself together again in order to return to his prestress level of functioning; and the *limited psychotherapy* model, which considers the individual as decompensating as a result of the reactivation of old conflicts. Treatment consists in interpreting and helping him understand some of these earlier conflicts.

Similarly, Sifneos (167) distinguishes between *anxiety-suppressive* treatment, for disturbed persons with weakened egos, which aims to decrease or eliminate anxiety through the use of supportive techniques and environmental manipulation during the acutely traumatic phase of the situation, and *anxiety-provoking* treatment, for persons with some ego strengths and capacities, which makes use of rapport and transforms treatment into a learning experience. It challenges past actions and teaches the client to anticipate situations likely to produce unpleasant consequences. By stimulating a certain degree of new anxiety, the worker motivates the person to understand his emotional conflicts, recognize and deal with his reactions, and engage in a corrective emotional experience.

As part of treatment planning, time limits may be set by using the three dimensions— number of interviews, spacing of intervals, and total span of time—flexibly as the situation demands. Some services specifically limit intervention to a set number of meetings—say, six, eight, or ten.

Implementation of Treatment

As mentioned, the implementation phase of crisis intervention usually deals with setting up and working out specific tasks, primarily by the client, but also by the worker and significant others, designed to solve specific problems in the current life situation, to modify previous inadequate or inappropriate ways of functioning, and to learn new coping patterns. Treatment becomes keyed to the achievement of limited goals previously decided upon or implied by the nature of the initial contract. These may be simply relief from the pressures built up during the development of the crisis or arriving at a clearer understanding of what has been going on and what are the options open.

The concept of *task* opens up many possibilities. In crisis intervention, tasks are specifically couched in terms of what must be done in order to achieve reequilibration, the equivalents of Rapoport's "useful next steps." Golan sees them as divided into two categories, which may be carried out concurrently, the *material-arrangemental tasks* concerned with the provision of concrete assistance and services, and *psychosocial tasks* concerned with dealing with clients' feelings, doubts, ambiv-

alences, anxieties, and despairs, which arise while trying to carry out what both worker and client agree needs to be done.

Treatment techniques are, for the most part, similar to those used in other types of social work practice (82), with the terminology determined largely by the worker's frame of reference. During the initial phase, sustainment techniques, designed to lower anxiety, guilt, and tension and to provide emotional support, are frequently employed, with *reassurance, encouragement,* and the *offering of "gifts of love,"* to use Hollis' term, predominant. Procedures of direct influence, designed to promote specific kinds of change in the client's behavior, are probably used more often in crisis work than in other types of direct treatment. Of these, *giving advice,* particularly when the client is feeling overwhelmed and needs help in choosing a course of action, *advocating a particular course of action,* and *warning clients of the consequences* of maladaptive resolutions of the situation, are most often used. In extreme situations, where suicide may have been threatened or attempted or where the client is deteriorating rapidly, *direct intervention* may be necessary. As the client becomes more integrated, techniques of *reflective discussion,* particularly of his current and recent past situation and patterns of interaction, are appropriate.

Techniques geared to learning how to change behavior become important tools. *Anticipatory guidance, role rehearsal,* and *rehearsal for reality* are three closely allied procedures which emphasize the learning component in crisis treatment. Among behavioral modification techniques, those aimed at *positive reinforcement* and *shaping* of new behavior through a step-by-step approximation of the desired action are probably the most frequently used, as well as *modeling, teaching, coaching,* and *prompting.* (These last tools have long been used by social workers under different labels.) Employment of *assertive training* and *desensitization* programs have also been reported, and, most recently, *provision of feedback and instruction.* In recent years, a number of gestalt and transactional analysis techniques have added a new vocabulary to treatment (19, 124), although the usefulness of some of the devices may be questioned. In general, the level of effectiveness tends to reflect the particular commitment of the advocators of the technique.

An integral part of treatment in a crisis situation, as part of the "broad push" to achieve rapid reintegration, is *environmental work* and *activity with collaterals*—within the agency itself, with other professionals in the community, and with various types of natural and mutual support systems. Sometimes the worker may choose to leave direct treatment to others and to act as consultant to other elements in the total ecological system (37).

Termination of Intervention

In crisis work, termination of a case assumes unique importance. Worker and client, once the agreed-upon time limit approaches, review their progress since the client first came in in terms of key themes and basic issues with which they struggled. Emphasis is placed on the tasks accomplished, the adaptive coping patterns developed, and the ties built with persons and resources in the community. Future activity, when the client will be on his own, is planned. Often the case ends on an "as needed" basis as the worker closes the door but leaves a crack open for further reapplication, should the situation change or new crisis situations develop. (This is based on the presupposition that crises are part of the normal life pattern of individuals and families and can be expected to recur episodically.)

Throughout the case, the worker's stance is active, purposive, and committed, conveying the message that he knows what he is doing and is willing to take risks. However, as the client becomes more integrated, he tends to become more active in seeking his own solution. At such points, the worker becomes correspondingly less active. A fairly frequent occurrence is for the

client to take the lead and inform the worker, even before the time limit is used up, that he is ready to "take charge of himself" once more, thus terminating on his own.

Types of clients best treated

If we look upon the crisis approach as a formulation to be used selectively, as one of a variety of interventive strategies, a central question to be posed is: For whom? What should be the criteria for its application?

The answer is complex since two separate issues are involved: who experiences the crisis and who needs help in dealing with the situation created. As mentioned, crisis theory states that anticipated crises, of both the developmental and transitional kinds, can arise throughout the life span; thus crisis intervention would seem appropriate for everyone at some point. From another angle, unanticipated crises are so varied and unpredictable that, unless the service is available at points where such situations, by definition or prediction, can be expected to turn up—such as the emergency ward of a general hospital or the waiting room of a police station—the crisis aspects of the situation may come to light only after a different type of intervention has been started or the client has been sent away.

Some years ago, it was recommended that the crisis orientation might be appropriate for the very strong or the very weak, for those requiring only short periods of help or for those not motivated for continued service (126, p. 279). Since then we have become much more flexible in its application and more broad-based in our outlook. If we use the nature of the request for service and the extent to which the applicant wants to change as the criteria, we would probably find that a large majority of clients asking for help at moments of stress are asking for relief of discomfort and reduction of external pressures—two of the goals of crisis treatment.

One of the after-the-fact sets of criteria

which might have some bearing could be to look at those persons or families that have demonstrated ability to cope with crisis-producing events in the past. Successful crisis coping was found to be associated with behavioral adaptability and flexibility within a family, affection among family members, good marital adjustment between husband and wife, companionable parent-child relationships, family members' participation in decision making, wife's participation in husband's social activities, nonmarginal economic status, individual or family previous experience (direct or vicarious) with the type of crisis encountered, objective knowledge of the facets of a specific crisis before it occurs, and established patterns of interaction with the extended family, neighbors, and friends (131, p. 74). The obvious difficulty in using such a checklist is that precisely these types of clients are not usually the ones who come to the attention of professionals. Probably, would-be clients would have a negative prefixed to each attribute.

An extension of this approach might be to ask, along with Rapoport (141), for which clients would the crisis approach not be appropriate? It has been found that the large group of clients frequently seen in social agencies who seem to live in a chronic state of crisis are not good candidates since, to them, a self-generated crisis state is a lifestyle. While they manifest the overt symptoms of urgency, disordered affect, disorganized behavior, and ineffectual coping, closer examination shows that the basic character structure may have suffered severe and chronic ego depletion and damage. To many in this group, the crisis appearance is not a reaction to the original hazardous event, but a maladaptive attempt to ward off underlying personal disturbance or even psychosis. Such persons, often classified as borderline personalities or character disorders, may need help in emergencies but do not seem to be able to engage in the active participation and task resolution involved in the crisis approach. A typical example of this type of personality are

those clients seen in Travelers Aid offices who engage in "crisis flight" (78).

As a corollary to this group of clients, some persons may or may not themselves demonstrate overt symptoms of disequilibrium but lead such disordered, chaotic lives that they tend to produce crisis states in others—in their families, neighbors, teachers, public health nurses, and police with whom they come in contact and, eventually, in the professionals to whom they are, often unwillingly, referred. Those who tend to exhibit this "crisis-inducing" syndrome are usually quite resistant to change.

A further group of clients who may not be amenable to this approach are those persons who exist marginally in a state of chronic inability to cope with life's demands, such as the discharged mental patient, the physically or mentally handicapped, and the aged ill. Providing continuous support is probably a necessary attribute to their continued functioning, even in a limited way. Nevertheless, even this group can probably respond to short-term crisis support (123).

Although we broadened our concept of crisis to include a large proportion of life events, we have probably merely sketched out the outlines of the possibilities for use of this approach. Practically, it seems that the three pivotal indicators that can offer keys to the extent to which it should be offered as the treatment of choice are: *evidence of a clearcut hazardous event* that has direct bearing on the client's present state of disequilibrium; *a high level of anxiety or pain,* coupled with demonstrated motivation and potential capacity for change; and *evidence of breakdown in problem solving in the recent past* (61).

Implications for work with families, groups, and communities

Crisis situations, by definition, usually involve family role networks; in fact, much of the basic theory dealt with families in disequilibrium

(1, 59, 158). In terms of its application, most of the Harvard Public Health studies concentrated on the family as the basic unit of service (29). Langsley and Kaplan (100) see the family as experiencing a crisis when an important role is not being filled. If agreement cannot be reached as to who should fill the role, family pressures build up and the susceptible member may choose to escape through psychotic symptoms, seemingly irrational behavior, suicide attempts, or a request for sanctuary in a hospital. His refusal to undergo role change may be enough for the family to demand hospitalization for him as a maladaptive way of maintaining their equilibrium. Thus the goal of intervention becomes the restoration of the entire family unit to an acceptable level of functioning without the need to resort to hospitalization of the "sick" member.

In general, whether the family is considered initially to be in a state of collective crisis because of some role disruption of a member, or whether the state of crisis in one member acts as a hazardous blow to the rest of the family, disrupting their usual balance, the total upset situation calls for careful examination. An evaluation of the family's strengths and weaknesses, their capacities and motivation for change, and the resources at their disposal builds the foundation for treatment planning and execution. Restoring and augmenting family communication patterns becomes a particularly important treatment goal. Recently, entire family networks, actual or simulated, have been activated as a treatment strategy to enable distressed persons to regain their equilibrium (156, 174).

In addition to use of the crisis approach with nuclear and extended families, which are natural small groups, it has also been applied to friendship and common interest groups, including gangs and clubs that are not family-related (44). According to Parad (127), crisis intervention can be applied to a broad spectrum of formed groups as well, including groups of children and teachers in school settings, work groups, and therapy groups.

Groups are also being used as treatment tools when a number of people are simultaneously experiencing a common crisis. In the case of community disasters, the group provides a quick, economical means of reaching large numbers of victims to provide psychological first aid and to inform them of the details of the catastrophe, the resources available, and the means of minimizing disruptive after effects, as in the case of the Chicago train crash (67) and the San Fernando Valley earthquake (16). Recent developments include the use of crisis intervention groups in protective service settings and the rapid spread of self-help groups for a wide range of problem situations, some of which reach crisis proportions. After the 1973 war in Israel, social interest groups were used to help widows of soldiers share their experiences in learning to overcome the transitional problems of widowhood (63).

One of the first uses of crisis groups occurred at the Rush Center in Los Angeles, where they still form one of the main instruments for treatment (178). Opinion as to their utility, however, fluctuates. People seem willing to accept help in a group who might not otherwise do so. Support to members, particularly from disadvantaged elements, appears to be significant; social relationships often grow out of group contacts; and the group provides a vehicle for encouraging expression of significant feelings and developing desensitization to disturbing topics. Members often suggest new coping mechanisms to help others overcome their own difficulties. On the other hand, some individuals find it difficult to focus on resolution of their own crises in the open-ended group setting, where each member may be at a different stage of grappling with his specific situation. Sometimes coping mechanisms may be suggested that are more maladaptive than adaptive. Groups are often hard to fill, and much time must be spent on matching and sorting out membership. Finally, little professional treatment time seems to be gained (117).

On the community level, use of the crisis approach in widespread disasters has already been discussed. In many instances the hazardous event and the collective reactions of shock, loss, and concern for others have resulted in the breakdown of defensive barriers of race prejudice and economic self-interest and the development—for a short while—of altruistic communities of voluntary cooperation and mutual good will (172, pp. 281-282). Professional activity at this level is frequently linked with programs for primary prevention or early intervention; recent enabling federal legislation has provided the impetus to develop imaginative, far-reaching approaches. While social workers have long been experts in building up to-and-from referral systems within their communities, they are only now beginning to envisage the possibility of viewing the community as a client in its own right. Crisis and disasters may thus provide the springboard for increased cooperation or even restructuring of welfare services.

Much of the current research interest in crisis intervention is practice oriented and aimed at answering the basic question, "Do crisis services work?" (113). An allied interest has been to study the specific conditions, in terms of presenting problems, client populations, and structure of services, which provide the maximal return. In addition to the basic research in life span psychology and stress situations cited earlier, some work is being done on examining specific types of crisis situations (138) and on developing new tools by which to measure crisis dimensions (69). Unfortunately, the rapid pace of crisis intervention and the committed, partisan dedication of staff members tend to run counter to the careful, meticulous planning and rigorous controls needed to carry out well-conceived and well-executed research projects.

Implications for further use

Several years ago, when the first edition of this volume was written, it was felt that, despite its wide dissemination and general acceptance, the application of crisis theory seemed to have approached the boundaries of its usefulness, that a lull had occurred in its application. Since then, a resurgence of interest and the taking over of the approach by multidiscipline crisis teams and suicide prevention centers seem to have given it new life; certainly its usage appears to be increasing and spreading into new types of settings. Restructuring of services has overcome the built-in difficulty of not having crisis intervenors posted in places and at times when crisis-pressured clients can make quick use of them.

The separation of crisis treatment from other forms of services in an agency, however, brings about an artificial distinction between treatment offered during periods of high anxiety and increased pressure and other forms of service, and runs counter to the historical foundations upon which the social work profession has been built. If crisis intervention is to become a viable practice modality, it must be considered part of the practice repertoire of *all* social workers, to be offered differentially and as the treatment of choice under conditions where it appears to promise the maximal return. It should be usable at specific periods in long-term cases of chronic and recurrent crises as well as in short-term, limited problem situations.

The key may very well lie in the extent to which students in schools of social work are being taught the principles of crisis theory and its application along with other treatment modalities. Baldwin (6) has pointed out that the skills of the professional practitioner are developed at three levels: the *conceptual skills* that provide the framework for understanding problems and for developing strategies for change; the *clinical skills* and techniques for implementing an effective therapeutic strategy, which are an extension of the conceptual framework; and the *communication skills* that are necessary to enhance information exchange in the therapeutic relationship and to create a nonthreatening open bond. Effective crisis intervention requires training at each of these levels. Crisis therapy training, he feels, can provide unique opportunities to learn to set limits on therapeutic contacts, to negotiate specific, achievable goals, to focus on the present stress, to accept appropriate outcomes, to devise strategies at a practical and concrete help level, to learn to make rapid assessments, to become more direct and active, to gain experience in managing difficult patients, and to learn termination and disposition skills.

Despite the frequent objection that the crisis approach demands a level of autonomy and rapid decision making that is too advanced for many students, its integration into methods courses could serve to overcome the gap between clients in crisis and workers, committed to serve them but feeling poorly equipped to meet their special needs at times of heightened stress and pressure.

References

1. Ackerman, Nathan W. *The Psychodynamics of Family Life.* New York: Basic Books, 1958.
2. Aguilera, Donna C., Janice M. Messick, and Marlene S. Farrell. *Crisis Intervention: Theory and Methodology.* St. Louis: Mosby, 1970.
3. Alevizos, Peter N. and Robert P. Liberman. "Behavioral Approaches to Family Crisis Intervention," in Howard J. Parad, H. L. P. Resnik, and Libbie G. Parad, eds. *Emergency and Disaster Management: A Mental Health Sourcebook.* Bowie, Md.: Charles Press, 1976, pp. 129-143.
4. Alexander, Franz. "Psychoanalytic Contributions to Short-Term Psychotherapy," in Lewis R. Wolberg, ed. *Short-Term Psychotherapy.* New York: Grune and Stratton, 1965, pp. 84-126.
5. Babcock, Charlotte G. "Inner Stress in Illness and Disability," in Howard J. Parad and Roger R. Miller, eds. *Ego-Oriented Casework: Problems and Perspectives.* New York: Family Service Association of America, 1963, pp. 45-64.
6. Baldwin, Bruce A. "Crisis Intervention in Professional Practice: Implications for Clinical Training." *American Journal of Orthopsychiatry,* 47, October 1977, pp. 659-670.
7. Baldwin, Katherine A. "Crisis-Focused Casework in a Child Guidance Clinic." *Social Casework,* 49, January 1968, pp. 28-34.
8. Bartlett, Harriett M. *The Common Base of Social Work Practice.* New York: National Association of Social Workers, 1970.
9. Barton, Allen. *Communities in Disaster.* New York: Doubleday, 1969.
10. Bates, Paul B. and K. Warner Schaie, eds. *Life Span Developmental Psychology: Personality and Socialization.* New York: Academic Press, 1973.
11. Beatt, Earl J. "The Family Developmental Approach: A Program for Coping with Transitional Crises," in Parad, Resnik, and Parad, *Emergency and Disaster Management,* 1976, pp. 395-406.
12. Beck, Dorothy F. *Patterns in Use of Family Agency Services.* New York: Family Service Association of America, 1962.
13. —— and Mary Ann Jones. *Progress on Family Problems: A Nationwide Study of Clients' and Counselors' Views on Family Agency Services.* New York: Family Service Association of America, 1973.

14. Bergman, Anne. "Emergency Room: A Role for Social Workers." *Health and Social Work,* 1, February 1976, pp. 32-44.

15. Birnbaum, Freda, Jennifer Coplon, and Ira Scharf. "Crisis Intervention After a Natural Disaster." *Social Casework,* 54, November 1973, pp. 545-551.

16. Blaufarb, Herbert and Jules Levine. "Crisis Intervention in an Earthquake." *Social Work,* 17, July 1972, pp. 16-19.

17. Bloom, Bernard L. "Definitional Aspects of the Crisis Concept." *Journal of Consulting Psychology,* 27, 1963. Reprinted in Howard J. Parad, *Crisis Intervention: Selected Readings.* New York: Family Service Association of America, 1965, pp. 303-311.

18. Borgman, Robert D. "Crisis Intervention in Rural Community Disasters." *Social Casework,* 58, November 1977, pp. 562-567.

19. Brechenser, Donn M. "Brief Psychotherapy Using Transactional Analysis." *Social Casework,* 53, March 1972, pp. 173-176.

20. Brill, Naomi I. *Working with People: The Helping Process.* Philadelphia: Lippincott, 1973.

21. Brook, Bryan D., Michael W. Kirby, Paul R. Polak, and Rita Vollman. "Crisis Hostel: An Alternative to the Acute Psychiatric Ward," in Parad, Resnik, and Parad, *Emergency and Disaster Management,* 1976, pp. 67-73.

22. Burgess, Ernest W. "Family Living in the Later Decades," in Marvin B. Sussman, ed. *Sourcebook on Marriage and the Family,* 2nd ed. Boston: Houghton Mifflin, 1963, pp. 425-431.

23. Burnett, Bruce B., John J. Carr, John Sinapi, and Roy Taylor. "Police and Social Workers in a Community Outreach Program." *Social Casework,* 57, January 1976, pp. 41-49.

24. Cain, Lillian P. "Casework with Kidney Transplant Patients." *Social Work,* 18, July 1973, pp. 76-83.

25. Caldwell, J. M. "Military Psychiatry," in A. M. Freedman, H. I. Kaplan, and H. S. Kaplan, eds. *Comprehensive Textbook of Psychiatry.* Baltimore: William and Wilkins, 1967.

26. Caplan, Gerald. "A Public Health Approach to Child Psychiatry." *Mental Health,* 35, 1951, pp. 235-249.

27. ———. *Principles of Preventive Psychiatry.* New York: Basic Books, 1964.

28. ———. *Support Systems and Community Mental Health.* New York: Behavioral Publications, 1974.

29. ———, Edward A. Mason, and David M. Kaplan. "Four Studies of Crisis in Parents of Prematures." *Community Mental Health Journal,* 2, Summer 1965.

30. Carter, Robert D. and Richard B. Stuart. "Behavior Modification Theory and Practice: A Reply." *Social Work,* 15, January 1970, pp. 37-50.

31. Chapman, Dwight W. "A Brief Introduction to Contemporary Disaster Research," in George W. Baker and Dwight W. Chapman, eds. *Man and Society in Disaster.* New York: Basic Books, 1962, pp. 3-22.

32. Churchill, Sallie R. "Preventive Short-Term Groups for Siblings of Child Mental Hospital Patients," in Paul Glasser, Rosemary Sarri, and Robert Vinter, eds. *Individual Change Through Small Groups.* New York: Free Press, 1974, pp. 364-374.

33. Clark, Eleanor. "Round the Clock Emergency Psychiatric Services." *Social Work Practice, 1973.* New York: Columbia University Press, 1963. Reprinted in Parad, *Crisis Intervention,* 1965, pp. 261-273.

34. Coelho, George V., David A. Hamburg, and John E. Adams, eds. *Coping and Adaptation.* New York: Basic Books, 1974.

35. Cohen, Nathan E. *Social Work in the American Tradition.* New York: Holt, Rinehart, and Winston, 1958.

36. Cohen, Shlomo I. and Leopold O. Walder. "An Experimental Analog Derived from Crisis Theory." *American Journal of Orthopsychiatry,* 41, October 1971, pp. 822-829.

37. Collins, Alice H. and Diane L. Pancoast. *Natural Helping Networks.* Washington, D.C.: National Association of Social Workers, 1976.

38. Cumming, John and Elaine Cumming. *Ego and Milieu.* New York: Atherton Press, 1966.

39. Datan, Nancy and Leon H. Ginsberg, eds. *Life-Span Developmental Psychology: Normative Life Crises.* New York: Academic Press, 1975.

40. Dohrenwend, Barbara S. and Bruce P. Dohrenwend. *Stressful Life Events: Their Nature and Effects.* New York: Wiley, 1974.

41. Dublin, Louis I. *Suicide: A Sociological and Statistical Study.* New York: Ronald Press, 1963.

42. Duckworth, Grace L. "A Project in Crisis Intervention." *Social Casework,* 48, April 1967, pp. 227-231.

43. Einstein, Gertrude. *Learning to Apply New Concepts to Casework Practice.* New York: Family Service Association of America, 1968, pp. 9-49.

44. Epstein, Norman. "Techniques of Brief Therapy with Children and Parents." *Social Casework,* 57, May 1976, pp. 317-323.

45. Erikson, Erik H. *Childhood and Society.* New York: Norton, 1950.

46. ———. *Identity, Youth and Crisis.* New York: Norton, 1968.

47. Escalona, Sibylle K. *The Roots of Individuality: Normal Patterns of Development in Infancy.* Chicago: Aldine, 1968.

48. Ewalt, Patricia L. "The Crisis Treatment Approach in a Child Guidance Clinic." *Social Casework,* 54, July 1973, pp. 406-411.

49. ———. "The Case for Immediate Brief Intervention." *Social Work,* 21, January 1976, pp. 63-65.

50. Family Service Association of America. *Scope and Method of Family Service.* New York: Family Service Association, 1953.

51. Fantl, Berta. "Preventive Intervention." *Social Work,* 7, July 1962, pp. 41-48.

52. Fischer, Joel and Harvey L. Gochros. *Planned Behavioral Change: Behavior Modification in Social Work.* New York: Free Press, 1975.

53. Fox, Sandra S. and Donald J. Scherl. "Crisis Intervention with Victims of Rape." *Social Work,* 17, January 1972, pp. 37-42.

54. Frank, Jerome. "The Role of Hope in Psychotherapy." *International Journal of Psychiatry,* 5, May 1968, pp. 383-395.

55. Freud, Anna (1936). *The Ego and Mechanisms of Defense.* New York: International Universities Press, 1946.

56. Freud, Sigmund (1923). *The Ego and the Id.* London: Hogarth Press, 1961.

57. Getz, William, Allen E. Weisen, Stan Sue, and Amy Ayers, *Crisis Counseling*. Lexington, Mass.: Heath, 1974.

58. Gill, Merton M. *The Collected Papers of David Rapaport*. New York: Basic Books, 1967.

59. Glasser, Paul H. and Lois N. Glasser, eds. *Families in Crisis*. New York: Harper and Row, 1970.

60. Glick, Ira A., Robert S. Weiss, and C. Murray Parkes. *The First Year of Bereavement*. New York: Wiley, 1974.

61. Golan, Naomi. "When Is a Client in Crisis?" *Social Casework*, 50, July 1969, pp. 389-394.

62. ———. "Crisis Theory," in Francis J. Turner, ed. *Social Work Treatment: Interlocking Theoretical Approaches*. New York: Free Press, 1974, pp. 420-456.

63. ———. "Wife to Widow to Woman." *Social Work*, 20, September 1975, pp. 369-374.

64. ———. "Work with Young Adults in Israel," in William J. Reid and Laura Epstein, eds. *Task-Centered Practice*. New York: Columbia University Press, 1977, pp. 270-284.

65. ———. *Treatment in Crisis Situations*. New York: Free Press, 1978.

66. Grinker, Roy R. and John P. Spiegel. *Men Under Stress*. New York: Blackeston, 1945.

67. Grossman, Leona. "Train Crash: Social Work and Disaster Services." *Social Work*, 18, September 1973, pp. 38-44.

68. Grumet, Gerald W. and David L. Trachtman. "Psychiatric Social Workers in the Emergency Department." *Health and Social Work*, 1, August 1976, pp. 114-131.

69. Halpern, Howard A. "The Crisis Scale: A Factor Analysis and Revision." *Community Mental Health Journal*, 11, Fall 1975, pp. 295-300.

70. Hamilton, Gordon (1940). *Theory and Practice of Social Case Work*, 2nd ed. New York: Columbia University Press, 1951.

71. Hansen, Donald A. and Reuben Hill. "Families Under Stress," in Harold T. Christensen, ed. *Handbook of Marriage and the Family*. Chicago: Rand McNally, 1964, pp. 787-792.

72. Hardgrove, Grace. "An Interagency Service Network to Meet Needs of Rape Victims." *Social Casework*, 57, April 1976, pp. 245-253.

73. Harris, F. G. and R. W. Little. "Military Organizations and Social Psychiatry." *Symposium of Preventive and Social Psychiatry*. Washington, D.C.: Walter Reed Army Institute of Research, 1957, pp. 173-184.

74. Harshbarger, Dwight. "An Ecologic Perspective in Disaster Intervention," in Parad, Resnik, and Parad, *Emergency and Disaster Management*, 1976, pp. 271-280.

75. Hartmann, Heinz (1939). *Ego Psychology and the Problem of Adaptation*. New York: International Universities Press, 1958.

76. ——— (1947). *Essays in Ego Psychology*. New York: International Universities Press, 1964.

77. Henderson, Howard E. "Helping Families in Crisis: Police and Social Work Intervention." *Social Work*, 21, July 1976, pp. 314-315.

78. Hiatt, Catherine C. and Ruth E. Spurlock. "Geographical Flight and Its Relation to Crisis Theory." *American Journal of Orthopsychiatry*, 40, January 1970, pp. 53-57.

79. Hill, Reuben. "Generic Features of Families Under Stress." *Social Casework,* 39, February–March 1958, pp. 139–150. Reprinted in Parad, *Crisis Intervention,* 1965, pp. 32–52.

80. Hirsch, Josephine S., Jacquelynne Gailey, and Eleanor Schmerl. "A Child Welfare Agency's Program of Service to Children in Their Own Homes." *Child Welfare,* 55, March 1976, pp. 193–204.

81. Hoffman, David L. and Mary L. Remmel. "Uncovering the Precipitant in Crisis Intervention." *Social Casework,* 56, May 1975, pp. 259–267.

82. Hollis, Florence. *Casework: A Psychosocial Therapy,* 2nd ed. New York: Random House, 1972.

83. Holmes, Thomas H. and Richard H. Rahe. "The Social Readjustment Rating Scale." *Journal of Psychosomatic Research,* 11, 1967, pp. 213–218.

84. Holt, Robert R. "Ego Autonomy Revisited." *International Journal of Psychoanalysis,* 46, 1965, pp. 151–167.

85. Jacobson, Gerald F. "Programs and Techniques of Crisis Intervention," in Silvano Arieta, ed. *American Handbook of Psychiatry,* v. 2. New York: Basic Books, 1974, pp. 810–825.

86. ———, Martin Strickler, and Wilbur E. Morley. "Generic and Individual Approaches to Crisis Intervention." *American Journal of Public Health,* 58, February 1968, pp. 338–343.

87. ———, D. M. Wilner, W. E. Morley, S. Schneider, M. Strickler, and G. J. Sommer. "The Scope and Practice of an Early Access Brief Treatment Psychiatric Center." *American Journal of Psychiatry,* 121, June 1965, pp. 1176–1182.

88. Jaffe, Ruth. "Psychoanalytic Implications of Reactions of Israeli Soldiers to the Six-Day-War," in Heinrich Z. Winnik, Rafael Moses, and Mortimer Ostrow, eds. *Psychological Bases of War.* New York: Quadrangle, 1973, pp. 89–110.

89. Janis, Irving. *Psychological Stress.* New York: Wiley, 1958.

90. ——— and Leon Mann. *Decision Making.* New York: Free Press, 1977.

91. Kalis, Betty L., M. R. Harris, A. R. Prestwood, and E. H. Freeman. "Precipitating Stress as a Focus in Psychotherapy." *Archives of General Psychiatry,* 5, September 1961, pp. 219–226.

92. Kaplan, David M. "A Concept of Acute Situational Disorders." *Social Work,* 7, April 1962, pp. 15–23.

93. ———. "Observations on Crisis Theory and Practice." *Social Casework,* 49, March 1968, pp. 151–155.

94. ———, Aaron Smith, Rose Grobstein, and Stanley E. Fischman. "Family Mediation of Stress." *Social Work,* 18, July 1973, pp. 60–69.

95. Kasius, Cora, ed. *A Comparison of Diagnostic and Functional Casework Concepts.* New York: Family Service Association of America, 1950.

96. Keith-Lucas, Alan. "Structures in Traditional Agencies for Crisis Intervention to Aid the Dependent Child in Trouble." *Child Welfare,* 48, July 1969, pp. 420–422, 431.

97. Klein, Donald C. and Erich Lindemann. "Preventive Intervention in Individual and Family Crisis Situations," in Gerald Caplan, ed. *Prevention of Mental Disorders in Children.* New York: Basic Books, 1961, pp. 283–305.

98. Korner, I. N. "Crisis Reduction and the Psychological Consultant," in

Gerald A. Specter and William L. Claiborn, eds. *Crisis Intervention*. New York: Behavioral Publications, 1973, pp. 30-45.

99. Lang, Judith. "Planned Short-Term Treatment in a Family Agency." *Social Casework*, 55, June 1974, pp. 369-374.

100. Langsley, Donald and David M. Kaplan. *Treatment of Families in Crisis*. New York: Grune and Stratton, 1968.

101. Lazarus, Richard S. *Psychological Stress and the Coping Process*. New York: McGraw-Hill, 1966.

102. ——, James R. Averill, and Edward M. Opton, Jr. "The Psychology of Coping: Issues of Research and Assessment," in Coelho, Hamburg, and Adams, *Coping and Adaptation*, 1974, pp. 249-315.

103. Lebow, Grace H. "Facilitating Adaptation in Anticipatory Mourning." *Social Casework*, 57, July 1976, pp. 456-465.

104. LeMasters, E. E. "Parenthood as Crisis." *Marriage and Family Living*, 19, 1957. Reprinted in Parad, *Crisis Intervention*, 1965, pp. 111-117.

105. Lieberman, Morton A. "Adaptive Processes in Late Life," in Datan and Ginsberg, *Normative Life Crises*, 1975, pp. 135-159.

106. Lindemann, Erich. "Symptomatology and Management of Acute Grief." *American Journal of Psychiatry*, 101, September 1944. Reprinted in Parad, *Crisis Intervention*, 1965, pp. 7-21.

107. Lowenthal, Marjorie F., Majda Thurnher, David Chiriboga, and Associates. *Four Stages of Life: A Comparative Study of Women and Men Facing Transitions*. San Francisco: Jossey-Bass, 1975.

108. Lucas, Rex A. *Men in Crisis: A Study of a Mine Disaster*. New York: Basic Books, 1969.

109. Lukton, Rosemary C. "Crisis Theory: Review and Critique." *Social Service Review*, 48, September 1974, pp. 384-402.

110. McCubbin, Hamilton I., Barbara B. Dahl, Philip J. Metres Jr., Edna J. Hunter, and John A. Plag, eds. *Family Separation and Reunion: Families of Prisoners of War and Servicemen Missing in Action*. San Diego: Center for Prisoners of War Studies, Naval Health Research Center, 1974.

111. McGee, Richard K. *Crisis Intervention in the Community*. Baltimore: University Park Press, 1974.

112. Maluccio, Anthony N. "Action as a Tool in Casework Practice." *Social Casework*, 55, January 1974, pp. 30-35.

113. Maris, Ronald and Huell E. Connor. "Do Crisis Services Work? A Follow-Up of a Psychiatric Outpatient Sample." *Journal of Health and Social Behavior*, 14, December 1973, pp. 311-322.

114. Merbaum, Michael and Albert Hefez. "Some Personality Characteristics of Soldiers Exposed to Extreme War Stress." *Journal of Consulting and Clinical Psychology*, 44, 1976, pp. 1-6.

115. Meyer, Carol H. *Social Work Practice*, 2nd ed. New York: Free Press, 1976.

116. Moos, Rudolf H., ed. *Coping with Physical Illness*. New York: Plenum, 1977.

117. Morley, Wilbur E. and Vivian B. Brown. "The Crisis Intervention Group: A Natural Mating or a Marriage of Convenience?" *Psychotherapy: Theory, Research, and Practice*, 6, Winter 1969, pp. 30-36.

118. Morris, Betty. "Crisis Intervention in a Public Welfare Agency." *Social Casework*, 49, December 1968, pp. 612-617.

119. Murphy, Lois B. *The Widening World of Childhood*. New York: Basic Books, 1962.

120. ———. "Preventive Implications in the Preschool Years," in Caplan, *Prevention of Mental Disorders in Children*, 1961, pp. 218-248.

121. ——— and Alice E. Moriarty. *Vulnerability, Coping, and Growth: From Infancy to Adolescence*. New Haven: Yale University Press, 1976.

122. Nelson, Zane P. and Dwight D. Mowry. "Contracting in Crisis Intervention." *Community Mental Health Journal*, 12, September 1976, pp. 37-44.

123. Normand, William C., Herbert Fensterheim, and Susan Schrenzel. "A Systematic Approach to Brief Therapy for Patients from a Low Socioeconomic Community." *Community Mental Health Journal*, 3, Winter 1967, pp. 349-354.

124. O'Connell, V. F. "Crisis Psychotherapy: Person, Dialogue, and the Organismic Event," in J. Fagen and I. L. Shepherd, eds. *Gestalt Therapy Now*. New York: Harper and Row, 1970.

125. Parad, Howard J. "Preventive Casework: Problems and Implications." *Social Welfare Forum, 1961*. New York: Columbia University Press, 1961, pp. 178-193. Reprinted in Parad, *Crisis Intervention*, 1965, pp. 284-298.

126. ———. "The Use of Time-Limited Crisis Intervention in Community Health Programming." *Social Service Review*, 40, September 1966, pp. 275-282.

127. ———. "Crisis Intervention," in John B. Turner, ed. *Encyclopedia of Social Work*, 17th issue, v. 1. Washington, D.C.: National Association of Social Workers, 1977, pp. 228-237.

128. ——— and Libbie G. Parad. "A Study of Crisis-Oriented Short-Term Treatment." *Social Casework*, 49. Part I, June 1968, pp. 346-355. Part II, July 1968, pp. 418-426.

129. ———, H. L. P. Resnik, and Libbie G. Parad, eds. *Emergency and Disaster Management: A Mental Health Sourcebook*. Bowie, Md.: Charles Press, 1976.

130. ———, Lola Selby, and James Quinlan. "Crisis Intervention with Families and Groups," in Robert W. Roberts and Helen Northen, eds. *Theories of Social Work with Groups*. New York: Columbia University Press, 1976, pp. 304-330.

131. Pasewark, Richard and Dale A. Albers. "Crisis Intervention: Theory in Search of a Program." *Social Work*, 17, March 1972, pp. 70-77.

132. Pavenstedt, Eleanor and Viola W. Bernard. *Crises of Family Disorganization*. New York: Behavioral Publications, 1971.

133. Paykel, E. S. "Life Stress and Psychiatric Disorder," in Dohrenwend and Dohrenwend, *Stressful Life Events*. New York: Wiley, 1974.

134. Perlman, Helen H. *Social Casework: A Problem-Solving Process*. Chicago: University of Chicago Press, 1957.

135. ———. "Some Notes on the Waiting List." *Social Casework*, 44, April 1963, pp. 200-205. Reprinted in Parad, *Crisis Intervention*, 1965, pp.193-201.

136. ———. "In Quest of Coping." *Social Casework*, 56, April 1975, pp. 213-225.

137. Piaget, Jean. *The Origins of Intelligence in Children*. New York: Norton, 1963.

138. Polak, Paul R., Donald J. Eagan, Richard L. VandenBergh, and Vail Williams. "Crisis Intervention in Acute Bereavement: A Controlled Study of Primary Prevention," in Parad, Resnik, and Parad, *Emergency and Disaster Management*, 1976, pp. 443-457.

139. Rapoport, Lydia. "The State of Crisis: Some Theoretical Considerations." *Social Service Review*, 36, June 1962, pp. 211-217. Reprinted in Parad, *Crisis Intervention*. 1965, pp. 22-31.

140. ———. "Crisis-Oriented Short-Term Casework." *Social Service Review*, 41, March 1967, pp. 31-42.

141. ———. "Crisis Intervention as a Mode of Brief Treatment," in Robert W. Roberts and Robert H. Nee, eds. *Theories of Social Casework*. Chicago: University of Chicago Press, 1970, pp. 267-311.

142. Rapoport, Rhona. "Normal Crisis, Family Structure, and Mental Health." *Family Process*, 2, 1963, pp. 68-80. Reprinted in Parad, *Crisis Intervention*, 1965, pp. 75-87.

143. ——— and Robert N. Rapoport. "New Light on the Honeymoon." *Human Relations*, 17, 1964, pp. 33-56.

144. Raymond, Margaret, Andrew E. Slaby, and Julian Lieb. "Familial Responses to Mental Illness." *Social Casework*, 56, October 1975, pp. 492-498.

145. Reid, William J. and Laura Epstein. *Task-Centered Casework*. New York: Columbia University Press, 1972.

146. ———, eds. *Task-Centered Practice*. New York: Columbia University Press, 1977.

147. Reid, William J. and Ann W. Shyne. *Brief and Extended Casework*. New York: Columbia University Press, 1969.

148. Resnik, H. L. P. and Harvey L. Ruben, eds. *Emergency Psychiatric Care: The Management of Mental Health Crises*. Bowie, Md.: Charles Press, 1975.

149. Reynolds, Bertha C. *An Uncharted Journey*. New York: Citadel Press, 1963.

150. Rhodes, Sonya L. "A Developmental Approach to the Life Cycle of the Family." *Social Casework*, 58, May 1977, pp. 301-311.

151. Rich, Margaret E. *A Belief in People*. New York: Family Service Association of America, 1956.

152. Ripple, Lilian, with Ernestina Alexander and Bernice W. Polemis. *Motivation Capacity, and Opportunity: Studies in Casework Theory and Practice*. Chicago: School of Social Service Administration, University of Chicago, 1964.

153. Rosenbaum, C. Peter and John E. Beebe III. *Psychiatric Treatment: Crisis Clinic, Consultation*. New York: McGraw-Hill, 1975.

154. Rosenberg, Blanca N. "Planned Short-Term Treatment in Developmental Crises." *Social Casework*, 56, April 1975, pp. 195-204.

155. Rossi, Alice S. "Transition to Parenthood." *Journal of Marriage and the Family*, 30, 1968, pp. 26-39.

156. Rueveni, Uri. "Network Intervention with a Family Crisis." *Family Process*, 14, June 1975, pp. 193-203.

157.   Russell, Betty and Sylvia Schild. "Pregnancy Counseling with College Women." *Social Casework,* 57, May 1976, pp. 324-329.

158.   Scherz, Frances H. "The Crisis of Adolescence in Family Life." *Social Casework,* 48, April 1967, pp. 209-215.

159.   ——. "Maturational Crisis and Parent-Child Interaction." *Social Casework,* 52, June 1971, pp. 362-369.

160.   Schulz, David A. *The Changing Family: Its Function and Future.* Englewood Cliffs, N.J.: Prentice-Hall, 1972.

161.   Selye, Hans. *The Stress of Life.* New York: McGraw-Hill, 1956.

162.   Shader, Richard I. and Alice K. Schwartz. "Management of Reaction to Disaster." *Social Work,* 11, April 1966, pp. 99-105.

163.   Shaw, Robert, Harry Blumenfeld, and Rita Senf. "A Short-Term Treatment Program in a Child Guidance Clinic." *Social Work,* 13, July 1968, pp. 81-90.

164.   Sheridan, Mary S. and Doris R. Johnson. "Social Work Services in a High-Risk Nursery." *Health and Social Work,* 1, May 1976, pp. 86-103.

165.   Shneidman, Edwin S., Norman L. Farberow, and Robert E. Litman. *The Psychology of Suicide.* New York: Science House, 1970.

166.   Sifneos, Peter E. "A Concept of Emotional Crisis." *Mental Hygiene,* 44, April 1960, pp. 169-179.

167.   ——. "Two Different Kinds of Psychotherapy of Short Duration." *American Journal of Psychiatry,* 123, March 1967, pp. 1069-1073.

168.   ——. *Short-Term Psychotherapy and Emotional Crisis.* Cambridge, Mass.: Harvard University Press, 1972.

169.   Silverman, Phyllis R. "Widowhood and Preventive Intervention." *Family Coordinator,* January 1972, pp. 95-102.

170.   Simonds, John F. "A Foster Home for Crisis Placements." *Child Welfare,* 52, February 1973, pp. 82-90.

171.   Siporin, Max. *Introduction to Social Work Practice.* New York: Macmillan, 1975.

172.   ——. "Disaster Aid," in *Encyclopedia of Social Work,* 1977, v. 1, pp. 277-288.

173.   Small, Leonard. *The Briefer Psychotherapies.* New York: Brunner/Mazel, 1971.

174.   Speck, Ross V. and Carolyn L. Attneave. *Family Networks.* New York: Pantheon Books, 1973.

175.   Specter, Gerald A. and William L. Claiborn, eds. *Crisis Intervention.* New York: Behavioral Publications, 1973.

176.   Stotland, Ezra. *The Psychology of Hope.* San Francisco: Jossey-Bass, 1969.

177.   Strickler, Martin. "Applying Crisis Theory in a Community Clinic." *Social Casework,* 46, March 1965, pp. 150-154.

178.   —— and Jean Allgeyer. "The Crisis Group: A New Application of Crisis Theory." *Social Work,* 12, July 1967, pp. 28-32.

179.   —— and Margaret Bonnefil. "Crisis Intervention and Social Casework: Similarities and Differences in Problem Solving." *Clinical Social Work Journal,* 2, Spring 1974, pp. 36-44.

180.   Taplin, Julian R. "Crisis Theory: Critique and Reformulation." *Community Mental Health Journal,* 7, March 1971, pp. 13-23.

181. Taylor, James B., Louis A. Zuicher, and William H. Key. *Tornado: A Community Responds to Disaster.* Seattle: University of Washington Press, 1970.

182. Titchener, James L., Frederic T. Kapp, and Carolyn Winget. "The Buffalo Creek Syndrome: Symptoms and Character Change after a Major Disaster," in Parad, Resnik, and Parad, *Emergency and Disaster Management,* 1976, pp. 283-294.

183. Towle, Charlotte. *Common Human Needs.* Washington, D.C.: Federal Security Agency, 1945. Reissued, New York: National Association of Social Workers, 1957.

184. ——. "Reinforcing Family Security Today." *Social Casework,* 31, February 1950. Quoted in Rich, *A Belief in People,* 1956.

185. Townsend, Gladys E. "Short-Term Casework with Clients Under Stress." *Social Casework,* 34, November 1953, pp. 392-398.

186. Tyhurst, James. "The Role of Transition States—Including Disaster—in Mental Illness." *Symposium on Preventive and Social Psychiatry.* Washington, D.C.: Walter Reed Army Institute of Research, 1957, pp. 149-169.

187. Vogel, Ezra F. and Norman W. Bell. "The Emotionally Disturbed Child as the Family Scapegoat," in Bell and Vogel, eds. *The Family.* New York: Free Press, 1960, pp. 382-397.

188. Wasserman, Sidney. "The Middle Age Separation Crisis and Ego Supportive Casework Treatment." *Clinical Social Work Journal,* 1, September 1973, pp. 38-47.

189. Weakland, John H., Richard Fisch, Paul Watzlawick, and Arthur M. Bodin. "Brief Therapy: Focused Problem Resolution." *Family Process,* 13, June 1974, pp. 141-168.

190. White, Robert W. "Motivation Reconsidered: The Concept of Competence." *Psychological Review,* 66, September 1959, pp. 297-333.

191. ——. *Ego and Reality in Psychoanalytic Theory.* Psychological Issues No. 11. New York: International Universities Press, 1963.

192. Wilson, Robert S. *The Short Contact in Social Case Work,* v. 1. New York: National Association for Travellers Aid and Transient Service, 1937.

193. Wiseman, Reva S. "Crisis Theory and the Process of Divorce." *Social Casework,* 56, April 1975, pp. 205-212.

194. Woolf, Donald A. and Marvin Rudman. "A Police-Social Service Cooperative Program." *Social Work,* 22, January 1977, pp. 62-63.

195. Zastrow, Charles and Ralph Navarre. "Help for Runaways and Their Parents." *Social Casework,* 56, February 1975, pp. 74-78.

Annotated listing of key references

CAPLAN, Gerald. *Principles of Preventive Psychiatry.* New York: Basic Books, 1964.
  Basic presentation of Caplan's approach to crisis intervention, with emphasis on various levels of intervention, according to public health model. Important reference, although the theory has moved beyond this point.

CAPLAN, Gerald. *Support Systems and Community Mental Health.* New York: Behavioral Publications, 1974.
  First essay is extremely important, signifying basic change in Caplan's orientation, with increased emphasis on use of natural and mutual help systems.

GOLAN, Naomi. *Treatment in Crisis Situations.* New York: Free Press, 1978.
  Attempts to place crisis intervention within framework of social work practice and presents a basic treatment model to be used flexibly in different settings. This is an outgrowth of task-centered model.

KAPLAN, David M. "Observations on Crisis Theory and Practice." *Social Casework,* 49, March 1968, pp. 151–155.
  Discussion of early Harvard studies, using public health framework. Presents important concept of acute situational disorder and psychological tasks to be mastered, with implications for agencies and practitioners.

PARAD, Howard J. "Crisis Intervention," in *Encyclopedia of Social Work,* 17th issue. Washington, D.C.: NASW, 1977, pp. 228–237.
  Crisp, concise presentation of basic crisis theory and its current research and practice applications, including future trends.

PARAD, Howard J., H. L. P. Resnik, and Libbie G. Parad, eds. *Emergency and Disaster Management.* Bowie, MD.: Charles Press, 1976.
  Important sourcebook of recent developments in the field, including reports of disaster work. While the quality of articles is uneven and some are repetitious, it reflects current emphases and preoccupations in crisis area.

RAPOPORT, Lydia. "Crisis Intervention as a Mode of Brief Treatment," in Robert W. Roberts and Robert H. Nee, eds. *Theories of Social Casework.* Chicago: University of Chicago Press, 1970, pp. 267–311.
  Presents Rapoport's last analysis and interpretation of crisis theory and its application to the field of practice. Excellent historical summary and perspective.

SIPORIN, Max. "Disaster Aid," in *Encyclopedia of Social Work,* 17th issue. Washington, D.C.: NASW, 1977, pp. 277–285.
  Careful, detailed analysis of recent developments in this area, including review of theory and discussion of governmental policies and programs.

STRICKLER, Martin and Margaret Bonnefil. "Crisis Intervention and Social Casework: Similarities and Differences in Problem Solving." *Clinical Social Work Journal,* 2, Spring 1974, pp. 36–44. *Interesting effort to compare traditional casework practice and crisis intervention, pointing out commonalities and changes in direction, including that of goals, techniques, and worker's stance.*

21

Interlocking Perspective for Practice

by

FRANCIS J. TURNER

In beginning this endeavor several years ago, it had been my intention that in the final chapter I would attempt to compare the spectrum of practice systems discussed in the book along a profile of identified variables. It was hoped that in so doing it would be possible for practitioners to make more effective use of each system by being able to identify similarities, differences and applicabilities between and among the thought systems.

It is clear that we are not yet ready for this for several reasons. Certainly one of the most important of these is the wide variation in the systems from the perspective of their being fully developed theories. As several of the authors mention, the term "theory" can be applied to few if any of the systems discussed in each chapter except in an imprecise way. Many of the various systems are at different levels of abstraction and have varying orders of forms and applicability.

A second reason why it is difficult to make detailed comparisons stems from the fact that each chapter was written by a different person. One of the things I learned early in this endeavor was the tremendous challenge and difficulty involved in attempting to write about these various topics from a common framework that would facilitate comparisons. Apart from the personal idiosyncrasies of the authors, who, understandably, would have preferred to develop their own outline rather than follow someone else's, it was clear that the task of ordering material in a common framework was virtually impossible, given the wide differences in development and focus of each topic. The spectrum of thought systems covered range from theories that attempt to explain the structure of personality and the effect of various phenomena on subsequent psychosocial development, to systems that direct strategies of intervention in specific circumstances. Thus, it is difficult to try to compare existential theory, which is both a philosophy of life as well as a base for therapy, with a chapter on communications concepts that deal with a specific, albeit essential, component of human interaction. Evidently it could be argued that, rather than depend on an academy of authors, surely a book such as this should be written by a single author who would then write from a common outline and thus facilitate comparison. I think that the day is coming when in fact this is what should be done. But it is still too early for this, as many of the topics are still developing and their place in social work is still emerging. Because of this, it was thought better to let those most identified with them to write about them.

The third reason that we are not yet ready for a definitive practitioner oriented comparison is that as yet the variables that one would use are still not fully apparent. We still need to know more about the differences in practice emerging from each system related to practice setting, client type, presenting problem or treatment objectives; that is, more clarity is needed about the operational differences between and among the systems.

But different as are both the structure of the various chapters and the content discussed within them, it is interesting that there are similarities both in content and theme that appear. As I read and reread the various chapters, I was struck by the clarity with which a common perception of social work was evident. Even though some authors begin with a conviction that a major focus of their chapter is to identify differences in their systems from those of their colleagues, there is in fact much similarity in their content. This observation of an intercommonality raises the speculation that there would be much similarity in direct work with clients by practitioners who held different theoretical positions. The differences that would be observed would focus more on practitioners' explanations and descriptions of human behavior and its reciprocal influences than on the actual processes and methods they would use in working with them. This, clearly, is a gratuitous statement that

needs to be tested in a rigorous fashion. Testing it would greatly aid our understanding of how theory influences practice.

Since the first edition to the book and with the addition of new chapters, several emerging themes can be observed across these writings in particular and in the periodical literature of the last few years. Certainly, there is much less faddism about new theories. We now seem to be much more comfortable in that the possibility of major theoretical breakthroughs is remote. There will not be any great theoretical panacea. This has resulted in a much more cautious approach to theory building and utilization. As mentioned in the Preface to this edition, we seem to be more interested in discussing precise application of parts of theory rather than in discussing new theories. This is a mature and welcome development. This is not to suggest that there will not be any new thought systems, only that there seems to be more emphasis now on making better use of what we currently have.

In a similar vein, an increasing comfort with an interlocking concept can be observed; that is, there is a growing awareness that each emerging theory need not stand alone, but can be enriched by seeking and developing areas of intervention with other systems. This, either as cause or effect, has resulted in a diminution of the intensity of some of our holy wars. We are much more comfortable with the perception that each system does have something to offer and that it is possible to function from a pluralistic theory base. Along with this maturing trend can be observed a growing appreciation of the need for theory as a basis for practice. This is especially important as the pressure for evaluation of practice continues.

Related to this are two further themes: one, the awareness of the complexity of the task of developing and testing theory in an evaluative mode; second, a growing awareness that all research need not be of an experimental nature; that is, we are once again at a point of appreciating the utility of phenomenological research, as used so richly by both Freud and Rogers. This is a further advantage of practicing from an interlocking perspective.

Certainly, the above is not to suggest that there are not different viewpoints expressed by the authors. Several describe areas in which their systems represent a divergence from other viewpoints. But frequently their description of the position of the other viewpoint is not what that school would say about itself. It appears we still have a number of long-enduring straw men that we need to attack to support our own positions. I suggest it is time that these be put to rest as they no longer seem to have a crucial place in practice—if, indeed, they ever did.

Two straw men that were frequently cited were the place of unconscious material in treatment and the content of assessment and diagnosis. In these two areas one might still observe a conviction that some of the theoretical approaches to practice insist on a constant, omnipresent, heavy and detailed focus on early history from which to formulate a diagnosis, and an assumption that unconscious components of human behavior are the principal focus of attention and the content of interventive processes. In view of this presumption on the part of some authors, it is remarkable how minimal is this stress anywhere in this book. Certainly, there are different views on the importance of material that is not conscious, as well as different views on the need to understand anything more about the client than what is immediately presented by him. But over and over again, the emphasis on treatment in all the chapters is on the present, on understanding the current life situations of the client, of using their reasoning capacities to learn new patterns of behavior and of involving the client in the total process. This is not exclusive, of course, and it would be incorrect to overemphasize the similarities, just as it is incorrect to overemphasize differences.

A third straw man that seems to persist is the continuing misconception that treatment for some schools of thought is by definition long term. Certainly some of the cases mentioned as examples implied a course of treatment that existed over several months, but no author suggests that this is the mode of all treatment. The more general assumption seemed to support a treatment process that was not extensive in length.

A prevalent theme throughout the book is that the focus of treatment should be on the client and his psychosocial situation and not exclusively on his inner psychic functioning. Not that the instinctual and inner life of man is overlooked, but that this component of the human situation is only a part of man. Thus much of the necessary framework for understanding the person in the treatment situation is related to his current situation, rather than the necessity of a detailed understanding of the past. Of course the latter is not excluded as a component of treatment, only that it is not given the stress that some critics of other systems presumed to exist. One emerging theme, not as apparent in the first edition, is the growing awareness of the biological component of our clients. Gestalt and its awareness of body language and mediation and its emphasis on body and mind have certainly helped bring this aspect of the person back into focus.

Thus, again, we see an emphasis on man in his present reality, his inherent search for growth, his health and strength, his ability to reason, to take responsibility, to change as well as adjust, to reflectively plan his present and future life and to be accountable for his functioning. Undoubtedly, there are differences in the weighting of these components of man's potential, but again there is more consensus than disagreement on the importance of the components and their intermixture.

In examining each approach to practice, one observes marked differences in the range of assumptions that each author makes about the nature of man, the components of personality, the nature and sources of change and, I think most importantly, the basic value orientations that underlie the theory about man, his worth and destiny.

It may well be that this is an area where the various authors take for granted that consensus exists or that value orientations are separate from a body of theory, and hence not the material for this type of project. I think it is important to continue to be more explicit about our values and assumptions. This, from a conviction that our values do influence our theory and the modes and settings in which we put our theories to practice.

It was the awareness that one variable along which the various systems differed was in their perception of the essence of basic human nature that gave a beginning idea on how to develop a system or a framework to serve as a basis for intersystem comparison. As I continue to struggle with the awareness of the similarities and differences between systems, I have begun to realize that since each approach to psychotherapy is attempting to do something similar— help people become more human—it may be that the differences are different perceptions of similar phenomena. Thus, it is possible that every approach to practice has to come to terms with the same components of the process, and that the systems will vary along an identifiable continuum for each component of the therapeutic process. With this in mind, I turned to the various systems as well as to the practice world and attempted to identify the questions that the practitioner needs to ask or answer about an approach to practice.

This approach proved fruitful and, with the assistance of several graduate students, the first drafts of an outline are emerging.* This is not yet ready for publication but hopefully will be in the near future. To date, I have identified six areas that appear to differentiate thought systems in practice. Each of these areas has several

subtopics that will not be listed here as they are still in development.

1. Each system has to be assessed from the viewpoint of its overall attributes, including its historical origins and the nature of its specificity and its empirical base.
2. Each system also has to be examined from the perspective of its perception of the individual and the nature of his rationality.
3. In addition, each therapeutic approach has to take a position about the nature of behavior, the determinants of behavior and the nature of personality change.
4. Thought systems must also identify the characteristics of the therapeutic process and the nature of change agents.
5. A system needs also to identify the required knowledge and the skills of a therapist.
6. Lastly, a system needs to identify the characteristics of its applicability and to provide a description and identification of its essential components.

It is hoped that further work on this outline will permit us to develop a system that could be of great utility to practitioners interested in electing different therapeutic approaches for different clients.

In the chapters it is evident that we continue to focus more attention on the understanding and utilization of direct work with clients than on indirect work: the psychotherapeutic activities rather than the sociotherapeutic activities. I do not suggest that we are ignoring the latter. What I think is happening is that we are continuing to take the environmental component of our practice responsibility for granted and focusing on the other; that is, stressing the "direct work" over the "indirect work," to use Richmond's terminology. Many of us in social work clinical practice underestimate the extent to which working effectively within the client's external significant systems is a part of our practice. We also underestimate the profile of differential skills we develop and the spectrum of roles in which we function in this component of practice. Re-

---

*In this process the assistance of Diane Kochendorfer has been indispensable. She has used the outline on several of the thought systems and has found it applicable and useful.

gardless of our theoretical base, we all could strengthen our understanding of practice and increase our precision and effectiveness if we began to focus the same attention on the environmental component of our practice as we do on our direct work with clients.

It is interesting that virtually all of the theoretical presentations, including the psychoanalytic school, where one might least expect it, presume the twofold thrust of practice on person and situation. Yet it is equally interesting that conceptually we have still not given this component the emphasis that it requires; this to the detriment of our conceptual base and ultimately to the detriment of our clients and communities. Undoubtedly, with ongoing theoretical development, a shift will take place. Clearly psychosocial therapy, systems theory, task-centered practice and problem-solving theory inherently espouse the importance of milieu work. As conceptualization in these systems continue, we can expect an increasing affirmation of the importance of work with the "situation" as well as the person.

Related to the focus on the interpersonal component of practice, I think a legitimate point of criticism of this collection could be made about an overemphasis on one-to-one treatment rather than work with groups and communities. Families appear to be in a somewhat different category; that is, we seem to take as given that all of our theoretical bases presume we can work with families, as well as individuals. But most of the chapters put a heavier focus on one-to-one intervention than on groups and communities. This has been a disappointment, as I began with a conviction that we have indeed moved further toward incorporating a multimethod based practice than the writings seem to indicate. I do not think that the fact that persons do not emphasize these other components indicates or suggests that there is no interest or concern in them. What I think it does suggest is that we still significantly reflect our tradition of "one man, one method." Undoubtedly, we have made progress in the direction of emphasizing multi-

competences in individual practitioners. Nevertheless, our writings still reflect a tendency to emphasize that methodology in which we are most comfortable, be it individual, family, group or community. Perhaps we shouldn't be too concerned about this because we do know that many practitioners in recent years have been able to practice comfortably with several methodologies and this trend appears to be continuing and growing. It is hoped that the number of practice-based articles and papers that emphasize a plurality of methodologies will increase. The appeal here is not to a unitary practice method or even to imply that we are approaching a point where we can realistically discuss a general theoretical system as a basis for all practice. What is being advocated is the need to continue to be open to influence from all seriously presented bodies or systems of thought and to be more comfortable as individual practitioners with a multimethod, multitheoretical armamentarium.

In 1964, Charlotte Towle wrote: "Certainly a profession does not come of age until it develops its own theory. The oversimplification at the root of shoddy practice is more likely to occur through the annexation of theory from other disciplines" (13, p. vii). With the marked dissolution of professional boundaries and areas of responsibility that has taken place during the decade that has passed since Towle wrote the above, the criticism of cross-fertilization is not as valid; nevertheless, the need for careful and conscious assimilation of material is still as important.

Although a tendency for enthusiasm about the content of each particular theory can be noted and fully understood, it is of particular importance also to note how each author has sought to consider the implications of his theory for practice. I think we are well beyond the point of easily adopting a body of thought in an unquestioning way, or applying it in the cliché-ridden style about which Dr. Towle warns us. Each author struggles with the strengths and limitations, the uses and gaps in his or her systems. Most identify the process of search, the concept of incompleteness, the necessity of seeing the theory in transition rather than as a final word, and are far from the point where they could be seen as "theory imperialists."

Each author subscribes to the necessity of individual practitioners having their own theoretical base, as well as the necessity of continued search for linkages between theories and new theories. No one suggests that we are approximating the emergence of a general theory, or even wonders if we should aspire to it. There are suggestions about connections between theories and the utility of theories serving as bases on which other theories can be developed or integrated. There is general consensus on the function of theory and on the utility of theory in giving direction and understanding to responsible practice.

In evaluating these approaches to theories, from the practitioners' viewpoint, a key question for the searcher to ask is one of utility. How will this approach help me to know what to do in practice? Few of the systems discussed could be called practice theory—that is, theories that give precise direction to the practitioner as to what to do in a particular situation to achieve a specified behavioral change or response. Some of the components of crisis theory, behavior modification, and to some extent transactional analysis, as here presented, approach practice theory. The need for such practice theory has been long advocated, and I suggest that we do have the conceptual base from which to begin to identify and test out some of the practice principles that would derive from these systems (11). The abstracting of such practice principles offers a potentially productive way of testing for differences or similarities between the various orientations presented in this book.

Most of our systems at this point conceptualize practice at a middle-range level or beyond. Most are seen by their promoting authors as being in development. Some are seen to be derivatives from earlier theories and others' efforts to translate material from other fields into concepts relevant for our practice. Thus, cognitive theory is presented as a development from earlier functional thinking, and systems concepts have been brought to our profession from other disciplines. As the content of each chapter is considered, we can see how early differences between theories disappear and new differences emerge as progress is made; that is, the multiplicity of thought systems in social work practice is seen as an enriching phenomenon, given the present state of practice and the demands on it.

It isn't that the existence of a multifaceted conceptual base is a desirable thing any more than is the existence of a unitary base. What is important is that there exists a multiple-theory-based practice that is not isolated. Thus one of the exciting observations that can be made on examining the various chapters is the lack of isolation in each approach to practice. It is intriguing to see to what extent each writer indicated how his approach is compatible with, developed from or influenced by other systems presented in this book. No one presented his theory in an exclusive approach independent of the others. Most indicated the areas where their approach was compatible or identified linkages between other theories. Both the chapter on functional theory and that on cognitive theory mention how the ego psychological development in the psychodynamic tradition aided in bringing the thought systems closer to the dynamic tradition.

Clearly, some of the systems do stand more by themselves than others either because of their specificity or their origins. This varying quality of observed affinity presented great difficulty in deciding what order to use in presenting the chapters. Several approaches were considered, including a simple alphabetical one, a historical one, a spectrum ranging from most abstract to most concrete, or one ranging from the most particular to the most general. Each of these seemed deficient in one way or another. It was finally decided to present the chapters in groupings where there was an observable common tradition or set of characteristics. This order was selected after the original outline was formulated. The original plan had also used a grouping approach that divided the chapters into traditional approaches, indigenous approaches, exogenous approaches, and approaches that served as linkages between other theories.

In the second edition it was decided not to attempt a formal division of the chapters into sections. Some clustering of chapters was done, where there was some obvious connection, but apart from that there is not a precise basis on which the order of the chapters was built. In a way, there is some satisfaction to be taken from this difficulty in ordering for it seems to underscore the phenomenon of cross-fertilization between systems that is an essential assumption of the book.

Presuming that there is a higher degree of consensus among different thought systems than is usually considered, important questions to be faced are: What are the implications for practice of this multifaceted, interlocking conceptual base? To what extent can and should a practitioner be knowledgeable about and comfortable with the range of systems here presented, as well as others not considered or still to emerge? In the first chapter it was pointed out that we do not really know at this point how extensive is the influence of this spectrum on practice. It was clearly advocated that responsible practice should be theory based, but it was also acknowledged that we didn't know if it is or not. It would be cynical in the extreme to speculate that these theories have no influence on practice, but I think it would be equally naive to imply that practitioners consciously, deliberately and consistently formulate their interventive strategies from a specific conceptual base.

I began this project from a conviction that all of the various thought systems influencing current practice were important and that it was our responsibility to be aware of each, to strive to understand it and deliberately try to put some of the concepts of each system into practice. In

approaching the project's conclusion I am even more convinced of the soundness, yet the challenge, of this approach to practice. Too long have we labored under the impression that adherence to one approach to practice by definition excluded others; that there was some component of disloyalty or some quality of Machiavellian manipulation to attempt to move from one approach to practice to another, depending on the situation, the setting, the resources, the persons or the request. Probably this would be more true if one held that the various approaches were mutually exclusive and contradictory, but clearly less true if one is convinced of a large element of interconnectedness and interinfluence.

One of the areas in which each author was asked to comment, if it seemed appropriate, was the kind of clients, situations or settings in which his or her system seemed most relevant or most appropriate.

In general, the authors tended to indicate a broad base of applicability rather than a specific one and preferred not to have the applications of a particular viewpoint seen in too restricted a way. For example, Donald Krill's chapter on existentialism suggests that this approach is useful for persons where problems of alienation exist, but hastens to add that this is not the only application of his approach.

Nevertheless, I think it appropriate to speculate briefly on some of the particular applications that one could make in using the various approaches. The implication of this discussion is that one of the components of the differential diagnostic component of practice is to speculate on which of the various approaches, or which combination of approaches, appears most relevant to a presenting situation. Practice from this viewpoint would suggest a more conceptually open approach than is the case where one has a more strongly fixed theoretical base. In no way am I suggesting support for a nontheory approach to practice, nor even for a theoretically neutral approach, but rather for an open approach in a period in our history when we are still very much in transition. As mentioned in the Preface, it is necessary for a person to develop as firm a theoretical base as is possible; however, in this process it is necessary to keep all options and all alternatives open. It seems that if this was a more prevalent approach to practice there would appear a greater and richer opportunity to develop linkages and integrative structures between the various theories that are already emerging. Such an approach would also provide richer opportunities for our clients. In considering the possibility of a clearer awareness of the differential utility of each system, it is important not to forget the concept of equifinality from general systems theory. This concept emphasizes that there are frequently many ways of achieving similar goals; that is, it may well be that many of the therapeutic systems under consideration, different though they may be, are capable of achieving the same outcomes. Nevertheless, this does not rule out the possibility of specific use for each approach.

In looking at the various theories it is possible to identify situations where each system can be seen as having a specific utility. Most have important implications in understanding large segments of practice. Thus, anyone who is working to improve his practice skills and effectiveness cannot overlook the importance of better understanding the dimensions and components of effective human *communications*. But beyond the general implications, these concepts have particular relevance in situations where there are marked differences between the clients and the social worker, be they cultural, value, or related to intellectual capacity.

Systems theory, as well as providing us with an essential framework for understanding and ordering the multifaceted milieus of our practice, can also be particularly helpful in those situations where the client's milieu is complex and where in a critical way a range of significant environments are involved. Such situations are frequently seen in many of our multiproblem clients.

The *Life model* or *ecological approach* has some similarities to systems theory. But it provides the practitioner with a richer understanding of the potential for growth that can take place both in the client and in the environment, when properly understood, than does systems theory. It is also an approach to practice that has a particular relevance for many of the cases we meet in general practice where the problems are essentially boundary problems.

Role theory similarly helps us understand many aspects for our client's life beyond the particular role in which we become involved with him throughout the life of the case. I find it particularly helpful for people in situations where the stress they are experiencing originates in role transitions in their life—be it newly married or separated persons, new arrivals to an area, or changes associated with status such as retirement or employment. Often the concepts of role theory are useful for clients in helping them order the alternatives open to them and the possible outcome of these alternatives.

Learning theory and the vast range of behavioral techniques related to it have opened up for practitioners a range of resources for achieving specified behavioral changes in clients. Apart from the increased understanding of the processes involved in the acquiring and modification of general behavior traits, learning theory has particular relevance for helping clients alter specific problem areas of functioning when it is assessed that such changes will achieve the identifiable goals, without the necessity of understanding causes or interconnectedness between behaviors. Thus, a man who can be helped to modify his eating habits in a manner that permits him to retain his health and continued employment can be significantly helped without his having to understand some of the reasons for his eating patterns.

Crisis theory also helps us to better understand the dynamics and expected behavior of people in various life traumas. This theory gives us an orientation to the early assessment of clients at intake as well as providing us with discrete objectives and procedures for dealing with those situations diagnosed as crises; that is, crises concepts orient us to speculate in treatment situations whether we have a person in crisis or not and if so, what to do about it.

Task-centered treatment has some similarities to crisis theory in that it focuses very much on brief, time-limited intervention. It is a particularly useful approach in situations where a parsimonious use of resources is essential. It is also a form of treatment of special utility for therapists who want to maximize the client's involvement in the process and to enhance the client's sense of autonomy and right to self-determination. It is also useful for practitioners who are looking for an approach that stresses their responsibility to set clear, identified and attainable goals.

Family theory clearly has a specific focus for practitioners and like most other orientations is an important anchoring concept to aid in understanding and managing many of the problems with which we are presented, often in the guise of individual adjustment or behavioral problems. As with all orientations, it can be overapplied and situations are at times diagnosed and managed in treatment from a family therapy orientation that could be better handled from a different perspective.

Existential theory, as mentioned earlier, is not a system of therapy as much as a framework for understanding oneself, others and the human experience. I would consider that it is virtually impossible to be a responsible practitioner in today's world without some type of existential framework. Nevertheless, I think there are some specific practice situations that we can encounter where an existential stance helps us both to understand the clients and to formulate a perspective from which to help them. I have an impression that we are seeing an increasing number of people whose problems emerge mainly from questions about their own identity and sense of alienation. Here we can be of considerable help to them by using a framework of existential thinking.

Meditation is the approach to practice that

perhaps is least understood by practitioners who have not examined it carefully. Certainly, it has much to offer many clients and appears to have particular utility for some. It appears to be useful for many of those clients suffering from confusion about themselves and their place in the universe, not unlike existentialism. In addition, it is also useful for clients who need and want to achieve a greater sense of self-mastery, and a disciplined approach to life.

Cognitive theories are obviously strongly influencing current practice in an overall fashion, as mentioned earlier in this chapter. In a specific way I think they are particularly important in those situations where our objectives are to help people work their way out of situations when they are capable of doing so. Here the focus on responsibility, ability and more effective use of one's executive functions are prime and assist clients to make better use of themselves in life situations beyond treatment.

Client-centered therapy, similarly, is particularly important and useful in practice situations where one's focus is to help the client regroup his own resources, begin to come to terms with himself more effectively and satisfyingly and pursue the life goals he has established.

Functional theory, like the previously mentioned ones, focuses on the client's self-resources and the healthy and developmental component of all functioning. In current practice I think if has a particular relevance in reminding us how to use the helping process within the structures of our established agencies. Too often in the past decade, we have tended to see the agency as a necessary, or even not so necessary, evil. The functionalist concept of using structure, time, policies and the resources of the agency as a part of the helping process, is a resource in treatment not sufficiently utilized. As Dr. Yelaja points out, this has particular ramifications for settings where authority is an important factor and the structure and policies of the agency are clearly specified, structured and fixed.

Gestalt theory is, of course, a popular movement in current society. It is a theory that frees up the therapist to be himself, to be innovative, creative and imaginative in practice. It is an approach to practice that fits readily with clients interested in a total and integrated sense of self and use of self. Thus it is useful for those situations where a significant component of our goal is to help the client get in better touch with himself in a manner that fosters conscious contact with self and life.

Transactional Analysis, like Gestalt theory, is very much a treatment approach that has strong popular support. Because of this, it is an approach of utility to those clients who do not see themselves or want to be seen as needful of or recipients of traditional psychotherapy. Like Gestalt, it is health oriented and emphasizes the positive. This in itself is therapeutic for many of our clients. It places great stress on the grave responsibility to decide on the kind of life that we will lead and, again, like many of the newer therapies, stresses autonomy. It also puts special emphasis on working in groups, a modality that appeals to many clients.

The problem-solving approach, like some of the above-mentioned theories, leads us to use our own problem-solving processes in seeking to understand the client and his reality, and then to partialize his situation. Further, it aids us to help the client find the optimum available route to the identified goals that he has established. I think it is a particularly useful framework for us in those situations where there is a risk of the areas of focus and the objectives of intervention becoming diffuse and unfocused.

Psychosocial therapy, like many of the others discussed, has a vast spectrum of applicability, and because of its commitment to openness, encourages utilization of several approaches. Specifically, it helps us focus on the dual components of persons and is essential in those cases where understanding of oneself and one's relationship with his significant environment is important.

Ego psychology leads us to keep focused on both the conscious and unconscious components of human behavior and personality. It focuses on the importance of understanding the external and social components of a client's life as well as his inner life. Although the subject of current criticism, this body of knowledge has essential relevance in situations where growth and movement for the client require a recognition and understanding of self, patterns of behavior and their derivatives. Important as are the reality approaches to practice, there are still numbers of clients who want and need to be understood in developmental terms and can only be helped by a sensitive understanding of their personality, history and development.

The current "bête noire" of clinical practice is of course *psychoanalytic theory*. Few writers or students in recent years would consider they had done their duty if they failed to attack this school of thought and its lack of relevance for current practice. Nevertheless, it is manifestly evident that the influence of this school has been pervasive, universal and continuing. It is also clear that there are clients who can only be fully understood, involved in treatment and helped by treatment from a psychoanalytic focus. The real-life problems created by transference problems and developmental fixations and regressions are great, and many can only be touched in this manner. In spite of the current emphasis on the present, there are many persons who in seeking a clearer and less alienated self-concept want to understand their emotional and developmental history and have a right to this treatment.

It is clear from the broad scope of most of the approaches to practice that a colleague could be a responsible and effective practitioner who fully understood the dimensions and limitation of any one of the approaches to practice discussed in this book. But I believe it is more certain that a person can be even more effective, imaginative, economical and responsible in practice through an ongoing commitment to understanding and striving to integrate an interlocking theoretical approach to social work treatment.

There is one additional observation to be made about the material presented in this volume. I have kept it to the last as I consider it a key and essential observation from the project. It is evident from each chapter that there is need for much ongoing interconnected research to test the implied hypotheses in the system and assess the therapeutic implications of the concepts. Yet it is equally evident that little progress has been made in this direction. We are now at the end of a decade in which considerable progress was made in establishing the need for better research, in developing competent researchers and in producing some excellent research. But we still have not made dramatic progress in beginning to develop a practice theory or a theory of practice based on the development of explicit operational hypotheses. I am not discouraged about this, nor do I wish to add to the already long list of exhortations and recriminations about our failures in this area. Clearly, there is a new spirit of scholarly commitment and practice responsibility within the professions. It is evident from these writings that there is a growing identification with an interlocking perception of practice. This is observable in the rippling effect taking place between systems. In recent years everyone has become more behaviorally oriented, we have all become more existential, all are systems sensitive and most are family centered. Practice is very much in the here and now, yet no one has put aside completely psychodynamic theory and a developmental approach to practice. More ministudies, single case models and phenomenological approaches are needed, as well as the continued use of the wisdom and discipline of the large sample control-based experiments to move these practice trends to transmittable bodies of knowledge.

Conclusion

Clinical social work practice remains an essential part of the profession's practice endeavors. The big wave of criticisms and challenges of clinical practice is over. Like God, it has once again been accepted that clinical practice is neither dead nor hiding out in archaic or outmoded agencies. It has been discovered, though, that clinical practice that seeks to understand and dares to intervene in the process of human growth and psychosocial development is indeed an overwhelmingly difficult task, replete with risks and uncertainties, but equally enriched with satisfactions and achievements. There is not to date, nor indeed will there be, a single theory of clinical social work practice. There are, and will continue to be, a range of understandings and tested findings about effective and planned change. Such findings will in some instances complement each other and help further interrelate theories; others will contradict, necessitating additional conceptualization and testing. Throughout, the practice of social work treatment will be from a base of interlocking theoretical approaches.

References

1. Baldwin, Alfred S. *Theories of Child Development.* New York: Wiley, 1968.
2. Bartlett, Harriett. *The Common Base of Social Work Practice.* New York: National Association of Social Workers, 1970.
3. Carkhuff, Robert R. and Bernard G. Berenson. *Beyond Counseling and Therapy.* New York: Holt, 1967.

4. Hall, Calvin S. and Gardiner Lindzey. *Theories of Personality*, 2nd ed. New York: Wiley, 1970.

5. Hollis, Florence. "Letter to the Editor," *Social Casework*, 52 (December, 1971), 652-653.

6. Murray, Henry A. and Clyde Kluckhohn. "Outline of a Conception of Personality," Kluckhohn, Murray and Schneider (eds.) *Personality in Nature and Society*. New York: Knopf. 1956.

7. Patterson, C. H. *Theories of Counseling and Psychotherapy*. New York: Harper and Row, 1966.

8. Roberts, Robert W. and Robert H. Nee. *Theories of Social Casework*. Chicago: University of Chicago Press, 1970.

9. Segalman, Ralph. *Theories of Personality*. A comparative schematic chart. El Paso, 12, Texas, 1964.

10. Simon, Bernice K. "Relationship between Theory and Practice in Social Casework, *Social Work Practice in Medical Care and Rehabilitation Settings*, Monograph 4. New York: National Association of Social Workers, 1960.

11. Stanton, John Ormond. "A Social Work Model for Developing and Empirically Testing Practice Principles in Marital Counseling." Unpublished doctoral dissertation. University of Toronto, Faculty of Social Work, 1972.

12. Stevenson, O. "Problems in the Use of Theory in Social Work Education," *The British Journal of Psychiatric Social Work*, 9, No. 1 (1967), 27-29.

13. Towle, Charlotte. "Preface," in F. Hollis (ed.) *Casework: A Psychosocial Therapy*. New York: Random House, 1964.

Index

Ackerman, Nathan W., 45, 387, 455, 476
Acting-out, 44
Action, in role theory, 393-94
Action therapy, 433-35
Active listening, 216
Actualizing tendency, 190-91
Adams, Jane, 36
Adams, John E., 383
Adaptation, in life model, 362-64
Adjustment, problem-solving approach to, 121-22
Adler, Alfred, 127, 243-45, 251-53, 256, 257, 262
Administration, client-centered principles and, 187
Adolescence, 23, 365
    identification and, 20
Agency function, 129-31, 134
Aggression:
    Adler's ideas about, 256
    cognitive view of, 244, 256-57
    Freudian view of, 256
Aggressive drives, 18
Albers, Dale, A., 515
Alcoholics, 416
    client-centered therapy with, 206
    meditation and, 321
Alevizos, Peter N., 511
Alexander, Franz, 501, 511
Alienation, 167
Allan, Eunice F., 13-28, 72
Alland, Alexander, Jr., 256-57
Allen, Frederick, 179, 201, 203
Allport, Gordon, 126, 152
Altman, Irwin, 369
Ambivalence, 41, 42
Analogistic method of theory building, 343
Anderson, R. E., 336, 339
Anderson, W., 221-23

Angyal, Andras, 126, 132, 152, 275
Anomie, 170-71
Ansbacher, Heinz L., 253, 256, 258
Antecedents of behavior, identifying the, 437-39
Antipsychiatry, 152
Anxiety, 509
    client-centered therapy and, 193
    cognitive view of, 257
    crisis intervention and, 516-17
    existentialist view of, 154
    meditation and, 319-22
    signal, 509
Aponte, Harry, 384
Armidale workshops, 208
Armstrong, Patricia M., 344n, 345
Arnold, Magda B., 255
Aronson, Harriet, 392
Asch, Solomon E., 388
Assertive counseling component, 120, 248
    problem-solving theory and, 95, 113
Atherton, Charles R., 398-99
Attention, focusing, 314, 315
Austin, Lucille, 16, 38
Authoritarianism, 355
Authority, functional approach and, 135
Autonomy, in life model, 365-66
Awareness-excitement-contact cycle, 281-84
Awareness process (or continuum), 277
Axline, Virginia, 201-4
Ayllon, Teodoro, 448
Azrin, Nathan H., 448

Bad faith, 153, 159
Baldwin, Alfred L., 3
Baldwin, Bruce A., 521
Bales, R. F., 415

Bandler, Louise, 16
Barnes, Graham, 310
Barnes, Hazel, 176
Barrett-Lennard, G. T., 177-241
Barry, E., 203
Bateson, Gregory, 155, 462, 463
Beatman, F. L., 45
Bebout, James, 214
Beck, A. M., 209, 214
Beck, Aaron T., 247, 272, 321
Behavior role as a synonym for, 386
Behavioral assessment, 435-42
Behavior change, *see* Change
Behavior disorders, 44
Behaviorism, cognitive theory and, 253, 254
Behavior modification, 164, 167, 402, 433-48
    annotated listing of key works on, 448
    crisis intervention and, 502, 511, 517-18
    environmental engineering and, 444-46
    Gestalt therapy and, 282
    Haley's strategies and, 156
    of personality, 158
    phobias and, 266
    process of, 442-46
    structure of intervention and, 442-44
Belief system, defensive, 159
Bell, John, 168
Bell, Norman W., 502
Benedict, Ruth, 386, 390
Benjamin Rush Center for Problems of Living, 504, 507
Berdyaev, Nikolai, 169
Berne, Eric, 293-300, 305, 310
Bernstein, Arnold, 392, 393, 407
Bernstein, Basil, 419
Bertalanffy, Ludwig von, 336-38
Berzon, Betty, 206n, 209, 214
Betz, Barbara J., 119
Betz, E. J., 93
Biddle, Bruce J., 391, 407
Bierman, Ralph, 120, 248
Birdwhistell, Ray L., 411, 416, 424, 430, 463
Blanck, Gertrude, 43
Blanck, Rubin, 43
Bloom, Martin, 339
Blugerman, Michael, 273-92
Bolman, William M., 56
Bolter, Agnes, 344n, 345, 348
Bonnefil, Margaret, 506, 532
Borderline, 43, 45
Borenzweig, Herman, 251
Boszormenyi-Nagy, Ivan, 462, 465, 476
Boulding, Kenneth, 338
Boundary, social work as work on, 350-52
Braaten, L. J., 209
Bradford, Kirk A., 152, 176
Brage, George, 384
Brenner, Charles, 253
Brief treatment, *see* Crisis theory
Brill, A. A., 293-94
Brill, Eugene, 344-45, 347
Brill, Naomi, 512
Brown, Michael, 298, 311

Bruch, Hilde, 413
Buber, Martin, 149, 158, 159, 169, 176, 275
Buckey, W., 337, 353-54
Buddhism, meditation and, 315-18
Burch, Noel, 216
Bureaucratic organization, 367-68
Burgess, Ernest, 502
Burian, W. A., 354
Burton, Arthur, 152, 166, 168
Butler, John, 184
Byers, Paul, 417-18

Cantor, N., 210
Capacity-to-communicate scale, 413
Caplan, Gerald, 499-501, 503-4, 509, 510, 515, 532
Carlson, Virginia, 344n, 348
Carter, I. E., 336, 339
Castaneda, Carlos, 356
Cause and effect, 316
Center for Studies of the Person, 217
Change, 164, 220, 227
    cognitive view of, 244, 245, 250-51, 261
    existentialist view of, 153-54, 160-61
    functional theory and, 125-27, 131
    Gendlin's theory of, 197-98
    general systems approach to, 346-47
    Gestalt theory and, 275
    meditation and, 318-20
    reality therapists' view of, 155
    social, 169-70
    See also Behavior modification; Growth; Process
Channel of communication, 413-14
Character-disordered clients, 43, 45
    ego-oriented casework with, 47-56
Chassell, Joseph, 28
Cherry, Colin, 410, 430
Children (child therapy):
    client-centered therapy with, 201-4
    companionship therapy program and, 227
    in Life Model, 364-66
    Parent Effectiveness Training and, 227
    problem-solving work with, 96-97
    relationship therapy with, 179
    See also Family therapy; Infants
Choices (decisions), 129
    freedom of, *see* Freedom of choice
Christianity, 316
Clemence, Esther, 38
Client-centered therapy (or system or approach), 155, 177-241, 543
    with children and in families, 201-5
    community and, 217-20
    conditions of therapeutic personality change in, 185-86, 192-96
    conditions of worth in, 192-93
    congruence in, 185
    current work on personal process and change, 221-25
    dimensions of therapy and personal facilitation in, 192-95
    empirical research in, 181-83
    "equation of therapy" in, 185

existentialist social work and, 163
facilitator-change agent in, 229-30
helping interview in, 198-201
human nature in, 188
with individuals, 205-9, 213-15
with individuals in groups, 205-9, 213-15
information-processing theory and, 221-23
interview research in, 183
nontherapy applications of, 187-88
origins and early development of, 178-79
play therapy in, 201-4
as post-school movement, 212-30
process conception in, 186
with schizophrenics, 186-87
school phase of, 181-88
the self in, 191-92
self-theory and, 183-84
social crises and interpersonal cultural change and,
    225-29
in teaching and education, 209-12, 215-17
therapy outcome in, 184
unconditional positive regard in, 185, 192-94
Client-worker relationship, see Relationship, client worker;
    Therapeutic relationship
Closed systems, 335-37
Coburn, Denise Capps, 293-311
Coelho, George V., 383
Cognitive casework, 248-49
Cognitive deficiency, 249, 262
Cognitive theory (or therapy), 243-72, 502, 543
    annotated listing of key works in, 272
    case vignettes exemplifying treatment, 267-69
    counterindications for use of, 266
    emotions and, 253, 255-56
    gaps in, 267
    general therapeutic concepts of, 253-58
    historical origins of, 244-45
    language and, 253
    other theories' connection to, 252
    personality change in, 260-61
    principal proponents of, 245-47
    principal social work proponents of, 247-51
    psychoanalysis and, 251
    psychosocial history and diagnosis and, 261-63
    social work research implications of, 266-67
    summary of, 243-44
    therapeutic relationships in, 258-60
    treatment methods and techniques, 263-65
    treatment modalities and, 266
    types of clients, problems, and settings most appropriate
        for, 265-66
Coleman, Marie, 400
Colt, Ann, 44
Commitment, existentialist view of, 154
Communication, 409-32
    annotated listing of key works on, 430-32
    context of, 411
    definitions of, 409
    feedback and, 423
    major principles of, 423-25
    messages and, 418-21
    metamessages and, 420-21
    model of, 411-13
    noise and, 421
Communication theory, 155-56, 409, 410
    family therapy and, 454-56
    See also Information theory
Communicator A, 411-13
Communicator B, 421-23
Community:
    client-centered approach and, 217-20
    ego psychology and, 45
    existentialism and, 169-71
    psychosocial therapy and, 81-82
Community disasters, 503, 508, 520-21
Community growth principle, 220
Community organization:
    existentialist view of, 170
    functional theory and, 136
    role theory and, 398
Companionship therapy program, 227
Competence, 365
Complementarity of roles, 389
    family therapy and, 462-63
Computers in psychosocial therapy, 76
Concepts, 3
Conditionality of response, 194
Conditions of therapy, 185-86, 192-96
Conditions of worth, 192-93
Confidentiality, general systems approach and, 345
Conflict, 132
    role, 390
Conflict resolution, 187-88
Confluence, 278
Confucianism, 316
Congruence, 193-95
Consciousness:
    client-centered view of, 190
    cognitive view of, 244, 245, 251, 257-58
    existentialist view of, 153, 159
    functional theory and, 252
    general systems theory and, 356
    therapeutic relationship and, 259
    See also Cognitive theory
Consequences of behavior, identifying the, 439-42
Contact analysis, 415
    general systems theory and, 344-45
Context analysis, 411
Context of communication, 411
Contracting:
    in task-centered treatment, 485-86
    in transactional analysis, 302-3
Coping:
    crisis theory and, 509-11
    in Life Model, 363-64
Corner, George W., 126
Cottrell, Leonard S., 386
Coulson, William, 216-17
Countertransference, 40
    psychosocial therapy and, 74
Counterwill, 132
Couples, treatment, 26-27
Courage, 259, 264
Creative force, 158

Crisis in Life Model, 372
Crisis groups, 520
Crisis theory (crisis intervention), 45, 499-533, 542
  annotated listing of key works on, 532-33
  assessment of the situation and, 514-16
  connection of other theories to, 509-11
  with families, groups, and communities, 519-21
  general therapeutic concepts of, 511-13
  generic vs. individual approach to, 516
  goals of treatment in, 516-17
  historical origins of, 501-4
  implementation of, 517-18
  implications for further use, 521-22
  implications for practice, 513-18
  introduction into social work, 504-6
  principal social work proponents of, 506-9
  in problem-solving work, 95
  summary of, 499-501
  termination, 518
  types of clients best treated by, 518-19
Crowding, 369, 370
Cultural change, interpersonal, client-centered movement
  and, 225-29
Cultural pattern, role as a, 386
Cumming, Elaine, 510
Cumming, John, 510
Curry, Andrew, 152, 176
Cybernetics, 410

Dalibard, Jill E., 415
Danehy, John J., 430-31
Davis, Barbara, 442
Deatherage, Gary, 318-19, 322-23, 331
Decontaminating, 302
DeCristoforo, Richard L., 344n, 345
Defenses (defense mechanisms), 18, 509
  client-centered view of, 192
  ego, 34-36
  existentialist view of, 153
Defensive belief system, 159
Degaming, 302
Dehumanization, social, 160-71
Denial phase, separation-termination and, 57-58
Dependency-independence, 41-42
Depression:
  cognitive treatment of, 264-65
  meditation and, 321, 322
  problem-solving approach to, 108-9
Descriptions, 392
Desensitization, meditation and, 314, 315, 319, 321
Deutsch, Morton, 387
Developmental stages, 21
  superego and, 21-23
  treatment as affected by, 23-24
Devonshire, Charles, 213-14
Dewey, Edith A., 261
Dewey, John, 279
Diagnosis:
  cognitive approach to, 261-63
  ego psychology and, 39
  in existential social work, 161
  functional approach to, 128-29

  Gestalt approach to, 280-81
  meditation and, 323
  problem-solving and, 94
  in psychosocial therapy, 78-79
  role theory and, 396-99
  transactional analysis and, 298
Diagnostic school, 124, 128; see also Psychoanalytic
  theory; Freudian approach
Dialectical psychology, 462
Dialogue, existentialist view of necessity of, 154
Dibs: In Search of Self (Axline), 204
Dinitz, Simon, 392
Directional change in existential therapy, 164
Direct reference phase of focusing, 197-98
Disasters, 503, 508, 520-21
Discomplementarity of roles, 389
Discounts, 301
Disequilibrium, role theory and, 400-401
Disillusionment, 155
  existentialist view of, 153
Distance, personal, 369, 370
Distress-relief quotient, 415
Dollard, J., 415
Dorfman, Elaine, 202-3
Double-bind, 463
Dreams, cognitive view of, 257-58
Drucker, Peter, 125, 126
Dual personalities, 258
Dublin, Louis, 504
Dubos, Rene, 226, 362, 366, 370, 383
Dunbar, Flanders, 305
Duncan, Starkey D., Jr., 415
Durkin, Helen E., 168, 349-50
Dusay, Jack, 299, 310
Dynamic formulations in existential social work, 162

Early recollections (ER), 261, 262
Eastern religious philosophy, 275
Ecological perspective, *see* Life Model
Ecology, 361; *see also* Life Model
Education (educational system):
  client-centered principles and, 187, 209-12, 215-17,
    225, 227
  social work programs, 172
Ego, 14, 17, 27
  defense mechanisms, 34-36, 38
  Freud's concept of the, 33-35
  identification and, 19
  meditation and, 318
  strengthening the, 37-38, 41
Ego development, 16-19, 32-35
  crisis resolution and, 510
  identification and, 19
  preoedipal, 21
  superego development and, 20-21
  See also Personality development
Ego-oriented casework, 38-40
  case examples of, 47-62
  with character-disordered clients, 47-56
  gaps in knowledge and implications for research in,
    46-47
  See also Ego psychology

Ego psychology, 15-17, 33-62, 125, 159, 251, 509, 544
  annotated listing of key works on, 67
  diagnosis and, 39
  historical origins and development of theory of, 33-36
  implications for individuals, families, groups, and communities, 45-46
  implications for types of clients and treatment approaches, 43-45
  social work and, 36-39
  treatment process and, 39-43
  See also Ego-oriented casework
Ego states, in transactional analysis, 297-99
Ego-supportive treatment, 45
Eldred, Stanley H., 415
Ellinwood, Charlotte, 203-4
Ellis, Albert, 152, 155, 166, 245-46, 248, 251, 255-56, 264, 272
Emerging persons, Rogers' view of, 225-27
Emerging theme in existential therapy, 165-66
Emery, F. E., 354-55
Emotions, cognitive view of, 244, 245, 253, 255-56
Empathy (empathic understanding):
  in client-centered therapy, 193, 194, 199-200, 202, 206, 207
  meditation and, 324
Encounter groups (encounter group movement), 152, 155, 166, 208-9
  community and, 217-20
  educational system change and, 215-16
  recent theory on, 213-15
Ends, E. J., 206
English, Fanita, 310
Enright, John, 281
Entropy, 335-36, 351
Environment:
  ecological concepts and, 362-70
  in existential therapy, 164
  general systems theory and, 350-55
Environmental engineering, 444-46
Epstein, Laura, 479, 497
Epstein, Nathan B., 414
Epstein, Norman, 249-50
Equifinality, 337
Equilibrium, 336
  role tyeory and, 400-401
Erikson, Eric, 34-36, 45, 70, 127, 293, 365-67, 371, 422, 501, 509, 510
Ernst, Franklin, 297
Escalona, Sibylle, 501
Evaluations in role theory, 394
Exhaustion crisis, 512
Existentialism (existential philosophy), 147-53
  basic stance of, 148-49
  bond with others in, 150-51
  change in, 153-54, 160-61
  client-centered approach and, 163
  the community and, 169-71
  freedom of choice in, 153-54
  Perls and, 274-75
  personality in, 158-60
  professional literature of, 151-53
  subjectivity in, 148-50

transactional analysis and, 297-99
Existentialist hero, 148-49
Existential psychology and psychotherapy, 152
  cognitive theory and, 252-53
Existential social work (or therapy), 147-76, 543
  annotated listing of key works on, 176
  case example of, 168-69
  diagnosis in, 161
  emerging theme in, 165
  goal formulations in, 163-65
  methods and principles of treatment in, 163-68, 171
  other therapeutic approaches related to, 154-55
  process of change in, 160-64
  research and knowledge gaps in, 171-72
  results of, 171-72
  therapeutic concepts of, 153-54
  therapeutic relationship in, 156-58
  values of, 157, 166-67
Expectation, crisis theory and, 512
Experience (experiencing):
  client-centered approach to, 188-92, 195-201
  existentialist view of, 160, 166
  scale of rating of, 197
  See also Subjectivity
Experiential psychotherapy, 224
  cognitive theory and, 250
Experiment in Gestalt therapy, 282
Extinction, 441

Faatz, Anita, 134
Facilitator-change agent, 229-30
Facts, 3
Fagan, J., 280-82, 291
Families, 26-27
  client-centered system and, 187
  ego psychology and, 45-46
  in Life Model, 371
  meditation for, 326
  psychosocial therapy and, 79-80
  role concept and, 397-98
  See also Family therapy
Family atmosphere, cognitive view of, 261
Family crisis, 502-3
Family group sessions, 464-69
Family process, 459-63
Family service agencies, crisis situations and, 507-8
Family therapy, 449-77, 543
  aims of, 469-71
  annotated listing of key works on, 476-77
  behavior as seen by, 451-52
  boundaries of the family and, 457-59
  communication theory and, 155, 454-56
  complementarity of roles and, 462-63
  content analysis of, 415
  crisis theory and, 519-20
  existentialist approach to, 168
  family group sessions and, 464-69
  Gestalt approach to, 286
  indications and contraindications to, 471-72
  integrating the elements of, 455-57
  integrational or eclectic approach to, 454-57
  present and future perspectives of, 472-73

Family therapy (cont.)
  problem-solving component in, 120
  social and historical content of, 449-51
  schools of thought, eclectics, and integration in, 452-55
  task-centered, 489
Fanshel, David, 413
Farberow, Norman, 504
Farrelly, Frank, 164, 168
Farson, Richard, 208, 227-28
Fauber, L., 44
Fears, 509
Federn, Paul, 34, 293
Feedback:
  communications theory and, 423
  general systems theory and, 337, 348
Feldman, Yonata, 38, 41, 67
Fenichel, Otto, 19
Figure-background formation, 277
Filial therapy, client-centered approach to, 204
Findlay, Barbara, 416
Fischer, Joel, 3
Fisher, George A., 344n, 345
Fixed causality, 126, 127
Flynn, J. P., 354
Focusing, 197-98
Focusing attention, meditation and, 314, 315
Force, creative, 158
Fox, Evelyn, 56
Frailberg, Selma, 402
Framo, James L., 476
Frankl, Viktor E., 152, 155, 166-68, 176
Freedom:
  client-centered view of, 188-89
  existentialist view of, 169
  individual, 148
  subjectivity and, 148-50
Freedom of choice (free choices):
  existentialism and, 153-54, 159, 166
  in functional approach, 134
Friedlander, S., 274, 275
Freud, Anna, 18, 31, 34, 36, 509
Freud, Sigmund, 14, 18, 19, 31, 124, 158, 159, 244,
    245, 253, 254, 256, 257, 293-94, 393, 400,
    509, 537
  ego psychology and, 33-35
Freudian approach:
  functional theory and, 124-27
  meditation and, 318, 319
  See also Diagnostic school; Psychoanalytical theory
Frohberg, Marjory, 152
Fromm, Erich, 171
Functional theory (for social work practice), 123-140, 543
  agency function and, 129-31
  annotated listing of key works on, 144-45
  authority and, 135
  cognitive theory and, 252
  community organization and, 136
  current and future perspectives for, 136-40
  diagnosis and, 128-29
  freedom of choice in, 134
  generic principles for, 129-31
  group work and, 136

  historical origins of, 124-29
  institutional context for practice and, 138
  integrated conception of social work practice in, 137-38
  major concepts of, 133-35
  structure and form of delivery and, 134-35
  time in, 128, 129, 133-34
  unitary theory and, 139-40
Functional unity, 337
Furst, Joseph, 245
Future, general systems theory and, 355

Game analysis, 300
Gardner, John W., 126
Garrett, Annette, 15-16, 31, 37-39, 67
Gautama, Siddhartha, 316
Gendlin, E. T., 186, 187, 191, 195-201, 214, 220,
    222-24, 227, 228
General systems theory, 333-59, 542
  basic concepts of, 335-38, 340
  building theory within framework of, 340-50
  in historical perspective, 338-39
  new world view and, 353-56
  professional response to, 348-49
  social work domain and, 352-53
  social work experience with, 339-40
  systems construct in, 335-38
  teaching, 349-50
Generic form of the general systems approach, 343-44
Gerard, Ralph, 338
Germain, Carel B., 361-78, 383, 384
Gervais, Jacquelyn M., 416
Gerz, Hans O., 266
Gestalt theory (or therapy), 152, 155, 166, 273-92, 544
  annotated listing of key works on, 291-92
  counterindications for the use of, 286-87
  historic origins of, 274-76
  history taking and diagnosis and, 280-81
  impact on social work practice, 276-77
  implications for practice, 285-86
  as an orienting principle, 281
  principal proponents of, 276
  social work research implications of, 287-88
  general therapeutic concepts of, 277-80
  treatment methods and techniques of, 281-85
Getzels, J. W., 388
Gitterman, Alex, 361-78, 384
Glaser, K., 220
Glasser, William, 155, 161, 246, 251, 264, 272
Glover, Edward, 35
Glueck, Bernard C., 320, 323, 326, 331
Goals:
  cognitive view of, 244, 245, 261, 263
  in existential social work, 163-65
Goble, Frank G., 254
Goffman, Erving, 411
Golan, Naomi, 499-522, 532
Goldman, Alvin I., 481
Goode, William J., 3
Goodman, Gerald, 227
Goodman, Paul, 276, 291
Gordon, Barry, 214
Gordon, Thomas, 187, 205, 207-208, 216, 227, 228

Gordon, William E., 349n, 350-51, 383
Gorlow, L. E., 206
Gottlieb, Werner, 247-48
Goulding, Mary, 303, 305-306, 310
Goulding, Robert, 303-306, 310
Great Depression of the 1930s, 504
Greenson, Ralph, 400
Grief, 503
    ego-oriented casework and, 56-62
Grinker, Roy, 338
Gronfein, Berthe, 267
Gross, Neal, 390. 407
Grossbard, Hyman, 44
Group meditation, 325
Groups:
    client-centered approach to, in educational system
        change, 215-17
    content analysis of, 415
    crisis intervention in, 520
    ego psychology and, 46
    encounter, see Encounter groups
    in Life Model, 371, 372
    psychosocial therapy and, 79-80
    role defined as participation in a specific, 386
    transactional analysis and, 304
    treatment, 26-27, 168
Group therapy, 304
    client-centered approach to, 205-9, 213-15
    cognitive approach to, 249-50
    task-centered, 490-91
Group work, functional theory and, 136
Growth:
    client-centered approach to, 190-92
    existentialist view of, 153-159
    functional theory and, 126, 131-32, 134
    Gestalt approach to, 278, 279
    See also Ego development
Guba, E. G., 388
Guerney, Bernard, 204
Guilt, existentialist view of, 154
Gyarfas, Mary, 152

Habituation effect, 316-17
Haigh, G. V., 183, 184
Haley, Jay, 93, 119, 155-56, 164, 166, 168, 171
Halkides, G., 193
Hall, Edward T., 416-18, 430
Hallowitz, David, 93-122, 248
Hamburg, David A., 383
Hamilton, Gordon, 4, 5, 31, 37, 38, 70, 91, 93, 504
Hankins, Frank, 70
Harper, Robert A., 246
Harrison, Grace P., 120, 248
Hart, J. T., 209
Hartman, Ann, 339
Hartmann, Heinz, 18, 34-36, 70, 501, 509
Harvard School of Public Health, 504
Hatcher, C., 291
Hearn, Gordon, 3, 6, 333-58
Hefez, Albert, 503
Hefferline, R. F., 291
Hellenbrand, Shirley, 397

Helping process, 127-28
    in Life Model, 373-75
    time in, 133
    See also Therapeutic process
Hendrick, Ives, 501
Here and now, 277
Hilgard, Ernest, 258
Hill, Reuben, 502
Himelstein, P., 291
Hinduism, 316
Hobbs, Nicholas, 205-206
Hoch, E. L., 206
Hockett, Charles F., 430-31
Hoffer, Eric, 170
Hoffman, Banesh, 126, 183
Hoffman, David L., 515
Hoffman, Lynn, 384
Hofstein, Saul, 126
Holistic approach, 244, 251
    Perls and, 274
    See also Organismic theory
Holistic conception of social work, 348-53
Hollis, Florence, 5-7, 16, 38, 39, 67, 70, 72, 74, 77, 82,
        84, 91, 93, 415, 517
Holloway, Bill, 310
Holloway, Stephen, 384
Holmes, Thomas, 510
Homeostatic process, family therapy and, 460-62
Hooker, Carol, 321
Hope, crisis theory and, 512
Hora, Thomas, 252
Horney, Karen, 36, 126, 152, 160n
Hospital social workers, 508
Hughes, James W., 386-87
Huige, Kristyn, 298, 311
Human growth, see Growth
Humanistic psychology, 152
Human nature:
    client-centered view of, 188-91
    cognitive view of, 260
Human potential movement, 206
Human relatedness in Life Model, 366-67
Human relations training movement, 206
Hyxley, Julian, 126
Hypnosis, cognitive vs. Freudian view of, 258

Id, 14, 33, 158
Identification, 16, 42
    developmental stages and, 21-23
    ego development and, 19
    process of, 18-19
    security image patterns as, 160
    sublimation and, 18
    superego, 20, 21
    therapeutic relationship, 24-28
    treatment as affected by, 23-24
Identification phase, case example of, 51-53
Identity in Life Model, 364-65
Imagery, cognitive treatment and, 246-47
Imre, Roberta Wells, 152
Incest, problem-solving approach to, 102-103
Individual freedom, 148

Individual psychology, Adlerian, 244
Individual uniqueness, 148-51
Infants, identity of, 364-65; *see also* Children
Information theory, 409-411
    client-centered therapy and, 221-223
Information therapies, 433-35
Ingersoll, Hazel L., 393
Inner passions, 160
    security image patterns as, 160
Inquiry, 355
Insight:
    crisis theory and, 513
    Gestalt therapy and, 284
Insomnia, meditation and, 320
Instinctual drives, cognitive view of, 244, 245, 253, 254
Integrated conception of social work, 137-38
Integrative and creative force, existentialist view of,
    158-59
Integrity therapy, 167
Intergroup, tension and conflict, 187-88
Interlocking perspective for practice, 535-45
International Transactional Analysis Association, 294
Interpretation, 40
Interpretive therapy, 179
Intervention, therapeutic relationship and, 15-17
Interviews, 17
Introjection, 19, 34
    Gestalt view of, 278-79
Irrational ideas, emotional disturbances and, 255-56

Jackel, Merl M., 44
Jacobson, Allvar Hilding, 393
Jacobson, Edith, 19, 28
Jacobson, Gerald F., 500, 504, 516
Jaffe, Ruth, 503
Jahoda, Marie, 127
James, Muriel, 310-11
Janet, Pierre, 258
Janis, Irving, 502
Jehu, Derek, 6, 82
Jewish mysticism, 316
Jogan, R., 184
Jongeward, Dorothy, 310-11
Jourard, Sidney, 315
Jung, Carl Gustav, 127, 152, 167
Juvenile delinquency, problem-solving approach to,
    106-108

Kahn, Alfred, J., 339
Kahn, Eugene, 293
Kanfer, Frederick H., 448
Kaplan, David M., 500, 506, 515, 516, 520, 532
Kardiner, Abraham, 501
Karpman, Stephen, 303
Katz, Robert, 166
Kaufman, Irving, 38, 42, 44, 45
Kazantzakis, Nikos, 149
Keefe, Thomas, 313-31
Kees, W., 431
Kernberg, Otto, 14, 31-32, 44
Kierkegaard, Soren, 148, 149, 151, 160
Kinesics (kinesis analysis), 416, 463
Klein, Alan, 152, 168

Knowledge, social uses of, 188
Koestler, Arthur, 336
Kogan, J., 274
Kohler, Wolfgang, 338, 356
Kohut, Heinz, 14, 44
Komarovsky, Mirra, 386
Konopka, Gisela, 5-6
Korean conflict, 503, 505
Korner, I. N., 512
Krauss, Herbert H., 257
Krill, Donald F., 147-76, 254, 541
Krim, Alaine, 416
Kris, Ernst, 501

Lackie, Bruce, 43
Laing, R. D., 152, 157, 161, 167, 169
La Jolla Program, 217
Langsley, Donald, 516, 520
Language:
    cognitive theory and, 249, 253
    opposing forces of, 418
Latency, 23
Lathrope, Donald E., 349n
Laughlin, H. P., 34
Lazarus, Arnold, 247, 253-54, 323
Lazarus, Richard, 502
Leadership:
    client-centered principles and, 187
    group-centered, 207-208, 214
Learning, client-centered approach to, 210-12, 228
Learning theory, 502, 542
    crisis theory and, 510-11
    psychological therapy and, 82
Lechnyr, Ronald J., 327n
Lecky, Prescott, 126, 152, 275
Lee, Marjorie, 263
Lee, Porter, 137
Lennard, Henry L., 392, 393, 407
Leonard, G. B., 226
Lessening of threat, 40-41
Levenson, Edgar A., 451
Lewin, Kurt, 9, 335, 336, 338, 356
Lewis, Harold, 3, 136n, 144
Liberman, Robert P., 511
Life Model (ecological perspective), 361-84, 542
    annotated listing of key works on, 383-84
    client and worker roles in, 372-73
    definition of need/problem and the unit of attention in,
        370-72
    ecological concepts and, 362-70
    illustration of, 375-77
    of practice, 370-78
Life style, cognitive approach to diagnosis and, 262
Life transitions, in life model, 371-72
Lindemann, Erich, 43, 499-501, 503
Linguistic codes, 419
Linstone, Harold, 355
Linton, Ralph, 386
Lippitt, R., 344n, 346-48
Listening , active, 216
Living systems, general systems theory and, 347, 353-54
Lutz, Werner, 6
Litman, Robert, 504

Loewenstein, Rudolf, 501
London, Perry, 433
Lukton, Rosemary C., 506
Lyman, Stanford M., 430
Lynd, Helen Merrell, 126

McClendon, Ruth, 305, 310
McEachern, Alexander W., 390, 407
McLuhan, Marshall, 420
Mahl, George F., 415-16
Mahler, Margaret A., 19, 22, 32, 43
Maluccio, Anthony N., 512
Management, client-centered principles and, 187
Marcus, Lotte, 3, 409-25
Marital counseling, client-centered approach to, 205
Marital problems, problem-solving work and, 101-103
Maruyama, Magaroh, 337-38
Marx, Karl, 320
Maslow, Abraham, 126, 152, 188, 246, 252-54, 275,
    315, 501
Mason, Ward S., 390, 407
Masterson, James, 14, 32, 44
Material reinforcers, 440
Matson, Floyd W., 126
Maultsby, Maxie, 246-47
May, Rollo, 152, 166, 168, 257
Mayer, Herta, 45
Mayer, John E., 258-59
Mead, George Herbert, 131, 388
Mechanic, David, 364
Meditation, 313-31, 543
    annotated listing of key works on, 331
    Buddhism and, 315-18
    capacities learned in, 314-15
    case example of use of, 327-28
    cautions and counterindications for use of, 322-23
    description and explanation of, 313-14
    origins of, 316
    psychosocial history and diagnosis and, 323-24
    research implications of, 326
    settings and levels of interventions and, 325-26
    social work treatment and, 317-18
    teaching, 324-25
    therapeutic relationship and, 324
Meerlo, Joos A. M., 391
Melancholia, 19
Mental health clinics, community, 170
Mental imagery, cognitive treatment and, 246-47
Merbaum, Michael, 503
Merton, Robert K., 3, 28, 386, 389, 392
Messages, 418-21
Metamessages, 420-21
Meyer, Carol, 387
Military psychiatrists, 503
Miller, James G., 333-35, 338, 347, 348, 350, 354
Miller, Roger, 422
Milmoe, Susan, 416
Minahan, Anne, 339
Minuchin, Salvador, 384, 476
Mitchell, C., 45
Mitchell, Sandra T., 398-99
Mittlemann, Bela, 501
Model building, general systems approach to, 344-48

Montalvo, Frank, 344n, 348
Moreno, Joseph L., 386
Morita therapy, 166
Morphogenic processes, 337-38
Motives, 244; see also Goals
Moustakas, Clark, 126, 152, 203, 204
Mowrer, O. Hobart, 155, 166-67, 415
Murphy, Louis, 501, 509
Multifinality, 338
Mutual causal processes, 337
Mutuality, client-worker, 35, 372, 373

Narcissistic injury, 44
Natural helper, 368
Nature, sense of kinship with, 366-67
Nee, Robert H., 4, 6, 144
Needs, life model and definition of, 370-72
Negative reinforcement, 440-41
Neiman, Lionel J., 386-87
Nelson, Benjamin, 400, 407
Nelson, Marian A., 56
Nelson, Marie Coleman, 391, 393-94, 400, 407
Neurosis, 43, 44
    cognitive view of, 257
Neutralization of drives, 18, 20, 21, 34
Newcombe, Theodore, 389, 393
Nikelly, Arthur G., 246, 262, 272
Noise, 411, 421
Nondirective therapy, 181-83; see also Client-centered
    therapy
Northrup, F. C. S., 126
Nyswander, Dorothy, 343

Object relations, 19, 20
Observer self, meditation and, 314, 319
Obstacles, analyzing and resolving, 488
Oedipal conflict, 20, 23
One-pointedness-of-mind, 315
Open systems, 335-37
Organismic self-regulation, 275, 277
Organismic theory, Perls', 275
Organismic valuing process, 191
Ornstein, Robert, 317
Osmond, Humphrey, 417
Overall, Betty, 392

Page, C. W., 206
Parad, Howard J., 5, 6, 45, 91, 500, 506, 513, 516, 532
Parad, Libbie G., 532
Paralinguistic research, 415-16
Parent-child problems, 119-20
    problem-solving approach to, 99-101, 103-105, 113
    See also Child therapy
Parent Effectiveness Training, 227
Parsons, Talcott, 3
Pasewark, Richard, 515
Passions, inner, 160
Passons, W. R., 285
Pennsylvania School of Social Work, 123, 125
Perception:
    cognitive view of, 255, 263
    meditation and, 315
Peres, H., 206

Performance, in role theory, 393-94
Perlman, Helen Harris, 5, 6, 38, 93-94, 120-21, 387,
    388, 395, 407, 479, 483, 505
Perls, Frederick (Fritz) S., 152, 160n, 168, 273-78,
    281-82, 285, 286, 291
Perls, Laura, 276
Permission, 303
Personal distance, 369, 370
Personality:
    cognitive view of the nature of, 260-61
    existentialist view of, 158-60
    Freudian view of, 158, 159
    meditation and, 318-19
Personality change:
    cognitive view of, 261
    Gendlin's theory of, 197-98
    See also Change
Personality development, 14-17 see also Developmental
    stages; Ego development; Identification
Phenomenological movement, 188-89, 251; see also
    Cognitive theory
Phenomenology, Gestalt therapy and, 282
Phillips, Helen, 136n
Phillips, Jean, 448
Philo of Alexandria, 316
Philosophy, existential therapy and, 166-67
Phobic patients, cognitive treatment of, 264-66
Piaget, Jean, 39, 338, 501
Pincus, Allen, 339
Pittenger, Robert, E., 424n, 430-31
Platt, J., 121
Play therapy, nondirective, 201-204
Polansky, Norman A., 38, 413
Politics, client-centered movement and, 226-28
Pollution, 363
Polsky, Howard, 349n
Polster, E., 274, 275, 278, 282, 291-92
Polster, M., 274, 275, 278, 282, 291-92
Porter, E. H., 180
Positive regard, 191-92, 202
    unconditional, 185, 192-94
Positive reinforcements, categories of, 439-41
Power:
    existentialist view of, 169
    Rogers' view of, 226
Pray, Kenneth L. M., 123, 128, 130, 135, 136
Precipitating factor, 515
Prescriptions, 391-92
Prestwood, Rodney, 422
Pretheory, 5
Price, Douglas B., 415
Privacy, 369, 370
Private logic, 262
Problem identification, 220
Problems, life model and definition of, 370-72
Problem-solving (theory or work), 93-122, 544
    additional concepts in, 94-97
    annotated listing of key works on, 119-22
    assertive counseling component in, 95, 113
    broadening the treatment team and, 115-16
    contexts of, 112-13
    definition of, 111-12

diagnosis and, 94
    internalized emotional disturbances and, 106-107
    environmental problems and, 109-10, 116-17
    future planning and direction and, 110-11
    in individual treatment, 114
    intrafamilial relationship problems and, 97-99
    marital problems and, 101-103
    parent-child problems and, 99-101, 103-105, 113
    Perlman's concepts and, 93-94
    pitfalls and counterindications, 116-17
    in relationship conflicts, 113-14
    school and home behavior problem-solving work and,
        103-106
    symptomatic behavior and, 114-15
    the unconscious and, 94
    See also Task-oriented treatment
Process:
    functional theory and, 125-26, 129, 133
    general systems theory and, 355-56
    See also Change
Process conception, 186, 195-98
Process of change, in existential social work, 160-64
Programmatic reinforcers, 439-40
Progressive mechanization, 337
Progressive segregation, 337
Projection, 19
    Gestalt view of, 279
Protection, 303
Provocative contact, in existential social work, 163-64
Proxemics, 416-18
Psychoanalysis:
    cognitive theory and, 251, 253
    Perls and, 274, 276
Psychoanalytic psychotherapy, 166
Psychoanalytic (psychodynamic) theory, 4, 5, 13, 70,
    127, 148, 544
    annotated listing of key works on, 31-32
    causation in, 14-16
    conceptual problems in, 16-17
    Gestalt theory and, 281
    psychosocial therapy and, 73, 85
    See also Diagnostic school; Ego psychology; Freudian
        approach; Personality development
Psychodrama, 155
Psychological knowledge, social uses of, 188
Psychology:
    ego, 15-17, 33-62, 125, 159, 251, 509, 544
    existential, 152, 252-53
    humanistic, 152
    of self, 44
Psycometrics, 85
Psychoses (psychotic individuals):
    cognitive theory and, 266
    Gestalt theory and, 287
    meditation and, 322-24
Psychosocial history, cognitive approach to diagnosis and,
    251, 261-63
Psychosocial study, 78
Psychosocial therapy, 69-87, 544
    annotated listing of key works in, 91
    basic assumptions of, 71-73
    client worker relationship and, 73

community and, 81-82
definition of, 69
diagnosis in, 78-79
direct treatment procedures in, 74-76
historical origins of, 69-70
indirect work in, 76-78
modalities of treatment in, 79-81
other theories' connection to, 82
overall assessment of, 85-87
present status of, 82-85
psychoanalytic theory and, 73
settings in, 79
technical aids in, 76
theoretical base of, 70-73
the unconscious and, 72-73
value orientations of, 71
Psychotherapy, *see specific schools and types of psychotherapy*
Psychotherapy model for crisis treatment, 516
Public health model, crisis theory and, 504
Public welfare agencies, 508
Punishment, 440

Quinlan, James, 513

Rackets, 300
Rado, Sandor, 257, 501
Rahe, Richard, 510
Raimy, Victor, 181, 184
Rank, Otto, 124, 125, 127-30, 132-34, 152, 179, 252, 274, 275
Rapaport, David, 35, 501
Rape victims, 508
Rapoport, Anatol, 338
Rapoport, Lydia, 45, 500, 506, 509, 512-17, 519, 532
Rapprochement subphase, 43
Raskin, N. J., 182-84, 205, 224n
Rationale, establishing incentives and, 488
Rational-emotive psychotherapy, 152, 166, 245, 248, 264
Reality-oriented therapy, 155, 167, 264; *see also* Cognitive therapy
Reality principle, 35
Reciprocity, 362
Recompensation model for crisis treatment, 516
Redecision therapy, 303-304
Redfield, R., 218n
Reequilibration, 389-90
Reese, Ellen P., 448
Reflective psychotherapy, 182-83
Regression, 40, 42, 43
Reich, Charles, 169-70, 274
Reichian Character Analysis, Perld and, 274
Reid, William, J., 7, 479-94, 497, 507
Reik, Theodore, 422
Rein, Martin, 137
Reiner, Beatrix, 38, 42, 44, 45
Reintegration, 515
Rejection, parental, 119-20
Relatedness, human: in life model, 366-67
Relationship, worker-client:
    crisis theory and, 512-13
    in life model, 372-73

psychosocial therapy and, 73
    See also Therapeutic relationship
Relationship change, in existential therapy, 164
Relationship conflicts, problem-solving work in, 96, 113-14
Relationship inventory, 193-95
Relationship phase, case example of, 48-51
Relationships, existentialist view of, 150-51
Relationship therapy, 179, 180
Relaxation, meditation and, 320, 322
Remmel, Mary L., 515
Repetitive themes, 41
Resistance, 40, 41, 132
    Gestalt theory and, 274, 275
Resnik, H. L. P., 532
Retroflection, Gestalt view of, 279
Reynold, Bertha, 256, 504
Rice, L. N., 221, 223
Richmond, Mary E., 5, 15, 16, 36, 91, 251, 538
Ripple, Lillian, 7
Robbins Institute, 245
Roberts, Robert W., 4, 6, 144
Robinson, Virginia, 123-25, 127, 144
Roethlisberger, F. J., 187
Rogers, Carl R., 3, 152, 158, 164, 166-68, 177-97, 199, 200, 204-206, 208-18, 221-23, 225-28, 324, 537
Rogers, William, 219-20
Role ambiguity, 388-89
Role complementarity, 389
Role conflict, 390
Role discomplementarity, 389
Role enactment, 393-94, 400
Role expectations, descriptive, 392
Role inadequacy, 390
Role incongruency, 390
Role induction, 399-400
Role prescription, 391-92
Roles (role theory), 395-407, 542
    annotated listing of key works on, 407
    application to social work, 394
    concepts and constructs of, 387-94
    definitions of, 385-87
    diagnosis and, 396-99
    explicit and implicit, 390
    family therapy and, 454
    group work and community organization and, 398
    intervention and, 399-401
    learning of, 388
    social study and, 394-96
Role-set, 389
Role vigor, 388
Rosenblatt, Aaron, 392
Rubin, Gerald K., 152, 176, 339
Rubinoff, Lionel, 169
Ruesch, Jurgen, 155, 414, 422, 431

Salk, Jonas, 226
Salomon, Elizabeth, 152
Salzman, Leon, 268
Samples, Bob, 356
Sanctioning, in role theory, 392-93

Sandler, Joseph, 19
Sarbin, Theodore R., 257, 393
Sartre, Jean-Paul, 148, 149, 153, 159, 160
Satir, Virginia M., 155, 164, 166, 168, 413, 476
Scale of rating of experiencing, 197
Scapegoating, 463
Scarbrough, H. E., 264-65
Schamess, Gerald, 45
Scheflen, Albert E., 411, 431, 463
Scherz, Frances H., 44, 45, 515
Schien, Edna Biehl, 398-99
Schiff, Jacqui, 301, 305, 310
Schizophrenic persons, 370
    ambulatory, 44
    client-centered therapy with, 186-87, 197, 199
    cognitive theory and, 266
    meditation, 322-24
Schmideberg, M., 35
Schools, 228; see also Education
Schwartz, William, 6, 383-84
Schwitzgebel, Ralph, 391
Scientific determinism, 125
Scott, Marvin B., 430
Script analysis, 300, 302
Script matrix, 300, 301
Searle, Harold F., 366-67
Secondary process, 35
Security image configuration, 159-60
Seeman, Julius, 182, 183, 186, 203
Selby, Lola, 513
Self, the:
    client-centered view of, 191-92
    functionalist view of, 131-33
Self-actualization, 244
Self-awareness, meditation and, 320
Self-concept, client-centered view of, 191, 192
Self-determination, general systems
    approach to, 345
Self-experience, 191, 192
Self-exploration, in client-centered group therapy, 206
Self-identity, 42, 43
Self-identity-Autonomy phase, case example of, 53-55
Self-psychology, 44
Self-regard, 191-92
Self-regulation, organismic, 275, 277
Self-theory, 181, 183-84
Seligman, Martin E.P., 295, 321
Selye, Hans, 126, 502
Sensitivity-encounter group movement, 206-208
Separation, functional theory and, 132
Separation-individuation process, 19-20
Separation-termination phase, 43
    ego-oriented casework and, 56-62
    functional approach to, 133
Sex drive, 244
    cognitive view of, 260-61
Sexual identity, 22, 23
Sexual problems:
    problem-solving work and, 101-102
    psychosocial therapy and, 86
Shafer, Carl M., 349n
Shapiro, Dean H., 320, 331

Sheerer, E. T., 183
Shepard, Martin, 263, 276
Sheperd, I. L., 281-82, 286-87, 291
Sherman, Murray H., 394, 407, 431
Sherman, Sanford N., 449
Schlien, John M., 186-87
Shneidman, Edwin, 504
Short-term treatment, see Crisis theory
Shulman, Lawrence, 343, 349n
Shyne, Ann W., 7
Sifneos, Peter, 500
Signal anxiety, 509
Simon, Bernice K., 4-5
Simon, Thomas, 354
Simulation, in task-centered treatment, 488
Sinnot, Edmund, 126
Sinsheimer, Robert, 152, 176
Siporin, Max, 250-51, 339, 506, 508, 532
Situational perspective, cognitive theory and, 250-51
Skinner, B. F., 169, 171, 188, 448
Smalley, Ruth, 4, 123, 129, 131, 136, 144-45, 252
Smith, E. W. L., 274-76, 292
Smith, Henry Lee, 424n
Snyder, William U., 181, 182, 186, 196
Social agency function, 129-31, 134
Social change, existentialist view of, 169-70
Social crises, client-centered movement and, 225-29
Social environment, 367-70
Socialization, role and, 386
Social networks, 368-69
Social norm, role as, 386
Social study, role theory and, 394-96
Social uses of psychological knowledge, 188
Society, existentialist view of, 169-70
Sociology, 28
Solomon, L. N., 209, 214
Soul, existentialist view of, 149
Space:
    communication and, 416-18
    fixed-feature, 417
    informal, 417-18
    in life model, 369
    semifixed-feature, 417
Spark, Geraldine M., 476
Specific behavior (symptom) change, in existential therapy, 164
Spiegel, John P., 389
Spiro, M. E., 218n
Spitz, Rene, 295
Spitzer, K., 93, 121
Spivak, G., 93, 121-22
Stamm, Isabel, 38
Stamps, 301
Standal, S., 184-85
Stanley, Joe H., 247-48
Stasis-process continuum, 196-98
State of active crisis, 515
Status, definition of, 385-86
Staver, Nancy, 38
Steady state, 336
Stein, Irma, 338, 339
Stein, Joan W., 6

Steiner, Claude, 300
Stierlin, Helm 476-77
Stock, Dorothy, 183, 184
Stotland, Herbert F., 3, 4, 6, 40, 44
Strean, Herbert S., 385-402, 407
Stress:
    crisis theory and, 502, 503, 510
    in life model, 363, 369
Stretch, John, 152, 176
Strickler, Martin, 500, 506, 532
Stroebel, Charles F., 320, 323, 326, 331
Stroke-awareness grid, 296
Strokes, 295-97
Structural analysis, transactional analysis and, 297-98
Strupp, Hans H., 415
Stuart, Richard B., 44, 433-46
Student-centered teaching, 210-12
Studt, Eliot, 373, 479
Stulberg, Burta, 248
Stulberg, Burton, 119-20
Subjectivity, 148-50
Sublimation, 16, 18
Subsystems, 336
Suffering, existentialist view of, 154
Sufism, 316
Suicide prevention movement, 504
Sullivan, H. S., 36
Sunley, Robert, 248-49, 262
Superego, 14, 17, 28, 159
    content of, 21
    development of, 20-23
    identifications, 20, 21, 25
Sustaining relationship, in existential therapy, 164
Sutherland, John, 355-56
Sutherland, Richard, 166, 176
Sutherland, Robert L., 386
Suzuki, D. T., 316
Symmetrical mechanisms, 462
Symptomatic behavior, problem-solving and, 114-15

Taft, Jessie, 123-25, 127, 129, 131, 133, 144, 152, 179, 201, 203
Taoism, 316
Tape recording in psychosocial therapy, 76
Taplin, Julian R., 502, 511
Target behaviors, selection of, 435-37
Task-centered treatment, 479-97, 543
    annotated listing of key works on, 497
    with families and formed groups, 489-91
    model of, 481-91
    range of application of, 492-94
    studies of, 481-92
    theoretical foundations of, 480-81
Task planning, 486-87
Task review, 488-89
Tasks in crisis intervention, 517
Teaching:
    client-centered principles in, 209-12, 215-17
    See also Education
Teaching Effectiveness Training program, 216, 228
Teilhard de Chardin, Pierre, 159
Television, closed-circuit: in psychosocial therapy, 76

Telschow, E. F., 206
Tension between groups and social systems, 187
Termination phase:
    case example of, 55-56
    of crisis intervention, 518
    of task-centered treatment, 489
Terreberry, Shirley, 355
Territorial behaviors, 369-70
Tharp, Roland, 448
Theme, emerging, 165
Theory (theories), 1-10
    comparison between and among, 535-37
    definitions of, 3
    different approaches to, 5-8
    practical uses of, 8-9
Theory building, general systems approach to, 340-50
Thera, Nyanaponika, 315
Therapeutic alliance, 17
Therapeutic process (helping process), 127-28
    existentialist view of, 153-54
    in life model, 373-75
    time in, 133
Therapeutic relationship, 27
    in client-centered therapy, see Client-centered therapy
    cognitive view of, 258-60
    dimensions of a, 24-28
    existentialist view of, 156-58, 160-61, 166-67
    meditation and, 324
    psychoanalytic therapy and, 15-17
    transference and, 24-25, 28
    See also Relationship, client-worker
Thereapeutic success, 171-72
Therapy outcome, 184
Theresa of Avila, St., 316
Thinking, 243, 253; see also Cognitive theory
Thomas, Edwin, J., 6, 391, 407
Thought disorders, meditation and, 323
Tieryakian, Edward, 169
Time:
    in functional theory, 128, 129, 133-34
    in life model, 369
Time structuring, 295-97
    checking out, 303
Timms, Noel, 258-59
Tomlinson, T. M., 209
Towle, Charlotte, 38, 505, 539
Transactional analysis, 155, 293-311, 544
    annotated listing of key works on, 310-11
    basic assumptions of, 294-95
    confused, psychotic clients and, 305
    existential positions in, 297-99
    limitations on the effectiveness of, 306
    redecision therapy and, 303
    social research and, 306
    social treatment techniques of, 301-304
    in social work practice, 304-305
    theoretical concepts of, 295-301
    in training therapists, 305-306
    versatility of, 304
Transcendental Meditation (TM), 317, 320, 323-25
Transference, 15-16, 24-25, 28, 31, 40
    psychosocial therapy and, 74

Travelers Aid, 505
Treatment modalities, 266
Trist, E. L., 354-55
Truax, C. B., 193, 206
Trustworthiness, communication and, 412-13
Turner, Francis J., 1-10, 69-87, 91, 339, 499, 535-45
Tyhurst, James, 503
Type token ratio (TTR), 415

Ullman, Montague, 258
Unconditionally of response, 194, 202
Unconditional positiive regard, in client-centered therapy,
    185, 192-94
Unconscious, the, 14
    cognitive view of, 244, 245, 251, 257-58
    ego psychology and, 37, 38
    functional theory and, 125
    meditation and, 319
    problem-solving and, 94, 121
    psychosocial therapy and, 72-73, 85
Uniqueness, individual, 148-51, 154-55
    cognitive view, 265

Values, existential therapy and, 166-67
Valuing process:
    optimum, 197
    organismic, 191
Van der Veen, F., 187, 205
Van Kaam, Adrian, 252
Varley, Barbara K., 401
Verbal accessibility, 413
Verger, Don, 261
Videotape in psychosocial therapy, 76
Vietnam War, 503
Vogel, Ezra F., 502
Vulnerability, 192, 193, 514-15

Wallen, R., 274
Warding off, separation-termination and, 58-59
Wasserman, Harry, 138
Wasserman, Sidney L., 33-65
Watson, John B., 253, 344n, 346-48
Watson, David, 448
Watts, Allen, 316
Watzlawick, Paul, 424, 431
Weil, Andrew, 356

Weinberger, Jerome L., 44
Weiss, David, 152, 158, 176
Wellesley Human Relations Service, 503
Welsh, B., 93, 121
Welwood, John, 319, 331
Werley, H. H., 345n
Werner, Harold D., 5, 243-72
Westley, B., 344n, 346-48
Wexler, D. A., 221-23
Wheelis, Allen, 388
Whitaker, Carl, 168
White, Colby L., 250
White, Robert W., 365, 509
Whittaker, James, K., 339
Whorf, Benjamin Lee, 419
Wierner, Norbert, 410
Will, functionalist view of, 252
Williams, Frederick, 431-32
Winthrop, Henry, 171
Wood, John, 217-18
Wood, Katherine M., 39-40, 67
Woodward, Julian L., 386
Woolfolk, Robert L., 320
Woolams, Stanley, 298, 310, 311
Worker-client relationship, see Relationship, client-worker
Working through, 40, 41, 43
    grief and, 59-62
World view:
    existentialist view of client's, 161
    general systems theory and, 353-56
World War II, 503, 505
Wortis, Joseph, 245, 266
Wynne, Lyman, 463

Yelaja, Shankar A., 123-40, 543
Yoga, meditation and, 316, 324

Zalba, Serapio R., 6
Zen Buddhism, 275, 316, 323, 324
    meditation and, 315-18, 322
Zifferblatt, Steven M., 331
Zimring, F. M., 222-23
Zinker, J., 281-84, 292
Znaniecki, Florian, 386
Zuk, Gerald H., 463